Arthur J. Jewers

The Registers of the Parish of St. Columb Major, Cornwall

From the Year 1539 to 1780

Arthur J. Jewers

The Registers of the Parish of St. Columb Major, Cornwall
From the Year 1539 to 1780

ISBN/EAN: 9783337037741

Printed in Europe, USA, Canada, Australia, Japan

Cover: Foto ©Lupo / pixelio.de

More available books at **www.hansebooks.com**

The Registers

OF THE

Parish of St. Columb Major,

CORNWALL,

FROM THE YEAR 1539 TO 1780.

EDITED BY

ARTHUR J. JEWERS, F.S.A.

LONDON:
HAMILTON, ADAMS, AND CO., 32 PATERNOSTER ROW, E.C.
MITCHELL AND HUGHES, 140 WARDOUR STREET, W.

1881.

LONDON:
MITCHELL AND HUGHES, PRINTERS,
140 WARDOUR STREET, W.

UTRUMQUE PARATUS
GWIR YN ERBYN Y BYD

Dedicated,

BY PERMISSION,

TO

SIR FRANCIS WYATT TRUSCOTT, KT.,

ALDERMAN AND LATE LORD MAYOR OF THE CITY OF LONDON.

IN PUTTING FORTH THE FOLLOWING CONTRIBUTION TO THE HISTORY OF YOUR NATIVE COUNTY, A COUNTY RICH IN HISTORICAL MEMORIES, I FEEL IT CANNOT APPEAR UNDER BETTER AUSPICES THAN THAT OF YOURSELF, NOT ALONE FROM THE FACT OF YOUR NAME HAVING ADDED LUSTRE TO THE LONG LIST OF CORNISH WORTHIES, BY YOUR HAVING BEEN CALLED LAST YEAR TO HOLD THE OFFICE OF CHIEF MAGISTRATE OF THE MOST POWERFUL CITY OF THE WORLD, BUT ALSO FROM THE EVER READY ENCOURAGEMENT RENDERED BY YOU TO THE CAUSE OF LITERATURE AND ART.

SHOULD THE PROMINENCE WHICH YOUR NAME GIVES THIS WORK STIMULATE THE PUBLICATION OF OTHER REGISTERS, IT WILL RENDER YOU, I AM SURE, NO LITTLE SATISFACTION; AND AT THE SAME TIME GAIN YOU THE GRATITUDE OF A MUCH WIDER CIRCLE THAN THAT OF GENEALOGISTS ONLY, IN THE PRESENT AND IN COMING GENERATIONS, AS WELL AS THAT OF

YOUR MOST OBEDIENT SERVANT,

ARTHUR J. JEWERS.

PLYMOUTH, *April*, 1881.

PREFACE.

If the Parish Registers of St. Columb Major had any special claim to be printed, it was not from their being so decayed they were on the point of perishing altogether, but rather from their being unusually perfect from almost the earliest to which such Registers go back, and from the number of entries relating to prominent county families that it contains, and the lingering traces of the "older religion," shewn in the burial of chauntry priests and chrisomers contained in its pages, which, while it gives more general interest, it must be doubted whether it gives them a prior claim over some of the dilapidated and fast-decaying registers which I have had occasion to consult in the course of preparing this volume and other kindred works, the only hope for the preservation of which is their being printed, and that before very long, or they must be irreparably lost, there being no other means of recovering the valuable information they contain, information often going beyond the bare legal entries of baptism, marriage, or burial.

It has been urged by some that only extracts relating to the more important persons recorded should be printed, but surely the objections to such a plan are self-evident. Why select persons only who were particularly prominent? or who shall say what entries will be of no use? the probability being that all, sooner or later, will be needed, and further, for public utility and historical value they must be an entire and very careful copy of the original.

It is difficult for any one who has not actual knowledge of the state of the case to comprehend the risk of destruction to which both parish registers and the monumental records in our parish churches are exposed; of the latter, after carefully noting them from a number of churches, and then revisiting the same churches after they have undergone so-called restoration, it will be a matter of no small surprise how much has disappeared; in many cases this is unavoidable, from their being too dilapidated and obliterated to be preserved when once touched, though more often a matter of taste with the clergyman or architect.

Reverting to the St. Columb Major's Registers, it will be quite unnecessary to enter into any extended account of them or digest of their contents, beyond a few explanatory remarks. With the exception of the weddings for about twenty years, from about 1760 to 1780, the whole of the Register which has been printed is written on parchment, in three volumes. The first volume, a long narrow folio, is for a large part beautifully written by one hand, being a copy from an earlier book, but towards the end it seems to have been indifferently kept and worse written. The baptisms commence in 1540; the weddings in 1544; and the burials in 1539; the whole being continued down to 1653.

The second volume is a large square folio, beginning in 1653, and ends in 1757. At the end of this volume is a record of the briefs read in the church, with the object for which they were made, and the amount collected, in accordance with an Act of Parliament 4 & 5 Queen Anne. Their objects vary, from the repair of churches to the assistance of individuals visited by misfortune; although of much interest, they hardly come within the scope of the present work; and also the following:—

"A register of such children as have been borne in ye parish of St Columb Major, and not baptised, of whom notice has been given according to ye Act of Parliament.

"John ye son of Bernard and Mary Rowse was borne ye 25 Oct. 1705.
Joseph son of Oliver Basely was borne ye 28 of May 1706."

These are the only two entries under this head.

The third is a smaller volume, and contains baptisms and burials only, from 1758 to 1812. On the inside of the front cover is the following record:—

"Lady Frances Gifford, Relict of Sr John Gifford, Bart., died February the 28th and was buried the 21st of March, 1751. J. COLLIER, Curate.

"The above copy was taken from the Registers of St. Columb Major in the county of Cornwall on Thursday ye 15th day of February, 1787.

THO^s^ COLERICKE, Curate."

At the end of the same volume are the following entries:—

"Buried at St Wenn July ye 31 Joan Sandy, aged an hundred years and above, 1784.

"In ye year 1775 on ye 12 Day of February being Sunday, the Tower and church of this Parish were greatly damaged by Lightening at half an Hour past Four in the morning."

The remaining volumes are on paper, in printed forms.

Among singular entries may be noted, as shewing how slowly surnames came into general use in remote parts among the humbler classes, the burial, in 1584, of Anthonie the Smith; in 1586, Stephen the Myller; in 1589, John the Thacher; and, even as late as 1603, that of Robert the Farrier. Among the marriages we meet such entries as the following: William Reve and Jane, servant to Michaell Nanskevell, in 1545; in 1556, Luke and Margery, servants to John Spraye; in 1621, John Dayes man and mayde. Of centenarians we have, in 1611, Thomas Tior, said in the entry to be 122 years of age by common report; and on the 29 Jan. 1791 was buried William Hicks of Criftoe in this parish, who was baptised 14th Feb. 1689, as is recorded in the burial entry: the baptism was probably at some other church, possibly at St. Wenn, as the entry does not appear in these Registers.

We pass readily from the Registers themselves to the families recorded in them. Holding the foremost place we find the Arundells of Lanherne in the adjoining parish of Mawgan, who had a grant, 7 Edward I. 1279 (to John de Arundell), of the right to hold a fair in their manor of St. Columb Major on the feast of St. Columba the Virgin, 23 Oct. in each year, and a market on Thursday in every week. The heiress of Arundell of Lanherne carried the representation through the family of Bealing to that of Lord Arundell of Wardour, descended from Sir Thomas Arundell, second son of Sir John Arundell of Lanherne, by his first wife Lady Eleanor, daughter of Thomas Grey, Marquis of Dorset; thus uniting the two lines which are represented by John Francis, twelfth and present Lord Arundell of Wardour; and we are indebted to his lordship for the Arundell bookplate.

The Hoblyns, who resided for many generations at their seat of Nanswhyden, where Robert Hoblyn, Esq., M.P. (called by Davies Gilbert "that bright ornament of his family and county"), accumulated a magnificent library, which was taken to Bath and sold by auction by his successor in the property, the Rev. Robert Hoblyn, M.A., J.P., the sale lasting six weeks, catalogues 10s. 6d. each, one of which is in the British Museum. The mansion was burnt to the ground in 1803, and that part of the estate sold. Their present representative, William Paget Hoblyn, Esq., M.A., J.P., built a residence, "The Fir Hill," in the adjoining parish of Little Colan, where he chiefly resides with his family, and to whom we are indebted for the use of the armorial bookplate of the above Robert Hoblyn, Esq., M.P. The plate originally had the following inscription, as is shewn by old impressions, viz., "R. H., C.C.C., Oxon, Comm'," the above Robert Hoblyn, Esq., having been of Corpus Christi College, Oxford. I am indebted to the following, who have kindly acceded to my request for the loan of their respective bookplates, viz., William Hoblyn, Esq., M.R.C.S., for that of his father, the late Rev. Edward Hoblyn, M.A., Vicar of Mylor-cum-Mabe, and to Richard Armstrong Hoblyn, Esq., for the loan of his own plate.

The Vivians were originally of Trenouth, in St. Columb, and then at Truan in the same parish, where they still have a stately house. Their line terminated in an heiress married to Sir Richard Vyvyan, Bart., of Trelowarren, from which marriage descends the present Richard Henry Stackhouse Vyvyan, Esq., of Truan. The family of Retallick or Retallack, which for many generations held an honourable position in the neighbourhood, is continued in the person of the present Francis Retallack, Esq., J.P., of Chytane, in the adjoining parish of St. Enoder.

The name of Rowse, which occurs very frequently, almost from the commencement of the Registers, and often in a substantial position, is still represented in two branches by Mr. Henry Jenkyn Rowse of Carworgy, and Mr. John Rowse of Trebudanon, both in St. Columb.

In the parish, or its immediate vicinity, there appear to have been two distinct families of Hicks, one belonging to the Cornish family of Hicks or Hext, and bearing for arms, *Or, a tower triple turreted between three battle-axes sable,* of which family were Hicks of Luxilyan and Hext of Constantine, of whom brief pedigrees were entered at the Heralds' Visitation in 1620; and the same coat is depicted (impaling Vivian of Truan, viz., *Or, a chevron azure between three lions' heads erased proper, a chief gules*) on the monument of the Rev. Richard Hicks, Rector of St. Ervan, who died in 1708, aged sixty-five; and of Eleanor his wife, who died in 1705, which remains in the church of St. Ervan, the inscription almost obliterated. The other family of Hicks claim to be descended from the family of Sir Baptist Hicks, Viscount Campden. Of this family there are two distinct branches, namely, Hicks of Retallick, and Hicks of Lanhynsworth; of the latter line are Richard Hicks, Esq., J.P., of Hartley Lodge, Compton, Plymouth, and his son Francis Hicks, Esq., of Burrington Park, near Plymouth. In both these branches the traditional descent from the Gloucestershire stock is maintained, together with the arms of the Campden line, and given quite separately by both branches, viz., *Gules, a fesse wavy between three fleurs-de-lis or. Crest: a stag's head couped or, gorged by a chaplet of roses gules.* But there is difficulty in tracing back the descent to its spring, both branches having neglected to keep any record, and they consequently can supply little information for establishing the connection. The same tradition seems to have been held when Davies Gilbert wrote his 'History of Cornwall.'

The family of Nankivell, who entered their pedigree at the Heralds' Visitation of 1620, appear to be represented by John Hicks Nankivell, Esq., M.R.C.S., of York. The following have ceased to exist in the parish:—Carter, lords of the manor of St. Columb, represented by Hoblyn. Part of their property, known as the "Carter Rocks," lying off the adjacent coast, is possessed by the present W. Paget Hoblyn, Esq., descended from Mary, second daughter and co-heiress of John Carter, Esq., of St. Columb; the other co-heiresses being Honour, married to William Silly, gent., and Jane, married to Giles Riseden, gent.

Jenkyn of Trekenning became extinct in the direct line on the death of James Jenkyn, Esq., in 1658, who left five daughters his co-heiresses, viz., Ann, married Sir John St. Aubyn, Bart., and was mother of Sir John

St. Aubyn, second Bart.; Mary, third wife of Sir Nicholas Slanninge, Knt. and Bart., but left no issue; Katherine, married John Trelawny, Esq., son of Sir Jonathan Trelawny, Bart. (she died without issue); Elizabeth, married to Sir George Cary of Clovelly; and Frances, who died unmarried. The present representative of Sir John St. Aubyn, the Rev. St. Aubyn Hender Molesworth-St. Aubyn, of Clowance, has very kindly lent the Molesworth and Molesworth-St. Aubyn bookplates. The older St. Aubyn plates appear to have perished in the fires which occurred at Clowance in 1837 and 1843.

Kete or Keate. This family appears to have become extinct in the St. Columb lines long since. A younger branch, descended from Gilbert, fourth son of Ralph Kete, buried at St. Columb in 1602, were raised to the degree of baronets in 1660, which title became extinct on the death of the Rev. Sir William Keate, fourth baronet, without issue, in 1757.

The family of Crewse, who were for several generations connected with this parish, were probably a branch of the old Devonshire family of that name, but their connection has not been ascertained.

The probable connection of the Godolphins of St. Columb with the noble Cornish family of Godolphin is pointed out in the note at page 65.

The family of Brabyn, which held a good position and was connected by marriage with the families of Carter and Jenkyn, was probably a branch of Brabyn of St. Minver, who entered their pedigree at the College of Arms about 1635. (With these arms, viz., *Argent, on a fesse couped gules, three leopards' faces or.*)

The family of Day also held a fair position; but the name of Thomas Day of St. Columb Major appears in the list of those whose claim to use armorial bearings was disallowed by the Heralds at Truro, 6 October, 1620.

The Warnes seem to have flourished and multiplied in the neighbourhood between St. Columb and Padstow, and the name still continues; but the family formerly resident for several generations in St. Columb appear to have died out in the male line; the co-heiress married Rawlings and Dungey, as mentioned on page 172 and page 174. Towards the close of the seventeenth century two brothers (sons of Stephen Warne of St. Columb) settled in the neighbourhood of East Anthony; the elder, Mr. William Warne of Thanckes in East Anthony, left an only daughter, married to Captain Thomas Graves, R.N. (father by his second wife of the first Lord Graves), to whom she carried the estate of Thanckes. The other brother, Simon Warne, left a son Simon, who took the name of Ward, and had issue (see Register extracts, Maker) two sons, Simon, whose only daughter and heiress married John Friend, Esq.; and William, who died without surviving issue.

The foregoing brief notice of some of the more prominent names in these Registers may not be unacceptable, though far from complete, but the very carefully prepared and exhaustive pedigrees given by Colonel Vivian in his work 'The Visitations of Cornwall,' render it quite superfluous to enter into fuller particulars of them here. Many of the old names still exist in the parish, while some have disappeared as above. Before leaving this part of our subject it may be interesting to state that Mr. Nelson D. Adams, of Washington, considers that some members of the St. Columb family of Adams were among the early settlers in America, and ancestors of some of the present families of the name in that country, the evidences of which will doubtless be fully set forth in the work which that gentleman has in hand, and which will doubtless be as elaborate and exhaustive as some previous works of the same description by our American cousins.

Successive restorations and improvements (?) have swept away any monuments of the families of Carter, Jenkyn, or Keate, that may have existed. According to Davies Gilbert, when he wrote his 'History of Cornwall,' there was in the church a monument to some of the family of Moore, consisting of a slate slab with inscription and these arms, *Sable, a swan close within a bordure engrailed argent*; and the Arundell brasses were much more extensive than now. The monuments were certainly much reduced on the restoration of the church by the late Rector Dr. Walker, who offered a fine bust of Robert Hoblyn of Nanswhyden, Esq., M.P., taken from a monument to his memory by the Rev. Edward Hoblyn, M.A., Vicar of Mylor-cum-Mabe, and it remains in the possession of his daughters, the Misses Hoblyn of Pentrelew, while other portions of various monuments are said to have been buried in the churchyard. This will doubtless be considered sufficient reason for briefly recording what yet remains.

Commencing with the monuments of the Arundells as the most ancient, we find that contrary to the brasses at Mawgan-in-Pydar, which have been recently re-fixed, these at St. Columb remain firmly fixed to the stone slabs by apparently the original fastenings. They were originally in the Arundell chapel (a chauntry built by the Arundells on the south side of the chancel of the parish church), and were, early in the present century, covered with some pews which were then placed in the chapel; on the restoration of the church a few years since, the chapel being re-pewed, they were removed to their present position, which is an unfortunate selection, as it subjects them to a large amount of wear from the feet of persons passing over them, they being on the floor of the nave immediately below the chancel steps.

They are composed of two large slabs of grey marble; the one on the south side, which is the oldest by nearly one hundred years, is in memory of Sir John Arundell, father of Sir John Arundell with whom commences the pedigree of Arundell of Lanherne, in the Heralds' Visitation of

Cornwall in 1620, *vide* Harleian publications. The stone measures 7 feet 4 inches by 3 feet 9 inches; around it, 3 inches from the edge, is a plain fillet of brass bearing this inscription: "✠ John Arundell Knyght of ye Bath and Knyght Banneret Recey[ver of] ye Duchye of Cornwall ffirst ma[ryed y Lady] Elizabeth Grey daughter to the Lorde Marquis of Dorset & [Catherine] daughter of Syr Thomas Gr[enville Knyght & dyed ye ey]ght of ffebruary the xxxvi yere of the reigne of Kyng Henry the eyght An^o^ Domini 1545 and ye yere of his age."

The brass bearing those parts of the inscription enclosed in brackets has been lost. In the upper part of the stone are the figures in brass of Sir John Arundell and his two wives, whose parentage is given in the above inscription. They are finely cut. Sir John is in the military costume of that period; behind his right shoulder rises a staff bearing a square banner, but unfortunately the matrix alone tells us this, as the brass itself of this with the crest and a portion of the helmet and lambrequin, upon which the head of the knight rests, has long since disappeared; the banner was probably charged with the quartered coat of Arundell without any impalement. Over the lady on the right hand of the knight, and whose head rests on a square cushion, is a shield with the following arms, viz.: Per pale, the dexter quarterly of six,—1. Six swallows (Arundell); 2. Four fusils conjoined in fesse (Dynham); 3. In chief a double arch, in base a single one (Arches); 4. An escutcheon within an orle of martlets (Chideocke of Chideocke, co. Dorset); 5. A bend (Carminow); 6. As the first. Impaling, quarterly of eight,—1. Barry of six, in chief three roundels (Grey, Marquis of Dorset); 2. A maunche (Hastings); 3. Barry of ten, an orle of martlets (de Valence, Earl of Pembroke); 4. Seven mascles conjoined three, three and one (de Quincy, Earl of Winchester); 5. Gone, probably a cinquefoil, for Bellomont, Earl of Leicester; 6. Gone, probably a fesse and canton, for Widville, Earl Rivers; 7. Six mullets, pierced, three, two and one (Bonville); 8. A fret (Harrington); for Sir John and his first wife, who was Elizabeth, daughter of Thomas Grey, first Marquis of Dorset (by his second wife, Cecilia, daughter and heir of William, Lord Bonville and Harrington); Sir J. B. Burke calls this lady Eleanor, not Elizabeth, as on the brass.

Over the lady on the left hand of the knight is a shield, Arundell as before, impaling, 1 and 4, Three sufflues, or organ rests (Grenville); 2 and 3, on a bend three roundels (Whitleigh), for the second wife of Sir John, and daughter of Sir Thomas Grenville of Stowe, Knt.; beneath the principal figures, which measure 29 inches in height, are two shields, flanked on either side by a small figure with a fillet of brass over each for their names; both the fillets are gone, as are also the figure and shield on the right hand side; they probably represented Sir John Arundell and his arms, ancestor of the Arundells of Lanherne and Chideocke: the head of the remaining figure is also gone, the shield is charged with the arms of Arundell quarterly as above, impaling, quarterly of four, 1. Howard, Duke of Norfolk; 2. De Brotherton; 3. Warren; 4. Mowbray. These are for Sir Thomas Arundell, Knt., who married Margaret, daughter and co-heir of Lord Edmund Howard, third son of Thomas, Duke of Norfolk; she was sister to Catherine, fifth wife of Henry VIII.; Sir Thomas Arundell was the second son of Sir John by his first wife, Lady Elizabeth Grey, and was ancestor of the present Lords Arundell of Wardour.

Beneath these, again, are the matrixes of two groups of children, the only part of the brass of these remaining being the label over the group to the spectator's right, which bears the names, "Joan Eleanor Mary." Below these, and forming the lowest part of the monument, are four shields, the second of which is pointed out by the matrix only: they are as follows:—First shield, per pale the dexter quarterly, 1 and 4, on a bend ermines, cotised, three boars' heads couped (Edgcumbe); 2 and 3, Semée-de-lis, and a lion rampant gardant (Holland). Impaling Arundell quarterly of six as above. Elizabeth, daughter of Sir John Arundell, married Sir Richard Edgcumbe of Mount Edgcumbe, Knt., Sheriff of Devon 35 Henry VIII.; Sir Richard married, secondly, Winefred, daughter of William Essex, Esq. The second shield is gone, but was doubtless charged with the arms of Arundell as above, for Jane, daughter of Sir John Arundell, who died unmarried in 1577, her will dated 2 Sep. 1575, was proved 31 Oct. 1577. Third shield, per pale, the dexter quarterly of eight, 1. A bend engrailed (Ratcliffe); 2. A fesse between two chevrons (Fitz-Walter); 3. A lion rampant crowned within a bordure; 4. A saltire engrailed; 5. Gone; 6. Three bars; 7. Semée-de-lis; 8. An infant swaddled, thereon an eagle preying, wings addorsed. Impaling Arundell quarterly as above.

Mary, daughter of the said Sir John Arundell, married Robert Ratcliffe, K.G., Earl of Sussex, so created 8 December, 1529; she was his third wife, the first being Elizabeth, daughter of Henry, Duke of Buckingham, and the second was Margaret, daughter of Thomas, Earl of Derby; his lordship died in 1542, having issue by his third wife, a son, Sir John Ratcliffe, Knt., obiit sine prole. Fourth shield, per pale the dexter quarterly of four, 1. A lion rampant (Fitz-Alan); 2. Three bars; 3. A fesse and canton (Widville); 4. 1 and 4 a fret, 2 and 3 a chief (Maltravers); impaling Arundell quarterly as above. The last-named Mary Arundell, widow of Robert, Earl of Sussex, married secondly to Henry Fitz-Alan, 18th Earl of Arundell, K.G.; she was his second wife, the first being her cousin Lady Catherine Grey, daughter of Thomas, 2nd Marquis of Dorset, by which lady the Earl alone had issue, viz., a son, who died *sine prole*, and two daughters, his co-heirs, Joanna, married John, Lord Lumley, and died *sine prole;* and Mary, married Thomas Howard,

Duke of Norfolk, by which marriage the Earldom and Castle of Arundell came to the Howards.

The other brass, or rather series of brasses—for it consists, as does the one before noticed, of several separate pieces let into a large ledger stone measuring 6 feet 10 inches by 3 feet 5 inches—is in a very good state of preservation, and quite complete. At the top of the stone, in the centre is a shield per pale, six swallows (Arundell) impaling on a bend three bucks' heads caboshed (Stanley); over the dexter coat a helmet surmounted by the crest of Arundell, a wolf passant, on a wreath; over the sinister coat a helmet supporting the crest of Stanley, viz., on a wreath an infant swaddled, thereon an eagle preying, wings addorsed, all backed by a mantling. To the dexter of this shield is another, charged with six martlets (Arundell), and to the sinister a third shield with the arms of Stanley, as in the impaled coat. Beneath these are figures of Sir John Arundell, Knt., in the military costume of the period, and his lady; on the right of the knight two sons kneeling, and on the left of his wife are four daughters, also kneeling, all above an oblong brass with the following inscription in Roman characters:—

"D. O. M.

"In hoc Divi Colvmbi Magnorvm sepvltvra Arvndeliorvm vbi intemerata fvlgent sacra atrato hoc marmore tegitvr Depositvm Nobil^mj Ioannis Arvndelij ord. Eqvest. vna cvm sva conivge Anna Stanley filia Thomæ ill^mj Comitis Derbiensis. Horvm progenies dvo fvere filii Ioannes et Georgivs, filiæ vero qvinqve Dorothæ, Elizabetha, Cicilia, Margareta, Gertrvda.

"Depositarij hi vt sangvine ita et virtvtibvs Clavere, Amorque Patris in Ioannem Filium Parentibus, exemplo fvit vixere hic ad 60, illa ad 71 ætatis annvm et postmodvm hic positi svnt ad svos maiores, ille 17 Novem. illa 22° Sept. A° Salvtis ille 1590, illa 1602."

Below this are three more shields: first, Arundell alone, without any quarters; second, Arundell alone, impaling, three lozenge-shaped buckles, the points of the tongues to the dexter (Jarnegan or Jerningham), surmounted by two helmets, the one on the dexter side bearing the crest of Arundell as above, the other that of Jerningham, namely, from a crest coronet a falcon's head between two wings expanded, the whole surrounded by a mantling. The third shield, Jerningham, as in the impaled coat. These are followed by the figures of John Arundell, Esq., in armour, with the long leather boots then in use; on his right four sons standing; on his left his wife, who has on her left seven daughters standing. These figures surmount a second oblong plate of brass bearing the inscription that here follows:—

"D. O. M.

"Eodem svb marmore svnt etiam Deposita Nobil^mi viri Joannis Arvndelij filii hvivsce eqvitis, et Annæ Iarnegan svæ Conivgis fæminæ vt Religione præstantis; ita clarissimo orivndæ stemmate Illvstrissimorvm Baronvm de Dacres Partivm Borealivm.

"His filii qvatvor, Ioannes, Michæl, Thomas, Georgivs, filiæqve septem, Maria Magdalena, Maria, Anna, Catherina, Dorothea, Winefreda, vt in Ioanne Patre ita in Ioanne hic seprlto filio incalvit relativa affectio, adeo vt amori Paterno plene responsa dederit filij Pietas, qvi vt possessionvm, ita et virtvtvm amplam hæriditatem accepit, Obiit 22° Ivlij, Scalari svo A° septvagesimo nimirvm ascenden^s ad Reqviem laboribvs et doloribvs annorvm exemtvs salvtis vero hvmanæ 1633."

There is a small brass near the priests' door in the chapel on the north side of the chancel, 16 inches by 12, bearing the following inscription and these arms, viz., in a lozenge-shaped shield, with lines to shew the colours, surrounded by floral scrolls, quarterly, 1 and 4, Azure, three stirrups with leathers Or, within a bordure engrailed Argent pellettée; 2. Argent, two bars nebulée sable, on a canton gules, a mullet Argent, pierced; 3. Sable, three infants' heads couped below the shoulder, each environed round the neck with a snake; on an escutcheon of pretence, Sable, six swallows argent, three, two, and one (Arundell).

"Dame Frances Gifford
relict of
Sr Jno Gifford Bar^t
died Febr^y 28th 1752
aged 48 years."

The four following are from floor slabs in the south chancel aisle, or Lady Chapel:

(1.) Arms: Six swallows (Arundell) impaling a pale and three bucks' heads erased (Roper). In the centre of the dexter coat was originally the badge of a baronet, but it has been erased. Crest: a wolf passant, over a knight's helmet.

"Here lyeth inter'd ye Body of
Sr John Arundell K^{nt}
who died October the 13th 1701
Aged 78 years.
Requiescat in Pace."

This slab was originally inscribed "Bart.," over which "K^{nt}" is engraved.

(2) Arms: A cross between four crosses pattée fitchée (Bealing), on an escutcheon of pretence (Arundell); impaling Arundell. Crest: Over an esquire's helmet, on a wreath a demi lion rampant, holding between its paws a cross pattée fitchée.

"Here lyeth the Body of
Sr Richard Bealings
who died October the 30th 1716
Aged 94 years.
Requiescat in Pace."

(3.) Arms: quarterly 1 and 4, Arundell; 2 and 3, Bealing, impaling a cross saltire (Gage).

"Here lyeth the Body of
Mrs. Ann Arundell
who died August the 25th 1718
Aged 34 years.
Requiescat in Pace."

This lady was second daughter of Joseph Gage, Esq., of Sherborne Castle (fourth son of Sir Thomas Gage of Firle, second Bart., by Mary, eldest daughter and co-heiress of John Chamberlain, Esq., of Sherborne Castle, co. Oxford), by his wife Elizabeth, daughter and eventual heir of George Penruddock, Esq. She was sister of Thomas, first Viscount Gage.

(4.) Arms: Bealing, on an escutcheon of pretence, Arundell; impaling Arundell.

"Here lyeth the Body
of the Lady Frances Bealings
who died December the 16th 172 .
aged 63 years.
Requiescat in Pace."

A portion of this last slab is covered by a pew.

The remaining monuments are, with one exception, in the north chancel aisle, or Jesus Chapel, and are as follows:—

On a ledger stone (or floor slab) these arms: Three talbots passant, impaling a fesse between two flaunches ermine. Crest almost obliterated. It is in memory of Giles Hamley of St. Columb Major, second son of William Hamley of Trebelthicke, in Great Mabyn, co. Cornwall. He married first, Barbara daughter of Philip Hawkins of Pennance, gent., by whom he had no issue; and he married secondly, Grace, daughter of Thomas Hoblyn of Tresaddern, gent., who, with six children, survived him. The above Giles Hamley died 20 Sept. 1738, aged 41.

A floor slab for Grace Hamley, who died 20 Nov. 1786. (This slab is almost obliterated.)

Another partly obliterated floor slab for Grace, wife of Thomas Hamley, clerk, and daughter of the Rev. John Tregenna, Rector of Mawgan, by Elizabeth his wife. She died 19 April, 1761, aged 23. The above Thomas Hamley, clerk, died 9 June, 1766, aged 35.

Another floor slab for Johanna Hamley, daughter of Giles Hamley, gent., and Grace his wife, died 25 May, 1760, aged 32.

Ledger stone against the wall on the north side of the altar, for

Thomas Hoblyn of Nanswhyden, Esq., who died Dec. 1635, aged 69. On it are three shields, viz., in the centre, quarterly: 1, A fesse between two flaunches ermine; 2, On a bend three swallows volant, in chief a crescent for difference; 3, Per chevron, in base a lozenge; 4, On a fesse three escallops, in chief a crescent for difference. This is between two other shields, viz., on the dexter, a chevron between three trefoils (Trevalcois); on the sinister side four fusils ermine, within a border of the second (Dynham).

Mural tablet with a shield, from which the arms are quite gone. It is in memory of Robert Hoblyn of Nanswhyden, Esq., who married Jane, only daughter of Thomas Coster, Esq., of Bristol, and Jane (Rous) his wife. He died 17 November, 1756, aged 46.

Mural tablet in memory of Edward Hoblyn of Tresaddern, Esq., who died 20 May, 1778, aged 69. Also, Ann Hoblyn, relict of the above Edward Hoblyn, Esq., and daughter of John Peter of Harlyn, Esq., who died 30 April, 1791, aged 85.

Floor slab, nearly obliterated. Robert Hoblyn, youngest son of the above Thomas Hoblyn. (The remainder of the inscription quite illegible.)

A mural tablet, surmounted by the arms of Vivian, with helmet, crest, and mantling, viz., 1 and 4, or, a chevron azure between three lions' heads erased proper, a chief gules; 2 and 3, argent, a chevron between three Moors' heads couped at the neck sable. Crest: A lion's head erased proper, collared azure, thereon three annulets, or. It sets forth that Robert Hoblyn of Nanswhyden, clerk, M.A., Rector of Ludgevan, and a Justice of the Peace, died 1 Feb. 1705, aged 47, having married Judith, daughter of Francis Burges of St. Earth, gent., and had issue, Francis Hoblyn of Nanswhyden, Esq., who married Penelope, daughter of Sidney Godolphin, Esq. He died 7 Nov. 1711, aged 25, leaving an only son, Robert Hoblyn, Esq., who inherited the estates of his ancestors. In the same vault lies Richard, only son of Richard Pendarves of Pendarves, Esq., by Elizabeth his wife, daughter of Mr. Thomas Corbit of London, merchant, who died 4 June, 1706, aged 21. This monument was erected by William Pendarves of Pendarves, his cousin-german. Thomas Pendarves, M.A., Rector of this parish and Vicar of Mawgan, son of Richard Pendarves of Pendarves, by Catherine, daughter of William Arundell of Menedarva, Esq., married Grace, second daughter of Robert Hoblyn of Nanswhyden, Esq., and had issue one son, William, and a daughter, Grace. He died 16 March, 1703, aged 59. A monument was erected by the widow of the above William Pendarves, daughter of Sidney Godolphin, and who was knighted by Queen Anne in the twenty-third year of his age, and died 13 March, 1726, aged 37, and was buried in Camborne church by his sister, the wife of Mr. Robert Coster.

The arms of Vivian have evidently no right to be attached to this monument; but when the church was restored the monuments were moved and broken, and many destroyed. The inscription itself is almost illegible.

Mural tablet for Edmund Hearle, gent., who died 16 Dec. 1796, aged 39.

Mural tablet for Rev. John Trefusis, M.A., who was for forty-two years Rector of this church, and who died Feb. 14, 1843, aged 69. (There is, also, a small brass plate to this Rev. J. Trefusis.)

A slate slab much carved, and with these arms: First shield, a chevron between three lions' heads erased, a chief. Crest: on a wreath a lion's head erased, gorged with a collar, charged with three annulets (Vivian). Second shield, ermine, a calf passant gules. Crest: on a wreath a savage, holding in his right hand an oak sapling torn up by the roots (Cavell). It records that beneath lies buried Charles Vivian, Elizabeth Vivian, and one son, unbaptised, of the six sons and one daughter of John Vivian of Trewan, Esq. Charles was aged five years, Elizabeth was aged one year and a-half. John Vivian died 17 Sept. 1630.

A mural tablet in memory of Thomas Vivian and Ann, for forty years his wife. He died 18 May, 1616. She died 25 March, 1635. John Vivian, their son and heir, married Frances, daughter and heir of Francis Buller, Esq. She died 6 Nov. 1613, and he married secondly, Mary, daughter and co-heiress of William Cavell, Esq., and their son and heir John Vivian married Anne, daughter of Sir John Trelawny, Knight and Baronet. She died 17 March, 1638, having had issue John and Elizabeth.

Mural tablet for Anne, daughter of Sir John Trelawny, Bart., and wife of John Vivian, eldest son and heir of John Vivian and Mary his wife, daughter and co-heir of William Cavell, Esq. She had issue John and Elizabeth, and died 17 March, 1638.

Mural monument, carved and coloured after the style of the period, surmounted with the arms with helmet and mantling, viz., Per pale, or, a chevron azure between three lions' heads erased proper, a chief gules impaling or, two bends engrailed sable. Crest: a lion's head erased proper, gorged with a collar azure, charged with three annulets argent. In memory of Frances, wife of Thomas Vivian of Trewan, Esq., and one of the sisters of William Blathwayt of Ditham, co. Gloucester, who died 16 March, 1707.

In the Churchyard.

Against the outside of the north wall is a large monument with three shields, the centre one, Per pale, on a bend three lions passant gardant, in chief a crescent for difference; on the shield to the dexter side are three falcons' heads erased (Sawle); on that to the sinister side, a chevron between three lions' heads erased, and a chief (Vivian). James Beauford, M.A., sometime Rector of Lanteglos; he married, first, Ann, daughter of Joseph Sawle, Esq[r] of Penrice. He married secondly, Jane, daughter of John Vivian, and died 19 March, 1720, aged 69.

Another mural tablet near the last, for Samuel Nicholls Nankivell, died 22 Aug[t] 1816, aged 34. James Stevens Nankivell, died 12 Feb. 1806, aged 4 months. James Stevens Nankivell, died 18 April, 1808, aged 14 months. Frances Nankivell, died 25 Feb. 1819, aged 14 years and 8 months. Catherine, wife of the above Samuel Nankivell, died 26 June, 1853, aged 71.

Also, inscriptions for—

John Hicks of Retallick, in this parish, died 11 Sept. 1818, aged 62.

John Hicks, son of the late John Hicks of Retallick and Betty his wife, died 15 June, 1832, aged 42.

Joseph Hicks Rowe, son of James Rowe and Betsey his wife, of Trevithick in this parish, died 20 June, 1847, aged 31.

Sarah Tregenna, youngest daughter of the Rev. John Tregenna, Rector of Mawgan and Roach, died 10 May, 1807, aged 61.

The above Samuel Nicholls Nankivell was the youngest of the six children of Thomas Nankivell, Esq., Surgeon, of Wadebridge (born in 1736 and died in 1822). S. N. Nankivell lived at St. Columb, and had five children, of whom the only survivor is the present John Hicks Nankivell, Esq., M.R.C.S., etc., of York, of whose six children four sons survive, the eldest being Herbert Nankivell, Esq., M.D., of Bournemouth, Hants. The name Nankivell is pure Keltic, and means the "Glen of Woodcocks;" a glen so-called (generally spelt Nanskevall), with its fine old oak wood, lies about two miles from St. Columb.

For the imperfections of the Work I must crave the forbearance of those who consult it. The transcript was made with great care, and it was intended to have read the proof sheets with the original Register; but notwithstanding the ready permission to transcribe these Registers for printing accorded by the Rector, the Rev. H. L. Ventris, M.A., and the Churchwardens, George Browne Collins, Esq., and Henry Whitford, Esq., when it was decided to issue the Work in a periodical form, the Rector took such an objection to the alteration, that he refused permission for the comparison to be made, and that must, therefore, be the excuse for any errors or omissions; but such, I believe, will be found to be few and unimportant.

Circumstances have prevented any variations or additions being made from the Archdeacon's transcripts at Bodmin, as was at first intended, and the notes being otherwise extended.

The opportunity is here taken to acknowledge the thanks due for the facilities given by the Clergymen of the various parishes from whose Registers extracts have been made for the purpose of annotating this Work, and also the cordial assistance rendered by other gentlemen, especially by Col. J. L. Chester, LL.D., and Colonel Vivian.

The thanks of Genealogists are due to the publishers, Messrs. Mitchell and Hughes, for the careful manner in which they have carried out the printing and embellishment of the Work, and in having taken upon themselves the responsibility of the heavy expense of making the experiment as to whether this class of work can be made to pay its own way, the result of their enterprise in the present instance being a loss, chiefly arising from the bulk of the work.

The elaborate Index, involving considerable labour, has been prepared, with his usual care and skill, by Mr. W. Wood Davis, M.A., of Plymouth.

Plymouth, January, 1881.

TO FACE "BAPTISMS" PAGE 1.

Richard A. Hoblyn.

Edward Hoblyn.

The Registers

OF

St. Columb Major, Cornwall.

BAPTISMS.

ANNO 1540.*

1 Jan. Wylliam s. of Dronisye Cresye
17 Jan. Richard s. of Thomas Kartert†
18 Jan. John father Walter Jenken
20 Jan. William s. of John Melhynnocke
23 Jan. Olyff d. of Henry Arthur
25 Jan. Elizabeth d. of Richard Nanconan
30 Jan. Margerie d. of Rawlinge Typpett
7 Feb. Elizabeth d. of John Knight
8 Mar. Columbe s. of John Trehare
17 Mar. Phillep d. of Thomas Tomeow (?)‡
20 Mar. John s. of John Pears
23 Mar. Ursula d. of James Nanskevell

ANNO 1541.

17 April Jane d. of Richard Grose
18 April Henrie s. of Robert Sexton
19 April Jane d. of John Crickbie
20 April Katherine d. of William Hawke
20 April Jannett d. of John Edward
8 May Ursula d. of Thomas Poythe (?)
15 May John s. of Edward Geyne
16 May Alse (Alice) d. of John Hetherd
17 May Stephen s. of William Smyth

* There have evidently been some leaves torn out at the beginning of the book, and being sewed in pairs, probably eight pages are gone; compare with first entries of burials.

† This is the Richard Carter with whom the pedigree of Carter in the 'Visitation of Cornwall, 1620,' commences.

‡ Names marked thus (?) were too illegible to make out clearly.

8 May *John s. of John Clerke
25 May George s. of William Mayhow
26 May Alson d. of Richard Tremaine
22 June Agnes d. of Robert Gwynnow
23 June Johane d. of John Coward
12 July Henrie s. of Robert Torway
13 July Maude d. of Luke Pollard
19 July Margaret d. of Richard Osborne
23 July Jane d. of Pears Marten
4 Aug. Robert s. of John Pabe
6 Aug. Tamson d. of Thomas Nanskevell
18 Aug. Tamson d. of John Clemow
23 Aug. Katherine d. of John Hawke
12 Sep. Alson d. of Marke Wylliams
14 Sep. Jane d. of Stephen Lawrie
14 Sep. John s. of Edward Myll
8 Oct. Jannett d. of Richard Rowse
9 Oct. Richard s. of William Sprey
1 Nov. Jane d. of John Sandowe
1 Nov. Margaret d. of John Sandowe
18 Dec. Jane d. of John Hockie
20 Dec. Emblenn d. of William Mayhow
22 Dec. Agnes d. of Thomas Treluddrow
25 Jan. Margaret d. of Nicholas Lyscott
15 Jan. Richard s. of Edmond Braye
29 Jan. Richard s. of John Davie
8 Feb. Humphrey s. of Marke Jolie
25 Feb. Richow d. of John Chaplayn
25 Feb. Thomas s. of Stephen Knight
2 Mar. Thomas s. of John Stephen
5 Mar. Constance d. of Richard Adam

* There are several instances besides this one of entries omitted in their proper place and afterwards inserted.

Anno 1542.

2 April Jane d. of Richard Watt
3 April Edwarde s. of Manuel Roger
11 April Jane d. of Edward Meryfeild
14 May John s. of Wm Ryse
23 May Luke s. of Remfrey Carter
29 May Robert s. of William Safroyne
17 June Thomas s. of Agnes Heatherd
27 June Richard s. of John Melhynnocke
6 July James s. of John Knight
12 July Ursula d. of Richard Typpett
15 July Richard s. of John Morthe
23 July Margaret d. of John ffraunce
10 Aug. Phillep d. of Richard Nicholls
10 Aug. John s. of James John Jane*
14 Aug. Agnes d. of Thomas Meryfeild
14 Aug. John s. of Bennett Bone
18 Aug. Thomas s. of William Bennett
19 Aug. James s. of Marke Williams
21 Aug. Jane d. of Nicholas Stephen
21 Aug. Henry s. of James Typpett
3 Sep. James s. of Henry Typpett
3 Sep. Margerie d. of Thomas Powyll
4 Sep. Thomas s. of Richard Reve
22 Sep. Otes s. of William Prowse
27 Sep. Thomas and John bastards to Rowland Brytaine
4 Oct. Ursula d. of John Willm Elsabeth
9 Oct. Jane d. of Harrie Clickett
17 Oct. Stephen s. of Allen Whytte
20 Oct. John s. of John Cowarde
10 Dec. Margerie and Jane ds. of Thomas Spreybond
. . . . . Richard s. of John M . . ll .†
21 Dec. John s. of John Tom
28 Dec. James s. of John Howe
10 Jan. Jane d. of Thomas Penyse
11 Jan. Jane d. of John Cryckbie
13 Jan. Jane d. of John Copithorne
14 Jan. Jane d. of one Wylmot
17 Jan. Pascow d. of Henrie Yolde
22 Jan. Henry s. of John Phillep
6 Feb. Robert s. of John Bennett
5 Feb. John s. of Pascow Hey
10 Feb. Marie d. of Remfrey William
13 Feb. Ursula d. of William ffoore
22 Feb. Remfrey s. of Jenken Adam
25 Feb. John s. of William Sprey
2 Mar. John s. of John Sandow
21 Mar. Elizabeth d. of Thomas Rowe

Anno 1543.

29 Mar. Margaret d. of Thomas Toabe
2 April Henry s. of William Smyth
4 April Phillep d. of John Hocken
6 April Jane d. of James Rosoyan
15 April Jane d. of Nicholas Dyar
20 May Katherine d. of John Clerke
23 May John s. of William Phillep
27 May Richard s. of John Sprey
30 May Thomas s. of Richard Tremaine
9 June John s. of Robert Tregonna
13 June Tamson d. of Richard Watte
16 June Rawlinge s. of Richard Torker
28 June Jane d. of Thomas Carter
30 June Richard and Katherine children of Stephen Jenyn
5 July Agnes d. of Robert John
5 July Antonie s. of John Bryton
9 July Jane d. of John Davie
29 July Marie d. of Thomas Beare
3 Aug. Katherine d. of Richard German
4 Aug. Tamson d. of John Olver
8 Aug. Richard s. of John James
11 Aug. Elizabeth d. of Robert Gwynnow
17 Aug. Agnes d. of John Jenyn
28 Aug. Jane d. of Robert Udy Symon
16 Sep. Helyn d. of John ffraunce
1 Oct. William s. of John Knight
2 Oct. Lawrence s. of Alexander Siblie
4 Oct. ffraunce s. of Richard Nancarow
23 Oct. William s. of John Hetherd
23 Oct. Bennett his mother named Johane
28 Oct. Jane d. of John Pears
22 Nov. Phillep d. of John Trehar
26 Nov. Jane d. of John Stephen
20 Dec. Thomas s. of John Treluddrowe
29 Dec. Thomas s. of John Edwarde
9 Jan. Katherine d. of John Bennett
12 Jan. Tamson d. of John Pabe
21 Jan. William s. of Thomas Meryfeild
28 Jan. Ursula d. of John Jenken
8 Feb. Ursula d. of Nicholas Lyscott
8 Feb. John s. of an Irish begger
18 Feb. John s. of Stephen Lawrie
23 Feb. Agnes d. of Thomas Trinckler
1 Mar. John and Margaret the children of John Gylbert

* The three names are so in the Register; a person with two Christian names appears in Oct. this same year, namely, John Wm Elsabeth. Jane has long continued a surname in the parish.

† This entry is at the foot of a page in the original, and has been cut out; this is the only instance in the whole Register of a part of a leaf being cut out. The name is evidently Moylle. The entry on the other side is quite cut out, which was the one, doubtless, which it was desired to suppress.

2 Mar. Columb s. of Thomas Treluddrowe
3 Mar. Margerie d. of John Bosse
4 Mar. Pastha d. of Thomas Dasowe
7 Mar. Tamson d. of Robert Brokre
8 Mar. Alse d. of John Olyver
11 Mar. Richard s. of Richard Watte
17 Mar. Alsone d. of James John

ANNO 1544.

26 Mar. Edwarde s. of Henry Jobe
8 April Jannett d. of Marke Jobe
10 April Vivian s. of John Browne
1 May Remfrey s. of John Clemmowe
17 May Henry s. of Henry Artur
2 June Jane d. of John Menhire
7 June John s. of Walter Blake
13 June William s. of John Moyle
10 July Johane d. of Otes Nanow
28 July Vivian s. of Edward Merifeild
30 July Pasca d. of John Torker
15 Aug. Otes s. of Walter Merifeild
23 Aug. Richard s. of William ffreere
27 Aug. George s. of John Tome
4 Sept. Richard s. of John Sandowe
16 Sept. Richard s. of John Teake
16 Sept. Emblen d. of John Chapleyne
19 Sept. William s. of Richard Adam
23 Sept. Johane d. of John Cowarde
23 Sept. Tamson d. of Thomas Jenken
9 Oct. Vivian s. of Jenken Nancarow
11 Oct. Bawden s. of John Jane
17 Oct. James s. of Sawndrie John
30 Oct. Vivian s. of Luke Pollard
4 Nov. Winnifred d. of Humphrey Tyfford
8 Nov. Johane d. of Richard Tom
23 Nov. Richard s. of Richard Rist
23 Nov. Alson d. of James Horken
8 Dec. Jane d. of John Rosewarne
20 Dec. Nowell s. of William Mayhowe
4 Jan. Jane d. of Henrie Rowse
20 Jan. Jane d. of John Clerke
22 Jan. Agnes d. of Robert Tregonna
31 Jan. Richard s. of Thomas Jenyn
22 Feb. Petronell d. of Thomas Merifeild
22 Feb. Johane a bastard to Udy Brytton
25 Feb. Margarett d. of Thomas Tynckler
4 Mar. William s. of Christopher Trevithan
9 Mar. John s. of John Moylle
9 Mar. William s. of Thomas Carter
12 Mar. Jane d. of Otes Bennett

ANNO 1545.

19 Mar. Humphrey s. of Emanuell Roger
28 Mar. Richard s. of Udie Myll
28 Mar. Marie d. of Thomas Scryvener
29 Mar. Tamson d. of William Bennett
5 April Constance d. of John Jeffery
14 April Emblen d. of James Vincent
15 April Alson d. of John Jenynge
23 April Humphrey s. of Richard Bere
26 April Jane d. of John Copithorne
29 April John s. of Allen Whytte
17 May Henrie s. of Richard Typpett
1 June John s. of Thomas Dasowe
1 June Marie d. of John Trehare
2 June John s. of Thomas Nanscarow
18 June John s. of James Rosegan
20 June John s. of Richard Sprey
1 July Tamson d. of Richard Gascoyne
3 July Pascatte d. of Marke Bennye
30 July Jane d. of John Stephens
30 July John s. of Thomas Williams
4 Aug. Katherine d. of William Trenowth
6 Aug. John his mother named Christian
13 Aug. Tamson her mother named Jane Symon
14 Aug. Jane d. of Mark William
3 Sept. John s. of John Davie
16 Sept. John s. of Henrie Pluegie
23 Sept. William s. of Robert Gwynnowe
1 Oct. Thomas s. of William Prowse
3 Oct. Alson d. of James John Jane
16 Oct. John s. of John Menhire
25 Oct. Jane d. of Udie Hodge
27 Oct. Margaret d. of Richard Trenuyrth
27 Oct. Richard s. of Edward Meryfeild
16 Nov. Richard s. of John Norton
8 Dec. Jane d. of Richard Osborne
8 Dec. Richard s. of Pascow Anhey
17 Dec. Thomas s. of Thomas Berd
20 Dec. John s. of John James
10 Jan. Jane d. of Jenken Adam
16 Jan. Thomas s. of Thomas Teake
27 Jan. Elizabeth d. of Robert Jolliff
26 Jan. William s. of John Sprey
7 Feb. Thomas s. of Thomas Tinckley
10 Feb. Henrie s. of John Teake
11 Feb. Henrie his mother Margerie Pynnocke
20 Feb. Richard s. of John ffraunce
24 Feb. Thomas s. of John Pabe
12 Mar. Remfrey s. of William Ryst
17 Mar. Antonie s. of John Edward
25 Mar. Elizabeth d. of Robert Jobham

ANNO 1546.

4 April Elizabeth d. of John Clymowe
12 April Henrie s. of John Sampson
13 April Pascow s. of John Bennett
18 April John s. of Stephen Jenyne
20 April William s. of Walter Merifeild
24 April Ursula d. of Thomas Rawe
9 May Jane d. of Remfrey Grosse
10 May Thomas s. of John Hetherd
21 May Jane d. of Otes Dyar
10 June ffraunce s. of William Phillep
12 June John s. of Christopher Darr
13 June Robert s. of Stephen Pascowe
8 Aug. John s. of Marke Williams
8 Aug. Marie d. of John Darr
15 Aug. Elizabeth d. of John Jenken
25 Aug. Ursula d. of Richard Nanscarow
31 Aug. Henrie s. of William Hawke
3 Oct. John s. of Jenyne
4 Oct. Tamson d. of John Perse
15 Oct. William s. of Raff Kerne *alias* Michell
17 Oct. Jane d. of Henrie Rowse
20 Oct. Richard s. of William Jolliff
6 Nov. Elizabeth d. of Robert Sexton
16 Nov. Jane d. of Richard Osborne
23 Nov. William s. of Robert Vages
2 Dec. Richard s. of John Calway
10 Dec. John s. of Richard Rawlinge
30 Dec. Richard s. of John Warren
11 Jan. Tamsone d. of John Lawry
22 Jan. John s. of John Clerke
23 Jan. John s. of Udie Geyne
17 Feb. Jane d. of John Manhire
15 Mar. William s. of John Jane
18 Mar. Margerie d. of William Sprey
23 Mar. Katherine her mother Agnes Henssoocke

ANNO 1547. E. SIXTH.

1 April Emblen her mother named Elizabeth
2 April John and John the children of John Pabe
13 May Antonie s. of Richard Torker
24 May Scelie d. of John Moylle
13 June Jane d. of Thomas Nanscaven
19 June Thomas s. of Otes Dyer
26 June Richard s. of John Harrie
5 July James s. of Richard Typpett
20 July Bennett s. of Thomas Treluddrowe
21 July William s. of John Davie
11 Aug. Richard s. of John Copithorne
15 Aug. William s. of Stephen Pascowe
28 Aug. Adam s. of Otes Jeffery
8 Sep. Phillep d. of Robert Tregona
10 Oct. Elizabeth and Jane the children of Richard Rawe
21 Oct. Jane d. of John Chaplaine
12 Nov. Remfrey s. of James Vyncent
15 Nov. John s. of Christopher Darr
16 Nov. Johane d. of William Hawke
23 Nov. Pethroke s. of John Trevenan
15 Dec. Margerie d. of John Teake
16 Dec. Walter s. of Richard Ryst
20 Dec. Johane d. of Henrie Anhey
23 Dec. Marie d. of John Sprey
28 Dec. Alse d. of John Cowarde
4 Jan. Jane d. of John Stephen
7 Jan. Elizabeth d. of Jane Rosegan
10 Jan. Marten s. of John Hyndyrorke
12 Jan. Richard s. of Robert Vicar
16 Jan. Udie s. of one Campie
22 Jan. Thomas his mother named Johane
18 Jan. Humphrey s. of Henrie Udie
23 Jan. Henrie s. of John Hawke
3 Feb. Henrie s. of Thomas Jenyn
3 Feb. James s. of Manuell Roger
12 Feb. Robert s. of Robert Jolliffe
14 Feb. Johane d. of Henrie Jolliff
15 Feb. Richard s. of John Brytaine
28 Feb. John the mother Elizabeth Marten
9 Mar. Henrie s. of Thomas Teake
16 Mar. Jane d. of John Pabe
18 Mar. Jane d. of Thomas Bennye

ANNO 1548.

1 April Jane d. of Stephen Benny
4 April Thomas s. of Edward Merifeild
2 May Jane d. of Allen Whytte
11 May John s. of Richard Cregon
19 May Thomas s. of John Nanskevell
2 June Agnes d. of William Bennett
4 June Jane d. of John Melvis
11 June Jane the mother Elizabeth Marke
11 June Henrie s. of Pascowe Anhey
13 June William s. of Robert Gwynnowe
24 June John s. of Henrie Pluysie
24 June Jane d. of Walter Meryfeild
21 June Pastha bastard the mother Jane Marke
21 June John s. of James Halwoyer
8 July Henrie s. of John Illerie
9 July John and Bennett the children of John Joppe
19 July John s. of John Illarie
22 July Alson d. of Jenken Rowse
22 July Robert s. of John Treluddrowe

13 Aug. Lawrence the mother called Katherine
18 Aug. Dorothie d. of Udie Typpett
19 Aug. John s. of Marten Dyer
4 Sep. John s. of Thomas Tyler
8 Sep. Henrie bastard the mother named Margerie Alm
20 Sep. John s. of John Nicholls
17 Sep. Jane d. of John Rowse
18 Sep. John s. of Marke William
21 Sep. John s. of John Bennett
21 Sep. Margaret d. of Thomas Rogers
21 Sep. Alse d. of Thomas Rawlinge
3 Oct. Olyff d. of Richard Spraye
10 Oct. James s. of Edward Lawrence
22 Oct. Jane d. of Richard Rawe
21 Oct. Marke s. of Stephen Lawrie
4 Nov. Richard s. of John Milhynnyck
8 Nov. Jane d. of John Horkey
8 Nov. William s. of John Jane
9 Nov. Jane d. of Richard Kinge
11 Nov. Emblen d. of Richard Sampson
14 Nov. Margerie d. of Harrie Leven
16 Nov. John s. of Richard ffasher
10 Dec. Margerie d. of William Jolliff
30 Dec. Katherine d. of John Sadler
2 Jan. Jane d. of John Briham
4 Jan. Robert s. of John Sewalsters
24 Jan. Jane d. of John Robyn
30 Jan. Marie a bastard the mother Elizabeth Weaver
8 Feb. Margerie d. of Raff Mirkett
12 Feb. Richard s. of one Cardewe
14 Feb. Jane d. of Stephen Jenyn
17 Feb. Jane d. of John Manhire
22 Feb. James the father John Carwethuff
4 Mar. John s. of William Bawden
10 Mar. Elizabeth d. of Robert Sexton
19 Mar. Elizabeth d. of William Phillep
22 Mar. William bastard the father John Willm Elsabeth
25 Mar. James s. of Marten Clyston

ANNO 1549.

26 Mar. Constance d. of Richard Nicholl
28 Mar. John s. of Richard Torker
6 April Agnes d. of Thomas Treluddrowe
7 April Robert s. of John Calwaie
17 April Phillep d. of Thomas Jenyne
17 April Richard s. of Richard Rawlinge
25 April Jane d. of Robert Jenyne
23 May Margerie d. of John Temple
30 May Tamson d. of John Bettie
9 June Thomas s. of John Jenyne
30 June Stephen s. of Richard Reve
4 July James s. of Richard Nanconan
6 July John s. of William Mayhoue
8 July Elizabeth d. of John Spraye
21 July Olyff d. of Thomas Dasone
30 July Henrie s. of James Younge
30 July John s. of James Younge
2 Aug. Johane d. of William Probose
10 Aug. Johane d. of Harrie Harter
13 Aug. Johane d. of Robert Gwynnowe
21 Aug. George s. of James Weaver
15 Sep. Thomas s. of Robert Tregona
21 Sep. John s. of Humphrey Staple
10 Oct. John the father Lallie Jolle
20 Oct. Pacience d. of William Haygar
19 Nov. Ursula d. of Thomas Richard
27 Nov. Robert s. of Christopher Darr
1 Dec. John s. of John Teake
1 Jan. Alse d. of Harrie Opie
8 Jan. John s. of Stephen Pascowe
8 Jan. Harrie s. of Stephen Pascowe
11 Jan. Jane d. of John Cardewe
15 Jan. Katherine d. of James Rosegan
1 Feb. Thomas s. of John Davie
2 Feb. Henrie s. of John Nanskevell
3 Feb. William s. of Walter Merifeild
3 Feb. Thomas s. of John Campie
5 Feb. Tamson d. of John Pabe
15 Mar. Johane d. of James Vyncent
18 Mar. William s. of Thomas Marke
22 Mar. Agnes d. of Mathew Dyar
25 Mar. William s. of Marke Bennett

ANNO 1550.

30 Mar. Jane the mother Bresitie ffolett
13 April William s. of John Copithorne
8 May Jane d. of Richard Rawlinge
8 May Margarett d. of Richard Rawlinge
25 May Margaret d. of John Eplett
24 June Jane d. of John Yedd
30 June Jane d. of John Chaplaine
17 July Blanch d. of Richard Osborne
19 July Bawden d. of John Moyle
19 July Alise d. of John Moyle
1 Aug. Robert s. of John Hetherd
2 Aug. Emblen d. of Thomas Scryvener
23 Aug. Alse the father John Clemow
30 Aug. Katherine d. of John Stephen
31 Aug. Agnes bastard the father Walter Creppe
7 Sep. Blanch d. of Richard Nicholl
24 Sep. Elizabeth d. of John Clemowe
28 Sep. Elinor d. of Edward Meryfeild
1 Oct. Thomas s. of John Dyar
9 Oct. John ffather William James
23 Oct. Jane d. of Harrie Laven
29 Oct. Jane d. of Richard Nicholas

8 Nov. Harrie s. of William Jolliff
9 Nov. ffraunce s. of Richard Fysher
21 Nov. Harrie s. of John Nicholas
27 Nov. Margaret d. of James Younge
30 Nov. John s. of John Melhynnocke
22 Dec. William s. of Edward Richard
28 Dec. Christopher s. of Manuell Roger
6 Jan. Richard s. of John Hawke
17 Jan. Robert s. of Udie Hodge
21 Jan. Thomas s. of Thomas Dyar
22 Feb. Marg. d. of John Sprey
24 Feb. John s. of Henrie Rowse
5 Mar. Richard s. of Udie Lawrence
10 Mar. John s. of John Vyvian
15 Mar. John s. of John Menhire
15 Mar. Jane d. of ffraunce Adam
18 Mar. Thomas s. of Thomas Bennye

ANNO 1551.

29 Mar. Pasthue d. of Richard Sprey
6 April Harrie s. of John Strongman
9 April John s. of Richard Rawe
11 April John s. of John Jane
16 April James s. of Panscow Anhey
17 April Scipriau s. of John Treluddrow
22 April Thomas s. of John Bryhand
25 April Johane d. of John Sutton
26 April John s. of John Calwaye
26 April Johane d. of John Weaver
8 May Jane d. of John Nanskevell
23 May William s. of Richard Nancouan
31 May Udie father John Adam
8 June Richard s. of Richard Kinge
18 June Umphrey s. of Thomas Ollye
26 June Thomas s. of Stephen Bennye
2 July Katherine s. of John Davie
12 July Phillep s. of William Hodge
19 July Honor d. of Robert Sexton
25 July Tamson d. of James Rawe
26 July Johane d. of Robert Udie
6 Aug. Christopher s. of Richard Rawlinge
23 Aug. Richard s. of Richard Nicholl
24 Aug. Mariett d. of John Braye
30 Aug. John s. of John Horkie
30 Aug. John s. of John Belkie
31 Aug. Richard s. of John Batt
2 Sep. Harrie s. of Harrie Haycrefte
2 Sep. Alse d. of Thomas Calwaie
16 Sep. Alse d. of William Bawden
20 Sep. Richard s. of Richard Tarker
22 Sep. Stephen s. of Stephen Lawrie
4 Oct. Harrie s. of Thomas Jenyne
4 Oct. Stephen s. of Antonie Rawe
21 Oct. William s. of Cost Cardew
26 Oct. Remfrey s. of Harrie Phluyesie

1 Nov. Stephen s. of Stephen Abraham
9 Nov. John s. of Robert Gwynnowe
29 Nov. Margaret d. of Jendgken Adam
29 Nov. John s. of Raff Bishopp
6 Nov. John s. of Richard Typpett
18 Dec. Alse d. of Richard Ryst
1 Jan. Richard s. of Martyn Clyston
3 Jan. ffraunce s. of Christopher Darr
7 Jan. William s. of Harrie Opie
24 Jan. Alse father one Davy
24 Jan. Tamson d. of Thomas Jenken
28 Jan. James s. of Richard John Richard
4 Feb. Remfrey s. of William Pears
22 Feb. Jane d. of Richard Rysowas
5 Mar. Anne d. of Richard ffysher
13 Mar. Thomas s. of William Toake
24 Mar. William s. of William Bennett

ANNO 1552.

1 April Harrie s. of John Campie
3 April Johane d. of John Ornoll
3 April Margerie d. of John Ornoll
20 April Richard s. of John Jenyne
20 April Robert s. of John Jenyne
22 April John s. of John Wylbie
5 May Alse d. of Marke Williams
6 May Robert s. of Humfrey Staple
6 May Johane d. of Humfrey Staple
11 May Richard s. of John Pabe
12 May John s. of ffraunce Adam
16 May Phillep d. of John Richard
20 May James s. of William Phillopp
21 June Harrie s. of ffraunce Typpett
11 July Mellior d. of John James
8 Aug. ffraunce s. of Remfrey Grosse
10 Aug. John s. of Thomas Bond
5 Sep. Johane d. of Bennett Mowne
22 Oct. John s. of John Edye
23 Oct. Phillep d. of Jefferie Allan
5 Nov. Johane d. of Harrie Rosogan
7 Nov. Katherine d. of Robert Tregona
7 Nov. Thomas s. of Robert Tregona
20 Nov. Johane d. of Harrie Lavein
27 Nov. James s. of John Stephen
30 Nov. Richard s. of James Younge
18 Dec. Mylson d. of Robert Gwennowe
31 Dec. John s. of John Copithorne
22 Jan. John s. of John Bettie
2 Feb. Agnes d. of Richard Pearse
12 Feb. Tamson d. of Stephen Bennye
12 Feb. Sciprian s. of Stephen Baker
13 Feb. Margerie d. of John Waren
16 Feb. Jane d. of John Hawke
20 Feb. Katherine d. of John Trewen
23 Feb. Richard s. of John Skrevenor
23 Feb. Jane d. of John Eplett

23 Feb. Margerie d. of John Torwaye
5 Mar. Katherine d. of John Wene
19 Mar. John s. of Richard Nicholas

ANNO 1553.

9 April Jane d. of John Trenowth
1 May Katherine d. of Robert Jenyne
7 May Jane d. of John Nicholas
11 May Constantine s. of Richard Nanconan
20 May Marian d. of Thomas Jenyne
23 May John s. of Marke Williams
29 May Honor d. of Robert Sexton
9 June John s. of Harrie Pollard
10 June John s. of William Marten
23 June John s. of Antonie Rawe
11 June Jane d. of Ots Bennett
2 July Agnes d. of John Merifeild
23 July Tamson d. of Pascowe Anhaye
30 July Richard s. of Lallow Jolle
7 Aug. Harrie s. of Edward Merifeild
23 Aug. ffraunce s. of Richard Rawe
30 Sep. Jane d. of John Vyncent
9 Oct. Katherine d. of Richard Blake
13 Oct. Thomas s. of John Chaplaine
15 Oct. Harrie s. of Thomas Hawke
16 Oct. Richard s. of Henrie Rowse
25 Oct. Barbara d. of John Naukevell
1 Nov. Margerie d. of John Anhey
15 Nov. Peternoll d. of William Ager
20 Nov. Jane d. of John Carter
27 Nov. Jane d. of William Estas
27 Nov. Jane d. of Richard Ryssewas
2 Dec. John s. of William Cocke
7 Dec. Grace d. of John Browne
14 Dec. John s. of Remfrey Hawke
17 Dec. Elizabeth d. of John Braye
17 Dec. Olyff d. of John Braye
25 Nov. Nowell s. of John Tom Robert
2 Jan. John s. of Harrie Heycrefte
7 Jan. John s. of James Younge
16 Jan. Julian s. of Harrie Artor
18 Jan. Margerie d. of Thomas Benny
21 Jan. Elizabeth d. of Harrie Artor
31 Jan. Jane d. of Richard Sprey
2 Feb. John s. of Thomas Tyer
7 Feb. John s. of William John Thomas
24 Feb. William s. of John Warron
28 Feb. William s. of Mathew Dyar
11 Mar. John s. of William John
4 Mar. William s. of John Strongman
11 Mar. Tamson d. of William Hodge
16 Mar. John s. of Thomas Jenken
18 Mar. Johane d. of John Nancolas

ANNO 1554.

1 April Harrie s. of Regnolde Laven
5 April William and Thomas sons of Udie Skeberen
6 April John s. of Robert Gwynnowe
11 April Humphrey s. of James Vyncent
13 April Olyff d. of Richard Torker
30 April Richard s. of Manuell Roger
9 May Tamson d. of Richard Bylky
15 May John s. of Phillep Rosegan
18 May Emblen d. of John Jenynye
18 May Thomas s. of Robert Udie
23 May Agnes d. of Richard Rowe
28 May Jane d. of Thomas Calwaye
2 June Christopher s. of John Batt
2 June John s. of John Calwaye
11 June Robert s. of John Pabe
7 July Elizabeth d. of John Menhynnycke
9 July Alse ffather Thomas Watte
13 July Jenefer d. of Robert Bosowarne
13 Aug. John s. of George Horkie
18 Aug. John s. of Thomas Ollye
28 Aug. John s. of Udie Hodge
4 Sep. Elizabeth d. of Symon John
16 Sep. Richard s. of Jenken Adam
20 Sep. Richard s. of Marke Williams
12 Oct. *G : ...... s. of Pascowe Clalyne
14 Oct. Johane d. of Harrie Laven
16 Oct. *H : ...... s. of John Treludrowe
20 Oct. *J : ...... s. of Stephen Abraham

[*The names of those who were baptised in the rest of the year 1554 were lost or not registered, and from that yere untill the theirteen yere of the reigne of our most gracious Sovereign Ladie Quene Elizabeth that nowe is were lykwise lost or not wryten. But here followe the names of those that were baptised sythence the yere of our Lord God* 1571.]

ANNO 1571.

2 April Thomas s. of Richard Toker
4 April Alse d. of Richard Tremaine
16 April Honor d. of Richard Browne
22 April Pascowe s. of John Langdon
2 May Pascowe s. of John Langdon
20 May Richard s. of Richard Calwaie
6 July Robert s. of Robert Clobert
10 July Richard s. of George Mayhewe
14 July Thomas s. of Thomas Rawe
14 Aug. Marye d. of Ots Meryfeild
10 Sep. Constanc d. of Harrie Typpett
19 Sep. Richard s. of Richard Vyvian
23 Sep. Agnes d. of Richard Teake
23 Sep. Thomas s. of Thomas Jenkyn

* Sic.

8 Oct. Elizabeth d. of Alexander Pawlle
1 Nov. Columba d. of Thomas Stephen
5 Nov. Johane d. of Thomas Pell
3 Nov. Columba d. of Richard Rysewas
10 Nov. Alse d. of Thomas Locke
20 Dec. Alse d. of William Vivian
4 Jan. Honor d. of Harrie Sexton
12 Jan. Johane d. of John Clarke
29 Jan. James s. of George Marke
25 Feb. Katherine d. of Richard Gylle
27 Feb. Alse d. of John Randell
10 Mar. Honor d. of Richard Lukye
12 Mar. Katherine d. of Humphrey Edward
14 Mar. Johane d. of Thomas Hyxt

ANNO 1572.

1 April Edward s. of John Bennett
3 April Humphrey s. of John Skynner
4 April John s. of John Adam
6 April John s. of Richard Pearse
12 April Richard s. of Jefferie Allen
12 April Johane d. of William Tamlen
3 May John s. of Robert Calwaye
10 May Thomas s. of Roger Maben
2 June Richard s. of James Williams
2 June Robert s. of Robert Phillep
6 July Molliar d. of Robert Anhaye
6 July John s. of Richard Norton
24 July Johane d. of John Lyttacott
19 Aug. John s. of John Langdon
28 Aug. Gregorie s. of John Darr
2 Sep. Johane d. of Nicholas Cardewe
10 Sep. Johane d. of Robert Jenyne
22 Sep. Antonie s. of William Rawe
24 Sep. Elizabeth d. of Harrie Geyne
25 Sep. Thomas s. of Humphrey Knight
12 Oct. John s. of John Baylie
22 Oct. Elizabeth d. of Robert Sadler
2 Nov. Richard s. of Richard Oxenham
10 Dec. John mother Margerie Marten
10 Jan. Alse d. of Harrie Laven
28 Jan. Ursula d. of George Marke
10 Feb. Johane d. of John Nicholas
12 Feb. John s. of John Roscorla
16 Feb. Elizabeth d. of Harrie Adam
20 Feb. John s. of Thomas Stephen
26 Feb. John s. of Thomas Vesey
7 Mar. John mother Anlyff Torker
8 Mar. Mylson d. of Alexander Pawll
9 Mar. Thomas s. of Humphrey Vyncent
11 Mar. Elizabeth d. of Nowell Mayhew
20 Mar. John s. of Thomas Nicholas

ANNO 1573.

27 Mar. John s. of John Pabe
28 Mar. William s. of Richard Blake
12 April Hugh s. of Thomas
24 Mar. Olyf d. of Richard Nicholas
3 May Dorothie d. of John Strongman
24 May Phillep d. of John Retallecke
18 June Robert mother Margerie Edwarde
19 June Thomas s. of George Mayhowe
12 July Elizabeth d. of John Vallyes
15 July John s. of Richard Vivian
23 July Johane d. of Otes Merifeild
2 Aug. Elizabeth d. of Humphrey Rowse
7 Aug. Paciene d. of John Cocken
9 Aug. John s. of John Ryse
15 Aug. Malachie mother Anne Edward
20 Aug. Lowdie d. of Thomas Trelawgan
2 Sep. Tamson mother Johane Jenken
18 Sep. William s. of John Langdon
18 Sep. John s. of John Collinges
21 Oct. John s. of Roger Maben
22 Oct. Johane d. of Thomas Tyfford
23 Oct. John mother Richowe Chaplinge
18 Nov. John s. of Richard Nanconan
4 Dec. Oliffe d. of John Peane
18 Dec. Honor d. of John Sprey
7 Jan. Harrie s. of Thomas Tyer
14 Jan. *Syx... d. of ffrance Nanconan
22 Jan. Polhoricke mother Honor Toaker
8 Feb. Johane d. of John Torker
14 Mar. Thomas s. of Robert Phillepp

ANNO 1574.

10 April Richard s. of Richard Oxenham
30 April Tamson mother Anne Robyn
2 May John s. of John Cardew
10 May Johane d. of Robert Marke
9 June Thomas s. of Humphrey Manuell
20 July William s. of Thomas Hawke
30 July Olyff d. of John Geyne
23 Aug. Olyff d. of Richard Vyvian
26 Aug. John s. of John Retallacke
30 Aug. James s. of Nowell Mayhowe
20 Sep. William s. of John Pearse
3 Oct. ffraunces and John sons of Nicholas Treman
3 Oct. John s. of Richard Teake
14 Oct. Mellior d. of John Baylie
20 Oct. Richard s. of Roger Maben
20 Oct. Johane d. of Robert Roger
20 Oct. Richard s. of John Skynner

* Sic.

7 Nov. Peter s. of John Ryse
1 Dec. Johane d. of John Nuttle
5 Dec. Tamson d. of John Adam
5 Dec. Johane d. of Bennett Roskeen
20 Dec. Margerie d. of John Engrosse
27 Dec. John s. of Thomas Jenken
12 Jan. Reginold s. of Richard Scryvenor
20 Jan. Peternell d. of John Langdon
21 Jan. John s. of William Pell
29 Jan. Grace d. of John Runnell
30 Jan. Ursula d. of Richard Pearse
21 Feb. Johane d. of Humphrey Vyncent
3 Mar. ffloreno d. of William Rawe
5 Mar. Alse d. of Richard Nicholas
10 Mar. Thomas s. of Thomas Stephens
20 Mar. Nicholas s. of Thomas Hawke

Anno 1575.

29 Mar. Margerie d. of Nicholas Cardewe
2 April William s. of Richard Julle
5 April Joyce d. of John Lyttacott
25 May Johane d. of Thomas Howell
3 June Johane d. of Thomas Teake
7 June Robert s. of George Mayhowe
10 June Trystram s. of Henrie Gwynnowe
10 June John s. of Robert Anbey
12 June Barnabas s. of Harrye Sexton
20 June Alse d. of Robert Kent
6 July Johane d. of John Cardewe
8 July Susan d. of Robert Calwaye
12 July Margerie d. of Thomas Tyer
14 Aug. Agnes d. of Robert Calwaie
20 Aug. Richard s. of Harrie Adam
20 Aug. Thomas s. of ffraunce Rawe
31 Aug. Johane d. of Harrie Geyne
20 Sep. Tamson d. of Remfrey Rowse
3 Oct. Johane d. of Otes Meryfeild
9 Oct. Alse d. of Reynold Pawlle
16 Oct. Robert s. of John Darr
22 Oct. Robert s. of Jefferie Allen
10 Nov. Thomas s. of James Williams
20 Nov. Elizabeth mother Eme Nicholas
1 Dec. Honor d. of Robert Cornishe
8 Dec. Nicholas s. of George Marke
26 Dec. Harrie mother Anne Rawe
5 Jan. Marie mother Jane Calwaie
15 Jan. William s. of John Valleyes
21 Jan. Marke s. of John Scorler
25 Jan. Bennett s. of John Langdon
17 Feb. Harrie s. of Thomas Cocken
24 Feb. Raff s. of Thomas Nickes
24 Feb. Johane d. of Thomas Rowe
25 Mar. John mother Alse Edward

Anno 1576.

4 April William s. of Richard Ibbett
6 April Richard s. of Robert Locke
18 April Richard s. of John Carter gent.
18 May Alse d. of Thomas Trelowgan
24 May Mylson d. of Harrie Gascoyne
30 May Maude d. of Richard Sprey
7 June William s. of Richard Bennye
18 June Peternell mother Tamson Dymont
12 July Edward s. of Roger Maben
23 July ffraunces s. of John Ryse
24 July Johane d. of John Knight
30 July William s. of Thomas Merifeild
10 Aug. Isott d. of Richard Moylle
10 Aug. Robert s. of Richard Lawrence
11 Aug. Johane mother Johane Steven
12 Aug. Symon mother Anne Edward
19 Aug. Elizabeth d. of Richard Oxenham
12 Sep. Michaell son of Humphrey Manuell
2 Oct. Margarett d. of John Peane
3 Oct. Alse d. of Otes Meryfeild
1 Nov. Emblen d. of Petherick Pernell
1 Nov. ffraunces s. of John Snell
10 Nov. Thomas s. of Thomas Hawke
27 Nov. Phillep d. of John Lyttacott
2 Dec. Brigett d. of John Davie
22 Dec. John s. of Thomas Treblesende
23 Dec. Johane d. of John Knight
26 Dec. Jane mother Agnes Jane
30 Dec. Susan d. of Sampson Morcombe
6 Jan. Harrie s. of William Browne .
12 Jan. Elizabeth d. of Walter Rawe
24 Jan. William s. of Richard Hawke
30 Jan. Harrie s. of Richard Nicholas
31 Jan. John s. of Thomas Nuttle
4 Feb. Elizabeth d. of Robert Calwaie
8 Feb. John s. of John Cocken
20 Feb. Richard s. of Thomas Jenken
28 Feb. Avis d. of Robert Kent
3 Mar. Richard s. of Harrie Sampson
3 Mar. Bennett s. of John Horwell
10 Mar. Tamson d. of George Mayhowe
21 Mar. Margarett d. William Tredynycke
21 Mar. Thomas s. of Thomas Howett
24 Mar. Ibbett bastard mother Kateryne Collys

Anno 1577.

8 April Johane d. of Humphrey Vyncent
9 April Richard s. of John Adam
14 April Harrie s. of Harrie Roam
20 April Olyffe d. of Robert Moyses
7 May Katherine d. of Thomas Hawke

14 May Elizabeth d. of Richard Edye
21 May John s. of Robert Williams
25 May Marie d. of Robert Rosegan
25 May Pentecost d. of said Robert Rosegan
30 May Richard s. Robert John
10 June John s. of Richard Ryst
4 June John s. of ffraunces Naneonan
11 June John s. of Humphrey Tremayne
22 June Elinor d. of George Marke
30 June John s. of Nicholas Trehemban
30 June Pascow s. of Nicholas Trehenban
8 July Richard s. of John Mathew
12 July Katherine d. of William Rawe
30 July Elizabeth d. of Thomas Teake
24 Aug. Mylson d. of Henrie Gwynnowe
30 Aug. Thomas s. of John Skynner
1 Oct. ffraunce s. of John Vyon
3 Oct. Marie d. of Nicholas Cardew
26 Oct. Thomas s. of Richard Blake
1 Nov. Richard s. of Thomas Vesey
12 Nov. John s. of James Wylliams
16 Dec. Peter s. of John Serybende
20 Dec. Phillep s. of John Knight
1 Jan. Jenefer d. of John Cardewe
8 Jan. Phillep d. of John Tresawell
12 Jan. John s. of Richard Teag
14 Jan. Tamson d. of Robert Jolle
10 Feb. John s. of Richard Moylle
15 Feb. Johane d. of John Payne
3 Mar. Johane d. of Harrie Hawke
15 Mar. Thomas s. of John Toker
24 Mar. Katherine mother Christian Hydon

ANNO 1578.

4 April Johanne d. of John Nankevell
20 April Johane d. of Harrie Meryfeild
1 May John s. of John Moyle
28 May John s. of James Chapleyne
28 May Christopher s. of James Chapleyne
30 May Johane mother Agnes Putford
31 May Richard s. of John Calwaye
9 June Syslie d. of Harrie Sexton
12 June Temperance d. of Nicholas Treylian
20 June Petherick s. of John Snell
9 July Lovdie d. of Thomas Jenkin
21 July Richard s. of George Marke
6 Aug. Thomas s. of John Langdon
22 Aug. Harrie mother one Jane
31 Aug. William s. of Wylliam Grosse
7 Sep. William mother Jane Chapleyne
15 Sep. Thomas s. of John Adam
20 Sep. Molliar d. of Richard Torken
21 Sep. Honor d. of Richard Screvener
21 Sep. Dorothie d. of John Menhire
25 Oct. Ursula d. of Jefferie Allen
26 Oct. Margarett d. of Thomas Clarke
7 Nov. Elizabeth d. of Thomas Vyvian

[*In December, Januarie, ffebruarie, Anno p'dicte, theire were none baptysed or ells not regystered.*]

10 Mar. Olyffe d. of Thomas Meryfeild
21 Mar. Margerie d. of John Nicholas
23 Mar. John mother Johane Symon

ANNO 1579.

29 Mar. John s. of John Rescott
29 Mar. Emblen d. of Humphrey Manuell
12 April Katherine d. of Robert Cornish
25 April Agnes d. of William Clarke
26 April Olyffe mother Olyff Tooker
4 May Edward s. of Richard Hawke
20 June Margarett d. of John Nicholl
29 June John s. of John Carter gent.
26 July John son of John Adam
20 Aug. Pethericke s. of John Snell
15 Sep. Ibbet d. of Richard Sprey
25 Sep. John s. of John Nicholl
8 Oct. Olyffe d. of Thomas Meryfeild

[*In November and December Anno p'dict there were none baptysd or ells none regystered.*]

22 Jan. Richard the mother Emblen Roode
2 Feb. John s. of John Moylle
13 Feb. Maude d. of Robert Calwaie
13 Feb. Elizabeth d. of Robert Jollyff
9 Mar. ffraunce s. of Sampson Morcombe

ANNO 1580.

31 Mar. Emblen d. of Thomas Vivian
6 April Barbara d. of Richard Williams
8 April Richard s. of John Bonython gent*
6 May William s. of Lawrence Jobb
23 May John s. of Robert Moyses
2 June Johane d. of ffraunce Typpett
11 June Raffe s. of Stephen Abraham
11 July John s. of Richard Abraham
26 July Thomas s. of John Davie
21 Aug. George s. of Humphrey Nankevell
4 Sep. Johane d. of one Bastylen
7 Sep. Nicholas s. of one Bastien
8 Sep. Thomas s. of Pethericke Pernell
18 Sep. Elizabeth d. of Water† Stephens
17 Oct. John s. of a certan power begger

* By his wife Eleanor dau. and co-heir of Wm. Myllyton.
† Sic for Walter.

21 Oct. Agnes d. of John Lukie
25 Oct. Johane d. of Humphrey Edward
17 Nov. John s. of Humphrey Vyncent
25 Nov. Richard s. of Richard Blake
11 Dec. Honor d. of John Retallecke
12 Dec. Johane d. of a certen power begger
17 Dec. John and Johane children of Michell Harrie
3 Jan. Margarett d. of Thomas Daye
18 Feb. Pethericke s. of Richard Renolds
20 Feb. William s. of Harrie Hawke
25 Feb. William s. of Renolde Pawle
25 Feb. Anne d. of John Younge
1 Mar. James s. of Nowell Mathew
2 Mar. James s. of John Carter gent.

Anno 1581.

2 April William s. of Remfrey Rowse
14 May John s. of Richard Norton
28 May John s. of John Norton
4 June John s. of Marke Lowry
18 July Alse d. of James Scrarraborow
22 July Johane d. of Davie Congdon
3 Aug. William s. of John Mayhow
6 Aug. John s. of John Horkie
8 Aug. Harrie s. of John Rawe
20 Aug. Robert s. of ffraunce Calwaie
1 Sep. Elizabeth d. of ffraunce Nanconan
10 Sep. Marye d. of Robert Calwaye
12 Oct. Jane d. of George Marke
22 Oct. William base borne the mother Barbara Eplett
3 Nov. Barbara d. of Nicholas Whyte
30 Nov. John s. of William Wylls
18 Dec. Nicholas s. of Thomas Rowe
21 Dec. John s. of Richard Copithorne
23 Dec. Christopher s. of Humphrey Manuell
28 Dec. Alse d. of John Calwaye
8 Jan. Katherine d. of John Adam
10 Jan. Elizabeth d. of John Maye
13 Jan. G^e s. of Robert Lantell
24 Jan. Elizabeth d. of William Clarke
27 Jan. Anne d. of John Langdon
30 Jan. John s. of Thomas Vyvian
31 Jan. Harrie s. of Robert Roger
5 Feb. Roger s. of Thomas Davie
17 Feb. Olyff d. of Degorie Stubbs
26 Feb. Thomas his mother sister of Thomas Tyer
5 Mar. Thomas s. of Bennett Calwaye
7 Mar. Elizabeth d. of John Rowse
10 Mar. William s. of Humphrey Vyncent
12 Mar. Elizabeth d. of James Jenken
12 Mar. Honor d. of John Pollard
18 Mar. Antonie s. of John Davie
19 Mar. Thomas s. of Remfrey Grosse

Anno 1582.

1 April Nicholas s. of Richard Hame
8 April Zenobia d. of Thomas Meryfeild
11 April John s. of Robert Custoller
12 April Katherine d. of Humphrey Nankevell
22 April Richard s. of Nicholas Tonken
3 May John s. of Robert Jollyffe
13 June Marie d. of Pascow Pokynhorne
14 June Johane d. of Thomas Olver
14 June Richard s. of Richard Spraye
14 June Pascow s. in law of Pascowe John
16 June Henrie s. of William Trethynnocke
21 July Johane d. of John Jolle
3 Aug. Marie d. of John Lawrie
5 Aug. John s. of John Brabyn
10 Aug. Johane d. of John Torken
23 Aug. Johane d. of Richard Cardew
20 Sep. Warne s. of Sampson Morcombe
5 Oct. Emblen d. of John Snowe
9 Oct. John s. of Nicholas Drew
13 Oct. John the mother Katherine Grosse
14 Oct. Charles s. of John Carter gent.
15 Oct. Marten s. of John Valleys
28 Oct. Ambrose s. of Richard Hawke
1 Nov. Tamson d. of Richard Hodge
8 Nov. Richard s. of Marten Behednoe
11 Nov. Johane d. of Harrie Meryfeild
22 Nov. Johane d. of Robert Darr
30 Nov. John s. of Wylliam Wylls
1 Dec. Richow and Eliz. daus. of John Menhire
3 Dec. Johane the mother Johane Rousovelle
7 Dec. Walter s. of John Roskeen
10 Dec. Thomas s. of John Phelpp
9 Jan. Marie d. of Lawrence Jobbe
11 Jan. Edmond s. of Robert Moyses
16 Jan. Margerie d. of Marke Lawrie
18 Jan. Margerie d. of Davye Congdon
18 Jan. Johane d. of Thomas Tennye
11 Feb. Richard and Pascow sons of John Younge
12 Feb. James and Richard sons of Thomas Jenyne
16 Feb. Thomas s. of William Braye
3 Mar. John s. of John Rowse
5 Mar. ffraunce s. of John Lukie

Anno 1583.

18 April John s. of John Moyllo
3 May Richard s. of John Retallacke
4 May John s. of Pethericke Pernell
9 May Edward s. of Thomas Torken
12 May Scylie and one other bastarde to two women unknowen
25 May John s. of Gregorie Lyttacotte
9 June Robert the mother a woman that was to Luke Lyttacotte
15 June James and Emblen the children of Robert Calwaye
10 July G . . . . (*sic*) d. of Nicholas Tresylian
10 July E . . . . (*sic*) d. of Richard Gyllard
17 Aug. Anne d. of Thomas Vyvian
17 Aug. Honor d. of Nowall Mayhow
19 Aug. Anne d. of John Rawe
24 Aug. Honor d. of Thomas Teage
10 Oct. Johane d. of John Staple
27 Oct. Richard s. of William Rawe
28 Oct. Elizabeth d. of ffraunce Nanconan
22 Nov. Arthur s. of John Carter gent.
1 Dec. John the mother Wyllmott Scobeld
4 Jan. Margerie d. of Stephen Harvie
12 Jan. Marie d. of Thomas Reve
20 Jan. Olyff d. of John Sprey
26 Jan. Anne d. of John Langdon
30 Jan. Jane d. of John Cardewe
1 Feb. John s. of Digorie Stubbs
6 Feb. Marye d. of a strange woman
9 Feb. Thomas s. of Richard Reve
11 Feb. Johane d. of James Lawrence
12 Feb. Jane d. of Marke Lawrie
26 Feb. John s. of John Adam
26 Feb. John and Johane the children of John Leverton
27 Feb. fflorence d. of Kennell Calway
7 Mar. Henrie s. of James Jenkin
7 Mar. Petronill d. of John George
15 Mar. John s. of Robert Jolly

Anno 1584.

4 April Marke s. of Rychard Williams
11 April Elizabeth d. of William Copithorne
18 April Charity d. of John Knight
26 April Mary d. of John Davy
17 May Elizabeth d. of James Cornish
19 May Barbara d. of Remfrey Rowse
23 May Willmott d. of William Trethinnocke
28 May Pethericke s. of Reignold Engrosse
2 June William s. of Rychard Horky
4 June Thomas s. of John Skinner
11 June Sisle d. of William Engrosse
16 June Thomas s. of Thomas Jenkin
21 June John s. of Antonie Smyth
14 June John s. of John Trembeth
11 July Thomas s. of Richard Copithorne
14 July Alse d. of ffraunce Calwaye
18 July Colomb s. of John Pollard
19 July Elizabeth d. of Richard Nuttle
26 July Barbara d. of Robert Roger
2 Aug. Jane d. of John Kowalls
2 Aug. John s. of Stephen Abraham
2 Aug. Richard s. of John Peane
5 Aug. Honor d. of John Paver
6 Aug. John s. of Thomas Cocken
14 Aug. Johane d. of Thomas Dyer
5 Aug. Katherine d. of Thomas Dansone
16 Aug. Elizabeth d. of Marten Rawe
26 Aug. Susan d. of John Calway
1 Sep. John s. of John Tennye
2 Sep. Marie d. of Humphrey Vyncent
6 Sep. G^or s. of Harrie Hawke
23 Sep. Richard s. of Christopher Tresawlle
24 Sep. Alse d. of John Snowe
27 Sep. Anne d. of John Rowse
3 Oct. Richard s. of John Tresawlle
6 Oct. Lawrenc s. of John the Sadler
8 Oct. Richard s. of John Younge
9 Oct. Thomas s. of John Jenyne
30 Oct. John s. of William Upcott
25 Nov. Johane s. of William Braye
28 Nov. Richard s. of John Langdon
10 Dec. Olyffe d. of Thomas Vyvian
12 Dec. John s. of John Nankevell
17 Dec. Thomas s. of Robert Calwaie
19 Dec. Richard the mother Margerie Trevythan
7 Jan. Pascow and Hester children of Richard Norton
8 Jan. Katherine d. of Nicholas Whytte
12 Jan. John s. of Nicholas Rawe
13 Jan. Mylson bastard child to the young Cocken
14 Jan. George s. of Thomas Hodge
26 Jan. D (*sic*) d. of Richard Michell
1 Feb. Jane d. of John Bennett
9 Feb. Emannuell s. of John Phillepp
12 Feb. Peter and Arthur sons of Sampson Narren
14 Feb. John s. of Robert Moyses
18 Feb. Katherine d. of Younge Laven
18 Feb. Marke s. of Marke Laurie
20 Feb. John s. of Thomas Vivyan
20 Feb. Johane d. of Richard Sprey

23 Feb. Margerie d. of Thomas Daye
25 Feb. Jane d. of John Baylie
28 Feb. Edward s. of Thomas Meryfeild
7 Mar. Pascoe d. of Margerie Tresony

ANNO 1585.

31 Mar. Jane d. of Thomas Olver
20 April Olyffe d. of Thomas Meryfeild
12 May John s. of John Brabyn
14 May Jane d. of John Moylle
18 May Richard s. of Harrie Meryfeild
19 May Jane the mother Grace Kneebone
4 June Johane d. of Christopher Manuell
9 June Emblen d. of ffraunce Calwaye
20 June Elizabeth d. of Robert Kentall
28 June Peter the mother Mary Screvener
4 July Thomas s. of Marten Behedno
9 July Katherine d. of John Grace
7 Aug. Elizabeth d. of William fforgett
11 Aug. Nicholas s. of John Phillep
11 Aug. Pascae s. of John Darr
12 Aug. William s. of Marten Hamblie
18 Aug. James s. of William Cooke
12 Sep. Richard s. of Richard Reyve
20 Oct. Johane d. of John Judde
30 Oct. William s. of John Rawe
1 Nov. Honor d. of John Carter gent.
3 Nov. Jane d. of Richard Williams
7 Nov. Thomas the father John Loybbie
20 Nov. Thomas s. of Gregorie Lyttacott
30 Nov. John s. of Harrie Hawke
30 Nov. Arthur s. of Richard Pollard
30 Nov. Katherine d. of Robert Locke
13 Dec. John s. of Harrie Typpett
26 Dec. Elizabeth d. of Richard Oxnam
1 Jan. John s. of a power Irish begger
3 Jan. Johane d. of Nicholas Tucker
9 Jan. Johane d. of Johane Luky widowe
10 Jan. Susan d. of John Snowe
12 Jan. Harrie s. of John Rowse gent.
18 Jan. William s. of John Warren
6 Feb. John s. of William Trethnnycke
7 Feb. Dorothie d. of John Moylle
7 Feb. Barbara d. of Humphrey Edye
10 Feb. Harrie s. of John Lyttacott
11 Feb. Thomas s. of Richard Marten
16 Mar. William s. of William Clarke
25 Mar. Emblen d. of Thomas Horkie

ANNO 1586.

6 April Thomas s. of John Retallecke
17 April John s. of Thomas Daye
1 May Harrie s. of William Wills
6 May John s. of Remfrey Rowse
12 May Zenobia d. of Petherick Pennell
15 May Elinor d. of ffraunce Nanconan
31 May Harrie s. of Robert Jolliffe
10 June Ursula d. of Thomas Vyvian
12 June William s. of John Brabyn
18 June John s. of Thomas Myll
4 July Marie d. of Marke Lawrie
10 July Agnes d. of Nowall Mayhowe
19 July Johane d. of Antonie Batten
20 July Elizabeth d. of Richard Edii
15 Aug. Jane the mother Elizabeth Coover
1 Sep. William s. of John Peane
5 Sep. Thomas s. of Thomas Teage
15 Sep. John s. of Richard Rowse
23 Sep. John s. of Stephen the myller
30 Sep. John s. of Richard Hawke the younger
2 Oct. Robert s. of John Bennett
9 Oct. Jane d. of William Copithorne
1 Nov. Marie d. of Richard Gylland
12 Nov. Katherine d. of Martyn Rowe
11 Dec. Jane d. of John Heydon
15 Dec. John s. of John Younge
21 Dec. John the father Robert Davie
31 Dec. ffraunce d. of Richard Daston,
2 Jan. Marye d. of John Phillepp
21 Jan. Margarett d. of George Horkie
22 Jan. Anne d. of John Toker
26 Jan. Honor d. of John Adam
26 Jan. John s. of John Grace
2 Feb. Marie d. of John Staple
25 Feb. William s. of Richard Copithorne
27 Feb. Jane d. of John Sprey
20 Mar. Emblen d. of John Jerman
24 Mar. Elizabeth the mother Olyff Hoper

ANNO 1587.

13 April Johane d. of John Cocke
13 April William s. of Robert Calwaie
13 April Thomas s. of John Phillep of Lanevett
14 April Marie the mother Johane Luky
29 April Thomas s. of James Cornish
1 May Dorothie d. of John Phillep
15 May Julean s. of Richard Moylle
21 May Josias s. of Richard Pollard
1 June John s. of Renold Grosse
3 June Elinor d. of Henrie Daye
12 Aug. Thomas s. of Robert Moyses
12 Aug. Jane d. of John Knight

18 June Thomas s. of Sampson Morcombe
8 Oct. Katherine d. of Thomas Myll
8 Oct. Agnes d. of ffraunce Angrosse
9 Oct. Thomas s. of James Hawke
24 Oct. Margarett d. of John Rawe
7 Nov. Remfrey s. of William Engrosse
16 Nov. Hughe s. of Mark Lawrie
23 Nov. Grace d. of John Rowse
25 Nov. Elinor d. of John Carter gent.
26 Nov. Alse d. of Thomas Baylie
8 Dec. Thomas s. of William Upcott
9 Dec. Thomas s. of William Lukie
10 Dec. Robert s. of John Pollard
16 Dec. Agnes d. of John Lane
25 Dec. Thomas s. of John Brabyn
18 Jan. James s. of Richard Moylle
23 Jan. Katherine d. of John Moylle
31 Jan. Jane d. of John Heydon
7 Feb. Phillep d. of James Lawrance
25 Feb. Tamson d. of John Bennett
27 Feb. Elinor d. of Harrie Meryfeild
6 Mar. Agnes d. of Richard Sprey
13 Mar. William s. of John Snowe

Anno 1588.

3 April Pacyence d. of Richard Oxnam
3 April Christopher the mother Margery Rowe
7 April ffraunce s. of Henrie Hadoke
12 April Richard s. of Robert Rodger
15 April Johane d. of Martan dyer
21 April Roger s. of Degory Stubbs
3 May Mary d. of Nicholas Olver
5 May Henry s. of Richard Hawke
15 June Mary d. of Richard Williams
14 July Mary d. of Petherick Pernell
14 July Catherine d. of John Moile
14 July Thomas s. of John Rensavell
16 July William the mother Margaret Rowe
25 Aug. Dallirywer s. of boden Moyle
26 Aug. Mari d. of John Tubb
2 Sep. John s. of John Nankevell
15 Sep. Richard the mother one Elizabeth Chaplain
8 Oct. Barbara d. of Thomas Vivian
19 Oct. John s. of John Grace
28 Oct. William s. of Richard Gylberd
14 Nov. Richard s. of Rawe glover
16 Nov. Jane d. of Marke Retallecke
18 Nov. Elizabeth d. of John Cardewe
24 Nov. John s. of Gregorie Lyttacott
25 Nov. Gregorie s. of John Vanson
20 Dec. G. s. of John Staple
22 Dec. Emanuel s. of a poure begger
23 Dec. Jane child of young Kent
24 Dec. E. & G. children to Netherton
19 Jan. Elizabeth d. of William Wylls
10 Feb. Johane d. of Pawlie Rawe
1 Mar. Richard s. of Nicholas Perken
11 Mar. Emblen d. of Richard Pollard
15 Mar. Richard s. of Thomas Teage
15 Mar. Phillep d. of John Younge
25 Mar. John s. of John Jollyffe

Anno 1589.

4 April Honor d. of John Lyttacott
7 April Henrie s. of Richard Oxnam
14 April John s. of Thomas Meryfeild
16 April K. the mother Johane Engrosse
20 April Agnes d. of Christopher Batt
28 April Marie d. of Thomas Troblefeild
4 May Anne d. of John Brabyn
8 May Harrie s. of Richard Rowse the elder
22 May Phillep d. of John Skinner
17 May William s. of William Copithorne
25 May Humphrey s. of John Marke
4 June Antonie s. of John Mayhowe
22 June Katherine d. of Richard Lovis
23 June Marten s. of Robert Dar
29 June Susan d. of John Davye
2 July John s. of John Rowe the younger
9 July Elizabeth d. of John Rowlyn
11 July Anne d. of Richard Copithorne
12 July E. s. of James Vallys
26 July Alse d. of John the thecher
27 July John s. of Phillep Thomas
3 Aug. Honor d. of John Geyne
10 Aug. Elizabeth d. of George Collings
20 Aug. Katherine d. of Henrie Trehenban
15 Aug. Richard s. of John Retallacke
20 Sep. Michell s. of John Carter gent
27 Sep. John and Tamson children of Richard Scrivener
8 Oct. Jane d. of Denys Wescott
16 Oct. Jane d. of Thomas Bennett
17 Oct. John s. of Harrie Dyar
18 Oct. Jane d. of Robert Jolliff
8 Nov. Elizabeth d. of John Jenyne
11 Nov. Richard bastard the mother Jane Hengroke
16 Nov. Richard s. of Harrie Hawke
11 Dec. John s. of Thomas Daye
19 Dec. John s. of Thomas Brabyn
4 Jan. Margarett d. of James Cornish
6 Jan. Elizabeth d. of John Philleps
12 Jan. John s. of Thomas Baylie
* Jan. Elizabeth d. of Reynold Grosse

* Obliterated.

20 Jan. Jane d. of Robert Jolliffe
29 Jan. ffraunce s. of Richard Hawke
31 Jan. Edward s. of William Upcott
7 Feb. Tamson the mother Johane Lukie
11 Feb. Emblen d. of Marke Slogett
17 Feb. Robert s. of Richard Moylle
20 Feb. Jane d. of William Luke
24 Feb. William s. of Thomas Cocke
28 Feb. Katherine d. of William Gylland
2 Mar. Harrie s. of John Tubb
9 Mar. William the mother Tamson Stoibey
11 Mar. John s. of Johane Maye
24 Mar. Jane d. of Sampson Morcombe

ANNO 1590.

5 April Jane d. of Stephen Harveye
19 April Margerie d. of John Rowe
21 April Barbara d. of Richard Pollard
21 April John s. of John Rosogan
30 April William s. of Thomas Olver
27 April Andrew s. of Thomas Symon
12 May Richow d. of ffraunce Rowe
4 June John s. of John Hyden
14 June John s. of Richard Spray
15 June Charety d. of William Rendall
3 July Humphrey s. of John Pollard
6 July John s. of Richard Drew
13 July Jane d. of Stephen Myllard
9 Aug. John s. of William Strongman
9 Aug. Thomas s. of ffraunce Grosse
10 Aug. Rose d. of Thomas George
11 Aug. Roger s. of Robert Williams
26 Aug. Honor d. of Robert Calway
8 Sep. James s. of John Moylle
8 Sep. Thomas s. of John Snowe
9 Sep. Maud d. of Thomas Symon
17 Sep. Thomas s. of William Roskodgian
15 Sep. Elizabeth d. of Christopher Marifeild
20 Sep. Henrie s. of Richard Moylle
16 Oct. Peternell d. of John Grace
17 Oct. Agnes d. of William Braye
19 Oct. Thomas s. of Nicholas Tonkin
20 Oct. Rowlen s. of Henrie Meryffeilde
26 Oct. Paskow s. of Thomas Vivian
21 Dec. William s. of Abraham Stephin
4 Jan. Susanna d. of John Lawrence
26 Dec. Reygnold s. of Richard Hawke
27 Jan. Jane d. of ffraunce Grosse
12 Feb. Reygnold s. of John Troblefeild
25 Feb. Mathy s. of William Wills
28 Feb. Harrie s. of John Haycroft
1 Mar. James s. of John Harding

ANNO 1591.

3 April Paskow s. of Marten Dier
18 April Richow d. of Beden Moylle
18 April Elizabeth d. of Henry Dier
19 April Richard s. of Richard Cardew
19 April Thomas s. of John Younge
30 April Richard s. of Richard Rowse
2 May Elizabeth d. of Marke Lawry
9 May Harry s. of Nicholas Drew
12 May Anne d. of John Carter gent.
27 May Fraunce s. of Thomas Daye
29 May Constance d. of John Pears
6 June Robert s. of Robert Jolly
13 June Jane d. of James Hawke
26 June John s. of John Tyer
30 June Nowell s. of John Cornish
8 July Olly d. of Nicholas Vallis
15 July Richow d. of Richard Stephin
15 July Thomas s. of Sampson Braye
27 July John s. of John Tubbe
29 July John s. of Pawle Rawe
29 July Jane d. of William Copithorne
3 Aug. Richard s. of Thomas Hodge
11 Aug. Blanch d. of William Treludder
12 Aug. Rempfrey s. of John Rowse
15 Aug. Agnes d. the father Robert Davie
15 Aug. Marie d. of Richard Copithorne
19 Aug. Richard s. of William Jolliff
20 Aug. Sycilie d. of John Horkie
25 Aug. Blanch the mother Elizabeth Whyte
27 Aug. Elizabeth d. of John Nicholl
30 Aug. Stephen s. of Richard Lovies
21 Sep. John s. of John Kent
21 Sep. Harrie s. of Richard Pollard
9 Oct. Richow d. of Gregorie Lyttacott
9 Oct. John s. of Robert Williams
10 Oct. Jane d. of Dennys Wescott
13 Oct. Thomas the father John Morcombe
17 Oct. Marten s. of Richard Dunacombe
25 Oct. Marie the father John Tregeneder
25 Oct. John s. of John Hydon
27 Oct. John s. of Richard Rowse
27 Oct. Thomas s. of Richard Williams
14 Nov. Pascow s. of Thomas Lange
14 Nov. John s. of Richard Seryvenor
25 Nov. Thomas s. of Thomas Myll
26 Nov. Collumba d. of John Davie
29 Jan. Richard s. of Thomas . . . .*
15 Feb. Valetyne the mother Margery Calway

* A blank left.

16 Feb. Elizabeth d. of Bennett Reskean
12 Mar. Honor d. of John Blake

ANNO 1592.

1 April Elizabeth d. of John Moylle
22 April Anne d. of John Geene
30 April Thomas s. of John Pathicke
11 May Katherine d. of John Grace
24 May Jane d. of John Marke
2 June Robert s. of Stephen Trussall
14 June Margery d. of Willam Gilberd
20 June Elizabeth d. of Nicholas Perken
3 July Honor d. of John Braye
25 July D (*sic*) d. of John Nankevell
31 July Richard s. of John Heycrafte
5 Aug. Richard s. of Richard Copithorne
8 Aug. Elizabeth d. of Hughe Sexton
15 Aug. Thomas s. of Nicholas Drewe
16 Aug. James s. of Marke Retallecke
27 Aug. Marye d. of Marten Dyar
29 Aug. Richard s. of Thomas Daye
21 Sep. Phillep d. of ffraunce Yeoman
24 Sep. Thomas s. of Thomas Symon
29 Sep. Richard s. of John Tonken
30 Sep. Margery d. of William Edward
2 Oct. John s. of James Vallyes
17 Oct. John s. of William Reskigian
7 Nov. Bennett s. of John Mayhow
12 Nov. Thomas s. of Ambrose Lawrye
20 Nov. Jane d. of Richard Hawke
26 Nov. William s. of Thomas Naparrow
14 Dec. Richard s. of Antonie Pynnow
16 Dec. Robert s. of William Lukie
19 Dec. Honor d. of John Rawe
19 Dec. Janne d. of Richard Moylle
22 Dec. Eliz'ath Dier d. of Henrie Dier
9 June Nicholas s. of John Bennett
12 June James s. of John Cullocott of St. Annes*
14 June John the mother Margarett Trusoe
13 June John s. of Marten Bishoppe
20 Feb. Edward s. of John Carter gent.
19 Feb. John s. of G. . . D. . . .†
28 Feb. Thomas the mother Margarett Calway
3 Mar. Gyllian d. of Harrie Hawke
18 Mar. John s. of Augustine the myller
18 Mar. Alse the mother Jennye Dyar
19 Mar. Nicholas the mother Johane Truscott
25 Mar. James s. of Edwarde Teage

* This is really St. Agnes, commonly called in this neighbourhood St. Anne's.

† Sic.

ANNO 1593.

29 Mar. Elizabeth d. of Will'm Kendall
11 April Will'm s. of Will'm Upcott
11 April John s. of Antonie Burlace
17 April Agnes d. of Thomas Meryfeild
28 April John s. of Reynolde Grosse
28 April Elizabeth d. of Bawden Moylle
30 April John s. of John Pollard
5 May Katherine d. of John Sprey
16 May Balthaser s. of Dennys Wescott
24 May Harrie s. of James Cornish
6 June John s. of Paskowe Tyfforde
10 June Richard s. of Richard Stephen
17 June Thomas s. of Thomas Brabyn
3 July Emblen d. of John Nicholas
14 July Thomas s. of John Pearse
20 July Elizabeth d. of Richard Hawke
22 July Marye d. of Richard Pearse
25 July Marie d. of John Copithorne
7 Aug. Martyn the mother Margarett Poll
9 Aug. Elizabeth d. of Thomas George
18 Aug. Harrie s. of John Heycrafte
5 Sep. Jane d. of Stephen . . . .
6 Sep. Robert s. of Thomas Myll
22 Sep. Johane d. of Alexander Hendra
29 Sep. Mychaell s. of Thomas Vyvian
2 Oct. Elizabeth d. of Robert Tynner
13 Oct. Johane d. of William Gilberd
24 Oct. Marten s. of Richard Rowse
30 Oct. Hughe s. of John Lae
20 Nov. Johane d. of John Phillep
9 Dec. Robert s. of Harrie Trehemben
27 Dec. Johane d. of John Wylliams
13 Jan. Harrie s. of John Tyer
31 Jan. Margaret d. of Richard Lovey
2 Feb. Harrie s. of John Younge
4 Feb. Thomas s. of Thomas Baylyff
7 Feb. Agnes d. of John Nankevell
8 Feb. Johane d. of Will'm Rawlinge *alias* Wylls
8 Feb. Barbara d. of John Moylle
24 Feb. James s. of Richard Wylliams
3 Mar. Joyce d. of John Thacher
3 Mar. Honor the mother one Jsett a poore woman
8 Mar. Will'm and Richow the children of John Maye
14 Mar. Margerie d. of John Davye
20 Mar. Will'm s. of James Hawke

ANNO 1594.

20 Mar. Thomas s. of Robert Mylland
25 Mar. Alson d. of Richard Letha
25 Mar. Cheston d. of Richard Rowse
27 April Thomas s. of Thomas Daye
29 April Joyce d. of Edward Teage
30 April Richard s. of Will'm Edward

1 May Robert s. of Will'm Jolliffe
1 May Richard s. of Will'm Thomas
12 May Elizabeth d. of Thomas Meryfeild
23 May Richard s. of ffrance Engrosse
7 June Bennett s. of John Rowse
7 June Maude d. of John Kent
28 July Alse d. of Will'm Gylberd the elder
1 Aug. Edward the mother Marie Karke *alias* Cluton
6 Aug. Grace d. of Richard Copithorne
11 Aug. Robert s. of Gregorie Lyttacott
11 Aug. Michaell s. of Rawlyn Cary
13 Aug. Thomas s. of Antonie Hoskyn
18 Aug. Henrie s. of Nicholas Thomas
28 Aug. John s. of Stephen Trusscott
28 Aug. Johane d. of John Hydon
30 Aug. Will'm s. of John Heycrefte
5 Sep. John s. of Thomas Bennett
1 Nov. Henrie s. of Thomas Lange
7 Nov. Henrie s. of Stephen Myllerd
7 Nov. Typhenie d. of Sampson Braye
23 Nov. Dorothie d. of Pawlie Rawe
25 Dec. John s. of John Geene
13 Jan. Honor d. of John Rawe
25 Jan. John s. of John Braye
27 Jan. Jane d. of Water Smyth
2 Feb. Pascow d. of Thomas Myll
21 Feb. John s. of Martyn Dyar
27 Feb. George s. of Sampson Morcombe
14 Mar. Charitie d. of Hughe Sexton
14 Mar. John s. of John Staple
25 Mar. Honor d. of Martyn Bishoppe

ANNO 1595.

21 April Richard s. of Richard Carter
22 April Roger s. of Thomas Wythell
4 May Pascowe s. of Richard Hawke
20 May John s. of Lallow Nicholas
15 June George s. of Stephen Tubbe
28 June Thomas s. of Harrie Hawke
29 June Elizabeth d. of John Torker
5 July Honor d. of John Younge
14 July Honor d. of Nicholas Pearse
17 July Thomas s. of John Lae
18 July Barbara d. of Henrie Dyer
18 July Thomas s. of Bawden Moylle
20 July Anne d. of John Knight
28 July Margaret d. of John Geene
3 Aug. Elinor d. of Nicholas Drewe
17 Aug. Richard s. of Thomas Vivian
17 Aug. Nicholas s. of Thomas Daye
23 Aug. Martyn s. of John Mayhowe
28 Aug. Marie d. of John Grace
31 Aug. Will'm s. of John Tubbe
2 Sep. Marten s. of Edward Teage
18 Sep. Elizabeth d. of Thomas Lavyn
26 Sep. Harrie s. of John Heycrafte
28 Sep. Nicholl d. of William Kendall
28 Sep. Richard s. of John Marke
9 Oct. Thomas s. of Stephen Trussell
1 Nov. *J . . . . d. of Marke Retallecke
12 Nov. Elizabeth d. of John Browne
12 Nov. Richard s. of Thomas Bennett
16 Nov. Peter s. of John Pollard
16 Nov. John s. of William Edward
13 Nov. Marye d. of George Collinge
26 Nov. *L . . . . s. of John ffraunce
30 Nov. *J . . . . d. of Pascow Tyfford
14 Dec. Elizabeth d. of John Copithorne
14 Jan. Johane d. of John Kent
14 Jan. *R . . . . s. of John Sprey
15 Jan. William the mother Jane Yeo
12 Feb. *J . . . . s. of Reynolde Grosse
16 Feb. Rempfrey s. of Will'm Gylberd
25 Feb. James s. of Richard James
8 Mar. Alse d. of Richard Hawke
13 Mar. Agnes d. of James Cornish
14 Mar. Roger d. of Thomas Mylle
20 Mar. Thomas s. of James Valleys
20 Mar. Johane d. of Bennett Pollard

ANNO 1596.

9 April Will'm s. of John Nicholas
10 April Will'm s. of John James
10 April Alse d. of John Moylle
12 April Will'm s. of John Randell
12 April Harrie s. of Richard Bowell
13 April Honor d. of John Nowell
25 April Thomas s. of Will'm Richard
26 April Nicholas s. of Harrie Trehemban
1 May Alse d. of John Hydon
5 May Johane d. of Robert Ryse
6 May Thomas s. of Will'm Coale
13 May Prissylla d. of Richard Moylle
15 May Will'm s. of Will'm Wylliams
20 May William s. of John Thomas
29 May John s. of Will'm Lukye
29 May Marie d. of Richard Lovell
15 June Jane d. of John Genynge
15 July Honor d. of Will'm Strongman
18 July Thomas s. of John Allen
8 Aug. Marie d. of ffraunce Yoeman
9 Aug. Will'm s. of John Torker
21 Aug. Marie d. of Humphrey Hyllary
1 Sep. *J . . . . . . of Nicholas Weaver
12 Sep. Thomas s. of John Hawke
1 Oct. Sampson s. of Will'm Tennye
3 Oct. Pacience d. of Marten Tome
Oct. *L . . . . of John Rowse

* The initial only is given in the original as explained in the introductory chapter.

16 Oct. Elizabeth d. of Richard Kendall
24 Oct. Edward s. of John Knight
10 Nov. James s. of Nicholas Thomas
9 Nov. John s. of Stephen Trussell
22 Nov. John s. of Christopher Stradford
13 Dec. Elizabeth d. of William Wylls
16 Dec. Roger s. of Lallow Nicholas
19 Dec. Johane d. of Will'm Troblefeild
21 Dec. Harrie s. of John Tanken
10 Jan. Grace d. of William Gylberd
11 Jan. Marten the mother Elizabeth Edwards
19 Jan. Katherine d. of Thomas Bennet
23 Jan. James s. of Will'm Tremayne
26 Feb. Harrie s. of Henrye Marten
27 Feb. James s. of John Daye
29 Feb. Alse d. of Nicholas Holman
16 Mar. Marye d. of Thomas Carthewe

ANNO 1597.

30 Mar. Elizabeth d. of John Lacollas
17 April Edward s. of George Tubbe
19 April John s. of John Troblefeild
20 April Johane d. of John Nankevall
23 April Marie d. of Thomas Myll
30 April Emblen d. of John Pearse
3 May Thomas s. of Thomas Daye
6 May John s. of George Collinge
18 May Marten s. of John Tyer
25 May John s. of Will'm Jolliff
17 June George s. of John Younge
28 June Richard s. of John Rawe
17 July Tamson d. of Richard Rowse
18 July Thomas s. of John Menhire
23 July Barbara d. of Henry Meryfeild
30 July Marten s. of Will'm Edward
23 Aug. John s. of Bennett Pollard
26 Aug. *L. . . . s. of Reynolde Grosse
28 Aug. Constance d. of Richard Scryvener
† Sep. Susan the father one Bettye
8 Nov. Elizabeth d. of Thomas Stephen
9 Nov. Agnes d. of Marten Dyer
12 Nov. John s. of Richard Carter
13 Nov. Elizabeth d. of John Grene
29 Nov. Johane d. of Harrie Woffe
3 Jan. Johane d. of Richard Oxenham
5 Jan. Richard s. of Will'm Bodie
16 Jan. Peter s. of Edward Teage
2 Feb. †Richard s. of . . . . Stribly
20 Feb. William s. of Gregorie Lyttacott

* Initial only in the original. † Blank.

24 Feb. Johane d. of John Marke
2 Mar. Henrie s. of Harrie Hawke
6 Mar. Nicholas s. of Thomas Lange
14 Mar. Elizabeth d. of Nicholas Bonsoll
16 Mar. Elizabeth d. of Sampson Morcombe
25 Mar. Hugh s. of Harrie Rowse

ANNO 1598.

25 Mar. Marie d. of Harrie Norton
1 May John and Elizabeth the children of Lallow Nicholas
8 May Elizabeth d. of John Hercraft

[*These followinge were not registered by ye Curate w^h did baptise them.*

18 May James s. of James Pollard
14 Oct. Hughe s. of John Rise
15 Oct. Edward s. of Robert Rosewas
15 Oct. Thomas s. of Richard Pollard
21 Oct. Alice Carpenter *alias* Williams d. of Roger Carpenter *alias* Williams

By STEVEN BATT, *Curate.*]

26 Nov. Elenour d. of Richard Cornishe
3 Dec. Thomasine d. of Thomas George
10 Jan. Amye d. of Thomas Dassawe
14 Jan. Thomas s. of Thomas Cardew
14 Jan. Johane d. of Richard Blake
18 Jan. Augustine s. of Augustine Hoskinne
27 Jan. John s. of Ralphe Newton
28 Jan. James s. of John Rowse
30 Jan. Mary d. of Dennys Wescott
8 Feb. Elizabeth d. of John Hidon
3 Mar. Barbara d. of Will'm Cole
3 Mar. Emblen d. of John Kente
4 Mar. Thomas s. and Jane d. the mother Jane Rogers
14 Mar. Cicely d. of William Strongman
17 Mar. Richard s. of Will'm Gilbert
21 Mar. John s. of Humphrey Illary
22 Mar. Alice d. of John Maihow

ANNO 1599.

27 Mar. Elizabeth d. of Edward Teage
27 Mar. William the mother Amye Jhinkine
3 April Patience d. of John Valles
28 April Alice d. of Richard Moyle
4 May Elizabeth d. of Thomas Withell
8 May John s. of Will'm Tennye
25 May Henry s. of John Williams
9 June Joice d. of Henrie Dier
12 June Grace d. of Reinold Hawkinge

14 June Humphrey s. of John Law
5 July Germane s. of John Day
5 July Johane d. of same John Day
7 July Thomas s. of John Nicholas
9 July Thomas s. of Richard Hawke
21 July Dorithy d. of John Phillip
26 July John s. of Richard Polkinhorne
29 July James s. of John Pinnow
29 July Johane d. of Will'm Jane
24 Aug. Will'm s. of Bastian Trevithan
25 Aug. John s. of Pascow Tyfforde
2 Sep. Johane d. of John Roscarlow
12 Sep. Margery d. of William Upcott
17 Sep. John Oxname s. of Thomas Oxname
19 Sep. Christopher Knight s. of John Knight
22 Sep. Grace James d. of Edward James
23 Sep. Katherine Parrow d. of Nicholas Parrow
29 Sep. Elizabeth Tonkinge d. of John Tonkinge
7 Oct. John Tubb s. of Steven Tubb
16 Oct. Honory Jhinken d. of James Jhinken
28 Oct. Thomas Jolly s. of Henry Jolly
31 Oct. Justance d. of Richard West
2 Nov. Elonour Mill d. of Thomas Mill
7 Nov. Thomas Carter s. of Richard Carter
10 Nov. Joane d. of Thomas William
15 Nov. Marton s. of Thomas Stevens
11 Dec. Humphrey s. of James Hawke
14 Dec. Nicholas base s. of Elizabeth Jhinken
17 Dec. William s. of William Torkinge
20 Dec. William s. of Nicholas Bounshall
8 Jan. Patience d. of Diggory Stubs
12 Jan. Thomasine d. of John Geene
13 Jan. Richard s. of Thomas James
25 Jan. Hary s. of John Sexton
26 Jan. Hary s. of Marten Dyer
15 Feb. Mary base d. of Jane (bastard) Vinson
2 Mar. Hary s. of William Strongman
3 Mar. Nicholas s. of John Tibbett
9 Mar. Joane Pell the base d. of Margaret Pell
13 Mar. Sara the base d. of Elizabeth Edwards
21 Mar. Elizabeth d. of John Nankevell
23 Mar. Katherine d. of James Roskigion

ANNO 1600.

26 Mar. Mary d. of John Tier
8 April Ronald s. of Thomas Lavin
9 April Thomas s. of John Jullian
9 April John s. of Robert Rise
9 April Tamson d. of Benet Polard
17 April James s. of George Collins
22 April Margery d. of Will'm White
25 April James s. of Thomas Marke
30 April Nycollas s. of Richard Lovis
20 May Ane d. of John Guinowe *alias* Skygen
21 June Tiffeny d. of Hary Hake of Hallione
30 June Elizabeth d. of Thomas Martyn
6 July Elizabeth d. of Henry Daffe
10 July Joane d. of William Jane
13 July John s. of Richard Rowse
16 Aug. Henry s. of Henry Rowse
24 Aug. Josias s. of James Day
25 Aug. Paschaw d. of John Tucker
1 Sep. Thomas s. of John Baylie
9 Sep. Thomas the mother Dorothey Lenke
21 Sep. Elizabeth d. of Richard Williams
28 Sep. Bridgett and Agnes the daughters of John Allen
29 Sep. Michaell s. of John Moyle
30 Sep. James s. of Will'm Tenny
4 Oct. Thomas s. of Richard Kayther
5 Oct. John s. of John Thomas
9 Oct. Joane d. of James Cornishe
14 Oct. Sampson s. of Roger Carpenter
15 Oct. Elizabeth d. of . . . .* Hollman
26 Oct. John s. of William Lukye
6 Nov. Grace d. of John Day
14 Nov. Patience d. of Richard Rowse *alias* Jenkyn
22 Nov. ffrances the base son of Margaret Bowden
4 Dec. Richard base son of Katherine Teage
4 Dec. Marten s. of Davie Rawe
20 Dec. John s. of Antony Hawke
28 Dec. William s. of William Blake
30 Dec. Walter s. of John Browne
31 Jan. Jane d. of John Rise
6 Feb. Avice d. of Thomas Bennett

John Trenowth bapt. the 13 and Johane bapt. at home by the midwife the 9 of Feb. the children of Humphrey Trenouth and were buried the same day

* Obliterated.

13 Feb. David the base son of Margerie Nicholas *alias* Groaes
21 Feb. Mary d. of John James
21 Feb. Richard s. of Thomas Bennett
22 Feb. John the base son of Joane Nicholls
23 Feb. Edward s. of Edward Teague
26 Feb. John s. of John Browne
27 Feb. Mary d. of Antony Nicholl
2 Mar. Margerie d. of William Gilbert
17 Mar. Richard s. of John Frenche
18 Mar. Hughe s. of Richard Blake
21 Mar. Elizabeth d. of William Williams

ANNO 1601.

25 Mar. Richard s. of William Copithorne
11 April Richard s. of Richard Cornishe
18 April Susanna d. of John Rowse
20 May Thomas s. of Anthony Burlace
28 May Hughe s. of Edward Bray
3 June Anne the base daughter of Anne Littacott
13 June Hughe s. of ffraunce Trehymban
14 June Hughe s. of Dronise Wescott
20 June Mellison d. of David ffyne
24 June John s. of Nicholas Parkyn
3 July Phillippe s. of Thomas Nicholls *alias* Nacallen
4 July John the bastard son of Margaret Will'm widow (a stranger)
22 July Ebbett d. of Sampson Morcombe
26 July Ursula d. of Thomas Gardener of Locdington in the county of Wiltes travaylinge by pasport wth his wife
10 Sep. John s. of John Moyle the younger
24 Sep. Thomas s. of Thomas Williams of Scogy
8 Oct. Henrie s. of John Roscorla
10 Oct. Honor d. of Ralphe Robyns
16 Oct. Oliver s. of Richard Pollarde
17 Oct. William s. of Thomas Cocke ye younger
4 Nov. Thomas the bastard son of Bridgette Buseley
5 Nov. Humphrey the bastard son of Margaret Rogers
6 Nov. Pascowe d. of John Browne
8 Nov. John s. of William Jollye
14 Nov. Anne d. of Thomas Merifeild
8 Dec. John s. of James Hawke
9 Dec. Cecily d. of William Jane
13 Dec. Elenore d. of Richard Hawke of Trevarrian
24 Dec. Katherine d. of Reynolde Hawkye
27 Dec. Thomas the bastard sone of Lowdye Trelogan
8 Jan. John the bastard sone of Ollye Moyses
22 Jan. Nicholas s. of Steven Tubbe
23 Jan. Jane d. of James Roskigian
26 Jan. John s. of William Lukye
24 Feb. Thamsine d. of Nicholas Bownshall
28 Feb. Thomas s. of Richard Polkinghorne
18 Mar. Cicely d. of Renneld Engrosse
24 Mar. Joane d. of Thomas Stevens the younger
24 Mar. Joane d. of Thomas Martyn ✕

ANNO 1602.

4 April Oliver s. of William Strongman
8 April John a base childer ye puue of Joane Luke widow*
11 April John Marke s. of John Marke of Nanswhiddon
12 April Anstice d. of John Nanskevell
25 April Richard Trenowth d. of Humphrey Trenowth
16 May Thomas Cocken s. of William Cocken
13 June Marye Hoskyn d. of Augustine Hoskyn
27 June Joane Carter d. of Richard Carter gent.
22 July Alice Dawe d. of George Dawe
27 July William Browne s. of John Browne *alias* Roe
29 July Elizabeth White d. of William White
2 Aug. Thomas Abraham s. of John Abraham
8 Aug. Richard Moyell s. of Richard Moyell of Awstell gent.
9 Aug. John Thomas s. of Richard Thomas
19 Aug. John Dyer s. of Martine Dyer
9 Sep. Urias Guylbert s. of Will'm Guylbert
9 Sep. Margaret Lawry d. of Thomas Lawry
9 Sep. Mary Tucker d. of John Tucker
10 Sep. Jane (a bastard child) d. of Thomasine Trevyth

* Sic.

12 Sep. Phillippe Harrye s. of Renneld Harrye
16 Sep. Elizabeth Lawrey d. of James Lawrey
1 Nov. Thomas James s. of Richard James
9 Nov. Julian West d. of Richard West
17 Nov. Manuell Tucker s. of John Tucker
29 Nov. Edward Teague s. of Edward Teague
7 Dec. Richard Meryfeild s. of William Meryfeild
11 Dec. ffraunsce Robyns s. of Thomas Robyns
12 Dec. Susauna Williams d. of Richard Williams
1 Jan. Elizabeth Bennett d. of Edward Bennett
2 Jan. ...... Hawke d. of Henry Hawke
(*Part rubbed off.*)
9 Jan. Thomas Oxenham s. of Thomas Oxenham
16 Jan. Elizabeth Rawe d. of Anthony Rawe
18 Jan. Martyn Trescott s. of Gwalter Trescott
24 Jan. Nicholas Withell s. of Thomas Withell
6 Feb. John Dey s. of John Dey
10 Mar. William Callway s. of Thomas Callway
12 Mar. Elizabeth Valleys d. of James Valleys
20 Mar. Martyne Jeynkun s. of John Jeynkun
20 Mar. Janyfer Tenny d. of Wm. Tenny

ANNO 1603.

21 April Ambrose Hawke s. of James Hawke
23 April William Norten s. of Nich'as Norten
21 May German Kent s. of John Kent
16 June Richard Williams s. of Roger Williams
18 June Hughe Tippett s. of William Tippett
9 July John Mayhow s. of James Mayhow
10 July Joane Body d. of John Body
30 July John Keate s. of Ralphe Keate
31 July John Hickes s. of John Hickes
31 July Jane Hickes d. of the said John Hickes
6 Aug. Anne Tregheare d. of Thomas Tregheare
13 Aug. Thomas Reeve s. of John Reeve
21 Aug. Martine Blake s. of Will'm Blake
31 Aug. John Lawrey s. of James Lawrey
28 Sep. Michell Strangman s. of Martine Strangman
6 Oct. John Ryce s. of John Ryce
9 Oct. Joycce Hollman d. of Nich'as Holman
27 Oct. Henry Rowse s. of Richard Rowse
9 Nov. Honor Trestaine d. of Otes Trestaine
.....* William James (?) s. of Will'm James
.....* Thomas a base childe ......
19 Nov. Robert Bennett s. of Thomas Bennett
4 Dec. John Browne s. of John Browne potter
7 Dec. Hughe Norton s. of Henrye Norton
13 Dec. Alice Symons d. of Thomas Symons
3 Jan. Anne d. of Richard Moyle
3 Jan. Jane d. of John Rouse
3 Jan. Thomas Steevens s. of Thomas Steevens
5 Jan. Hugh s. of John Rescorla
10 Feb. Jane d. of John Stribly
12 Feb. Charitie d. of Thomas Williams
20 Feb. Jane d. of John Williams *alias* Ristugion
24 Feb. Henry s. of Richard Cornish
28 Feb. Honor d. of Henry Sprey
5 Mar. Thomas s. of Benet Pollard

ANNO 1604.

10 April Adam s. of Thomas Martin
20 April Renfreid s. of John Moyle Jun[r]
26 April Anne d. of Thomas Day
30 April Jane d. of William Williams
6 May Hugh s. of Richard Browne
25 May James s. of Stevan Tubb
2 June Sislie d. of Sampson Marcom
17 June Richard a base son of Jane Nankervall
25 June Ronfreid a base child
29 June Elizabeth d. of Thomas Merifeild
29 June Peeter s. of James Jenkine
11 Aug. John s. of Paskow Langdon

* Much obliterated here and stained.

12 Aug. William s. of John Barrett
19 Aug. Martin s. of Martin Dier
28 Aug. Lawance base son of Alice Roe

THO. SMALLRIDGE, *Curate.*

21 Sep. Penkerest d. of John Geene
22 Sep. James s. of John Haycraft
27 Sep. William s. of Rainold Hawkin
7 Oct. William s. of John Allin
9 Oct. Jane d. of Anthony Rowe
17 Oct. John s. of Peirce Penhale
8 Nov. Agnes d. of John Bodie
12 Nov. Nicholas s. of John Nankevall
18 Nov. William s. of John Trenbeath
19 Nov. Grace d. of Randell Harvy
28 Nov. John Lawrie s. of Ambrose Lawrie
25 Nov. Sampson Grose s. of Reynald Grose
30 Nov. Katherine Straugman d. of William Strangman
11 Dec. Paskoe s. of Thomas Dugoe
1 Jan. Henrye s. of Richard Hawke Junr
20 Jan. Richard s. of Richard Hawke of Trevedaw
7 Feb. Margaret d. of John Philipe
11 Feb. Agnis d. of Nicholas Bounsell
12 Feb. Agnis d. of Thomas Cocke
18 Feb. Honor d. of Edward Teage
26 Feb. Elizabeth d. of John Teilour
28 Feb. Adam s. of John Day

THO. SMALLRIDGE, *Curate*,* 1604.

2 Mar. Thomas s. of Ralph Hooper
9 Mar. Thomas s. of Thomas Lavin
11 Mar. Nicholas s. of Henry Hawke

ANNO 1605. T. S.†

28 Mar. Richard s. of John Teage
11 April Petronell d. of Richard Carter
22 May Catherine d. of Henrye Rowse
25 May Elizabeth d. of William Tresotherine
26 May Thomas s. of William White
1 June ‡John Lilius matieri Hiberniæ
2 July Adam s. of William Gilberte
5 June Pethericke s. of John Dar
5 June Anne d. of Richard Polkinhorne
18 July Thomas s. of William Tippett
4 Aug. Richard s. of William Blacke
18 Aug. James s. of John Abraham
20 Aug. Ralph s. of Richard Williams *alias* Marke and Petronell his d. were bapt‡

26 Sep. Jane d. of Richard Jolley
14 Oct. Thomas s. of Nicholas Naparoe
18 Oct. Luke s. of Edward Bennett
23 Oct. Margery d. of William Roscorlor
10 Nov. William s. of John Hix
17 Nov. John s. of Richard Bowyer
19 Nov. Johane d. of Thomas Chappell
4 Dec. Elizabeth d. of Robert Williams
7 Dec. §. . . . s. of John Nutting
14 Dec. §. . . . d. of Christopher Pedler
20 Dec. Elizabeth d. of Ralph Kett||
12 Jan. James s. of Thomas Steevens
12 Jan. Margerye d. of John Trembeth

THO. SMALLRIDGE, *Curate.*

13 Jan. Margerye d. of John Williams
15 Jan. Richard s. of Henrye Callaway
17 Jan. John s. of William Jane
22 Jan. Thomas and Henrye sons of John Reeve
24 Jan. Anthonie s. of Thomas Calaway
30 Jan. Joane d. of Martine Strangman
7 Feb. Constance d. of Thomas Benet *alias* Danis
23 Feb. Reskimer s. of Henrie Sprey
27 Feb. Sampson s. of John Roscorlor
27 Feb. Thomas s. of Henery Norten
13 Mar. Thomas s. of John Rice
23 Mar. Petronell d. of Robert Rice

ANNO 1606.

30 Mar. Joane d. of Thomas Tregeare
30 Mar. Nicholas s. of Tobias Hancocke
1 April Elizabeth d. of Brigget Roode
6 April Elizabeth d. of Edmund Nicholas
8 April Jane d. of Rainold Grose
10 April Fraucis s. of John George
11 April ¶. . . . d. of James Roskaegian
4 May William s. of John Jenken
4 May Melissa d. of Thomas Merifeild gent.
10 Mar. Ambrose base son of Constance ¶. . . .
30 Mar. John s. of Roger Young
30 Mar. Joyce d. of Robert Allen
30 Mar. Philep d. of Paskell Langdon
5 June Alexander s. of Michaell Harrie
9 July Archibald s. of John Rowse
12 July Melissa d. of Bennett Pollard

THOMAS SMALLRIDGE, *Curate*

* His signature here and after occurs at the foot of the pages in the original.
† Tho. Smallridge. ‡ Thus in the original.

§ Left blank in the original.
|| Probably Keate. ¶ Obliterated.

3 Aug. John a base son of Mary Pascow
7 Aug. Henery s. of Sampson Bray
14 Aug. Alice d. of William Rowse
22 Aug. Nicholas s. of John Gwyne
14 Sep. Margerie d. of Ambrose Lawrie
7 Sep. Alice d. of John Philipp
17 Sep. John s. of Francis Jones
18 Sep. Thomas s. of Robert Tippett
2 Oct. Henry bastard son of Anne Lyttycott
13 Oct. Giles s. of Walter Truscott
23 Oct. John s. of Robert Darr
9 Nov. Thomas s. of Reinold Littycott
5 Dec. Charity d. of John Wills
7 Dec. John & Richard sons of Will' Tenny
11 Dec. John s. of John Body
25 Dec. Richard s. of John Stribly
31 Dec. Reskimer s. of John Pecarse
31 Dec. Marie the base daughter of Honor Sprey
5 Jan. Alise d. of Thomas Carthew
8 Jan. Mary d. of Thomas Bennett
10 Jan. John s. of John Allen
17 Jan. James the base son of Wilmot & of Henry Dyer
6 Feb. Nicholas bastard son of Thamason Havent

THO. SMALLRIDGE, *Curate.*

15 Feb. Joyce d. of William Strangman
15 Feb. Agnes d. of William Roscorlor
18 Feb. Patience d. of Reinold Hawkine
25 Feb. James s. of John Trembeath
1 Mar. John the base son of Elizabeth Benny
1 Mar. Jane d. of William Williams
17 Mar. Elizabeth d. of John Williams
24 Mar. Elizabeth d. of Thomas Bennet

ANNO 1607.

27 Mar. Margerie d. of John Nankevell
29 Mar. Barbarer d. of Will' Gilbert
2 April Grace d. of Richard Tonkin
6 April Agnis d. of William Williams *alias* Roscudgion
8 April Henry s. of John Trublofeil
26 April Alice d. of William Cocking *alias* Tremain
6 May Elizabeth d. of John Roscudgion *alias* Williams
6 May Charitie a base daughter of Jane Vincent
10 May Richard s. of Stephen Tubb
13 May Thomas s. of Anthony Raw
8 May John s. of Richard Addam *alias* Rowse
15 May Agnis d. of Thomas Martin
26 May Elizabeth d. of Richard Browne
3 June James s. of Thomas Oxnam

THO. SMALLRIDGE.

8 June Jone d. of Anthony Burlace
14 June Grace d. of John Retallack Junr. gent.
14 June John s. of John Reeve
14 June Jane d. of Nicholas Parkin
27 June Charitie d. of . . . .* Huckey
29 June Charitie d. of Tobias Hancocke
2 Sep. Elenor d. of Thomas Wimboke
6 Oct. Thomas s. of Deamice Westcott
1 Nov. William s. of Tho. Basly
8 Nov. James s. of Edmond ffrench
18 Nov. Arthur the bastard son of Joane Miller
27 Nov. Petronell d. of Richard Williams
30 Nov. Maximilian a base son of Marg. Grose
10 Dec. Barbara d. of Martin Dier
11 Dec. John s. of ffrancis Lill *alias* Lion
18 Dec. Stephen s. of Thomas Hanin
28 Dec. *. . . . s. of Will'm Trekein
29 Dec. Margaret d. of Reinold Grose
6 Jan. Margerye d. of Richard Pascowe
7 Jan. Philip d. of Pascall Kentall
26 Jan. John s. of John Smith gent.
2 Feb. Nicholas s. of William Jane
10 Feb. Joane d. of Thomas Cocke
14 Feb. James s. of John George
14 Feb. William s. of William Peream
17 Feb. Elizabeth d. of John Drewe
17 Feb. Elizabeth d. of Walter Cocke
19 Feb. Grace & Elizabeth d. of John Nutting
28 Feb. Joane d. of William Black

THO. SMALLRIDGE, *Curate.*
. . . .* CORNISH } *Wardens.*
ROGER DONACUMBE }

3 Mar. Mary d. of Henry Rowse
3 Mar. Nicholas s. of Emanuel Harvey
10 Mar. John s. of William Trasaddery
21 Mar. Richard s. of Thomas Williams
23 Mar. Joane d. of William Tippett

ANNO 1608.

25 Mar. Katherine d. of James Maihow
17 April Avice d. of Richard Jollife

* Obliterated.

27 April John s. of Thomas Duggoe
30 April Gilbert s. of Ambrose Lawry
30 April Grace d. of Richard Cornish
2 May Colome s. of John Menheare
9 May Edward s. of Thomas Merifeild gent.
14 May Margerye d. of Edward Littlejohn
30 May Dewnes the base daughter of Mary Cocke
3 July Richard s. of Nicholas Napparoe *alias* Rowe
4 July Mark s. of Richard Bennett
3 Aug. Thomas s. of John Gaine
5 Aug. Richard s. of Paskell Langdon
7 Aug. Anna d. of Thomas Callway
11 Aug. Agnis d. of Ralph Rolt
25 Aug. Mary d. of John Rescorlow
18 Sep. Thomas s. of John Davie *alias* Benett
28 Sep. William s. of Robert Williams
30 Sep. Grace d. of John Trembeath
12 Oct. William the base son of Mary Gale *alias* Mayway
12 Oct. Constance d. of Thomas Barnett
16 Oct. William s. of Alexander Jollye
16 Oct. Anne d. of John Mill
27 Nov. Alice d. of John Roe
13 Dec. John s. of Edward Benett
25 Dec. Susanna d. of Richard Browne

THOMAS SMALLRIDGE, *Curate.*
*JOHN L . . . . & } *Wardens.*
*FRANCIS . . . . }

5 Jan. Katherine d. of Alexander Warne
7 Jan. Susanna d. of ffrancis Jones
13 Jan. Francis s. of Christopher Pedler
24 Jan. Darathe d. of Humphrey Hawke
12 Feb. Renfreid s. of William Rowse
20 Feb. Elizabeth d. of William Bewes
26 Feb. Honor d. of William Bond
9 Mar. Ann d. of Thomas Carthew
16 Mar. Dorathea d. of John Willes
16 Mar. Joane d. of Henery Sprey
19 Mar. Renfreid s. of Richard Bowen

ANNO 1609.

2 April Henery s. of Thomas Tregeare
12 April Nicholas s. of John Philip
24 April Jane d. of Richard Adams *alias* Rowse
30 May Agnes the base child of Jane Holman

* Obliterated.

11 June James s. of Richard Carter
24 June Grace d. of Thomas Cocke
25 June William the s. of Robert Hambly
2 July John s. of Martine Strangman
3 July Mary d. of John Burlace
15 July Grace d. of Walter Cocke
30 July Barbara d. of John Reeve
30 July John s. of Bennett Polard

In August an° 1609 were none baptised.

21 Sep. John s. of Edward Merifeild
2 Oct. Mary d. of William Trekeine
5 Oct. John s. of Richard Hawke of Trevarrian
28 Oct. fflorence d. of Thomas Lawry
2 Nov. Lucrosse the base child of Jane Vincent
11 Nov. John s. of Walter Bishopp
3 Nov. Katherine d. of Reskimmer Sprey
10 Nov. Olife the base daughter of Lame Rettor

THO. SMALLRIDGE, *Curate.*
JOHN ALLEN & } *Wardens.*
RICHARD BENETT }

16 Dec. Henry & William sones of Michaell Key
17 Dec. John s. of Oliver Binnie
23 Dec. John s. of John Boddy
24 Dec. Margerie d. of John Willes
27 Dec. Barbara d. of William Tresaddary
13 Jan. Alice d. of Richard Retallack
24 Jan. William s. of William Strangman
29 Jan. George s. of Thomas Lane
31 Jan. James s. of James Rescudgion
18 Feb. ffrancis d. of Thomas Steephens
18 Feb. Ananias s. of William Williams *alias* Reskudgion
23 Feb. Mathew s. of John Smith gent.
27 Feb. John s. of Richard ffowler
4 Mar. Tamazen d. of William Rowse
17 Mar. William s. of John Bond
18 Mar. Melissa d. of Reinold Hawkens
18 Mar. Patience a base daughter of Katherine Hawke
25 Mar. William s. of Henery Addams
25 Mar. Olyf d. of John George

ANNO 1610.

1 April John s. of John Hockin
8 April John s. of John Jewell
7 May John s. of Emanuell Harvey
13 May fflorence d. of John Lawry

19 May Katherine d. of Thomas Merifeild
20 May John s. of John Bayly
27 May Pentecost d. of William Tremain
10 June fflorence d. of Reinold Litticott
26 June Peeter s. of John Hugh
29 June Petronell d. of Ambrose Lawry
30 June William s. of Thomas Varcowe

Thomas Smallridge, *Curate.*
Anthony Hawke & John Trobellfeild } *Wardens.*

3 July Martine the base s. of Tamazon Hambly
25 July James s. of John Browne
11 Aug. Nicholas s. of Thomas Bash
12 Aug. Colome s. of Paskell Kentall
18 Aug. John s. of Thomas Horckey
21 Aug. ffrancis the base s. of Jane Oliver
24 Aug. Joane d. of Richard Benett
16 Sep. Joane d. of Walter Cocke
22 Sep. Philip d. of Richard Dyer
30 Sep. Paskell s. of Richard Williams
7 Oct. Katherine d. of ffrances Dazow
10 Oct. William s. of John Cocking
12 Oct. William s. of James Mayho
21 Oct. John s. of Richard Hand
4 Nov. John s. of Richard Jolly
17 Nov. Anthony s. of Anthony Rawe
17 Nov. Humphry the bastard s. of Ann Littycott
25 Nov. Alice d. of Henery Calway
13 Dec. Peeter s. of Thomas Calway
18 Dec. John s. of William Poleame
19 Dec. Paskell s. of Paskell Langdon
11 Jan. Thomas s. of . . . .* Treloggan
12 Jan. Wilmot base d. of Wilmot
19 Jan. William s. of William Jane
19 Jan. Elizabeth d. of John Smith gent.
19 Jan. John s. of Robert Darr
27 Jan. John s. of John Williams
27 Jan. Barbara d. of Edmund ffrench
27 Jan. John s. of William Bewes

Thomas Smallridge.

2 Feb. Constance d. of Walter Bishop
4 Feb. Richard s. of Jerman Retallack
5 Feb. William the base son of Bridget Bash
10 Feb. Elizabeth d. of Edward Littlejohn
20 Feb. Henery s. of Renfreid Hawke
20 Feb. Louisia the base daughter of Joyce Darr

* Obliterated.

20 Feb. Aradice the base daughter of Alice Amy
22 Feb. Henery s. of John Rowe
24 Feb. Jane the base daughter of Margery Grosse
28 Feb. Elizabeth d. of Edward Benett
7 Mar. John s. of Henrye Sprey
9 Mar. Patience d. of Thomas Wyet
25 Mar. Mary d. of William Copithorne

Anno 1611.

26 Mar. John s. of William Tippett
27 Mar. Thomas s. of John Day
29 Mar. Pascall s. of John Dawe
29 Mar. Edward s. of John Langdon
3 April Honor d. of Humphrey Hawke
20 April Katherine d. of Richard Helyer
27 April Jane d. of Richard Pascow *alias* Pokinghorne
30 April John s. of John Roscorlow
9 May John s. of John Trembeath
23 May Ann d. of Richard Duggo
4 July Honor d. of Robert Allen
6 July Will'm & Susanna s. & d. of Stephen Tubb
29 July An & Oliff daughters of Richard Cornish
11 Aug. John s. of Henry Adam

Thomas Smallridge.

15 Aug. Honor d. of Robert Tippett
30 Sep. Luke s. of Anthonie Burlace
31 Oct. James s. of Willia' Bond
13 Nov. Dorothie d. of John Band gent.
13 Nov. Ralph s. of Ralph Keat
13 Nov. Richard s. of Alexander Jolley
1 Dec. Alice d. of John Rowe
2 Dec. Joane d. of Francis Hill *alias* Lill
2 Dec. George s. of Reskimmer Sprey
3 Dec. John s. of Richard Williams
7 Jan. Richard s. of ffrancis Benny
7 Jan. Agnes d. of William Creede
26 Jan. Grace d. of John Staple
31 Jan. John s. of Thomas Jane
13 Feb. Margaret d. of Thomas Barnet
20 Feb. Francis s. of John Rice
22 Feb. Hanibal s. of Francis Treere
22 Feb. Mary d. of Richard Retallack
1 Mar. Mary d. of John Horkye
15 Mar. John s. of John Cockin *alias* Tremaine
19 Mar. Hugh s. of Benett Pollard
22 Mar. Judeth d. of Edward Hobline gent.

Thomas Smallridge, *Curate.*

ANNO 1612.

28 Mar. Mary d. of John Cundy
29 Mar. William s. of Richard Hawke of Trevarren
26 April Denas d. of John Drewe
26 April Margaret d. of John Taylor
27 April Mary d. of Thomas Benett *alias* Davie
19 May Agnes d. of John Harvey

THOMAS SMALLRIDGE, *Curate.*
HENRIE COCKE & SAMPSON MORCOMBE } *Wardens.*

14 June Agas d. of Ambrose Lawry
18 June Peeter the base son of Mary Dyer
1 July Margerye d. of John Cowry
6 July Richard s. of Henrye Addam *alias* Rowse
15 Aug. John s. of Rainold Litticott
15 Aug. Mary d. of Thomas Stephens
6 Sep. Richard s. of Thomas Litticott
20 Sep. Joan d. of John Rowe
21 Sep. Robert s. of Christopher Pedler
22 Sep. George s. of Reinard Hawkin
4 Oct. Boatona d. of John Heicroft
18 Oct. Ann d. of Nicolas Bonasall
30 Oct. Joane d. of Richard Rawlinge
31 Oct. Theodorus son of Emanuell Harvey

In November were none baptized.

17 Dec. John s. of William Rowse
3 Jan. Darathe d. of Thomas Husband
17 Jan. William s. of William Trekeine
31 Jan. Thomas s. of Nicolas Duggoe
6 Feb. Emmanuell s. of John Dawe
14 Feb. William s. of Thomas Hawkin
28 Feb. Agnes d. of John Hawke
2 Mar. Peeter s. of Martine Strangmen
3 Mar. Henrye s. of John Upcott
4 Mar. John s. of Thomas Wyatt

THO. SMALLRIDGE, *Curate.*

ANNO 1613.

27 Mar. Mary d. of Thomas Lawry
28 Mar. Olif d. of Robert Berry
28 Mar. Elizabeth d. of Richard Bowen
5 April Sydnath s. of German Retallack
18 April Henrye s. of Richard Jolly
18 April Agnes d. of Thomas Merifeild gent.

THO. SMALLRIDGE, *Curate.*
JOHN HEICROFT JOHN YOUNG } *Wardens.*

21 April Thomas s. of Thomas Nattallen
6 June John s. of Nicolas Martine
20 June Grace d. of John Browne
6 July John s. of John Hugh
7 July Joan d. of John Drew
11 July Olife d. of James Mayhoo
12 July Henrye s. of William Jane of the towne
15 July Katherine d. of Thomas Davies *alias* Benett
1 Aug. Gilbert s. of Thomas Hockey
12 Aug. John s. of William Copithorne
28 Aug. Francis d. of John Strangman
28 Aug. Joane d. of John Treneage
5 Sep. John s. of Henrye Calway
19 Sep. John s. of William Truscott
3 Oct. Anne d. of John Vivean gent
9 Oct. Henry s. of Thomas Rawe
9 Oct. William s. of John Trebenbane
14 Oct. Robert s. of Humphrey Marke
14 Oct. Alice d. of Anthony Randle
15 Oct. John s. of John Cundy
18 Oct. Ann d. of Renfred Michell
30 Oct. Agnes d. of John Roskorloe
14 Nov. Henry s. of John Trembeth
14 Nov. Elizabeth d. of Richard Paskow *alias* Polkinghorne
28 Nov. John a base son of Joane Poade
29 Nov. Andrew s. of Thomas Chappell
13 Dec. James base son of Joane Edy

THOMAS SMALLRIDGE.
JOHN MAY & NICHOLAS CRUSE } *Wardens.*

8 Jan. Alice d. of Henry Sprey
22 Jan. George & Francis s. & d. of John Smith gent
27 Jan. John s. of John Bond gent
5 Feb. John s. of Reskimmer Sprey
12 Feb. Christian d. of Thomas Calway
16 Feb. Agnes d. of Walter Keysa
20 Feb. Margaret d. of John Stribly
25 Feb. Mary d. of Richard Smith iun^r

THO. SMALLRIDGE, *Curate.*

ANNO 1614.

8 April William s. of John Tremaine *alias* Cocking
11 April John s. of Thomas Steephens
21 April William s. of George Juell
3 May Robert s. of Paskall Kentall
22 May John s. of John Wills
29 May Dorathe d. of Richard Dazoe
13 June John s. of . . . .* ffrench
15 June Beaton d. of Richard Cornish
2 July Jane d. of Thomas Cocke
9 July Elizabeth d. of Joell Jewell
12 July Priscilla d. of Thomas Kent
4 Aug. Jane d. of Robert Cocking

* Obliterated.

11 Aug. Anne d. of Oliver Nymise
14 Aug. Alice d. of John Langdone
14 Aug. Avice d. of Francis Benny
20 Aug. John s. of Thomas Littycott
7 Sep. John s. of John Dawe iuni[r]
15 Sep. Genifore d. of Alexander Jolley

THOMAS SMALLRIDGE.
JOHN MAY & NICOLAS CRUSE } *Wardens.*

25 Sep. Alice d. of William Peleane
3 Oct. Martine d. of William Bewes
6 Oct. Elizabeth d. of Anthony Borlas
9 Oct. Richard s. of Richard Hawke of Trevarren
18 Oct. Benimin s. of John Harvey
21 Oct. Richard s. of Thomas Bash
23 Oct. Thomas s. of Thomas Barnett
20 Nov. Redagon d. of John Rice
22 Nov. George s. of Henrye Addam
18 Dec. John s. of William Bond
27 Dec. William s. of William Gillingame
8 Jan. James s. of John Strangman
16 Jan. John the base son of Margaret Michell
17 Jan. Anne d. of John Carthewe
1 Feb. Henrye s. of Henrye Addam *alias* Rowse
1 Feb. George s. of George Champion
19 Feb. Anne d. of Edward Hoblyn gent
19 Feb. Honor d. of John Smith gent
19 Feb. Gawen s. of John Kent
19 Feb. Jane d. of John Medders
26 Feb. Katherine d. of Richard Jolly
8 Mar. Mathewe s. of Thomas Allen
9 Mar. Genifore d. of Reskimmer Sprey
11 Mar. Jane d. of Robert Allen
19 Mar. John s. of Thomas Benett *alias* Danys

THO. SMALLRIDGE, *Curate.*

ANNO 1615.

29 Mar. Jane d. of Nicolas Yeo
12 April ffrances the base son of Elizabeth Vallies
17 April Thomas s. of Humphrey Trenowth
20 April John s. of John Hawkyn

THOMAS SMALLRIDGE, *Curate.*
JOHN SMITH & JOHN BRABYN } *Wardens.*

20 April Mathewe s. of Thomas Husband
20 April Anne d. of John Bayly
1 May Tamson base d. of Joane Cocke
27 May John s. of John Dawe
22 June Peeter s. of Nicolas Bonsall
23 June Bernard s. of William Rowse
27 July Joane d. of Robert Berry
11 Aug. Charles s. of Christopher Pedler
13 Aug. Nicolas s. of Richard Williams
3 Sep. Christiana d. of William Black
12 Sep. Mary d. of Reinald Hawkyn
17 Sep. Agnes d. of John Row
17 Sep. Rebecca d. of Robert Cockinge
21 Sep. John s. of Richard Hellyer
8 Oct. Richard s. of Thomas Nantallyn
19 Nov. Grace d. of Hugh Lawry
21 Nov. Richard s. of Robert Typpett
24 Dec. Agnes d. of John Hawke
28 Dec. John s. of John Taylor
7 Jan. Anna d. of John Lawry
7 Jan. Marian d. of Emmuell Harrice
9 Jan. Dorathe base d. of Katherine Moyle
2 Feb. Dorathe d. of Richard Retallack
2 Feb. William s. of Robert Bowen
2 Feb. Joyce d. of Robert Bowen
5 Feb. Honora d. of Lucke Pollard
11 Feb. Jerman s. of Jerman Retallack
11 Feb. John s. of Richard Carveth

THOMAS SMALLRIDGE, *Curate.*
THOMAS OXENHAM & JOHN CARTHEW } *Wardens.*

11 Feb. Joane d. of Nicholas Duggoe, late Dewsod
20 Feb. Jane d. of James Mayhoe
21 Feb. Jane d. of Thomas Lawry
28 Feb. Honor d. of John Ruorden
14 Mar. Wilmot d. of Steephen Knight
20 Mar. Henrye s. of Emmanell Harvey

THOMAS SMALLRIDGE, *Curate.*

ANNO 1616.

29 Mar. William s. of Thomas Wyett
2 April Katherine d. of John Cocking the elder
10 April Olif d. of John Mayhoe
12 April Elizabeth d. of Richard Smyth jun.
14 April Dorathe d. of ffrances Thomas
25 April Honor d. of Anthony Rawe
28 April Thomas s. of John Beard gent.
11 May John s. of John Drew
26 May Anna d. of Thomas Rowe
28 May Elizabeth d. of Thomas Brabyn
9 June John s. of John Vivian gent.*

* 9 June, 1616, by his wife Mary dau. and coheir of Wm. Cavell, whom he mar. at St Kew, 18 Ap., 1615.

10 June Thomas s. of Thomas Hocky
23 June John s. of Thomas Cardew
28 June Peeter s. of Barnabas Betty
13 July John s. of William Dankester
23 July Anna d. of John Cockyn *alias* Tremayne
28 July Dorathe d. of Oliver Jagoe
31 Aug. Honor d. of Thomas Calway
8 Sep. Frances s. of Thomas Jane
13 Sep. Honor d. of John Moyses
22 Sep. Mary d. of Edward Hoblyn gent.
22 Sep. Richard s. of James Moyle

THOMAS SMALLRIDGE, *Curate.*
THOMAS OXNAM, JOHN CARDEW } *Wardens.*

29 Sep. Renatus s. of Renatus Byllett gent.
29 Sep. Jane d. of John Hawkey
6 Oct. Christian d. of Henry Calway
14 Oct. Elizabeth bastard d. of Elizabeth Chapman
26 Nov. Bethsaida d. of Humphrey Trenouth
11 Dec. Richard s. of William Pelleane
16 Dec. Judeth d. of John Harvey
29 Dec. William s. of William Creede
9 Jan. Ebete d. of Thomas Skynner
12 Jan. Robert s. of Paskoe Tregellas
29 Jan. Donate vel Deonata d. of Martyne Donnacombe
2 Feb. Nicolas s. of Robert Trehenbane
2 Feb. Cyssill d. of John Treneage
7 Feb. Richard s. of John Bond gent.
11 Feb. Ann d. of William Bewes
13 Feb. John s. of John Haycroft
21 Feb. Mary d. of John Williams
27 Feb. Sibilla d. of John Evans
12 Mar. Nicolas s. of Edmond ffrench
16 Mar. Steephen base s. of Jane Tubby *alias* Benett

THOMAS SMALLRIDGE, *Curate.*

ANNO 1617.

6 April John s. of Henry Litticott
6 April Nicolas s. of John Trehenbane
13 April John s. of William Beuford
17 April Mary d. of John Cardwe
18 April William s. of John Metherell
19 April Joane d. of Thomas Steephens

THOMAS SMALLRIDGE, *Curate.*
JOHN DREWE & HUGH LAWRY } *Wardens.*

29 May Christian d. of Thomas Davies *alias* Benett
9 June Joane d. of Francis Benny
12 June Hester d. of John Addam
15 June Nicolas d. of Paskall Polkinghorne
15 June Joane d. of James Mayhoe
29 June William base s. of Wilmote Litticott reputed father Robert Pollard
4 July John bastard s. of Elizabeth Behednoe, the reputed father John Hugh
5 June Dorathe d. of Henry Willes
8 June George s. of John Smith gent.
28 June John bastard s. of Beaton Strangman widow
3 Aug. Adria d. of John Mayhoe
3 Aug. Agnes d. of Paskell Keutall
10 Aug. Thomas s. of John Vivian gent.
11 Aug. Thomas s. of William Gillingame
24 Aug. Richard s. of Richard ffowler
27 Aug. John s. of John Staple
30 Aug. Thomas s. of Raynold Weekes
31 Aug. John s. of Henry Rowse *alias* Addam
31 Aug. John s. of John Retallack jun.
7 Sep. Richard s. of George Hodge
7 Sep. Edward s. of Richard Behednoe
16 Sep. ffrances s. of Thomas Husband
2 Oct. Dorathea d. of Thomas Bayly
5 Oct. Philip d. of Richard Jollife
8 Oct. John s. of Beniamin Strangman
25 Oct. Cisly d. of George Jewill
26 Oct. John s. of William Trekeyn
5 Nov. Marke s. of Walter Bishop

THOMAS SMALLRIDGE, *Curate.*
JOHN DREWE & HUGH LAWRY } *Wardens.*

9 Nov. Thomas s. of John Dawe
27 Nov. Gartride d. of William Bond
30 Nov. Thomas s. of John Hockyn
14 Dec. John s. of Gilbert Rawe
20 Dec. Grace d. of Thomas John
21 Dec. Peeter s. of John Rescorlow
5 Jan. Elizabeth d. of Edward Hoblyn gent.
10 Jan. Elizabeth d. of John Rice
11 Jan. Lawrde d. of Reskymmer Sprey
14 Jan. Henry s. of John Dyer
29 Jan. Thomas s. of John Cockyn the yelder
8 Feb. John s. of Luke Pollard
8 Feb. Beniamyn s. of Richard Willams of Tregasoe

15 Feb. William s. of Robert Berry
16 Feb. Phillippe d. of Steepben Knight
26 Feb. Christopher s. of John Hendy
1 Mar. Cisly d. of Richard Carvith
1 Mar. Petronell d. of Thomas Jenning
4 Mar. Joane d. of Reinold Hawkyn
8 Mar. George s. of Thomas Allen

THOMAS SMALLRIDGE, *Curate.*

ANNO 1618.

26 Mar. ffrancis d. of Thomas Littacott
28 Mar. Marian d. of Thomas Wyett
29 Mar. John s. of John Langdon
4 April Alice d. of John Cockinge *alias* Tremaine
7 April Joane d. of Christopher Pedler
9 April Jane d. of Robert Pollard

THOMAS SMALLRIDGE, *Curate.*
ROBERT DRUE & NATHANIELL CREEDE } *Wardens.*

11 April Ann d. of Robert Cockyn
3 May Elizabeth d. of John Beard gent.
7 May Paskall s. of Thoms Natallen
10 May Christopher s. of John Drewe
23 May Elizabeth d. of John Lawry
14 June Richard s. of Nicolas Bounsall
18 June ffrances s. of John Hawkey
29 June Joane d. of John Skrinner *alias* Martyn
5 July Elizabeth d. of John May
10 July Joyce d. of John Bayly
30 July Hugh s. of Emmanuell Harvey
4 Aug. Dorathe d. of Henry Helston
8 Aug. Jane d. of John Kent
9 Aug. Richard s. of John Carter jun. gent.*
13 Aug. John bastard s. to Jane Moyle
30 Aug. Honor d. of John Bond gent.†

In September were none baptized.

4 Oct. Thomas s. of James Cockyn
8 Oct. Henry s. of William Rowse
10 Oct. Stephen s. of Thomas Hawke
1 Nov. William s. of John Vivian gent.
20 Nov. Henry s. of Reinold Peeter
29 Nov. Anna d. of Oliver Jagoe
14 Dec. Benyamyn s. of William Dankester

* This John Carter was mar. at St. Breock, 13 Sept., 1617, to Mary, dau. of Robt. Moyle, of St. Germans, Esq.

† This John was son and heir of Wm. Bond, of Earth, near Saltash. *See* his mar. in 1609.

27 Dec. Mary d. of John Body
30 Dec. Robert s. of Robert Tippett

THOMAS SMALLRIDGE, *Curate.*
ROBERT DRUE & NATHANIEL CREEDE } *Wardens.*

14 Jan. Jerman s. of Richard Bowen
4 Feb. Thomas a base son of Elizabeth Merrifield
21 Feb. Honor d. of William Beuford
21 Feb. Katherine d. of Robert Trehenban
24 Feb. Richard s. of Richard Rowse
25 Feb. Robert s. of Benyamyn Strangman
3 Mar. Katherine d. of John Moyle
8 Mar. John a base s. of Honor Duggoe
15 Mar. Henry s. of Henry Moyle
15 Mar. Thomas s. of Henry Calaway
18 Mar. Joane d. of Mathew Wills

THOMAS SMALLRIDGE, *Curate.*

ANNO 1619.

26 Mar. William s. of John Brabyn
7 April Dorathe d. of Marke Tyer
10 April Richard s. of ffrances Treere
11 April John s. of Edward Hoblyn gent.
16 April John the base s. of Barbara Moyle
22 April Thomas s. of Edmund ffrench
4 May Patience d. of Gilbert Roe
29 May William s. of William Tresaddarn
14 June Gilbert s. of Thomas Caleway
23 June Peeter s. of Thomas Jane
3 July Petronell d. of Thomas Mantall
11 July Elizabeth d. of Martyne Donnacombe
11 July Henry the base s. of Oliva Merrifield was buried same day, reputed father John Jolley jun^r
5 Aug. Bernard s. of William Saltow
14 Aug. Richard s. of John Copithorne
1 Sep. John s. of John Addams
1 Sep. Peeter s. of Thomas Retallack

THOMAS SMALLRIDGE, *Curate.*

5 Sep. Joane d. of Robert Pollard
5 Sep. Emblyn d. of William Jane
11 Sep. Jane d. of John Cardwe
19 Sep. John s. of Robert Drewe
19 Sep. Richowe d. of Richard Dunne
3 Oct. Margarethe d. of Henry Wills
7 Oct. Alice d. of John Harvey

7 Nov. Mary d. of Hugh Lawry
18 Nov. Patience d. of Thomas Lawry
19 Dec. Mathewe s. of John Trembeath
30 Dec. John s. of John Dyer
12 Jan. Richard s. of John Tenny
16 Jan. Remfrey s. of Thomas Hocky
23 Jan. Rosa d. of Robert Cocke
30 Jan. Robert s. of Thomas Husband
30 Jan. Adam s. of John Metherell
3 Feb. Mary d. of Richard Smyth
9 Feb. Ann d. of Pascow John
10 Feb. Christopher s. of Henry Rowse
10 Feb. Eleanor d. of Jonathan Juell
16 Feb. Susan d. of Walter Bishopp
23 Feb. Jone d. of Henrye Davy
19 Mar. Richard s. of John Vyvian

ANNO 1620.

29 Mar. Tamsyn d. of John Mayhow
18 April Patience d. of Henry Litticott
12 May Thomas s. of Thomas Skynner
13 May Richard s. of Reskymer Spraye
17 May Henry s. of William Beacose
18 May Nicholas s. of John Cocken junr.
21 May Elizabeth d. of William Gillingame
25 May Mathewe s. of James James
1 June James s. of John Bond gent.
3 June Susan d. of Luke Pollard
4 June John s. of Rob'te Beuye
11 June Judeth d. of Edward Hoblyn gent.
11 June Jane d. of William Bond
24 June Humphrey s. of John Cocking
20 July John s. of William Brabyn
23 July Robert s. of Thomas Bennet
30 July William s. of Mathewe Wills
4 July Samuell s. of Thomas Steevens
9 July Honoria d. of Thomas Wyett
11 July Margerye d. of John Dane
24 July John s. of John Lawrye
8 July John s. of Richard Rouse
26 July Grace d. of John Brabyn
23 Sep. Remphrey s. of John Jolle
2 Oct. Mary d. of John Smith gent.
15 Jan. William s. of Marteyne Trusteyne
24 Oct. Reskymmer s. of Thomas Allen
25 Oct. Ellis s. of Jobb Pollard
25 Oct. Grace d. of William Rawling
11 Mar. Jane d. of John Vivian gent.
14 Mar. Thomasine d. of Reginald Peter
16 Mar. Nicolas s. of Nicolas Bounsell
17 Mar. Grace d. of James Moyle
25 Mar. Symon s. of John Trewman

ANNO 1621.

20 April Richard s. of Thomas Husband
3 May Elizabeth d. of Richard Edwards
20 May Thomas s. of John Daye
6 June Richard s. of William Dancaster
23 June Robert s. of ffrances George
2 July John s. of Paschow John
6 July Thomasine d. of John Langdon
11 July Dorcas d. of John Copithorne
24 July Grace d. of Thomas Bayly
2 Aug. Anne d. of Reynoll Hawkyn
5 Aug. Elizabeth d. of John Carter gent.
7 Aug. Mary d. of Jo. Martyn
19 Aug. Humphrey s. of Richard Behedoe
26 Aug. Grace d. of John Medderne
9 Sep. Philip d. of John Hawkye
15 Sep. Johane d. of Gilbert Rowe
16 Sep. Marye d. of Charles Trubodye gent.
16 Sep. Philip d. of William Rouse
16 Sep. John s. of Thomas Hawkye
30 Sep. Loveday d. of William Terkeene
6 Oct. Cecila d. of John Williams
25 Oct. Anne d. of Alexander Penfounde
2 Nov. Grace d. of Richard Smyth
11 Nov. Richard s. of Jeromm Kent
22 Nov. Andrey d. of Reskimmer Sprey
30 Nov. Rose d. of Henrye Moyle
16 Dec. Thomas s. of William Salter
9 Jan. Thomas s. of John Harvey
9 Jan. Grace d. of Richard Pynnowe
10 Jan. Walter s. of John Tyre
13 Jan. John s. of John Cocking
20 Jan. Peter s. of John Adams
2 Feb. Richard s. of Richard Crawleigh
6 Feb. Emblyn d. of Edward Hoblyn gent.
16 Feb. William s. of Reynoll Weeks
20 Feb. Thomas s. of Thomas Paynter
3 Mar. John s. of Thomas Calway
6 Mar. Richard s. of John Cocke
6 Mar. Nicholas s. of William Blake
6 Mar. Susanna d. of Thomas Body
10 Mar. Thomas s. of John Tynney
17 Mar. John s. of Mathewe Wills
24 Mar. John s. of John Brabyn

NICHOLAS COB, *Cu.*

ANNO 1622.

6 April John s. of John Mayhoe
7 April Thomas s. of Nicholas Lang
13 April Thomas s. of John Bayly

22 April Honor d. of Martin
28 April William s. of William Williams
28 April Thomas s. of John Kent
26 May Katherine d. of William Brabin
9 June Margaret d. of Martin Phit
22 June Mary d. of Thomas Trimbeen
30 June Richard s. of Thomas Husband
3 July Elizabeth d. of John Pook
14 July John s. of Robert Bery
18 July Henrye s. of Pascha Hawke
4 Aug. Mary d. of Robert Cockin
18 Aug. Jane d. of James Cockin
25 Aug. Peter s. of Charles Trewbody gent.
17 Sep. John s. of John Martin
29 Sep. John s. of John Drew
20 Oct. Jane d. of John Carter
21 Oct. Beniamin s. of John Dyer
1 Nov. William s. of Thomas Skinner
24 Nov. Mary d. of John Lawry
7 Dec. William s. of William Beford
29 Dec. John s. of Thomas Wiat
19 Jan. Elizabeth d. of William Jolly
7 Feb. Petronell d. of Richard Hitchings
13 Feb. John s. of Charles Conner
23 Feb. James s. of Beniamyn Strangman
26 Feb. Jane d. of Alexander Penfound
12 Mar. Jane d. of John Hendry
21 Mar. Joyce d. of Richard Hawke

ANNO 1623.

27 Mar. Cathering d. of Henry Rowse
30 Mar. John s. of Thomas Benet
31 Mar. Mary d. of Robert Pollard
6 April Ann d. of John Rowse
25 April Margaret d. of Richard Edwards
27 April Hugh s. of Thomas Retallack
28 April Jane d. of Nicolas More
2 May Patience d. of John Smith gent.
3 May Umphry s. of Alexander Lange
8 June James s. of Robert Litticot
. .* June Christian d. of Steven Loves
17 June Mary d. of Thomas Brabinne
22 June Henrye s. of Richard Rowse
9 July Margerye d. of Henry Moyle
10 July Gartruet d. of Philla Bond
20 July Simon of Robert Trehenben
. .* Aug. Thomas & Nicholas sons of Thomas Jane
. .* Sep. Mary d. of Rynald Peter
24 Sep. Thomas the base son of Emblen Scantlebury
28 Sep. Peter s. of William Tresaddarn
28 Sep. Joane d. of William Williams
28 Sep. Grace d. of Nicolas Stribley
. .* Oct. Mary d. of John Copithorne
. .* Oct. Adam s. of Martine Tristeane
2 Nov. Thomas s. of John Adams
7 Nov. Jane d. of Luke Pollard
22 Nov. William s. of Thomas Hockey
14 Dec. Dorathy d. of William Libbey
14 Dec. Humphrey s. of John Harvey
22 Dec. Richard s. of Richard Williams
23 Dec. Grace d. of William Thomas
12 Jan. ffloraunce d. of Jerman Retallacke
1 Feb. ffrances s. of John Vivian gent.
20 Feb. Edward s. of William Dunkester
14 Mar. Mathew s. of Mathew Wills
. .* Mar. ffrances d. of Nicolas Bounsall

ANNO 1624.

. .* Mar. Elizabeth d. of Gilbert . . . .*
. .* April John s. of John Day gen. & Audry his wiffe
. .* April ffrancis s. of Thomas Tom & Martha his wiff
12 April Grace d. of John & Petronell Treningwas
24 April William s. of John & Elizabeth Mill
25 April Joane d. of Richard & Susanna Cavith
12 May Julian d. of Thomas & Elizabeth Wart
17 May Patience d. of John & Jane Mederne
18 July John s. of John & Mary Carter gent.
25 July Jane d. of William & Margaret Keat gent
2 Aug. John s. of John & Elenor Cockinge
1 Aug. Dorathey d. of William & Jane Salter
8 Aug. John s. of John & Jane Joll
8 Aug. Giles s. of John & Jane Williams
29 Aug. Honor d. of John & Honer Darr
29 Aug. Dorathy d. of Thomas & Jane Paynter
9 Sep. John s. of John & Phillipp Bayly
12 Sep. Patience d. of John & Elizabeth Tenny
12 Sep. Ann d. of John & Elizabeth Dow

* Obliterated.

21 Sep. ffrancis d. of Henrye & Anne Brabyn
26 Sep. Elizabeth d. of William & Elizabeth Cock
13 Oct. Richard s. of John & Alice Poole
29 Oct. John s. of Henrye & Anne Moyl
7 Nov. Elinor d. of Thomas & Thomasine Skinner
30 Nov. John s. of Thomas & ffowrance Husband
12 Dec. Emblen d. of Arthur & Alice Jolly
19 Dec. Penelope d. of Mark Tyre & Katherine Tyre
1 Jan. Archibald the base sone of Jone ffranncis
26 Jan. Katherine d. of Robert & Jone Litticott
6 Feb. Alice d. of Osithies and Jone Gummow
13 Feb. Edward s. of Martin Dunacombe & Badgett his wieff
27 Feb. Grace d. of Henrye & Jone Naparroe
3 Mar. Humphrey s. of Alexander & Margaret Penfound
13 Mar. William a base sone of Susan Lae

Anno 1625.

27 Mar. ffraunces s. of ffrances George & Jone his wieff
3 April John s. of Robert & Jone Pollard
3 April Julyan d. of Robert & Julyan Higgins
4 April William s. of Pachawe & Katherine John
9 April Henrye s. of Reynoll & Hester Weekes
19 April Stephen s. of Stephen & Helinor Knight
11 April Honor d. of John and Anne Bayly
25 April Humphrey s. of John & Elizabeth Trewman
8 May William s. of Richard & Rose Edwards
8 May Jane d. of William & Elizabeth Bond
22 May William s. of John & Jane Cocking
26 May Jane d. of Immanuell & . . . .* ffranc

* Obliterated.

29 May William s. of Thomas & Thomazine Bayly
10 May John s. of James & Thomasine Cocking
12 June William s. of Humphrey Arthur & . . . .* his wife
12 June Richard s. of John Martyne & Joane his wieff
13 June Richard s. of Paskall Hawke & Anna his wieff
10 July Elizabeth d. of Thomas & Christian Calway
17 July John s. of Nicholas & Margery Bounsoll
17 July Elizabeth d. of Thomas & Jane Trembeath
4 Aug. Thomas s. of Robert & Katherine Trehenban
22 Aug. William s. of William Keat gent & Margaret his wieff
22 Aug. William s. of William Bond & Jone his wieff
28 Aug. Mathew s. of John Vivian gent & Mary his wieff
28 Aug. Jayes d. of Beniamyn & Jone Strongman
17 Sep. Dorathie d. of Imannuell & Sarah Harvey
2 Oct. Anthony s. of John & Elizabeth Lawry
9 Oct. Grace d. of Thomas & Margaret Tom
9 Oct. Margerye d. of Reskymer & Jane Spray
30 Oct. Richard s. of Richard & Barbara Rowze
30 Oct. Mary d. of Henrye & Elizabeth Harvey
30 Oct. Cecilia the bastard dau. of Elizabeth Browne
18 Nov. Martyn s. of Martyn Tristeane and Patience his wiffe
19 Nov. Johan d. of John & Richewe Myhoe
20 Nov. Mary d. of John & Grace Spraye
23 Nov. Julyan d. of John & Julyan Lugge
25 Nov. Alce d. of Thomas & Katherine ffranc
27 Nov. Thomas s. of Henrye & Susan Riche
27 Nov. Grace the d. of Thomas & Mary Body
21 Dec. William the bastard sone of Avis Benett
26 Dec. Thomas s. of Thomas & Jane Merifield

26 Dec. Richard s. of Richard & Susan Carveath
15 Jan. Margaret d. of John & Helinor King
22 Jan. William s. of Nicolas Moore & Phillip his wieff
13 Feb. Gyles s. of Martyn & Thomasyn Edwards
16 Feb. Katherine d. of Christopher Cocke & Dorathie his wieff
26 Feb. Helenor d. of Alexander & Margaret Penfound
5 Mar. John s. of John & Jone Harvey
5 Mar. Honor d. of Thomas & Elizabeth Bennett
12 Mar. ffrances d. of Luke & Jone Pollard
19 Mar. Elizabeth d. of Henry Blighe gent. & Margaret his wieff
22 Mar. Edward s. of John & Elizabeth Copithorne
25 Mar. John s. of Henrye & Ann Moile

ANNO 1626.

26 Mar. William s. of John Wickett & Christian his wieff
29 Mar. Phillip d. of John & Phillip Bayly
1 April William the base sone of Avis Bennett
3 April William & John the bastard sons of Jane Ellerye
14 May Phillip d. of James Moyle & Elizabeth his wieff
22 May Mary d. of John & Jone Rouze
30 May Martin s. of German & Alice Retallack
4 June Thomas s. of John Brabyn & Grace his wieff
4 June Anne d. of Robert Litticott & Jone his wieff
8 June Andrew the s. of William & Jone Bonsall
8 June *. . . . s. of Anthonye & Grace Baufore
14 June *. . . . d. of William & Elizabeth Litticott (?)
9 July Richard s. of John Carter gent. & Mary his wieff
26 July William s. of John Cocking & Jone his wieff
July *. . . . s. of John & Honor . . . .*
6 Aug. Richard s. of David & Jone Grosse
13 Aug. Edward s. of Rawlyn & Alice Merifeild
31 Aug. John s. of John Moyle & Florance his wieff
9 Sep. James s. of Thomas Wyatt & Elizabeth his wieff
13 Sep. Alice d. of William & Constance Turbarvile
21 Sep. Joyce d. of Thomas & Jane Penwith
29 Sep. Thomasine d. of William & Margerye ffith
6 Oct. William s. of William Keat gent. & Margarett his wieff
15 Oct. Arthur s. of George Levithon & Jane his wiffe
28 Oct. Dorothye d. of Thomas & Mary Luky
22 Nov. Arthur s. of Arthur Jollye & Alice his wieff
3 Dec. Grace d. of Stephen Loveis & Jennifer his wieff
3 Dec. Mellerye d. of John Williams & Mary
10 Dec. Donnatt the base daughter of Penticost Geene
14 Dec. Peter s. of John Adam & Thamason his wieff
6 Jan. Anne d. of Nicholas Tresteane and . . . .* his wieff
7 Jan. Mary d. of Henrye Hervey & Elizabeth his wieff
14 Jan. Pacience d. of Nicholas Peter & Peternell his wieff
15 Jan. Marke the base son of Grace Mutton
15 Jan. Margerye d. of John Mill & Elizabeth his wieff
28 Jan. Anne d. of Gilbert Rowe and Margerye his wieff
11 Feb. Charity d. of William Salter & Jane his wieff
18 Feb. Thomas s. of Nicholas Bounsoll & Margerye his wieff
18 Feb. Julian s. of John Kinge & Ellen his wieff
11 Mar. Avis d. of John Williams
21 Mar. Anne the base daughter of Elizabeth Hill

ANNO 1627.

1 April Edward s. of Robert Pollerd & Jane his wieff
1 April James s. of Robert Lukey & Margerye his wieff
1 April Priscilla d. of William Libbye & Katherine his wieff
15 April Mary d. of Christopher Cocke and Dorothy his wieff
22 April Alice d. of Robert West & Jane his wieff

* Obliterated.

6 May Theophilus s. of Thomas Lac and Margarett his wieff
6 May Edward s. of Henrye Moyell and . . . .* his wieff
27 May Honor d. of John Metherell and Jone his wieff
24 June Henrye s. of Thomas Skynner and Thomasyn his wieff
29 June Anne d. of John Trencage & Patience his wieff
1 July Edward s. of John Vivian gent. & Mary his wieff
8 July William s. of Edward White and Elizabeth his wieff
28 July Henrye the base sone of Henrye Husband & Alice Cocke
26 Aug. Honor d. of Marke Tyer & Joan his wieff
9 Sep. Richard s. of Water Currite & Elizabeth his wieff
15 Sep. John s. of Thomas Tom & Margaret his wieff
15 Sep. Honor d. of Sampson Lawry & Mary his wieff
3 Sep. John s. of Thomas Merifeild
24 Oct. John s. of William Calway & Jane his wieff
26 Oct. John s. of John Legg and Julian his wieff
26 Oct. Joan d. of Beniamin Strongman & Joane his wieff
26 Oct. Elizabeth d. of Williams & Elizabeth his wieff
10 Nov. Sicilla d. of Henery Bligh & Margaret his wieff
15 Dec. William s. of John Dyer & Honor his wieff
16 Dec. Elinor d. of William and Margaret Keate
16 Dec. Thomas s. of Nicholas and Katherine Stribley
23 Dec. Richard s. of John Moile
23 Dec. Richard s. of Henrye & Johane Nanparrow
6 Jan. Abraham s. of Thomas & fflorances Husband
20 Jan. Humphrey s. of Richard & Rose Edwards
27 Jan. John s. of Richard Whitford & Grace his wieff
27 Jan. Grace d. of Mathew & Mary Willis
3 Feb. Jane d. of James Rouse & Mary his wieff
18 Feb. Edward s. of William and Johan Granfford

* Obliterated.

23 Feb. Tamsyn the base daughter of Cicilie Morcom
2 Mar. Henrye s. of John Haicroft & Jane his wieff
2 Mar. Radigan d. of Henrye and Elizabeth Lidacoate
8 Mar. Ann d. of Thomas & Elizabeth Alleyn
10 Mar. Honor d. of John & Tamsyn Adams
16 Mar. James s. of John & Elizabeth Tenny
22 Mar. John s. of Robert Trebenbann & Katherine his wieff

ANNO 1628.

30 Mar. Colan s. of William & Elizabeth Doncaster
30 Mar. Beaton d. of Thomas & Rebecca Bailye
3 April James s. of Richard & Ann Merifeild
8 April Joane d. of John & Elizabeth Lawry
10 April Grace d. of William & Ann May
14 April Margarett d. of John & Jane Thorne
20 April Mary d. of John & Catheryne Mayhowe
25 April Issabell d. of Thomas & Jane Stephins
27 April Jane d. of Richard & Susan Carveathe
4 May John s. of John & Phillipp Barlosse
11 May Martyn the base sone of Phillipp Yeonam & Johan Luke
7 May Constantine s. of Chesson . . .* & Charity his wieff
18 May James s. of James & Alice Cocke
22 May Elizabeth a base daughter of Elizabeth . . . .*
8 June Honor d. of John & Grace Sprey
8 June Mary d. of Thomas & Mary Bodye
22 June Robert s. of Robert Litticott & Jone his wieff
29 June Hughe s. of Henry & Phillip Sexon†
13 July Gilberd Rowe s. of Gilbert Rowe
9 Aug. Thomas s. of German & Susan Kent
19 Aug. Skinner d. of John & Johane Harry
. . . .* Martyn s. of Phillipp Yamon

* Obliterated. † Sexton, see p. 37, 25 May, 1631.

7 Sep. Mary d. of Nicholas & Philip More
14 Sep. Jane d. of Pascowe & Anne Hawke
19 Sep. Paciens the base daughter of Mary Perse
14 Sep. Henrye s. of Richard & Elizabeth Black
28 Sep. John s. of Lennard and Elizabeth May
28 Sep. Catherine d. of William and Mellery Williams
28 Sep. Ruth d. of Steeven & Jiniver Lovell
4 Sep. John s. of David & Jane Walkie
12 Oct. Honor d. of John & Leah Arter
5 Nov. Phillepp s. of John & Helinor King
10 Nov. John d. of Digory & Grace Marshell
30 Nov. Richard s. of Martyn & Tamsyn Edwards
30 Nov. Barbara d. of John & Jone ...*
.........* Nicholas s. of William & Marg[t] Keate
1 Jan. John s. of Henrye & Margarett Blighe
11 Jan. John s. of John & Mary Williams
18 Jan. Jone d. of Alexander & Margaret Penfound
18 Jan. Anne d. of Luke & Jane Pollard
8 Feb. Grace d. of John & Elizabeth Copithorne
8 Mar. Thomas s. of Robin & Alice Merifeild
9 Mar. Anne d. of William Cocken and Honor his wieff
20 Mar. Robert s. of Thomas & Tamson Skinner

ANNO 1629.

29 Mar. Nathaniel s. of John & Tamson Adam
Mar. Grace d. of George & Jane Leverton
29 Mar. Martyn s. of Thomas & Margarett Tom
6 April Elizabeth d. of John & Honour Dyer
12 April John s. of Abraham & Elizabeth Martine
12 April Christian d. of Reskemer & Jane Sprey
17 May John s. of William & Johan Boand
26 May Davyd s. of William & Enstis Thomas
31 May Peter s. of Robert & Johan Pollard
17 June John s. of Arthur & Alice Jolly
21 June Marye d. of Henry & Alice Husband
5 July Jane d. of Robert & Johan West
12 July James s. of Marke & Katherine Tyre
19 July Tamsyn d. of Thomas & Mary Lukye
26 July Adam s. of Martyn & Pacience Tresteane
2 Aug. Thomas s. of Thomas & Anne Bayliffe
9 Aug. Humphrey s. of John & Elizabeth Lawry
12 Aug. Charles s. of Michell & Mary Davy
23 Aug. Johane d. of Martyn & Bridget Donnicombe
23 Aug. Peter the base son of Pentecost Greene
24 Aug. William the base son of Ancety Hicks
28 Aug. Johan d. of ffrancis & Julian Rescarrock
6 Sep. Mote d. of Henry & Jease Rouse
13 Sep. Henry s. of Henry & Ann Martyn
13 Sep. John s. of James & Elizabeth Moyle
18 Sep. Grace the base daughter of Barbara Merrifeild
27 Sep. Edward s. of Thomas & ....* Steephens
4 Oct. Richard s. of Mathew & Mary Wills
4 Oct. Alice d. of Thomas & Elizabeth Wyett
11 Oct. Henry s. of William & Jone Beauford
11 Oct. Lenes s. of William & Jane Salter
16 Oct. Thomasyne d. of Robert & Elizabeth Bosparva
18 Oct. Symon s. of Thomas & Margaret Lae
25 Oct. James s. of Peter & Anne Jenkyn gent
4 Nov. Thomas base s. of Anne Harvey
15 Nov. Elizabeth d. of John & Julian Legge
29 Nov. William s. of Beniamin & Jone Strangman

* Obliterated.

26 Dec. Susanna d. of William & Jane Calway
27 Dec. John s. of Thomas & florence Gilbert
27 Dec. Christopher s. of Henry & Anne Moyell
3 Jan. John s. of John & Katherine Mayhowe
17 Jan. Thomasyne d. of Nicholas & Anne Buckingham
24 Jan. ffrances d. of John & Leah Artor
14 Feb. George s. of William & Margarett Kete
21 Feb. Jane d. of John & Jane Poole
21 Feb. florence d. of Walter & Elizabeth Coriton
7 Mar. Charity d. of Robert & Charity James
14 Mar. William s. of Richard & Anne Merifeild
21 Mar. Josiah s. of John & Pacience Greymes
21 Mar. Elizabeth d. of Thomas & Jane Merifeild
24 Mar. William s. of John & Eleanor King

ANNO 1630.

11 April Grace d. of Arthur & Elizabeth Crawly
16 April John s. of Thomas & Constance Thomas
18 April Marye d. of Robert & Alse Drew
20 April John s. of John & Margaret Grace
2 May Thomas s. of Thomas & Grace Williams
30 May John s. of John & Elizabeth Copithorne
30 May John s. of George & Anne Humphry
6 June John s. of Jeames & Marye Rowse
20 June Thomas s. of Thomas & Marye Pearse
4 July Marye d. of William & Elizabeth Dancaster
18 July Prudence d. of Ollyver & Agnes Jago
23 July John s. of Nicholas & Katherine Peter
25 July Richard s. of Robert & Agnes Dunken
1 Aug. Marke s. of Jerman & Agnes Retallack
15 Aug. Jane the base daughter of Johane Williams
22 Aug. Jeames s. of John & Jane Metherell
29 Aug. Phillipp d. of Richard & Mary Leytie
10 Sep. Margaret & Christian the children of Robert & Katherine Trehenban
12 Sep. *Weeter s. of John & Mary Vivian
29 Sep. Rachell d. of Nicholas & Joane Laugdon
10 Oct. Agnes d. of Thomas & florence Husband
17 Oct. Jane d. of Ralient & Agnes Williams
14 Nov. Robert s. of Robert & Joane Pollard
14 Nov. Ollyver s. of William & Joane Basey
21 Nov. Beaton d. of Thomas & Rebecca Bayloife
12 Dec. Henry s. of Edward & Elizabeth Blake
22 Dec. John s. of John & Anne Kent
28 Dec. Margery d. of Robert & Joane . . . .
3 Jan. Marye d. of Thomas & Joane Arrundell
9 Dec. Christopher s. of Anthony & Jane Jenkyn
9 Dec. Richard s. of Richard & Rose Edwards
16 Jan. Thomas s. of William & Joane Beaford
13 Feb. Richard s. of Richard & Jane Winn
13 Feb. John s. of Gylbert & Margery Rowe
17 Feb. Gilliam d. of Degory & Grace Marryall
20 Feb. Jeames s. of John & florence Rowse
20 Feb. Anne d. of John & Martha Young
28 Feb. Wilmott d. of Richard & Elizabeth Blake
6 Mar. Elizabeth d. of Adam & Jane Daie
14 Mar. Robert a base son of Anne Littycott
20 Mar. John s. of Henry & Alice Husband

ANNO 1631.

11 April Edmond s. of Danyel & Jane Walkey

* Walter, see entries relating to him hereafter.

11 April Jeneffre d. of Henry & Margarete Bligh
11 April Richard s. of Richard & Alse Cornishe
12 April John s. of Martyn & Patience Treasteane
8 May Hester d. of John & Margery Lukye
25 May Charitye d. of Henry & Phillepp Sexton
27 May Grace d. of Anthonye & Alice King
5 June George s. of Martyn & Thomasin Edwards
5 June Rebecca d. of John & Phillip Bayly
5 June Mary d. of Thomas & Elizabeth Bennett
12 June Raphe s. of Leonard & Elizabeth Maho
17 June Margaret d. of William & Margaret Kete gent.
24 July John s. of John & Elizabeth Tenny
22 Aug. Anne d. of Robert & Anne Dunkyn
4 Sep. Henry s. of John & Helynor Knight
4 Sep. John s. of Henry & Anne Martyn
11 Sep. Johane d. of William & Austis Thomas
18 Sep. Thomasin d. of James & Thomasin Cocking
25 Sep. William s. of Arthur & Alice Jollye
25 Sep. Elizabeth d. of Thomas & Margarett Lae
29 Sep. Agnes d. of John & Mary Williams
29 Sep. Mary d. of Henry Olliver & Phillep his wife
2 Oct. John s. of John & Margery Grace
9 Oct. Katherine d. of John & Julian Legge
9 Oct. Grace d. of Thomas & Grace Williams
26 Oct. Henry s. of Beniamyn & Jane Strangman
26 Oct. Anne d. of Henry & Alice Roscorlo
18 Oct. John s. of Thomas & Mary Body
23 Oct. Digory s. of John & Honor Dyer
29 Oct. Charles s. of John & Mary Vivian
6 Nov. James s. of John & Mary Carter
13 Nov. William s. of William & Lowdye Cocking
13 Nov. William d. of Patient & Anne Williams
27 Nov. William s. of Henry & Elizabeth Martyn
27 Nov. John s. of Thomas & Elizabeth Allyn
11 Dec. Gilbert s. of William & Katherine Libby
11 Dec. Mary d. of Aneas & Jane Tacye
18 Dec. John s. of Thomas & Anne Bayliffe
1 Jan. Richard s. of Edward & Elizabeth White
29 Jan. James s. of John & Jone Lawry
26 Feb. Ann d. of William & Elizabeth Dancaster
11 Mar. Alice d. of William & Jane Calway
18 Mar. Tiffenye d. of William & Jane Salter
18 Mar. Phillip d. of Richard & Jane Langdon
24 Mar. Temperance d. of Thomas & Grace Stephens

Anno 1632.

25 Mar. James s. of John & Katherine Mayhow
25 Mar. Jane d. of Edward & Anne Ash
25 Mar. Elizabeth d. of James & Marye Rouze
8 April Jane d. of David & Jane Stribleye
16 May Jane d. of Thomas & Marye Lukye
27 May Grace d. of John & Elizabeth Dawe
3 June Jane d. of Christopher & Dorothie Cocke
21 June Jane d. of Robert & Joane West
17 June Henry s. of Nicholas & Anne Buckingham
17 June Honor d. of Henry & Joyce Rouze
17 June Mary d. of John & Leah Arthur
8 July John s. of Thomas & Jane Pearce
15 July Richard s. of George & Jane Lunye

5 Aug. Josuah s. of William & Joane Bewford
5 Aug. Elizabeth d. of Mathew & Mary Wills
5 Aug. Jane d. of Martyn & Bridgett Dunnacombe
12 Aug. John s. of Thomas & Beaton Hawke
12 Aug. John s. of Marke & Katherine Tyre
17 Aug. Hester a base child to Susanna Hawke
6 Sep. Julian d. of Nicholas & Katherine Stribleye
6 Sep. Jane d. of George & Anne Humphry
10 Sep. Joane d. of Luke & Jane Pollard
23 Sep. Anthonye s. of Anthonye & Anstis Whiteford
30 Sep. Daniell s. of Robert & Charity . . . .*
14 Oct. Grace d. of Abraham & Elizabeth Husband
28 Oct. Peter s. of John & Grace Kendall
9 Nov. Grace d. of Thomas & Joane Arrundell
18 Nov. Ebbott d. of Walter & Elizabeth Cayter
25 Nov. Priscilla d. of Robert & Joane Bary
9 Dec. Edward s. of Richard & Elizabeth Crawly
16 Dec. Barbara d. of John & Honor Dyer
16 Dec. Joane d. of John & Mary Retallack
27 Dec. Henry s. of John & Anne Kent
1 Jan. Mathew a base child to Anne Moyle
6 Jan. Barbara d. of Nicholas & Petronell Peter
9 Jan. Mary d. of Robert & Anne Dunkyn
13 Jan. Stephen s. of John & Ellinor Kynge
13 Jan. Grace d. of Alexander & Margaret Penfound
13 Jan. Jane d. of Robert & Alice Drewe
20 Jan. James s. of Reynoll & Mary Hawkye
27 Jan. Mary d. of Martyn & Anne Rowe

* Obliterated here; it is James, see 2 Dec. 1634.

5 Feb. Grace d. of Digory & Grace Marshall
10 Feb. George s. of Thomas & Anne Bayliffe
17 Feb. Mary d. of John & Mary Vivian
24 Feb. Jane d. of Adam & Jane Daye
24 Feb. John s. of John & Joane Bennett
17 Mar. Elizabeth d. of Henry & Alice Husband
21 Mar. Oliff d. of John & Elizabeth Dar

Anno 1633.

31 Mar. Joell s. of Hugh & Elizabeth Blake
7 April Thomas s. of Thomas & Rebeccha Baylye
7 April Johane the bastard daughter of Elizabeth White
21 April John s. of Æneas & . . . .† Tacye.
28 April Honor d. of William & Honor Terkeane
5 May Henry s. of Robert & Keteren Trehembam
19 May Tyffeney d. of Reynald & An Hawke
19 May Mycaell s. of Richard & Alice Cornish
19 May Elizabeth d. of Marten & Elizabeth Tresteau
2 June Peter s. of Robert & Johane Pollard
9 June James s. of James & Elizabeth Moyell
16 June Elizabeth d. of Henry & Phylip Saxton
23 June Elizabeth d. of Thomas & Mote Kestlack
31 June Margery d. of John & Ann Horswell
14 July Johon d. of John & Grace Marshall
14 July Catheren d. of John & Prissilla Jane
17 July Peter s. of Thomas & Margaret Tome
. . . . . .† Barbara & Beaten daus. of John and Martha Lowry
21 July Phylyp d. of Willm & Johon Bound
28 July James s. of Henry & Mary Tregeare
20 Aug. Degory s. of John & Johon Metherell

† Obliterated.

8 Sep. John s. of Thomas & Elizabeth Pockenhorn
22 Sep. Joane d. of William & Jane Calway
29 Sep. Anne d. of Nicolas & Elizabeth Jane
6 Oct. Rachell d. of Henry & Alse Rescorlow
6 Oct. Mary d. of Henry & Joane Marten
13 Oct. Thommasen d. of William & Joane Basly
13 Oct. Elizabeth d. of Richard & Elizabeth Blake
20 Oct. Joane d. of John & Phylyp Baylife
17 Nov. John s. of Richard & Mary Carter
17 Nov. Margery d. of Richard & Margery Hopper
...* Dec. William s. of William & Joane Way
...* Dec. Anstes d. of Arthur & Alice Jolly
8 Dec. John s. of Henry & Honor Lee
8 Dec. Christopher s. of Rawling & Alce Merefeild
22 Dec. Richard s. of Benzamen & Johan Stranman
22 Dec. John s. of William & Anstes Thomas
29 Dec. Edward s. of John & Elizabeth Lawry
1 Jan. John s. of Richard & Ann Meryfeild
6 Jan. Marye d. of Henry & Marye Elizabeth Marten
6 Jan. Dorcus the d. of Edward & Elizabeth White
12 Jan. Barbara d. of Thomas & Beten Hawke
12 Jan. Marrien d. of William & Lowdy Cocking
19 Jan. Jonathen s. of James & Mary Rowse
26 Jan. Marke s. of John & Elizabeth Tenny
9 Feb. Nycolas s. of Edward & Agnes Ash
9 Feb. John s. of Marten & Tamson Edwards
16 Feb. Thomas s. of Thomas & Mary Body

ANNO 1634.

30 Mar. Zenoby d. of Thomas & ffiorence Gylbert

* Day of the month not given.

7 April Gilbert s. of Henry & Margaret Bligh
20 April John s. of Archibald & Jone Rowse
20 April Elizabeth d. of John & Jone Lawry
27 April Robert s. of Nicholas & Ann Bucingame
4 May Garterell d. of John & Grace Kendell
8 May Rebecke d. of John & Honner Dier
8 May Christopher s. of Pacience & Ann Wills
27 May Elizabeth d. of John Vivian gent. and Mary his wife
27 June Robert s. of Lenard & Elizabeth Way
31 July Ollive d. of Thomas & Elizabeth Alen
17 Aug. Elizabeth d. of Thomas & Grace Williams
24 Aug. Nathan s. of John & Katherine Mayhow
24 Aug. Mary d. of Walter & Elizabeth Coriton
22 Sep. Emblen d. of Josias & Darryty Day
24 Sep. Thomas s. of William & Elizabeth Cruse
5 Oct. William s. of James & Tamson Cocken
29 Oct. George s. of Antheny & Entis Whitford
9 Nov. Phillipp d. of John & Elyne King
24 Nov. Darriti d. of Mary Borlace
2 Dec. Mary d. of Robert & Cheryty James
28 Dec. Margery d. of Henry & Alce Husband
2 Jan. Henry d. of Henry & Joyce Rouse
2 Jan. Emblen d. of John & Lea Arter
18 Jan. Hester d. of Sampson & Hester Rescorla
2 Feb. Peter s. of Luke & Jone Pollard
2 Feb. An d. of William & Jane Salter
2 Feb. Olly d. of John & Mary Williams
8 Feb. Garthered d. of Thomas & Jane Nanparrow
25 Feb. John s. of John & Anish Luky
28 Mar. Elynor d. of Adam & Jane ....†

† Obliterated; the name is Day, see 1 Oct. 1637.

28 Mar. Jane d. of Thomas & Mary Wescot
15 Mar. Thamson d. of Digory & Grace Marshall

ANNO 1635.

29 Mar. Anne d. of Thomas & An Baylefe
5 April Jane d. of William & Joane Beaford
3 May Ann d. of Abraham & Elizabeth Husband
10 May Constance d. of John & Mary Retallack
29 June Peter s. of John & Grace Martiall
2 July Ann d. of Michell & Mary Davye
9 July German s. of John & Ann Kent
31 July Luke s. of Thomas & Greson Harvey
3 Aug. John s. of Martyn & Ann Row
4 Aug. William a bastard of Mary Horswell
16 Aug. John s. of Thomas & Margery Hawke (?)
16 Aug. . . . d. of Reynell & Ann . . .*
23 Aug. Honor d. of Thomas & Elizabeth Pokinghorne
13 Sep. John s. of Davye & Sicily . . .†
13 Sep. Honor d. of John & Anne Horswell
27 Sep. Marke s. of John & Margery Grace
8 Oct. Edward s. of Thomas & Alce Hoblyn
8 Oct. Marke s. of Marke & Elizabeth Tire
21 Oct. Lowdy d. of George & Johane Lombe
15 Nov. Margaret d. of Richard & Joane Langdon
23 Nov. Joane d. of Hugh & Katherine (illegible)‡
15 Nov. Ann d. of Thomas & Constance Thomas
22 Nov. William s. of Henry & Mary (illegible)§

. . . . LEGGE, *Rector*.
JOHN DAVE &
THOMAS RU . . . . (illegible)

* Obliterated; Hawke, see 19 May, 1633.
† Obliterated; Hambly, see 19 August, 1638.
‡ Spray, see 7 March. 1639.
§ Tregeare? see 30 Sep. 1638

6 Dec. Margaret d. of John & Pentecost Gryms
20 Dec. Anthony s. of George & Anne Humphrey
10 Jan. Honor d. of John & Katherine Mayowe
17 Jan. John s. of William & Jane Calway
30 Jan. James s. of John & Prissilla Jane
7 Feb. Marye d. of Beniamyn & Johan Strangman
19 Feb. Hannibell s. of Henry & Elizabeth Martyn
22 Feb. Thomas a bastard s. of Patience Wyatt

ANNO 1636.

11 April Philip s. of George & Mary King
22 Mar. William s. of John & Elizabeth Darre
22 Mar. Henry s. of John & Johane Lyttycott
22 Mar. Elizabeth d. of Johane Beslye
22 Mar. Barbara d. of Ananyas & Johane Tacye
24 Aug. Maude d. of William & Anstes Thomas
22 May Janne d. of Thomas & fflorence Gylbartt
16 May Marke s. of William & Lowdy Cockyn
31 May John s. of John & Alls Pears
3 June Thomas s. of Thomas & Elizabeth Allyn
6 June William s. of Giles & Elizabeth Truscott
19 Jan. Honnor d. of Henry Lee & Honnor his wieff
22 June Thomas & Ann children of John & Elizabeth Copithorne
24 July Edmond s. of Thomas & Ann Penandrea
4 Sep. James s. of Nicholas & Petternell Petter
4 Sep. Mary d. of Thomas & Grace Williams
16 Sep. Mary d. of Henry & Margaret Bligh
25 Sep. William s. of John & Phillip Baylye
25 Sep. Marye d. of John & Honnor Dyar
14 Oct Jane d. of Henry & Alles Rescorla

23 Oct. ffrances d. of Richard & Jane Bawden
13 Nov. Robert s. of Richard & Wilmott Hawke
13 Nov. Petter s. of Thomas & Mary Bodye
13 Nov. Thomas s. of Christopher & Dorothie Cocke
22 Nov. Anthonye s. of John & Ellynor Kinge
22 Nov. Remphry s. of Archibald & Joane Rowse
11 Dec. Ralphe s. of Richard & Elizabeth Crawlye
11 Dec. Levys s. of Margery Hawkyn *alias* Trenbeard
18 Dec. Martyn s. of John & Alls Strangman
10 Jan. Mary d. of John & Ebett Jollye
8 Jan. Honnor d. of John & Elizabeth Williams
15 Jan. Henry s. of Jozias & Dorothie Daye
22 Jan. Honnor s. of Abraham & Elizabeth Husband

ANNO 1637.

29 Mar. Mary d. of Lennard & Elizabeth May
7 April Jane d. of Thomas & Dathony Common
16 April Lawdee d. of Patience & Ann Williams
17 April Jellian d. of Sampson & Hester Rescorla
23 April Ann d. of Ralfe & Garteret Keate
23 April Mary d. of Richard & Ann Meryfild
14 May Mathew the base s. of Elizabeth Wills
21 May Jane d. of Luas & Emlyn Godfrey
29 May Johane d. of William & Jane Calway
29 May Honor d. of John & Pentecost Gennis
30 May Maud d. of Anthony & Barbara Michell
11 June William s. of Robert & Cherety James
11 June Beaten d. of John & Ann Hoswell
12 June Jonathan s. of John & Mary Vivian
9 July Margery d. of Robert & Johane Grose
23 July Jacob s. of Thomas & Ann Baylife
23 July Mary d. of Thomas & Mary West
30 July Rebecka d. of John & Johane Lawry
30 July Elizabeth d. of Digory & Grace Marshall
30 July Elizabeth d. of Walter & Elizabeth Corniton
6 Aug. William s. of William & Jane Salter
13 Aug. John s. of Anthony & Janaver Pollowin
20 Aug. Elizabeth d. of Henry & Joyce Rowse
20 Aug. John s. of John & Presilla Jane
20 Aug. Mary d. of Ambrose & Peternall Randall
28 Aug. Peternell d. of John & Elizabeth Tynne
3 Sep. John s. of Richard & Elizabeth Blacke
11 Sep. Joyce d. of John & Leath Arthur
17 Sep. Grace d. of Barnabas & Constance Betty
24 Sep. John s. of John & Sibella Rescorla
1 Oct. John s. of Adam & Jane Day
8 Oct. John s. of George & Mary Kinge
8 Oct. Joyce d. of Henry & Tamson Bray
15 Oct. Ralph s. of John & Mary Williams
2 Nov. Richard s. of John & Katherine Mayhow
20 Dec. John s. of Stephen & Ann Renell
28 Dec. John s. of Giles & Elizabeth Truskat
21 Jan. Edward s. of William & Elizabeth Cruse
21 Jan. Honour d. of Henry & Alse Husband
2 Feb. Margaret d. of Thomas & Ann Hamly
4 Feb. Margaret d. of Thomas & Margaret Law
6 Feb. Honour d. of James & Mary Rowse
18 Feb. George s. of Bengeman & Johan Strongman
11 Mar. Katteren and Adrea daughters of John & Ann Jenkyen

ANNO 1638.

30 Mar. Henry s. of Henry & Jane Nanparow
5 April Jane a base child of Jane Jolley
22 April Honor d. of Martyn & Ann Raw
13 May George s. of Josias & Dorothe Day
13 May Elizabeth d. of Thomas & Mary Nanparow
10 June Peter s. of Henry & Margaret Bligh
10 June John s. of Hugh & Elizabeth Blake
17 June Richard s. of Richard & Wilmott Hawke
5 July Mary d. of Samson & Hester Rescorla
5 Aug. Peter s. of James & Temson Cockyn
12 Aug. ffrances d. of Henry & Ann Martyn
15 Aug. Edward s. of Thomas & Margaret Michell
19 Aug. David s. of David & Seseley Hambly
1 Sep. Bernard s. of John & Mary Vivian
1 Sep. Dorothey d. of Michell & Ann Davey
9 Sep. Charles s. of Henry Thomas & Jenefrey his wiffe
20 Sep. Jane d. of John & Jane Jane
30 Sep. Richard s. of Henry & Mary Tregeare
30 Sep. Jone d. of John & Olive Cundy
7 Oct. John s. of John & Avise Lukey
9 Oct. Emblyn d. of John & Barbara Oxnam
14 Oct. Christopher s. of George & Ann Humphrey
21 Oct. Jouslin d. of John & Ann Kent
21 Oct. Nicholas s. of William & Constance Thomas
28 Oct. Jone d. of Henry & Tamson Bray
8 Nov. David s. of Marke & Catherine Tyer
25 Nov. John s. of John & Ann Vivian jun.
5 Dec. John base s. of Olive Thomas
16 Dec. Marke s. of Thomas & Ann Nicholas
1 Jan. Jenefrey d. of Archibald & Jone Rowse
13 Jan. Henry s. of Henry & Honor Lee
13 Jan. Agnes d. of Thomas & Moale Reslake
13 Jan. Beaton d. of Thomas & Beaton Hawke
7 Feb. Tamson d. of John & Alse Strongman
17 Feb. Mary d. of Anthony & Barbara Michell
27 Feb. Ann d. of John & Ann Horswell
19 Mar. John and Martyn children of Martyn & Jane Stevens
24 Mar. John s. of John & Mary Retalack
25 Mar. Abigall d. of Arthur & Alse Joley

ANNO 1639.

31 Mar. Gertrud d. of Ralph & Gertrud Keate
31 Mar. Honor d. of Ralph & Barbara Williams
6 April Denies s. of Richard & Jane Langdon
7 April Melier d. of Thomas & Mary Boday
16 April Avis d. of William & Lowdy Cocking
21 April Honor d. of Lewes & Emblyn Godfrey
25 April Mary d. of William & Margaret Ward
28 April *. . . . s. of Abraham & Margaret Husband
29 April Stephen s. of John & Anne Stephens
16 June Lewes s. of William & Margery Hawkyn
7 July Dennis s. of Thomas & Mary Westcot
7 July Jane d. of John & Margaret Brint
21 July Anne d. of Anthony & Beaton Ellery
28 July Margery d. of Thomas & fflorance Gilbert
4 Aug. Margaret d. of John & Johane Lawry
18 Aug. William s. of Robert & Grace Cock
25 Aug. Joyce d. of Regnold & Anne Hawke

* Obliterated.

29 Aug. John s. of John & Ebbet Jolleye
3 Sep. Anne d. of Stephen & Anne Lovell
29 Sep. Richard s. of Richard & Wilmot Hawke
29 Sep. Richard s. of Luke & Constance James
6 Oct. William s. of Walter & Lowdy Vivian
6 Oct. Joane d. of Christopher & Elizabeth Wallcot
20 Oct. Elizabeth d. of George & Mary King
12 Nov. Tamson d. of James & Emlyn Jollye
17 Nov. John s. of Richard & Alse Cornishe
8 Dec. Margery d. of John & Patience Gennis
22 Dec. William s. of Authony & Jenefer Pollowin
29 Dec. Henry s. of William & Elizabeth Cock
1 Jan. Walter s. of Barnabas & Constance Betty
6 Jan. Margaret d. of Thomas & Mary Michell
19 Jan. Anthony s. of John & Martha Jolly
26 Jan. Robert s. of Robert & Charity Jane
9 Feb. Emlyn d. of John & Phillip Baylie
9 Feb. Jane d. of Henry & Paskas Row
19 Feb. George s. of Richard & Elizabeth Crawlyn
27 Feb. Methusala s. of Thomas & Ann Williams
1 Mar. John s. of John & Barbara Oxnam
1 Mar. Mary d. of Ambrose & Petronell Randall
7 Mar. Ollife d. of Hugh & Katherine Spray
7 Mar. Jane d. of Beniamyn & Ebbett Harvy
6 Mar. Tamson d. of Sampson & Hester Rescorla

ANNO 1640.

29 Mar. John s. of Richard & Aves Williams
12 April Bettews d. of Henry & Goyse Rowse
16 May Thomas s. of Thomas & Margaret Law
25 May Thomas s. of James & Mary Rowse
7 June Phillip s. of Henry & Alice Husband
9 June Honor d. of Nicholas & Elizabeth Jane
14 June Thomas s. of William & Jane Callwaye
21 June John s. of Patience & Ann Williams
24 June Joane d. of John & Mary Williams
21 June Elizabeth d. of John & Learth Arthur
11 July Richard s. of Rawlyn & Mary Edwards
12 July Margaret d. of Richard & Joane Langdon
19 July James s. of Adam & Jane Daye
19 July Joane d. of William & Elizabeth Crewse
2 Aug. John s. of John & Elizabeth Williams
6 Sep. William s. of John & Presilla Jane
20 Sep. Mathew s. of Mathew & Mary John
20 Sep. Edmond s. of Annanias & Joane Barne
27 Sep. Ellis s. of John & Grace Gendall*
4 Oct. Grace d. of Henry & Jane Nanparrow
4 Oct. Joane d. of Humphrey & Julyan Bearde
5 Oct. ffrances d. of Diggory & Grace Marshall
18 Oct. Benjamin s. of ffaythfull & Marg. Bishopp
18 Oct. Elizabeth d. of John & Elizabeth Myll
25 Oct. ffrancis s. of Benioymyn & Joane Strongman
27 Oct. Henry s. of John & Ebbett Jollife
1 Nov. Barbara d. of William & Margery Trembeaw
6 Nov. Honner d. of John & Elizabeth Darr
15 Nov. ffrancis s. of Hugh & Elizabeth Blake
18 Nov. William s. of John & Ann Jenkyn
4 Dec. John s. of Richard & Ann Troth†
13 Dec. Margery d. of Thomas & Ann Bayly

* Kendall, see p. 45, 10 Aug. 1645.
† Original entry signed Ri. Troth.

20 Dec. William s. of Josyas & Dorothe Daye
27 Dec. John s. of Martyn & Joane Stephens
27 Dec. Richard s. of John & Joane Stapell
24 Jan. Edward s. of Rawlyn & Alice Merifeild
24 Jan. William s. of John & Jane Jane
27 Jan. Henry s. of Henry & Jenever Thomas
21 Feb. Elizabeth d. of David & Sissilla Hambly
28 Feb. Abraham s. of Henry & Honor Lee
20 Mar. Avis d. of Thomas & Joan Hockey
24 Mar. James and Robert children of James & Mary Rouse

ANNO 1641.

3 April Mary d. of John and Ann Jenkyn
4 April Mary d. of Henry & Margaret Bligh
1 Sep. Richard s. of Richard & Jane Troth (was Borne Sep. 1 1642*)

ANNO 1642.†

4 Feb. William s. of William & Elizabeth Lanyon

ANNO 1643.

10 April Elizabeth d. of John & Elizabeth Lawry

ANNO 1641.

3 Mar. Mary d. of John & Mary Retallock
3 Mar. Phillipp d. of Thomas & Constance Thomas
11 Mar. Thomas s. of Barnabas & Constance Betty
22 Mar. John s. of Ralph & Barbara Williams

ANNO 1642.

9 May Julyan d. of Lewis & Emblen Godfrey
23 May James s. of Marten & Barbara Row
9 June Peter s. of Nicholas & Ann Bounsell
14 June Jane d. of Will. & Susan James
14 June Sibell d. of Thomas & Mary Law

* Entered thus, and signed Ri. Troth.

† The Registers are very irregular and ill-kept about this period.

15 June Peter s. of John & Oliffe Cundy
20 June Roger s. of Anthony & Beaton Ellery
27 June Joane d. of Thomas & Amy Williams
4 July Susan d. of Henry & Mary Bray
6 July John s. of John & Ellenor Lang
28 July Thomas s. of Nicholas & Jane Baseley
28 July Joane d. of Stephen & Ann Lovell
4 Aug. Phillis d. of John & Elizabeth Blake
8 Aug. Henry s. of Reskemer & Joane Spray
8 Aug. Ann d. of Thomas & Beaton Hawke
8 Aug. Avis d. of John & Ann Kent
22 Aug. John s. of Mathew & Grace Allen
12 Sep. William s. of Richard & Wilmett Hawke
12 Sep. Mary d. of Thomas & Ann Pearse
12 Sep. ffrances a base d. of Agnes Harvey
16 Sep. Winifred d. of Thomas & Patience Bawden
20 Sep. Rose d. of John & Elizabeth Tenny
25 Sep. Honor d. of Sampson & Hester Rescorla
6 Oct. Richard s. of Robert & Grace Cocke
3 Nov. Joan d. of Bennett & Joan Perden
15 Nov. William s. of Anthony & Barbara Michell
28 Nov. Christopher s. of Christopher & Cristian Woolcock
5 Dec. Joan d. of James & Joan Skaberic
5 Dec. Richard s. of Cristian Burke
8 Dec. Jane d. of Thomas & Mary Westcott
2 Jan. John s. of Peter & Emblen Betty
2 Jan. William s. of Archibald & Joan Rouse
9 Dec. Mary d. of William & Elizabeth Cock
30 Dec. Gilbert s. of Thomas & Mary Richards
30 Dec. Henry s. of Henry & Mary Treger

30 Dec. Joan d. of Walter & Joan Corington
6 Feb. ffrancis s. of Luke & Constance James
6 Feb. William s. of William & Constance Thomas
13 Feb. Sara d. of John & Joan Lawry
20 Feb. Elizabeth d. of Thomas & Honor Treven
26 Feb. John s. of Richard & Joan Withell
26 Feb. Mary d. of Thomas & Ann Bailie
3 Mar. . . . .* s. of Anthony & Ann Pollowin
6 Nov. Thomas s. of Richard & Anne Troth† (6 Nov. 1644)‡

The names of such as have ben baptised sethence the 25th of April, 1644.

Anno 1644.

2 May Ann d. of John Vivian Esq.
5 May John s. of Henry Trulerford
12 May Abigall d. of Walter Vivian
18 June Anthoney s. of Robert James
22 June John s. of Barbara Bettey
23 June Thomas s. of James Jeabiis§
7 July William s. of John Hervey
14 July Jane d. of John Browne
21 July Ralph s. of Ralph Williams
24 July Joane d. of Anthoney Ellerey
10 Aug. Peter s. of Peeter Callaway
25 Aug. John s. of Henerey Brey
22 Sep. Jane d. of John Allen
29 Sep. George s. of Gilbert Remphrey
6 Oct. Frances d. of John Horswell
13 Oct. Thomas s. of Anthoney Pellowin
15 Oct. Thomas s. of Thomas Hawke
1 Nov. Elizabeth d. of Nicholas Bounsell
6 Nov. Thomas s. of Richard Troth
7 Nov. Elizabeth d. of Thomas Westcott
2 Dec. John s. of John Geene
25 Dec. Emblem d. of Nicholas Jane
5 Jan. Philipp d. of John Browne
19 Jan. Frances d. of William Crues

* Obliterated.

† End of the regular entries of baptisms in the first volume, the following being entered among some weddings and burials at the end of the first volume.

‡ This entry is signed Ri. Troth. § Sic.

26 Jan. Pacience d. of Luke James
2 Feb. Daniell s. of Daniell Hambley
16 Feb. Michaell s. of Michaell Davie
16 Feb. George s. of James Cocken
23 Feb. Richard s. of Richard Retallacke
2 Mar. Margaret d. of Henry Tregeare
23 Mar. James d. of Marten Stephens
23 Mar. Peeter s. of Mathew John

Anno 1645.

30 Mar. Thomas s. of Thomas Nicholas
5 April Joane d. of Rescemer Sprey
5 April William s. of John Stephens
10 April Dorothy d. of Thomas Rowe
25 April Penticost d. of John Grimes
27 April Richard s. of John Kent
27 April Joane d. of Pascoe Langdon
4 May Philip s. of Nicholas Withell
18 May Nicholas s. of Robert Cocke
18 May Emblin d. of George Champion
26 May David s. of Thomas Naparra
8 June Thomas s. of Richard & Jane Littacott
8 June Mary d. of Abraham & Elizabeth Husband
15 June John s. of John & Martha Jolliffe
18 June Honour & Elizabeth daughters of Samson & Hester Rescorla
20 June John s. of Nicholas & Jane Basely
20 June Henery s. of Richard & Frances Jollye
10 Aug. Charles s. of Edward & Em. Hockyn
10 Aug. John s. of John & Grace Kendall
31 Aug. Elizabeth d. of John & Ebott Jollye
21 Sep. Joane d. of Richard & Joane Copithorne
28 Sep. John s. of Gilbert & Elizabeth Launder
5 Oct. Alice d. of John & Mary Williams
13 Oct. Thomas s. of John & Elizabeth Vivian
6 Jan. John s. of John & Susanna Hendra
30 Jan. John base s. of Anne Veale the reputed father John Teage
8 Feb. Henry s. of John & Grace Miller

15 Feb. Frances d. of John & Elizabeth Darre
15 Feb. Richard s. of Thomas & Amy Williams
22 Feb. Andrean d. of John & Ann Stephens
4 Mar. Catherine d. of Martyn Rowe
4 Mar. John s. of Luke & Constance James
13 Mar. Thomas s. of William & Lowdy Cockinge

ANNO 1646.

5 April William s. of William Langdon
12 Mar. Ruth d. of Jermyn Retallacke
24 April Marke base s. of Jane Tacye
3 May Peter s. of Henry & Alice Husband
7 May Thomas s. of Richard & Florence Rowse
10 May George s. of Stephen & Ann Lovell
10 May Sibella d. of Reskimer & Joane Spray
31 May Richard s. of John Littacott
31 May Honor d. of Benjamin & Ebbott Harvey
14 June Richard s. of Hugh Sprey & Katherine his wife
14 June Grace d. of Thomas & Beaten Hawke
12 July Lewis s. of Lewis & Emlyn Godfrey, borne 8 July
25 July Florence d. of Josiah & Dorathie Day, borne 9 July
25 July John base s. of Elizabeth Gillingham
1 Aug. Richard s. of Richard & Avice Wiiss, borne 30 July*
22 Aug. James s. of James & Honour Oxnam, borne 16 Aug.
30 Aug. John s. of Robert & Ebbott Husband, borne 24 Aug.
30 Aug. Hugh base s. of Mary Carter, borne 29 Aug.
12 Sep. George s. of Henry & Honour Lee, borne 4 Sep.
13 Sep. John s. of Peter & Florence Rescorla, borne 10 Sep.
22 Sep. Jane d. of Henry & Jenniver Thomas, born 19 Sep.
30 Sep. John s. of Richard & Joane Copithorne, borne 26 Sep.
1 Oct. Judeth d. of Francis & Ann Burgess, borne 28 Sep.

* Wise, see p. 48, 23 Feb. 1649.

1 Oct. Francis & Archibald sons of James & Mary Rowse, borne 1 Oct.
2 Nov. Tristram s. of Peter Betty, borne 1 Oct.
7 Nov. Charles s. of Nicholas & Ann Bounsell, borne 4 Nov.
8 Nov. John s. of John & Elizabeth Browne, borne 7 Nov.
15 Nov. John s. of John & Elizabeth Mill, borne 14 Nov.
22 Nov. Mary d. of John & Joane Lawry, borne 15 Nov.
22 Nov. Elizabeth d. of John & Joane Jane, borne 20 Nov.
22 Nov. Thomas s. of William & Lowdy Cockin, borne 23 Nov.
29 Nov. Charytie d. of Thomas & Joane Hockey, borne 21 Nov.
29 Nov. Mary d. of Richard & Ann Bounsell, borne 26 Nov.
7 Dec. Rebecca d. of Jerman & Honour Retallack, borne 4 Dec.
20 Dec. Grace d. of John & Katherine Brewer, borne 14 Dec.
3 Jan. Frances d. of William & Susan James, borne 26 Dec.
17 Jan. Mary d. of Anthony & Jenniver Pollowyn, borne 15 Jan.
31 Jan. Joane d. of Anthony & Beaten Ellery, borne 24 Jan.
6 Feb. James s. of Anthony & Barbara Roe, borne 6 Feb.
10 Mar. Frances d. of Rich. & Jane Littacott, borne 8 March
21 Mar. George s. of George & Honour Champion, borne 15 March
21 Mar. Joane d. of Rich. & Wilmott Hawke, borne 15 March

ANNO 1647.

4 April John s. of John & Elizabeth Gwiñow, borne 28 March
19 April Joane d. of Luke & Constance James, borne 12 April
19 April George s. of Rich. & Ann Troth, borne 13 April
19 April Jane d. of John & Ann Hoswell, borne 19 April
28 April Thomas s. of William & Margery Trembeare, borne 26 April
9 May John s. of John & Ann Stephens, borne 4 April
27 June Mary d. of William & Elizabeth Crows, borne 21 June

25 July Ann d. of Humphrey & Sibell Harvey, borne 21 July
25 July Thomas s. of Adam & Jane Day, borne 22 July
15 Aug. Mary d. of Thomas & Mary Westcott, borne 14 Aug.
5 Sep. Mary d. of Robert & Mary Strongman, borne 31 Aug.
19 Sep. Jane d. of Henry & Pascoe Roe, borne 8 Sep.
19 Sep. Catherine d. of Guilbert & Avice Remphrey, borne 16 Sep.
26 Sep. John s. of Thomas & Joane Langdon, borne 25 Sep.
10 Oct. Mary d. of Edward & Em. Hockin, borne 9 Oct.
27 Oct. Mary d. of Reskimer & Joane Sprey, borne 25 Oct.
6 Nov. John s. of John Vivian Esq. & Mary his wife, borne 31 Oct.
7 Nov. Tamson d. of Francis & Mary Richard, borne 31 Oct.
7 Nov. John s. of Christopher & Peternell Hendy, borne 6 Nov.
3 Dec. Mary d. of John & Patience Grace, borne 28 Nov.
8 Dec. Honour d. of William & Lowdey Cockin, borne 7 Dec.
10 Dec. Thomas s. of Theophilus & Mary Law, borne 7 Dec.
2 Jan. John s. of Thomas Nicholls, borne 28 Dec.
9 Jan. Anne d. of John Beauford Rector & Anne his wife, borne 2 Jan.
16 Jan. Thomas s. of Mathew & Grace Allen, borne 12 Jan.
23 Jan. Elizabeth d. of Jo. & Peternell Thorne borne 19 Jan.
4 Feb. Richard s. of Stephen & Ann Lovell, borne 30 Jan.
6 Feb. Ellenor d. of Martyn & Joane Stephens, borne 30 Jan.
6 Feb. Grace d. of ffrances & Ann Burges, borne 1 Feb.
13 Feb. David s. of Richard & Honor Retallack, born 6 Feb.
13 Feb. Anthony s. of Isack & Eliz. Jenkyn, borne 8 Feb.
13 Feb. Stephen base s. of Thomazine Harvey, born 8 Feb.
14 Feb. . . . . .* s. of Jo. & Alice Strongman, borne 10 Feb.
5 Mar. Barbara d. of Anthony & Winifred Pollowyn, borne 27 Feb.

* Obliterated.

11 Mar. Tho. s. of John & Grace Miller, borne 4 March
11 Mar. ffrancis base s. of Precilla Jane, borne 7 March
15 Mar. Katherine & Honor daughters of Henry & Mary (?) Tregeere, borne 14 March
17 Mar. James s. of Bennett & Jone Cardew, borne 8 March

ANNO 1648.

16 April *. . . . s. of Guilbert & Elizabeth Lawnder, borne 5 April
7 May *. . . . liam d. of Thomas & Ann Baylie, borne 3 May
21 May Margery d. of Edward & Priscilla Chaplain, borne 18 May
28 May Peter s. of Peter & ffrances Rescorla, borne 21 May
28 May John s. of John & Jane Jane, borne 25
9 June Jasper s. of Mathew & Mary Tresaderne, borne 4 June
2 July James s. of Robert & Grace Cocke, borne 26 June
30 July Nathaniel, s. of George & Honor Champion, borne 25 July
13 Aug. John s. of Emanuell & Thomazine Hawke, borne 5 Aug.
20 Aug. Charles s. of Jerman & Honor Retallack, borne 13 Aug.
20 Aug. Grace d. of John & Sara Littacott, borne 19 Aug.
10 Sep. Mary (?) d. of Richard & ffrances Jolley, borne 5 Sep.
1 Oct. Olive (?) d. of Thomas & Mary Pearse, borne 26 Sep.
8 Oct. Alice (?) d. of Nicholas & Jane Basely, borne 6 Oct.
11 Oct. Jam' s. of Robert Hoblyn gent. & Grace his wife, borne 30 Sep.
15 Oct. Jane d. of Henry & Jone Rowse, borne 14 Oct.
22 Oct. Honor d. of John & Cleere Arthur, borne 15 Oct.
5 Nov. William s. of Martyn & Anne Roe, borne 4 Nov.
12 Nov. Jane d. of Richard & Agnes Moyle, borne 5 Nov.
24 Nov. John s. of John Carter gent. & Honor his wife, borne 19 Nov.
26 Nov. Richow d. of Richard & Joane Copithorne, borne 23 Nov.

10 Dec. Jane d. of Giles & Eliz. Williams, borne 1 Dec.
6 Jan. Christopher s. of Christopher & Peternell Hendy, borne 5 Jan.
7 Jan. Gregory s. of John & Elizabeth Browne, borne 29 Dec.
14 Jan. Margaret d. of Anthony & Joice Pawly, borne 6 Jan.
2 Feb. ffrancis s. of John & Anne Stephens, borne 31 Jan.
4 Feb. ffrances d. of Josias & Dorothy Day
16 Feb. John s. of Humphrey & Sibella Harvey, borne 9 Feb.
24 Feb. Nicholas s. of Nicholas & Anne Bunsell, borne 20 Feb.
4 Mar. Constance d. of Tho. & Barbara Hawke, borne 25 Feb.
13 Mar. William s. of George & Grace James, borne 9 Mar.

ANNO 1649.

26 Mar. Tho. s. of Henry & Alice Husband, borne 17 Mar. 1648
20 April Richard s. of Henry Lee, borne 13 April
22 April Jo. s. of Jo. & Catherine Brewer, borne 20 April
6 May James s. of Reskimir & Elizabeth Allen, borne 28 April
13 May Mary d. of James & Joane Scriven[r], borne same day
14 May Barnabas s. of Peter & Em. Betty, borne 9 May
30 May Jo. s. of William & Dorathy Langdon, borne 27 May
3 June Anthony s. of Peter Callaway borne 31 May
10 June Alice d. of Walter & Judeth Vivian, borne 5 June
24 June ffran. s. of Jo. Beauford Rector & Anne his wife, borne 15 June
24 June Alexander s. of John & Jane Jane, borne 17 June
1 July John s. of Richard & Wilmott Hawke, borne 23 June
17 July Philip d. of Richard & Anne Troth, borne 13 July
23 June John s. of Beniamyn & Ebott Harvey, borne 17 July
29 June ffran. s. of ffran. Burges gent. & Anne his wife, borne 27 June
1 Aug. Judeth d. of Tho. & Margaret Roe, borne 27 June
3 Sep. John s. of Theophilus & Mary Lawe, borne 29 Aug.
18 Sep. Alice d. of Tho. & Anne Pollard, borne 16 Sep.
6 Oct. ffran. s. of Jo. Vivian Esq. & Mary his wife,* borne 4 Oct.
21 Oct. Edward s. of ffran. & Honor Richards, borne 15 Oct.
27 Oct. Beaton d. of Anthony & Beaton Ellery, borne 21 Oct.
18 Nov. Grace d. of Luke & Constance James, borne 14 Nov.
23 Nov. Stephen son of Stephen & Anne Lovell, borne 17 Nov.
30 Nov. Judeth d. of Robert Hoblyn gent. and Grace his wife borne 26 Nov.
9 Dec. Samuell s. of John & Margery Jolley, borne 4 Dec.
16 Dec. Jacob s. of Isack & Elizabeth Jenkyn, borne 4 Dec.
21 Dec. Anne d. of William & ffrances White, borne 16 Dec.
23 Dec. Samuel s. of John & Elizabeth Mill, borne 18 Dec.
31 Dec. Honor d. of Humphrey & Honor Pawle, borne 26 Dec.
6 Jan. Mary d. of John & Bridget England, borne 1 Jan.
13 Jan. James s. of James & Jone Stephens, borne 8 Jan.

* This Francis Vivian mar. in 1677 Anne, only dau. and heir of Hen. Maynard of Cosworth in Little Colan, by Bridget, dau. and heir of Samuel Cosworth of Coswarth, and his dau. and heir Mary mar. Sir Richard Vyvyan of Trelowarren, Bart.

Little Colan Parish Register.

Nic. Cosworth of C. Esq., bur. 5 Dec. 1680.
Margt. Cosoworth bur. 24 Jan. 1683.
Anna wife of Francis Vivian of Cosworth, Esq., bur. 8 Sept. 1685.
Mrs. Bridget Maynard of Cosworth bur. 8 Oct. 168[?].
Mary dau. of Francis Vivian Esq. and Ann his wife bapt. 28 Sept. 1681
Sr. Samuel Cosoworth Kt. bur. 6 May 1666.
Henry Maynard gent. bur. 21 April 1670.
Mrs. Julian Maynard of St. Enoder bur. 26 Jan. 1670.
Wm. Cosoworth gent. bur. 14 Dec. 1673.
Rob. Cosoworth of Cosoworth, Esq., bur. 27 May 1678.
Francis Vivian of Cosoworth, Esq., bur. 2 Aug. 1690.
John Cosoworth, gent., bur. 29 Feb. 1707.

St. Eval Parish Register.

Sir Richard Vyvyan and Mrs. Mary Vivian mar. 9 Nov. 1697.

19 Jan. Mary d. of William & Elizabeth Crewes, borne 12 Jan.
20 Jan. Mary d. of James & Mary Rowse, borne 15 Jan.
27 Jan. John s. of John & Susan Hendra, borne 21 Jan.
28 Jan. Emblyn d. of Lewis & Emblyn Godfrey, borne 26 Jan.
2 Feb. Robert s. of Richard & Jane Littacott, borne 24 Jan.
2 Feb. Mary d. of Edward & Cissely Chapple, borne 30 Jan.
12 Feb. Grace d. of William & Elizabeth Crewes, borne 3 Feb.
23 Feb. Joane d. of Richard & Barbara Wise, borne 16 Feb.
24 Feb. Jane d. of Richard & Mary Langdon, borne 19 Feb.
24 Feb. Joane d. of John & Susan Lawry, borne 16 Feb.*
10 Mar. William s. of Thomas & Mary Rickerds, borne 9 Mar.
24 Mar. Mathew s. of Robert & Ebott Husband, borne 23 Mar.

ANNO 1650.

21 April Jane d. of Henry & Pasias Roe, borne 14 April
28 April John s. of John & Anne Hoswell, borne 19 April.
28 April Elizabeth d. of Jacob & Mawde Puncher, borne 24 April
28 April Nicholas s. of William & Anne Tresteane, borne 17 April
6 May Anne† d. of James Jenkyn gent. & Jane his wife, borne 1 May
17 May John s. of Peter & ffrances Rescorla, borne 10 May
23 June Anthony s. of Thomas & Joane Langdon, borne 18 June
7 July Jacob s. of Abraham & Elizabeth Husband, borne 4 July
14 July Richard s. of Thomas & Mary Nanparrow, borne 6 July
19 July Grace d. of Christopher & Peternell Hendey, borne 18 July
21 July Jane d. of John & Grace Miller, borne 13 July
21 July ffrances d. of Henry & Alice Littacott, borne 17 July
11 Aug. Anne d. of John & Anne Stephens, borne 4 Aug.

* John Lawry appointed Sexton in 1645, and in 1642 John Lawry paid £1 6s. 8d. rent of Roserrons for two years. (Green Book.)
† She mar. John St. Aubyn. See note, p. 60.

11 Aug. Mary d. of John & Mary Williams, borne 5 Aug.
11 Aug. John s. of Humphrey & Cissely Trehemban, borne 7 Aug.
22 Aug. John s. of Anthony & Barbara Roe, borne the same day
15 Sep. Elizabeth d. of William & Margery Hawkyn, borne 10 Sep.
22 Sep. Arthur s. of John & Sara Littacott, borne same day
29 Sep. John s. of John & Peternell Thorne, borne 22 Sep.
27 Oct. John s. of Richard & Agnes Moyle, borne 20 Oct.
29 Oct. Honor d. of John Carter gent & Honor his wife, borne 21 Oct.
10 Nov. Richard s. of Pascho & Cissely Williams, borne 6 Nov.
8 Dec. Elizabeth d. of Rich. & Joane Copithorne, born 2 Dec.
29 Dec. Ebott d. of Mathew & Mary John, borne 28 Dec.
9 Feb. Pascow s. of John & Elizabeth Browne, borne 2 Feb.
16 Feb. Edward s. of Anthony & Joane Pawley, borne 15 Feb.
26 Feb. Honor d. of George & Honor Champion, borne 22 Feb.
2 Mar. Elizabeth d. of Anthony & Jainfer Pollawyn, borne 1 Mar.
21 Mar. Grace d. of John & Thomazine Arthur, borne 12 Mar.
21 Mar. Joane d. of Martyn & Joane Stephens, borne 18 Mar.

ANNO 1651.

6 April Martin s. of Martin & Anne Roe, borne 5 April
13 April Elizabeth d. of Henry & Thomazine Bray, borne 6 April
15 April John s. of Edward & Em. Hockyn, borne 13 April
20 April James s. of William & Mary Bone, borne 17 April
3 May Philip s. of John & Katherine Browne, borne 23 April
3 May Mary d. of William & Lowdy Cockyn, borne 2 May
18 May Mary* d. of James Jenkyn gen. & Jane his wife, borne 15 May

* She mar. Sir Nicholas Slanning, Bart., and died s.p.

16 May Honor d. of Henry & Alice Husband, borne 8 May
26 May James s. of Guilbert & Eliz. Lawnder, borne 24 May
1 June Thomas s. of Nicholas & Anne Bounsell, borne 29 May
1 June John s. of William & Susan James, borne 31 May
25 June John s. of Gilbert & Judeth Calaway, borne 20 June
25 June fflorence d. of Robert & Ebott Husband, borne 21 June
12 July Thomas s. of Thomas & Beaton Hawke, borne 8 July
15 July Christian d. of Peter & ffran. Calaway, borne 10 July
15 July Jane d. of Stephen & Anne Lovell, borne 13 July
30 July Cissely d. of Thomas & Mary Westcott, borne 29 July
19 July Margaret d. of John & Susan Hendra, borne 16 July
20 July Mary d. of George & Grace James, borne 17 July
1 Aug. Thomas s. of Mathew & Grace Allen, borne 29 July
12 Aug. Sibella d. of Humphrey & Sibella Harvey, borne 10 Aug.
18 Aug. Elizabeth d. of John Vivian Esq[r] & Mary his wife, borne 16 Aug.
3 Sep. Katherine d. of Thomas & Mary Rickerd, borne 2 Sep.
5 Sep. Elizabeth d. of Giles & Mary Edwards, borne 2 Sep.
7 Oct. Elizabeth d. of John & Margery Tyack, borne 4 Oct.
28 Oct. Rich. s. of Jo. & Ann Stephens, borne 26 Oct.
9 Nov. Tho. s. of Robert Hoblyn gent. & Grace his wife, borne 7 Nov.*
30 Nov. Henry s. of Robert & Grace Cock, borne 27 Nov.
22 Dec. Jane d. of ffran. & Honor Richard, borne 16 Dec.
27 Dec. John s. of John & Phillip Moyle, borne . . Dec.
31 Dec. James s. of Richard & Avis Kebbull, borne 28 Dec.

* This Robert was son of Edw. Hoblyn of Nanswhyden in St. Columb Major, Esq., by Mary, dau. and coheir of Rob. Apley of Barnstaple, co. Devon, Esq. He mar. Grace, dau. and coheir of John Carew of Penwarne, Esq., second son of Ric. Carew of Anthony.

7 Jan. Grace d. of James & Joane Stephens, borne 5 Jan.
11 Jan. Susan d. of W[m] & Joane Richards, borne 10 Jan.
21 Jan. William s. of Richard & Eliz. Hardin, borne 16 Jan.
14 Feb. Eliz. d. of W[m] & Grace Edwards, borne 10 Feb.
20 Feb. ffrancis s. of Peter* & ffrances Rescorla, borne 14 Feb.
8 Mar. Dorothey d. of John & Christian Roe, borne 6 Mar.
13 Mar. Joane d. of Henry & Mary Tregeare, borne 11 Mar.
24 Mar. Peter s. of George & Honor Champion, borne 20 Mar.

ANNO 1652.

12 April Dorathy d. of Josias & Dorathy Day, borne 6 April
17 April Peter s. of Gabriell & Elizabeth Cocke, borne 16 April
23 April Pasco s. of Richard & Mary Langdon, borne 21 April
23 April John s. of John & Pentecost Grimes, borne 21 April
9 May . . . .† s. of Bennett & Joane Purthew, borne 10 May
2 June Martin s. of John & Jane Jane, borne 27 May
4 June Thomas s. of Richard & ffrances Jolley, borne 30 May
14 June Roger s. of John & Prudence Watt, borne 6 June
12 July Ellinor d. of Ben. & Ebott Harvey, borne 2 July
24 July Roger s. of Roger & Olive Jonas, borne 21 July
28 Aug. Jacob s. of Jacob & Mawde Puncher, borne 24 Aug.
30 Aug. Hendy d. of Thomas & Joane Langdon, borne 27 Aug.
25 Sep. Mary d. of Thomas & Beaton Hawke, borne 22 Sep.
30 Sep. Thomas s. of Anthony & Joane Pawle, borne 23 Sep.
5 Oct. Peter s. of Richard & Anne Mayle, borne 29 Sep.
12 Oct. Oliver s. of Edward & Jone Best, borne 5 Oct.
28 Oct. John s. of Stephen & Anne Lovell, borne 22 Oct.
20 Nov. Walter s. of Walter & Judeth Vivian, borne 15 Nov.

* Peter Rescorla was one of the parish wardens this year. (Green Book.)
† Obliterated.

30 Nov. Robert s. of John & Thomsyn Berry, borne 27 Nov.
3 Dec. Arthur s. of William & Elizabeth Crews, borne 30 Nov.
16 Dec. Mary d. of John Vivian* Esqr & Mary his wife, borne 14 Dec.
.. Dec. Thomas s. of James & Philip Witts, borne ...† Dec.
31 Dec. Anthony s. of Simon & Mary Trehemban, borne 26 Dec.
11 Jan. Eliz. d. of Andrew & Eliz. Jenkyn of St. Dennis, borne 1 Jan.
28 Feb. John s. of John & Thomazine Arthur, borne 20 Feb.
3 Mar. Anne d. of Edward & Anne Barker, borne 27 Feb.
10 Mar. Rebecka d. of John & Elizabeth Mill, borne 3 Mar.
14 Mar. John s. of John & Anne Merrifeild, borne 6 Mar.

ANNO 1653.

25 Mar. Mary d. of Thomas & Clary George, borne 24 Mar.
30 Mar. Peter s. of Peter & Elizabeth Jane, borne 28 Mar.
2 April Sampson s. of Humphrey & Cissely Trehemban, borne 30 Mar.
15 April Katherine d. of Pascho & Katherine Laugdon, borne 2 April
30 April ffrances d. of James & ffrances White, borne 25 April
25 May Thomas s. of Thomas & Susanna Lawry, borne 28 April
9 May John s. of George & Honor Champion, borne 6 May
16 May Robert s. of Richard & Wilmott Hawke, borne 8 May
31 May Joane d. of John & Martha Jolly, borne 24 May
31 May Vivian s. of Thomas & Elizabeth Salter, borne 21 May
6 June Mary d. of Martin & Mary Retallack, borne 1 June
8 June Henry s. of John & Elizabeth Browne, borne 4 June
13 June Thomas s. of Christopher & Peternel Hendy, borne 5 June
13 June Thomazine d. of James & Mary Rowse, borne 7 June
2 July John s. of W^m^ & Joice Cundy, borne 27 June
5 July William s. of William & Mary Bone, borne 2 July
8 July Mawde d. of James & Joane Stephens, borne 4 July
9 July Peter s. of William & Joane Richards, borne 7 July
6 Aug. Jone d. of William & Mawde Strongman, born 31 July
2 Sep. Isabella d. of Peter & ffrances Rescorla, borne 25 Aug.
8 Sep. George s. of Robert & Ebbot England, borne 31 Aug.
8 Sep. Peter s. of John and Anne Hoswell, borne 5 Sep.
9 Sep. Honor d. of Nicholas & Anne Bounsell, borne 18 Aug.
22 Sep. Katherine* d. of James Jenken gent. & Jane his wife, borne 15 Sep.
28 Sep. Tho. s. of Robert & Mawde Skynner, borne 22 Sep.
1 Jan. Grace† d. of Pascowe & Jane Brabyn
27 Jan. Anthony s. of Anthony & Jenefer Pollawyn
27 Jan. Mary d. of John England
22 Feb. Katherine d. of Peter & ffrancis Calway
20 Mar. Mary d. of John & Anne Slade
24 Mar. James s. of Gabriel & Elizabeth Cock

ANNO 1654.

9 April Jane d. of Henry & Alice Heycroft
21 April Grace d. of Edward & Ursula Chapell
22 May Mary d. of Richard & Thomasin Martyn
17 June John s. of Robert & Maude Skynner
22 June John s. of Walter & Joane Tyer
10 July Grace d. of Stephen & Ann Lovell
10 July John son of Simon & Honor Lee

* This John Vivian was son and heir of John Vivian, Esq., of St. Columb, by Mary, dau. and coheir of Wm. Cavill of Treharrock, Esq., and mar. at Tavistock 18 Oct. 1642, Mary, dau. of Sir John Glanville.

† Obliterated.

* She mar. John Trelawny, Esq., son and heir of Sir Jonathan Trelawny, 2nd Bart., but who died s.p. before his father.

† From this entry to that on 23 Oct. 1660, each entry has "was borne;" the date of baptism is reverted to after the latter date.

12 July William s. of Richard & Jane Dancaster
17 July Robert s. of ffrancis & Mary Manuell
18 July Jane d. of William & Susan Bennett
3 Aug. George & Margarett the s. & d. of George & Jane Humfry
16 Oct. ffrancis d. of Richard & ffrancis Jolly
17 Oct. Mark s. of John & Susan Lawry
27 Oct. Joane the d. of Reskymer & Joane Sprey
5 Sep. Luke s. of Arthur & Ann Jolly
9 Sep. ffayth d. of Richard & Emblyn Troth
16 Sep. James s. of Richard & Agnes Moyle
21 Sep. Edward s. of George & Honor Champion
25 Oct. John s. of Daniell & Ellinor Couch
28 Oct. Martyn s. of Edward & Emme Hocken
7 Nov. Avis d. of John & Ann Beaufford
13 Nov. Joane d. of Henry & Elizabeth Blake
29 Nov. Elizabeth d. of Theophilus & Mary Lae
6 Dec. Katherine d. of Grace & John Lukye*
10 Dec. Agnes d. of Hugh & Grace Treneson
13 Dec. Mary d. of James & Mary Merifeild
21 Dec. Ann d. of John & Ann Merifeild
28 Dec. Elizabeth d. of John & Thomasin Berry
12 Jan. Phillipp d. of Robert & Grace Hoblyn
24 Jan. Jenefer d. of Anthony & Jenefer Pollawyn
31 Jan. Janet† d. of John Vivian, Esqre.
2 Feb. Nicholas s. of Emanuel & Thomasin Hawke
8 Feb. Elizabeth d. of Richard & Elizabeth Harding
10 June Ann d. of Jacob & Maude Puncher
24 Feb. John s. of James & Philipp Wyatt

* Sic.

† She mar. the Rev. James Beauford, M.A., Rector of St. Columb.

2 Mar. Joane s. of William & Mary Bone
4 Mar. Henry s. of William & Maude Strongman

ANNO 1655.

1 April Grace d. of John & Gertrude Kent
29 April Philipp s. of James & Joane Stevens
30 April William s. of Will'm & Thomazin Mill
4 May Edward s. of Thomas Michell
11 May Honor d. of Gabriell & Eliz. Cock
13 May Samuel s. of Will'm & Ann Hawkins
26 May Thomas s. of Thomas & Eliz. Salter
27 May Beniamyn s. of Beniamyn & Ebbott Harvye
30 May Elizabeth d. of John & Anne Slade
27 June Mary d. of Will'm & Joane Richards
14 June Will'm s. of Thomas Rickard
20 July Michael s. of John Tynny
7 Aug. Henry s. of James Rous
8 Aug. John s. of ffrancis Manuell
29 Aug. Richard s. of Thomas George
9 Sep. Will'm s. of John Browne
9 Sep. Jane d. of Elias Pollard
10 Sep. Sara d. of John Litticott
8 Oct. Thomas s. of Josias Dey
8 Oct. Thomasine d. of Robert Skynner
28 Oct. Henry s. of Henry Heycroft
6 Nov. Margarett d. of Symon Trehembam
13 Nov. Olive d. of Richard Revill
30 Nov. Isabella* d. of Thomas Travers Re'or
8 Dec. Mathewe s. of Thomas Wills
16 Dec. Joane d. of Daniell Couch
22 Dec. Richard s. of Richard Troth
4 Jan. Philip s. of John Mill
4 Jan. Joane d. of Anthony Hawky
6 Jan. Symon s. of Symon Lae
9 Jan. Elizabeth d. of James Jenkyn gent.
17 Jan. Anthony s. of Thomas Rowe
19 Jan. Mary d. of William Bone
25 Jan. Joane d. of William Bryn
27 Jan. Mary d. of Henry Tregere
28 Jan. Elizabeth d. of Thomas Merifield

* She is named in the will of Samuel Travers, Esq., M.P. See Introductory Chapter.

30 Jan. Hester d. of George Crapp
30 Jan. Joane d. of John Hendra
6 Feb. Peter s. of Nicholas Bounsell
6 Feb. John* s. of Robert Hoblyn Esquire
15 Feb. Mary† d. of John Carter gent.
21 Feb. Peter s. of Henry Trehembam
26 Feb. Margarett d. of William Edwards
3 Mar. Gilbert s. of Humfry Oxnam

Anno 1656.

7 April Henry s. of Henry Blake
11 April John s. of Anthony Ellery
12 April Joane d. of William White
12 April James s. of Thomas Bounsell
22 April ffrancis d. of Peter Calway
6 May Richard s. of Richard Langdon
10 May Mary d. of James Wyett
9 May Joane d. of John Beafford clerke
17 May Ruth d. of John Richards
16 May John s. of John Tyack
18 May Thomas s. of Humfry Harvye
20 May Mary d. of John Browne
29 May Ebbott d. of Christopher Hendey
2 June Elizabeth d. of John Lawry
2 Jau.‡ Elizabeth d. of William Crewse
24 Jan.‡ John s. of John England
5 July Dorothy d. of John Rowe
14 July George s. of Stephen Lovell
21 July ffrancis s. of William Beauford
24 July Nicholas s. of Thomas Langdon
12 Aug. Edward s. of John Horsewell
19 Aug. Abigall d. of Arthur Jolly
22 Aug. Henry s. of John Kent
11 Sep. Daniell s. of Daniell Ropson
17 Sep. Elizabeth d. of Richard Moyle
4 Oct. Jonathan s. of William Cundye
15 Oct. Barbara d. of Richard Jolly
17 Oct. Thomas s. of Thomas Tremayne
21 Oct. Abigall d. of George Humfrye
1 Nov. Ralph s. of Humfry Trehembam
10 Dec. Mary d. of Robert Coade
28 Dec. ffrancis d. of ffrancis Richards
10 Jan. Margarett d. of Reskymer Sprey
14 Jan. Elizabeth d. of John Berry
5 Feb. Ann d. of Anthony Michell
5 Feb. Richard s. of James Merifeild
13 Feb. Thomas s. of William Richards
19 Feb. Edward s. of William Sampson
28 Feb. Mark s. of Walter Tyer

* Buried in 1656.
† She mar. Tho. Hoblyn of Tresaddern. See Weddings, 1 Sep. 1688.
‡ Sic.

4 Mar. Margery d. Henry Trehembam
6 Mar. Pascowe s. of Pascowe Brabyn
20 Mar. Anne d. of William Mill
24 Mar. Robert s. of Robert Husband

Anno 1657.

14 April Elizabeth d. of John Merefield
2 May Mary d. of Thomas Merefield
2 May Martha d. of ffrancis Manwell
3 May Thomas s. of Mathew Allyn
8 May Richard s. of Richard George
27 May Humfry s. of Humfry Oxnam
10 June Anthony s. of Anthony Pollawyn
11 June Anne d. of John Beauford clerke
17 June Ann d. of Richard Troth
26 June Henry s. of John Tenny
28 June John s. of William Strongman
3 July Anne d. of Gabriell Cock
5 July Elizabeth d. of Arthur Broad
31 July John s. of James Stevens
24 Aug. Christian d. of Hugh Retallack
25 Aug. Mary* d. of Robert Hoblyn Esq[r]
31 Aug. Thomas s. of Stephen Lovell
15 Sep. John s. of Robert May
11 Sep. Margarett d. of John Vivian Esq[r]
18 Sep. Joane d. of John Richards
30 Sep. John s. of Christopher Inch
9 Oct. Elias s. of Elias Pollard
12 Oct. Mary d. of Theophilus Lae
16 Oct. Richard son of Thomas Calway
20 Oct. Elizabeth d. of Robert Skynner
6 Nov. Jane d. of Daniell Couch
17 Nov. John s. of John† & Elizabeth Legg
21 Nov. Stephen s. of Humfry Harvye
27 Nov. Jone d. of Anthony Paule
3 Dec. Jonathan s. of Symon Lae
4 Dec. Wiliam s. of William Beafford
24 Dec. Edward s. of George Nation
29 Dec. Thomas s. of Thomas Langdon
1 Jan. Honor d. of Ralph Chenowith
18 Jan. James s. of Peter Calway
23 Jan. ffrances d. of James Jenkyn Esquire
2 Feb. Ruth d. of John Slade
4 Feb. Rebecca d. of William Brenton
19 Feb. James s. of William Bone
14 Mar. Thomas s. of Thomas George
24 Mar. Thomas s. of John Lawry

* Buried in 1658.
† He was a son of the Rev. John Legge, and mar. Eliz. dau. of John Hicks, gent. See Weddings, 1656.

ANNO 1658.

31 Mar. William s. of William Bennett
1 April John s. of John Kent
15 April Rose d. of William Edwards
18 April Thomas s. of Richard Dancaster
24 April Henry s. of John Browne
25 April Peter s. of John Merifeild
10 May John s. of Nathaniel Adams
10 May Patience d. of Henry Bruer
30 May Richard s. of Robert Code
5 June Jane d. of John Beauford
15 June Margery d. of Gyles Edwards
18 June Christopher & Jenefer s. & d. of Henry* Warne
29 June Alice† d. of Thomas Travers clerke
30 June William s. of John Gillbert
7 July George s. of Anthony Pollawyn
12 Aug. Anne d. of Thomas Tremayne
16 Aug. John s. of Thomas Richard
21 Aug. Rachell d. of Emanuel Hawke
25 Aug. Samuel s. of George Champion
30 Aug. Henry s. Peter Rescorla
1 Sep. Philip s. of Peter Kendall
17 Sep. Robert‡ s. of Robert Hoblyn Esquire
28 Sep. John s. of John Carter gent.§
5 Oct. Anne d. of William White
5 Oct. Elizabeth d. of Henry Blake
17 Oct. Anne d. of Arthur Broade
1 Nov. John s. of Thomas Wills
25 Dec. Christopher s. of Nicholas Withiel.
29 Dec. Richard s. of John Jolly
9 Jan. Martyn s. of John Ingland
13 Jan. John s. of Robert May
1 Feb. Elizabeth d. of John Day
2 Feb. Nehemiath s. of John Best
4 Feb. Nicholas s. of Nicholas Basely
11 Feb. George s. of George Crapp
12 Feb. William s. of William Richards
16 Feb. Grace d. of Pascow Brabyn
23 Feb. John s. of John Davys
24 Feb. Margery d. of Margery Horsewell
24 Mar. George s. of John Luke

* He was son of John Warne and Ann Flamock (mar. at Padstow, 21 July, 1638). These children were by his first wife (see Weddings, 1656). Jennefer died the Oct. following.

† Named in the will of Samuel Travers, Esq., M.P.

‡ He mar. the dau. and heir of Burgess of Truro, and was father of Francis Hoblyn of Nanswhyden, Esq.

§ Buried the next year.

ANNO 1659.

31 Mar. ffrances d. of Richard Hardyn
2 April Constance d. of Richard Troth
3 April Richard s. of Edward Crawlye
3 April Ralph s. of Ralph Chenoweth
4 April Stephen s. of John Legg
5 April Mary d. of John Mill
8 April James s. of Josias Day
10 April Elizabeth d. of George Luney
12 April John s. of John Richards
21 April Anne d. of John Kent
26 April Richard s. of Daniell James
27 April ffrances d. of Thomas Michell
24 May James s. of John Rowse
3 June Love d. of Gabriel Cock
4 June John s. of James Merifeild
4 June Bridgett d. of William Crewse
10 June Avis d. of Christopher Thomas
4 June Henry s. of Robert Skynner
22 June Jone d. of William Jolly
12 July ffrances d. of Humfry Oxnam
21 July John s. of Nathaniell Adams
3 Aug. Anne d. of George Humfry
9 Aug. Jane d. of John Stevens
11 Aug. Mary d. of John Beauford clerke
17 Aug. Henry s. of William Mill
2 Sep. Anne d. of Richard Jolly
7 Sep. Margarett d. of Jacob Pancher
12 Sep. William s. of Christopher Inch
23 Sep. Mary d. of John Berry
5 Oct. James s. of William Strangman
14 Oct. Jane d. of John Tynny
16 Oct. William & Richard two sonnes of John Vivian Esquire
20 Oct. Mary d. of Jonathan Rowse
5 Nov. Barbara d. of Thomas Prestredge
21 Nov. Honor d. of Daniel Couch
26 Nov. Sislye d. of Avis Burlace
9 Dec. John s. of John Gregor
10 Dec. Anne* d. of Robert Hoblyn Esquire
14 Dec. William s. of Symon Lae
31 Dec. Walter s. of Richard Moyle
31 Dec. Peternell d. of William Bone
17 Jan. Margarett d. of William Methe-rell
23 Jan. Jemmima d. of Richard Edwards
24 Jan. Mary d. of Henry Warne
29 Jan. Philipp d. of Peter Gibbs
10 Feb. Anne d. of John Slade

* Mar. to Rev. John Bishop, Rector of St. Columb Major.

15 Feb. William s. of Henry Trehembam
25 Feb. George s. of George Nation
26 Feb. Mary d. of John Pears
28 Feb. Edward s. of Thomas Merifeild
3 Mar. Mary d. of William Hawkey
8 Mar. William s. of William Edwards
12 Mar. Arthur s. of Arthur Broade
24 Mar. Jane d. of Oliver Basely

Anno 1660.

5 April Mary d. of Robert Coode
5 April Emblyn d. of Daniel Ropson
8 April ffrances d. of John Rowe
8 April Mary d. of John Lawry
13 April John s. of Anthony Rowe
18 April Elizabeth d. of Peter Kendall
26 April John s. of John Roe
30 April Henry s. of John Jolly
10 May Christopher s. of Peter Rescorla
15 May Edward s. of John Merrifield
21 May Arthur s. of Arthur Jolley
23 May Rebecca d. of Richard George
28 May John s. of Theophilus Lawe
30 May Christopher s. of John England
11 June Joane d. of Thomas Cockyn
1 July Meliar d. of Humfry Trehembam
12 July Margarett d. of Nicholas Bounsell
15 July James s. of Stephen Capell
12 Aug. Phillip s. of Humfry Oxnam
21 Aug. Peter s. of Elias Pollard
22 Aug. Elizabeth d. of John Legg
25 Sep. John s. of William & Alice Beauford was bapt.
9 Sep. Elizabeth d. of William Merrifield
25 Sep. Anthony & John sons of John Rowse were bapt.
25 Sep. Jane d. of Peter Callaway
29 Sep. Elizabeth d. of Ralph Crawley
2 Oct. Ruth d. of Henry Brewer
6 Oct. George s. of Giles Edwards
9 Oct. Henry s. of Thomas Wills
23 Oct. John s. of Edward Crawley
9 Nov. George s. of Mathew Allen*
12 Nov. Jane d. of Henry Blake
25 Nov. Elizabeth d. of Thomas Drew
25 Nov. Elizabeth d. of William Betty
24 Dec. Lewis s. of John & Jane Daye
28 Dec. John s. of John Merrifield of Halveor
4 Jan. Nathaniell s. of Nathaniell Adam

* With this entry the dates are those of baptisms, the date of birth being discontinued.

5 Jan. Elizabeth d. of Thomas Michell
12 Jan. Richard s. of Ralph Chenoweth
12 Jan. Joane d. of Arthur Commen
21 Jan. John s. of John Allen
29 Jan. Peter s. of John Guilbert
20 Feb. William s. of Paschow Brabyn
28 Feb. Thomas* s. of Robert Hoblyn Eq[re]
2 Mar. Susan d. of William Jolley
8 Mar. Temperance d. of Robert Skynner
15 Mar. John s. of Richard Thomas
22 Mar. Margery d. of Richard Troth

Anno 1661.

27 Mar. Richard s. of Richard Srea
15 April Joane d. of John & Gertrude Kent
16 April Dianna d. of Daniell & Joane James
16 April Margery d. of Thomas & Clary George
17 April Elizabeth d. of John & Elizabath Browne
26 April Jane† d. of John Carter gent. & Honour his wife
26 April Elizabeth d. of John & Jane Best
29 April Thomas s. of John & Honor Richards
29 April Honor d. of Henry & Elizabeth Jolley
30 April Honor d. of Ralph & Joane Lambe
3 May Jane d. of Thomas & Mellior Withell
14 May Mathew base s. of Avis Burlace
14 May James s. of Peter & Jane Daye
21 June Henry s. of Richard & Margery Veale
29 June Nicholas s. of Thomas and . . . . .‡ Langdon
7 July Anne d. of John Steephens
13 July Edward s. of Peter & Anne Kendall
20 July Jane d. of George & Mary Luney
22 July Elizabeth d. of Dennis & Agnes Westcott

* This Thomas Hoblyn mar. in 1688 Mary, dau. and coheir of John Carter, Gent., from which marriage descends the present William Paget Hoblyn of Nanswhyden and the Fir Hill, Esq.

† She mar. Giles Riseden. (See marriage 1684, also extracts from St. Breock Reg.)

‡ Obliterated. Joane. See 23 June, 1650.

26 July Philip d. of Guilbert & Melior Launder
2 Aug. Jane d. of William & ffrances White
2 Aug. Susana d. of John & Susana Lawry
4 Aug. Jane d. of Charles & Catherine Thomas
19 Aug. Mary d. of Gilbert & Joane Coade
1 Sep. Joane d. of Hugh & . . . .* Retallack
5 Oct. Constance d. of Henry & Hester Morcombe
19 Oct. Phillip s. of Humfry & Joane Oxnam
25 Oct. Jane d. of Richard & Mary Moyle
11 Nov. Anne d. of Arthur & Anne Jolley
15 Nov. Thomas s. of John & Beaton Merifeild
16 Nov. Mary d. of James & Izabell Hawke
22 Nov. Elizabeth d. of Edward & Margery Lawry
8 Dec. John s. of Peter & Joice Rescorla
11 Dec. Garthrude d. of William & Mary Bone
27 Dec. John s. of John & Anne Slade
1 Jan. John s. of Symon & Honor Lawe
1 Jan. Elizabeth d. of James & Joane Steephens
3 Jan. Robert s. of Henry & Joane Trehemban
3 Feb. Alice d. of William & Joane Merifield
7 Feb. ffrances d. of John Beauford, Rector, & Anne his wife†
11 Feb. Elizabeth d. of Ralph & Elizabeth Crawley
12 Feb. John s. of Nathaniell & Joane Adam
19 Feb. Michaell s. of Martyn & Joane Strongman
23 Feb. Christopher s. of Christopher Wolcock
9 Mar. Honor d. of Oliver Basely
19 Mar. Richard s. of Richard & Emblyn Slade

* Obliterated.

† His first wife dau. of Joseph Sawle, Esq., of Penrice.

ANNO 1662.

25 Mar. John s. of William & Agnes Metherell
31 Mar. Elizabeth d. of John & Anne Merifield
31 Mar. Anne d. of James & Mary Merifield
31 Mar. John s. of Thomas & Jaell Drew
19 April Olive d. of John & Thomazine Berry
25 April ffaithfull s. of John & Grace Luke
26 April John s. of John & Jane Best
6 May James s. of William & Mary Samwell
19 May Thomas s. of Thomas & Mary Rickard
7 June John s. of William & Joane Richards
8 June Katherine d. of John & Dorothy Davis
13 June Alice d. of Ralph & Eustis Chenowith
18 June William s. of Robert & Jane Coade
29 June Anne d. of John & . . . .* Retallack
29 June Alice d. of William & Thomasin Mill
6 July Anne d. of Walter & Joane Tyer
18 Aug. Grace d. of Robert Hoblyn Esq. & Grace his wife
23 Aug. Joane d. of Peter & Anne Kendall
30 Sep. Peter s. of Peter & Joane Gibbs
19 Sep. William s. of Edward & Ruth Crawly
26 Sep. Peter s. of Christopher & Joane Inch
5 Oct. Steephen s. of Steephen & Elizabeth Capell
10 Oct. Arthur s. of Thomas & Thomazin Michell
12 Oct. John s. of Henry & Elizabeth Jolley
17 Oct. Thomas s. of Thomas & Dorothy Benny
31 Oct. James s. of John & Peternell Rowse
2 Nov. John s. of William & Joane Bettyson

* Obliterated. Christian. See 26 Jan. 1677.

7 Nov. Sarah d. of Theophilus & Mary Law
9 Nov. Thomas s. of William & Grace Edwards
9 Nov. Thomas s. of Guilbert & Mellior Launder
10 Nov. Grace d. of John & Mary Tynny
9 Dec. Joane d. of Paschow & Jane Brabant
19 Dec. Grace d. of George & Alice Daye
28 Dec. Charles s. of Anthony & Christian Rowe
1 Jan. Elizabeth d. of Daniell & Elinior Couch
1 Jan. Thomas s. of Jonathan & Grace Rowse
. . . . * Elizabeth d. of Thomas & Grace Wills†
21 Jan. John s. of Daniell & Hester Ropson
21 Jan. Isack s. of John & Elizabeth Mill
23 Jan. Thomas s. of John & Alice Pieror
1 Feb. Isack s. of Humfry & Sibella Harvey
24 Feb. Mathew s. of Richard & Emblyn Troth†
3 Mar. Thomas s. of Giles & Margery Edwards
. . . . . Mary d. of John & Honour Richards
18 Mar. Henry s. of John & Elizabeth Rowse
20 Mar. Jane d. of Thomas & Hester Merifield
21 Mar. Jane d. of John & Bridgett England
23 Mar. John s. of John & Jane Daye

ANNO 1663.

27 Mar. Symon s. of Humfry & Sisley Trehemban
29 Mar. Presilla d. of Peter & ffrances Callaway
20 April John s. of William & Honor Jolley
21 April Agnes d. of Henry & Barbara Brewer

* Obliterated.
† "Paid Tho. Wills 20s. rent of his house that Richard Troth lives in." 1661. (Green Book.)

5 June Hannah d. of John & Thomazin Berry*
8 June Joane d. of John & Margery Burne
9 June William & Peter the sons of Richard & Margrett George
15 June Alice d. of Henry & Elizabeth Blake
20 June John base son of Dorothy Burlace
28 June Thomas s. of William & Joane Merifield
28 June Elizabeth d. of John & Anne Rowe
2 Aug. William s. of Thomas & Margarett Cockyn
9 Aug. James s. of Arthur & Alice Comon
16 Aug. Thomas s. of John & Joane Gilbert
6 Sep. Thomazin d. of Henry & Hester Morcombe
6 Sep. Eliz. d. of John & Joane Loggett
2 Oct. ffrances d. of Martin & ffrances Strongman
17 Oct. Eliz. d. of Thomas & Grace Crewes
18 Oct. Elizabeth d. of Stephen & Eliz. Capell
25 Oct. Jane d. of Edward & Alice Merifield
6 Nov. Thomas s. of George & Mary Luney
7 Nov. Giles s. of Giles & Elizabeth Williams
8 Nov. Richard s. of Ralph & Elizabeth Crawley
13 Nov. John s. of Luke & Honor Giles
15 Nov. Mary d. of Robert & Maude Skynner
18 Nov. Temperance d. of James & Isabell Hawkey
22 Nov. Peter s. of Christopher & Joane Inch
5 Dec. John s. of William & Mary Bone
11 Dec. William s. of William & ffrances White
11 Dec. Thomas s. of William & Anne Viguers
20 Dec. ffrancis s. of Elias & Joane Pollard
11 Jan. Emblyn d. of John & Margarett Truscott

* John Berry paid rent of his shop 12s. 6d. 1651. (Green Book.)

16 Jan. Richard s. of Nicholas & Anne Bounsell
16 Jan. Jonathan s. of John & Abigall Udey
20 Jan. Joane d. of Dennis & Agas Westcott
2 Feb. James s. of William* & Alice Beauford
20 Feb. John s. of Peter & Anne Kendall
26 Feb. ffrances d. of James & Jane Stephens
11 Mar. Richard s. of Paschoe & Jane Brabyn
24 Mar. Theophilus s. of Symon† & Honor Lawe

ANNO 1664.

30 Mar. William‡ s. of Thomas & Eliz. Warne
1 April John s. of Edward & Margery Lawrey
6 April James s. of Nathaniell & Joane Adam
1 May John s. of Morgan & Mary Oliver
5 May Mary d. of Robert Hoblyn Esq. & Grace his wife
6 May Richard s. of Thomas & Joane Langdon
19 May Elizabeth d. of Richard & Beaton Thomas
30 May Elizabeth d. of Stephen & Peternell Wolcock
10 June Samuell s. of Edward§ & Anne Crewes
19 June Katherine d. of William & Mary Samble
25 July Anne d. of Thomas & Clary George
19 Aug. Stephen s. of Stephen & Jone Stephens
4 Sep. Anne d. of Richard & Jane Dancaster
18 Sep. James s. of James & Mary Merifield
18 Sep. Richard s. of Richard & Barbara Brewer
25 Sep. frances d. of John & Catherine Retallack
5 Oct. Emblyn d. of John & Mary Allen
18 Oct. Anne base childe of Dorothy Launder
21 Oct. Alice d. of Ralph & Annastatia Chenowith
21 Oct. Mary d. of John & Ellinor Rowse
22 Oct. Stephen s. of Arthur & Joane Jenkyn
9 Nov. John s. of John & Precilla Stephens
13 Nov. William s. of Giles & Margery Edwards
13 Nov. Ralph s. of Ralph & Elizabeth Crawley
27 Nov. Mary d. of Peter & Joane Gibbs
9 Dec. Emblyn d. of John & Anna Merefield
14 Dec. Anne d. of Thomas & Dorothy Benny
14 Dec. George s. of Oliver & Catherine Basely
16 Dec. William s. of George & Mary Lucey
26 Dec. James s. of Peter & Honor Cockin
29 Dec. Phillip s. of Daniell & Joane James
6 Jan. Elizabeth d. of William & Mary Bone
9 Jan. Christopher s. of Christopher & Joanna Inch
12 Jan. Mary d. of John & Abigall Edey
15 Jan. Bitreon s. of Richard & Emblyn Slade
8 Feb. Thomas s. of Richard & Maude Skyner
11 Feb. ffrances d. of Guilbert & Melior Launder
4 Mar. Elizabeth base d. of Olive Williams
6 Mar. Henry s. of William & Anne Hawkey
19 Mar. Joseph s. of William & Joane Merifield
22 Mar. Anne d. of John & Joane Daye
22 Mar. Robert s. of Remphrey & Jane Rowse

ANNO 1665.

26 Mar. Mary & Udey daughters of Thomas & Grace Wills

* Wm. Beauford elected Treasurer in place of James Jenkyn, Esq., deceased, 1659. (Green Book.)

† Symon Lawe paid rent of his shop 16s. 8d., 1652, Tho. Lawe, surety. (Green Book.)

‡ This Wm. mar. Ann dau. of Arthur Broad. See mar. 4 June, 1686.

§ He paid 7s. 4d. rent of the higher shop in 1661. (Green Book.)

9 April John s. of John & Grace Luke
23 April Thomas s. of John & Dorothy Davis
3 May John s. of John & Jone Daye
4 May Walter s. of Walter & Jone Tire
7 May Jane d. of Thomas & Thomazin Michell
15 May Richard s. of William & Anne Viguers
15 May Mary d. of Humfry & Sibella Harvey
16 May Margaret d. of John & Sibella Lee
26 May Henry s. of John & Honor Richards
2 June John s. of James & Issabell Hawkey
11 June Elizabeth d. of John & Mary Tenny
18 June Samuell s. of Henry & Elizabeth Jolley
24 June Thomas s. of Richard & Margery Williams
1 July John s. of Ralph & Joane Lambe
1 July Thomas s. of Isack & Elizabeth Nicholls
23 July James s. of John & Alice Pearse
6 Aug. Susan d. of Daniell & Hester Ropson
6 Aug. Arthur s. of Richard & Margery Veale
6 Aug. Henry s. of William & Honor Jolley
11 Aug. Pascow s. of John & Elizabeth Browne
27 Aug. Richard s. of John & Joane Gilbert
1 Sep. Henry s. of John & Anne Burnard
22 Sep. Jane d. of John & Jenefer Watts
1 Oct. Joane d. of Edward & Alice Merifield
4 Oct. Hannah d. of Josiah & Elizabeth Grimes
7 Oct. Peter s. of John & Elizabeth Rowse
7 Oct. Edward s. of Edward* & Ruth Crawly
28 Oct. Mary d. of John & Marrian Peters

* Edw. Crawley paid the rent of his shop, 9s. 6d., in 1659. (Green Book.)

28 Oct. Peter s. of Peter & Anne Kendall
29 Oct. Anne d. of Daniell & Marrian Phillips
4 Nov. Richard s. of James & Joane Stephens
8 Nov. Mary d. of George & Alice Daye
21 Nov. John s. of Robert Hoblyn Esq. & Grace his wife
3 Dec. William s. of Henry & Elizabeth Blake
3 Dec. Anthony s. of Anthony & Christian Rowe
9 Dec. Symon s. of Henry & Joane Trehemban
13 Dec. Joane d. of John & Jane Rowe
25 Dec. Marriett d. of Pascow & Jane Brabyn
25 Dec. John s. of John & Margery Williams
26 Dec. Bernard s. of Bernard & Elizabeth Rowse
26 Dec. Jane d. of John & Jane Best
27 Dec. John s. of John & Honor Jane
6 Jan. Maudlyn d. of William & Honor Tenny
26 Jan. Ralph s. of Reskimer* & Gartred Allen
2 Feb. Honor d. of Richard & Mary Moyle
4 Feb. Mary d. of Richard & Elizabeth Wills
4 Feb. Elinor d. of Jonathan & Grace Rouse
14 Feb. ffrancis s. of Thomas & Hester Merifield
14 Feb. Emblin d. of Peter & Joane Gibbs
7 Mar. Joane d. of Martin & ffrances Strongman
16 Mar. Thomas s. of Nathaniell & Joane Adam
18 Mar. Honor d. of Arthur & Anne Jolley

ANNO 1666.

28 Mar. Mary d. of Gilbert & Jane Richards
16 April Thomas s. of Christopher & Peternell Woolcock
17 April Grace d. of William & Grace Edwards
25 April Anne d. of William & ffrances White

* Reskymer Allen paid rent of his shop 42s. 6d.

4 June Joane d. of Stephen & Eliz. Capell
4 June Isack s. of David & Alice Pearse
15 June John s. of Robert & Jane Litticott
23 June Honor d. of Richard & Emblyn Edwards
24 June Joane d. of Henry & Mary Gill
11 July Mary d. of Dennis & Agatha Westcott
13 July Edward s. of Edward & Anne Crewes
13 July James s. of William & Mary Lanion
16 July Jane d. of Thomas & Grace Wills
20 July Honor d. of Henry & Hester Morcombe
29 July John s. of William & Mary Samble
29 July Richard s. of John & Abigall Udey
10 Aug. John s. of William & Jane Evelyn
12 Aug. John s. of Daniell & Elinor Couch
12 Aug. John s. of John & Joane Lockett
12 Aug. Jane d. of Giles & Margery Edwards
15 Sep. Thomas s. of Thomas & Grace Crewes
19 Sep. John s. of John Beauford Rector & Anne his wife
21 Sep. John s. of John & Jane Oxnam
21 Sep. Edward s. of Edward & Margery Lawry
29 Sep. Thomas s. of George & Christian Crapp
7 Oct. Mary d. of John & Catherine Retallack
28 Oct. Anne d. of Isack & Eliz. Nicholls
7 Nov. Eliz. d. of Ralph & Anstis Chenoweth
14 Nov. Phillip d. of Gidion & ffrances Cockyn
25 Nov. William s. of James & Mary Merifield
8 Dec. George s. of Josias & Eliz. Grimes
16 Dec. Henry s. of Charles & Joane Thomas
19 Dec. John s. of John* & Jane Daye

* John Day, gent., one of the twelve men in 1672. (Green Book.)

26 Jan. John & Eliz. s. and d. of John & Jane Best
29 Jan. Catherine d. of John* & Alice Brabyn
2 Feb. Lanceloit s. of Richard & Beaton Thomas
2 Feb. Thomas s. of Thomas & Joane Callaway
10 Feb. Thomas s. of Stephen & Jane Stephens
17 Feb. John s. of John & Sibella Lee
23 Feb. Hughe s. of William & Agnes Cockyn
1 Mar. John s. of John & Eliz. Kinge
8 Mar. Joane d. of John & Jenefer Watts
10 Mar. Mary d. of Oliver & Catherine Basely

ANNO 1667.

29 Mar. Humfry s. of Humfry & Sissilly Trehemban
31 Mar. Jane d. of Ralph & Elizabeth Crawley
3 April James s. of Methusala & Sarah Williams
8 April Honor d. of Symon & Joane Lae
9 April James s. of John & Jane Daye
13 April Honor d. of John & Anne Merifield
14 April Lowdy d. of Thomas & Marrett Cockyn
27 May Ralph s. of John & Margarett Williams
21 May James s. of Henry & Barbara Brewer
18 June Anne d. of John† Seyntaubyn Esq. & Anne his wife
21 June Thomas s. of John & Thomazine Whitford
14 July George s. of George & Alice Day
9 July Phillip s. of Reskimer & Garthred Allen

* John Brabyn, gent., one of the twelve men in 1650. (Green Book.)

† This John Seyntaubyn was son of John St. Aubyn, Esq., of Clowance, by his wife Catherine, dau. and coheir of Francis Godolphin of Treveneage. Anne his wife was dau. and coheir of James Jenkyn of Trekynning in St. Columb Major, mar. 14 Nov. 1665. Their dau. Anne mar. first, George, son and heir of Sir Peter Killigrew of Arwennick; and secondly, Tho. Goslyn of Westminster, Esq.

19 July Jane d. of William & Mary Bone
26 July Richard s. of John & Honor Richards
11 Aug. Peter s. of William & Mary Samble
25 Aug. Phillip s. of John & Joane Gilbert
20 Sep. Elizabeth d. of John & Abigall Udye
4 Oct. John s. of William & Jane Evelyn
1 Nov. Elizabeth d. of John & Margary Burne
20 Nov. John s. of Stephen & Rachell Banger
24 Nov. ffrances d. of Gideon & ffrances Cockyn
27 Nov. Nathaniell s. of Edward & Margery Lawrye
6 Dec. Phillip s. of Thomas & Thomazin Michell
13 Dec. William s. of Wm & Joane Merifield
15 Dec. Henry s. of Henry & Mary Gill
20 Dec. Nicholas s. of Nathaniell & Joane Adam
22 Dec. George s. of Henry & Barbara Lee
27 Dec. Richard s. of Edward & Ruth Crawly
6 Jan. John s. of Thomas & Joane Rouse
6 Jan. James s. of James & Joane Moyle
6 Jan. Elizabeth d. of George & Mary Luny
6 Jan. Temperance base d. of Dorothy Launder
10 Jan. Mary d. of Phillip & Jone Kinge
19 Jan. William s. of Peter & Honour Cockinge
19 Jan. Elizabeth d. of John & Anne Burnard
1 Feb. Thomas base s. of Joane Inch
5 Feb. Oliver base s. of Katherine Rowe
9 Feb. Stephen* s. of Thomas & Elizabeth Warne
12 Feb. Mary d. of Ralph & Anastatia Chenoweth
14 Feb. Elias s. of Peter & Anne Kendall
26 Feb. Paschow s. of James & Jone Stephens

* His mother was Elizabeth Lovell. For his own marriage, see wedding, 8 Dec. 1693.

1 Mar. John s. of John & Alice Pierce
6 Mar. John s. of James & Emblyn Methwell
12 Mar. ffrancis and Carew sons of Rob Hoblyn Esq. & Grace his wife
14 Mar. Archiball s. of Remphrey & Joane Rouse

ANNO 1668.

1 April John s. of James & Margarett Rouse
12 April Richard s. of Edward & Alice Merifield
1 May Honour d. of John & Alice Rouse
11 May William s. of William & Honour Jolly
11 May John s. of Christopher & Peternell Woolcock
31 May Mathew s. of Daniell & Hester Ropson
5 June John s. of Arthur & Joane Jenkyn
20 June Edward s. of John & Marrian Peter
24 June Joell s. of Stephen & Elizabeth Capell
24 June Mary and ffrances daughters of John and Mary Tenny
25 July ffrances d. of Robert & Jane Litticott
9 Aug. John s. of John & Honour Husband
16 Aug. John s. of John & Alice Blake
22 Aug. Edward s. of Wm & Mary Lanion
23 Aug. ffrances d. of Thomas & Grace Wills
23 Aug. Christian d. of John & ffrances Buckthorpe
29 Sep. John s. of John & Margarett Truscott
4 Oct. Honour d. of Ralph & Mary Lambe
4 Oct. Richard s. of Josias & Elizabeth Grimes
4 Oct. Richard s. of Jonathan & Grace Rouse
4 Oct. Henry s. of William & Honour Tinney
27 Oct. Elizabeth d. of John & Alice Brabyn
30 Oct. George s. of Charles & Joane Thomas

30 Oct. Phillippa d. of Thomas & Grace Crewes
1 Nov. Judeth d. of Richard & Margery Edwards
29 Nov. Luke s. of Luke & Honour Giles
18 Dec. Richard s. of Richard & Emblyn Edwards
20 Dec. William s. of Edward & Anne Crewes
28 Dec. Richard s. of John & Margery Williams
17 Jan. Ruth d. of Richard & Emblyn Slade
22 Jan. Elizabeth d. of Tho. & Hester Merifield
30 Jan. Temperance d. of Stephen & Anne Stephens
31 Jan. Jane d. of John & Catherine Retallack
7 Feb. Joane d. of Ralph & Elizabeth Crawly
14 Feb. Charles s. of John & Abigall Udye
19 Feb. Jenefer d. of Richard & Elizabeth Wills
20 Feb. Sarah d. of John* & Elizabeth King
21 Feb. Abell s. of John & Joane Logget
21 Feb. Elizabeth d. of Anthony & Christian Rowe
24 Feb. Mary d. of John & Jenifer Watts
7 Mar. Isabell d. of Hugh & Thomazin Richards
21 Mar. Elizabeth d. of Arthur† & Anne Jolley

ANNO 1669.

13 April John s. of John & Anne Merifield
14 April Emblin d. of John & Jane Daye
9 May Jane d. of Patherick & Joane Gilbert
21 May Elizabeth d. of Henry & Hester Morcombe
30 May ffrancis s. of Elias & Anne Pollard
11 June John s. of William & Honour Delbridge
18 June James s. of Christopher & Anne Blake

* Mr. John Kinge paid for the rent of his shop 23s. in 1672. (Green Book.)
† Arthur Jolly was one of the Wardens of the parish in 1651. (Green Book.)

20 June Edward s. of James & Mary Merifield
24 June Elizabeth d. of Richard & Margery Williams
2 July Richard s. of Nath. & Joane Adam
9 July Samuell s. of Robert Hoblyn Esq., & Grace his wife
11 July Edward s. of Oliver & Catherine Basely
16 July William s. of Wm. & Jane Evelyn
17 July Anne d. of Henry & Honour Brush
1 Aug. Mary d. of John & Grace Trebilcock
20 Aug. John s. of Isack & Elizabeth Nicholls
3 Sep. Reskimer s. of Reskimer & Grace Allen
5 Sep. Jone d. of James & Emlyn Metherill
11 Sep. Peter s. of John & Thomazin Bale
17 Sep. William s. of Ralph & Anastatia Chenoweth
2 Oct Honour d. of John & Sibella Lee
10 Oct. William s. of Wm. & Honour Jolley
15 Oct. Grace d. of Giles & Margery Edwards
10 Dec. Peter s. of John & Jane Best
12 Dec. George s. of John & Precilla Stephens
9 Jan. Jane d. of Thomas & Eliz. Scaberio
13 Jan. John s. of John Seyntaubyn,* Esq. & Anne his wife
14 Jan. John s. of John & Margery Burne
22 Jan. Henry s. of Thomas & Thomazin Michell
22 Jan. John s. of John & Joane Gilbert
23 Jan. William s. of Richard & Beaton Thomas
5 Feb. ffrancis s. of Edward & Anne Crewes
11 Feb. Ralph s. of George & Mary Luney
11 Feb. Anne d. of Thomas & Grace Crewes
24 Feb. Anstis d. of Thomas & Elizabeth Warne

* John St. Aubyn, Esq., was created a Baronet in 1671, and was succeeded by this son, who became the second Baronet.

26 Feb. Gilbert base s. of ffrances Crewes
27 Feb. John s. of John & Thomazin Whitford
9 Mar. Sampson s. of Wm. & Agnes Cocke
16 Mar. Stephen s. of Richard & Mary Lovell
16 Mar. Elizabeth d. of John & Mary Williams

Anno 1670.

26 Mar. John s. of Thomas & Elizabeth Callaway
9 April George s. of Phillip & Joane Kinge
8 May William s. of Walter & Joane Tyer
21 May William s. of Robert & Maude Skynner
4 June Joane d. of Methusalah & Sarah Williams
25 June Henry s. of James & Margarett Rouse
17 July Roger s. of Gidion Cockyn & ffrances his wife
22 July John s. of John & Alice Brabyn
7 Aug. Anthony s. of Thomas & Joane Calloway
7 Aug. Mary d. of Christopher & Peternell Woolcock
17 Sep. Thomas s. of Stephen & Elizabeth Capell
2 Oct. Joane d. of James & Joane Moyle
8 Oct. Elizabeth d. of William & Honour Delbridge
16 Oct. Mary d. of John & Alice Blake
18 Oct. Patience d. of Josias & Eliz. Grimes
21 Oct. George s. of Richard & Emblyn Edwards
23 Oct. Mary d. of Thomas & Joane Rowse
19 Nov. Anne d. of Henry & Honour Brush
23 Nov. Thomas s. of Dennis & Agatha Westcott
4 Dec. John s. of James & Anne Hendra
4 Dec. Agnes d. of John & ffrances Buckthought*
9 Dec. Edward s. of Edward & Margery Lawry

* This name is spelt in the Registers sometimes Buckthorpe, but it exists at the present time (1880) in the parish as Buckthought.

14 Dec. Elizabeth d. of George & Jane Reynolds
27 Dec. Joane d. of Ralph & Eliz. Crawly
14 Jan. Ralph base son of Mary Awdridge
29 Jan. Elizabeth d. of John & Catherine Retallack
10 Feb. William s. of William & Joane Darre
12 Feb. Mary d. of Wm. & Honour Tenny
15 Feb. Richard s. of Henry & Anne Jolley
19 Feb. Jane d. of Michaell & Jane Cowlinge
8 Mar. Mary d. of Peter & Anne Kendall
17 Mar. Elizabeth d. of Nath. & Joane Adams
24 Mar. Thomas s. of Tho. & Grace Wills
24 Mar. Elizabeth d. of Wm. & Mary Lanion

Anno 1671.

25 Mar. Richard s. of Michaell & ffrances Cornish
2 April Leah d. of Ralph & Mary Lambe
12 April Alice d. of Remphrey & Jane Rowse
16 April Margery d. of Daniell & Hester Ropson
25 April John s. of Petherick & Joane Gilbert
1 May Lawrence s. of Peter & Honour Cockyn
29 May Avis d. of Thomas & Marriott Cockyn
9 June Elizabeth d. of John & Eliz. Kinge
12 June Elizabeth d. of John & Janifer Watts
13 June Emblyn d. of John & Jane Daye
13 June Thomas s. of ffrancis & Mary Mannell
2 July Mary d. of Henry & Mary Gill
26 Aug. John s. of John & Mary Tenny
15 Sep. ffrancis and William sons of Robert Hoblyn Esq. & Grace his wife
14 Oct. John s. of John & Joane Trustcott*

* Sic.

29 Sep. Thomas s. of William & Agnes Cock
11 Nov. John s. of Charles & Joane Thomas
19 Nov. James s. of Robert & Jane Littacott
1 Dec. Elizabeth d. of Thomas & Elizabeth Chaple
2 Dec. Thomas s. of Thomas & Elizabeth Callaway
3 Dec. Thomas s. of Edward & Alice Merifield
3 Dec. John s. of Tho. & Elizabeth Scaberio
6 Jan. Henry s. of Henry & Barbara Lee
24 Jan. Phillip s. of Phillip & Jone Kinge
26 Jan. Prudence d. of John & Abigall Udye
2 Feb. Thomas s. of Thomas & Thomazin Tom
2 Feb. fflorence d. of Isack & Eliz. Nicholls
9 Feb. Joane d. of Richard & Emlyn Slade
17 Feb. Gilbert s. of John & Honor Richards
24 Feb. Henry s. of John & Sibella Lee
3 Mar. Oliver s. of Oliver & Catherine Basely
17 Mar. Henry s. of John & Joane Loggett
24 Mar. Jane d. of Hugh & Thomazin Richards

Anno 1672.

25 Mar. Honor d. of Arthur & Joane Jenkyn
25 Mar. Honor d. of John & Honor Husband
29 Mar. Eliz. d. of Thomas & Eliz. Warne
29 Mar. Dorothy d. of James & Emblin Metherall
6 April Sarah d. of Christian Michell Wid.
9 April James s. of George & Mary Luny
12 April Anne d. of Thomas & Hester Merifield
20 April John s. of John & Matilda Dunkin
26 April Elizabeth d. of William & Honor Delbridge
4 May William s. of Richard & Emblin Richards
10 May John s. of Peter & Jane Bligh
27 May Honor d. of Nath. & Margarite Champion
27 May John s. of John & Thomazin Bale
19 July James and Elizabeth s. and d. of John & Joane Gilbert
21 July Richard s. of Richard & Mary Edwards
28 July Robert s. of James & Mary Merifield
2 Aug. Matilda d. of Reskimer & Gartrid Allen
18 Aug. Mary d. of Henry & Mary Gill
18 Aug. Joane d. of John & Kath. Retallack
28 Aug. Richard s. of Richard & Mary Lovell
7 Sep. John s. of William & Joane Darre
21 Sep. Dorothy d. of Richard & Beaton Thomas
22 Sep. Alice d. of Wm. & Honor Jolly
24 Nov. Elizabeth d. of Wm. & Joane Merifield
1 Dec. Judeth d. of Christopher & Peternell Wolcock
20 Dec. Jane d. of Thomas & Grace Crewes
26 Dec. Elizabeth d. of James & Mary Cocke
18 Jan. Luke s. of Luke & Honor Giles
2 Feb. Charity d. of Stephen & Elizabeth Capell
7 Feb. Mary d. of Wm. & Jane Eveling
12 Feb. James s. of Robert & Joane Litticott
21 Feb. Joane d. of John & Joane Truscott
28 Feb. Mary d. of Ralph & Elizabeth Crawley
28 Feb. Bridgett d. of Michaell & Jane Cowling
2 Mar. ffrances d. of John & ffrances Buckthought
7 Mar. John base s. of Grace Tonkyn
8 Mar. Elizabeth d. of John & Thomas Whitford
9 Mar. Wm. s. of John & Honor Richards

Anno 1673.

23 April Richard s. of John & Matilda Dunking

26 April Thomas base s. of Millson Merefield
17 May Thomas s. of Richard & Mariery Williams
17 May Elizabeth d. of Mathuselah & Sara Williams
23 May John s. of Henry & Honor Brush
31 May Ann d. of Josias Grymes
7 June William s. of Charles & Dorcas Retallack
14 June William s. of William & Honor Tynne
28 June Anthony s. of ffrancis* & Grace Godolphin
23 July James s. of James & Gartrid Peeters
8 Aug. John s. of Edward & Mariery Lawry
9 Aug. John s. of John & Junerfer Watts
10 Aug. Henry base child of ff.orence Trenines
17 Aug. Susanna d. of William & Agnes Couch
23 Aug. Inigo base s. of Joane Inch Widd
5 Sep. William s. of Ralfe & Constice Chenoweth
6 Sep. John s. of John & Ann Merefeld
6 Sep. Ann d. of Peeter & Ann Kendall
14 Sep. Archibald s. of Jonathan & Grace Rowse
20 Sep. Margarite d. of Richard & Emblyn Edwards
3 Oct. Edward base s. of Thomazin Richards
4 Oct. Robert s. of Thomas & Joane Rowse
12 Oct. Thomas s. of John & Abegall Udye
17 Oct. James s. of Daniell & Hester Ropson
24 Oct. Aurthur s. of Richard & Elizabeth Jolly
14 Nov. Richard s. of Henry & Alice Rowse

* This Francis is presumed to have been the son of John Godolphin of St. Kew (by his wife Honor, dau. of John Molesworth). See Colonel Vivian's 'Visitations of Cornwall,' p. 187, where Anthony is suggested as the Christian name of his wife's father, but his wife was doubtless the Grace, dau. of Wm. and Eliz. Crewes, bapt. 12 Feb. 1649. See p. 49 *ante*. For their marriage see Weddings, 4 Nov. 1672.

21 Nov. Will'm s. of Will'm & Mary Lanyon
3 Dec. Will'm s. of Thomas & Elizabeth Calvey
7 Dec. Phillip s. of Peeter & Ann Husband
20 Dec. Henry s. of Phylip & Joane Kinge
6 Jan. John s. of Petherick & Joane Gilbert
9 Jan. Peeter s. of John & Frances Allen
9 Jan. Gartrid d. of Reskymer Allen
10 Jan. Thomasin d. of Peeter & Honor Cockin
17 Jan. Charles s. of Nycholas & Jane Bounsell
8 Feb. Thomas s. of Thomas & Elizabeth Scaberio
21 Feb. Jane d. of Charles & Joane Thomas
22 Mar. Thomas s. of Nathaniell & Joan Adams

Henry Jolly & Phillip Oxnam } *Wardens.*

Anno 1674.

11 April Henry s. of Will'm & Joan Darr
12 April John s. of Anthony & Gartory White
17 May Julian d. of James & Jane Moyle
8 June Thomas s. of John & Honor Husband
20 June Edward s. of Thomas & Elizabeth Warne
28 June Ralph s. of Ralph & Mary Lambe
11 July John s. of John & Catherine Retallack
12 July James s. of Isaak & Elizabeth Nicholls
12 July Mary d. of George & Mary Luney
25 July Francis s. of John & Matilda Dunkyn
2 Aug. Richard s. of John & Mary Tenny
15 Aug. Thomas s. of Thomas & Florence Lawe
16 Oct. Jane d. of Richard & Mary Lovell
17 Oct. Emblyn d. of Nathaniell & Margarite Champion
21 Oct. Catherine d. of John & Johan Sprey

23 Oct. William s. of Thomas & Frances Nicholls
20 Nov. William s. of William & Joice Dennis
27 Nov. John s. of John & Frances Browne
30 Nov. James s. of Richard & Emblyn Edwards
29 Jan. Peter s. of John & Jane Daye
6 Feb. Richard s. of John & Sibella Lee
13 Feb. Johan the base d. of Marrien Luke
14 Feb. John s. of Stephen & Johan Stephens
6 Mar. Margery d. of Christopher & Peternell Wolcock
19 Mar. James s. of James & Mary Rowse
23 Mar. John s. of James & Johan Daye
14 Mar. Elizabeth d. of Anthony & Mary Callaway

ANNO 1675.

6 April Thomas s. of Bartholomew & Jane Trethewy
7 April Zacharius s. of Ralph & Enstis Chenoweth
17 April John s. of William & Johan Launder
24 April John s. of John & Catherine Moyle
1 May Nicholas s. of Nicholas & Jane Bounsell
1 May Margaret d. of James & Emblyn Metherell
21 May Jane d. of Thomas & Alice Stephens
22 May Richard s. of John & Joan Truscot
29 May William s. of Richard & Emblyn Slade
18 June Isaac s. of John & Joane Gilbert
25 July Mary d. of Thomas & Mary Nicholls
1 Aug. Mary d. of Samuell & Jane Pryn
6 Aug. Nathaniell s. of John & Thomazin Bale
6 Aug. Mary d. of John & Elizabeth Kinge
13 Aug. Alice d. of George* & Jane Champion

* George Champion, gent., one of twelve men in 1693. (Green Book.)

12 Sep. William s. of John & Jennefer Watts
2 Oct. Jane d. of James & Mary Cock
16 Oct. Mary d. of Robert & Jane Litticott
1 Nov. William s. of John & Abigall Udy
13 Nov. Peter s. of Thomas & Elizabeth Callaway
19 Dec. Tobias base s. of Christian Roe
31 Dec. Thomas s. of Richard & Jane Hawk
7 Jan. Christian d. of Edward* & Margery Bluet
15 Jan. John s. of Thomas & Florence Lawe
22 Jan. Elizabeth d. of Richard & Christian Retallack
5 Feb. Emblyn d. of Richard & Emblyn Edwards
19 Feb. Honor d. of Josias & Elizabeth Grimes
25 Feb. Peternell d. of John & Thomas Whitford
26 Feb. William s. of Edward & Alice Rawling
27 Feb. Joell s. of John & Alice Blake
13 Mar. Grace d. of John & Frances Allyn
19 Mar. Thomas s. of Richard & Elizabeth Jolley

ANNO 1676.

27 Mar. Henry s. of Peter & Ann Husband
27 Mar. Paterick s. of Paterick & Johan Gilbert
2 May Pentecost d. of Nicholas & Frances Woodman
22 May Philip d. of Henry & Barbara Lee
27 May John s. of John & Matilda Dunkyn
27 May Mary d. of William & Johan Merifield
15 July Francis s. of Thomas & Grace Crewes
23 July Joice d. of William & Jane Eveling
29 July Humphry s. of Thomas & Johan Rowse

* This Edw. was probably son of Edw. Bluett and Christian Arthur, who were mar. at St. Enoder 19 Nov. 1649. St. Enoder P. R.

30 July Nicholas s. of Thomas & Mary Cocking
26 Aug. John s. of Philip & Johan Kinge
2 Sep. Anne d. of Thomas & Elizabeth Scaberio
9 Sep. Edward s. of John & Julian Harvey
7 Oct. Isaac s. of Isaac & Elizabeth Nicholls
7 Oct. Frances d. of Thomas & Alice Stephens
8 Oct. John s. of John & Frances Buckthought
20 Nov. Peter s. of Peter & Johan Pollard
14 Nov. Elizabeth d. of John & Frances Browne
25 Nov. Peter s. of Nicholas & Jane Bounsell
22 Nov. Sarah d. of Methuselah & Sarah Williams
5 Dec. Gilbert s. of James & Mary Merifield
5 Dec. Mary d. of Nathaniell & Jane Gliddon
26 Dec. Arthur s. of William & Honor Tinney
1 Jan. Edward s. of Edward & Mary Lawry
12 Jan. Allice d. of John & Johan Sprey
13 Jan. Richard s. of Daniell & Hester Ropson
16 Jan. John s. of William & Mary Rowe
10 Feb. Grace d. of Arthur & Johan Jenkyn
17 Feb. Honor d. of Thomas & Elizabeth Warne
25 Feb. William s. of William & Agnes Cock
26 Feb. Ralph s. of John & Jane Daye
16 June *Jane d. of Anthony & Mary Callaway
17 June *Dennis s. of Dennis Agatha Westcott
23 June *Mary d. of William & Mary Lanyon
19 Mar. John s. of Richard & Emblin Edwards

ANNO 1677.

30 Mar. William s. of Marke & Anne Tyer

* These three names were omitted in their right place. (Thus entered, with the explanation, in the original Register.)

30 Mar. Honor d. of Richard & Jane Pollard
7 April Elizabeth d. of Nathaniell & Margaret Champion
4 April W^m s. of Anthony & Gertrude White
16 April W^m s. of W^m & Johan Launder
17 April Mary d. of Richard & Johan Clemmas
5 May Thomas s. of Thomas & Marriet Cocking
8 May Arthur & Johan s. & d. of W^m & Hono^r Jolly
12 May John s. of Robert & Grace Litticott
12 May Elizabeth d. of Charles & Ann Bownsell
12 May Grace d. of Henry & Johan Cock
19 May Anthony s. of Hendy & Dinah Langdon
28 May George s. of George & Mary Luney
24 June John s. of Christopher & Peternell Wolcock
30 June Jacob base s. of Ann Puncher
25 July Richard s. of Richard & Audrid Hawke
12 Aug. Mark s. of Richard & Christian Retallack
13 Aug. Sampson s. of John & Thomazin Bale
13 Aug. George s. of George & Elizabeth Reynold
20 Aug. Mary d. of Jacob & Mary Husband
1 Sep. Anne d. of Richard & Emblin Slade
5 Sep. Hono^r d. of Thomas & Catharine Hendy
5 Sep. Jane d. of John & Honor Husband
6 Oct. James s. of Robert & Honor Harris
6 Oct. Margarite d. of John & Thomazin Tom
6 Oct. Mary d. of John & Alice Benallack
20 Oct. John s. of Michell & Frances Cornish
20 Oct. Jane d. of Frances & Grace Godolphin
1 Nov. John & Thomas s. of John & Mary Langdon
10 Nov. Bligh s. of Henry & Margarite Haycroft

13 Nov. John s. of John & Johan Truscott
16 Nov. Jane d. of George & Jane Champion
23 Nov. Elizabeth d. of John & Elizabeth Cocking
22 Dec. Peter s. of Wm & Johan Darre
12 Jan. Abraham s. of Isaac & Emblin Husband
19 Jan. John s. of Beniamin & Millicent James
26 Jan. Catharine d. of John & Catharine Retallack
26 Jan. Margarite d. of Simon & Alice Rawling
1 Feb. Edward s. of Thomas & Frances Michell
2 Feb. Peter s. of Peter & Honor Cocking
9 Mar. Mary d. of Wm & Joice Dennis

ANNO 1678.

7 April Jane d. of Thomas & Jone Wilking
20 April Johan d. of Wm & Rose Hoskin
20 April Catharine d. of John & Thomasin Whitford
29 April Elizabeth d. of Richard & Elizabeth Jolly
4 May Jane d. of Robert & Jane Litticott
11 May Elizabeth d. of Philip & Johan Kinge
31 May Anne d. of Thomas & Alice Stephens
2 June Isaac s. of Isaac & Elizabeth Nicholls
2 June Charles s. of Thomas & Elizabeth Seaberie
2 June Stephen s. of Richard & Mary Lovell
4 June Samuell s. of Samuell & Elizabeth Maye
14 June Thomas s. of John & Jennefer Watts
19 June John s. of Nicholas & Jane Bownsell
13 July Mary d. of John & Johan Mill
13 July Mary d. of Peter & Anne Husband
8 Aug. Matilda & Eliz. d. of John & Sibella Lee
9 Aug. Margarite d. of Nathll & Margarite Champion
16 Aug. Philip s. of Leonard & Jane Brewer
16 Aug. Thomas s. of Petherick & Johan Gilbert
17 Aug. John s. of John & Frances Allyn
18 Aug. Dorothy d. of George & Alice Daye
31 Aug. Mary d. of Nathll & Johan Adams
7 Sep. Eliz. d. of Peter* & Eliz. Champion
7 Sep. Anne d. of Thomas & Jane Minnow
16 Sep. Richard s. of Nicholas & Frances Woodman
12 Oct. Robert s. of Henry & Johan Cock
19 Oct. John s. of James & Margarite Rowse
11 Nov. John s. of Josias & Elizabeth Grimes
29 Nov. Grace d. of John & Elizabeth Kinge
29 Nov. Anthony s. of Edward & Margery Lawry
2 Dec. Wm s. of John & Frances Browne
2 Dec. John s. of John & Alice Benallack
7 Dec. Eliz. d. of Anth. & Elizabeth Callaway
20 Dec. Matthias s. of ffaith Troth
18 Jan. fflorence d. of Philip & fflorence Harris
19 Jan. Catharine d. of John & Mary Langdon
25 Jan. Anne d. of Nathll & Jane Gliddon
25 Jan. Humphry base s. of Honor Bounsell
31 Jan. Michaell s. of Michaell & Jane Cowling
1 Feb. Ralph s. of Reskimer & Gertrude Allen
8 Feb. Ebbot d. of John & Dorothy Jolly
11 Feb. Philip s. of Humphry & Mary Sloggett
21 Feb. Honor d. of James & Emblin Metherell
6 Mar. Richard s. of James & Mary Cock

ANNO 1679.

5 April Johan d. of Dorothy Daye

* This Peter Champion mar. Elizabeth, dau. of William Arundell, of Falmouth; they had issue Peter, Elizabeth, Ann, Margery, Mary.

20 May Marke s. of John & Johan Truscot
1 June Marye d. of William & Honor Jollye
8 June Phillipp s. of James & Avis Michell
8 June Ann d. of John & Joane Sprey
4 July George s. of Mr. George* & Mrs. Jane Champion
10 Aug. Grace d. of William & Agnes Cock
17 Aug. Dennis s. of Thomas & Joane Rowse
23 Aug. John s. of William & Mary Minnow
19 Sep. John s. of John & Mary Ingland
21 Sep. Thomas s. of William & Audrye Hawke
28 Sep. Richard s. of William & Mary Rowe
6 Oct. Sacielie d. of Isick† & Emblin Husband
7 Oct. ffrancis s. of Mr. Hammauell & Mrs. Elizabeth Maye
18 Oct. John s. of Thomas & Mary Cockin
19 Oct. Patience d. of Richard & Jane Pollard
8 Nov. John s. of Thomas & Katherin Hendye
21 Nov. Mary d. of John & Ann Chenoweth
22 Nov. Elizabeth d. of Mr. James & Mrs. Ann Edwards
8 Dec. Jane d. of John & Elizabeth Cockin
14 Dec. Richard s. of Richard & Honor Harris
19 Dec. Hester d. of Benjamin & Millison James
28 Dec. Ann d. of Peter & Ann Richards
29 Dec. Ann d. of John & ffrances Allin
2 Jan. Lowdye d. of Simon & Alice Rawling
19 Jan. Samuell s. of William & Joane Launder
24 Jan. John s. of John & Joane Mill
24 Jan. John s. of Humfrey & Mary Sloggett
25 Jan. Mary d. of Thomas & Florence Lawe

* His wife was Jane Haycroft, see Weddings, 26 June, 1674.

† Isaac Husband paid rent of shop 10s., in 1633. (Green Book.)

26 Jan. Mary d. of Anthony & Mary Callway
1 Feb. Beaton base d. of Joane White
2 Feb. Margery d. of Nicholas & Jane Bounsell
13 Feb. Thomas s. of Robert & Grace Litticott
14 Feb. Jane d. of Richard & Christian Retallack
2 Mar. John s. of Mr. Henry & Margarite Haycroft
12 Mar. Ann d. of Peeter & Elizabeth Champion
13 Mar. John s. of James & Mary Nicholls
20 Mar. Martin s. of Richard & Elizabeth Jollye

ANNO 1680.

26 Mar. Thomas s. of Thomas & Alice Steevens
30 Mar. Edward s. of Anthony & Elizabethe Michell
13 April Elizabethe d. of Michell & ffrances Cornish
13 April Garthered d. of John & Honor Husband
17 April Thomas s. of Thomas & Elizabeth Scibberio
15 April Mary d. of John & Allice Beenallack
29 May Steephen s. of Marke & Ann Tyer
29 May William s. of John & Allice Blake
25 June Henry s. of Henry & Alice Rowse
17 July Elizabth d. of Jacob & Mary Husband
24 July Martha d. of William & Joyce Dennis
7 Aug. Joseph s. of John & Matilda Dunkin
8 Aug. Joice d. of George & Mary L . . . .*
10 Aug. Jane d. of Roger & Joan Ellery
14 Aug. Richard d. of John & Joan Sprey
4 Sep. Emblyn d. of Richard & Katherine Troth
8 Oct. Joan d. of John & frances Buckthought
9 Oct. Beaton d. of Philip & Joane King
21 Nov. Thomas s. of Thomas & Joane Wilkin

* Obliterated. Luney. See 20 July, 1661.

2 Dec. Honor d. of William & Honor Tinnye
3 Dec. George base s. of ffaith Troth
7 Dec. Robert s. of Leonard & Jane Brewer
11 Dec. Willmott d. of William & Audrye Hawk
27 Dec. Mathew s. of Peter & An Husband
18 Jan. Peter s. of Patrick & Joan Gilbert
8 Jan. Eliz[th] d. of Isaack & Eliz[th] Nicholls
22 Jan. Honor d. of Josias & Elizab[th] Grimes
28 Jan. Joseph s. of Samuell & Eliz[th] May
31 Jan. Nicholas s. of Thomas & Sarah Hockin
19 Feb. Jonathan s. of Jonathan & Grace Rouse
19 Feb. Symon s. of Thomas & Elizab[th] Warn
26 Feb. Joyce d. of Joseph & Joyce Row
14 Mar. ffrancis s. of Robert & Mary Mannuell
14 Mar. Julian d. of William & Rose Hoskyn

Anno 1681.

23 April Mary d. of Anthony & Garthred White
29 April Jane d. of John & Thomasin Whitford
30 April Hugh s. of John & Mary Langdon
30 April Mary d. of John & Honor Tyer
6 May James s. of James & An Edwards
15 May Joan d. of Thomas & Elizab[th] Skibberow
23 May Honor d. of Peter & Honour Cockyn
28 May Elizab[th] d. of francis & Grace Godolphin
29 May Thomas s. of John & Mary Pakinhorn*
11 June Grace d. of James & Elizabeth Steevens
18 June Thomas s. of Charles & An Bounsell
18 June John s. of Anthony & Mary Callway
1 July Nathan s. of Rob[t] & Jane Litticott

* Sic.

12 July Methuselah s. of Methuselah & Sarah Williams
. . . . . .* Elizabeth d. of Edward & . . . .
3 Aug. Grace d. of Robert & Mary Retallock
7 Aug. John s. of William & Agnis Cock
7 Aug. Elizab[th] base child of Jane Moyle
13 Aug. Samuell s. of William & Joan Launder
20 Aug. Henry s. of Henry & Joan Cock
26 Aug. Joan d. of John & Alice Benallack
2 Sep. An d. of Roger & Joane Ellery
3 Sep. Henry s. of William & Joan Dennis
.. Sep. Julian d. of Humphry & Jane Harvey
10 Sep. Junefer d. of John & Jenefer Watts
23 Sep. Mary d. of Michaell & Jane Cowling
29 Sep. Mary d. of Bernard & Jane Lobb
3 Oct. Mary d. of John & Joan Truscott
7 Oct. Mary d. of Richard & Susan Williams
23 Oct. John s. of Hendy & Dinah Langdon
17 Nov. Elizabeth d. of Nicholas & Dorothy Hawk
8 Nov. An d. of John Bishop Rector and An his wife
10 Nov. Honor d. of Nathan & Jane Gliddon
16 Dec. Elizabeth base child of An Jolley
26 Dec. Margery d. of Peter & Elizab[th] Champion
6 Jan. James s. of Nicholas & Jane Bounsell
17 Jan. Grace d. of Nathan & Margaret Champion
24 Jan. John s. of ffrancis & Maud Dungye
18 Feb. Anthony s. of John & Margaret Pill
3 Mar. Edward s. of Daniell & Margaret May
8 Mar. Elizab[th] d. of Jacob & Margaret Husband

* So in the original, surname and date left blank.

11 Mar. Robert s. of John & Mary England
24 Mar. Thomas s. of William & Elizab[th] Bazely

ANNO 1682.

26 Mar. Sampson s. of John & Joan Mill
1 April Alice d. of John & Dorothy Jolly
7 April John s. of Peter & An Richards
17 April Leah d. of Thomas & Mary Cockyn
18 April Hester d. of Beniaman & Millson James
22 April Henry s. of John Jolly
16 May Henry s. of John & ffrances Brown
6 June Elizab[th] d. of Isaack & Emblin Husband
16 June Sarah d. of Samuell & Elizab[th] May
24 June Philip s. of William & Joane Minnow
24 June Joan d. of Thomas & Jane Hendy
6 Aug. Mary d. of James & Mary Cock
19 Aug. John s. of William & Honour Arundle*
8 Sep. Martin s. of Michaell & Elizab[th] Strongman
27 Sep. Richard s. of James & Avis Michell
30 Sep. Anthony s. of Anthony & Elizab. Michell
6 Oct. Philip s. of Charles & Thomazin Allen
7 Oct. Elizab[th] d. of Philip & fflorence Harris
23 Oct. James d. of Thomas & Alice Stephens
4 Nov. William s. of W[m] & Avis Moor
10 Nov. Tiffany d. of Richard & Elizab[th] Jolley
13 Nov. Nathan s. of Nathan & Margaret Champion
25 Nov. Peter s. of Robert & Hono[r] Harris
2 Dec. Grace d. of John & ffrances Allen
26 Dec. An d. of William & Audry Hawke

* Honour Pollard. See their marriage 21 Nov. 1681. This Wm. is supposed to be grandson of Wm. son of Tho., grandson of Sir John Arundell of Lanherne, by Eliz. Dauet. See Col. Vivian's 'Visitations of Cornwall,' p. 5.

26 Dec. Peter s. of Peter & Elizab[th] Champion
1 Jan. Mary d. of Nicholas & Jane Bounsell
6 Jan. Thomas s. of Isaac & Elizab[th] Nicholls
6 Jan. An d. of Littleton & Elizab[th] Weymont
6 Jan. Mary d. of James & Martha Nettle
28 Jan. Margaret d. of Nicholas & Dorothy Hawke
28 Jan. Elizab[th] base d. of An Puncher
2 Feb. William s. of William & Elizab[th] Bone
6 Feb. Philip s. of Humphry & Jane Oxnam
20 Feb. Robert s. of Robert & Mary Mannuell
24 Mar. John s. of John & Elizab[th] Cockyn

ANNO 1683.

7 April William s. of William & Rose Hoskyn
13 April Robert s. of John Bishop Rector & An his wife
17 April Henry s. of John & Jane Grimes
21 April Henry s. of John & ffrances George
24 April John s. of John & Joan Rows
18 May Nicholas s. of Nicholas & ffrances Woodman
20 May Thomas s. of Thomas & Elizab[th] Skibberiow
8 April Anthony s. of Roger & Joane Ellery
10 June ffaithful s. of John & ffrances Buckthorpe
16 June Alice d. of Will[m] & Joice Dennis
22 June Elizab[th] d. of Thomas & Elizab[th] Tibb
23 June Daniell d. of Daniell & Margery May
23 June Robert d. of William & Margaret Michell
24 June Mary d. of John & Mary Langdon
30 June Joane d. of Petherick & Joane Gilbert
8 July James s. of Peter & Ann Husband
21 July Giles s. of John & Joane Truscott
17 Aug. Ann d. of John & Jane Lawarren

19 Aug. Susanna d. of John & Alice Benallack
1 Sep. William s. of Will'm & Mary Minnow
2 Sep. Thomas s. of Richard & Susanna Williams
15 Sep. Grace d. of William & Joane Launder
21 Sep. John s. of Arthur & Mary Broad*
21 Sep. Timothy s. of James & Elizabeth Stevens
30 Sep. ffaithfull s. of William & Ann Cock
13 Oct. Thomas s. of John & Alice Blake
20 Oct. Anthony s. of Philip Kinge & Joane his wife
27 Oct. George s. of George & Mary Tom
2 Nov. Ann d. of William & Jane Penhellick
3 Nov. Alice d. of Robert & Mary Retallack
12 Nov. Mary d. of Thomas & Mary Richards
13 Nov. Mary d. of John & Katherine Brabyn
16 Nov. James s. of James Beauford Clerk & Jane his wife†
23 Nov. Ann d. of Samuell & Eliz. May
12 Dec. John s. of John & Joan Sprey
18 Dec. Damoris d. of Edward Hoblyn Esq.‡ & Damoris his wife
23 Dec. Margarett d. of Nathaniell & Margarett Champion
23 Jan. John s. of George & Jane Champion
22 Feb. Phillip s. of Richard & ffrances Callaway
23 Feb. John s. of Robert & Elizabeth Elford
15 Mar. Charity d. of John & Lydia Champion
15 Mar. Elias s. of Henry & Joane Cock
25 Mar. Elizabeth d. of Bernard & Jane Lobb
25 Mar. Joane d. of Hendy & Diana Langdon

* See their mar. in 1682. He was son of Arthur Broad and Margery Blake of Mawgan.

† This Jane was his second wife, and dau. of John Vivian, Esq., of Trewan in St. Columb.

‡ He was of Croane; his father, Edw. Hoblyn of Bodmin, was third son of Edw. Hoblyn of Nanswhyden, by Mary Apley. The dau. Damoris mar. Wm. Bickford of Dunsland.

ANNO 1684.

13 April Timothy s. of Anthony & Gartherude White
19 April John s. of Dorothy Day
1 May Joan d. of Thomas & Joan Wilkey
2 May Elizabeth d. of William & Rose Hoskyn
7 May Anthony s. of Anthony & Mary Callaway
8 May John s. of John & Abigall Edye
28 June James s. of Josias & Joice Row
5 July Remphrey s. of Thomas & Elizabeth Skeberrioe
5 July Margarett d. of Mark & Ann Tyer
5 July Thomas s. of Jane Merifield
19 July John s. of James & Ann Edwards
26 July ffrancis and William sons of Margarett England
9 Aug. Michaell s. of Michaell & ffrances Cornish
10 Aug. Ann d. of Peter & Ann Cockyn
12 Sep. Eliz. d. of Peter & Ann Richards
20 Sep. Jane d. of Humphry & Dorothy Benny
8 Oct. ffrancis s. of ffrancis & Maud Dungye
17 Oct. William s. of William & Eliz. Basely
25 Oct. John s. of Michaell & Elizabeth Strongman
10 Nov. Martyn s. of John & Mary England
18 Nov. Mary d. of William Richards
22 Nov. William s. of Beniaman & Millicent James
30 Nov. Marke s. of John Tyer
2 Jan. Thomas s. of Samuell & Elizabeth May
13 Jan. Dorothy d. of Humphry & Jane Oxnam
24 Jan. William s. of John & Margery Dunkyn
30 Jan. Mary d. of Jacob & Mary Husband
2 Feb. Joane d. of Thomas & Eliz. Adams
2 Feb. Mary d. of Anthony & Eliz. Michell
7 Feb. Gilbert s. of Gilbert & Grace White
14 Feb. Mary d. of Richard & Elizabeth Jolly

14 Feb. Elizabeth d. of John & Alice Benallack
15 Mar. Isaack s. of Anthony & Jane Jenkyn
22 Mar. Mary d. of James & Avis Michell
25 Mar. Richard s. of Arthur & Mary Broad

ANNO 1685.

3 April Joice d. of Isaack & Emblyn Husband
3 April Mary d. of William & Joane Dennis
7 April William s. of John & Joan Rowse
10 April Mary d. of Thomas & Alice Stephens
11 April William s. of Roger & Joane Ellery
11 April John s. of William & Audry Hawke
22 April Henry s. of Samuell & Lydia Champion
2 May John s. of John & Margarett Pill
9 May Charles s. of Robert & Grace Litticott
9 May Mary d. of Richard & Constance Kestell
10 May Mary d. of Robert & Honor Harris
16 May Mary d. of Robert & Mary Manuell
1 June ffrancis s. of Peter & Elizabeth Champion
8 June William s. of Isaack & Elizabeth Nicholls
8 June John s. of Michaell & ffrances Cowling
23 June John s. of Daniel & Margery May
4 July Samuell s. of Phillip & fflorence Harris
12 Aug. Elizabeth d. of Thomas & Elizabeth Day
29 Aug. William s. of John & ffrances Drew
31 Aug. Reskimer s. of Charles & Tamsin Allen
18 Sep. Ann d. of George & Jane Champion
20 Sep. George s. of Thomas & Cicily Typpett
27 Sep. Honour d. of Symon & Tamsin Lawe
9 Oct. Thomas s. of Robert & Mary Retallack
17 Oct. Grace d. of Thomas & Mary Cocken
24 Oct. Grace d. of Thomas & Elizabeth Skeberriow
31 Oct. Jane d. of James & Mary Cocken
7 Nov. Josias s. of John & Joan Truscott
16 Nov. William s. of John & Lydia Champion
19 Nov. Honnour d. of Joan Couch
27 Nov. Joan d. of Dinah & Morgan Roberts
1 Dec. Mary d. of Walter & Ann Vivian
4 Dec. Phillip d. of William & Mary Browne
10 Dec. John s. of Nicholas & ffrances Woodman
25 Dec. Joseph s. of John & Ruth Tucker
1 Jan. Philip s. of Elizabeth Woolcock
22 Jan. Elizabeth d. of James & Temperance Harris
23 Jan. ffrances d. of Humphry & Dorothy Benny
23 Jan. Mary d. of William & Joan Minoe
30 Jan. Enstice d. of John & Dorothy Jolly
12 Feb. Johan d. of John Bishopp Rector & Ann his wife
16 Feb. Richard s. of Henry & Grace Blake
24 Feb. Margery d. of Honnour Jolly
1 Mar. Avis d. of John & Jane Lawarren
13 Mar. James s. of Philip Kinge & Joane his wife

ANNO 1686.

27 Mar. Ann d. of Bernard & Jane Lobb
4 April Arthur s. of William & Mary Michell
17 April Elizabeth d. of Nicholas Bounsell
8 May Rebecca d. of William & Grace Lae
25 May Robert s. of Robert & Elizabeth Elford
27 June Epiphany d. of William & Joice Dennis
3 July Elizabeth d. of Roger & Joan Ellery
10 July John s. of John & ffrances Tom

10 July Thomas s. of Thomas & Elizabeth Tybb
17 July ffaithfull s. of James & Merryn Nettle
17 July Jane d. of Nicholas & Jane Hawke
24 July Elizabeth d. of John & Mary Polkinhorne
6 Aug. Jane d. of Samuell & Lydia Champion
14 Aug. Mary d. of William & Joane Dennis
28 Aug. Arthur s. of Luke & Elizabeth Jolly
18 Sep. William s. of William & Jone Dancaster
18 Sep. Anne d. of William & Anne Cundye
19 Sep. Sampson s. of William & Anne Cock
15 Sep. Grace d. of John & Katherine Brabyn
9 Oct. Phillip d. of John & Lydia Champion
10 Oct. Joane d. of Jonathan & Anne Daw
11 Oct. Elizabeth d. of Anthony & Elizabeth Michell
16 Oct. James s. of George & Jane Champion
16 Oct. Nathaniell s. of Thomas & Launder
1 Nov. John s. of John & Alice Benallack
5 Nov. William s. of Thomas & Honnor Benny
9 Nov. William s. of William & Rose Hoskyn
14 Nov. Elizabeth d. of George & Elizabeth Hix
20 Nov. James s. of James & Elizabeth Stephens
27 Nov. Mary d. of Humphry & Jane Oxnam
3 Dec. Michaell s. of Michaell & Eliz. Strongman
11 Dec. Maleor d. of John & Rebecca Richards
Phillip d. of Thomas & Philip Reynolds
27 Dec. Robert s. of John & Julian Strongman
. . . . . John s. of Thomas & Joan Wilkye
5 Jan. Henry s. of ffrancis & Elizabeth Hoblyn
14 Jan. Timothy s. of Thomas & Eliz. Eudeane
22 Jan. Symon s. of Daniell & Margery May
29 Jan. Philip s. of George & Mary Tom
31 Jan. Joane d. of Richard & ffrances Callaway
2 Feb. Arthur s. of Gilbert & Grace White
19 Feb. William s. of William & Joane Launder
15 Mar. Arthur s. of William & Anne Warne
24 Mar. Honour d. of Isaack & Emblyn Husband

ANNO 1687.

28 Mar. Rachell d. of Henry Langdon
1 April Petherick s. of Petherick & Joan Gilbert
2 April Phillippi d. of Edward & Barbara Rickard
16 April Richard s. of John Buckthorpe
26 April Ann d. of John & Joane Rowse
29 April Elizabeth d. of Morgan & Dinah Roberts
20 May Edward s. of ffrancis & ffrances Godolphyn
21 May Katherine d. of Peter & Elizabeth Champion
10 June Elizabeth d. of Will'm & Eliz. Basely
11 June Joice d. of John & Elizabeth Harris
2 July . . . . s. of Humphry & Dorothy Benny
16 July Elizabeth d. of John & ffrances Drew
19 Aug. Dorothy d. of Mary Wills
26 Aug. Anthony s. of Anthony & Mary Martyn
26 Aug. Grace d. of Thomas & Grace Day
17 Sep. Elizabeth d. of John & Avis Michell
24 Sep. Peter s. of Peter & Ann Richards
. . . . . Lydia d. of John & Lydia Champion, eodem die
22 Oct. Mary d. of Jacob & Mary Husband
4 Nov. Edward s. of John Bishopp Rector & Anne his wife
6 Jan. John s. of John Tyer
20 Jan. Daniell d. of Mary Woolcock
28 Jan. Elizabeth d. of Henry & Grace Blake

4 Feb. Blanch d. of Symon & Tamsin Law
6 Feb. Joan d. of Richard & ffrances Callaway
10 Feb. Thomas s. of Mark & Mary Penny
12 Feb. Jane d. of John & Mary England
14 Feb. Ann d. of Edward & Sarah Crews
18 Feb. Philip s. of Charles & Tamsin Allen
16 Feb. Ann d. of Walter & Vivian
25 Feb. Ann d. of Bernard & Jane Lobb
3 Mar. Elizabeth d. of James & Elizabeth Cowling
5 Mar. Richard s. of Thomas & . . . . Phillips
9 Mar. Edward s. of George & Jane Champion
11 Mar. Tamsin d. of James & Mary Cocken
17 Mar. Elizabeth d. of Thomas & Elizabeth Skeberrio
19 Mar. Mary d. of Thomas & Mary Launder

ANNO 1688.

31 Mar. Martyn s. of Martyn & Dorothy Tom
31 Mar. Ann and Mariey daughters of Jonathan & Ann Daw
1 April . . . . d. of John & Jane Le Warren
6 April Mary d. of Thomas & Mary Parken
14 June Robert s. of Mary & Robert Retallack
9 June ffrancis s. of John & ffrances Tom
15 June Elizabeth d. of William & Mary Browne
29 June Henry s. of Arthur & Ruth Veale
14 July Richard s. of Honor & Robert Harris
21 July John s. of James & Katherine Bone
21 July Elizabeth d. of Richard & Mary Mannell
6 Aug. Nicholas s. of Thomas & Mary Trevithick
12 Aug. Susanna d. of Thomas & Jone Tonkyn
13 Aug. William s. of Robert & Elizabeth Blake
8 Sep. Martyn s. of James & Elizabeth Stephens
17 Sep. Margarett d. of John & Lydia Champion
10 Sep. Anne d. of John & Elizabeth Cocken
5 Sep. Elizabeth d. of George & Grace Hix
13 Sep. Anne d. of Luke & Elizabeth Jolly
1 Nov. James s. of James & Avis Michell
3 Nov. Elizabeth d. of John & Jenifer Grimes
4 Nov. Grace d. of John & Rebecca Richards
10 Nov. Henry s. of Humphry & Jane Oxnam
14 Nov. Mary d. of John & Mary Lifford
17 Nov. Honor d. of Thomas & Joane Langdon
1 Dec. Jane d. of John & Elizabeth Harris
1 Dec. Mary d. of Nathaniell & Rebecca Adams
14 Dec. William s. of William & Elizabeth White
24 Dec. Katherine d. of John & Kath. Brabyn
13 Jan. Ann d. of William & Joane Dancaster
26 Jan. Mary d. of Thomas & Grace Day
2 Feb. Nathaniell s. of Samuell & Lydia Champion
9 Feb. ffrancis s. of Isaack & Emblyn Husband
14 Feb. Henry s. of William & Rose Hoskyn
24 Feb. James s. of William Luny
2 Mar. William s. of Thomas Wilken
9 Mar. Sarah d. of Peter & Elizabeth Champion
10 Mar. Margarett d. of Thomas & Margarett Hawke
15 Mar. ffrancis s. of Daniell & Margery May

ANNO 1689.

1 April Jane d. of Michael Cowling
13 April Thomas s. of Nicholas Hawke
13 April Elizabeth d. of Thomas & ffrances Drew
13 April Elizabeth d. of Thomas & Honor Benny
. . . . . Mary d. of Thomas & Rose Crapp

15 April Edward s. of Anthony Martyn
27 April Nathaniell s. of James Olliver
29 April Jane d. of John & Jane Oxnam
4 May Thomas s. of Peter Kendall
5 May Jane d. of William & Mary Michell
10 May Rebecca d. of Prudence Jacob
15 June Honner d. of Beniaman & Honor Berry
26 July Garthered d. of Mark & Garthered Lawry
31 Aug. William s. of George & Mary Tom
12 Sep. Thomas* s. of John Vivian, Esq., & Mary his wife
16 Sep. William s. of Henry Michell
15 Oct. ffrances † d. of ffrances Godolphyn
19 Oct. ffrancis s. of Martyn Tom
19 Oct. John s. of Thomas Cocke
26 Oct. Stephen s. of John Tyre
26 Oct. John s. of Beniaman James
9 Nov. Anne d. of ffrancis Pollard
23 Nov. Elizabeth d. of Willian Baseley
30 Nov. John s. of John Strongman
23 Dec. John s. of John & Elizabeth Champion
26 Dec. Robert s. of Robert Husband
27 Dec. William s. of Thomas Phillips
30 Dec. Anne d. of Charles Thomas
11 Jan. Edward s. of John & Dorothy Dunkyn
20 Jan. Joane & Rose daughters of Robert Elford
20 Jan. Humphry s. of John England
30 Jan. ffrancis s. of James Harris
7 Feb. Henry s. of Edward Rickard
8 Feb. Elizabeth d. of Robert & Elizabeth Barry
15 Feb. Peter s. of Peter Bounsell
22 Feb. Anne and Sarah daughters of Phillip & Joane Kinge‡
24 Feb. John s. of Thomas Trevithicke
14 Mar. Thomas s. of Thomas Whitford, Curat
22 Mar. Jane d. of Peter Michell

ANNO 1690.

29 Mar. Susanna d. of William & Joice Dennis
29 Mar. Phillipa d. of Thomas Launder

* This Thomas died unmarried; his mother, Mary, dau. of Joseph Sawle of Penrice, Esq., was the second wife of John Vivian of Trewan, Esq.

† She mar. James Champion.

‡ Philip Kinge paid rent of shop £2, 1703, and John Kinge, gent., one of the twelve men, 1678-93. (Green Book.)

16 April William s. of James Tremaine *alias* Cockin
16 April Arthur s. of Arthur Broade
19 April Henry s. of William & Joane Dennis
21 April Elizabeth d. of ffrancis Tom
7 May James s. of John Bishop, Rector & Mary his wife
17 May Henry s. of Thomas Reynold
25 May ffrances d. of Mary Strongman
9 June Honor d. of Elias Pollard
13 June Gartrude d. of Charles Allin
4 July Henry s. of Nicholas Grigg
4 July Jonathan s. of John Lewarne
19 July Katherine d. of Peter & Elizabeth Champion
25 July Jane d. of Richard Langdon
27 July Walter s. of Phillip Harvey
1 Aug. Mary d. of Thomas Adams
16 Aug. Mary d. of Robert & Mary Retallack
12 Sep. William s. of William Minnow
19 Sep. John s. of Thomas & Grace Day
26 Sep. Rose base child of Annis Martyn
5 Oct. John s. of Edward Peters
1 Nov. Samuell s. of Samuell & Lydia Champion, borne the 7th of October
2 Nov. Ann d. of John Strongman
8 Nov. Thomas s. of James Stephens
10 Nov. William s. of James Nettle
10 Nov. Jane d. of Richard Callaway
10 Nov. Anne d. of Peter Kendall
11 Nov. Humphry s. of Humphry Oxnam
12 Nov. Jane d. of Mathew Davye
15 Nov. John s. of John Harris
18 Nov. Matilda d. of Robert Dunkin
5 Dec. John s. of John Lifford, borne the 30th of October
6 Dec. William s. of William Luney
13 Dec. Mary d. of William Hornabrook
20 Dec. Mary d. of James Bond
23 Dec. Elizabeth d. of Thomas Tomkin
29 Dec. John s. of William Lambe
1 Jan. Jane d. of Humphry Harvey
15 Jan. Jane d. of Richard Brabyn
24 Jan. Katherine d. of Jonathan Day
27 Jan. John s. of Nicho. Woodman
10 Feb. John s. of John Huddy
10 Feb. Elizabeth d. of Bernard Rouse
14 Feb. Mary d. of George Champion
14 Feb. Mary d. of John Drew
20 Feb. John* s. of Thomos Hoblyn, gent.

* This John was the only son of Tho. Hoblyn by his first wife. See marriage 1688, and note, p. 55 *ante*.

20 Feb. John s. of William & Jane Penhellick
7 Mar. Mary d. of Robert Berry
8 Mar. Anne d. of Nathaniell Adams
13 Mar. Mary d. of Mark Penny
14 Mar. Richard s. of Peter Archer
16 Mar. John s. of William Browne
17 Mar. Richard s. of John & Ann Oxnam

ANNO 1691.

25 Mar. Elizabeth d. of Arthur Beale
28 Mar. William s. of Thomas & Ann Parkin
5 April Jacob s. of Jacob Husband
10 April Mary d. of Anthony May & Mary his wife
13 April Susanna d. of Gilbert White
24 April Honnor d. of Cecily Lee
27 April Luke s. of Luke Jolley
2 May Marey d. of Thomas Mannell
2 June . . . d. of John Abram
27 June Mary d. of Theophilus Betty
30 June Ann d. of William Hosken
13 July Grace d. of Philip Kendall
31 July William s. of William Rowe
1 Aug. Elizabeth d. of James Cowling
8 Aug. Ann d. of Giles Williams, jun.
9 Aug. Mary d. of William Cockaine
30 Aug. Honor d. of Edward Richards
2 Sep. John s. of John Sprey
5 Sep. Charles s. of Charles Thomas
12 Sep. Anthony s. of Anthony White
19 Sep. Robert s. of Edward Ede
21 Sep. Mathew s. of James Olliver
27 Sep. Charles s. of Ezekiell Thomas
3 Oct. Junipher d. of Edward Rickard
9 Oct. Courtenay d. of Richard Williams, gent.
2 Nov. ffrances d. of ffrancis & Jone Tom
5 Nov. Elizabeth d. of Thomas Scaberrian
9 Nov. Thomas s. of Thomas Benny
9 Nov. Elizabeth d. of Peter Bounsall
22 Nov. John s. of ffrancis & Jone Tom
22 Nov. Loveday d. of Nicholas Hawke
29 Nov. Honor d. of Robert Mannell
29 Nov. Mary d. of Henry Langdon
6 Dec. Thomas s. of Thomas Callaway
22 Dec. Samuell s. of John Bishop, Rector, & Mary his wife
25 Dec. Ann d. of Daniell May
26 Dec. John s. of George Jolley
29 Dec. George s. of John Dunkin,* gent.

* In the list of Dunkyn wills at Bodmin none are styled of St. Columb.

13 Jan. Katherine d. of John Brabyn
22 Jan. Mary d. of Philip Harvey
23 Jan. Ruth d. of Richard Langdon
26 Jan. Richard s. of John Champion
30 Jan. William s. of James Brewer
30 Jan. Margaret d. of Henry Rouse
14 Feb. fflorence d. of Thomas Trevethick
27 Feb. Margarett d. of Henry Blake
4 Mar. Ann d. of Thomas Tremaine
5 Mar. John s. of William White
8 Mar. Petronel d. of Henry Brewer

ANNO 1692.

2 April Katherine d. of John Huddy, gent. & Mary his wife
3 April Alice d. of John Strongman
3 April Mary d. of Richard George
15 April Mary d. of Peter Champion, gent.
16 April Samuell s. of John Bonallack
16 April Susanna d. of ffrancis Pollard
25 April Michell s. of Michell Strongman
24 May Stephen s. of William Minnow
28 May Elizabeth d. of John Rouse
18 June Thomas s. of Thomas Minnow
30 July Edward & Margaret* children of ffrances Godolphin
12 Aug. Benjamyn s. of Benjamin James
13 Aug. Ann d. of James Merefield
20 Aug. Grace d. of Thomas Day
31 Aug. Paschow s. of Peter Browne
25 Sep. Ruth d. of Dorothy Lauder
9 Oct. Thomas s. of Lancelott Clemence
15 Oct. William s. of Joell Cabell
22 Oct. Mary d. of Henry Cock
6 Nov. Edward s. of Edward Peters
7 Nov. Richard s. of Thomas Whitford
19 Nov. Ann d. of Peter Husband
23 Nov. Junipher d. of Robert Dunkin
25 Nov. Elizabeth d. of John Lewarne
9 Dec. John s. of Humphrey Oxnam
9 Dec. Joyce d. of William & Joyce Dennis
2 Jan. ffrancis d. of John & ffrances Tom
2 Jan. Mary d. of Peter Richards
3 Jan. Richard s. of Richard Williams gent., and Eliz. his wife
6 Jan. Mary d. of John Bishop rector & Mary his wife
. . . . .† . . . . .† of William Baseley

* The dau. mar., in 1720, John Bolitho of Redruth.

† A blank left in the original.

13 Jan. Richard & Thomas sons of Richard Calway
15 Jan. George s. of George Jolley
15 Jan. Thomas s. of Thomas Lander
4 Feb. Richard & ....* children of Samuell Champion, buried same day
5 Feb. Humphry s. of ffrancis & Mary Merefield
12 Feb. Mary d. of John Cockaine
19 Feb. Mary d. of John Endye
26 Feb. Richard s. of Thomas Mannell
11 Mar. Mathew s. of Thomas Reynolds
2 July† Petter s. of Petter Michell
17 Mar. John s. of John Oxnam

ANNO 1693.

31 Mar. Margret d. of Martine & Dorothy Tom
2 April Jane d. of Charles Thomas
7 April Theoder s. of John Issabell
13 April Honor d. of Edward Champion
17 April Dorothy d. of James Bone
18 April Robert s. of Mr Robert Berry
14 May James s. of James Olliver
24 May John s. of James Michell al's Rowe
12 June Elizabeth d. of John England
15 July William s. of Isaack Pearse
16 July William s. of William & Jone Dennis
22 July Elizabeth d. of Charles Allen
24 July Ralph s. of Philip Allen
29 July William s. of Mr John Lifford
2 Sep. Thomas s. of Thomas Pearse
3 Sep. John s. of Peter Kendall
15 Sep. John s. of Mr James Day
23 Sep. Edward s. of Joseph Jane
6 Oct. Elizabeth d. of Mr Anthony Martyne
14 Oct. Katherine d. of Richard Brabyn
7 Nov. John s. of John Day clerk, borne 15 Oct.
11 Nov. Philip s. of James Stephens
11 Nov. Elizabeth d. of Mr John Champion
15 Dec. Grace d. of Sampson Burt
25 Dec. Mary d. of William Cockaine
25 Dec. Mary d. of Anthony Callaway
30 Dec. Jonathan s. of John Lewarne
10 Jan. Jenipher d. of Humphry Benny
20 Feb. John s. of John Davies
20 Feb. Richard s. of Nicholas Gregg
12 Mar. Ursula d. of Mr John Huddy
13 Mar. ffrances d. of William White

* A blank left in the original. † Sic.

ANNO 1694.

14 April Elizabeth d. of Wm Hornabroke
21 April Charity d. of Joell Capell
21 April Temperance d. of Henry Cock
4 May James s. of Richard Williams gent.
4 May William s. of Mr Peter Champion
5 May Joseph s. of Thomas Day
12 May William s. of Thomas Adams
17 May Ollife d. of Richard Cowle
29 May Thomas s. of John Bishop rector & Mary his wife
2 June Margret d. of Arthur Veale
7 July Michaell s. of William Basley
20 July Daniell s. of Daniell May
20 July Ann base child of Elizabeth Michell *al's* Rowe
22 July Jone d. of Henry Blake
29 July Mary d. of Thomas Seabeerian
29 July Elizabeth d. of John Buckthought
12 Aug. Ann d. of Edward Ede
18 Aug. John s. of Henry Thomas
26 Aug. John s. of Isaack & Jane Nicholls
1 Sep. Daniell s. of Thomas & Sarah Tremeane
12 Sep. Elizabeth d. of Mary Davies
28 Sep. Thomas s. of Lancelott Clemens
6 Oct. Mary d. of Stephen Warne
6 Nov. Elizabeth d of Richard Rouse gent.
11 Dec. Jone d. of John Issabell
26 Dec. Elizabeth d. of Samuell Champion
1 Jan. Jone d. of Thomas Trevethick
5 Jan. Mary d. of Josias Merefield
22 Jan. John s. of Edward Champion
26 Jan. ffrances d. of Richard Callaway
1 Feb. Mary d. of John Lewarne
2 Feb. John s. of Jacob Husband
2 Mar. Dorothy d. of Charles Thomas
3 Mar. Margret d. of John Pill
5 Mar. John s. of Robert Dunkyn
5 Mar. Catherine d. of Nicholas Woodman
8 Mar. Henry s. of Mr Henry Haycroft
8 Mar. Henry s. of Henry Brewer
9 Mar. Hugh s. of Mr John Huddy
13 Mar. Jane d. of Mr James Day
19 Mar. John s. of Mr Anthony Martyne
19 Mar. ....* d. of ....* Lawry

* A blank left in the original.

ANNO 1695.

26 Mar. Mary d. of Samuel Batten gent.
6 April Jane d. of Giles Williams jun^r^
15 April Richard son of Richard George
21 April James s. of Henry Rows
5 May Margret d. of Nathaniell Adams
11 May William s. of John Husband
18 May Mary d. of William Luney
26 May Ann d. of George Jolley
9 June Edward s. of James Mercfield
21 June Humphry s. of Philip Harvey
22 June Jane d. of John Grimes
30 June Dennis s. of Nicholas Strongman
2 July Charles s. of William Hosken
11 Aug. John s. of Edward Peters
26 Aug. John s. of John Day clerk
31 Aug. Ann d. of Martyne & Constance Tom
8 Sep. Jonathan & Grace children of John Bishop Rector & Mary his wife
5 Oct. ffrancis s. of Thomas Peirce
6 Oct. Jone d. of Richard Langdon
6 Oct. Jane d. of Isaack Nicholls
27 Oct. John s. of Thomas Manuell
10 Nov. Richard s. of John Hicks
11 Nov. Katherine d. of Thomas Whitford
7 Dec. Charity d. of William Rowe
14 Dec. Elizabeth d. of Thomas Tom & Joane his wife
29 Dec. John s. of Humphry Harvey
1 Jan. Ann d. of ffrancis Godolphin
1 Jan. Alice d. of William Cocking
19 Jan. John s. of John Drew
26 Jan. Ann d. of James Stephens
18 Feb. Martha d. of Samson Burt
21 Feb. John s. of Thomas Tremeane
21 Feb. Epiphency d. of Humphry Oxnam
22 Feb. Joseph s. of Henry Cock
26 Feb. John s. of John England
8 Mar. Ann d. of Thomas Williams
17 Mar. Richard s. of Richard Cornish
18 Mar. Walter s. of John Lewarne

ANNO 1696.

24 April Dorothy* d. of Thomas Hoblyn gent. & Jone his wife, borne 23 Mar.
24 April Elizabeth d. of James Bone
13 June Dennis s. of Michaell Strongman
24 July Ezekiell s. of Ezekiell Retallack

* This Dorothy married Mr. Phillip Sparnon, see Mar., 1719.

28 July Bernard s. of Bernard Rouse
11 Aug. Grace d. of Thomas Pendarves* Rector & Grace his wife
15 Aug. Richard s. of John Davies
4 Sep. Ekekiell s. of Samson Gerrans
12 Sep. Mary d. of Thomas Benny
3 Oct. Sarah d. of Thomas Daye
11 Oct. Dorothy d. of John Banger
13 Oct. Henry s. of Mr Richard Rouse
7 Oct. William s. of Lancelott Clemens
6 Nov. Agnes d. of Mr John Lifford
9 Nov. Elizabeth d. of Joell Capell
5 Nov. Michaell s. of Edward Richards
20 Nov. Paschow s. of Richard Brabyn
27 Nov. Mary d. of Daniell May
4 Dec. Jane d. of Thomas Solomon
5 Dec. Nathaniell s. of Mr John Champion
26 Dec. Richard s. of Thomas Callaway
3 Jan. Mary d. of Richard Webber
13 Feb. Honor d. of William Tenny
5 Feb. Thomas s. of John Husband
21 Feb. James s. of John Rapson
2 Mar. Jone d. of Robert Dunkin
5 Mar. Elizabeth d. of Thomas Adams
7 Mar. John s. of John Drew
9 Mar. Mary d. of Mr Robert Berry
12 Mar. Jone d. of William Minnow
15 Mar. James s. of Mr Peter Champion
23 Mar. John s. of Stephen Buckingham

ANNO 1697.

2 April William s. of Oliver Rowe
5 April Henry s. of Henry Thomas
6 April Ann d. of Joseph Jane
18 April Edward s. of Edward Stephens
24 April Samuell s. of John Grimes
25 April Judeth d. of Bernard Lobb
14 May Catharine d. of John Day clerk
18 May Ann d. of Mr James Day
22 May Alice d. of Isaack Nicholls
30 May William s. of Mathew Davies
5 June Elizabeth d. of Richard Cornish
10 July Benjamin s. of Thomas Issabell
17 July Richard s. of Samuell Champion
17 July Johan d. of Thomas Merefield

* He was son of Richard Pendarves, Esq., of Pendarves, by Catherine, dau. of Wm. Arundell of Menedarva, Esq.; and was rector of St. Columb Major and vicar of Mawgan in Pyder: at the latter church he was mar. (see extracts from Mawgan Registers, 1688) to Grace dau. of Rob. Hoblyn, Esq., of Nanswhyden, by whom he had Sir William Pendarves, knighted by Queen Anne, who died s. p., and Grace, baptized as above. She mar. first, Mr. Robert Coster, of Truro, and secondly Samuel Percival of Clifton, Bristol, but died s. p. She left as her heir John son of the Rev. Dr. Stackhouse, whose son Edward Wm. Wynne took the name and arms of Pendarves.

1 Aug. Mary d. of George Jolley
8 Aug. Mary d. of John Buckthought
10 Aug. Thomas s. of Thomas Trevethick
28 Aug. Remfrey s. of Archiball Rowse
28 Aug. Arthur s. of Richard Callaway
24 Sep. Mary d. of Hugh Pollard
27 Sep. Elizabeth d. of John Thomas
23 Oct. John s. of John Lewarne
30 Oct. Honor d. of Henry Cock
2 Nov. ffrancis s. of Richard Rowse
15 Nov. Thomas son of Thomas Day
19 Nov. fflorence d. of Henry Rowse
4 Dec. Daniell s. of Richard James
7 Dec. Ebbott d. of John Lamb
11 Dec. Henry s. of Stephen Warne*
29 Dec. John s. of Henry Brewer
9 Jan. Daniell s. of Charles Thomas
15 Jan. Mathew s. of Phillip King
23 Feb. Grace† d. of Thomas Hoblyn Esq[re]
26 Feb. John s. of John Banger
5 Mar. Elizabeth d. of Thomas Tremeane
7 Mar. Honor d. of Thomas Whitford
8 Mar. Thomas s. of John Merefield

ANNO 1698.

26 Mar. Mary d. of William Michell
26 Mar. Edward s. of Edward Richards
3 April Elizabeth d. of Oliver Basley
11 April ffrances d. of Edward Lawry
26 April John s. of Thomas Callaway‡
30 April John s. of Giles Williams
21 May William s. of William Cockaine
28 April John s. of Thomas Peirce
14 June Jonathan s. of William Law
16 July Jane d. of Richard Cockaine
16 July Catharine d. of Edward Basley
25 July Thomasine d. of William Rowe
31 July Jone d. of Michaell Cowlyn
26 Aug. Arthur s. of Henry Michell
8 Oct. Richard s. of John Parkyns
9 Oct. Thomas s. of M[r] John Lifford
11 Nov. William s. of Henry Darr
11 Nov. Jane d. of William Youlton
16 Dec. Stephen s. of Stephen Buckingham
22 Dec. Catharine d. of Oliver Rawe
30 Jan. Solomon s. of William Basley
11 Feb. Elizabeth d. of John Ropson & Elizabeth his wife
25 Feb. Grace d. of William Hornabrooke
11 Mar. James s. of James Brewer

ANNO 1699.

24 June Charles s. of John England
21 July Amy d. of James Adams
22 July Mary d. of John Tenny
22 July Ann d. of John Symons
23 July fflorence d. of Isaack Nicholls
25 July Honor d. of M[r] Henry Blight
7 Aug. Judeth* d. of M[r] Thomas Hoblyn
12 Aug. Anne d. of Nathaniell Adams
2 Sep. Elizabeth d. of Joell Capel
16 Sep. Martha d. of Thomas Sollomon
22 Sep. John s. of Enoder Inch
23 Sep. Mary d. of James Bone
24 Sep. Alice d. of Archibald Peters
27 Sep. Abraham s. of Grace . . . .†
30 Sep. Mary d. of John Davies
18 Oct. Thomas s. of M[r] Thomas Wills
21 Oct. Henry s. of Christopher Warne
15 Nov. Edward s. of Thomas Merefield
6 Jan. Lewis s. of John Daye clerke
31 Jan. John s. of John Clemens
2 Feb. Ann d. of Thomas Benny
6 Feb. Luce d. of Hugh Pollard‡

ANNO 1700.

26 Mar. Symon§ s. of Stephen Warne
27 Mar. John s. of Charles Thomas
1 April Jane d. of Thomas Issbell
27 April Mary d. of Joseph Merefield
30 April Ann d. of John Parking
4 May Henry s. of Joseph & Jane Jane
1 June William s. of John Lawry
2 June Jane d. of Bernard Lobb
22 June Elizabeth d. of John Lewarne
29 June Jenifer d. of Richard James
9 July Richard s. of Richard & ffrances Webber
15 July Scicily d. of John England
5 Aug. Michaell s. of Richard Cornish
10 Aug. Ann d. of Thomas Parking
11 Aug. James s. of James Day mer. & Martha his wife
17 Aug. Richard s. of Henry Brewer
8 Aug. Charles s. of Henry Thomas
24 Aug. John s. of John Lifford
15 Oct. John s. of John Lamb
19 Oct. John s. of Thomas Tippett
1 Nov. William s. of William Row
3 Nov. Thomazin d. of William Dennis

* By his wife Mary Jack Andrew, see mar. 1693.

† She died young.

‡ Tho. Callaway paid rent of a shop 10s. in 1683. (Green Book.)

* She died young.

† Blank.

‡ Hugh Pollard was treasurer of the parish in 1711. (Green Book.)

§ Married in 1728 Hannah Bilkey, see mar.

9 Nov. Ann d. of William Michell *al's* Row
12 Nov. Grace* d. of Mr Thomas Hoblyn & Jone his wife
19 Nov. Dorothy d. of Henry Rowse
26 Nov. Richard s. of Richard Rowse
2 Dec. John s. of William Eveling
11 Dec. Jane d. of James Stephens
26 Dec. Rebecka d. of William Lawry
28 Dec. John s. of Thomas Whitford
6 Jan. John s. of Thomas Varkoe
11 Feb. Grace d. of Stephen Buckingham
15 Feb. Margret d. of Thomas Tanner mercer & Emlyne his wife
15 Feb. Avics d. of William Cockaine
1 Mar. John s. of Robert Merefield
9 Mar. Joseph s. of Robert Dunkin
16 Mar. Robert s. of Edward Eade
23 Mar. Jone d. of George Thomas

ANNO 1701.

14 April John son of Richard Edwards & Elizabeth his wife
28 April Jane d. of Henry & Honor Michell
31 May Ann d. of Nathaniel Wood
9 June Catharine d. of Isaack Nicholls
9 June Charity d. of Oliver Basley
15 June Robert s. of John Symons
27 June Jane d. of Thomas Hawke
29 June Elizabeth d. of Thomas Polkinhorne
8 July Jane d. of Hugh Pollard
28 July Mary d. of Henry Blight
28 July Martine s. of John England
20 Sep. John s. of Charles Tresteane
22 Sep. Elizabeth d. of William Youlton
24 Sep. Pentecost d. of Henry Darr
6 Oct. Gregory d. of Archibald Rowse
1 Nov. George s. of Thomas Cockaine *al's* Tremeane
11 Nov. Jenifer d. of Mathew Battrell
17 Nov. Peter s. of William Callaway
29 Nov. Charles s. of John & Jenifer Richards
5 Dec. ffrances d. of John Best
26 Dec. John s. of Richard Rawe
1 Jan. Jone d. of John Drew
5 Jan. John s. of John & Jenefir Parking
18 Jan. Symon s. of William Lawe
24 Jan. Elizabeth d. of Bernard Rowse
30 Jan. Ann d. of William Hornabrooke
2 Feb. John s. of John Gummow

* This dau. mar., as his second wife, Giles Hamley of St. Columb, second son of William Hamley of Treblethic, Esq.

8 Feb. John s. of Bernard Lobb
17 Feb. Thomas & James sons of Thomas Adams
21 Feb. Margret d. of John Tenny
22 Feb. Jane d. of ffrancis Phillips
1 Mar. William s. of Inigoe Inch
23 Mar. Elizabeth d. of Thomas Tibb

ANNO 1702.

28 Mar. William s. of Richard Brabyn
7 April Richard s. of Arthur Veale
10 May Anthony s. of Tho. Callaway
24 May William s. of Thomas Merefield
29 May Jenifer d. of Oliver Rowe
18 June Jonathan s. of Jonathan Daw
1 July John s. of Peter Best
10 July Phillip s. of Thomas Benny
20 Aug. John s. of Peter Bounsell
5 Sep. William s. of Stephen Warne
6 Sep. John s. of Thomas Inch
1 Oct. Luke s. of John Lifford
24 Oct. Joel s. of Joel Capell
24 Oct. Jane d. of Marke Lawrey
7 Nov. Edward s. of Thomas Pearse
12 Nov. Philip s. of Philip Kinge
14 Nov. Elizabeth d. of William Dennis junr
14 Nov. Richard s. of George Thomas
3 Dec. Elizabeth d. of Richard Webber
3 Dec. Joan d. of Archibald Rowse
15 Dec. Robert s. of Thomas Hoblyn gent. & Joan his wife
16 Dec. Nathaniell s. of John Tanner Mercer & Emblyn his wife
16 Dec. Richard s. of George Basely
18 Dec. John s. of Richard Rawe junr & ffrances his wife
22 Dec. John s. of John Parking
10 Jan. Jane d. of John Lewarne
16 Jan. John s. of Charles Thomas
2 Feb. Ann d. of Richard James
9 Feb. Richard s. of Thomas Hawke
12 Feb. John s. of John Symons
5 Mar. Grace d. of Richard Rowse
10 Mar. Richard s. of Richard Cornish
13 Mar. Joseph s. of Thomas Issabell

ANNO 1703.

30 Mar. Mary d. of Joseph Jane
3 April Alice d. of Joseph Merefield
10 April Thomasin d. of John Gummow
10 April Joseph s. of John Best
10 April Mark s. of Edward Basely
14 April William s. of John & Lydia Clemens
17 April Thomas s. of John & Mary Davis

15 May Genefer d. of Robert & Jane Merifield
22 May Mary d. of Philip & Martha Slockett
29 May Charity d. of Olliver Basely Junr
12 June Jane d. of Ralph & Mary Allen
19 June William s. of William Eveling Junr
18 July Elizabeth d. of Nathaniell Adams
6 Aug. Alice d. of Hugh & Elizabeth Pollard
7 Aug. Edward s. of John Lawry
11 Aug. Thomas s. of Thomas & Mary Whiteford
4 Sep. Jane d. of William Basely
6 Sep. Genefer d. of Edward Lawry
12 Sep. Gartrude d. of Edward Eade
9 Oct. Elizabeth d. of Mathew Battrell
9 Oct. Susanna d. of Charles & Elizabeth Tresteane
9 Oct. Jane d. of Henry Thomas
16 Oct. Mary d. of John Symons
16 Oct. Nathaniell s. of Nathaniell & ffrances Wood
19 Dec. John s. of John & Martha Bulling
1 Jan. Reginald s. of Stephen Buckingham
1 Jan. Edward & Michaell sons of Edward Richards
16 Jan. Mary d. of Giles Pell
28 Jan. Mary d. of Abraham Husband
2 Feb. Ann* d. of Thomas Hoblyn Atturney & Joan his wife
2 Feb. ffrances d. of Henry & Honor Michell
5 Feb. Phillip s. of Phillip Harris†
14 Feb. Jane d. of Henry Blight
19 Feb. John s. of John Richards
29 Feb. Joan d. of Inigo Inch
22 Mar. Jane d. of William & Emblyn Rosuggan

ANNO 1704.

9 April Thomas s. of William Cocking *alias* Tremaine
18 April Robert s. of John Drew
22 April Mary d. of Isaack Nicholls
29 April Eliz. d. of Mr James Daye
29 April Anne d. of Mary Reading

* She married George Keigwin.
† Philip Harris was one of the way wardens in 1710. (Green Book.)

20 May Mary d. of Richard & Eliz. Brabyn
27 May Mary d. of John & Ebatt Lamb
5 June Mary d. of John & Christiana Symonds
10 June Pentecost d. of Thomas & Sarah Cocking *alias* Tremain
17 June John s. of John & Temperance Tinney
24 June Joan d. of Richard & Joan Pascoe
5 Aug. Richard s. of John & Anne Harris*
12 Aug. Coningsby d. of Coningsby Packington Norbury a Lieutenant in Her Majesty's Service & Mary his wife
14 Aug. James s. of Philip & Mary King
10 Sep. Mary d. of John & Margret Perkins
23 Sep. Frances d. of Nath^ll & ffrances Woods
4 Oct. Anne d. of Mr Hugh & Elizabeth Pollard
8 Oct. Jane d. of William & Jone Williams
14 Oct. Mark s. of Peter & Margret Tremaine
15 Oct. Thomas s. of Thomas & Jone Merryfield
21 Oct. James s. of Tho. & Jane Polkinhorne
21 Oct. Mary d. of Richard Gilbert
25 Oct. Samuel s. of Sam^ll & Honor Williams
28 Nov. Grace ye base daughter of Joan Rowe
4 Dec. Eliz. d. of Peter & Susa'na Best
16 Dec. Grace d. of Mr John & Emeline Tanner
26 Dec. Jane d. of John & Jane Best
30 Dec. Alice d. of Tho. & Jane Pearse
13 Jan. John s. of George & Jane Baseley
20 Jan. John s. of Richard & Frances Callway
26 Jan. Eliz. the base daughter of Jane Hodge
27 Jan. Mary d. of George & Jane Thomas
2 Feb. Eliz. d. of Philip Collier Rect^r & Eliz. his wife

* John Harris was one of the overseers in 1715. (Green Book.)

2 Feb. Michaell s. of Jonathan & Catherine Barrett
2 Feb. John s. of Wm & Catharine Blake
2 Feb. Lewis s. of Robt & Florence Cock
6 Feb. Eliz. d. of James & Anne Moreshead
12 Feb. Matthias s. of Matthias & Mary Battrell
17 Feb. Philip s. of Wm & Anne Hornabrook
24 Feb. John s. of John & Grace Issable
3 Mar. Mary d. of of Thomas & Mary Hawke
12 Mar. Agnes d. of John & Agnes Lifford

ANNO 1705.

30 Mar. Anne d. of Will. & Eliz. Youlton
10 April Eleanor d. of Tho. & Eliz. Adams
15 April Eliz. d. of Anthony & Eliz. Hoskin
23 April Philip s. of John & Jennefair Parkyn
23 April Thomas s. of Degory & Pent Keast
23 April Mary d. of Robt & Joan Husband
5 May Mary d. of Stephen & Mary Warren*
12 May Wm s. of Wm & Temperance Bone
12 May Mary d. of John & Grace Gum'owe
12 May Agnes d. of John & Mary Metherill
4 June Mary d. of James & Jone Gilbert
9 June Mary d. of William & Joan Dennys
10 June Anne d. of Richd & Joan Pascoe
20 June John s. of Philip & Martha Sloggett
23 June Eliz. d. of Oliver & Jane Rawe
29 June Mary d. of Mr Richard Rowse
29 July Nathaniell s. of Charles & Jane Thomas
4 Aug. Mary d. of John & Eleanor Opey

* This should be Warne not "Warren," see other entries.

5 Aug. Catharine d. of John & Dinah Gilbert
11 Aug. John s. of John & Joan Lawrey
2 Sep. Elizabeth d. of Thomas & Elizabeth Inch
15 Sep. Mary d. of Wm & Grace Lae
22 Sep. Honr s. of Peter & Mary Pollard
22 Sep. Eliz. d. of Tho. & Candacea Litticoat
24 Sep. Dorothy d. of Wm & Dorothy Roe
6 Oct. Anne d. of Tho. & Elizabeth Couch
20 Oct. John s. of Richd & Frances Webber
3 Nov. Eleanor d. of Wm & Jane Wilkin
12 Nov. Riche s. of John & Lydia Clemows
24 Nov. Joane d. of Peter & Jane Bounsall
11 Dec. Mary d. of Wm & Jane Evelinn
15 Dec. Florence d. of Charles & Eliz. Trestain
26 Dec. John s. of Archibald & Mary Rowse
27 Dec. Samuell s. of Joell & Eliz. Capell
5 Jan. Eliz. d. of Tho. & Mary Whitford
12 Jan. Honor d. of John & Susa'na Jane
12 Jan. Susa'na d. of Tho. & Sarah Tremayn
19 Jan. Mary d. of Philip & Anne Harris
26 Jan. John s. of Tho. & Florence Issable
26 Jan. Matilda d. of John & Temperance Tinny
9 Feb. Richard s. of Richard & Thomazin Cowle
20 Feb. Jeremy s. of Philip Collier Rectr, borne 4 Feb.
24 Feb. Matthias s. of Matthias Battrell & Mary his wife
12 Mar. Henry s. of Mr Henry & Mary Blight

ANNO 1706.

25 Mar. Thomas s. of Robt & Jane Merrifield
15 April Anne d. of Edward & Mary Lawrey
21 April Eliz. d. of Philip & Philippa Michell

4 May John s. of Roger & Mary Reading
13 May Thomas s. of Thomas & Julian Polkinhorn
16 June Frances d. of Isaack & Jane Nicholls
27 June Eliz. d. of Philip & Martha Sloggett
28 June Thomas s. of Jonathan & Catharine Barrett
5 July Peternell d. of Henry & Honor Michell
19 July Daniell s. of Nathaniell & ffrances Wood
27 July Jane d. of Thomas & ffrances Baseley
9 Aug. Dinah* d. of Christopher & Jane Warne
17 Aug. Francis s. of Anthony & Mary Godolphin
17 Aug. John s. of Rich^d & Thomazin Gilbert
30 Aug. John s. of Edward & Anne May
3 Sep. William s. of Rich[d] & Anne Hicks
2 Oct. Loveday d. of James & Loveday Rowse
5 Oct. Rachel d. of W[m] & Margret Trembeath
26 Oct. John s. of James & Anne Moarshead
10 Nov. John s. of Edward & Jane Burne
12 Nov. Philip s. of Richard & Philippa Cornish
15 Nov. Jane d. of Bernard & Eliz. Lobb
16 Nov. Anne d. of Peter & Mar Tremain
14 Dec. William s. of John & Martha Bulleyn
14 Dec. Charles s. of George & Jane Thomas
18 Dec. Anthony s. of Anthony & Eliz. Hoskin
31 Dec. Edward s. of M[r] James & Martha Day
7 Jan. John s. of John & Grace Gum'owe
30 Jan. Jenefair d. of Thomas & Joan Tom
3 Feb. Mary d. of Popham & Catharine Morricet†

* She married John Merifield, see marriages 1732. Her father Christopher Warne was married at St. Enoder, 31 Dec., 1698, to Jane Hichens

† See marriages 1705.

8 Feb. Jane d. of Henry & Jane Thomas
22 Feb. Anne d. of John & Dinah Gilbert
23 Feb. Giles s. of Giles & Jane Williams
8 Mar. John s. of John & Anne Harris
8 Mar. John s. of Robert & Joan Husband
12 Mar. Abraham s. of Abraham & Mary Husband
13 Mar. Jane d. of M[r] Thomas Hoblyn & Joan his wife
18 Mar. Anthony s. of M[r] John & Emeline Tanner

ANNO 1707.

18 April Mary d. of Degory & Pentecost Keast
28 April Eliz. d. of W[m] & Joan Callaway
3 May Sam[ll] s. of Peter & Susa'na Best
10 May Eliz. d. of Rich[d] & Jane James
29 May Methuselah s. of Methuselah & Mary Williams
31 May Robert s. of Thomas & Candace Litticoat
20 June John s. of Richard & Ursula Arnold
22 June Philippa d. of W[m] & Jane Wilkin
22 June W[m] s. of W[m] & Jane Evelyn
28 June Eliz. d. of Joseph & Jane Jano
27 July Joan d. of Tho. & Prudence Gilbert
16 Aug. John s. of John & Mary Metherill
17 Aug. Margret d. of William & Joan Williams
22 Aug. Hono[r] d. of Henry & Eliz. Lee
23 Aug. William s. of John & Joan Lawrey
8 Oct. Thomas Pollawin s. of John & Jenefaire Parkin
25 Oct. Grace d. of Richard & Thomazin Cowle
10 Nov. John s. of Robert & Jane Merrifield
14 Nov. ffrances d. of Dorothy Rowse, wid., by Edward Champion
15 Nov. Peter s. of Peter & Mary Pollard
22 Nov. Tho. s. of Richard & Joan Pascoe
2 Dec. William s. of Philip & Mary King

5 Dec. John s. of William & Sarah Baseley
12 Jan. Humphrey s. of Phillip & Martha Sloggett
17 Jan. John s. of Stephen & Mary Warne
16 Feb. Eliz. d. of Archibald & Mary Rowse
17 Feb. Jane d. of James & Jane Gilbert
16 Mar. Eliz. d. of Philip & Anne Harris
18 Mar. John & Tho. sons of Oliver & Jane Rawe
19 Mar. Rich[d] s. of Abraham & Eliz. Husband
20 Mar. Anne d. of Tho. & Eliz. Inch
20 Mar. Eliz. d. of John & Mary Parkin
23 Mar. Eliz. d. of Tho. & Eliz. Cornwall

ANNO 1708.

6 April Joane d. of Joseph & Jane Merifield
8 April Benjamin s. of Charles & Jane Thomas
19 April Robert s. of John & Jane Best
22 April W[m]* s. of Philip Collier rector & Eliz. his wife, borne April 2
25 April Eliz. d. of Isaac & Jane Nichols
27 April Mary d. of Philip & Philippa Michell
30 April George s. of Edward & Jane Burne
1 May Mary d. of Mich[ll] & Jane Cornish
29 May John s. of John & Joan Harris
5 June Mary d. of Peter & Susan'a Best
7 Aug. W[m] s. of M[r] Richard & Eliz. Rowse
7 Aug. Anne d. of W[m] & Eliz. Youlton
8 Aug. Ralph s. of John & Ebatt Lamb
15 Aug. Isaac s. of Robert & Florence Cock
15 Aug. Elizabeth d. of John & Dorothy Arscott
21 Aug. Reskymer s. of Philip & Anne Allen
21 Aug. Sarah d. of Tho. & Mary Hawke
3 Sep. Florence d. of Tho. & Florence Issable
3 Sep. Anne d. of Edward & Anne May
25 Sep. W[m] s. of Joell & Eliz. Capell

* This William was a lawyer at St. Austle, and married Ann Toller of Fowey.

2 Oct. Henry s. of Anthony & Eliz. Hoskyn
16 Oct. Anne d. of W[m] & Temperance Bone
5 Nov. Anne d. of W[m] & Joan Dennys
9 Nov. Edward s. of M[r] Tho. & Joan Hoblyn
12 Nov. Anne d. of M[r] Hugh & Eliz. Pollard
27 Nov. Eleanor d. of Philip & Honor Callaway
27 Dec. Sam[ll] s. of John & Mary Perkins
27 Dec. Mary d. of Richard & Ursula Arnold
27 Dec. Susan'a d. of Timothy & Mary Stephens
27 Dec. Thomas s. of Arthur & Cath[ne] Jolley
28 Dec. Mary base child of Mary Oliver
8 Jan. W[m] s. of Anthony & Mary Godolphin
8 Jan. Richard s. of Thomas & Mary Whitford
10 Jan. Anne d. of James & Anne Moreshead
15 Jan. Honor d. of George & Jane Thomas
15 Jan. Eliz. d. of Thomas & Jenefaire Richards
17 Jan. William s. of Henry & Joan Champion
22 Jan. Frances d. of Richard & Frances Webber
5 Feb. Mary d. of W[m] & Mary Brewer
19 Feb. John s. of John & Dinah Gilbert
26 Feb. Ann d. of Jonathan & Catharine Barrett
5 Mar. John s. of John & Temperance Tinny
8 Mar. W[m] s. of John & Anne Harris
12 Mar. Richard s. of Richard & Anne Hicks
19 Mar. Ursula d. of John & Martha Chapell

ANNO 1709.

25 Mar. Tibitha d. of Stephen & Margaret Tyer
26 Mar. Mary d. of Richard & Jane Lovell
1 April Grace d. of M[r] John & Anne Edwards
2 April John s. of W[m] & Margaret Trembeath
3 April Roberts s. of John & Joan Rice

18 April Mary* d. of Philip Collier Rector & Elizabeth his wife, borne 29 March
7 May Eliz. d. of Tho. & Eliz. Couch
14 May Rich[d] s. of Rich[d] & Eliz. Brabyn
14 May Tho. s. of John & Mary Parkyn
14 May Catharine d. of Degory & Pentecost Keast
21 May Henry s. of Benjamin & Eli. Chalway
21 May Peter s. of Henry & Mary Blight
28 May Sampson s. of John & Philippa Hicks
25 June Peter s. of Peter & Mary Cockyn
2 July Nathaniell s. of Nathaniell & ffrances Wood
29 July Frances d. of Michaell & Grace Cornish
30 July Mary d. of Thomas & El. Cornwall
30 July Nicholas s. of William & Catherine Blake
5 Aug. John & Thomazine children of John & Eliz. Remphry
13 Aug. Anne d. of John & Joan Hawke
19 Aug. Catherine d. of Christopher & Jane Warne
18 Sep. Margaret d. of W[m] & Jane Wilkin
20 Sep. Grace d. of Edward & Dorothy Champion
22 Oct. Edward s. of Edward & Jane Burne
4 Nov. Thomas s. of Henry & Honor Michell
7 Nov. Nicholas s. of Robert & Joan Husband
7 Nov. Charles s. of Thomas & Candace Litticott
9 Nov. Hon[r] d. of Methuselah & Mary Williams
3 Dec. John s. of John & Mary Meudon
28 Dec. Eliz. d. of Faithfull & Joan Cock
7 Jan. Rich[d] s. of Joan Pascoe
21 Jan. Grace d. of Henry & Eliz. Lee
22 Jan. Eliz. d. of John & Jenefair Parkins
9 Feb. Elizabeth d. of John & Mary Hawke
11 Mar. W[m] s. of Philip & Anne Harris
11 Mar. W[m] s. of John & Mary Metherill
11 Mar. Joan base child of Mary Dennys

* She married Tho. Trethewey of Lostwithiel.

12 Mar. John s. of John & Philippa Michaell

ANNO 1710.

5 April Charles s. of Peter & Mary Pollard
15 April Jenefair d. of Oliver & Jane Rawe
22 April W[m] s. of Stephen & Mary Warne
30 April Anastatia d. of John & Ebbat Hendy
5 May Robert s. of Francis Hoblyn Esq[r] & Penelope* his wife
6 May John s. of Archibald & Mary Rowse
7 May James s. of William & Jane Evelyn
29 May Robert s. of Robert & Jane Merrifield
29 May Catherine d. of Rich[d] & Ursula Arnold
29 May Susanna d. of Charles & Olimpia Trestain
17 June Edward s. of Henry & Jane Thomas
24 June Mary d. of Thomas & Elizabeth Inch
8 July Abraham d. of Abraham & Eliz. Husband
8 July Dorothy d. of M[r] John & Emelin Tanner
15 July Judeth d. of Thomas & Jane May
19 Aug. Hon[r] d. of Peter & Anne Allen
26 Aug. Walter s. of John Harris & Joan his wife
7 Oct. W[m] s. of Thomas & Sarah Tremayn
8 Oct. Rebecka d. of W[m] & Joan Williams
5 Nov. Mary d. of Tho. & Catherine Merrifield
6 Nov. Emeline d. of M[r] John & Anne Edwards
7 Nov. Edward s. of Edward & Anne May
18 Nov. Anthony s. of Anthony & Eliz. Hoskyn
19 Nov. Jane d. of Rob[t] & Eliz. Brewer
27 Dec. John s. of John & Eliz. Dingey
27 Dec. John s. of John & Philippa Eudy

* This Penelope was daughter of Sidney Godolphin, created in 1706 Earl of Godolphin. The Robert above was their only son, and married Jane only dau. of Rob. Coster, Esq., of Bristol. See also his burial in 1756.

5 Jan. Thomas s. of Thomas & Eliz. Cornwall

13 Jan. Robt s. of Mr Tho. Hoblyn & Johan his wife

20 Jan. James s. of James & Jane Gilbert

21 Jan. Frances d. of John & Joan Hawke

27 Jan. Eli. d. of Benjamin & Eliz. Chalwell

6 Feb. Philip s. of Philip Collier Rector & Eliz. his wife

10 Feb. Luke s. of Arthur & Catharine Jolly

11 Feb. Lydia d. of Henry & Joan Champion

2 Mar. Thomas s. of John & Philippa Hawke

11 Mar. Jenefaire d. of Wm & Eliz. James

17 Mar. Mary d. of John and Dorothy Arscott

23 Mar. John s. of Michaell & Grace Cornish

Anno 1711.

2 April William s. of John & Dinah Gilbert

2 April Alice d. of Francis & Joan Vivian

3 April Eliz. d. of Mr Richd Rouse

28 April Grace d. of Timothy & Mary Stephens

21 May Walter s. of Samuell & Eliz. Harris

22 May James s. of Gilbert & Mary Merrifield

26 May Jennefair d. of John & Susanna Jane

2 June Mary d. of James & Anne Moreshead

3 June Thomas s. of John & Joan Tom'

9 June Thomas s. of James & Alice Stephens

9 June Eliz. d. of Henry & Thomasine Cock

16 June Degory s. of Degory & Pentecost Keast

16 June Sarah d. of Wm & Eliz. Brewer

23 June Susanna d. of Philip & Sarah Brewer

14 July George s. of Philip & Mary King

14 July Tho. s. of Tho. & Mary Tonkin

22 July John s. of Wm & Eliz. Wilkin

17 Aug. Tho. s. of Richd & Elizabeth Brabyn

18 Aug. Eliz. d. of John & Joan Mill

19 Aug. Jonathan s. of Jonathan & Catherine Barrett

19 Aug. Mary d. of John & Martha Chapell

1 Sep. Elizabeth d. of Henry & Florence Oxnam

9 Sep. Catherine d. of Wm & Joan Dennys

16 Sep. Stephen s. of Charles & Jane Thomas

12 Oct. Richd s. of Henry & Honr Mitchell

18 Oct. Margaret d. of Peter Cockyn *al's* Tremain

14 Oct. Eliz. d. of John & Mary Parkyn

21 Oct. Susanna d. of George & Jane Thomas

12 Nov. Jane d. of Edward & Jane Burne

12 Nov. Anne d. of Wm & Catherine Blake

13 Nov. Joan d. of Thomas & Julian Polkinhorne

25 Nov. Charles s. of Oliver & Jane Rawe

26 Dec. Grace* d. of Anthony & Mary Godolphin

5 Jan. Thomas s. of Thomas & Jane May

12 Jan. Mary d. of Thomas & Frances Tilly

1 Feb. Eliz. base child of Margaret Roch

9 Feb. Anne d. of Richd & Jane Lovell

16 Feb. Eliz. d. of Thomas Baseley

23 Feb. Richd s. of John & ~~Philip~~ Hicks Philippa

1 Mar. James s. of Nathaniel & Sarah Oliver

4 Mar. Sarah d. of Richd & Ursula Arnold

8 Mar. John s. of John & Joan Lawrey

23 Mar. Dorothy d. of Philip & Philippa Mitchell

Anno 1712.

9 April Jane d. of John & Joan Hawke

12 April John s. of Philip & Jane Harris

12 April Philippa d. of Philip & Anne Allen

21 April Mary d. of Tho. & Candace Litticott

22 April Mary d. of Faithfull & Joan Cock

29 April Catherine d. of Mr Hugh & Eliz. Pollard

* She married John Buckingham, see mar. 1736.

10 May Thomas s. of Robert & Jane Merrifield
7 June Mary d. of Nicholas & Joan Broad
9 June Eliz. d. of Robert & Eliz. Brewer
10 June Johan d. of John & Jane Richards
11 June Elizabeth d. of Philip Collier Rector & Eliz. his wife, borne 16 May
5 July John s. of Thomas & Catherine Merrifield
2 Aug. Francis s. of Thomas & Eliz. Hicks
26 Aug. John Arundell s. of Mr John Tanner* & Emelyn his wife
9 Sep. Richd s. of Mr Richd & Jane Edwards
13 Sep. John s. of James Trenery
29 Sep. Eliz. & Mary daughters of Roger & Mary Reading
5 Oct. Florence d. of Samuell & Eliz. Harris
11 Oct. Wm s. of Wm & Mary White
14 Oct. Francis s. of John & Elizabeth Dingey
14 Oct. Anne d. of Tho. & Eliz. Cornwall
18 Oct. Mary d. of James & Grace Callaway
22 Nov. Richd s. of Michaell & Grace Cornish
22 Nov. Francis d. of Edward & Dorothy Champion
3 Jan. John s. of Charles & Olympia Trestain
12 Jan. John s. of Thomas & Honr Marks
20 Jan. Mary d. of Francis & Johan Vivian
2 Feb. Johan d. of Richd & Anne Hicks
9 Feb. Benjamin s. of Benjamin & Eliz. Chalwell

* Descended from Anthony Tanner, gent., who mar. at St. Enoder, 5 Feb. 1630, Dorothy, dau. of Zachary Arundell of St. Enoder, gent. Among other monuments to the family of Tanner, at St. Enoder, is one for Anthony Tanner, gent., who died May, 1708; also Arundell Tanner his son buried 2 June, 1708, which bears the following shield of arms, viz., quarterly 1 and 4, on a chief three blackamores' heads couped, a crescent for difference; Tanner. 2, six martlets, a mullet for difference. 3, Fretty, a martlet for difference. Crest, a talbot's head couped, in the mouth a bird-bolt. The arms are carved on the slate slab forming the monument, consequently, no colours are given, and it may be noted that the martlets of Arundell are 3 and 3, and Tanner in the fourth quarter is placed on a lozenge.

13 Feb. John s. of John & Mary Chapman
28 Feb. William s. of Wm & Margaret Trembeath
28 Feb. Philip s. of Henry Thomas
14 Mar. Stephen s. of Stephen & Margaret Tyer
15 Mar. Richd s. of Richd & Johan Harris
21 Mar. Wm s. of Wm & Eliz. James

ANNO 1713.

7 April John s. of John & Philippa Udy
19 April Richd s. of Tho. & Prudence Gilbert
25 April Eliz. d. of Gregry & Wilmot Nance
26 April Judeth d. of Mr Tho. Hoblyn & Joan his wife
6 June Eliz. d. of Gilbert & Mary Merrifield
27 June Thomazine d. of Anthony & Elizabeth Hoskyn
28 June Edward s. of Philip & Martha Sloggett
18 July John s. of Philip & Mary Kinge
18 July Richd s. of Wm & Jane Evelyn
9 Aug. John s. of Oliver Baseley
29 Aug. Martha d. of Wm Youlton
20 Sep. John s. of John & Joan Tom
26 Sep. Samll s. of Mr Francis & Mary May
29 Sep. Thomasine d. of James & Grace Callaway
3 Oct. John s. of John & Martha Chapell
10 Oct. Nathll s. of Nathll & Sarah Oliver
17 Oct. Anne d. of John & Mary Mewdon
24 Oct. John s. of Tho. & Jane May
24 Oct. Edwd s. of Tho. & Sarah Tremain
9 Nov. Eliz. d. of Wm Blake
10 Nov. Richd s. of Peter & Honor Callaway
11 Nov. Frances d. of Degry & Pentecost Keast
24 Nov. John s. of John & Philippa Hawke
26 Dec. John s. of Henry & Mary Rows
29 Dec. Wm s. of Robt & Eliz. Brewer
23 Jan. Thomas s. of John & Eliz. Dingey
23 Jan. Eliz. d. of Henry & Eliz. Lee
23 Jan. Catherine d. of Arthur & Catherine Jolly

2 Feb. John s. of Rich[d] & Ursula Arnold
2 Feb. W[m] s. of John & Dinah Gilbert
14 Feb. John s. of W[m] & Joan Williams
20 Feb. Eliz. d. of Rich[d] & Frances Webber
20 Feb. Tho. s. of Edm[d] & Dinah Varcar
25 Feb. Mary d. of Michaell & Grace Cornish
25 Feb. Grace d. of Christopher & Jane Warne
28 Feb. Anne d. of Philip & Anne Allen
4 Mar. Eliz. d. of John & Joan Lawrey
13 Mar. Rich[d] s. of Rich[d] & Catherine Cundy
15 Mar. Patience base child of Prudence Parnell

ANNO 1714.

29 Mar. James s. of James & Alice Stephens
29 Mar. Anne d. of Philip & Anne Harris
29 Mar. Eliz. d. of Henry & Thomasine Cock
10 April Anne d. of John & Joan Mill
17 April John s. of John & Dorothy Arscot
17 April Susanna d. of Faithfull & Joan Cock
24 April Samson s. of John & Philippa Hicks
8 May Jane d. of Jonathan & Catherine Barret
17 May Margaret d. of Rob[t] & Jane Merrifield
18 May Frances d. of Henry & Hon[r] Michell
29 May Joan d. of Sam[ll] & Hon[r] Bussow
5 June John s. of Rich[d] & Thomasine Cowle
5 June Charles s. of Arthur & Rebecka Rawe
18 June Gilbert s. of Henry & Mary Blight
24 July Rob[t] s. of M[r] Rich[d] & Jane Edwards
30 July John s. of M[r] Rob[t] & Grace Carthew
1 Aug. W[m] s. of Giles & Jane Williams
20 Aug. Anne d. of M[r] Rich[d] & Eliz. Rows
2 Oct. Sarah d. of Methuselah & Mary Williams
3 Oct. James s. of Philip & Philippa Michell
10 Oct. Jane d. of James & Anne Moreshead
16 Oct. Charles s. of W[m] & Joan Dennis
2 Nov. Susanna d. of M[r] James & M[rs] Anne Paynter
8 Nov. W[m] s. of Tho. & Eliz. Hicks
9 Nov. James s. of M[r] John & Emeline Tanner
9 Nov. Francis s. of Edward & Anne May
13 Nov. Michael s. of Martyn & Joan Strongman
26 Nov. Catherine d. of John & Ebat Hendy
27 Nov. James s. of Timothy & Mary Stevens
27 Nov. John s. of Sam[ll] & Eliz. Harris
27 Nov. Anne d. of John Tinney
4 Dec. Tho. s. of John & Mary Metherill
11 Dec. Petronell d. of Rich[d] & Petronell Peters
1 Jan. Temperance d. of John & Susanna Jane
5 Jan. Jane base child of Elizabeth Bounsell
15 Jan. Philip s. of Henry & Florence Oxnam
26 Jan. Abell s. of Rob[t] & Eliz. Walkey
28 Jan. Alice d. of Francis & Joan Vivian
2 Feb. Tho. s. of Tho. & Candace Litticott
16 Feb. Rich[d] s. of John Turner
1 Mar. Anne d. of W[m] & Mary White
4 Mar. Charles s. of John & Mary Whedon
8 Mar. Eliz. d. of W[m]* Demonfryart
14 Mar. Joan d. of W[m] & Mary Tub

ANNO 1715.

2 April Philippa d. of Thomas & Hon[r] Marks
9 April Tho. s. of Francis & Anne Solomon
18 April Mary d. of Tho. Rawlyn
24 April Mary d. of Oliver & Jane Rawe
7 May Antony Henry s. of Robert Cock
14 May Philip s. of Antony & Catherine Kendall
10 June Edward s. of John Richards
11 June Jane d. of John & Joyce Hambly

* This William was probably son of George Demonfryart, physician, mayor of Bodmin, 1691, 1694, 1700, 1712, 1716, whose son William was born in 1689.

24 June John s. of Robert & Eliz. Strongman
6 July Richd s. of Mr Richd & Jane Edwards
16 July Antony s. of Antony White
24 July James s. of James Trenery
24 July Jane d. of Tho. May, deceased
30 July Joseph s. of Nathaniel & Sarah Oliver
2 Aug. Frances d. of John & Philippa Udy
3 Sep. John s. of Antony & Eliz. Hoskin
2 Oct. Wm s. of Wm & Eliz. Wilton
15 Oct. James s. of James & Grace Callaway
5 Nov. Anne d. of Humphry & Eliz. England
14 Nov. Degory s. of Degory & Pentecost Keast
26 Nov. Philip s. of John & Anne White
12 Dec. William base child of Epiphany Oxnam
26 Dec. William s. of Richd & Ursula Arnold
26 Dec. Wm s. of Richd & Catherine Cundy
26 Dec. Eliz. d. of Tho. & Eliz. Hicks
27 Dec. Tho. s. of Robt & Jane Merrifield
27 Dec. Robt s. of Robt & Eliz. Brewer
6 Jan. Tho. s. of Samuell & Honr Bussow
24 Jan. Margery base child of Margery Pooll
2 Feb. Thomasine d. of Henry & Thomasine Cock
17 Feb. Philip s. of Philip Collier Rector & Eliz. his wife, borne 4 Feb.
18 Feb. Tho. s. of Wm & Eliz. James
19 Feb. Saml s. of James & Margaret Barston
25 Feb. Philip s. of Henry & Florence Oxnam
28 Feb. Mary d. of John & Mary Metherill
11 Mar. Tho. s. of Tho. & Prudence Gilbert

ANNO 1716.

26 Mar. Francis s. of John & Eliz. Dingey
3 April Jane d. of Arthur & Rebecka Rawe
7 April Florence d. of Philip & Anne Harris
16 April Henry s. of Henry & Honr Mitchell
21 April Francis s. of Mr Francis Paynter* & Mary his wife
21 April James s. of Tho. & Julian Polkinhorn
21 April Joan d. of Edmd & Dinah Varcar
... April Richd base child of Eliz. Polkinhorn
24 April Robt s. of John & Philippa Hawke
19 May Anne d. of Arthur & Catherine Jolly
26 May James s. of John & Philippa Hicks
21 July Eliz. d. of John & Joan Tom
22 July James s. of James & Frances Champion
11 Aug. Josias s. of Tho. & Honr Callaway
11 Aug. John s. of John & Ebbat Hendy
12 Aug. Anne d. of Henry & Mary Garland
25 Aug. Saml s. of Saml & Eliz. Harris
25 Aug. Mary d. of John & Mary Meudon
25 Aug. Joan d. of Martin & Joan Strongman
7 Sep. Edward, Mary & Jennifaire† children of Anthony & Mary Godolphin
7 Sep. James s. of James & Mary Cowling
17 Sep. Tho. & Eliz. s. & d. of Tho. & Eliz. Cornwall
2 Oct. Eli. d. of Abraham & Eliz. Husband
14 Oct. John s. of John & Mary Wheedon
20 Oct. Eliz. d. of Edward & Mary Creeber
20 Oct. Michaell s. of Michll & Eliz. Rundle
27 Oct. Mary d. of Robt & Mary Mannell
30 Oct. Philip s. of Wm & Anne Benny
12 Nov. Thomas s. of Robt & Anne Hambly
12 Nov. Wm s. of Samll & Jane Litticott
12 Nov. John s. of Wm & Eliz. Bone
13 Nov. Tho. s. of John Harris
20 Nov. Eliz. d. of Mr Richd & Jane Edwards

* Francis Paynter, gent., and Mrs. Mary Hawkey, widow, married Aug. . . . . 1713, at Little Colan. (Colan Par. Reg.)

† Probably born at one birth, and the only instance of this rare occurrence in these Registers.

8 Dec. Wm s. of Stephen & Margaret Buckingham
8 Dec. Anna d. of Faithfull & Joan Cock
9 Dec. Wm s. of Gregory & Wilmot Nancey
11 Dec. Francis s. of Richd & Philippa Peters
4 Jan. Eliz. d. of John & Jane Bone
5 Jan. John s. of Anthony & Catherine Kendall
19 Jan. Anne d. of James & Alice Stephens
19 Jan. Mary d. of Humphry & Eliz. England
2 Feb. Philip s. of Philip & Philippa Mitchell
2 Feb. Loveday d. of Tho. & Honor Mark
9 Feb. Eliz. d. of John & Johan Mill
14 Feb. Archibald base child of Johan Green
16 Mar. Wm s. of Richd & Anne Hicks
16 Mar. Eliz. d. of Robert Cock
23 Mar. Rachell d. of Tho. Solomon

ANNO 1717.

7 April Wm s. of Tho. & Mildred Basely
8 April James s. of Anthony & Dinah Coad
22 April Methuselah s. of Methuselah & Mary Williams
23 April Mary d. of John & Margaret Brenfield
27 April Anthony s. of Tho. & Candace Litticott
18 May Mary d. of Edward & Anne May
7 June Mary d. of Wm & Margaret Trembeath
11 June Mary d. of Gilbert & Joyce Meales
22 June Mary d. of Christopher & Jane Tabb
23 June William s. of Peter & Eliz. Pollard
21 July Martha d. of Nichs & Joan Broad
11 Aug. Ruth d. of Wm & Joan Dennis
11 Aug. Mary d. of Archibald & Mary Rows
17 Aug. Richd s. of Stephen & Jane Warne
17 Aug. Eliz. d. of Nathaniell & Sarah Oliver
6 Sep. Robt s. of Robt & Eliz. Walkey
21 Sep. Nichs s. of Wm & Jane Opie
21 Sep. Wm s. of Wm & Mary Woolcock
24 Sep. Mary d. of John Turner
28 Sep. John s. of John & Eliz. Cowling
1 Oct. James s. of Mr Richd & Jane Edwards
12 Oct. Jane d. of Richd & Catherine Cundy
19 Oct. John s. of John & Mary Gilbert
9 Nov. Ralph s. of Saml & Honr Bussow
11 Nov. Isaac s. of Wm & Margaret Blake
11 Nov. Anne d. of John & Dinah Gilbert
11 Nov. Honor d. of John & Philippa Udy
12 Nov. Dorothy d. of John & Dorothy Arscot
16 Nov. Mark s. of Roger & Alice George
16 Nov. Bridget base child of Joyce Dennis
14 Dec. John s. of Martyn & Joan Strongman
20 Dec. Francis s. of Mr John & Emeline Tanner
26 Dec. Richd s. of John Langdon
27 Dec. Richd s. of Robt & Mary Mannell
30 Dec. George s. of Arthur & Frances Strongman
1 Jan. Tho. s. of Thomas Tilly
4 Jan. Henry s. of Henry & Thomasine Cock
11 Jan. Eliz. d. of Robt & Eliz. Strongman
18 Jan. Philip s. of Wm & Anne Benny
21 Jan. Jane d. of Robt & Eliz. Brewer
10 Feb. Richd d. of John & Anne Sprey
28 Feb. Tho. s. of Robt & Anne Hambly
28 Feb. Philippa d. of John & Philippa Hicks
1 Mar. James s. of John & Jane Bone
1 Mar. George s. of James & Frances Champion
7 Mar. George base child of Jane Sowden
12 Mar. Anne d. of Mary Porter, wid.
15 Mar. Charles s. of Philip & Mary Rickard
19 Mar. William s. of John & Eliz. Dingey

ANNO 1718.

23 April Benjamin s. of John & Catherine Harris

26 April John s. of Timothy & Mary Stephens
10 May Frances d. of Tho. & Honor Callaway
11 May Honor d. of John & Ebat Hendye
18 May Wm s. of James & Margaret Barston
23 May Philip s. of John & Philippa Hawke
24 May John s. of John & Catherine Goss
2 June Anne d. of Dennys & Mary Tremaine
5 July Frances d. of Richd & Frances Webber
26 July Honr d. of Philip & Anne Harris
26 July Mary d. of James Trenerry
29 July Thos s. of Thomas & Eliz. Hicks
2 Aug. Anthony s. of Anthony & Catherine Kendall
16 Aug. Shadrach s. of Shadrach & Jane Tremaine
23 Aug. Richd s. of Michaell & Eliz. Rundle
13 Sep. Francis s. of Francis & Anne Solomon
13 Sep. Jane d. of Charles & Frances Thomas
13 Sep. Martha d. of John & Martha Chapell
25 Sep. Prudence d. of Thomas & Prudence Gilbert

. . . . Collier, *Rector*.

11 Oct. John s. of Humphry & Eliz. England
11 Oct. William s. of Tho. & Eliz. Williams
21 Oct. Mary d. of John & Joan Hawke
25 Oct. Penelope d. of Mr Richd & Mrs Eliz. Incledon
10 Nov. John s. of Richd & Philippa Peters
10 Nov. John s. of John . . . . Turner
15 Nov. Thomas s. of Samuell & Jane Litticott
25 Nov. Anne d. of Tho. & Susanna Wills
29 Nov. Fishlake s. of Joseph & Jane Chubb
29 Nov. James s. of Edward & Anne May
8 Dec. Prideaux base child of Jane Lewarne
21 Dec. John s. of John & Anne Sprey
27 Dec. Wm s. of Wm & Mary Rawe
27 Dec. Wm s. of Philip & Philippa Mitchell
3 Jan. Mary d. of Nathaniell & Sarah Oliver
6 Jan. Mary d. of Henry & Mary Rows
10 Jan. Tho. d. of Faithfull & Joan Cock
31 Jan. Grace d. of Samll & Eliz. Harris
2 Feb. Wm s. of John & Mary Mewdon
21 Mar. Jane d. of Robt & Eliz. Cock

Anno 1719.

11 April Catherine d. of William & Margaret Blake
18 April Dorothy d. of Degory & Pentecost Keast
24 April Edward s. of Tho. & Margaret Kestle
23 May Anne d. of Tho. & Mary Litticot
. . May Eliz. d. of Mr Robt & Eliz. Quarme
6 June Nicholas s. of Roger & Anne George
7 June Richd s. of Gregory & Wilmot Nancey
20 June Eliz. d. of George Tippet
22 June Samuell base child of Anne Rawe
4 July Wm s. of William & Anne Benny
4 July Frances d. of Arthur & Frances Strongman
31 July Wm s. of Anthony & Dinah Coad
8 Aug. Dorcas d. of Peter & Dorcas Pidwell
22 Aug. Jane d. of Richard & Anne Rawe
29 Aug. Mary d. of Arthur & Catherine Jolly
11 Sep. James d. of Robert & Jane Merrifield
26 Sep. Thomas d. of John & Blanch George
26 Sep. Jennefaire d. of Richd & Thomasine Cowle
3 Oct. Wm s. of Wm & Joan Dinnis
10 Oct. Wm s. of William & Mary Gilbert
10 Oct. Mary d. of Thomas & Joan Solomon
23 Oct. Richard s. of Richd & Anne Whitford

4 Nov. Samuel-Champion s. of Joseph & Jane Chubb
6 Nov. John s. of Michaell & Eliz. Cornish
7 Nov. Margaret d. of John & Alice Stephens
9 Nov. Jane d. of John & Jane Bone
9 Nov. Rich[d] s. of Methuselah & Mary Williams
10 Nov. Thomas s. of Thomas & Mildred Baseley
11 Nov. Jane d. of ffrancis & Mary Cowling
14 Nov. Jenefaire d. of Thomas & Eliz. Cornall
14 Nov. Eliz. d. of Michaell & Eliz. Rundell
21 Nov. W[m] s. of Gilbert & Joyce Meals
22 Nov. Eliz. d. of John & Joan Hawke
14 Dec. Susanna d. of Peter & Grace Best
26 Dec. Joan d. of Martyn & Joan Strongman
29 Dec. Thomas s. of John & Catherine Hockyns
16 Jan. Nicholas s. of W[m] & Mary Woolcock
30 Jan. George s. of Christopher & Jane Warne
30 Jan. Grace d. of Robert & Mary Litticoat
6 Feb. Stephen s. of Richard & Jane Lovell
20 Feb. Philip s. of Robert & Elizabeth Brewer
27 Feb. Richard s. of W[m] & Elizabeth Wilton
27 Feb. Jane d. of Thomas & Eliz. Hicks
2 Mar. Henry base child of Mary Betty
4 Mar. Edward base child of Honner Pollard
12 Mar. James s. of Peter & Elizabeth Pollard
12 Mar. Mary d. of John & Philippa Hicks
12 Mar. Ann d. of John & Alice Langdon
13 Mar. Peter s. of James & ffrances Champion
15 Mar. John s. of Roger & Mary Tippett
18 Mar. Anne d. of Robert & Anne Hambley
19 Mar. Mary d. of Robert & Mary Mannell

Anno 1720.

5 April Charles base child of Prudence Parnell
9 April W[m] s. of Shadrach & Jane Tremean
15 April Jonathan s. of Archibald & Mary Rowse
25 April W[m] s. of Samuell & Honner Bussow
6 May Susanna d. of ffrancis & Joan Vivian
6 May Petronell d. of Henry & Mary Brewer
7 May Rich[d] s. of Thomas & Honner Callaway
6 June Mary d. of Dennis & Mary Tremean
7 June Eliz. d. of W[m] & Susanna Blake
7 June Grace d. of John & Eliz. Cowling
18 June Sarah d. of Nathaniell & Sarah Oliver
21 June Alice d. of John & Philippa Hawke
24 June Margaret d. of Henry & Mary Garland
13 July John s. of John Hockyns, deceased, & Catherine his wife
16 July W[m] s. of Anthony & Catherine Kendall
27 Aug. John s. of John & Mary Tomm
3 Sep. John s. of Philip & Anne Harris
10 Sep. Arthur s. of Arthur & Frances Strongman
16 Sep. Mary d. of W[m] & Anne Pearce
21 Sep. W[m] s. of Anthony & Dinah Coad
27 Sep. Rich[d] s. of Rich[d] & Philippa Peters
15 Oct. Anne d. of Philip & Philippa Michell
16 Oct. Tho. s. of W[m] & Anne Benny
21 Oct. Jane d. of M[r] Philip Spernon & Dorothy* his wife
22 Oct. Grace d. of John & Mary Buckingham
22 Oct. Elizabeth d. of Thomas & Honor Mark
7 Nov. John s. of W[m] & Mary White
7 Nov. James s. of John & Dorothy Arscott
12 Nov. W[m] s. of James & Epiphany Trenerry

* Dorothy, dau. of Tho. Hoblyn of Tresaddern, gent. See Marriages, 1719.

19 Nov. Eliz. d. of Wm & Honor Roberts
21 Nov. Thomas s. of Wm & Mary Rawe
17 Dec. Henry s. of Faithfull & Joan Cock
2 Jan. John s. of Roger & Alice George
2 Jan. Olive d. of John & Anne Sprey
21 Jan. Wm s. of Henry & Mary Rows
31 Jan. John s. of John & Jane Bone
25 Feb. Mary d. of Richd & Anne Rawe
4 Mar. John s. of Wm & Ursula Tom'
4 Mar. Joseph base child of Eliz. Minnow
11 Mar. John s. of Richd & Catherine Cundy
21 Mar. Grace d. of Thomas & Margaret Kestle

ANNO 1721.

25 Mar. Joan base child of Judith Lobb
28 Mar. James s. of John & Joan Hawke
4 April Eliz. d. of Humphry & Eliz. England
7 April Saml s. of John & Mary Mewdon
10 April Benjamin s. of Robt. & Eliz. Strongman
10 April Jane d. of Francis & Anne Solomon
29 April John s. of James & Mary George
6 May Philip s. of Saml & Eliz Harris
13 May Eliz. d. of Robt. & Eliz. Cock
29 May Frances d. of Jonathan & Mary Law
10 June Aaron s. of Anthony & Mary White
10 June Richd s. of Wm & Margaret Trembeth
17 July Thomas s. of Richd & Anne Hicks
22 July Patience d. of Ezekiel & Anne Retallock
23 July Eliz. d. of Gregory & Wilmot Nance
8 Aug. Eliz. d. of Mr Joseph Chubb & Jane his wife
9 Aug. Eliz. & Mary daus. of John & Mary Gilbert
13 Aug. Joseph base child of Eliz. Baseley
19 Aug. Catherine d. of John & Ebbat Hendey
30 Aug. Joan d. of John & Mary Turner
3 Sep. Mary d. of Thomas & Mary Litticot
8 Sep. Elizabeth d. of Wm & Jane Stevens
9 Sep. Henry s. of Henry & Anne Veale
23 Sep. Grace d. of Michl & Eliz. Cornish
3 Oct. Robt s. of Mr Richd Edwards & Jane his wife
14 Oct. Jane d. of Francis & Catherine Pearce
17 Oct. Mary d. of Mr John Lawrence* & Mary his wife
20 Oct. Gregory ye s. of Thomas & Ebbat Litticot
8 Nov. Peter s. of Peter & Dorcas Pidwell
2 Dec. Eliz. d. of Arthur & Frances Strongman
2 Dec. Eliz. d. of Martin & Joan Strongman
3 Dec. Wm s. of Timothy & Mary Stephens
9 Dec. Anne base child of Margaret Champion
31 Dec. Margaret d. of Wm & Margaret Blake
15 Jan. James s. of John & Grace Burges
20 Jan. Anne d. of John & Martha Chapell
29 Jan. Henry s. of John & Elizabeth Oxnam
2 Feb. John s. of Tho. & Eliz. Polkinhorn
10 Feb. Mary d. of Philip & Mary Rickard
17 Feb. John s. of Nathaniell & Sarah Oliver
17 Feb. Jane d. of James & Frances Champion
17 Feb. Anne d. of Wm & Mary Rawe

* This family were descended from John, second son of Humphry Lawrence, who died 9 June, 1669, and to whose memory there exists a mural monument in the chancel of Cubert Church, erected by his brother, Thomas Lawrence, Vicar of St. Winnow for forty-five years, and died s. p. in 1722, having brought up Arthur, John, and Jane, the three infant and orphan children of his brother Humphry above, by his wife Jane, dau. and heir of John Davies of Carines in the parish of Cubert, gent. Arthur became an Attorney-at-Law, died 19 April, 1699, whose great-grandson, Northmore Lawrence of Launceston, cleaned and repaired the above monument. John was ancestor of Lawrence of St. Columb, now extinct in the male line. Jane mar. . . . . Berzey of Fowey, merchant.

The inscription on the above monument sets forth the particulars here given.

24 Feb. Richard s. of W[m] & Susanna Blake
25 Feb. John s. of Richard & Anne Whitford
3 Mar. Richard s. of John & Jane Buckingham
13 Mar. W[m] s. of John Bone dec[d] & Jane his wife
17 Mar. John s. of John & Philippa Hicks

ANNO 1722.

27 Mar. Eliz. d. of Henry & Mary Brewer
31 Mar. Eliz. d. of Nicholas & Jane Opie
7 April Mary d. of John & Amie Tremain
14 April John s. of John & Catherine Hockin
14 April Mathias s. of Mathias & Grace Grose
14 April Cæcilia d. of Rich[d] & Philippa Peters
14 April Elizabeth d. of Sam[ll] & Honor Bussow
21 April Rich[d] s. of Thomas & Melior Baseley
21 April Jennefair d. of Rob[t] & Mary Litticot
22 April Peter s. of. Anthony & Catherine Kendall
30 April Frances d. of Rich[d] & Jane Grig
14 May Pentecoste d. of George & Eliz. Tippet
15 May Eliz. d. of W[m] & Ursula Tom'
19 May Mary d. of Rob[t] & Anne Hambly
27 May Thomas & Samuell sons of Tho. & Joane Solomon
2 June Tho. s. of John & Catherine Goss
6 July Sam[ll] s. of M[r] Joseph Bishop & Loveday his wife
21 July James s. of Arthur & Catherine Jolly
22 July Mary d. of John & Eliz. Cowling
23 July James s. of Methuselah & Mary Williams
27 July Anne d. of Mary Tubb
1 Aug. James s. of Rob[t] & Jane Merrifield
11 Aug. W[m] s. of Tho. & Eliz. Hicks
11 Aug. Mary d. of Methuselah & Mary Williams
19 Aug. Richard s. of Archibald & Mary Rows
4 Sep. Frances d. of John & Joan Hawke
9 Sep. Hendy s. of John & Mary Langdon
9 Sep. Anne d. of Mich[ll] & Eliz. Rundle
25 Sep. Andrew s. of M[r] Beltezar Williams & Eliz. his wife
24 Oct. Eliz. d. of W[m] & Anne Benny
27 Oct. John base child of Margaret Pill
3 Nov. Thomas s. of Thomas & Eliz. Williams
13 Nov. Michaell s. of Mich[ll] & Eliz. Cornish
1 Dec. James s. of Faithfull & Joan Cock
8 Dec. Thomas s. of Henry & Judeth Knight
8 Dec. George base child of Mary Betty
21 Dec. Anne d. of Roger & Mary Tippet
27 Dec. George & Peter sons of John & Philippa Hawke
1 Jan. Henry s. of M[r] Henry & Mary Rows
1 Jan. Mary d. of Philip & Philippa Michell
4 Jan. John s. of M[r] John Lawrence & Mary his wife
7 Jan. Tho. s. of Tho. & Margaret Kestle
16 Jan. Eliz. d. of Gilbert & Joyce Meale
19 Jan. Eliz. d. of Jonathan & Mary Law
2 Feb. Edw[d] s. of Francis & Catherine Pearce
20 Feb. Margaret d. of John & Amye Brewer
22 Feb. Peter s. of Peter & Grace Best
23 Feb. Grace d. of John & Anne Peters
2 Mar. Catherine d. of Rich[d] & Catherine Cundy
9 Mar. Eliz. d. of W[m] & Honor Roberts
23 Mar. Jane d. of John & Jane Buckingham
24 Mar. Tho. s. of W[m] & Eliz. Wilkin

ANNO 1723.

11 April Samuel s. of Sam[ll] & Eliz. Harris
16 April John s. of Samuel Grimes & Eliz. his wife

16 April Thomas s. of John & Catherine Hockin
16 April Eliz. d. of Robt & Eliz. Brewer
27 April John s. of Thomas & Mary Drew
4 May John s. of Mr James Bishop & Sarah his wife
4 May Margaret d. of Wm & Mary Bear
10 May Jane d. of Wm & Jane Stephens
19 May Mary d. of Shadrach & Jane Tremain
23 June Mary d. of Gregry & Wilmot Nancey
30 June Thomas s. of Mr Thomas Shepherd & Mary his wife
10 Aug. Eliz. d. of John & Mary Thomas
15 Aug. Humphry s. of Humphry & Eliz. England
17 Aug. Anne d. of Ezekiell & Anne Retallock
17 Aug. Anne d. of Stephen & Margaret Tyer
24 Aug. John base child of Mary Hailbron
25 Aug. Johanna d. of Mr Joseph Bishop & Loveday his wife
22 Sep. Mary d. of Daniell & Eliz. May
26 Sep. Jane d. of Nichs & Eliz. Coad
5 Oct. Wm s. of Thomas & Anne Rawling
12 Oct. Alice d. of Henry & Anne Veall
14 Oct. Henry s. of Richd & Anne Whitford
11 Nov. Thomas s. of Philip & Anne Harris
11 Nov. Samuel s. of Francis & Anne Solomon
11 Nov. Susanna d. of John & Susanna Willyams
23 Nov. Mathew s. of Nathaniell & Sarah Oliver
23 Nov. Elizabeth d. of Richd & Anne Rawe
30 Nov. Mathew s. of Mathew & Grace Grose
30 Nov. William s. of Philip & Philippa Mitchell
1 Dec. Richd s. of Michaell & Elizabeth Rundle
26 Dec. John s. of James & Frances Champion
27 Dec. John s. of John & Ursula Tom
27 Dec. Eliz. d. of John & Catherine Clemows
10 Jan. John s. of Mr Giles Hamley* & Barbara his wife
17 Jan. Eliz. d. of Joseph & Joyce Glanfield
20 Jan. William Withers s. of Mr John Lawrence & Mary his wife
5 Feb. Richd s. of John & Anne Sprey
15 Feb. Mary d. of Tho. & Mary Litticot
25 Feb. Anne d. of John & Joan Hawke
29 Feb. Jane d. of Nichs & Jane Opie

ANNO 1724.

29 Mar. Richd s. of John & Eliz. Cowling
30 Mar. Edmond s. of Edmond & Dinah Varcoe
7 April Henry s. of John & Margaret Trembeath
14 April Mary d. of Mr James Bishop & Sarah his wife
18 April John s. of Wm & Eliz. Olver
28 April Eleanore d. of John & Grace Burges
5 May Joan d. of Wm & Jane Dancaster
11 May John s. of Patience & Margaret Williams
14 May James base child of Joyce Denys
20 May Robt s. of Robt & Catherine Mannell
25 May Edwd s. of John & Martha Chapell
14 June Mary d. of John & Mary Turner
7 July Mary d. of Peter & Dorcas Pidwell
31 July Wm s. of William & Mary Worth
8 Aug. Richard s. of John & Mary Mewdon
8 Aug. Anne d. of Martin & Joan Strongman
22 Aug. Eliz. d. of Wm & Eliz. Rawe
5 Sep. Mary d. of Robt & Eliz. Cock
14 Sep. John s. of John & Eliz. Oxnam
19 Sep. Richd s. of Michll & Eliz. Cornish
19 Sep. Wm s. of Wm & Mary Lanyon
27 Sep. Anne d. of Mr Tho. Shepherd & Mary his wife
17 Oct. Wm s. of Arthur & Catherine Jolly

* Mr. Giles Hamley was second son of William Hamley, of Treblethick, Esq.; this John, who died an infant, was his only child by his first wife Barbara, dau. of Philip Hawkins of Pennence.

17 Oct. Richd s. of James & Epiphany Trenerry
24 Oct. Mary d. of Wm & Mary Bear
25 Oct. Wm s. of Wm & Eliz. Luney
31 Oct. George base child of Avice Nichols
9 Nov. Wm s. of Wm & Jane Pound
9 Nov. Sarah d. of Robt & Eliz. Brewer
10 Nov. Amye d. of John & Amye Brewer
21 Nov. John s. of John & Mary Lewarne
18 Dec. James s. of Arthur & Mary Callaway
27 Dec. Thomas s. of Francis & Catherine Pearce
29 Dec. John s. of Wm & Deborah Gatty
1 Jan. Nicholas s. of John & Anne Peters
6 Jan. Thomas s. of Thomas & Ebat Leddicot
9 Jan. Benjamin s. of Arthur & Frances Strongman
7 Feb. Catherine d. of Anthony & Catherine Kendall
13 Feb. Mary d. of Samuel & Mary Glanvill
22 Feb. Jane d. of Saml Grimes & Mary his wife
27 Feb. Avice d. of John & Mary Michell
20 Mar. George s. of George & Eliz. Tippet

Anno 1725.

3 April Gertrude d. of John & Dorothy Arscot
14 April John s. of Mr James Bishop & Sarah his wife
19 April Anne d. of Robt & Mary Litticot
24 April John s. of Joseph & Joyce Glanfield
22 May Richard s. of Richd & Jane Grigg
23 May Richd s. of John & Philippa Hawke
9 June Eliz. d. of William & Catherine Antron
12 June Grace d. of John & Jane Buckingham
12 June Mary d. of Methuselah & Mary Williams
13 June Jane d. of Gilbert & Joyce Meals
27 June Susanna d. of Mr Joseph Bishop & Loveday his wife
6 July John s. of John & Joan Hawke
7 Aug. Martha d. of John & Catherine Hockin
11 Aug. Anthony s. of Anthony & Dinah Coad
14 Aug. Margaret d. of Petherick & Margaret Williams
29 Aug. Dorothy d. of Daniel & Eliz. Thomas
18 Sep. Benjamin s. of Nathaniel & Sarah Oliver
18 Sep. Henry s. of Henry & Gertrude Pollard
18 Sep. Jane d. of Edward & Catherine Inch
25 Sep. Isabella d. of Wm & Jane Stephens
30 Sep. Wm s. of Wm & Jane Parkyn
2 Oct. Jane d. of Shadrach & Jane Tremain
4 Oct. Anne d. of Mr George Mapowder & Jane his wife
9 Oct. Francis s. of Robt & Catherine Mannell
16 Oct. Samuel s. of Samuel & Honor Bussow
16 Oct. Susanna base child of Mary Merifield
30 Oct. Anne d. of Edwd & Eliz. Merifield
5 Nov. John s. of John & Mary Langdon
6 Nov. John s. of Bernard & Temperance Rows
8 Nov. Thomas s. of Thomas & Eliz. Hicks
10 Nov. Charles s. of Mr Thomas Shepherd & Mary his wife
20 Nov. Mary d. of Tho. & Mildred Baseley
25 Nov. Henry s. of Henry & Mary Brewer
27 Nov. Emelyn base child of Emelyn Neill
7 Dec. Sarah d. of Roger & Mary Tippet
12 Dec. Humphry s. of Humphry & Elizabeth England
14 Dec. Mary d. of Mr John Lawrence & Mary his wife
18 Dec. Elizabeth d. of Wm & Eliz. Woolcock
31 Dec. Sampson s. of Isaac & Eliz. Husband
1 Jan. Nathaniel s. of Robert & Anne Strongman
15 Jan. Jane d. of Wm & Eliz. Olver

16 Jan. Hugh s. of John & Anne Williams
17 Jan. W^m^ s. of George & Joan Bond
29 Jan. Hugh s. of Mr Beltezer Williams dec^d^ & Eliz. his wife
7 Feb. Mary d. of Jacob & Mary Grigg
18 Feb. Margery d. of James & Frances Champion
19 Feb. Rich^d^ s. of Henry & Anne Veall
19 Feb. Ezekiel s. of Ezekiel & Anne Retallock
5 Mar. Thomasine d. of Solomon & Mary Baseley
12 Mar. Robert d. of Joseph & Mary Dunkin

ANNO 1726.

31 Mar. Mary d. of John & Mary Tom
3 April William s. of Arthur & Frances Strongman
9 April Mary d. of Nicholas & Jane Opie
30 April Catherine d. of William & Jane Dancaster
14 May Mary d. of William & Honor Roberts
28 May Edward s. of William & Joan Merifield
31 May James s. of Samuel & Elizabeth Harris
31 May Mary d. of William & Jane Pound
4 June Jane d. of John & Grace Whitford
19 June James s. of James & Mary George
1 July James s. of Mr Wm Williams & Jane his wife
2 July Susanna d. of John & Anne White
9 July William s. of Henry & Honor Barnicot
15 July Anne d. of Mr Giles Hamley & Grace* his wife
15 July John s. of Thomas & Elizabeth Williams
22 July Mary d. of Robert & Jane Merifield
14 Aug. Anne d. of Richard & Anne Whitford
16 Aug. William s. of William & Deborah Gatty

* By his second wife Grace, dau. of Thomas Hoblyn, of Tresaddern, gent., mar. at St. Wenn by licence, 20 Aug. 1725. The dau. died an infant.

27 Aug. Anne d. of Hugh & Mary Bullock

P. COLLIER, *Rect^r^*.

1 Sep. Thomas s. of John & Catherine Gass
1 Sep. Philip s. of Robert & Mary Kent
10 Sep. Samuell s. of Thomas & Joan Solomon
17 Sep. Jane d. of William & Jane Drew
19 Sep. Jennefair d. of Thomas & Margaret Kessell
7 Oct. Elizabeth d. of John & Eliz. Rapson
9 Oct. Eliz. d. of Mr Joseph Bishop & Loveday his wife
14 Oct. John s. of John & Anne Peter
17 Oct. Michaell s. of Edward & Grace Richards
25 Oct. Henry s. of William & Margaret Blake
17 Nov. William s. of John & Phillippa Hawke
19 Nov. John s. of Martin & Joan Strongman
21 Nov. Eliz. d. of James & Epiphany Trenerry
4 Dec. Jane d. of John & Amy Brewer
17 Dec. Jane d. of John & Martha Chaple
18 Dec. Nicholas s. of Thomas & Mary Litticot
31 Dec. Philip s. of Michaell & Elizabeth Cornish
6 Jan. John s. of Robert & Anne Hamley
6 Jan. John s. of W^m^ & Eliz. Luney
9 Jan. Anne d. of W^m^ & Catherine Antron
18 Jan. James s. of Francis & Patience Cowling
29 Jan. Jane d. of Mr George Mapowder & Jane his wife
31 Jan. Sarah d. of Mr James Bishop & Sarah his wife
4 Feb. John s. of W^m^ & Mary Stephens
4 Feb. Avice d. of Jonathan & Mary Law
6 Feb. Frances d. of Nicholas & Marg^t^ Gewens
18 Feb. Anne base child of Eliz. Best
20 Feb. Frances d. of Arthur & Mary Callaway
25 Feb. Eliz. d. of John & Mary Mewdon

28 Feb. John s. of Francis & Catherine Pearce
1 Mar. James s. of Mr Thomas Shephard & Mary his wife
7 Mar. Philip s. of Arthur & Catherine Jolley
13 Mar. Susanna d. of John & Joan Hawke
18 Mar. Elizabeth d. of John & Eliz. Oxnam
24 Mar. Elias s. of Anthony & Catherine Kendall
24 Mar. Abraham s. of Isaac & Elizabeth Husband

ANNO 1727.

3 April Frances d. of John & Mary Whedon
12 April Richd s. of Richard & Anne Rawe
3 June Eliz. d. of Samll & Mary Glanfield
10 June James s. of Samll & Mary Grimes
8 July John s. of John & Mary Lewarn
15 July John s. of Humphry & Mary Harvey
15 July Catherine d. of Methuselah & Mary Williams
23 July Eliz. d. of John & Grace Turner
4 Aug. Wm s. of Mr John Lawrence & Mary his wife
16 Aug. Jane d. of John & Jane Buckingham
18 Aug. John s. of George & Joan Bond
18 Aug. Eliz. d. of Francis & Joan Vivian
19 Aug. Mary d. of Philip & Mary Rickard
21 Aug. Honor d. of Thomas & Ebat Litticot
27 Aug. Anne d. of Wm & Jane Drew
1 Sep. Mary d. of Henry & Mary Brewer
1 Sep. Martha d. of Edward & Elizabeth Merifield
2 Sep. Wm s. of Wm & Eliz. Olver
8 Sep. John s. of John & Mary Best
21 Oct. Elizabeth d. of Daniell & Eliz. Thomas
27 Oct. Anne d. of John & Anne Sprey
29 Oct. Wm s. of Wm & Mary Bear
11 Nov. Jane d. of Joseph & Mary Dunkin
12 Nov. Robert s. of Rob. & Catherine Mannell
18 Nov. William s. of Nathaniel & Sarah Oliver
19 Nov. Loveday d. of Mr Joseph Bishop & Loveday his wife
25 Nov. Eliz. d. of John & Philippa Hicks
25 Nov. Margaret d. of Henry & Gertrude Pollard
27 Nov. Frances d. of Richard & Jane Grigg
1 Jan. Catherine d. of John & Philippa Hawke
13 Jan. Wm s. of Ezekiel & Anne Retallock
20 Jan. Susanna d. of Wm & Eliz. Rawe
27 Jan. Robt s. of Robert & Mary Litticot
2 Feb. John s. of Thomas & Temperance Davies
3 Feb. Eliz. d. of Bernard & Temperance Rows
5 Feb. Joanna* d. of Mr Giles Hamley & Grace his wife
5 Feb. Jane d. of John & Catherine Hockyn
27 Feb. Jane d. of Mr Wm Williams & Jane his wife
3 Mar. Robert s. of John & Elizabeth Cowling
15 Mar. Jane d. of Jane Lewarne
16 Mar. Mary d. of Arthur & Frances Strongman
18 Mar. Thomas s. of Wm & Deborah Gatty
23 Mar. Robt s. of John & Elizabeth Gummow

ANNO 1728.

30 Mar. James s. of Thomas & Eliz. Hicks
30 Mar. John s. of John & Grace Whitford
23 April Elizabeth d. of James & Frances Champion
18 May Jane d. of Samll & Elizabeth Harris
25 May Wm s. of Solomon & Eliz. Baseley
11 June Jennefair d. of Samll & Honor Bussow
28 June Jane d. of Shadrach & Jane Tremain
4 July Grace base child of Anne Benny

* She died unmarried in 1760.

5 July Petherick John s. of Petherick & Margaret Williams
12 July Anne d. of Mr James Bishop & Sarah his wife
13 July Hugh s. of Hugh & Mary Bullock
11 Aug. Eliz. d. of Wm & Jane Pound
17 Aug. James s. of Humphry & Elizabeth England
17 Aug. Anne d. of Robt & Eliz. Symonds
18 Aug. Dorcas d. of John & Dorcas Whetter
18 Aug. Anne d. of John & Mary Tippett
8 Sep. Alice d. of John & Mary Langdon
16 Sep. Wm s. of Wm & Florence Hicks
21 Sep. Elizabeth d. of Thos & Eliz. Glanfield
3 Oct. Grace base child of Mary Helborn
9 Oct. Frances d. of Wm & Jane Drew
12 Oct. Wm base child of Mary Tubb
13 Oct. Mary d. of Mr George & Jane Mapowder
19 Oct. Mary d. of Richard & Mary Davies
11 Nov. Dinah d. of John & Dorothy Arscott
13 Nov. Jane d. of Anthony & Catherine Kendall
15 Dec. John s. of John & Amy Brewer
19 Jan. Thomasine d. of Wm & Jane Parkyn
7 Feb. Robt son of Richd & Eliz. Austyn
15 Feb. Thomas s. of Peter & Eliz. Hornabrook
17 Feb. John s. of Mr Wm Williams & Jane his wife
18 Feb. Henry s. of Henry & Philippa Barnicot
24 Feb. Pascow s. of Thomas & Margaret Kessell
8 Mar. Mary d. of William and Mary Stephens

Anno 1729.

25 Mar. Jane d. of William & Anne Davies
8 April Thos s. of Edwd & Eliz. Merifield
19 April Jane d. of Jacob & Mary Grigg
19 April Eliz. d. of Joseph & Joyce Glanfield
26 April Mary d. of Wm & Jane Stephens
29 April Samuel s. of John & Mary Johns
17 May Elizabeth d. of Wm & Honor Lanion
24 May Anne d. of Richd & Anne Rawe
27 May Sarah d. of Wm & Eliz. Olver
7 June James s. of Francis & Patience Cowling
7 June Wm s. of Robt & Anne Hamley
7 June Mary d. of Nicholas & Jane Opie
16 June Thos s. of Nathanll & Sarah Oliver
16 June Jane d. of Samll & Mary Grimes
25 June Wm s. of John & Margaret Jackson
19 July Wm s. of John & Catherine Gass
9 Aug. Grace d. of Martin & Joan Strongman
13 Sep. Wm s. of John & Jane Inch
20 Sep. John s. of John & Jane Buckingham
27 Sep. Peter s. of John & Mary Best
1 Oct. William s. of Mr Giles Hamley & Grace his wife
5 Oct. Mary d. of Wm & Elizabeth Wilcock
11 Oct. Wm s. of Wm & Honor Roberts
11 Oct. Elizabeth d. of Robert & Catherine Mannell
10 Nov. Benjamin Thomas s. of Mr Philip Spernon & Dorothy his wife
10 Nov. John s. of John & Amy Brewer
10 Nov. Mary d. of John & Grace Whitford
29 Nov. Philippa d. of Simon & Alice Lawe
2 Dec. Henry s. of Henry & Mary Brewer
4 Dec. Grace d. of Thos & Mary Litticot
11 Jan. Nicholas s. of Mr John Bishop & Loveday his wife
17 Jan. Sarah d. of Thos & Anne Pearce
20 Jan. Sarah base child of Catherine Rundle
24 Jan. Eliz. d. of Philip & Mary Rickard

24 Jan. Jane d. of Henry & Gertrude Pollard
2 Feb. John s. of William & Joan Bullen
22 Feb. Anne d. of George & Joan Bond
1 Mar. John s. of Joseph & Mary Dunkin
3 Mar. Eliz. d. of Humphry & Anne Oxnam
10 Mar. Wm s. of John & Joan Hawke

ANNO 1730.

30 Mar. Eliz. d. of Richd & Jane Rows
31 Mar. Anne d. of Thos & Temperance Davies
4 April Anne d. of John & Philippa Hicks
19 April Margaret d. of Mr George Mapowder & Jane his wife
19 April Mary d. of Wm & Joan Merifield
24 April Jane d. of John & Eliz. Oxnam
26 April Frances d. of John & Mary Whedon
2 May Richd s. of Thos & Ebat Litticot
9 May James s. of Thos & Elizabeth Williams
18 May Wm s. of Robt & Anne Strongman
29 May Humphry s. of Mr John Lawrence & Mary his wife
30 May Thos s. of Francis & Catherine Pearce
2 June Richd s. of Mr Wm Williams & Jane his wife
4 June Anne d. of John & Anne Sprey
6 June Richard s. of John & Catherine Hockin
23 July Charles s. of Benjamin & Margaret Thomas
9 Aug. Mary d. of Wm & Jane Drew
9 Aug. Joseph s. of Wm & Jane Rawe
14 Aug. Edward s. of Edward & Eliz. Merifield
21 Aug. John s. of Wm & Jane Pound
22 Aug. Wm s. of Solomon & Jane Baseley
30 Aug. Anne d. of Wm & Mary Bear
12 Sep. Richd s. of Robt & Eliz. Bilkey
3 Oct. Thos s. of Richard & Eliz. Austin
10 Oct. Wm s. of Wm & Ursula Tom
23 Oct. Thos s. of Mr Gyles Hamley & Grace his wife*
7 Nov. Wm s. of Robert & Anne Hamley
7 Nov. John s. of Nichs & Jane Opie
9 Nov. John s. of John & Blanch Husband
9 Nov. George s. of Charles & Dorothy Retallock
9 Nov. Eliz. d. of Wm & Anne Davis
9 Nov. Mary d. of John & Mary Tippet
23 Nov. Mary d. of John & Mary Johns
28 Nov. Richard s. of John & Martha Chapell
1 Jan. Peter s. of James & Frances Champion
8 Jan. Wm s. of Henry & Gertrude Pollard
18 Jan. Jane d. of Humphry & Eliz. England
20 Jan. Robert s. of John & Margaret Jackson
30 Jan. John s. of Robt & Eliz. Symonds
3 Mar. Edward s. of Bernard & Temperance Rows

ANNO 1731.

27 Mar. Joanna d. of Wm & Jane Stephens
29 Mar. Eliz. d. of John & Grace Whitford
1 April Henry s. of Arthur & Mary Mitchell
3 April Simon s. of Simon & Alice Lawe
17 April Elizabeth d. of Wm & Florence Hicks
19 April Joan d. of John & Dorcas Whetter
21 April Henry s. of Patherick & Margaret Williams
27 April Mary d. of John & Rebekah Thomas
14 May Mary d. of Humphry & Mary Harvey
16 May Wm s. of Wm & Anne Benny
17 May Wm s. of Robt & Mary Litticot

* He was in holy orders and died in 1766, having married first 17 May, 1758, Grace, dau. and co-heir of Rev. John Tregenna, rector of Mawgan in Pydar, by whom he had one son, Tho. Tregenna Hamley, see bapt. 1759. The Rev. Tho. Hamley married secondly Mary, dau. of ...... by whom he had Edw. and Giles.

27 May Edward s. of M[r] John Bishop & Loveday his wife
7 June Jane d. of Thos & Eliz. Warne
7 June Eliz. d. of Ezek[ll] & Anne Retallock
11 June John s. of Giles & Eliz. Williams
12 June Abraham s. of Thos & Margery Best
20 June Mary d. of Henry & Constance Blight
29 June Eliz. d. of Sam[ll] & Eliz. Pearce
10 July Eliz. d. of W[m] & Eliz. Peters
17 July Mary d. of Anthony & Eliz. Rawe
18 July John s. of W[m] & Eliz. Olver
30 July Thos s. of M[r] Thos Shepherd & Mary his wife
8 Aug. Mary d. of John & Mary Lamb
15 Aug. Peter base child of Mary Chapell
22 Aug. Richard s. of John & Mary Langdon
4 Sep. Nathaniel s. of Nath[ll] & . . . . . Gill
7 Sep. Rob[t] base child of Mary Hailbron
9 Sep. Sarah d. of W[m] & Sarah Jane
18 Oct. Richard s. of Thos & Joan Solomon
8 Nov. Pascow s. of Pascow & Margaret Kessell
8 Nov. Eliz. d. of W[m] & Mary Stephens
8 Nov. Mary d. of Henry & Martha Sanders
9 Nov. W[m] s. of M[r] W[m] Williams & Jane his wife
27 Nov. Grace d. of Rich[d] & Anne Rawe
9 Dec. W[m] s. of W[m] Saundry of Maugan & Susanna his wife
14 Dec. Anne d. of M[r] Giles & M[rs] Grace Hamley
29 Dec. Mary d. of John & Catherine Hockin
8 Jan. Joan d. of W[m] & Jane Drew
22 Jan. Mary d. of Hugh & Mary Bullock
5 Feb. W[m] s. of Humphry & Anne Oxnam
12 Feb. Sarah d. of W[m] & Mary Langdon
16 Feb. Philippa d. of Benjamin & Margaret Thomas
21 Feb. Elizabeth d. of John & Jane Inch
4 Mar. Sarah d. of Philip & Mary Rickard
6 Mar. Crispin s. of Thomas & Mary Litticot
7 Mar. Margaret d. of John & Amy Brewer
17 Mar. Pasca s. of W[m] & Anne Davis, living 31 March 1821
19 Mar. Mary base child of Rebekah Ellerey

ANNO 1732.

28 Mar. Agns d. of Arthur & Frances Strongman
14 April John s. of John & Mary Best
18 April Will[m] Rapson s. of Denys & Mary Tremain
28 April Henry s. of Arthur & Mary Michell
28 April Eliz. d. of Edward & Eliz. Merifield
29 April William s. of Richard & Anne Rowse
27 May Grace d. of John & Joan Martyn
29 May John s. of Thomas & Ebat Liddicot
13 June Robert s. of Humphry & Eliz. England
21 July W[m] s. of M[r] John Thomas & Rebekah his wife
29 July W[m] s. of Joseph & Joyce Glanfield
31 July Gilbert base child of Eliz. Jeffery
5 Aug. Robert s. of Thomas & Rachell Keam
7 Aug. Richard s. of M[r] George Mapowder & Jane his wife
19 Aug. Richard s. of Rich[d] & Eliz. Austin; living 24 Feb. 1825
20 Aug. Margery d. of William & Honor Roberts
24 Sep. Grace s. of Martin & Joan Strongman
21 Oct. Catherine d. of Christopher & Honor Warne*
23 Oct. Mary base child of Susanna Tinney
6 Nov. Thomas s. of George & Joan Bond

* Honor Lee, see marriages 1731. This dau. Catherine married 13 Sept., 1756, William Rawlings, Esq., of Padstow, an eminent merchant; for their descendants see *The Landed Gentry*, by Sir J. B. Burke, Kt., Ulster King of Arms.

6 Nov. Thomas s. of Wm & Eliz. Luney
6 Nov. Robert s. of John & Blanch Husband
6 Nov. Blanch d. of Charles & Dorothy Retallock
29 Dec. Wm s. of John & Margaret Jackson
8 Jan. Grace d. of John & Jane Parnall
13 Jan. Arthur & Abraham sons of Thomas & Margery Best
27 Jan. Wm s. of William & Anne Pearce
27 Jan. James s. of Philip & Eliz. Gilbert
2 Feb. Michaell s. of Solomon & Mary Basely
17 Feb. Mary d. of Robt & Anne Hamley
17 Feb. John base child of Margaret Congdon
24 Feb. William s. of John & Mary Lewarn
28 Feb. Jennefaire d. of Wm & Jane Pound
3 Mar. Loveday d. of John & Philippa Hicks
3 Mar. John s. of Robert & Anne Pascow
6 Mar. Grace d. of Mr Giles & Mrs Grace Hamley
16 Mar. Henry s. of Thos & Eliz. Basely
17 Mar. Mary d. of John & Jane Buckingham

ANNO 1733.

26 Mar. Mary d. of Giles & Eliz. Williams *al's* Pell
27 Mar. Grace d. of John & Grace Whitford
27 Mar. Mary d. of Henry & Mary Brewer
7 April Jennefaire d. of Robert & Catherine Mannell
7 April Eliz. d. of Mr John Lawrence & Mary his wife
5 May Honor d. of John & Ebat Lamb
12 May Walter s. of John & Isabella Harris
25 May Robt s. of Robt & Eliz. Bilkey
26 May Arthur s. of Arthur & Mary Michell
26 May Wm s. of John & Catherine Hockin
8 June Eliz. d. of Wm & Sarah Jane
5 July Gertrude d. of Petherick & Margaret Williams
7 July Agns d. of Arthur & Frances Strongman
18 Aug. Nicholas s. of Nicholas & Jane Opie
27 Aug. Richard s. of John & Dorcas Whetter
3 Sep. John s. of John & Anne Sprey
16 Sep. Thomas s. of William & Elizabeth Olver
1 Oct. Mary d. of Robert & Mary Litticot
6 Oct. Robert s. of Robert & Elizabeth Symonds
20 Oct. Richard s. of Wm & Grace Evelyn
12 Nov. Elizabeth d. of Mr John & Rebekah Thomas
24 Nov. Elizabeth d. of John & Mary Tippet
18 Dec. Catherine d. of Benjamin & Margaret Thomas
25 Jan. Mark base child of Elizabeth Blake
16 Feb. Wm s. of Philip & Mary Rickard
23 Feb. Wilmot d. of Wm & Florence Hicks
3 Mar. Honor d. of George & Anne Mapowder
8 Mar. James s. of John & Amye Brewer
16 Mar. John base child of Abigaill Corner

ANNO 1734.

27 Mar. Elizabeth d. of Robt & Anne Hamley
30 Mar. Wm s. of Wm & Emeline Mitchell
30 Mar. Eleanor d. of Thomas & Mary Tamlyn
13 April Elizabeth d. of Richard & Eliz. Austin
6 May Jane d. of Philip & Mary King
7 May Mary d. of Thomas & Catherine Merifield
18 May Mary d. of Wm & Matilda Retallock
25 May Samuel s. of Joseph & Mary Dunkin
3 June Eleanore d. of William & Mary Stephens
3 June Grace d. of Simon & Alice Law

7 June Hugh s. of Mr Wm Williams & Jane his wife
16 June Anne d. of Adam & Mary Thomson
6 July John s. of Henry & Constance Blight
20 July Elizabeth d. of John & Martha Chappell
26 July Jane d. of Mr John Lawrence & Mary his wife
26 July Susanna d. of Richd & Mary Veall
24 Aug. John s. of John & Susanna Husband
24 Aug. Anne d. of John & Jane May
29 Aug. Thomas s. of John & Grace Whitford
21 Aug. Richd s. of John & Mary Best
3 Sep. Edward s. of John & Catherine Hocken
19 Sep. Mary d. of Thomas & Rachell Keam
28 Sep. Anne d. of Richard & Jane Rowse
28 Sep. Gilbert s. of Humphry & Mary Harvey
30 Sep. Elizabeth d. of Wm & Anne Davis
4 Oct. Jane base child of Elizabeth Hicks
5 Oct. Margaret d. of Wm & Joan Bullen
12 Oct. Samson s. of Anthony & Eliz. Rawe
12 Oct. Elizabeth d. of John & Isabella Harris
19 Oct. Anne d. of Thomas & Anne Keast
11 Nov. Thomas s. of Denys & Mary Tremain
13 Nov. Grace d. of Christopher & Honor Warne*
30 Nov. Dorothy d. of Charles & Dorothy Retallock
14 Dec. Thomas s. of Wm & Joan Merifield
24 Dec. James s. of James & Eliz. Oliver
26 Dec. William s. of Giles & Eliz. Williams *al's* Pell
1 Jan. Joan d. of John & Jane Inch
18 Jan. Mary d. of John & Damaris Trebilcock
3 Feb. Samuel s. of Ezekiell & Anne Retallock

* She married John Dungey, see marriages, 1766, by whom she had several children, and died his widow in 1789; see burials.

15 Feb. Mary d. of John & Joan Martyn
21 Feb. Philip & William sons of Philip & Eliz. Gilbert
25 Feb. Elizabeth d. of Mr John Collier & Mary his wife*

ANNO 1735.

5 April Ebat d. of John & Mary Lamb
8 April Stephen s. of Henry & Mary Brewer
8 April Solomon s. of Solomon & Mary Baseley
8 April Thomas s. of James & Eliz. Trenerry
12 April Jane d. of John & Margaret Trembeth
12 April Grace d. of Wm & Honour Lanyon
23 April Elizabeth d. of Nathaniel & Mary Locket
25 April Henry s. of John & Alice Tamlyn
26 May Catherine d. of Robt & Catherine Mannell
8 June Mary d. of John & Amye Brewer
18 June John s. of Susanna Tinney
23 June James s. of James & Dorothy Jenkin
30 June John s. of Thomas & Catherine Merifield
5 July William s. of Richd & Anne Rawe
19 July Robert s. of Robt & Elizabeth Merifield
19 July Anthony s. of Mr George Mapowder & Anne his wife
26 July Grace d. of Humphry & Eliz. England
3 Aug. Mary d. of Thomas & Mary Tamlyn
16 Aug. James s. of Willm & Jane Pound
16 Aug. Mary d. of Richard & Mary Carne
23 Aug. Mary d. of John & Blanch Husband
5 Sep. Anne d. of John & Mary Lewarne
8 Sep. Willm s. of Thomas & Elizth Glanfield

* Rev. John Collier and Mrs. Mary Pollard (both of St. Columb Major) married at Colan by licence 8 Jan. 1733. Colan P. Reg. He became vicar of Colan.

21 Sep. Hugh s. of Mr Tho. Stephens & Eliz. his wife*
26 Sep. Edward s. of John & Anne Sprey
20 Oct. Thomas s. of Mr Wm Williams & Jane his wife
25 Oct. Matthias s. of Richard & Constance Plynt
10 Nov. Jane d. of William & Eliz. Luney
11 Nov. Jennefaire d. of John & Jane May
11 Nov. Arthur s. of Arthur & Mary Michell
19 Nov. Michell base child of Jane Tippet
28 Nov. Anne d. of Willm & Mary Rickard
5 Dec. Elizabeth d. of Thomas & Eliz. Baseley
6 Dec. Richard d. of Richd & Ruth Baseley
13 Dec. Jane d. of John & Anne Harris
13 Dec. Grace d. of Nicholas & Elizabeth Husband
19 Dec. Nancy d. of Mr John Thomas & Rebekah his wife
26 Dec. Anne d. of Richard & . . . . . Bennet
1 Jan. George s. of George & Joan Bond
6 Jan. William s. of Wm & Eliz. Harris
7 Jan. John s. of Mr John Collier & Mary his wife, born 12th Dec.†
8 Jan. John s. of John & Thomazine Rows
19 Jan. Arthur s. of Wm & Jane Capell
24 Jan. Jonathan s. of Jonathan & Sarah Barrett
28 Feb. Mary d. of Adam & Mary Thomson
28 Feb. Rose d. of Ezechiell & Anne Retallock
28 Feb. Mary d. of Wm & Mary Muffet
20 Mar. Elizabeth d. of Robert & Eliz. Bilkey
20 Mar. Anne d. of Philip & Mary Rickard

* Mr. Thomas Stephens and Mrs. Elizabeth Pollard (both of St. Columb Major) married by licence 16 Jan. 1733. Colan P. Reg.

† This son, John, became of Veryan and married a dau. of . . . . . Williams of Veryan.

ANNO 1736.

25 Mar. Mary base child of Petronell Michell
3 April Anne d. of Jonathan & Margaret Dawe
3 April Richd s. of Anthony & Eliz. Rawe
10 April Mary d. of Henry & Catherine Endean
26 April Humphry s. of Henry & Constance Blight
26 April Mary d. of Robert & Jane Pascow
27 April Mary d. of James & Rachell Johns
5 May Joseph s. of Thomas & Catherine Merifield
6 May Eliz. d. of Mr Giles Hamley & Grace his wife*
15 May Anne d. of Wm & Emeline Buckingham
2 June John s. of Thos & Margaret Best
6 June John s. of Joseph & Rebekah Pricket
8 June Jane d. of James & Elizabeth Oliver
14 June Catherine d. of Wm & Honor Robarts
19 June James s. of John & Dorcas Whetter
25 June John s. of Robert & Elizabeth Drew
16 July Elizabeth d. of Thos & Anne Keast
6 Aug. John s. of Richard & Elizth Husband
4 Sep. John s. of Willm & Sarah Jane
8 Nov. Mary d. of John & Mary Wilton
27 Nov. Mary d. of Danll & Mary Dunn
16 Dec. Peter s. of Michll & Margaret Hive
28 Dec. Elizabeth d. of Simon & Alice Lawe
7 Jan. Mary d. of John & Susanna Husband
11 Jan. Philippa d. of Mr Joseph & Mary Collier†
15 Jan. Robt s. of Stephen & Frances Carhart
7 Feb. Mary d. of John & Jane Inch

* She married in 1761 the Rev. Robert Bateman, D.D., rector of St. Columb.

† She married the Rev. Walter Elford, rector of Milton Damerel, Devon.

12 Feb. John s. of Philip & Eliz. Gilbert
19 Feb. Henry s. of Christopher & Honor Warne
28 Feb. Mary d. of Edward & Eliz[th] Merifield
22 Mar. Philip s. of M[r] Will[m] Williams & Jane his wife

ANNO 1737.

30 Mar. John s. of Thomas & Anne Perot
30 Mar. George s. of Rich[d] & Mary Austin
11 April Thomas s. of James & Dorothy Jenkin
22 April Eliz. d. of Petherick & Margaret Williams
23 April Catherine d. of W[m] & Anne Davis
30 May John s. of W[m] & Grace Buckingham
30 May Mary d. of Rich[d] & Jane Rows
3 June Rich[d] s. of John & Grace Whitford
3 June Eliz[th] d. of John & Catherine Hockyn
3 June Catherine d. of Thomas & Catherine Merifield
14 June Henry s. of Richard & Mary Carne
25 June Charles s. of David & Jane Fulton
25 June Grace d. of John & Anne Sprey
6 July Samuel s. of W[m] & Margaret Wilton
17 July W[m] s. of Rich[d] & Constance Flint
23 July Sarah base child of Mary Tippet
24 July Anne d. of John & Eliz[th] Helston
31 July Mary d. of George & Joan Bond
20 Aug. George s. of W[m] & Eliz[th] Waters
3 Sep. Grace d. of W[m] & Anne Jelbert
11 Sep. Philippa d. of Mich[ll] & Frances Cornish
17 Sep. Will[m] s. of W[m] & Joan Bullen
24 Sep. Solomon s. of Solomon & Mary Baseley
24 Sep. Loveday d. of W[m] & Jane Pound
1 Oct. Anne d. of Mich[ll] & Jane Barret
8 Oct. Temperance d. of W[m] & Matilda Retallock
8 Nov. Thomas & Samson sons of W[m] & Florence Hicks
9 Nov. Catherine d. of Thomas & Catherine Langdon
3 Dec. Mary d. of W[m] & Grace Evelyn
4 Dec. John s. of John & Jane Dungey
10 Dec. Samson s. of Henry & Mary Brewer
6 Jan. John s. of Robert & Mary Litticott
7 Jan. Margaret d. of Isaac & Eliz. Blake
19 Jan. Mary d. of M[r] John Collier & Mary his wife
22 Jan. Rich[d] & Margaret children of Tho[s] & Rachell Keam
28 Jan. Richard s. of Jonathan & Sarah Barret
29 Jan. Ebenezer & Heneman children of John & Eleanor Powell
4 Feb. Eliz d. of Henry & Constance Blight
4 Feb. Anne d. of John & Anne Harris
14 Feb. John base child of Abagaill Soper
18 Feb. W[m] s. of William & Emelyn Buckingham
27 Feb. Mary d. of M[r] Joseph Comes & Mary his wife
4 Mar. Eliz. d. of W[m] & Anne Capell
9 Mar. John base child of Mary Sandford

ANNO 1738.

3 April Jane d. of William & Mary Rickard
3 April Jane d. of Rob[t] & Eliz. Merifield
3 April Eliz[th] d. of John & Blanch Husband
4 April John s. of John & Jane May
4 April Eliz[th] d. of W[m] & Eliz[th] Olver
13 April W[m] s. of M[r] Giles Hamley & Grace his wife
15 April Mary d. of Adam & Mary Thomson
15 April Jane d. of Philip & Mary Rickard
17 April Anne d. of Peter & Petronell Wills
17 April Rachell d. of Charles & Margaret Litticot

20 April Eliz[th] d. of Jonathan & Margery Dawe
27 April Mary d. of Rich[d] & Eliz[th] Husband
29 April John s. of John & Mary Lamb
13 May John s. of James & Jane Sherry
14 May Eliz[th] d. of Rich[d] & Alice Pascoe
20 May W[m] s. of John & Thomazine Rows
3 June Nathaniel s. of James & Eliz[th] Oliver
6 June John s. of M[r] George Mapowder & Anne his wife
8 July Johanna d. of Rich[d] & Elizabeth Cundy
9 July Anne d. of John & Amy Brewer
9 July Jane d. of Henry & Isabella Donoson
16 July Mary d. of W[m] & Elizabeth Harris
22 July Mary d. of Henry & Catherine Endean
12 Aug. Jennefaire d. of Thomas & Anne Keast
19 Aug. W[m] s. of W[m] & Christian Ormond
25 Aug. Samuell s. of Thomas & Ebat Litticot
26 Aug. Margery d. of Thomas & Margery Best
3 Sep. Frances s. of W[m] & Sarah Jane
17 Sep. Edward s. of Edward & Eliz[th] Merifield
7 Oct. Eliz[th] d. of Robert & Anne Pascoe
24 Oct. Joan d. of Henry & Constance Tamlyn
6 Nov. Loveday d. of Mark & Loveday Nichols
22 Nov. John s. of Arthur & Mary Mitchell
6 Dec. Elizabeth d. of Michaell & Frances Cornish
11 Dec. John s. of Stephen & Frances Carhart
26 Dec. John s. of John & Joan Francis
6 Jan. John s. of John & Joan Thomas
6 Jan. Philippa d. of James & Dorothy Jenkin
1 Feb. Mary base child of Catherine Brenfield
23 Feb. William s. of William & Mary Cockyn
25 Feb. John s. of Rob[t] & Eliz. Bilkye
3 Mar. Elizabeth d. of Rich[d] & Anne Jane
17 Mar. Jane d. of Rich[d] & Elizabeth Evelin
21 Mar. Suzana base child of Honor Roberts

Anno 1739.

17 April Elizabeth d. of John & Jane Dungey
23 April Richard s. of Philip & Elizabeth Gilbert
28 April Mary d. of John & Jane Trescott
5 May Anne d. of William & Honor Roberts
11 May Richard s. of John & Grace Whiteford
11 May George s. of Daniel & Sarah Rice
12 May William s. of John & Ann Best
26 May Mary d. of Nathaniel & Mary Lockett
4 June John s. of Richard & Philippa Page
19 June Thomas s. of Thomas & Catherine Merifield
19 July Frances d. of Richard & Jane Rowse
19 Aug. Jonathan s. of Jonathan & Margery Daw
8 Sep. Judith d. of Jude & Elizabeth May
14 Sep. Jane d. of Anthony & Elizabeth Rawe
4 Oct. Frances base child of Ann Liddicote
14 Oct. John base child of Joyce Dennis
3 Nov. William s. of Robert & Elizabeth Drew
12 Nov. Mary d. of William & Ann Davis
12 Nov. Catherine d. of William & Ann Jolbert
28 Nov. Richard s. of Thomas & Rachell Keam
10 Dec. Elizabeth d. of James & Elizabeth Oliver
11 Dec. Richard s. of John & Joan Martyn
12 Jan. Richard s. of John & Margaret Hockyn
19 Jan. Richard s. of Thomas & Catherine Langdon
24 Jan. Jane d. of Christopher & Honor Warne
12 Mar. William s. of John & Joan Thomas

15 Mar. Frances d. of Adam & Mary Thomson
22 Mar. Margaret d. of Charles and Margaret Liddicote

ANNO 1740.

8 April Elizabeth d. of Anthony Benny & Thomazine Cock
8 April Elizabeth d. of Robert & Catherine Mannell
9 April Mary d. of Thomas & Ann Keast
22 April Sarah d. of Isaac & Eliz. Blake
26 April Sarah d. of William & Jane Pound
17 May Elizabeth d. of Rich[d] & Grace Brenton
26 May Rebekah d. of Simon & Alice Law
26 May Martha d. of Peter & Petronell Wills
26 May William s. of Richard & Mary Austin
27 May Elizabeth d. of Richard & Eliz. Cundy
9 June Elizabeth d. of Thomas & Catherine Merifield
9 June William s. of William & Eliz. Olver
12 June James s. of James & Ann Sykes
14 June Ann d. of Thomas & Joan James
27 June Richard s. of John & Jane Inch
5 Aug. John s. of Richard & Dorothy Wilton
5 Aug. Robert s. of Nicholas & Elizabeth Husband
8 Sep. Francis s. of John & Grace Buckingham
8 Sep. Susanna d. of John & Susanna Husband
9 Sep. Richard & Jane children of Rich[d] & Mary Carne
14 Sep. William s. of William & Jane Caple
22 Sep. Elizabeth d. of Charles & Dorothy Retallock
9 Oct. Mary d. of George & Joan Bond
14 Oct. William s. of John & Jane Dungery
21 Oct. Ann d. of John & Jane May
25 Oct. Ann d. of Philip & Mary Rickard
3 Nov. Elizabeth d. of William & . . . . James
10 Nov. Florence d. of William & Florence Hicks
10 Nov. Jane d. of Henry & Constance Blight
11 Nov. Grace d. of Michaell & Frances Cornish
11 Nov. Ann d. of William & Eliz. Harris
28 Nov. Thomas s. of M[r] John & Mary Burges
6 Dec. Mary d. of William & Mary Rickard
6 Jan. Mary d. of Jonathan & Sarah Barret
2 Feb. John s. of John & Mary Varcoe
9 Feb. John s. of William & Grace Evelyn
14 Feb. Stephen s. of Stephen & Ann Brewer
20 Feb. William s. of William & Ann White
21 Feb. Richard s. of William & Joan Bullen
24 Feb. Mary-Philippa d. of M[r] John Collier & Mary his wife
26 Feb. Lydia-Batten d. of Richard & Alice Pascoe
27 Feb. William s. of Edward & Ann Lawrey
3 Mar. Mary d. of Bernard & Eliz[a] Willsford
7 Mar. John s. of James & Dorothy Jenkyn
9 Mar. Nicholas s. of John & Joan Frances

ANNO 1741.

11 April Robert s. of George & Mary Sowden
15 April John s. of Richard & Eliz[a] Evelyn
25 April Mary d. of William & Mary Brabyn
8 May William s. of John & Amye Brewer
18 May John s. of Solomon & Mary Baseley
18 May Rich[d] Francis s. of Rich[d] & Philippa Page
18 May John s. of John & Ann Harris
23 May Eliza. & Jane children of William & Eliza. Baseley
13 June Thomas s. of Nathaniel & Mary Lockett
1 July William s. of James & Elizabeth Oliver

4 July Mary d. of Philip & Eliz[a] Gilbert
11 July Susanna d. of John & Dorcas Whetter
16 July Grace base child of Ann Liddicote
18 July Richard s. of Thomas & Margery Best
24 July Margaret d. of Joseph & Ann Robins
2 Aug. William s. of M[r] Thomas Merifield & Catherine his wife
9 Aug. Susanna d. of M[r] W[m] Williams & Jane his wife
13 Aug. Stephen base child of Mary Hailbourn
4 Sep. Margaret d. of Richard & Eliz[a] Husband
12 Sep. Temperance d. of John & Margaret Hockyn
12 Sep. Joseph s. of William & Eliz[a] Willis
19 Sep. Margaret d. of Will[m] & Luce Trembeth
20 Sep. Thomas s. of Thomas & Catherine Langdon
21 Sep. Henry s. of Henry & Constance Tamblyn
10 Oct. Mary d. of Stephen & Frances Carhart
3 Nov. Mary d. of William & Mary Mewdon
5 Nov. Arthur s. of Richard & Mary Austin
9 Nov. Sarah base child of Mary Tippett
16 Dec. Jane d. of John & Margaret Cundy
21 Dec. Grace d. of John & Mary Burges
1 Jan. John s. of William & Susanna Tremaine
11 Jan. Robert s. of Adam & Mary Thomson
12 Jan. William s. of John & Grace Buckingham
12 Jan. John s. of John & Grace Mewdon
16 Jan. Mary d. of Petherick & Margaret Williams
19 Jan. Richard s. of William & Ann Davies
12 Feb. John s. of John & Jane Trescote
20 Feb. Ann d. of John & Eliz. Tippet
6 Mar. John s. of John & Rebecca England
13 Mar. Mary d. of Robert & Elizabeth Bilkey
20 Mar. William s. of Richard & Dorothy Wilton

ANNO 1742.

2 April James s. of William & Margaret Couch of St. Lawrence Tinker
19 April John s. of Thomas & Rachael Keam
8 May William s. of William & Mary Dungey
13 May Henry s. of Anthony Henry & Thomazine Cock
19 May Elizabeth d. of Richard & Eliz. Evelyn
7 June Ann d. of Robert & Ann Pascoe
7 June Ann d. of Charles & Mary Dennis
20 June Thomas s. of William & Mary Cocking *al's* Tremain
30 June Eliz. & Mary children of John & Thomazine Rowse
3 July William s. of William & Ann Jelbert
17 July William s. of Thomas & Eliz. Glanville
17 July Sarah d. of Richard & Constance Plint
21 July Jennefaire d. of Will[m] & Jane Williams
24 July Loveday d. of Thomas & Ann Keast
26 July Sarah d. of James Stephens jun[r] & Sarah his wife
1 Aug. Elizabeth d. of John & Elizabeth Goodall
23 Aug. Francis s. of Richard & Elizabeth Cunday
19 Sep. Joseph s. of John & Joan Martyn
25 Sep. Elizabeth d. of George & Mary Sowden
26 Sep. Jennefaire d. of Edward & Jane Brokenshire
15 Oct. Johanna d. of John & Joan Thomas
1 Nov. William s. of William & Eliz[a] Willis
8 Nov. Mary d. of Richard & Elizabeth Husband
8 Nov. Mary d. of John & Prudence Merifield
11 Dec. Eleanor d. of Isaac & Eliz[a] Blake
27 Dec. James s. of Robert & Elizabeth Merifield

2 Jan. Mary d. of John & Jane Dungey
1 Feb. James s. of James & Ann Pollard
2 Feb. John s. of John & Mary Strongman
5 Feb. Anthony s. of John & Elizabeth White
5 Feb. Ann d. of William & Jane Pound
6 Feb. John s. of Mr Thomas Merifield & Cath. his wife
19 Feb. Elizabeth d. of William & Jane Capell
19 Feb. Mary d. of John & Mary Varcoe
24 Feb. William base child of Ann Lovell
26 Feb. John s. of Richard & Grace Brenton
6 Mar. Mathew s. of John & Frances Flamank*
7 Mar. Eliza d. of William & Mary Brabyn
23 Mar. Grace d. of John & Margaret Cundy

ANNO 1743.

25 Mar. Benjamin s. of Edward & Eliz. Tremayne
9 April John s. of John & Mary Varcoe
17 April Richard s. of Robert & Virtue Kitt
15 May Mary d. of a person unknown, being found at Trebadannon May 13th or 14th
4 June William s. of Thomas & Joan James
4 July Methuselah s. of Jonathan & Sarah Barrett
9 July Jane d. of John & Jane May
16 July Eliz. d. of Mark & Eliza Nichols
17 July Grace d. of Henry & Constance Blight
19 Aug. Henry s. of Christopher† & Honor Warne
30 Aug. John s. of Thomas & Catherine Langdon
3 Sep. Mary d. of Richd & Ann Hawke
3 Sep. Richard s. of Richd & Ann Jane
3 Sep. Jennefaire d. of Thos & Dorothy Salmon
10 Sep. Mary d. of William & Elizabeth Harris
12 Sep. Thomas s. of Henry & Constance Tamblyn
19 Sep. Jeremiah s. of Edward & Elizabeth Merifield
22 Sep. Jane d. of John & Susanna Husband
23 Sep. Joan d. of Bartholomew & Joanna Brown
15 Oct. Nathaniel s. of Nathaniel & Mary Lockett
7 Nov. Grace d. of William & Grace Evelyn
8 Nov. Jno s. of Jno Lee of Broad Hembry, Devon (now a marine in Coll. Cotterell's Regimen), & Ann his wife
18 Dec. Robert s. of James & Dorothy Jenkin
27 Dec. George s. of George & Eliza Tippet
27 Dec. Mary d. of John & Ann Harris
3 Jan. Eliza d. of Jude & Elizabeth May
24 Jan. William s. of James & Jane Coad, was born the 20th
24 Jan. Ann d. of James & Ann Pollard
27 Jan. Richard s. of Samuel & Mary Harris
30 Jan. William s. of John & Ann Hooper
9 Feb. Mary base child of Grace Olliver
3 Mar. Joan d. of William & Joan Bullen
8 Mar. Thomas s. of Thomas & Rachael Keam
10 Mar. John s. of Edward & Ann Lawrey

ANNO 1744.

26 Mar. Elizabeth d. of William & Susanna Tremaine
31 Mar. Jane d. of John & Jane Trescote
3 April Mary d. of James & Mary Hawke
14 May John s. of Richard & Mary Austin

* In the church at St. Enoder, painted on a board, are these arms, viz., per pale, dexter arg. a cross gu. betw. four mullets of the last pierced of the field, impaling quarterly 1 and 4 arg. a lion ramp. gu. 2 and 3 arg. a fesse emb. at the top betw. 3 annulets gu. Crest, a fore arm erect vested az., buttons or, cuff arg., in the hand ppr. a wreath vert fructed gu. Motto, Mors Juna Vitæ. Beneath them the following inscription: Frances, wife of John Flamank of Padstow, died 18 April 1785.

† He married Elizabeth Dungey. See Marriages, 1766.

29 May Elizabeth d. of John & Frances Flamank
31 May Eliz[a] base child of Abagail Conner
16 June Elizabeth d. of Thomas & Mary Sweet
16 June Elizabeth d. of John & Ann Best
27 July John base child of Ann Redda
4 Aug. Mary d. of Francis & Rebecca May
11 Aug. Richard s. of Richard & Grace Breuton
26 Aug. Elizabeth d. of Thomas & Caroline Parkyn
31 Aug. Ann d. of Richard & Eliz. Husband
8 Sep. Edward s. of James & Elizabeth May
7 Oct. Mary d. of John & Margaret Hockyn
15 Oct. John s. of Adam & Mary Thomson
20 Oct. Thomas s. of Thomas & Ann Keast
27 Oct. Jenefayre d. of William & Jane Capell
11 Nov. Thomas s. of John & Thomazine Rowse
12 Nov. Anthony s. of Thomas & Mary Troth
12 Nov. William s. of John & Grace Buckingham
12 Nov. William s. of Charles & Mary Dennis
12 Nov. Richard s. of John & Margaret Cundy
13 Nov. Mary d. of Solomon & Mary Baseley
15 Dec. Richard s. of Thomas & Catherine Langdon
28 Dec. Jane d. of Philip & Eliza Gilbert
25 Feb. Eleanor d. of Richard & Elizabeth Cundy
26 Feb. Ann d. of Richard & Alice Pascoe
26 Feb. Samuell s. of John & Elizabeth White
23 Mar. Daniel s. of John & Jane May

ANNO 1745.

25 Mar. Richard s. of George & Mary Sowden
28 Mar. Richard s. of Richard & Jane Veal
4 April Ann d. of John & Sarah Stephens
6 April Jane d. of Mark & Elizabeth Nichols
16 April William s. of Thomas & Rachael Keam
13 May Catherine base child of Elizabeth Strongman
21 June William s. of Joseph & Jane Trescote
30 June Mary d. of Richard & Elizabeth Evelin
7 July Robert s. of John & Elizabeth Helstone
14 July Dinah d. of William & Ann Gilbert
10 Aug. Robert s. of Robert & Elizabeth Bilkey
2 Sep. John s. of Christopher & Honour Warne
6 Sep. Richard & Ann children of William & Mary Brabyn
22 Oct. Nicholas Donithorne s. of M[r] Edward Arthur & Mary his wife
27 Oct. Grace d. of Richard & Ann Jane
10 Nov. Elizabeth d. of James & Honour Colwill
17 Nov. Damaris d. of William & Ann White
21 Nov. Philippa d. of Nicholas & Elizabeth Husband
14 Dec. Grace d. of John & Joan Martyn
17 Dec. Mary d. of William & Mary Cockyn *al's* Tremain
25 Dec. Henry base child of Joan Benny of Mawgan
27 Dec. John s. of Nathaniel & Mary Locket
10 Jan. James s. of James & Mary Hawke
11 Jan. Mary d. of Bartholomew & Joanna Brown
13 Jan. John s. of John & Mary Hicks
31 Jan. Mary d. William Withington (a drummer in Gen[ll] Wentworth's Regiment of Foot) & Mary his wife
10 Feb. Charles s. of John & Susanna Husband
8 Mar. Thomazine d. of John & Eliz[a] Tippet
15 Mar. James s. of James & Elizabeth May

ANNO 1746.

1 April Arthur s. of Gilbert & Ann Strongman

11 April John s. of Petherick & Margaret Williams
12 April William s. of William & Susanna Tremayne
19 April Ann d. of William & Ann Hooper
25 April Mary base child of Mary Quick
23 May Ann d. of John & Margaret Walkey
30 May Elizabeth d. of Th[s] & Dorothy Salmon
7 June Peter s. of James & Ann Pollard
7 July Jane d. of Anthony-Henry & Thomazine Cock
13 July Catherine d. of Jonathan & Sarah Barret
19 Aug. Alice d. of Edward & Alice Hicks
24 Aug. Francis s. of Francis & Rebecca May
7 Sep. Ann d. of Richard & Ann Hawke
12 Sep. Ann d. of John & Margaret Cundy
3 Oct. Adam s. of Adam & Mary Thomson
10 Oct. John s. of William & Elizabeth Harris
15 Oct. William s. of Jonathan & Elizabeth Daw
18 Oct. Matilda d. of John & Ann Harris
17 Nov. Elizabeth d. of Robert & Elizabeth Drew
25 Nov. Joan d. of James & Jane Coad
10 Dec. Joseph s. of Thomas & Mary Troth
26 Dec. Jenefayre d. of Samuel & Mary Harris
1 Jan. Richard s. of Richard & Mary Williams
3 Jan. Joanna d. of William & Jane Williams
6 Jan. Richard s. of Richard & Alice Pascoe
6 Jan. Joan d. of Richard & Jane Veal
6 Feb. Jenefayre d. of Jude & Elizabeth May
11 Feb. Dorothy d. of M[r] Edward Arthur & Mary his wife
14 Feb. William s. of William & Jane Lorrington
28 Feb. Mary d. of Mathew & Margaret Oliver
4 Mar. Thomas s. of Thomas & Mary Sweet
8 Mar. John s. of William & Grace Evelyn
20 Mar. Elizabeth d. of Richard & Mary Raw

ANNO 1747.

31 Mar. Ruth d. of Thomas & Catherine Langdon
20 April Joanna d. of Thomas & Ann Keast
21 April William s. of John & Grace Buckingham
21 April Richard s. of Richard & Catherine Carne
21 April Thomas s. of Thomas & Joan James
26 April Philippa d. of John & Elizabeth Rawlyn
2 May Mary d. of John & Thomazine Rowse
5 May Mary d. of Robert & Mary Grigg
8 May Charity d. of William & Jane Capell
15 May Elizabeth d. of Philip & Elizabeth Gilbert
3 June Mary d. of John & Jane Bullen
17 June Mary d. of Nath. Driver of St. Sydwell's Exon & Jane his wife
27 June Edward s. of Edward & Ann Lawrey
2 Aug. Thomas s. of Thomas & Caroline Parkin
2 Aug. James base child of Thomazine Baseley
23 Aug. Johanna d. of Anthony Henry & Thomazine Cock
2 Sep. Isaac s. of Mark & Elizabeth Nichols
17 Sep. Henry s. of Henry & Constance Blight
30 Sep. Bernard s. of John & Jane Trescote
9 Oct. Richard base child of Alice Angove
23 Oct. Elizabeth d. of John & Susanna Husband
26 Oct. Anthony s. of Thomas & Rachael Keam
6 Nov. William s. of Walter & Jane Petherick
9 Nov. Johanna d. of Henry & Constance Tamblyn
10 Nov. Catherine d. of Richard & Eliz. Cundy

20 Nov. Joan d. of James & Eliz. May
20 Nov. Elizabeth d. of John & Honor Collwell
26 Nov. Catherine d. of Thomas & Thomasine Gass
7 Dec. Elizabeth d. of John & Elizabeth White
21 Dec. Henry s. of Henry & Elizabeth Veal
27 Dec. John s. of John & Lovedy Cowling
8 Jan. John s. of Jonathan & Catherine Rowse
16 Feb. Robert s. of Thomas Vyvyan Esq. & Lovedy his wife*
28 Feb. Arthur s. of Thomas & Catherine Langdon
4 Mar. Thomas s. of John & Mary Hicks

Anno 1748.

1 April Edward s. of Mr Edward Arthur & Mary his wife
10 April Francis s. of John & Elizabeth beth Helstone
10 April Elizabeth d. of John & Jane May
11 April Mary d. of John & Ann Best
22 April Elizabeth d. of John & Mary Peters
1 May Robert s. of Robert & Mary Bilkey
10 May Nicholas base child of Mary Quick
15 May Sarah d. of William & Susanna Tremain
22 May Mary d. of James & Sarah Stephens
5 June William s. of Wm & Mary Williams
16 June Mary d. of James & Mary Hawke
23 June Benjamin base child of Elizabeth Brey
8 July John & Elizabeth children of John & Elizabeth Tippett
15 July James s. of William & Ann White
6 Aug. Henry & Casely children of Witten & Trephosa Whiteford
23 Aug. Elizabeth d. of John & Grace Best

* This Thomas was the fourth son of Sir Rich. Vyvyan, Bart. (see note p. 48 ante), and mar. Loveday, dau. and h. of Nicholas Bogan. This Robert was their third son and d. unm.

26 Aug. Thomas s. of Thomas & Dorothy Salmon
5 Sep. Joseph s. of John & Hannah Husband
13 Sep. Jane d. of William & Jane Lorrington
21 Sep. Joan d. of William & Ann Hooper
22 Sep. Ann d. of James & Jane Coad
26 Oct. Thomas s. of Thomas & Mary Troth
7 Nov. John s. of John & Margaret Cundy
7 Nov. John s. of William & Mary Brabyn
7 Nov. Mary d. of William & Jane Capell
25 Nov. Joseph s. of Bartholomew & Joanna Brown
2 Dec. Mary d. of James & Ann Pollard
30 Dec. John s. of John & Margaret Walkey
6 Jan. William s. of Matthew & Margaret Oliver
27 Jan. Mary d. of Richard Davis (a soldier) & Mary his wife
5 Feb. Stephen s. of John & Ann Harris
6 Feb. Margaret d. of Andrew & Amey Maubyn
8 Feb. Thomas s. of Mr Thomas Morris & Margaret his wife
8 Feb. Robert s. of Robert & Mary Grigg
19 Feb. Henry s. of Henry & Frances Oxenham
22 Feb. Richard s. of Richard & Ann Jane
24 Feb. Martin s. of George & Ann Strongman
24 Feb. Elizabeth d. of Jonathan & Sarah Barrett
26 Feb. Howard s. of John & Lovedy Cowling
10 Mar. William s. of Jonathan & Catherine Rowse
22 Mar. Elizabeth d. of Nicholas & Eliz. Husband

Anno 1749.

28 Mar. Mary d. of John & Elizabeth White
29 Mar. Ann d. of Richard & Elizabeth Husband
4 May Eliza d. of John & Elizabeth Rawling

12 May James s. of John & Thomasine Rowse
20 May Mary d. of Richard & Elizabeth Evelyn
26 May Ann Martyn base child of Ann Sprey now wife of Jn° Martyn ye reputed father
29 May Peter s. of Richard & Mary Raw
2 July Jane d. of John & Jane Bullen
6 Aug. Thomas s. of Francis & Rebecka May
20 Aug. Honor d. of James & Honor Collwell
20 Aug. Jane d. of William & Grace Evelyn
8 Oct. Ann d. of Richard & Elizabeth Cundy
10 Oct. Richard s. of Henry & Elizabeth Veal
29 Oct. Catherine d. of John & Mary Lamb
5 Nov. Jenefayre d. of Jude & Eliz. May
6 Nov. William s. of John & Ann Martin
26 Nov. Andrew s. of Andrew & Elizabeth Tomm
13 Dec. Catherine d. of Richard & Catherine York
15 Dec. William s. of James & Susanna Hunson
25 Dec. Susanna d. of Thomas & Caroline Parkyn
25 Dec. William s. of Richard & Mary Davis a soldier
15 Jan. Charles Jacob s. of John & Susanna Husband
26 Jan. William s. of Mr. Edward Arthur & Mary his wife
2 Feb. Elizabeth d. of Samuell & Mary Harris
4 Feb. William s. of Jonathan & Mary Chapman
4 Feb. Mary d. of Whiten Whiteford dec. & Trephosa his wife
26 Feb. Elizabeth d. of Benjamin & Elizabeth Jones
2 Mar. Elizabeth d. of Thomas & Thomazine Gass
8 Mar. John s. of Henry & Constance Tamblyn
14 Mar. Mary d. of Mark & Elizabeth Nichols
23 Mar. Hannah d. of John & Mary Tomm

ANNO 1750.

26 Mar. John s. of Christopher & Honour Warne*
4 April Mary d. of Robert & Mary Turner, a soldier
13 April Walter s. of Walter & Jane Petherick
16 April Ruth d. of Richard & Jane Veal
16 April Mary d. of Robert & Ann England
17 April Stephen s. of Thomas & Mary Sweet
22 April Grace d. of Thomas & Mary Westcote
25 April Benjamin s. of John & Mary Strongman
30 April Jennifayre d. of Ralph & Mary Bussow
5 June Joseph s. of Humphry & Elizabeth Toms
20 June Ann d. of William & Mary Skinner
27 June George s. of Jonathan & Elizabeth Daw
6 July George s. of Thomas & Catherine Langdon
5 Aug. John s. of John & Mary Treherr
7 Aug. Joseph Raddon s. of Petherick & Margaret Williams
31 Aug. Ann d. of Edward Harris (a soldier) and Ann his wife
14 Sep. William s. of Wm Hornbey (drummer in Coll. Conway's Reg^t) & Frances his wife
16 Sep. James s. of Thomas & Ann Keast
21 Sep. Elizabeth d. of William & Elizabeth Harris
28 Sep. Henry s. of Thomas & Joan James
1 Oct. Elizabeth d. of Thomas & Jane Giles
5 Oct. Mary d. of John & Mary Hicks
22 Oct. Benjamin s. of Benjamin & Jane Kent
12 Nov. Mary d. of Solomon & Mary Baseley
12 Nov. Ann d. of John & Florence Warne
12 Nov. William s. of William & Ann Brewer
12 Nov. Jane d. of Jonathan & Catherine Rowse

* Mr. Christopher Warne was elected one of the twelve men in place of Robert Hoblyn, Esq., deceased, 1757. (Green Book.)

13 Nov. Eleanor d. of Thomas & Frances Tamblyn
25 Nov. John s. of William & Jane Lorrington
30 Nov. James s. of William & Susanna Tremain
21 Dec. Mary base child of Elizabeth Nichols
30 Dec. Margery d. of John & Elizabeth Tippett
4 Jan. Francis s. of Francis & Grace Trelevin
8 Jan. Elizabeth Hawke d. of James & Elizabeth May
13 Jan. Joanna d. of Richard & Alice Pascoe
9 Feb. William s. of William & Hannah Harry
20 Feb. Ann d. of Francis & Grace Avery
22 Feb. John s. of Henry & Frances Oxenham
15 Mar. Honor d. of Thomas & Dorothy Salmon
17 Mar. John s. of John & Jane Pearce
23 Mar. Benjamin s. of Bartholomew & Joanna Brown

ANNO 1751.

8 April Michael s. of Richard & Elizabeth Cornish
28 April John Brewer s. of Andrew & Amey Maubyn
16 May Jennefayre d. of Richard & Ann Endyvean
27 May James s. of George & Elizabeth Champion
27 May Jane d. of John & Mary Tonkin
2 June James s. of John & Elizabeth Helstone
9 June Ann d. of Henry & Elizabeth Veal
4 July Thomas s. of Thomas & Sarah Drew
5 July Robert s. of Robert & Elizabeth Drew*
17 July Charles base child of Thomazine Basely
19 July Richard s. of Andrew & Elizabeth Tomin
30 July Michael base child of Elizabeth Blake
2 Aug. James s. of James & Honor Collwill
14 Aug. Henry s. of William & Ann Harvey
29 Aug. John s. of William & Mary Tremain *al's* Cockyn
17 Sep. John s. of William & Jane Liddicote *al's* Gregor
18 Sep. Mary and Sarah daughters of William & Ann Lanyon
21 Sep. Joanna d. of Mr Edward Arthur & Mary his wife
29 Sep. William s. of John & Elizabeth Rawling
29 Sep. Mary d. of Jonathan & Sarah Barrett
1 Nov. James s. of Robert & Mary Bilkey
11 Nov. Thomas s. of Thomas & Mary Westcote
18 Nov. Elizabeth base child of Elizabeth Rickard
10 Dec. Elizabeth d. of John & Mary Traer
16 Dec. Ann d. of John & Ann Harris
23 Dec. John & Nicholas sons of John & Florence Warne
1 Jan. William s. of John & Jane Bullen
6 Jan. Richard s. of Richard & Jane Veal
11 Jan. Mary d. of John & Hannah Husband
20 Jan. Ralph s. of Jude & Elizabeth May
31 Jan. Mary d. of John & Mary Strongman
2 Feb. Margaret d. of John & Margaret Cundy
14 Feb. John s. of Samuel & Mary Harris
14 Feb. Elizabeth d. of John & Elizabeth Crapp
21 Feb. Samuel s. of Ralph & Mary Bussow
21 Feb. Richard s. of Richard & Mary Dell (a soldier)
1 Mar. John s. of Edmund & Mary Varcoe

ANNO 1752.

27 Mar. John base child of Elizabeth Tomm
28 Mar. Benjamin s. of Bartholomew & Joanna Brown
30 Mar. Mary d. of Richard & Elizabeth Cundy
30 Mar. Mary d. of George & Ann Strongman

* Mr. Robert Drew was one of the twelve men in 1746. (Green Book.)

2 April Thomas s. of Thomas & Catherine Langdon
5 April Mary d. of Thomas & Jane Giles
7 April Nicholas s. of William & Jane Williams
17 April John s. of Michael & Elizabeth Richards
25 April Thomas s. of Henry & Constance Tamblyn
27 April Humphry s. of John & Ann Martyn
7 May Mary d. of James & Joan Tabb
7 May Richard s. of Richard & Elizabeth Evelyn
16 May Thomas s. of James & Sarah Stephens
18 May William s. of William & Mary Skinner
20 May James s. of James & Mary Callaway
23 May Benjamin s. of Benjamin & Elizabeth Jones
29 May Richard s. of William & Mary Hicks
3 June James s. of Humphry & Susanna England
21 June William s. of Andrew & Amey Maubyn
22 June Mary d. of Richard & Mary Raw
28 June Elizabeth d. of Francis & Rebeckah May
3 July Elizabeth d. of Robert & Mary Grigg
17 July William base child of Jane Hendy
29 July Elizabeth d. of Thomas & Susanna Brewer
1 Aug. John s. of John & Honor Pill
7 Aug. Humphry s. of Robert & Ann England
2 Oct. William s. of Richard & Elizabeth Luke
14 Oct. Susanna d. of Nicholas & Mary Liddicote
29 Oct. Martha d. of Wm & Jane Liddicote *alias* Gregor
1 Nov. John s. of Jonathan & Mary Chapman
1 Nov. Benjamin s. of John & Thomazine Rowse
8 Nov. Jane d. of Richard & Susanna Rowse
20 Nov. Joan d. of Isaac & Elizabeth Grigg
21 Nov. Humphry s. of Humphry & Elizabeth Tomms
25 Nov. Jane d. of William & Ann Harvey
27 Nov. Mary & Agnes children of Henry & Agnes Willsford
6 Dec. John base child of Ann Lovell
8 Dec. Jane d. of James & Mary Hawke
23 Dec. Thomas s. of Thos & Thomazine Gass

ANNO 1753.

9 Feb. Jane d. of Thomas & Ann Wilson
18 Feb. James s. of Francis & Grace Avery
23 Feb. John s. of Henry & Elizabeth Veal
6 Mar. John s. of James & Honor Collwill
9 Mar. Arthur s. of Andrew & Elizabeth Tomm
9 Mar. Ann d. of James & Elizabeth May
11 Mar. John s. of William & Mary Rawshaw
12 Mar. Jane d. of William & Mary Brabyn
21 Mar. Ann d. of Degory & Alice Trescote
3 April Frances d. of Geo. & Elizabeth Champion
6 April Mary d. of Richard & Ann Jane
15 April Mary d. of Thomas & Caroline Parkyn
21 April John s. of Pascoe & Elizabeth Davis
23 April Walter s. of John & Elizabeth Tippett
15 May William s. of John & Margaret Walkey
20 May Elizabeth d. of Richard & Mary Oliver of Probus
21 May Emy d. of Bartholomew & Joanna Brown
28 May James s. of Walter & Jane Petherick
1 June John s. of Thomas & Sarah Drew
1 June Anthony s. of Thomas & Honor Kneebone of Gwenapp
8 June John s. of John & Alice Cornish
11 June Alice d. of John & Ann Martyn
16 June Ann d. of Theophilus & Eliza Williams

24 June Nicholas s. of John & Mary Tonkyn
24 June Peter s. of Peter & Eleanor Parkinson (a soldier)
3 July Mary d. of James & Jane Coad
6 July Abraham s. of Mark & Elizabeth Nichols
8 July Robert son s. of Richard & Elizabeth Kent
10 July Jennefaire d. of Samuell & Mary Harris
20 July William s. of James & Ann Pearce
27 July Henry s. of Thomas & Joan James
2 Aug. Thomas s. of Philip & Mary Cornish
31 Aug. John s. of Humphry & Mary Luke
6 Sep. Frances d. of Henry & Frances Oxenham
12 Sep. Jennefayre d. of Richard & Mary Veal
14 Sep. Thomas s. of Thomas & Elizabeth Rundall
29 Sep. Mary d. of John & Florence Warne
13 Oct. James s. of James & Mary Callaway
19 Nov. Jane d. of John & Jane Pearce
2 Dec. Martha d. of John & Mary Traer
26 Dec. Catherine d. of Humphry & Susanna England
27 Dec. Thomas s. of Edmond & Mary Varcoe
27 Dec. Mary base child of Grace Hailborne

Anno 1754.

1 Jan. Anne d. of Andrew & Amey Mabyn
14 Jan. Er s. of Thomas & Jane Giles
19 Jan. Ann d. of William & Ann Lanyon
26 Jan. Richard s. of Richard & Elizabeth Cornish
26 Jan. Joseph & Benjamin children of John & Mary Strongman
30 Jan. Frances d. of William & Mary Ivey
2 Feb. Mary d. of William & Mary Retallock
22 Feb. William & Ann children of Thomas & Dorothy Salmon
4 Mar. Blanch d. of William & Ann Tubb
22 Mar. William s. of Nicholas & Mary Liddicote
11 April James s. of Jonathan & Sarah Barret
15 April William s. of Philip & Alice Mark
5 May William s. of William & Sarah Ellery
8 May William s. of William & Elizabeth Hicks
10 May Elizabeth d. of Charles & Elizabeth Pearce
13 May George & Elizabeth children of James & Ann Pollard
19 May Ann d. of Richard & Ann Endyvean
22 May Jane d. of Richard & Elizabeth Cundy
24 May Catherine d. of Thomas & Amey Solomon
3 June Jane d. of John & Elizabeth Rawlin
29 June William s. of Thomas & Catherine Langdon
5 July Ann d. of Philip & Margaret Harris
19 July John s. of Richard & Susanna Rowse
19 July John s. of Richard & Elizabeth Luke
18 Aug. Francis & Alice children of Degory & Alice Trescott
23 Aug. Mary d. of William & Mary Skinner
23 Aug. Sarah d. of John & Susanna Husband
22 Sep. Ann d. of Thomas & Mary Sweet
26 Sep. David s. of Benjamin & Elizabeth Joans
6 Oct. Mary Robarth d. of Humphry & Elizabeth Thoms
13 Oct. George s. of George & Ann Strongman
19 Oct. Johanna d. of Ralph & Mary Buse
20 Oct. William s. of John & Elizabeth Mean
25 Oct. Jane d. of Robert & Elizabeth Drew
27 Oct. Ebbott d. of James & Joan Tabb
1 Nov. Margaret & Johanna children of Bernard & Margaret Wilsford
18 Nov. Johanna d. of Isaac & Elizabeth Grigg

18 Nov. Jane d. of Robert & Mary Bilkey
19 Nov. William s. of George & Jane Hicks
20 Nov. John s. of Henry & Constance Tamblyn
12 Dec. Jane base child of Ann Ellery
12 Dec. Mary d. of Richard & Mary Jolly
25 Dec. Martha d. of Philip & Mary Harvey
27 Dec. Honor d. of James & Honor Colwill

ANNO 1755.

10 Jan. Frances d. of William & Elizabeth Dixson
19 Jan. William s. of Pascoe & Elizabeth Davies
2 Feb. Susanna d. of Jude & Elizabeth May
5 Feb. John s. of James & Ann Pearce
7 Feb. Mark s. of George & Elizabeth Raw
19 Feb. Benjamin s. of John & Thomasine Rowse
23 Feb. William s. of William & Jane Lorington
31 Mar. John s. of Humphry & Susanna England
12 April Ann d. of James & Elizabeth May
19 May Charles s. of Theophilus & Elizabeth Williams
19 May Elizabeth d. of John & Alice Cornish
25 May William s. of William & Mary Ivey
20 May Loveday d. of one Jane Wilmot not of ye parish
8 June Elizabeth d. of Richard & Mary Veall
22 June Michael s. of Michael & Elizabeth Richards
24 June John s. of Edward & Ann Pearce
29 June Mary d. of John & Margaret Cundy
5 July Mary d. of Thomas & Sarah Drew
6 July Rebecka d. of Richard & Elizabeth Evelyn
13 July Rose d. of Robert & Mary Grigg
10 Aug. James s. of John & Honour Pill
17 Aug. William s. of Charles & Elizabeth Pearse
31 Aug. William s. of William & Ann Brabyn
7 Sep. James s. of John & Elizabeth Typpet
17 Oct. William s. of John & Margaret Walkey
8 Nov. Philip s. of Philip & Mary Cornish
16 Nov. Thomas s. of John & Mary Trare
17 Nov. Margaret d. of Thomas & Mary Mill
17 Nov. Edmond s. of Edmond & Mary Varcoe
18 Nov. John s. of Ann England
10 Dec. Philip d. of Francis & Rebecka May
12 Dec. Joseph s. of George & Mary Sowdon
17 Dec. John s. of John & Dorkas Gill
27 Dec. Margaret d. of William & Sarah Ellery
31 Dec. Jonathan s. of Jonathan & Mary Chapman
31 Dec. Rachael d. of William & Jane Liddicot *al's* Grigor

ANNO 1756.

1 Jan. James s. of James & Sarah Stephens
6 Jan. Ann d. of Richard & Elizabeth Chapman
23 Jan. Christiana base child of Grace Cock
2 Feb. John s. of Richard & Elizabeth Cornish
2 Feb. Luke s. of Francis & Grace Avery
4 Feb. John s. of Richard & Mary Raw
6 Feb. William s. of Samuel & Thomasine Clymos
19 Feb. John & Joseph children of Thomas & Jane Giles
22 Feb. Thomas s. of Nicholas & Mary Liddicote
5 Mar. Elizabeth d. of Pascow & Eliz. Davies
7 Mar. Joseph s. of Joseph & Mary Tonkin
13 Mar. Mary d. of Degory & Alice Trescot
19 Mar. Mark s. of Mark & Elizabeth Nichols

20 Mar. Jane & Ann daus. of Philip & Jane Strongman

21 Mar. John s. of Philip & Mary Harvey

2 April John s. of William & Elizabeth Hicks

16 April Elizabeth d. of Bartholomew & Joanna Brown

12 May Martha d. of John & Grace Webber

14 May Frances d. of James & Jane Coad

26 May Henry s. of John & Susanna Husband

28 May John s. of Samuel & Mary Harris

28 May Susanna d. of Thomas & Susanna Brewer

5 June James s. of Robert & Eliz. Drew

7 June Jane Chub d. of George & Elizabeth Champion

9 June John s. of John & Mary Peters

12 June Ann d. of Richard & Jane Bullock

4 July Catherine base child of Ann Jolly

11 July Ann d. of John & Jane Bullen

16 July Joan d. of Henry & Constance Tamblyn

23 July John s. of Philip & Alice Mark

6 Aug. Elizabeth d. of Nicholas & Sarah Clymo

19 Sep. William s. of Richard & Ann Jane

20 Sep. Ann d. of M[r] Thomas Williams & Mary his wife

26 Sep. Elizabeth d. of James & Ann Pearce

3 Oct. Grace d. of Richard & Susanna Rowse

3 Nov. Elizabeth d. of Humphry & Mary Luke

19 Nov. Margaret d. of Andrew & Amey Mabyn

21 Nov. Elizabeth d. of William & Mary Skinner

21 Nov. Jane d. of Edward & Ann Pearse

22 Nov. Julyan d. of Richard & Catherine Morlyn

23 Nov. Florence d. of Philip & Margaret Harris

27 Dec. Mary d. of Edward & Abigal Merefield

ANNO 1757.

1 Jan. Ann d. of John & ffiorence Warne

3 Jan. James s. of William & Mary Ivey

13 Mar. Elizabeth d. of Thomas & Elizabeth Veryan

20 Mar. Ann d. of James & Honour Colwel

10 April Thomas s. of Ralph & Mary Buse

10 April John s. of George & Ann Strongman

17 April Samuel s. of Theophilus & Eliz. Williams

6 May Samuel s. of Thomas & Amey Soloman

11 May Joseph s. of John & Mary Trare

15 May Mary d. of William & Mary Pound

30 May Elizabeth Westlick d. of Richard & Elizabeth Kent

30 May Mary d. of James & Joan Tab

31 May William s. of Humphry & Susanna England

3 June John s. of John & Ann Arthur

17 June Sarah d. of Richard & Sarah Hawke

19 June Frances d. of John & Alice Cornish

25 June John s. of James & Joan Stephens

26 June Jane d. of Isaac & Elizabeth Grigg

10 July Henry s. of Thomas & Catherine Langdon

30 Aug. Arthur base child of Ann Jolly

2 Sep. Mary d. of Robert & Grace Ceame

17 Sep. John s. of John & Catherine Whitford

30 Sep. Samuel s. of Benjamin & Elizabeth Joans

7 Oct. Humphry s. of John & Ann Martin

7 Oct. Thomas s. of William & Catherine Rawlings*

* This Thomas succeeded his father at Saunder's Hill, Padstow. He was High Sheriff of Cornwall in 1803, and one of the deputy wardens of the Stannaries. He married in 1782 Margery eldest dau. and co-heir of Thomas Price, Esq., of Tregolds, by whom he had several children.

9 Oct. Catherine d. of Thomas & Mary Mill
25 Oct. Thomas s. of Mr Tho. & Amelia Naish
28 Oct. John s. of Degory & Alice Triscot
7 Nov. Martha d. of James & Jane Coad
7 Nov. Elizabeth d. of Rich. & Margaret Grigg
21 Nov. William s. of Peter & Margaret Retallick
21 Nov. Ann d. Thomas & Sarah Drew
21 Nov. Ann d. of Thomas & Thomazine Buckingham
23 Nov. Jane d. of William & Jane Lorrington
28 Dec. James s. of John & Mary Drew

ANNO 1758.

6 Jan. Elizabeth d. of John & Elizabeth Mill
6 Jan. Ann d. of Thomas & Dorothy Salmon

A NEW REGISTER OF BAPTISMS, BEGINNING JANUARY 1758.

3 Jan. Alice ye d. of John & Elizabeth Tippet
6 Jan. Elizabeth ye d. of John & Elizabeth Mill
6 Jan. Ann ye d. of Thomas & Dorothy Salmon
11 Feb. John ye s. of John & Susannah Bulling
15 Feb. Joseph ye base child of Jenefaire Retallack
15 Feb. Lewis base child of Mary Coombe
5 Mar. Ann ye d. of John & Mary Peters
24 Mar. Judeth d. of Richard & Elizabeth Tomm
27 Mar. John ye s. of William & Mary Retallack
27 Mar. Ann ye d. of Philip & Alice Mark
27 Mar. Margaret ye d. of John & Blanch Tamlyn
27 Mar. John ye s. of William & Elizabeth Perkin
28 Mar. Catherine ye d. of William & Ann Brabin
7 April Grace ye d. of Philip & Mary Cornish
12 April William ye s. of William & Jane Lyddacoat
23 April Martha ye d. of James & Honour Colwell
27 April Nicholas ye s. of Thomas & Jane Giles
15 May George ye s. of George & Elizabeth Champion
15 May Mary ye d. of Michaell & Elizabeth Tanner
9 May Richard ye s. of Richard & Susannah Rowse
26 May Thomas ye s. of William & Elizabeth Hicks
9 June Susannah Jane ye d. of James & Ann Pearse
9 June Mary ye d. of Richard & Ann Edevan
21 June Thomas ye s. of Thomas & Mary Williams
2 July Mary ye d. of Richard & Elizabeth Gummow
7 July Mary ye d. of Robert & Grace Pendeen
7 July Ann base child of Ann Ellery
28 July William ye s. of Edmund & Mary Varcove
30 July Francis ye s. of Henry & Constance Tamlyn
30 July Nicholas ye s. of Nicholas & Mary Lyddacoat
1 Sep. Grace d. of Richard & Jane Bullock
8 Oct. Mary ye d. of William & Thomazin Swan
16 Oct. Francis ye s. of Nicholas & Sarah Clemow
24 Sep. Johan ye d. of Mr Robert & Elizabeth Drew
11 Oct. Elizabeth ye d. of Richard & Elizabeth Chipman
13 Oct. John ye s. of John & Grace Webber
20 Oct. John ye s. of George & Eliza beth Rowe
19 Nov. Humphry ye s. of William & Mary Ivey
20 Nov. Joseph ye s. of Richard & Mary Rowe
20 Nov. John ye s. of Thomas & Susannah Brewer

21 Nov. William s. of William & Ruth Crapp
11 Dec. Loveday d. of Mr John & Loveday Soaper
12 Dec. James s. of John & Mary Trayer

ANNO 1759.

2 Jan. Arthur s. of Richard & Elizabeth Cornish
7 Jan. Mary d. of John & Honour Pill
12 Jan. James s. of Edmund & Grace Bullock
12 Jan. William s. of Pascoe & Elizabeth Davis
30 Jan. Henry s. of Richard & Elizabeth Basely
2 Feb. William s. of Hezekiah & Jane Bunt
5 Feb. Jane Warne d. of Mr Wm & Catherine Rawlings
5 Feb. Philip s. of John & Margaret Cundy
11 Feb. Margaret d. of Philip & Margaret Harris
16 Feb. Philip s. of Humphry & Susanna England
15 Mar. Francis s. of Francis & Grace Olver
25 Mar. John s. of Richard & Elizabeth Eveling
1 April Margaret d. of Philip & Mary Harvey
29 April Bridget d. of John & Elizabeth Stephens
9 May Andrew s. of Thomas & Jane Giles
20 May Richard Cowling s. of Richard & Mary Veale
25 May Elizabeth d. of Peter & Elizabeth Hawke
31 May John s. of James & Elizabeth Arscott
4 June Thomas s. of William & Elizabeth Hicks
1 July Richard s. of Edward & Ann Pearce
6 July James s. of Philip & Ann Strongman
4 Aug. Thomas Tregenna* s. of Mr Thomas & Grace Hamley
12 Aug. William s. of Bartholomew & Johanna Brown
2 Sep. Catherine d. of Thomas & Johan Williams
19 Sep. Joseph s. of Mr Joseph & Mary Merifield
12 Oct. Ann d. of John & Mary White
19 Oct. Jennefaire d. of John & Grace Jane
18 Nov. Paska d. of William & Ann Lunoine
18 Nov. James s. of James & Honour Colwell
19 Nov. Johan d. of Edward & Abigail Merifield
19 Nov. Anne d. of William & Mary Glanville
19 Nov. Grace d. of Richard & Catherine Martin
20 Nov. Ann d. of John & Catherine Whitford
30 Nov. James s. of Andrew & Amey Mason
30 Nov. John s. of William & Elizabeth Gass
11 Dec. Frances d. of Digory & Alice Triscott
26 Dec. Honour d. of Ralph & Mary Busso
30 Dec. Paska base child d. of Thomasine Clemo

ANNO 1760.

1 Jan. Ann d. of James & Joan Stephens
2 Jan. Sarah d. of William & Mary Pound
7 Jan. Charles s. of Nicholas & Sarah Clemmo
7 Jan. Philippa d. of John & Alice Cornish
9 Jan. Eleanor d. of Richard & Elizabeth Cundey
20 Jan. William s. of Humphrey & Elizabeth Tomms
17 Feb. Thomas s. of Thomas & Amey Solomon
17 Feb. Mary d. of Thomas & Mary Williams
20 Feb. John s. of Mr John & Loveday Soaper
20 Feb. John s. of Richard & Sarah Hawke
21 Feb. Mary d. of Peter & Margaret Retallack

* He was Vicar of St. Ervan and St. Eval and was buried at the former place, in which church is a stone inscribed to his memory by John Clode Braddon, gent. of Camelford, his wife's nephew, he having married Mary, dau. of John Braddon of Camelford, and sister of Henry Braddon of Skisdon Lodge. She died 12 Dec., 1813, aged 57, buried with an inscribed slab at St. Ervan; and he died without issue 23 Dec., 1818.

27 Feb. Jane d. of George & Grace Brown
12 Mar. William s. of Mr William & Katherine Rawlings
7 April Mary d. of Jonathan & Mary Chipman
8 April Elizabeth d. of Richard & Jane Rowse
8 April Mary d. of Edmund & Mary Varcoe
8 April John s. of Elizabeth Tippet
15 April Mary d. of John & Grace Francis
15 April Bridget d. of John & Grace Webber
23 April John s. of William & Jane Lydacote
2 May Thomas s. of Thomas & Mary Mill
4 May Elizabeth d. of Robert & Grace Keame
24 May Richard s. of James & Ann Pearce
27 May Rachael d. of William & Thomazine Swan
28 May Michael s. of James & Margaret Jane
31 May Joyce d. of John & Mary Luney
20 June Elizabeth d. of Richard & Elizabeth Gummow
10 July Mary d. of John & Margaret Walkey
20 July Ann Brown d. of John & Margaret Creveth
26 July Nance d. of Nicholas & Mary Lydacote
5 Aug. William s. of William & Mary Oliver
6 Aug. Humphrey s. of Humphrey & Susanna England
17 Aug. Michael s. of Benjamin & Elizabeth Jones
17 Aug. Dorothy Saundry d. of John & Blanch Tamlyn
24 Aug. William s. of William & Elizabeth Perking
31 Aug. William s. of Mr William & Frances Lawrence
28 Sep. Thomas s. of John & Joan Symmons
25 Oct. Philippa d. of Peter & Elizabeth Hawke
17 Oct. Walter s. of Philip & Margaret Harris
5 Nov. Wm s. of James & Mary Tabb
7 Nov. Dorothy d. of James & Elizabeth Arscott
16 Nov. Elizabeth d. of John & Mary Peters
17 Nov. James s. of Richard & Elizabeth Chipman
17 Nov. Avis d. of William & Ruth Crapp
17 Nov. James s. of James & Elizabeth May
19 Nov. William s. of William & Mary Retallack
7 Dec. Robert s. of William & Mary Ivey
28 Dec. Alice d. of James & Sarah Stephens

ANNO 1761.

6 Jan. Catherine d. of Richard & Alice Hicks
14 Jan. Francis s. of Francis & Grace Olver
18 Jan. Joseph s. of George & Elizabeth Champion
25 Jan. Richard s. of Pascoe & Elizabeth Davies
8 Mar. Mary d. of Robert & Grace Edeveon
11 Mar. Thomas s. of Thomas & Susannaha Brewer
24 Mar. Elizabeth d. of Peter & Mary Cornish
24 Mar. William s. of John* & Elizabeth Tippet
24 Mar. Frances d. of George & Ann Strongman
24 Mar. Joice d. of John & Mary White
25 Mar. Bernard s. of Henry & Constance Tamlyn
31 Mar. John s. of John & Mary Bond
11 May Mary d. of William & Mary Glanvill
11 May Elizabeth d. of Peter & Mary Hervey
11 May Mary d. of John & Elizabeth Lewarne
3 June William s. of Mr William† & Catherine Rawlings
9 June Digory s. of Digory & Charity Prout
21 June Mary d. of John & Elizabeth Stephens

* John Tippet, appointed Governor of the Workhouse in 1766.

† He was of Exeter Coll., Oxford, took his M.A., and was for fifty years vicar of Padstow. He married in 1787 Susanna, dau. of Peter Salmon, Esq., and died 20 Dec., 1836, leaving issue, for whom see Sir J. B. Burke's *Landed Gentry*.

1 July Margaret & Ann daughters of James & Honour Colwill
9 Aug. Angelet d. of Edward & Ann Pearse
16 Sep. Elizabeth d. of Richard & Mary Bettinson
27 Sep. Sarah d. of John & Grace Joell
22 Nov. William s. of John & Mary Tonking
23 Nov. Michael s. of James & Ann Pearce
27 Nov. Catherine d. of Richard & Elizabeth Basely
27 Nov. Joyce d. of John & Ann Martyn
1 Dec. Johanna d. of Mr William & Ann Hamley
7 Dec. John s. of Mr William & Frances Lawrence
8 Dec. Benjamin s. of James & Mary Snell
12 Dec. John s. of Richard & Catherine Murling
12 Dec. John s. of Edmund & Grace Bullock
18 Dec. Robert s. of Peter & Elizabeth Hawke
21 Dec. Ann d. of William & Elizabeth Hicks

ANNO 1762.

1 Jan. William s. of William & Thomasin Swan
25 Jan. Julian d. of Julian Davey of*
25 Jan. John s. of Jane Harris
30 Jan. Thomas s. of Thomas & Johan Williams
3 Feb. Mary d. of William & Elizabeth Ford
21 Feb. Grace d. of George & Grace Brown
24 Feb. William s. of William & Elizabeth Gass
26 Feb. Catherine d. of Humphry & Susanna England
27 Feb. John s. of William & Jane Lyddicott
5 Mar. John s. of Peter & Elizabeth Courtney
12 Mar. Catherine d. of Thomas & Jane Giles
15 Mar. Flore d. of Thomas & Wilmot Trethewey
1 April James s. of James & Johan Stephens

* Blank.

2 April Daniel s. of Richard & Mary Veal
8 April John s. of John & Elizabeth Stephens
12 April Honour d. of Ralph & Mary Busso
12 April Grace d. of William & Sarah Elworthy
13 April Thomas s. of John & Catherine Whitford
19 April Anthony s. of John & Honour Pill
25 April Joseph s. of William & Dorothy Harris
2 May Michael s. of John & Alice Cornish
5 May Jane d. of Mr John & Johan Simmons
16 May Richard s. of Peter & Margaret Retallack
5 June Ann d. of William & Mary Ivey
23 June Ann d. of Philip & Margaret Harris
21 June Elizabeth d. of Thomas & Catherine Langdon
18 July Mary d. of Joseph & Mary Merrifield
28 July John s. of William & Elizabeth Lewarne
13 Aug. Richard s. of Richard & Catherine Hicks
20 Aug. John s. of William & Mary Retallack
3 Sep. Gertrude d. of William & Mary Oliver
3 Sep. William s. of Richard & Susanna Rowse
16 Sep. Blanch d. of Thomas & Mary Williams
17 Sep. Richard s. of Richard & Elizabeth Chipman
20 Sep. Ann d. of John & Mary Bond
26 Sep. Robert s. of Robert & Mary Mannel
26 Sep. Elizabeth d. of William & Elizabeth Perking
1 Oct. Richard s. of John & Margaret Walkey
3 Oct. Rebecka d. of Bartholomew & Johanna Brown
10 Oct. James s. of James & Elizabeth Arscott
21 Nov. Margaret d. of Thomas & Mary Mill
21 Nov. Richard s. of Richard & Elizabeth Luke

22 Nov. John s. of John & Florence Warn
22 Nov. John s. of John & Elizabeth Morris
23 Nov. Martha d. of Michael & Martha Basely
24 Nov. Richard s. of Thomas & Amey Solomon
26 Nov. Elizabeth d. of Theophilus & Elizabeth Williams
27 Dec. Martha d. of Jonathan & Mary Chipman
29 Dec. William s. of William & Margery Thomas

ANNO 1763.

5 Jan. Alice d. of John & Hannah Rowe
11 Feb. John s. of Philip & Mary Cornish
11 Feb. Samuel s. of James & Margaret Jane
16 Feb. James s. of John & Mary White
19 Feb. Walter s. of Paskoe & Elizabeth Davies
4 Mar. William s. of John & Jane Pinch
5 Mar. Alice d. of Digory & Alice Truscott
6 Mar. James s. of James & Elizabeth May
25 Mar. William s. of William Midleton a soldier & Elizabeth his wife
4 April Charles & Richard sons of Hezekiah & Jane Bunt
5 April Ann d. of Thomas & Thomazine Gass
24 April John s. of Francis & Eudith Hawkey
21 May Richard s. of Robert & Grace Keame
23 May Richard s. of Richard & Elizabeth Gummow
11 June Elizabeth d. of Thomas & Mary Westcott
17 June Thomas s. of Mr. John Quick* & Jane his wife
19 June Ann d. of John & Elizabeth Stephens
24 June Richard s. of Richard & Sarah Bearsley
26 June Thomas & Anne children of Joseph & Patience Hancock

* John Quick, Esq., one of the twelve men in 1762: Green Book.

12 Aug. Grace d. of Edmund & Mary Varcoe
21 Aug. John s. of John & Blanch Tamlyn
21 Sep. Anne d. of James & Anne Pearce
1 Oct. John s. of Benjamin & Elizabeth Jones
2 Oct. Patience d. of William & Ruth Crapp
10 Oct. Catherine d. of Mr. William & Catherine Rawlings
28 Oct. Grace d. of Peter & Elizabeth Courtency
20 Nov. Thomas s. of Edward & Ann Pearse
20 Nov. John s. of John & Mary Peters
20 Nov. John s. of John & Margaret Buckingham
25 Dec. John Antren s. of John & Grace Jane
27 Dec. Elizabeth d. of John & Ann Martin

ANNO 1764.

4 Jan. Elizabeth ye d. of James & Mary Snell
6 Jan. Hannah ye d. of William* & Thomazin Swan
8 Jan. Sarah d. of William† & Mary Ivey
30 Jan. William s. of Nicholas & Sarah Clemowe
17 Feb. Richard s. of John & Catherine Whitford
27 Feb. Joseph s. of William & Elizabeth Hicks
9 Mar. John s. of Richard & Alice Hicks
30 Mar. Sarah d. of William & Ann Lanyon
13 April Elizabeth d. of William & Elizabeth Drew
18 April John s. of William & Ann Liddicoat
20 April James s. of James & Margaret Jane
20 April Ann d. of Peter & Elizabeth Hawke
23 April James s. of John & Elizabeth Morish
23 April Thomas s. of George & Elizabeth Rawe

* William Swanne was Churchwarden in 1770: Green Book.

† William Ivey was one of the parish overseers in 1780: Green Book.

23 April Elizabeth d. of William & Elizabeth Lewarne
23 April John s. of Philip & Ann Harris
18 May John s. of Richard & Elizabeth Chipman
17 May Nancy d. of William & Dorothy Blight
11 June John s. of William & Dorothy Harris
11 June Thomas s. of Richard & Mary Bettinson
20 June William s. of Thomas & Susan Brewer
3 July Edward s. of Edward & Martha Hodge
22 July Elizabeth d. of George & Grace Browne
14 July Lewis s. of William & Honour Blight
4 Sep. Philip s. of Philip & Mary Harvey
28 Sep. Reuben s. of William & Margaret Thomas
25 Oct. Edward s. of Thomas* & Mary Hamley
22 Oct. Mary d. of John & Joan Symonds
15 Nov. John s. of John & Hannah Rowe
18 Nov. Nancey d. of John & Elizabeth Stephens
19 Nov. John s. of William & Sarah Ellery
19 Nov. William s. of William & Ann Williams
19 Nov. Susanna d. of Richard & Catherine Murlin
19 Nov. Ruth d. of William & Sarah Basely
19 Nov. James s. of John & Mary Tonkin
19 Nov. Ann d. of William & Mary Retallack
19 Nov. Robert s. of John & Elizabeth Tippet
9 Dec. Jane d. of Mathew & Ann Hool
9 Dec. John s. of John & Mary Bond
18 Dec. Sarah d. of Arthur & Ann Capell

ANNO 1765.

11 Jan. Richard s. of John & Mary White

* This Thomas was in Holy Orders and son of Giles Hamley, see ante p. 101 : the above Mary was his second wife.

13 Jan. Margaret d. of Francis & Eudith Hawkey
20 Jan. William s. of Thomas & Ann Cocke
23 Jan. Martha d. of Richard & Elizabeth Basely
10 Feb. Dorcas d. of James & Joan Stephens
16 Feb. Ann d. of Thomas & Joan Williams
24 Feb. Joseph* s. of James & Elizabeth Arscott
3 Mar. Elizabeth d. of Philip & Mary Cornish
17 Mar. Elizabeth d. of William & Mary Lobb
7 April Ralph s. of Ralph & Mary Bewes
8 April William s. of William & Mary Glanville
3 May Mary d. of William & Elizabeth Ford
10 May Richard s. of Isaac & Elizabeth Grig
27 May John s. of Hezekiah & Jane Bunt
27 May Jane d. of William & Dorothy Blight
28 May Jane d. of George & Elizabeth Champion
3 June Ann d. of William & Thomazin Swan
11 June Mary d. of Thomas & Mary Williams
23 June Mary d. of Thomas & Mary Mill
28 June William s. of Thomas & Amey Solomon
30 June Abraham s. of Abraham & Elizabeth Waters
21 July Henry s. of Richard & Mary Veal
28 July Mary d. of John & Margaret Walkey
1 Sep. Mary d. of John & Jennifer George
1 Sep. Elizabeth d. of William & Mary Ivey
8 Sep. Jane d. of Digory & Alice Truscott
8 Sep. William s. of John & Blanch Tamlin
8 Sep. Johanna d. of Nicholas & Mary Liddicoat
4 Oct. Robert s. of William & Elizabeth Austin

* He mar. 16 May, 1807, Ann Meager.

6 Oct. Mary d. of Thomas & Thomazine Gass
18 Oct. Elizabeth d. of Thomas & Mary Hinch
18 Nov. William s. of John & Elizabeth Morris
18 Nov. Ann d. of John & Ann Martin
20 Nov. Robert s. of Edmond & Mary Varcoe
20 Nov. Mary d. of James & Elizabeth Houghton
22 Nov. William s. of Peter & Elizabeth Courtnay
26 Dec. William s. of Michael & Susanna Basely
27 Dec. Richard s. of Thomasine Tippet

ANNO 1766.

3 Jan. Mary d. of James & Mary Snell
6 Jan. Elizabeth d. of Nicholas & Jennefer Lakeman
10 Jan. Ann d. of Wm Prestridge, a soldier, & Mary his wife
24 Jan. Jane d. of Robert Belfour, a soldier, & Susanna his wife
26 Jan. Thomas s. of Digory & Elizabeth Davies
26 Jan. John s. of Richard & Elizabeth Gummow
21 Feb. Elizabeth d. of Jephthah & Grace Whilter
23 Feb. Mary d. of Richard & Elizabeth Chapman
12 Mar. William s. of Edward & Ann Pearce
21 Mar. William s. of Elizabeth Lobb
25 Mar. Giles s. of Thomas* & Mary Hamley
30 Mar. Elizabeth d. of William & Mary Bone
31 Mar. Francis s. of John & Grace Jane
5 April John s. of John & Joan Symons
6 April George s. of John & Mary Luney
2 June Elizabeth† d. of Rev. Dr. Robert Bateman & Elizabeth his wife
13 June William s. of William & Elizabeth Lewarn
29 June Frances d. of William & Dorothy Harris

* See note p. 101.
† See note p. 105.

6 July John s. of Richard & Lidia Battin James
6 July James s. of James & Catherine Lillycrop
13 July Joseph s. of Humphry & Susanna England
13 July John s. of Edward & Abigal Merrifield
23 July James s. of James & Ann Pearce
3 Aug. Winefred d. of John & Mary Buckingham
8 Aug. Peter s. of Peter & Elizabeth Hawke
10 Aug. Ann d. of William & Ann Lanyon
17 Aug. Richard s. of William & Ruth Crapp
24 Aug. Mary d. of Joseph & Patience Hancock
24 Aug. William s. of Robert & Grace Keam
14 Sep. Richard s. of Francis & Grace Avery
21 Sep. William s. of Philip & Mary Harvey
5 Oct. Mary d. of John & Mary Davy
6 Oct. Edward Bishop s. of John & Lovedy Soper
7 Nov. Damaris d. of John* & Mary White
16 Nov. John s. of John & Elizabeth Stephens
17 Nov. John s. of George & Grace Brown
17 Nov. Philip s. of Philip & Margaret Harris
10 Dec. Ann d. of John & Elizabeth Harden
14 Dec. Richard s. of William & Sarah Ellery
31 Dec. Mary d. of Richard & Elizabeth Best

ANNO 1767.

2 Jan. Hezekiah s. of Hezekiah & Jane Bunt
11 Jan. Robert s. of Robert & Elizabeth Mannell
11 Jan. Ann d. of John & Elinor Luke
25 Jan. Caroline d. of Thomas & Ann Cooke
4 Feb. Joan d. of John & Mary Bond
8 Feb. Mary d. of Benjamin & Elizabeth Jons

* John White churchwarden in 1770: Green Book.

13 Feb. Catherine d. of William & Elizabeth Hicks
22 Feb. William s. of William & Frances Baseley
22 Feb. Peter s. of Francis & Edith Hawkey
8 Mar. Ann d. of Francis & Elizabeth Simmons
15 Nov.* Elizabeth d. of Richard & Elizabeth Hawken
22 Mar. Jane d. of Philip & Mary Cornish
22 Mar. Elizabeth d. of Thomas & Jane Giles
22 Mar. Joan d. of James & Joan Tabb
17 April Richard s. of William & Elizabeth Austin
17 April John s. of John & Joan Higgs
19 April Jane d. of William & Mary Retallack
21 April Elizabeth d. of John & Mary Liddicoat
13 May William Thomas s. of Joan Dyer
24 May Temperance d. of William & Mary Glanville
31 May John s. of Grace Hailbron
3 June Elizabeth d. of Nicholas & Mary Liddicoat
5 June Mary d. of William & Michal Rowe
5 June John s. of Timothy Brammar, a soldier, & Catherine
19 June Richard s. of James & Joan Stephens
28 June Peter† s of James & Elizabeth Arscutt
1 July James & Thomas s. of William & Thomasine Swan
17 July Samson s. of Thomas & Prudance Hicks
21 July Sarah d. of William & Honour Blight
25 July William s. of Thomas & Mary Williams
26 July James s. of William & Margaret Benney
18 Aug. Elizabeth d. of Richard & Frances Samson
20 Aug. John s. of John & Grace Dungey
20 Sep. Ann d. of John & Jennifer George
30 Sep. Elizabeth d. of Richard & Elizabeth Tom of Bodmin

* Sic.
† This Peter was bur. 5 April 1797.

3 Oct. John s. of Nicholas & Sarah Clemoe
9 Oct. Jennifer d. of George & Elizabeth Colwill
9 Oct. Jennifer d. of William & Jane Liddicoat
16 Oct. Mary d. of Arthur & Ann Capple
25 Oct. Robert s. of Judith Howard
22 Nov. William s. of James & Elizabeth Houghton
22 Nov. Thomas* s. of Thomas & Mary Mill
23 Nov. William s. of Thomas & Amey Solomon
23 Nov. Ann d. of Richard & Elizabeth Baseley
4 Dec. Susanna d. of James & Margaret Jane
13 Dec. Susanna d. of William & Mary Ivey
27 Dec. Thomas Tregenna† s. of Thomas Rogers, Esq., & Margery his wife

ANNO 1768.

30 Jan. Methuselah s. of Methuselah & Mary Barret
5 Feb. William s. of John & Joan Symonds
7 Feb. Richard s. of John & Mary Cowling
12 Feb. Elizabeth d. of Thomas & Mary Rowse
14 Feb. James s. of John & Blanch Tamblin
27 Feb. Joseph s. of Joseph & Elizabeth Tinney
6 Mar. James s. of James & Mary Snell
16 Mar. Frances‡ d. of Rev. Dr. Robert Bateman, Rector of this Parish, & Elizabeth his wife
20 Mar. Sarah d. of Margaret Retallack
26 Mar. Bridget d. of Richard & Mary Bulling
4 April Jennifer d. of John & Elizabeth Stephens

* Thomas Mill and Mary Retallack of St. Wenn mar. 7 Oct. 1792. Elizabeth Caroline their daughter bap. in 1801.
† By dau. & coh. of Rev. John Tregenna.
‡ She mar. 8 Feb. 1797, by licence, Richard Paul, at St. Columb. Robert Bateman, son of the Rev. Richard Paul & Frances his wife, bapt. 22 March 1798. Frances, dau. of the same, bap. 27 Dec. 1799.

22 April John s. of Nicholas & Jennifer Lakeman
29 April Joseph s. of Richard & Elizabeth Chapman
1 May Elizabeth d. of John & Mary Peters
1 May James s. of Edmund & Mary Varcoe
6 May Temperance d. of Fra^s & Jane Jane
20 May Susanna d. of Michael & Susanna Baseley
23 May William s. of John & Grace Jane
24 May Elizabeth d. of Peter & Elizabeth Courtnay
31 May Margaret d. of Rev. Thomas Biddulph* & Martha his wife
2 June Jane d. of Joseph & Mary Merifield
19 June Susanna d. of Peter & Elizabeth Hawke
20 June Ann d. of Alexander McNight a soldier, 22nd Reg^t, & Frances his wife
12 July Samuel s. of William & Catherine Rawlings
17 July Thomas s. of Hezekiah & Jane Bunt
29 July Philippa d. of Thomas & Joan Williams
30 July Jennifer d. of Richard & Catherine Morlin
31 July Rose d. of William & Ruth Crapp
21 Aug. Jephthah s. of Jephthah & Grace Whiller
30 Sep. Robert s. of Robert & Ann Sowden
10 Oct. James s. of James & Grace Gilbert
11 Nov. Jane base child of Mary Budle
27 Nov. Jane d. of John & Constance James
23 Dec. Betsey Dungey d. of Henry† & Elizabeth Warne

* He was Vicar of Padstow. Martha was his second wife, and the dau. & coh. of the Rev. John Tregenna, Rector of Mawgan. See Mar. 1761.

† Henry Warne was one of the twelve men in 1764, and churchwarden in 1789, having been an overseer in 1787 while still one of the twelve men (Green Book). His daughter named above is recorded with others of her family on an altar tomb in the churchyard.

24 Dec. William s. of John* & Grace Dungey
30 Dec. William s. of Richard & Mary Langdon

ANNO 1769.

6 Feb. Alice d. of Francis & Edith Hawkey
11 Feb. Grace d. of Joseph & Elizabeth Tinney
24 Feb. George ye base child of Margaret Liddicoat
26 Feb. Cordelia d. of John & Margaret Buckingham
25 Mar. Catherine d. of Robert & Elizabeth Tabb
27 Mar. Mary d. of Methuselah & Mary Barret
27 Mar. James s. of Pascoe & Elizabeth Davis
2 April William s. of Francis & Elizabeth Simons
9 April Elizabeth d. of Philip & Margaret Harris
14 April Elizabeth d. of John & Mary White
16 April Mary d. of William & Elizabeth Austin
23 April William s. of William & Dorothy Harris
5 May James s. of John & Blanch Parkin
14 May Elizabeth d. of Thomas & Ann Cooke
16 May Mary d. of Robert & Elizabeth Mannel
29 May John s. of Nicholas & Elizabeth Guens
17 June Robert s. of James & Joan Stephens
20 July Frances d. of Richard & Frances Sampson
26 July John s. of Richard & Elizabeth Best
6 Aug. John s. of John & Elizabeth Harvey
27 Aug. James s. of Joseph & Barbara Dyer
27 Aug. Honor Stribley d. of Edward & Ann Pearce
31 Aug. John s. of John Barnard & Ann his wife
1 Sep. William s. of Robert & Jane Drew
10 Sep. Jane d. of George & Elizabeth Colwill

* See Mar. 1766. Mr. John Dungey, one of the twelve men in 1770. Green Book.

20 Sep. Jane d. of John & Mary Bond
4 Oct. Richard s. of Richard & Mary Williams
17 Oct. Elizabeth* d. of James and Elizabeth Arscutt
25 Oct. Ann d. of Richard & Elizabeth Basely
28 Oct. Samuel s. of William & Catherine Rawlings
3 Nov. Ann d. of Thomas & Prudence Hicks
12 Nov. Mary Varcoe d. of James and Elizabeth Houghton
4 Dec. Thomas s. of Richard & Elizabeth Hawken
15 Dec. Thomas s. of John & Jennefer George

Anno 1770.

1 Jan. Nancey d. of John & Catherine Whitford
6 Jan. Robert s. of John & Joan Seymons
10 Jan. Samuel base child of Elizabeth Brown of y[e] parish of Gluvias
16 Jan. Ann d. of William & Margaret Benney
18 Feb. Mary d. of Hezekiah & Jane Bunt
19 Feb. John s. of Richard & Mary Bulling
21 Feb. William s. of Mary Retallack widow
8 Mar. John s. of Jephthah & Grace Whitter
12 Mar. Robert s. of William & Frances Basely
14 Mar. Mary s. of Ephraim & Susanna Stephens
13 May John s. of John & Elizabeth Trescouthick
13 May Mary d. of Philip & Mary Cornish
8 June Thomas s. of William & Temperance Glanville
15 June John s. of James & Mary Snell
25 June Philip s. of James & Grace Gilbert
15 July Mary d. of William & Sarah Elery

* She mar. 25 May 1799, Benjamin Jones. Eliz., the w. of James Arscott, was bur. 11 Oct. 1803. Peter Arscott, s. of Benj. & Eliz. Jones, bapt. 1 Jan. 1802.

23 July William s. of Arthur & Ann Caple
5 Aug. Peter s. of Peter & Elizabeth Courtenay
12 Sep. Catherine d. of Richard & Ann Langdon
2 Oct. Jane d. of John & Grace Dungey
12 Oct. Allice d. of Peter & Elizabeth Hawke
31 Oct. Frances s. of Francis & Edith Hawkey
15 Nov. Grace d. of Robert & Grace Keam
18 Nov. Elizabeth d. of William & Elizabeth Lewarne
19 Nov. Mary d. of Michael & Susanna Basely
4 Dec. John s. of Solomon & Elizabeth Basely
14 Dec. John s. of Richard & Frances Sampson
27 Dec. Thomas s. of Francis & Jane Jane

Anno 1771.

21 Jan. Mary d. of Robert & Elizabeth Tabb
21 Jan. Sarah d. of John & Grace Jane
10 Mar. John & Luke sons of John & Jennefer George
10 Mar. Mary d. of George & Grace Brown
10 Mar. Ann d. of John & Constance James
1 April Robert s. of William & Elizabeth Austin
1 April Cordelia d. of Thomas & Ann Cooke
21 April Peter s. of Francis & Elizabeth Simons
1 May Johanna d. of Thomas & Mary Mill
9 May Elizabeth d. of Francis & Ann Hill
10 May Sarah d. of Elizabeth Harris
20 May Thomas s. of William & Ruth Crapp
20 May Mary d. of Methuselah & Mary Barret
22 May Charles s. of William & Jane Liddicoat
24 May Mary d. of John & Mary White
27 May John s. of John & Rebecca Julian
31 May Thomas s. of Robert & Jane Drew

31 May Jennifer d. of Richard & Mary Bettinson
31 May Sarah d. of John & Elizabeth Hardin
28 June Thomas s. of Thomas & Joan Williams
5 July Thomas s. of Thomas Tippin a soldier in y[e] 20th Regt. & Mary his wife
6 July John s. of John & Philippa Mewton
14 Aug. Richard s. of Richard & Lydia Batten James
25 Aug. James s. of James & Elizabeth Houghton
26 Aug. Joseph s. of Joseph & Mary Merrifield
27 Aug. Mary d. of Joseph & Barbara Dyer
3 Sep. Honor d. of John & Mary Liddicoat
29 Sep. Jennifer d. of John & Charity Tonkin
17 Oct. Rebecca & Elizabeth ds. of William & Honour Blight
1 Nov. Honour d. of Arthur & Elizabeth Strongman
2 Nov. Mary d. of George & Elizabeth Colwill
18 Nov. Philip s. of John & Elizabeth Stephens
18 Nov. Jennefair d. of Richard & Elizabeth Basely
18 Nov. Margaret d. of John & Margaret Buckingham
23 Nov. Ann d. of George & Mary Tippet
6 Dec. Jennefair d. of John & Hannah Hicks
27 Dec. Grace d. of Jephthah & Grace Whitter
29 Dec. Jane d. of James & Joan Stephens

ANNO 1772.

14 Jan. William s. of William & Margaret Benny
22 Jan. William s. of Nicholas & Dorothy Tamblyn
26 Jan. Nicholas s. of John & Elizabeth Harvey
28 Feb. Catherine d. of Hezekiah & Jane Bunt
9 April Harriot d. of John & Martha Jewel
12 April Samuel Hooker s. of James & Margaret Jane
20 April Catherine d. of Robert & Elizabeth Mannel
24 April Solomon s. of William & Frances Basely
25 April Betty d. of John & Grace* Dungey
17 May Thomas s. of James & Grace Gilbert
22 June James s. of John & Joan Symons
6 July Thomas s. of Thomas & Prudence Hicks
12 July Blanch d. of Peter & Elizabeth Courtney
12 July Elizabeth d. of Richard & Temperance Grigg
22 July Catherine d. of Pasco & Elizabeth Davis
2 Aug. Jennefair d. of Francis & Grace Cundy
16 Aug. Mary d. of John & Jane Martin
30 Aug. Archelaus s. of William & Dorothy Harris
6 Sep. William s. of Richard & Mary Bulling
25 Sep. James s. of James & Mary Dinnis
14 Nov. Ann d. of George & Grace Brown
23 Nov. Richard s. of John & Ann Gatley
4 Dec. Rebecca d. of William & Rebecca Monros, a soldier 23rd reg[t]
9 Dec. Robert s. of Robert & Grace Keam
21 Dec. William s. of John & Mary Pasco
22 Dec. Andrew White s. of Amy White
24 Dec. Edward s. of Nicholas Donnithorn & Jane Arthur his wife

ANNO 1773.

1 Jan. Elizabeth d. of Richard & Elizabeth Hawken
3 Jan. Mary d. of Peter & Jane Pollard
10 Jan. Rachel d. of Andrew & Sarah Austin
22 Jan. Harry s. of John & Elizabeth Oxenham
24 Jan. Richard s. of William & Mary Glanville

* Grace Dungey, wid., bur. 13 March, 1789.

31 Jan. Richard s. of Richard & Mary Williams
31 Jan. Margaret d. of James & Mary Snell
5 Feb. John s. of George & Mary Tippett
5 Feb. Elizabeth d. of Robert & Elizabeth Tabb
8 Feb. Jennefair d. of Philip & Margaret Harris
18 Feb. Mary d. of Mary Oliver
19 Feb. John s. of John & Blanch Parkin
3 Mar. George s. of James & Elizabeth Houghton
14 Mar. Elizabeth d. of John & Elizabeth Stephens
17 Mar. William s. of Solomon & Elizabeth Beasely
21 Mar. William s. of Nicholas & Dorothy Tamblyn
3 April Catherine d. of Peter & Elizabeth Hawke
12 April Mary d. of Richard & Ann Langdon
12 April Richard s. of William & Jane Henwood
19 April Ann d. of Robert & Ann Sowden
27 April Nicholas s. of John & Jennefair George
9 May Ann d. of William & Elizabeth Austin
1 June Elizabeth d. of William & Sarah Ellery
13 June Francis s. of Francis & Elizabeth Simons
14 June Amy d. of William & Elizabeth Brewer
27 June John s. of Joseph & Mary Kelly
4 July Henry s. of Philip & Mary Hervey
4 July John s. of John Morland a soldier in ye 3rd reg^t^ & Martha his wife
11 July Stephen s. of Francis & Jane Jane
16 July Jennefair d. of Michael & Susanna Beasely
19 July John s. of John & Charity Tonkin
25 July William s. of Thomas & Ann Ball
25 July William s. of William & Joan Trembeth
28 July Frances Tom. d. of William & Philippa Drew
6 Aug. Jane d. of Arthur & Ann Caple
7 Aug. James s. of John & Elizabeth Trescouthick
8 Aug. John s. of Peter & Grace Curtis
15 Aug. John s. of Samuel & Mary Keast
22 Aug. Cecilia d. of Edmund & Mary Varcoe
24 Aug. Elizabeth d. of Thomas & Elizabeth May
31 Aug. Nicholas s. of Nathaniel & Elizabeth Hender
15 Sep. Mary d. of John & Constance James
16 Sep. Sarah d. of William & Margaret Benny
25 Sep. John s. of William & Ruth Crap
25 Sep. Methuselah s. of Methuselah & Ann Barrett
28 Sep. Hugh s. of John & Grace Jane
4 Oct. John s. of Richard & Elizabeth Jane
26 Oct. Wm Chapman s. of Catherine Strongman
31 Oct. Thomas s. of Thomas & Ann Cook
22 Nov. William s. of Walter & Dorcas Knight
22 Nov. Elizabeth d. of William & Jane Flamank
29 Nov. Susanna d. of John & Martha Jewel
8 Dec. Ann d. of John & Lovedy Truscutt
8 Dec. Robert s. of Richard & Mary Kent
20 Dec. Timothy s. of John & Mary White
28 Dec. William s. of Arthur & Elizabeth Strongman

Anno 1774.

17 Jan. William s. of Edward & Elizabeth May
9 Feb. William s. of George & Mary Dawe
15 Feb. John s. of John & Mary Liddicot
17 Feb. Ann White d. of Thomazine Tippett
21 Feb. Ann d. of Peter & Jane Pollard
11 Mar. Elizabeth d. of John & Philippa Mewdon

25 Mar. William s. of William Carr a soldier in ye 22nd reg^t & Mary his wife
30 Mar. John s. of Nicholas & Ann Courtney
8 April William s. of Robert & Jane Drew
29 April Philip s. of James & Grace Gilbert
6 May Patsey Jane d. of Henry & Elizabeth Warne*
13 May Benjamin s. of John & Catherine Whiteford
26 June Anthony s. of Richard & Lydia Batten James
1 July Thomas s. of Francis & Ann Hill
3 July Wm Godolphin s. of John & Margaret Buckingham
14 July Elizabeth d. of Thomas & Mary Mill
14 July Elizabeth d. of John & Mary Stephens
19 Aug. Amy d. of Thomas & Prudence Hicks
25 Aug. Mary d. of John & Joan Simons
26 Aug. William s. of Francis & Jane Jane
29 Aug. Mary Tippet d. of Mary Thomas
4 Sep. Elizabeth d. of Richard & Mary Cundy
30 Sep. Mary d. of Anthony & Amy White
2 Oct. Thomas s. of Joseph & Mary Merifield
3 Oct. Sarah d. of Andrew & Sarah Austin
7 Oct. Richard s. of John & Blanch Parkin
7 Oct. Stephen s. of Stephen & Catherine Brewer
9 Oct. Thomas s. of Thomas & Ann Bullock
24 Oct. Richard s. of Richard & Mary Bulling
21 Nov. Thomas s. of Peter & Elizabeth Courtney
27 Nov. Ann d. of Hezekiah & Jane Bunt
4 Dec. William s. of James & Elizabeth Tabb
5 Dec. Elizabeth d. of John & Martha Jewel

* She died unmarried, and is recorded on an altar tomb in the churchyard, together with her parents and sisters.

10 Dec. Thomas s. of Robert & Elizabeth Maunel

ANNO 1775.

6 Jan. Joseph s. of Henry & Fanny Hoskin
14 Jan. Mary d. of Richard & Mary Bettinson
2 Feb. William s. of Rachael Liddicoat *alias* Gregor
3 Feb. Elizabeth d. of James & Elizabeth Houghton
8 Feb. Jenny d. of John & Jane Mill
19 Feb. Elizabeth d. of Thomas & Ann Ball
4 Mar. Jennifer d. of John & Lovedy Truscott
8 Mar. Joan d. of Robert & Elizabeth Tabb
16 Mar. Philip s. of Peter & Elizabeth Hawke
14 April William s. of William & Dorothy Harris
15 April John s. of William & Elizabeth Brewer
22 April Harry s. of John & Elizabeth Oxenham
23 April Jane d. of Peter & Jane Pollard
23 April Henry s. of James & Mary Snell
6 May Richard & Philippa s. & d. of Richard & Mary Kent
7 May Edward s. of John & Jennefair George
19 May Elizabeth d. of William & Jennefair Collins of the parish of Kenwen
25 May John s. of John & Frances Teppitt
2 June Philip s. of William* & Philippa Drew
7 June Thomas s. of Thomas & Elizabeth May
12 June Richard & Ruth s. & d. of Richard & Elizabeth Baseley
26 June John s. of Edward & Elizabeth May
2 July Mary d. of George & Mary Daw
9 July John s. of William & Elizabeth Austin
16 July Elizabeth d. of Francis & Elizabeth Symons

* William Drew of Bosworgey and Mr. William Drew of Resuggan were elected Twelve Men in 1785. Green Book.

17 July Jane d. of M[r] Nicholas Donithorne & Jane Arthur his wife
20 Aug. Nicholas s. of John & Charity Tonkins
3 Sep. William s. of Samuel & Mary Keast
4 Sep. Elizabeth d. of Ann Williams
8 Sep. William s. of William & Philippa Dancaster
23 Sep. Mary d. of William & Jane Flamank
22 Oct. John s. of John & Constance James
16 Nov. John s. of Walter & Dorcas Knight
29 Nov. John s. of Thomas & Johanna Salmon
3 Dec. James s. of Richard & Elizabeth Hawken
10 Dec. John s. of Francis & Jane Jane
29 Dec. Samuel s. of Anthony & Amy White

ANNO 1776.

1 Jan. George s. of Alexander & Mary Sharp
10 Jan. Francis s. of Francis & Ann Hill
31 Jan. Jane d. of Thomas & Jane Willoughby
6 Feb. John s. of John & Mary Pascoe
21 Feb. Ann d. of Richard & Ann Langdon
25 Feb. Jennefair d. of Pascoe & Elizabeth Davis
2 Mar. William s. of Richard & Lydia Batten James
3 Mar. Edmund s. of Thomas & Ann Bullock
4 Mar. Elizabeth d. of John & Prudence Roberts
8 Mar. Joseph s. of Joseph & Catherine Osborn
23 Mar. Ann d. of Richard & Mary Williams
26 Mar. Peter s. of John & Grace Jane
26 Mar. Jane Coad d. of Thomas & Joan Harvey
31 Mar. Jennefair d. of Joseph & Mary Kelley
16 May Frances d. of Peter & Elizabeth Hawke
20 May Fanny d. of Joseph & Susanna Rowe
2 June Ann d. of Methuselah & Mary Barrett
2 June James s. of Thomas & Ann Cooke
9 June Richard s. of Richard & Elizabeth Gummo
14 June Elizabeth d. of Michael & Susanna Basely
23 June Thomas s. of Robert & Jane Drew
13 July Thomas s. of Thomas & Prudence Hicks
21 July William Williams s. of Ann Aver
26 July James s. of Arthur & Ann Caple
5 Aug. Edward s. of Edward & Rachel Gummo
18 Aug. James s. of Peter & Jane Pollard
22 Aug. Mary d. of John & Martha Jewel
31 Aug. William s. of Richard & Elizabeth Jane
6 Sep. Richard s. of William & Sarah Ellery
8 Sep. Honour d. of John & Elizabeth Trescouthick
3 Oct. James s. of John & Mary White
11 Oct. Mary* d. of Henry & Elizabeth Warne
25 Oct. John s. of Richard & Mary Cundy
28 Oct. Joan d. of Edward & Jane George
10 Dec. Charles Thomas s. of Robert & Grace Keam
18 Dec. Richard s. of Richard & Mary Veal
18 Dec. Nicholas s. of Peter & Elizabeth Courtney
28 Dec. William s. of Thomas & Johanna Salmon

ANNO 1777.

3 Jan. William s. of Jane Basely
10 Jan. Elizabeth d. of John & Blanch Parkin
12 Jan. Thomas s. of Thomas & Ann Ball
25 Jan. Richard s. of William & Sarah Basely
28 Jan. Thomas s. of Francis & Catherine May

* She died unmarried 21 June, 1827. They had another dau. Sophia Grace, bapt. 15 July, 1782: married 22 Dec., 1808, to Nicholas Truscott Ball, of Mevagissy, and bur. 21 Oct., 1809.

31 Jan. Elizabeth d. of Arthur & Elizabeth Strongman
2 Feb. Dorothy d. of Nicholas & Dorothy Tamblyn
4 Feb. William s. of William & Margaret Benny
10 Feb. Tempe d. of Henry & Fanny Hoskin
16 Feb. John s. of Stephen & Catherine Brewer
17 Feb. Anne d. of James & Elizabeth Houghton
23 Feb. Philippa d. of John & Philippa Mewdon
25 Feb. Elizabeth d. of Francis & Edith Hawkey
9 Mar. Jennefaire d. of William & Philippa Dancaster
30 Mar. Elizabeth d. of John & Johanna Varco
30 Mar. Jonathan & Geo. sons of George & Mary Daw
31 Mar. Gregorye s. of James & Elizabeth Tabb
11 April William s. of John & Johanna Stephens
11 April William s. of Peter & Frances Rowe
19 May George s. of John & Frances Teppitt
23 May William s. of John & Charity Tonkin
8 June Charles s. of William & Dorothy Harris
19 June John s. of Peter & Elizabeth Hawke
23 June Thomas s. of Richard & Lydia Batten James
29 June Grace d. of James & Grace Gilbert
14 July Betsey d. of John & Elizabeth Oxenham
16 July James s. of Robert & Elizabeth Tabb
19 July John s. of Joseph & Mary Merifield
20 July Anthony s. of William & Mary Buckingham
17 Aug. Thomasine d. of Nichs* & Ann Courtuey
22 Aug. Thomas s. of Thomas & Joan Harvey
24 Aug. John s. of Anthony & Amy White

* Nicholas Courteney bur. 3 Oct., 1800; Peter Courteney and Elizabeth Maunell, both of St. Columb Major, mar. 8 Feb., 1783.

24 Aug. John s. of John & Amy Langdon
6 Sep. Mary d. of Henry & Mary Brower
21 Sep. Joseph s. of John & Mary Stephens
3 Oct. Mary d. of W^m^ & Dorothy Rounseval
3 Oct. Clarinda d. of Joseph & Susanna Rowe
26 Oct. William s. of John & Mary Drew
17 Nov. Margaret d. of Samuel & Mary Keast
24 Nov. James s. of James & Patience Champion
14 Dec. Ann d. of James & Mary Snell
25 Dec. Thomas s. of Edward & Elizabeth May

ANNO 1778.

18 Jan. John s. of Francis & Ann Hill
26 Jan. Peter s. of Peter & Grace Courtice
29 Jan. John s. of John & Prudence Roberts
19 Feb. Elizabeth d. of Edward & Rachael Gummo
5 Mar. John s. of Christopher & Jane Rheins
20 Mar. Patty d. of John* & Martha Jewell
2 April Ralph s. of Philip & Ann Brown
5 April Catherine d. of William & Elizabeth Austin
27 April John s. of William & Jane Rowse
1 May Richard s. of Andrew & Sarah Austin
8 May William s. of William & Mary Truscutt
26 June James s. of Martha Webber
12 July John s. of Francis & Elizabeth Simons
12 July Sarah d. of Methuselah & Mary Barrett
27 July John s. of Thomas & Joan Williams
29 July Mary d. of Thomas & Jane Willoughby
10 Aug. Martha d. of Richard & Mary Bulling

* John Jewell, surgeon to the parish in 1786. (Green Book). Denham Melanchthon, s. of Mr. John Jewell and Mary his wife, bapt. 20 May, 1785.

16 Aug. Ann d. of Thomas & Ann Bullock
23 Aug. Ann d. of Richard & Lydia Batten James
17 Sep. Edward s. of Thomas & Ann Cook
18 Sep. George s. of Richard & Mary Veal
20 Sep. Frances d. of John & Rosamond Carhart
20 Sep. Elizabeth d. of Peter & Ann Pollard
5 Oct. John s. of John & Elizabeth Morcomb
12 Oct. Mathew s. of Peter & Elizabeth* Courtney
1 Nov. Stephen s. of Walter & Ann Teppit
1 Nov. Thomas s. of John & Hannah Cock
8 Nov. Henry s. of John & Constance James
23 Nov. Elizabeth d. of Richard & Ann Langdon
24 Nov. Richard s. of Richard & Mary Cundy
1 Dec. Elizabeth d. of Arthur & Alice White
10 Dec. Phyllis d. of William & Philippa Dancaster
18 Dec. Jane d. of John & Mary White

1779.

1 Jan. Richard s. of Richard & Elizabeth Jane
12 Jan. Richard s. of Peter and Frances Rowe
17 Jan. John s. of Joseph & Catherine Osborn
22 Jan. John s. of Francis and Catherine May
7 Feb. John s. of Richard & Elizabeth Gummo
17 Feb. Mary d. of James & Elizabeth Pearce
5 Mar. Mary d. of Pasco & Elizabeth Davis
6 Mar. Jennefair d. of Joseph & Mary Kelly
16 Mar. Robert s. of Richard & Elizabeth Grigg
3 April Ann d. of Edward & Elizabeth May
5 April Samuel s. of Thomas & Ann Ball

* Elizabeth, wife of Peter Courtney, bur. 14 June, 1781.

11 April Thomas s. of Robert & Elizabeth Mannel
18 April James s. of John & Frances Teppit
16 May Francis s. of Richard & Mary Bettinson
7 June George s. of George & Mary Dawe
8 July Cordelia d. of John & Mary Buckingham
9 July Harry s. of Henry & Elizabeth Warne*
9 July Samuel s. of John & Martha Jewell
9 July Elizabeth d. of James & Grace Gilbert
11 July Grace d. of Richard & Grace Chaple
13 July Ann d. of Frances & Jane Jane
13 July Edward s. of Edward & Rachell Gummo
6 Aug. James s. of Robert & Elizabeth Tab
17 Aug. Betty† d. of William & Mary Buckingham
28 Aug. William s. of Edward & Jane George
29 Aug. Wm Hawke s. of Thomas & Grace Smith
30 Aug. George s. of John & Mary Drew
5 Sep. Tillane d. of William & Mary Hewett
13 Sep. Elizabeth d. of John & Joan Simons
17 Sep. James s. of James & Elizabeth Tabb
18 Sep. John s. of John & Elizabeth Oxenham
3 Oct. Joseph s. of Stephen & Rosamond Commons
16 Oct. Elizabeth d. of Anthony & Amy White
22 Oct. Elizabeth d. of James & Patience Champion
21 Nov. Mary d. of William & Jennefair Collins
5 Dec. Henry s. of Richard & Mary Veal
30 Dec. Henry s. of Peter & Jane Pollard

* Elizabeth, wife of Mr. Henry Warne, bur. 9 Dec., 1798.

† She married 19 Feb., 1802, James Teppet. Grace, d. of Wm. and Mary Buckingham, bapt. 5 May, 1781, married 28 Aug., 1802, to William Keast. Abraham, son of the same, bapt. 16 March, 1783, married 16 Aug., 1807, Grace Evelin.

ANNO 1780.

1 Jan. Mary d. of Arthur & Elizabeth Strongman
5 Jan. John s. of John & Rosamond Carhart
7 Feb. Elizabeth d. of John & Eliza-Hawke
11 Feb. Jane d. of William & Ruth Rawling
28 Feb. James s. of Arthur & Ann Caple
27 Mar. Richard s. of John & Philippa Mewton
27 Mar. William s. of Samuel & Elizabeth Johns
27 Mar. Mary d. of John & Ann Gass
27 Mar. Mary d. of Samuel & Mary Keast
24 April Temperance d. of Richard & Elizabeth Grigg
24 April James s. of Frances & Elizabeth Simons
24 April Francis s. of John & Mary Stephens
24 April Elizabeth d. of John & Elizabeth Trescouthick
1 May Sampson Stephens s. of Margaret Liddicoat
6 May Joan Liddicoat d. of Elizabeth Saundry
15 May Prudence d. of John & Prudence Roberts
15 May Thomas & John sons of William & Eliz. Trebilcock
16 May *Lucy d. of Richard & Mary Veal.

* She married 27 Feb., 1802, Richard Glanville.

27 May John s. of Methuselah & Mary Barret
19 June James s. of William & Margaret Benny
6 July Elizabeth d. of Stephen & Catherine Brewer
16 July Grace d. of Peter & Grace Cortis
16 July Elizabeth d. of George & Joyce Reynolds
12 Aug. Mary d. of Philip & Ann Brown
29 Aug. William s. of Christopher & Jane Rains
29 Sep. Elizabeth d. of Henry & Mary Brewer
22 Oct. Elizabeth d. of Thomas & Johanna Salmon
1 Nov. Elizabeth d. of William & Jane Taylor
3 Nov. Ann d. of Arthur & Alice White
6 Nov. Richard s. of William & Elizabeth Tremayne
8 Nov. Thomas s. of Thomas & Grace Smith
9 Nov. Elizabeth d. of William & Hannah Merifield
20 Nov. Mary d. of John & Mary Tomm
13 Dec. Ann d. of Stephen & Ann Brewer
19 Dec. John s. of James & Elizabeth White
27 Dec. William s. of Edward & Susanna Betterson
22 Dec. John s. of Richard & Elizabeth Jane
29 Dec. Elizabeth d. of Michael & Elizabeth Cornish

Hender Molesworth.

Molesworth St. Aubyn.

John Molesworth.

WEDDINGS.

Here followe the names of such as were and have byne maried sathene the theird daie of August in the six and theirteith yere of the raigne of Kinge Henrie the Eight wthin the saied p'ish of Ste Colombe.

ANNO 1544.

3 Aug. Robert Wyll & Jane Pawlie, widow

23 Aug. George Pelawyne & Maude Thomas

18 Jan. William Marke & Dorothey Stephen, widow

18 John Norton & Margaret Lukie

ANNO 1545.

7 June William Reve & Jane servant to Michaell Nanskevell

14 June Richard Osborne & Sysell servant to Thomas Nanskevell

20 June Thomas Rawlinge & Margaret Dawe

23 Aug. Stephen Pascow & Christian Moyses

19 Sep. William Pascow of St Denys* & Pascatte Vyvian

27 Sep. Richard Udie of Ruan & Alse Nanskevell

28 Feb. John Dyer & Alson Hycke, widow

28 Feb. Fransces Williams & Johane Rowse

28 Feb. John Rich & Margery Rothan, widow

ANNO 1546.

23 June James Young & Clarye Torwaie

1 July John Jenken & Phillep Vyvian

1 July William Bawden & Agnes Dyer, widowe

15 July Marten Clyscon & Alse Bodie

15 July John Adam & Johane Joliffe

22 July Harrie Butler & Johane Vincent, wydow

* St. Denys is an adjoining parish to St. Columb.

29 July John Vyvian & Ollyff* Tresaster

8 Sep. Nicholas Maben & Johane Rawe, widow

17 Sep. Humphrey Staple & Elizabeth Rawlinge, widow

1 Oct. John Epplett & Margaret his wife

14 Oct. John Bettye & Tamson Mawna, widow

29 Oct. Richard Sampson & Jane Potter, widow

4 Nov. Michaell Davie & Jane Gaye, widow

25 Nov. John Carthew & Margaret Tremaine

20 Jan. Harrie Opie & Alse his wife

27 Jan. Thomas John & Jane his wiffe

14 Feb. John Brihan & Alse Bone, widow

In three yeres now followinge there were none maried or omytted to be registered but here followe those that were maried in

ANNO 1549.

3 June Nicholas Lane & Elizabeth Oake

5 July John Richards & Katherine Laven

7 July John Strongman & Johane Mathew

29 Sep. ffransces Typpett & Pascoe his wiffe

13 Oct. Richard Nichlys & Syslie Edye

7 Dec. Thomas Jenken & Katherine Pabe

* She was dau. & h. of . . . . . Tresaster of St. Wenne. She survived her husband, being named in his will, dated 4 June, 1587, proved 1589; in it he is styled of Trenowth; it also names their children Thomas, John, Pascaux, sons, and Johane and Emlin, daughters. Johane mar. John Carter.

13 Dec. Phillep Rosogan & Agnes Hawke
31 Jan. Jefferie Thomas & the late wiffe of Rawlinge Calway
1 Feb. Harrie Gwynnowe & Margaret Strongman
3 Feb. William Pearse & Alse Rowse
9 Feb. William Teage & Alse Salisburie

ANNO 1550.

23 May William Hodge & Elizabeth Jane
6 June John Carwaye & Agnes Sandowe
27 June Richard Phillep & Margery Salpen
19 July Thomas Teage & Jane Nanconan
25 Oct. Renolde Laven & Jane Jollie
15 Nov. John Thomas *al's* Troblefeild and Jane his wiffe
29 Nov. George Hockey & Margaret Sylle
22 Dec. Richard Marten & Katherine Bawden
13 Feb. John Merifeild & Agnes Penrose

ANNO 1551.

29 May Raffe John & Margaret Mayhowe
26 June Richard Blake & Julian his wiffe
31 July Harrie Pollard & Elizabeth his wiffe
8 Aug. John the servient of Willm & Alse his wiffe
8 Aug. John Cocken & Ellen his wiffe
9 Aug. Remfrey Hawke & Denys his wiffe
5 Sep. William Estas & Jane Phillep
9 Oct. Harrie Gene & Pascal Rowse
23 Oct. John Carter & Elizabeth Pawlie
23 Oct. Thomas Hawke & Tamson Thomas
16 Nov. Harrie Hater & Elizabeth Dunstone
20 Nov. Thomas Hoskyn & Alse Typpett
20 Nov. Lallow Jolle & Margaret his wiffe
29 Nov. John Vyncent & Johane Nanskevell
21 Jan. Thomas Robert & Jane Wytte
21 Jan. John Nancollas & Jane Robert
28 Jan. John Browne & Jane Watte
12 Feb. John Wylcocke & Marie his wiffe
14 Feb. William Marten & Sycelie his wiffe

ANNO 1552.

16 April John Hicks & Jane Rosogan, widowe
12 Oct. Pascow Challen & Elizabeth Browne
19 Nov. Harrie Gascoyne & Jane Mayhow, widow
26 Nov. John Stonie & Alse Brabyn
26 Nov. Thomas Osborn & Tamson Typpett
2 Dec. Thomas Rawe & Margery Davie

ANNO 1553.

27 June Udie Putford & Elizabeth his wiffe
12 Nov. William Carter & Margery Nicholl
18 Nov. Thomas Teage & Syslie Tresoys
18 Nov. Thomas John Jane & Jane his wiffe
7 Feb. Thomas Jenyne & Margery Bennett
9 Feb. Stephen Michell & Jane Ager
9 Feb. Harrie Gwynnowe & Agnes Rosogan

ANNO 1554.

16 June John Grosse & Katherine his wiffe
3 Nov. John Roscorla & Johane Chapleman
11 Nov. Thomas Lewes & Elizabeth Udie
1 Feb. Harrie Jenyne & Jane Lukie

ANNO 1555.

5 May John Moylle & Johane his wiffe
2 June John Bawdie & Johane Taylor
22 Aug. Richard Crocker & Johane Typpett
20 Sep. John Mayhowe & Alse Typpett
4 Oct. Richard Nanskavell & Agnes Hamblie
2 Nov. John Edwarde & Johane his wiffe
2 Nov. John Will'm Elizabeth & Margerie his servant
9 Nov. John Thomas & Johane Grosse
15 Nov. Thomas Randell & Elizabeth Rawe

22 Nov. William Salpen & Elizabeth Barret
22 Nov. John Benny & Margaret Weever
4 Jan. John Phillep & Johane Scryffernor
30 Jan. Luke Lyttacott & Alse servant to Richard Nanconan
4 Feb. William Hamblie & Tamson ffeare
8 Feb. Thomas Lukie & Johane Adam

Anno 1556.

20 June John Roger & Marye Marke
21 June Richard Bawden & Johane servant to Christopher Bawden
12 Sep. Richard Teage & Elizabeth Randell
12 Sep. Bennet Briner & Johan Somer
12 Oct. Luke & Margery servants to John Spraye
31 Oct. Reynolde Rygge & Anne Bylkie, widow

Anno 1557.

5 Sep. John Dyar & Margery Robyne
15 Oct. Richard Michell & Kaye Coste
16 Jan. Richard Hetherd & Elizabeth his wiffe
20 Jan. Jefferie Allen & Johane Tregonye
20 Jan. John Dawe & Elizabeth John
2 Feb. John Spraye & Margery Sysse
2 Feb. John Hockie & Christian his wiffe

The names of those wth were maried in this said p'ish^e^ of St Colombe were not registered or els are lost from the yere above wryten 1557 unto the 27 daie of Maye then followinge, Anno 1571.

Anno 1571.

27 May Roger Maben & Mawde Pollard
28 May Andrewe Bonnfeild & Alse Nicoll, widow
20 June Robert Rosogan & Katherine Merfeild
23 June Robert Calwaie & Margaret Slade
1 July Hugh Gene & Margaret Marke
2 July John Collinge & Margery Will'ms
28 July Thomas Veysey & Jane Rowse
16 Sep. Alexander Pawlle & Jane Jerman
8 Oct. Harrie Gylls & Margaret Dyer
15 Oct. Thomas Rich & Elizabeth Remfrey
21 Oct. John Lyttacott & Johane Merifeild
24 Nov. James Younge & Amye Rose
3 Dec. Robert Lake & Katherine Dyer
10 Dec. Robert Lantell & Katherine Haye
6 Jan. Lallow Jolle & Elizabeth his wiffe
14 Feb. Richard Lawrence & Alse Bowarcke

Anno 1572.

2 July John Clemenc & Margaret Roch
6 July Pawlie Trenowth & Tamson Bruer
3 Aug. Thomas Roch & Elizabeth Bottresse
3 Aug. Richard Nicholas & Johane Jolle
2 Nov. John Tocker & Agnes Bligh
24 Nov. John Niclas & Agnes Treneage
10 Dec. Harrie Heycrafte & Dorothie Dyer
15 Jan. John Dobell & Amye Scryvener

Anno 1573.

28 April Richard Vyncent & Agnes Dawe
8 June Robert Trelawder & Johane Glanfeild
25 Oct. Thomas Tyer & Mathie Bennye
16 Nov. Thomas Merifeild & Pascae Spraye
16 Nov. William Nuttle & Margaret Nicholl
28 Nov. Newall Mayhow & Katherine Rosogan
25 Jan. Wyllm Bastian & Marie Wylls
25 Jan. James Jenken & Johane ffraunse
30 Jan. Thomas Jenken & Ursula Spraye
4 Feb. Richard Cocke & Johane Dobe
7 Feb. Thomas Yowell & Margaret Waller

Anno 1574.

11 Oct. Thomas Teage & Katherine* Warne

* This Katherine was daughter of John Warne of St. Columb.

17 Oct. John Troblefeild & Johane Carveth
24 Oct. Thomas Davie & Katherine Blake
24 Oct. Richard Davie & Alse Wylle*
1 Nov. John Richard & Johane Otes
5 Nov. John Hocken & Margery Whytte
27 Nov. Reynolde Pawllo & Elizabeth Marten
27 Nov. Richard Phillep & Margery Tregeare
29 Jan. Richard Tregeare & Margaret Rowse

ANNO 1575.

17 April John Carter & Jane Vivian†
30 May Thomas Cocken & Dorothie Pethericke
6 June John Knight & Honor Teage
25 June Walter Symon & Tamson Rawe
3 Oct. Richard Lawrence & Constance Cobb
30 Oct. John Mathew & Margarett Epplett
20 Nov. John Payne & Johane Collas
26 Nov. John Younge & Elizabeth Jane
28 Jan. Harrie Sampson & Johane Cundye
28 Jan. John Sampson & Johane Tome
29 Jan. Pethericke Pernell & Mary John
5 Feb. Nicholas Tanken & Alse Wylkie

ANNO 1576.

3 May Sampson Morcombe & Jane Lyttacott
9 July Richard Moylle & Johane Barne
20 Sep. George Carew & Elizabeth Tynner
20 Sep. John Lyttacott & Johane Laven
7 Oct. Nicholas Geunys & Johane Marke
3 Nov. William Grosse & Alse Bawden
29 Nov. Richard Ryse & Johane Jenyne
9 Dec. John Rawlinge & Katherine Tregonie
20 Jan. Harrie Hawke & Katherine Mayhowe

ANNO 1577.

22 April John Trembeth & Johane Tyfford*
9 May John Pearse & Nicoll his wife
8 July Harrie Merifeild & Phillip Edye
30 July John Moylle & Katherine Swete
14 Aug. Nicholas Kearne & Johane Hancocke
21 Oct. ffransces Williams & Agnes Gyll
27 Oct. Stephen Williams & Honor Valyes
19 Jan. Harrie Typpett & Margaret Bawdon
22 Jan. John Nankevell & Elizabeth Rowse
30 Jan. William Clerke & Agnes Davie
3 Feb. Michaiell Harrie & Margaret Collinges

ANNO 1578.

11 May Lawrence Jobbe & Johane Jollie
18 June Thomas Vyvian & Anne Lure†
12 July John Illarye & K.‡ Stephen, widow
12 July Marke Lawrie & Dorothie Bishoppe
27 Feb. James Nankevell & Peren Eves
10 Mar. Harrie Hawke & Mylson, servant to Mr. Lower

ANNO 1579.

23 April Richard Marten & Johane Menhire
23 April John Joulle & Anne Trenowth
5 June Thomas Daye & Katherine ffamack
5 June John Edie of S[t] Issie & Pascae Ryse

* This is the last entry on the page, and four pages of burials intervene between it and the next entry in the original, probably bound in by accident, the date of the burials being 1620-1625.

† This Jane was daughter of John Vivian of Trenowth, but her baptism does not appear in the register, the entries being lost from October, 1554, to April, 1571. See also note, p. 137.

* In 1585 Joan Trembethe, relict of John Trembethe, paid 3s. 4d. bequeathed to the poor of the parish by her said husband. Vide Green Book.

† He was son and heir of John Vivian and Alice Tresaster; see marriages 1546. His wife was dau. and heir of Peter Lower, of Truro. Tho. Vivian was buried 18 May, 1617; in his will he names his wife Anne, sons John, Pascowe, Michael, Thomas, and Richard; daughters Olive, Barbara, Ursula, and Emlin, who married Ric. Moyle of St. Austell, see marriages in 1601; also Rich. & John Vivian of St. Merryn.

‡ Thus in the original.

12 June Nicholas Gervice & Margaret Boscarnan*
14 June John Pollard & Jane Webber of St Kew†
4 July Humphrey Evans & Johane Sckynner
19 July Thomas Calwaye & Alse Lawrence
17 Sep. James Lawrence & Grace Braye
9 Oct. Davie Congdon & Margaret Norton
24 Oct. ffransces Calway & Margaret Gylland
25 Nov. John Lawrie & Jane Illaric
28 Nov. James Mayhow & Phillep Northey
28 Nov. Harrie Typpett & Jane Dungey

The names of those which were maried in Anno Dom. 1580 were lost or not registered.

Anno 1581.

8 Oct. Nicholas Whytte & Tamson Dymont
25 Oct. Richard Hand & Nicholl Heycraft
25 Oct. Thomas Olver & Tamson Kyttowe
22 Oct. Thomas Whytte & Aves Geffert
13 Nov. John Brabyn & Katherine Carter‡
13 Nov. John Manuell & Margaret Spray, widow
13 Nov. Richard Carthew & Margaret his wife
20 Nov. John Bonnet & Alse his wife
20 Nov. Robert Tenny & Jane Hockie
15 Jan. John Rawse & Ann Arscott
20 Jan. Thomas Hodge & Elizabeth Michell
29 Jan. ffransces Rawe & Amye Halle
29 Jan. Thomas Shomaker & Mary Atkyns

* He was probably Nic. son of Ric. Gerveis and Jane, dau. of Thomas Trefuses of Trefuses, and she Margaret, dau. of Hugh Boscawen by Phillip, dau. and co-heir of Nic. Carminow.

† She was probably a dau. of William Webber of Amell in St. Kew, by his wife, dau. of William Mathew of St. Kew.

‡ This John Brabyn, gent., was one of the Twelve Men in 1587, and died in 1593; his wife Katherine was dau. of James Carter, gent. of St. Columb, by his wife Honor, dau. and co-heir of John Newman; they had issue John, born 1582, died 1583, John, William, Thomas, and Ann. She re-married James Jenkin, gent.

10 Feb. Harrie Devonshire & Jane Merifeild

Anno 1582.

15 July John Snowe & Emblen Williams
4 Oct. William Upcott & Mary Illaric
14 Oct. Thomas Nankevell & Wilmot his wife
27 Oct. John Staple & Margaret his wife
13 Nov. Coste Batte & Emblen his wiffe
19 Nov. Richard Moylle & Marian Braye
19 Jan. John Spraye & Elizabeth Hengcocke
20 Jan. Richard Williams & Elizabeth Tregowlls

Anno 1583.

10 July William Copithorne & Marie Merifeild
12 July John George & Johane Bennye
20 July Marten Rawe & Marrian Richard
12 Sep. John Heyden & Agnes John
16 Sep. James Cornish & Margery Rowse
12 Oct. John Dobell & Phillep Cocken, widow
12 Oct. John Netherton & Margery Norton
20 Oct. Richard Bennet & Agnes Cornish
18 Nov. John Baylie & Alse Tryll
20 Nov. John Phillep & Tramson Loves
2 Jan. Thomas Tyfford & Agnes Crabe
13 Jan. Thomas Jagoe & Marye Sprey
10 Feb. John Skynner & Grace Service
11 Feb. John Thomas & Marren John, widow

Anno 1584.

1 June John Grace & Jane ffeare
13 July Thomas Myll & Honor fflamacke
31 Aug. William Calway & ffloренc Betty
4 Oct. Renold Laven & Johane his wiffe
11 Oct. John Darr & Jane Spraye
28 Nov. Marten, servant to John Cardew, & Ursula Typpett
10 Nov. Richard Rawlinge & Johane Tregonnowe
4 Feb. Antonie Batten & Clary Nowell
6 Feb. Rob. Menhinnyck & Lucye Vivian

ANNO 1585.

8 June William Collie & Katherine Tresawell
12 June John Jude & Elizabeth Laven
15 June Nicholas Holman & Jane Valleys
30 June John Moylle & Elizabeth Marsall
4 Oct. Walter Williams & Elizabeth Menhenisse
5 Oct. Humphrey Pearse & Johane Hasell
31 Oct. Richard Rowse & Elizabeth Hawke
14 Nov. Harrie Joliff & Katherine his wife
14 Nov. John Lane & Johane Jule
15 Nov. Richard Dasow & ffryswed Williams
23 Nov. George Hockey & Mary Sexton, widow
27 Nov. George Brown & Margaret Sheperd

ANNO 1586.

13 June William Lukye & Dorothie Williams
23 Oct. James Hawke & Margery Nuttle
24 Oct. Richard Vanson & Dorothie Cocken, widowe
7 Jan. ffransces Jane & Jane Engrosse

ANNO 1587.

17 Oct. Bawden Moylle & Jane Darr, widow
22 Oct. John Stickland & Jane Benye
24 Oct. Marke Retallacke & Jane Gene
24 Oct. John Chapman & Molliar Boswalloe *al's* Wise
26 Nov. John Rawe & Johane his wiffe
2 Dec. Remfrey Rowse & Jane Lawrie, widow*
17 Dec. John Rawe & Margaret Carwithie
28 Jan. Marten Dyer & Emblen Sexton

ANNO 1588.

22 April Richard James & Margaret his wiffe
20 May Richard Loves & Jane Daie *al's* Rosogan

* Son of John Rowse the elder. In 1585 he held certain 'copies' of the parish at the yearly rent of 13s. 4d., which his father held before. (Green Book.)

23 June John Hicks & Jane Strongman
1 July James Lawrence & Barbara Beny
25 Sep. John Marke & Peternell Coyett
22 Sep. John Kent & Jane his wiffe
6 Oct. James Valleys & Anne his wife
19 Jan. John Tyer & Johane Abbott
20 Jan. Richard Drew & Alse Jeffery
20 Jan. John Gene & Margaret Gylle
21 Jan. William Jolliff & Elizabeth his wife
22 Jan. ffransces Rawe & Alse Opie
25 Jan. John Pearse & Susan his wife
26 Jan. Harrie Dyer & Honor Hawke
27 Jan. George Collings & Jane Veasey
27 Jan. Edward Cardew & Johane Moyses
3 Feb. Thomas Bennett & Margaret his wiffe

ANNO 1589.

14 April John Hetherd & ffransces Gene
21 April John Wylls & Johane Sprey
9 June Richard Stephens & Jane Cowch
9 June Antonie Burlace & Johane his wife
28 Sep. John Patricke & Mary Anhey
6 Oct. William Randall & Mary Calwaye
6 Oct. Thomas Symon & Johane Grymcott
20 Oct. John Cornish & Ellen his wiffe
10 Nov. William Gylberd & Johane his wiffe
23 Nov. Robert Treluddrow & Elizabeth his wiffe
27 Nov. Richard Rowse & Johane his wiffe
11 Jan. Thomas Marten & Isett Darr
18 Jan. William Williams & Honor his wiffe
15 Feb. Richard Michell & Emblen his wiffe

ANNO 1590.

23 May John Lukie & Johane his wiffe
1 June Richard Cardewe & Jane his wiffe
22 Sep. Remfrey Rowse & Johane his wiffe
19 Oct. William Truscott & Elizabeth Treman
15 Nov. John Rowse & Elizabeth his wiffe
16 Nov. Thomas Lange & Elinor his wiffe

16 Nov. Sampson Bray & Elizabeth his wiffe
22 Nov. ffrancees Rawe & Alse his wiffe
24 Nov. Antonie Pynnowe & Elizabeth his wiffe
21 Jan. William Prydws & Johane his wiffe
26 Jan. William Jane & Elizabeth his wiffe
31 Jan. William Gylberd & Melliar his wiffe
7 Feb. Thomas Bennett & Jane Calwaye

ANNO 1591.

18 May John Nicholas & Alse Pernall
13 June John Rawe & Jane Hawke
27 June Richard Hawke & Cheston his wiffe
27 July William Cottye & Margery Brouwne
14 Aug. Hugh Sexton & Honor his wiffe
28 Sep. Stephen Trussell & Jane his wiffe
28 Sep. John Moylle & Jane his wiffe
20 Nov. Bawden Moylle & Johane his wiffe
29 Jan. John Maye & Alse his wiffe

ANNO 1592.

19 April Stephen Abraham & Alse his wiffe
5 May Nicholas Thomas & Katherine Rawe
2 July Thomas Cardewe & Anne his wiffe
17 July John Braye & Alse his wiffe
21 Aug. Pascow Tyfford & Susan Grosse
10 Oct. Robert Tynner & Johane his wiffe
7 Nov. Thomas Nicholas & Katherine his wiffe
27 Nov. William Knight & Anne his wiffe
28 Jan. John Thomas & Marye his wiffe
31 Jan. Edward Teage & Ollyffe Strongman

ANNO 1593.

26 April John Hawke & Marye his wiffe
16 July Thomas Daye & Tamson his wiffe
16 July Bennet Pollard & Johane his wiffe
21 Oct. John Troblefeild & J.* his wiffe

* Sic.

5 Jan. John Judde & Margaret his wiffe
5 Jan. Richard John & Grace his wiffe
21 Jan. Richard James & Agnes his wiffe
21 Jan. Austen Hosken & Johane his wiffe
26 Jan. Robert Trenance & Phillep his wiffe

ANNO 1594.

15 Sep. William Cocken & Marie his wiffe
27 Oct. Harrie Hawke & Alse his wiffe
23 Nov. James Daye & Blanch his wiffe
12 Jan. Thomas Gylle & Johane his wiffe
12 Jan. John Philleps & Ursula his wiffe
15 Feb. Water Williams & Alse his wiffe
3 Mar. William Cole & Marye his wiffe
3 Mar. John Nowell & Mary his wiffe

ANNO 1595.

12 May John S.* & Tamson his wiffe
1 June Robert Ryse & Syslie Strongman
17 June John Ramsey & Mylson his wiffe
30 June John Genynge & Elizabeth his wiffe
14 July William Rich & Susan his wiffe
16 Sep. John Nancollas & Elizabeth his wiffe
10 Nov. Thomas Cocke & Elizabeth his wiffe
17 Nov. John Allen & Johane Truscott
29 Dec. John Nankevell & Jane his wiffe
19 Jan. John Troblefeild & Johane his wiffe

ANNO 1596.

19 Oct. Richard Menhire & Brigot his wiffe
13 Nov. Marten Rawe & Elizabeth his wiffe
14 Nov. James Stephens & Elizabeth his wiffe
14 Nov. Thomas Dazow & Sara his wiffe
15 Nov. John Baylie & Agnes his wiffe
21 Nov. Thomas Oxenham & Elizabeth his wiffe
21 Nov. William Congdon & Grace his wiffe

* Sic.

22 Jan. Thomas Stephens & Ellen his wiffe
7 Feb. William Whyte & Johane Tyfford
7 Feb. Harrie Norton & Elizabeth his wiffe

ANNO 1597.

15 June John Compe & Elizabeth his wiffe
19 Sep. Harrie Rowse & Marye Webber
17 Oct. Richard Williams & Elizabeth his wiffe
24 Oct. Nicholas Bounsoll & Elizabeth Symon
29 Oct. Edward Carthew & Johane his wiffe
4 Jan. Nicholas Cornish & Elizabeth his wiffe

ANNO 1598.

3 July Roger Carpe'ter & Sedwell Service
26 Nov. Richard Daniell & Jane Vincente
13 Jan. John Brey & Joahne Evans
19 Feb. John Roscarlow & Honory Cornish

ANNO 1599.

16 April William Jane & Joane Sutton
4 June Richard Polkinghorne & Thomazine Luke
25 June Gregory Tome & Joane Bise
23 July John Gillian & Elizabeth Phillip
23 July James Reskigen & Joane James
11 Sep. ffraunces Triman & Margery Brey, widow
17 Sep. Humphrey Trenouthe & Elizabeth Adam
22 Oct. John James & Emblene Snowe
22 Oct. Robert Hamett & Joane Henod
5 Nov. William Williams & Ursuly Dungey
24 Nov. John Tibbett & Margaret Dirram
26 Nov. William Clerke & Cicely Jhinken
26 Nov. William Bennet & Elizabeth Hawkey
17 Jan. John Withall & Jane Sampson
17 Jan. Anthony Michell & Dorithy George

ANNO 1600.

31 Mar. Nichollas Borthy & Catterin Hamly
31 Mar. Wylliam James & Elizabeth Hake
12 April John Collis & Jone Braye
15 April Master Henry Pomory & Mysteris Elizabeth Bonythan*
5 July Digory Stubbes & Thomazine Marshall
13 July John Browne potter & Phillippe Lyll
20 July Marke Bennye & Jane Balye
1 Oct. John Brown *al's* Woe & Sisse Ingland
12 Oct. Oliver Rawe & Alice Norton
29 Nov. Edward Bray & Margery Cardue
19 Jan. Anthony Hawke & Mary Cornishe
4 Feb. Richard Williams & Jane Jenninge

ANNO 1601.

27 April William Tippett & Margery Jeffery
6 May David ffyne & Ebbet Collys
29 June Thomas Lawrye & Jennfer Cardew
13 July Thomas Callway & Christian Harrys
15 Aug. Gwalter Cocke & Rose ffrodde
17 Aug. Reynalde Engrouse & Elenore Bray
5 Oct. Walter Trescott & Elizabeth Cardew
2 Nov. James Lawrey & Alice Cocken
9 Nov. Richard Leigh gent. & Mrs. Eleanore Bonython†
11 Nov. Reynold Harryes & Alice Phillippes
26 Nov. William Hawke & Anstice Davye
28 Nov. Renfrey Hawke & Phillippe Taprell
10 Nov. John Abraham & Joane Cardew

* He was son of Hugh Pomeroy of Tregony, and grandson of Sir Edward Pomeroy of Bury Pomeroy, co. Devon. She was dau. of John Bonython of Bonython, by Elinor, dau. and coheir of William Mylyton.

† This Richard Leigh would appear to be a son of William Leigh of Leigh in Cornwall, by Mary, dau. of Andrew Pomeroy of Newton Ferrers, Devon; his wife was a dau. of John Bonython by Eleanor, dau. and co-heir of Wm. Mylyton, and sister of Elizabeth, wife of Mr. H. Pomeroy above. This Eleanor is not given in Col. Vivian's pedigree of Bonython.

15 Dec. Pascaw Vyvyan* gent. & Mary fflammacke gen. wid.
26 Jan. Richard Moyell gen.† & Emblen Vivian, gen.
10 Jan. James Mayhow & Margaret Sloggatt
30 Jan. Richard Rowse *al's* Adam & Joane Martyn
30 Jan. Thomas Tregheare & Joane Evan

ANNO 1602.

20 April John Jeinkyn & Elizabeth Nancannon
27 May ffrancisce Allen & Alson Cnabbe
10 July John Tucker & Joane Lynnye
1 Aug. William John & Grace Hawke
14 Sep. Thomas Symons the younger & Agnes Cocken
3 Nov. John Hicks & Mary Dungey
27 Nov. John Reeve & Margery Sobey
27 Nov. Nicholas Norton & Jane Marshall
27 Nov. Reynolde Littacott & Willmotte Gath
3 Feb. John Body of Dewstolke & Mary Callway
14 Feb. Richard Williams & Dorothy Kente
19 Feb. John Stribley & Alice Drewe
19 Feb. John Harvey of St. Tyves‡ & Susanna Morcombe

ANNO 1603.

6 June Martyne Straugman & Thamazine Addam
23 June John Rundell & Joane Bennett *al's* Reskeyn
5 Sep. Richard Browne & Susanne Callway
17 Oct. Robert Allen & Thamasine Jollye

* He was second son of Thomas Vivian of Trenowth and Ann Lower; and his wife, Mary, dau. of John Lipkencott of Wibberie, co. Devon, relict of Nic. Flamank of Boscarne, who died in 1599.

† He was son of Ric. Moyell of St. Austell, by Mary, dau. of Lawrence Kendall. He died in 1654, and was buried at St. Austell; in his will he names his daughters Olave Trebarfett (relict of John Harris of St. Issey) and Barbara Carlyon; his grandchildren Rich. Harris, Barbara Carlyon (she married Rich. Scobell of Menaguins), Rich. Moyle and Samuel Moyle, Jane, Ann, Philip, Mary and Emblen Moyle, also Rich. Moyle of St. Columb Major and John Moyle of the same place. His son David Moyle executor. His wife was dau. of Tho. Vivian and Ann Lower, see *ante*, p. 140.

‡ St. Ives.

10 Oct. John Tayler & Charity Knight
22 Oct. Martine Williams & Alice Rendall
24 Oct. John Nicholl *al's* Natallen & Brigette Colliver
24 Oct. John Smith & Mary Burrough
7 Nov. Ambrose Lawrye & Katherine Hawkyn
21 Nov. Richard Jollye & Joane Spearinge
26 Nov. Henry Sprey & Elizabeth Oxnam
6 Jan. Thomas Dugo*
12 Jan. John Allen & Mary Nuttle
8 Feb. Pascow Langdon & Johane Knight
10 Feb. Richard Hawke & Elanor Bray
William Riscugion†

ANNO 1604.

16 April Michaell Harrice & Margaret Rogers
24 April Richard Hawke & Cisely Clarke
30 Aug. William Bone & Joane Rogers
22 Sep. John Teage & Mawt Calway
2 Oct. John Retallack & Dorothy Randle
18 Nov. Robert Darr & Agnes Coals
28 Jan. German Retallack & Alice Moile
11 Feb. Robert Williams & Elizabeth fford

ANNO 1605.

29 April Richard Adam & Joane Yeoe
4 May Richard Bowen & Elizabeth Roch
27 May Henry Callaway & Philip his wife
22 Sep. William Rowse & Julian Bayliffe
23 Sep. John William & Alice Trelogan
12 Nov. Edmund Nicholles & Alice Roe
25 Nov. Tobias Handcocke & Alice Browne
26 Nov. Robert Tippet & Katherine Pabe
1 Dec. Thomas Benett & Jane Cockin
10 Feb. Thomas Rawe & Grace Williams
18 Feb. Henrie Tippett & Maria Sacombe
18 Feb. Richard Jenkens & Katherine Littecott

* Sic.

† The name is thus entered, but nothing more said.

ANNO 1606.

25 May John Cocke & Barbara White
16 June John Wills & Katherine Manoke
16 June John Gine & Mellior Peard
17 June Thomas Carthew & Alice Calaway
18 June John Bale & Katherine Addams
14 July John Hendra & Elizabeth Mayow
28 July Thomas Hockey & Maud Panier
29 July Anthony Burlance & Elinor his wife
18 Oct. John Peearce & Richow Michael
28 Oct. Thomas Withiell & Jane Eddy
2 Nov. William Trekyne & Honor Hawke
19 Jan. Thomas Mill & Elizabeth Truscott, vid.
26 Jan. ffrancis Lill & Elizabeth Henwoode
17 Feb. John Drue & Jane Pearce

ANNO 1607.

1 June John Menheare* & Ursula Allen
1 June Paskall Kentall & Katherine Williams
10 Oct. Stephen Harvey & Jane Cornell, vid.
12 Oct. John Cockey & Wilmote Beauch
12 Nov. Edward Littlejohn & Jane Moile
24 Nov. ffrancis Treer & Jane Vivean
24 Nov. Tho. Williams & Alice Lowry, vid.
17 Jan. Thomas Withiell & Elizabeth Brome
17 Jan. John Rowe & Oliffe Gine
17 Jan. Alexander Jollife & Barbara Oxnam

ANNO 1608.

2 June Richard Symons & Joane Dier
15 June Thomas Grose & Elizabeth ffine, vid.
28 June Edward Merifield & Petronel George
19 July William Jane & fflorence Tamkey
19 July Alexander Warne* & Joane Drewe
16 Aug. John Menheare & Petronell Miller
7 Sep. Thomas Barnett & Katherine Lavine
5 Nov. William Beawes & Elizabeth Langdon
8 Nov. Thomas Tanken *al's* Sparnell & Margery Daye
22 Nov. Richard Retallack & Agnes Doome
23 Nov. ffrancis Dazoe & Embline Alee
7 Feb. William Willes & Daratha Peearce, vid.

ANNO 1609.

2 May John Bond† gent. & Honor Carter
26 June Henry Addam & Elizabeth Lae
12 Sep. Thomas Jane & Mary Gale
30 Sep. John Saple & Jane Perkine
2 Oct. John Treneage & Petronell Benny
16 Jan. Richard ffowler & Jane Merifeild
23 Jan. George Nankevell & Honor Drewe
1 Feb. John Langdon gent. & Margery Mudon
1 Feb. John Dawe & Elizabeth Dawe
1 Feb. John Tippett & Katherine Crabbe
1 Feb. William Rendall & fflorence Paskow

ANNO 1610.

30 April John Rowe & Elizabeth Nutting
12 May Richard Moyses & Honor Carthewe
4 May Thomas Wyet & Elizabeth his wife
16 June William Copithorne & Margaret Sandowe
13 Sep. John Marshall & Jane Peerse

* John Menheere, in 1594, gave a silver ball to the parish. (Green Book.) The ancient practice of hurling the silver ball is still kept up with considerable spirit. The game consists of a contest between the male inhabitants of the town quarter, and those of the rural part of the parish; the one who can carry the ball to the appointed goal keeping it for the ensuing year. A preliminary hurl takes place on Shrove Tuesday, but the following Saturday week is the great day, when business is suspended, and all classes and ages take part in the contest.

* Son of John Warne of St. Ervan.

† He was son and heir of William Bond of Earth in St. Stephens by Saltash, by Margaret eldest dau. and co-heir of Hugh Fountaine of Ugborough, co. Devon. She was dau. of John Carter of St. Columb Major, gent., by Jane dau. of John Vivian of Trenowth, gent.: they had issue four sons and three daughters, viz.. William, John, James, Richard, Dorothea, Blanch, Honor.

29 Oct. Thomas Hawkin, Mr Hoblin's man
4 Nov. ffrancis George & Joane John
1 Dec. Richard Daue & Joane Baker
28 Jan. John Trehemban & Elizabeth Walter
28 Jan. Richard Hellier & Susan Snowe

Anno 1611.

16 April William Williams & Joane Hosken
27 April William Olver & Margaret Verren
3 June John Hawke & Katherine Burlace
5 Aug. William Williams & Treston Hoskine
10 Sep. Nicholas Bounsell & Margery Harvey
28 Oct. John Heicleft & Jane Marcombe
4 Nov. John Dawe & Mary Bilkye
12 Nov. Thomas Litticott & Grace Gradley
18 Nov. Thomas Stevens & Jane Copithorne
25 Nov. William Rawline & Margery Norten
25 Nov. William Truscott & Joane ffrancys
23 Feb. ffrancis Trehemban & Joane Richard

Anno 1612.

21 April Thomas Husband & fflorence his wife
14 Mar. John Harvey & Joane Holman
10 June John Day & Alice Berey
22 June John Cock & Elizabeth Caun
25 July Thomas Grose & Jane Thomas
7 Oct. Richard Smith gent. & Patience Broade
2 Nov. Richard Carveth & Susanna Calwaye
9 Dec. William Juth gent. & Ursulu Vivian*
15 Feb. Anthony Randell & Margaret Loves

Anno 1613.

14 April Nicholas Nicholls & Susan Cliffe
21 June Nicholas Cruse & Susanna Body
30 June Tho. Rowe & Honor Sprey

* This Ursula was a dau. of Thomas Vivian of Trenowth and Ann Lower his wife.

19 Sep. Thomas Kent & Catherine Meader
2 Nov. Mark Williams & Mary Olliver
16 Nov. Renfred Joll & Joane Randell
23 Nov. Richard Dayoe & Elizabeth Bate
25 Nov. John Merrifeild & Dorathe Prout
14 Dec. William Brabyn & Redagon Tankyn
3 Feb. John Cardewe & Philip Stepheens
8 Feb. John Bere gent.* & Margery Hoblyn
9 Feb. George Jewell & Joane Parking
14 Feb. William Beaford & Joane Caruannell
2 Mar. John Martyn & Olif Sprey

Anno 1614.

11 May Richard Boner & Elizabeth Blackaller
16 May Robert Cockinge & Margery Vivian
24 July Emanuell Harrice & Jane Hawke
20 July ffrancis Trehenbane & Jane Vincent
20 Sep. Lucke Pollard & Joane Webb
10 Oct. Thomas Jenning & Elizabeth Horrwell
9 Nov. John Kent & Ann Litticott
16 Jan. Hugh Lawry & Mary Copithorne
17 Jan. Paskowe Boden & Alice Dunston
20 Feb. William Dancaster & Elizabeth Phillipp

Anno 1615.

5 June Rob. Hambly & Petronell Skeberioe
1 July Richard Williams & Jane Trustll (?)
17 July Stephen Knight & Eleanor Muden
24 July John Evans & Susan Duggoe
18 Sep. John Cockinge & Jane Lucky
18 Sep. Oliver Jagoe & Annice Roger

* He was son of Sampson Bere of Lanteglos, by Philippa dau. of .... Ridgeway of Devon, and grandson of Tho. Bere of Trevedo, by Sibbell, dau. and heir of John Doyngell of Benethwood. He became of Trevedo; his wife Margery was dau. of Thomas Hoblyn of Nanswhydon by his first wife Judith, dau. of Edw. Trevalcois. They had issue Thomas, bap. in 1616; Eliz., bap. 1618; Judeth, and others.

9 Nov.	Thomas Brabyn & Tamazen Randall
27 Nov.	Henry Davie & Alice Gilbert
27 Jan.	Paskall Tifford & Barbara Jolly, vid.

ANNO 1616.

29 April	Robert Trehenban & Katherine Corington
25 June	John Blackcaller & Wilmote Husband
1 July	John Addams & Tamson Champion, vid.
1 July	James Moyle & Elizabeth Vivean
22 July	Henry Littecott & Elizabeth Trefrye
29 July	George Hodge & ffrances Angwyn
6 Aug.	John Day & Adria Colquite
7 Aug.	John Rowse & Joyce Strangman
16 Sep.	Martyne Donnacombe & Bridgett Clemoe
17 Sep.	Thomas Retallack & Elizabeth Parnell
23 Sep.	Henry Willes & Jane Day
14 Oct.	William Creele & Lawra Croppe
21 Oct.	Stephen Loves & Jenefred Benny
21 Oct.	Richard Behednow & Margery Nicholas
12 Nov.	Thomas Bayly & Rebecca Godfrey
17 Dec.	John Dyer & Honor Strangman
22 Jan.	Benyamin Strangman & Joanne Rowse
10 Feb.	Gilberte Roe & Margery Dowe
2 Mar.	Robert Drewe & Alice Heidon

ANNO 1617.

8 July	William Jolleye & Phillipp Mayhoe
15 July	John Copithorne & Elizabeth Heidon
12 Aug.	Thomas John & Elizabeth Drewe
20 Oct.	James Cockyn & Tamson George
20 Oct.	Marke Tyer & Katherine Pawlie
6 Nov.	John May & Joane Cocke
15 Jan.	Robert Pollard & Joane Hockaday
20 Jan.	Thomas Hawkey & Susanna Lae
26 Jan.	John Kent & Joane Waye
27 Jan.	John Brabyn & Anne Gwinnow
16 Feb.	Richard Rowse & Barbara Dyer

ANNO 1618.

1 June	Reinald Peeter & Joane Nynnise
20 July	Henry Helson & Katherine Moyle
26 Nov.	Thomas Retallack & Anne Ninnise
23 Jan.	Humphry Thomas & Joane Kettoe

ANNO 1619.

5 April	Thomas Simons & Elizabeth Trescott, vid.
29 May	Jonathan Jewell & Emblyn Peeke
9 Nov.	Nicholas Clemoe & Susan Rowse
15 Nov.	Michaell Thomas & Petronell Hambly
1 Feb.	John Williams & Jone Pell
28 Feb.	Pascowe Hawke *(blank)*
28 Feb.	James James & Honor Rowe

ANNO 1620.

24 April	Henry Husband & Jone Phillipp
24 April	Thomas Williams & Mary Snowe
26 April	Marten Tresteane & Pacience Tome
23 July	Richard Edwards & Rose Nankevall
3 Aug.	Charles Trubodye,* gent., & Agnes d. of Thomas Hoblyn, gent
21 Aug.	Robte Manuell & Bridget Baselye
2 Oct.	William Randoll & Elizabeth d. of Pascow John

ANNO 1621.

17 April	John Dayes man & mayde
13 April	John Spreye & Jane Hosken
28 May	Richard Crawleigh & Elizabeth Teeke
2 June	Jeremye Kent & Susan Bennett

* He was son and h. of Peter Trewbody, of Castle Lanlivery; his wife was a sister of Margery, wife of John Bere above, see note *ante*, p. 147.

2 July ffrancis Trewman *(blank)*
16 July William Williams & Mellerye Moyle
29 July Richard Pynnoe & Jane Carter
13 Aug. Alexander Penfound & Margery Kelwaye
27 Aug. Rawlyn Merefilde & Mr Vivian's mayde
8 Oct. Thomas Richards *al's* Bodye & Marye Tooker
30 Oct. Walter Spreye & Agnes Younge
18 Dec. Hugh Sprey & Susanna Browne

Anno 1622.

29 April John Rowse & Joane Tom
29 April Richard Hitchinge & Zenobia Merefeilde
26 Aug. Henry Trehemban & *(blank)* Cocke
25 Nov. William Thomas & Hester Nankivell
27 Nov. John Bayly & Phillip Langdon
3 Feb. George Nanskevell & Alles Skeberie
17 Feb. Henry Blight & Margaret Lawry

Anno 1623.

9 June Nicholas Stribley & Catherine Loves
9 June Thomas Law & Margaret Norton
22 Sep. John Luky & Petronell Trevethick
12 June Thomas Grosse & Jane Jenkyn
17 June David Walky & Jane Harvey

Anno 1624.

26 July James Dawe & Patience Smith, widdow
16 Aug. John James & Ann Cocke
8 Nov. Henry Richard & Susan the widowe of Richard Healier
7 Feb. Remphrey Jollye & Joane Jonas
12 Feb. Robert West & Joane Haydon
12 Feb. John Lawrye & Elizabeth Williams

1625.

13 June Henrichus Harvey vxarem dvxit Elizabetham Bounsall
4 July William Keete* & Elizabeth Beare
30 July John Moyle & Rebecca Carwitham
27 Oct. Christopher Cocke & Dorothie White
31 Oct. Martyn Edwards & Thomasin Bounsell

Anno 1626.

13 May William Calwaye & Jone Rouze
19 June ffrancis Rowse & May Michell
19 June Thomas Recorlake & Mawde his wiffe
18 July John Grace & Margery Upcott
21 Aug. Anthoney Jenkyn & Jane Bennett
25 Sep. Edward White & Eliz. Bosweage
10 Oct. Thomas Rouze & Anne Meihoe
11 Oct. Richard Copithorne & Priscilla Moyle
20 Nov. John Richard & Grace Coffyn
27 Nov. Walter Coryton & Elizabeth Williams
27 Nov. James Burlace & Alice Williams

Anno 1627.

17 April Robert James & Charity Wills
15 Jan. John Moydey & Jone Benny
23 April Peter Bond & Jane Olver
11 June Michaell Davy & Mary Retallack
16 July John Mayhow & Katherine Strangman
16 July Thomas Allen & Elizabeth Sexton
25 Aug. Lenard May & Elizabeth May
17 Sep. Thomas Tom & Constance Benat
15 Oct. Richard Merifeeld & Agnes Mayhow
29 Oct. Thomas Basly & Ann Richow
12 Nov. Nicholas Parkin & Catherine Grase
15 Jan. Henry Rowse & Joyse Strangman
19 Jan. Abraham Martyn & Elizabeth John
25 Feb. John Drewe & Mary Badcocke

* He was son of Ralph Kete, of St Columb, by his first wife Anne, dau. of William Arscott, of Holsworthy. His wife was a dau. of Thomas Bere, of Trevedo.

ANNO 1628.

9 June Richard Blake & Elizabeth Tankyn
8 July Patient Wills & Ann Cocking
17 Aug. John Broune & Honnour Cocket
27 Oct. Peter Jinking,* gent., & Anna Pomeroye
26 Jan. Thomas Pearse & Mary James
28 Jan. Thomas Williams & Grace Pudtegen

ANNO 1629.

21 April Thomas Gilbert & florence Juell
29 June John Grymes & Patience Rowse
6 July Richard Hawke & Jane Trenbeathe
6 July Nicholas Buckingham & Ann Tregeare
16 Jan. John Kent & Anne Trespettigo
21 Jan. Michaell Thomas & Ellenor Knight
23 Jan. John Day & Katherine Bawden

ANNO 1630.

18 April John Young & Mathow Hoswell
29 April John Rowse & florence Fare
7 June William Basly & Joane Cundy
15 June Walter Vivian & Lowdy Carlian
29 June Edward Knight & Joane Edye
25 July Richard Laugdon & Joane Case
2 Nov. Christopher Knight & Margery Langdon
17 Jan. Henry Rescorla & Alse Vivian
19 Jan. William Jeffery & Elizabeth Blake
24 Jan. Abraham Husband & Elizabeth John
6 Feb. Anthony Whittford & Constance Vounder

ANNO 1631.

18 April Renold Hawkey & Marye Adams
6 June William Williams & Joane Jollye
6 June Davye Stribleye & Jane Thomas

* He was the son of James Jenkin, of Trekenning, in St Columb Major, by Katherine, dau. of John Carter, of St Columb, and relict of John Brabyn, gent. She was the dau. of Andrew Pomeroy, of St Columb, by Jane, dau. and h. of Digory Hext, of Launceston.

8 June Edward Ashe,* gent., & Anne Kete
31 Oct. Thomas Carthewe & Grace Lawrye
14 Jan. Davye Walkye & Johane Peter
21 Jan. John Kendall & Grace Pedler

ANNO 1632.

11 June Rignold Hawke & Anne Ellerye
18 June Richard Hax & Margery Pokinhorne
24 July Richard Tregennowe & Jane Polkinhorne
4 Aug. Roger Browne & Blanche Scholler
10 Sep. Richard Carter & Marye Perse
26 Nov. Hearye Tregeare & Marye Olliver
21 Jan. John Darr & Elizabeth Arthur
4 Feb. John Hicks & Alce Hockyn
11 Feb. Josiah Daye & Dorothy Husband

ANNO 1633.

29 April John Horswell & An Bounsell
29 April John Jaen & Prissilla Lyll
8 July Archiball Rowse & Joane Steephens
15 July Nycholas Jane & Elizabeth Whyte
5 Aug. William Way & Johon Williams
9 Nov. George King & Mary White
20 Jan. Sampson Rescorlaw & Hester Addames
20 Jan. Thomas Harrys & Catheren Spray

ANNO 1634.

21 April Thomas Michell & Margaret Penendre
2 June Thomas Weskote & Mary Rescorly
27 Oct. John Gregory & Peternell Meryfeld
3 Nov. Theodorus Harvey & Chesson Richards
2 Nov. John Luky & Anish Daniell
24 Nov. John Strongman & Alse Simon
25 Nov. Hopson Baly & Elline Mahowe
23 Jan. John Oxman & Barbery Rouse

* He was son of Hen. Ash, of Sowton, Devon, by Loveday, dau. of Rich. Moyle, of St Austell, gent. His wife was a dau. of Ralph Kete, of St Columb, by Ann, dau. of William Arscott, of Holsworthy.

24 Jan. David Hambly & Sessely Morcome
27 Jan. James Pennow & Jone Landorig
27 Jan. Robert Grose & Jone Cornish

ANNO 1635.

6 April Martyn Stephens & Johan Martyn
3 Aug. Paschaw Browne & Margaret Cornish
5 Aug. William Ollyver & Elizabeth Trevethan
27 Aug. Barnabas Bettye & Katherine Pawlye
21 Sep. Richard Rouse & Amye Caparen
19 Oct. Giles Trescott & Elizabeth Harvye
26 Oct. George Spraye & ffLorence Rowse
10 Nov. Robert Nutting & Anne Dyer
12 Nov. Thomas Gwynian & Mary Heydon
1 Feb. Richard Hawke & Wilmott Berry
1 Feb. William Cocke & Elizabeth Davye
10 Feb. John Jolliffe & Ebett Priest

ANNO 1636.

26 April John Bettye & Jenneffer Bennye
27 April John Williams & Elizabeth Bettye
30 April Adam Dyer & Thomazin Cob
19 July John Roscorva & Sybella Evans
2 Aug. Mychell Strongman & ffrances Stevens
2 Aug. Anthoney Mytchell & Barbarowe Nycholl
20 Sep. Anthoney Pellawyn & Cenever Jollye
23 Nov. Henry Peers & Janne Daye
23 Nov. Barnabye Bettye & Constance Bishopp
23 Nov. Henry Braye & Thamazine Rowsse
12 Jan. Thomas Comon & Dorothie Phillippe
17 Jan. Steven Lovell & An Baylye
23 Jan. Mychaell Davye & An Bullen

ANNO 1637.

25 April Walter Noctover & Patience Vallis
25 June John Cundy & Ollife Vese
12 July John Jane & Jane Lenine
14 Aug. John Stephens & Ann Calway
2 Dec. Christopher Morcom & Elizabeth Thomas
15 Jan. Ralfe Williams & Barbara Dyer
3 April Beniamen Harvey & Ebat Sekyñr

ANNO 1638.

24 Sep. Christopher Wolcock & Christian George
25 Sep. John Brent & Margaret Phillipes
12 Nov. Hugh Sprey & Catherine Brabyn
1 Dec. John Strongman & Ann Harise
5 Jan. Henry Rowe & Passukis Jollye

ANNO 1639.

30 Sep. Thomas Boden & Patience Row
5 Oct. Christopher Parkyn & Mary Lawry
5 Oct. Robert Husband & Elizabeth Hamlyn
12 Nov. John Mill & Elyzabeth Peist
25 Nov. John Staple & Joane Pidler
28 Nov. Thomas Pollard & Ann Trenance
29 April John Davye & Jone Keant
13 May John Gillingame & Ann Hawke
22 Jan. Mathew John & Mary Burlas

ANNO 1640.

13 April David fflod & Mary Nottell
4 May Nicholas Basely & Jane Parkyn
8 June William James & Susan Robyns
4 Aug. John Notten & Katherine Parkyn
17 Aug. Reskimer Spreye & Joane Mayhow
8 Sep. Alexander Wills & Mary Lawry
28 Sep. John Hellyar & Alice Sandoe
27 Nov. Richard Troth & Ann Carthew
28 Nov. Bennett Perdew & Joane Pollard
18 Jan. Richard Nicholls & Jane Mellis
19 Jan. Peter Betty & Emlyn Davy
27 Jan. Nicholas Bounsell & Anr John
28 Jan. Thomas Hockey & Joane Stephens

17 Feb. ffrancis Burges* gen. & Ann Hoblyn
20 Feb. James Scabenyow & Joane Potter

ANNO 1641.

5 May Thomas Trevrin & Jane Vivian
22 Sep. John Bruar & Katherine Moore
5 Oct. Richard Jollyffe & ffrances Husband
19 Oct. Emanuell Hawke & Tamsin Landon
15 Nov. Richard Pinnow & Jane Marke
22 Nov. Richard Retallack & Honor Moses
25 Jan. William Lanyon & Elizabeth Graylyn

ANNO 1644.

13 May John Rouse & Jeneveetid Betty
17 June Peter Strongman & Ann Netten
28 Oct. Thomas Langdon & Joane Hendy
30 Oct. Christopher Hendy & Peternell Abraham
18 Nov. Richard Copithorne & Joan Mayhow
18 Nov. Richard Litticott & Jane May

ANNO 1645.

21 July Christopher Morcomb & Cheston Woolcock
12 Sep. John Williams & Grace John
13 Oct. ffrancis Littacott & Honor Callaway
20 July Theophilus Lawe & Mary Harvey

ANNO 1646.

29 Sep. John Cocke & Sibella Rescorla, vid.
8 Oct. Isack Jenkyn & Elizabeth French
2 Nov. Robert Strongman & Mary Edwards
7 Dec. Humphrey Harvey & Sibella Denning
9 Feb. Henry Knivett* gen. & Joane Hals
27 July Richard Hawke & Elizabeth Hill
4 Aug. James Stephens & Joane Kestlack
7 Sep. John Carter† gent. & Honour Lawry
28 Sep. Jo. Thorne & Peternell Williams
3 Nov. Barnabas Betty & Joane Rowse
15 Nov. Henry Rowse & Joice Rowse
29 Nov. Richard fford & Cissely Westerne
15 Dec. Thomas Nicholas & Joane Tome
25 Jan. John .... & Susan B...... ‡
27 Jan. Hugh Harvey & Mary Carter
28 Jan. Walter Vivian & Judeth Harvey

ANNO 1647.

7 Feb. Anthony Pawley & Joane Staple
14 Feb. William Crewes & Elizabeth Donacombe

ANNO 1648.

29 April Richard Moyle & Agnes Michell
2 Oct. Richard Langdon & Mary Robins
29 Oct. Henry Littacott & Alice Callaway
26 Dec. Thomas Callaway & Elizabeth Crawly
2 Jan. Wm. White & ffrances Pollard

* He was son of Humphry Burges of St. Erth, by Anne, dau. and heir of Richard Trenwith of St. Erth, and married first Grace dau. of John Molesworth of Pencarrow, Esq., by whom he had no issue; he married secondly as above, Ann dau. of Edw. Hoblyn of Nanswhyden, Esq., by Mary dau. and co-heir of Robert Apley of Barnstaple, Esq.; by this lady he had twelve children, of whom six survived him. viz., Thomas, Edward, Humphrey, Grace, Mary, Judeth. The latter, who became his eventual heir, married the Rev. Rob. Hoblyn, and was mother of Francis Hoblyn of Nanswhyden, Esq., J.P., who mar. Lady Penelope Godolphin. dau of Sydney, first Earl of Godolphin. He was buried 7th October, 1684, and his wife 31st Aug., 1688, at St. Mary's, Truro, where a monument to their memory was erected by their dau. Judeth Hoblyn.

* He was son and heir of Thomas Knyvett of Rosemeryn, by Ellen, dau. of Rich. Forster. He was buried at Budock as Henry Knyvett, gent., in 1671, and his wife was buried at the same place in 1669.

† He was son of John Carter, gent., of St. Columb, by Mary, dau. of John Moyle of St. Germans, gent. She was dau. of Sampson Lawry and Mary his wife (see bapt. 1627). They had issue. John who died young, and three daughters co-heirs. viz., Honour, married William Silly; Mary, married Thomas Hoblyn, of Tresaddern, gent.; and Jane married Giles Risedon.

‡ This entry is almost obliterated, and the man's name is without doubt Hendra (see bapt. 27 Jan., 1649); the wife's name commences with B, she probably being Susan, dau. of Walter Bishop, bapt. 16 Feb. 1619.

19 Mar. John England & Bridgett Donnacombe

ANNO 1649.

16 April William Cundy & Joice Baylie
7 May John Rickerd & Margery Powell
21 May Nicholas Williams & Cissely Trencage
29 May John Lawry & Susan Richards
June* Thomas Rickerd & Mary Blake
20 Aug. Hum. Trehemban & Cissely Browne
19 Sep. Marke William & Mary Coule
29 Oct. Edward Knight & Joane Morcombe
9 Jan. John Cockin & Eliz. Champion
11 Feb. Nicholas Rogers & Anne Buckinghame

ANNO 1650.

14 June John Arthur & Thomasin Daye
1 July Giles Edwards &Margery Mill
15 July William Hawkye & Anne Robins
27 July William Bone & Mary Copithorne
3 Aug. John Tyack & Margery Bishop
10 Aug. William Richards & Joane Jolly
2 Oct. Alexander Wills & Elizabeth Hals
22 Oct. William Edwards & Grace Richards
9 Nov. John Bligh & Elizabeth ffinch
2 Dec. Roger Jonas & Olive Thomas

ANNO 1651.

18 Nov. Richard Hawke & Grace Rawlin
29 Dec. Symon Trehemban & Mary Sprey
17 Jan. Richard Roope & Prissilla Coode
19 Jan. Christopher Jenkyn & Richoe Dunne
14 Feb. John Berry & Thomasin Coade

ANNO 1652.

5 July Thomas Salter & Elizabeth Lawrey
17 July John Strongman & Mawde Rowse
24 July Robert Skynner & Mawde Tenney
25 Sep. Richard Scrivenire & Thomas Nicholas
8 Jan. Walter Dyer & Joane Woulfe
14 Feb. Thomas Tremayne & Jane Pollard
21 Feb. George Couch and Barbara Cockinge

ANNO 1653.

13 April John Slade & Anne Hawkey
25 April Thomas Vincent & Olive Dancaster
17 May Arthur Jolly & Anne Rowatt
9 July ffrancis Manuell & Mary Richards
30 July Hugh Trenesell & Grace Thomas
1 Aug. Daniel Ropson & Hester Leekey
2 Aug. George Humphry & Jane Jane
8 Aug. Symon Law & Honour Bayley
26 Sep. Richard Dancaster & Jane Tremayne
27 Sep. John Dives Clerk & Eliz. Merrifeild*

* Blank.

* She was a dau. of Thomas Merrifield, gent.

SECOND VOLUME.

A New Register Booke, made the Second day of January, 1653, by Virtue of an Act of Parliament of the 24th of August last, in wth are Registered all the Contracts of Mariages and Publicacons thereof, Mariages, Births, and Burialls, wth have bin within the p'ish of Colombe Maior, in the Countye of Cornwall, since the said second day of January 1653, by George Kinge, elected by the p'ishioners to be Register for the said p'ish, and approved of and sworne by Richard Carter, Esquire, one of the Justices of the Peace of the said countye.

(Signed) RICH. CARTER.

PUBLICACONS AND MARRIAGES, 1653.*

ANNO 1653.

23 Jan. The contract of mariage betweene James Merefeild & Mary Code of this p'ish was the 8th day of January published the first tyme, 15th of January published the second tyme, the 22nd of January published the third tyme, and the 23rd of January the said James Merefeild & Mary Code were maried.

2 Feb. Mathew Handcock & Jane Bone 15 Jan., 22 Jan., 29 Jan.

6 Feb. Anthony Harvey & Margery Congdon 22 Jan., 29 Jan., 5 Feb.

6 Feb. Robte Emmett & Agnes Serjeant 22 Jan., 29 Jan., 5 Feb.

20 Feb. Daniel Couch & Ellinor Skynner 29 Jan., 5 Feb., 12 Feb.

17 April John Grace & Elizabeth Bray 12 Feb., 19 Feb., 26 Feb.

12 Mar. Nathaniel Adams & Marye Burne 20 Feb., 5 March, 12 March

15 May John Kent & Gertrude Kendall 5 March, 12 March, 19 March

* From this date down to 1659 the record of the marriages is contained in the same entry as the record of the publication of the contract of marriage; but beyond the first entry, which is given in full by way of example, it has been considered advisable to abbreviate the entries to nearly the usual form. The date preceding the entry is that of the marriage, following the entries are those of the publication of banns.

10 April Richard Symons & Anstis Stone of Columb Minor 26 March, 2 April, 9 April

ANNO 1654.

. . . . .* Thomas Harris & Joane Page of Columb Minor 30 April, 7 May, 14 May

28 June Maugan Cornish & Philippa Collins 25 May, 28 May, 11 June

3 July Henry Blake & Elizabeth Allyn 28 May, 4 June, 11 June

1 July Richard Troth & Emblyn Dale 11 June, 18 June, 25 June

14 Aug. Elias Pollard & Susan Calway 9 July, 16 July, 23 July

26 July Robert James & Maud George first in the Markett Place 13 July, the second tyme in the Church 16 July, the third tyme in the Markett Place 20 July

. . . . . Thomas John & Beatresse Somer of Columb Minor 3 Sep., 10 Sep., 17 Sep.

. . . . . Robert Slyman & Frances Greenaway 17 Sep., 24 Sep., 1 Oct.

5 Nov. John Tynnye & Mary Olver 8 Oct., 15 Oct., 22 Oct.

25 Nov. Henry Dyer & Katherine Hore 22 Oct., 29 Oct., 5 Nov.

. . . . . Richard Stephens & Ann Munday 22 Oct., 29 Oct., 5 Nov.

. . . . . Nighton Cock & Ann Soloman 22 Oct., 29 Oct., 5 Nov.

* Where the dots occur the date of marriage is omitted in the original.

James Morris & Mary Bennye 29 Oct. & 2 Nov. in the Market place
John Dingle & Jane Killston 5 Nov., 12 Nov., 29 Nov.
Philip White & Jone Baselye 12 Nov., 19 Nov., 26 Nov.
William Adam & Mary Wilton 12 Nov., 19 Nov., 26 Nov.
William Arthure & Dorothy Molcock of Columb Minor 3 Dec., 10 Dec., 17 Dec.
William Trewren of Madderne & Elizabeth Code of this p'ish 10 Dec., 17 Dec., 24 Dec.
Richard Andrewe of Crantock & Elizabeth Otes of Padstowe 31 Dec., 7 Jan., 14 Jan.
John Congdon of Columb Minor & Mary Sampson of the same 31 Dec., 7 Jan., 14 Jan.
John Jose & Diana Adams of Crantock 21 Jan., 28 Jan., 4 Feb.
Pascow Higgons of Crantock & Joane Williams of the same 4 Feb., 11 Feb., 18 Feb.

ANNO 1655.

William Troulson of Columb Minor & Isott Morris of Little Colan 15 April, 22 April, 29 April
Henry Trehembam & Joane Mill 22 April, 29 April, 6 May
Abel Williams & Katherine Jolly 6 May, 13 May, 20 May
6 July John Richards & Honor Rous, first 27 May in the Market place, 3 June, 10 June
Richard Lukys of Columb Minor & Thomasine Sconserne of the same 27 May the first tyme in the Markett place, 3 June, 10 June
Richard Jeffery of Columb Minor & Alice Wickett of Little Colan 27 May the first tyme in the Markett place, 3 June, 10 June
. . . . . Thomas Trenance of Withiell & Katherine Cock of this p'ish 27 May, 3 June, 10 June
9 July Christopher Blake & Anne Rescorla 10 June, 17 June, 24 June
10 July Thomas Wills s. of Mathewe Wills of this p'ish, deceased, & Grace Crowley, dau. of Richard Crowley of this p'ish, deceased 17 June, 24 June, 1 July
. . . . . Colan Blewett* s. of Colan Blewett, of Little Colan, Esq., deceased, & Elizabeth Wrey, dau. of Sir William Wrey, knight & bart., deceased Published in the Markett place 21 June, 28 June, 5 July
27 Sep. Thomas Nicklus & Dorcas Robarts of Columb Minor Published three tymes upon three several Lords dayes
18 Sep. William Beafford of this p'ish & Alice Hearle of Cubye, published three tymes upon three several Lords dayes ended 5 Aug., and were married by Richard Collins — (In the time of the Rebellion, and were fully maryed by the Minister the 10th day of Sept., 1656†).
. . . . . Robert Code & Jane Stephens published three tymes ended 2 Sept.
. . . . . Robert Moyle of this p'ish & Mary Thomas of Gwendron, published three tymes ended 25 Sept., and were maried by Richard Carter, Esq.
. . . . . Thomas Bounsell & Honor Strangman, published three tymes ended 22 Sep.
17 Nov. Thomas Cock s. of John Cock of Columb Minor & Mary Samon dau. of John Samon, published three tymes ended 10 June, & were maried by Richard Carter, Esq.

* Colan Blewett bap. at Colan, 14 Sep., 1630. He was a major in the army of King Charles I., and ob. s.p. His wife Elizabeth was a dau. of Sir William Wrey, second bart., by his wife Elizabeth, youngest dau. of Sir Edw. Chichester, created Earl of Donegal.

† This part in brackets is added between the lines by another hand.

Henry Endeen s. of Hen. Endeen of Colomb Minor, deceased & Philippa Roberts dau. of John Roberts of Columb Minor, published three tymes ended 18 Nov.

William Sampson & Audrey Lukye of this p'ish, published three tymes ended 16 Dec.

Arthur Breade of this p'ish & Margery Blake of Maugan, published three tymes ended 20 Jan.

Joseph Fittick of Colomb Minor & Jane Cock of the same, published three tymes ended 31 Jan.

Gabriell Newton of Mawgan & Maud Werringe* of Little Petherick, published in the Markett place on three several markett dayes ended 21 Feb., & maried by Richard Carter, Esq.

18 Feb. John Naparroe of this parish & Alice Pynnoe of this p'ish, published upon three several Lord's dayes end 17 Feb., & were maried by Richard Carter, Esq.

ANNO 1656.

27 May Oliver Baselye of this p'ish & Katherine Badge of Camborne, published the last time 24 Feb. Maried by Richard Carter, Esq.

Mathew Adams of this p'ish & Joan Fry of Bodmin, the last time 16 March

. . . . . John Blake of Maugan & Elizabeth Hawke of Colomb Minor, 3 April

26 April Stephen Sleepe of Ennoder & Margery Gammoe of Colomb Minor, 3 April. Mar. by Ric. Carter, Esq.

William Moore & Mary Dyer of this p'ish, 20 April

John Wise of Ennoder & Elizabeth Calway, 20 April

John Day s. of James Day, gent. & Jane Godfrey dau. of Lewis Godfrey, gent. 27 April

* This should be Warne.

21 June Anthony Michell & Christian Lukye of this p'ish, 8 June. Mar. by Ric. Carter, Esq.

Ralph Chenowith & Anstis Jolly of this p'ish, 17 Aug.

John Legge s. of John Legge, clerke, deceased & Elizabeth Hicks dau. of John Hicks, gent., deceased 23 Nov.

20 Dec. Thomas Calway & Joane Coppithorne of this p'ish, 30 Nov. Mar. by William Orchard, Maior of Bodmyn.

Robert May & Jane Kent of this p'ish, 18 Jan.

ANNO 1657.

7 April Christopher Inch & Joane Baylye, 29 Feb. Mar. by Tho. Gawen, Esq.

1 Mar. Edmund Hughes, clerke & Martha Bluett, 15 Feb. Mar. by Ric. Carter, Esq.

11 May Henry Warne & Diana Philpe 8 Feb., & mar. by William Orchard, Maior of Bodmyn

4 Mar. Richard Whitford of Little Colan & Ann Brabyn of this p'ish, 22 Feb. Mar. by William Opye, Justice in Bodmyn

John Werry of St. Wen & Charitye Salter of this p'ish 8 March

. . . . . Henry Watts of St. Stephens & Elizabeth Rowse of this p'ish, 5 April

. . . . . John Gilbert & Joane West of this p'ish, 5 April

. . . . . William Jolly & Joane Retallack, 19 April

. . . . . Henry Brewer & Barbara Rowse, 3 May

20 July William Lanyon & Emme Hockyn, 12 July, & mar. by Ric. Carter, Esq., one of the Justices

5 Aug. Richard Congdon & Margaret Sprey, 19 July, mar. by Thomas Travers, clerk

26 Oct. John Davis & Dorothy Libby of this p'ish, 2 Aug., mar. by Thomas Travers, clerk

6 Oct. Peter Kendall & Anne Williams 9 Aug. Mar. by Tho. Travers, clerk

. . . . . John Best & Jane Warne 23 Aug.

23 Oct. George Kinge & Mary Tucker 6 Sep., mar. by Edmund Hughes, clerk

Maugan Cock of Maugan & Milson Pollard, 13 Sep.

3 Nov. Peter Rescorlac & Joyce Strangman, mar. by Tho. Travers, clerk

17 Nov. John Rowse & Elizabeth Crase

30 Jan. Nicholas Basely & Ann Sprey

ANNO 1658.

27 Mar. John Merifield & Beaton Bayleiffe

4 June Daniell James & Joane Dun

8 June Thomas Michell & Thomasine Strongman

8 June Edmond Walkey & Ellinor Perry

21 June Phillipp Nicklas & Alice Rous

20 July George Luny & Mary May

22 July Peter Day & Jone Brabyn

21 July Edward Crawley & Katherine Lovell

24 July John Stevens & Presilla Libbey

13 Dec. Thomas Williams & Jone Peirse

29 Dec. William Metheroll & Agnes Moyle

29 Dec. Jonathan Rowse & Grace Cornish

ANNO 1659.

16 May Richard Edwards & Temperance Stephens

2 July Arthur Comon & Alice West

10 July Edward Hoblyn,* gent. & Bridgett Carewe

John Hicks & Zenoby Gilbert, published three times

10 July Henry Hobert & Sara Browne

10 July William Merifeild & Jone Westcote

5 Nov. Elias Pollard & Anne Allen

26 Dec. John Allen & Mary Williams

9 Jan. Ralph Crawley & Elizabeth Couth

17 Jan. William Jolly & Honor Woolcock

10 Feb. John Bourne & Margery Hatch

28 Feb. Thomas Drew & Jaell Darye

* He was the third son of Edw. Hoblyn of Nanswhyden, Esq., by his wife Mary, dau. and co-heir of Robert Apley of Barnstable; he was town clerk of Bodmin, and died 28 Dec., 1688, aged 62. His wife was one of the daughters and co-heiresses of John Carew of Penwarne; by her he was ancestor of Hoblyn of Penhargard, Colquite and Croane.

8 Mar. Thomas Withell & Mellior Richards

ANNO 1660.

23 April Henry Jolly & Elizabeth Skynner

17 Sep. Martyn Strongman & ffrances Steephens

6 Oct. Richard Williams & Margery Langdon

16 Oct. Dennis Westcott & Agatha Samble

29 Oct. Gilbert Lawnder & Melior Williams

10 Nov. John May & Grace Stribly

13 Nov. Henry Morcomb & Hester Rescorla

27 Nov. John Truscott & Margaret Lawry

27 Nov. James Hawkey & Issabell Steephens

18 Dec. Richard Veale & Margaret Wills

28 Dec. Lawrence Kendall & Junifell Pollowyn

1 Jan. Richard Slade & Emblyn Daye

5 Feb. John Bryant & Udye Wills

ANNO 1661.

16 April William Moore & Dorothy Wills

19 April Edward Lawry & Margery Grosse

14 May John Hawkey & Ann Dancaster

3 June Christopher Wilcock & Peternell Tenny

19 Aug. James Watts & Ann Bewes

22 Aug. John Rouse & Ellinor Penfound

4 Jan. John Thomas & Margery Reignold

ANNO 1662.

17 June William Dennis & Agnes Kestlack

9 Sep. Remfrey Rowse & Jane Drew

21 Oct. Bernard Rowse & Elizabeth Hawkey

10 Nov. John Loggett & Joane Nanparcow

13 Jan. Luke Giles & Honor Lee

20 Jan. Richard Wills & Elizabeth Coode

13 Feb. William Vigers & Anne Slade

ANNO 1663.

27 April John Smyth & Raddigan Littacott

12 May Edward Crewes & Anne Pollard
19 May Thomas Warne* & Elizabeth Lovell
15 June Morgan Oliver & Mary Sweete
4 July Thomas Hockyn & Agnes Williams
14 July Edward Merrifeild & Alice Sprey
4 Aug. Stephen Stephens & Anne Husband
8 Sep. George Bayley & Elizabeth Emett
10 Nov. Arthur Jenkyn & Joane Marshall
19 Jan. Peter Cockyn and Honor Williams
3 Feb. John Brabyn, gent. & Alice Daye

ANNO 1664.

26 April John Watts & Jenifer Rouse
21 June John Lee & Sibella Law
16 July John Lawrey & Maude Puncher
25 July Richard Hoblyn,† Esq., & Anne the daughter of John Carew of Penwarne, Esq.
16 Aug. John Barner & Ann Bayley
10 Sep. Isack Nicholl & Elizabeth Reede
17 Sep. John Jane & Honour Grace
17 Sep. Thomas Hendra & Jane Hicks
17 Sep. John James and Elizabeth Harris
19 Oct. William Evelyn & Jane Rescorla
16 Nov. Daniell Phillipp & Marion Knight
16 Jan. Robert Edwards & Emblyn Champion
17 Jan. John Peters & Marion Spry

ANNO 1665.

10 April John Williams & Margery Polkinghorne
29 April William Tenney & Honor Rowe
27 April Henry Gill & Mary Coriton

* Son of John Warne of St. Issey; she was dau. of Stephen Lovell by Ann his wife, dau. of John Bayly. They had several children, of whom Stephen left descendants.

† He was a son of Edw. Hoblyn, of Nanswhyden, Esq., by Mary, daughter and co-heir of Rob. Apley of Barnstaple; he was of Antron, and mar. one of the daughters and co-heirs of John Carewe of Penwarne, but ob. s. p. will proved in 1693.

1 Aug. Robert Litticott & Joane Brent
12 Aug. Thomas Rowse & Joane Trethewy
25 Oct. Stephen Banger & Rachell Rescorla
14 Nov. John Seyntaubin* the sone of John Seyntaubyn, Esq. & Anne the d. of James Jenkyn, Esq., deceased
29 Nov. Richard Edward & Margery Barber
2 Dec. Henry Lee & Barbara Basley
23 Jan. Gidion Cockyn & ffrances Husband
29 Jan. Charles Thomas & Joane Bray
26 Feb. David Pearse & Alice Nicholl

ANNO 1666.

16 April William Cock & Ann Richards
14 July John Whitford & Thomas Steephens
4 Jan. Thomas Littacott & Jane Harbor
16 Jan. James Moyle & Joane Thomas
2 Feb. James Metherell & Emblyn Arthur
4 Mar. Charles Retallack & Dorcas Hoskyn
5 Mar. Thomas Salter & Jone Vanson

ANNO 1667.

25 April James Rouse & Margaret Thomas
29 June John Westerne & Beaton Merifeild
24 July Thomas Geach & Ellinor Luney
26 July Richard Pinnowe & Mary Rowe
27 July John Husband & Honor May
5 Oct. Phillip Kinge & Joane Ellery
12 Nov. Edward Pollowyn & Elizabeth Hambly
30 Nov. Ralph Lamb & Mary Arthur
30 Nov. John Blake & Alice Hockey

ANNO 1668.

14 April John Buckthorpth & ffrances Littacott
4 July Thomas Scaberioe & Elizabeth Hockyn

* This John St. Aubyn was created a baronet in 24 Charles II., 1671; he married as above a dau. and co-heir of James Jenkyn of Trekynning in St. Columb, Esq., by whom he had Sir John, the second bart., and two daughters, Anne and Elizabeth; the latter mar. Tho. Northmore of Cleave, near Exeter. (See also note, p. 60.)

26 Sep. John Pollouwyn & Phillippa Langman
29 Sep. Henry Burgh & Honor Lovell
10 Oct. Arthur Comon & Phillippa James
26 Oct. John Bale & Thomazine Rescorla
10 Nov. Richard Lovell & Mary Jolly
13 Jan. Richard fforde & Audrye Sprey
15 Jan. John Cawdy & Joane Martin
6 Feb. Samuel Edwards & Joane Thorne

ANNO 1669.

10 May William Delbridge & Honour Williams
11 May Henry Jolly & Anne Rawe
11 June George Randle & Jane Basely
20 June Thomas Callaway & Eliz. Kestlack
15 June William Darre & Jone Callaway
22 June John Tome & Thomasine Peter

ANNO 1670.

20 June ffrancis Trebilcock & Pernell Levermore
22 June Nicholas Slanninge,* knt of the bath and baronett, & Mary the daughter of James Jenkyn, Esq., deceased
24 Jan. Edward Couch & ffrances Baylie

ANNO 1671.

1 Feb. Elias Heard & Dorothy ffountaine
19 Feb. Stephen Stephens & Joane Cornish

ANNO 1672.

16 April Phillip Oxnam & Epiphany Salter
21 May Edward Pollowyn & Jane Bewes
25 May Thomas Stevens & Dorothy Sleepe
15 June John Cock & Mary Seaberio
22 July Thomas Bennet & Margarite Grimes
2 Sep. Robert Clemow & Sara Prater
8 Oct. James Peters & Gartrid Spry
4 Nov. ffrancis Godolphin* & Grace Crewes
28 Jan. Peter Husband & Anne Chammin

ANNO 1673.

7 April Simon Rawling & Alice Cockin
7 April John Allen & ffrances Horswell
3 May Nycholas Bounsell & Jane Allen
13 June Theophilus Betty & Hester Hoge
24 June Henry Cock & Mary Cock
14 July Thomas Lawe & fflorence Husband
2 Sep. Henry Warne & Katherine Ivy
11 Sep. Thomas Michell & Frances Cruse
18 Nov. John Sprey & Joan Rowse
17 Jan. Charles Gummow & Joan Hawk
27 Jan. John Browne & Frances White
17 Feb. Frances Poole & Grace Dawe

ANNO 1674.

7 May John Sherman & Jane Short
26 June George Champion & Jane Haycroft
23 July Samuell Pryn & Jane Roe
4 Aug. William Minnow & Florence Rescorla
8 Aug. John Edwards & Charity Withell
29 Aug. Peter Pollard & Johan Humphrey
5 Sep. Charles Bownsell & Anne Lovell
22 Sep. Thomas Guilly & Mary Westcott
26 Sep. Christopher Reynold & Jane Brabyn
9 Nov. Richard Retallack & Christian Westerne
13 Jan. Richard Pollard & Jane Blake
3 Feb. George Reignolds & Elizabeth Williams

* Sir Nicholas Slanning was created a baronet 19 Jan., 1662-3. He married first Ann daughter of Sir George Carteret, bart., of St. Owen's in Jersey; secondly, Mary dau. of Sir Andrew Henley of Henley, co. Somerset, bart.; thirdly, the co-heir of James Jenkin, of Trekynning, as above; and fourthly, a dau. of Edmond Parker, of Borrington. He had issue by his second wife only, a son, Sir Andrew Slanning, 2 bart., who died s.p.

* He was probably son of John Godolphin of St. Kew by Honor, dau. of John Molesworth, who was third son of John Godolphin, second son of Sir Francis Godolphin of Godolphin. His wife was a dau. of William & Elizabeth Crewes of St. Columb (see her bapt. 1649). They had issue, three sons and six daughters; of these Anthony mar. twice, and left issue by both wives.

ANNO 1675.

27 April Richard Hawke & Jane Barber
29 April Robert Litticott *al's* Grigor & Grace Cundey
23 Oct. John Harvey & Julyan Trounsell
27 Nov. Francis Rescorla & Elizabeth Agre
5 Feb. George Sleepe & Philip Paynter

ANNO 1676.

27 Mar. William Silly,* Esq. & Honor the dau. of John Carter, Esq., deceased
8 April John Pill & Margarite Pawly
10 June Henry Langdon & Dinah Martyn
16 Sep. Jacob Husband & Mary Martyn
21 Oct. John Strongman & Elizabeth Crawley
21 Nov. Nicholas Hodge & Jane Farroe
4 Dec. William Hendra & Johan Hoskyn
3 Feb. John Benallack & Alice Williams

ANNO 1677.

16 June John Cocking & Elizabeth Pollowyn
4 July John Mill & Johan Congdon
16 July Ezekiell Gummow & Christian Pollard
27 July Christopher Bethick & Emblin Martyn
22 Sep. Wm. Hawkins & Sarai Reynolds

ANNO 1678.

17 June Henry Chapman & Avis Withiell
29 June William Minnow & Mary Richards
12 Sep. John Whitaker & Honor Darr
21 Feb. John Gibbs & Thomas Prater

ANNO 1679.

6 May John Polkinghorne & Mary Thomas
18 July Edward Rickard & Barber Jollye
29 July John Joynking & Charritye Pozowarne
16 Sep. Richard Williams & Susan Richards
23 Feb. Richard Cock & Joane Stibbert

ANNO 1680.

21 April William Moore & Avis Couch
8 May Robert Manuell & Marye Couch
1 May George Tom & Mary Hockin
17 Sep. Robert Retallack & Mary Edwards
2 Oct. John Tyer & Honor Launder
23 Oct. Humphrey Harvey, junr. & Jane Warne
30 Dec. John Bishop, rector, & An* the daughter of Robert Hoblyn, Esq.
15 Jan. John Sanders & Margaret Burlace
29 Jan. Stephen Hendy & Christian Callaway
5 Feb. Nicholas Hawk & Dorcas Barry
25 Feb. Anthony Robbins & Elizabeth Barry

ANNO 1681.

7 May Peter Bounsell & Mary Audredg
27 May William Bazely & Elizabeth Michell
18 June William Samble & Mary Mannell
2 July Bernard Lobb & Jane Williams
28 Oct. Henry Jolly & Hon^r Bounsell
21 Nov. William Arundell† & Honor Pollard
24 Nov. Thomas Tibb & Elizabeth Barry
26 Dec. Charles Allen & Thomas. Skinner
4 Feb. John Thern & Jane Couch
28 Feb. John Rouse & Joan White

ANNO 1682.

13 Oct. Arthur Broad & Mary Adams
4 Nov. John Harvy & Jone Stephens
6 Jan. William Richards & Joan Carne

* He was of Trevelver, son of John Silly of St. Wenn, afterwards of Trevelver in St. Minver, M.P. for Bodmin, by Jane dau. of William Cotton, Precentor of Exeter. Honor Carter, one of the co-heirs of John Carter of St. Columb, was his second wife, the issue of whom, two daughters, became co-heirs, viz., Jane, married Nathaniel Shepherd of Little St. Botolph, Bishopsgate, London, and Honour, married Anthony Tanner of St. Euoder, died s.p.

* Daughter of Rob. Hoblyn, of Nanswhyden, Esq., by Grace, dau. and co-heir of John Carew of Penwarne. They had issue Robert, Johanne, and Edward. The Rev. John Bishop mar. secondly Mary, dau. of Rev. Thomas Pendarves, rector of St. Columb and Mawgan, by whom he had several other children.

† See note p. 71, ante.

ANNO 1683.

8 July Thomas Bounsell & Grace Bawden
16 July Gabriell Glanvill & Honour Lawry
12 Nov. Richard Callaway & ffrances Michell
14 Nov. Emanell Tonkyn of the p'ish of St. Dennis & Mary Best of the p'ish of St. Wenn
26 Dec. Humphrey Benney & Dorothy Row
15 April Thomas Tonkyn & Jone Lawry

ANNO 1684.

28 April John Beauchamp,* Esq. & Emblyn Edwards
21 May William Beret† & Margaret Metherell
24 May John Drew & ffrances Retallack
30 June Samuel Champion & Lydia Batten
26 July Thomas Adams & Elizabeth Stephens
22 Sep. Giles Risedon, Esq. & Jane Carter‡
10 Nov. Symon Law & Thomasin Williams
26 Dec. Richard Bray & Ebbott John
1 Jan. Morgan Roberts & Diana James
9 Jan. John Abram & Judeth Williams
20 Jan. Walter Vivian & Anne Howe
14 Feb. Thomas Langdon & Joane Harvey
27 April William Lawe & Grace Rawlin

ANNO 1685.

9 May John Langdon & Entice Endean
16 May William Minnoe & Johane Paine
16 May James Cocke & Mary Michael
1 Aug. John Michell & Avis Mill

* Son of John Beauchamp of Chiton (Chytane) in St. Enoder. In a short pedigree of Beauchamp of Pengreep. in the *Herald and Genealogist*, vol. viii., p. 518, the above John and Emblyn are given as ancestors of Francis Beauchamp of Pengreep, who mar. Ellen Cranmer; this is evidently an error, the date of the mar. is given as 1584, instead of 1684. See also Col. Vivian's Visitations of Cornwall; ped. Beauchamp of Benerton and Beauchamp of Chiton.

† He was probably a son of Geo. Bere of St. Ervan.

‡ She was youngest dau. and co-heir of John Carter of St. Columb.

8 Aug. William Dancaster & Joan Harden
3 Oct. Jonathan Daw & Ann Thomas
31 Oct. Luke Jolly & Elizabeth Bone
17 Nov. George Hicks & Grace May
19 Nov. ffrancis Bedella & Elizabeth Law
21 Nov. John Strongman & Julian Bilky
26 Dec. Thomas Launder & Mary Hawkey

ANNO 1686.

17 April Marke Lawry & Gartherude Bone
4 June William Warne* & Anne Broad
21 Aug. William Tucker & Mary Goade
7 Sep. Thomas Bolitho & Anne Jolly
16 Sep. Thomas Day & Grace Kent
25 Sep. Thomas Smith & Joane Callaway
25 Sep. James Olliver & Margery Chapell
16 Oct. James Callaway & Rebecca Martyn
27 Nov. John Leverton & Mary Stephens
15 Jan. Martyn Tom & Dorothy Luke
20 Jan. Edward Cruse & Sarah Bishopp

ANNO 1687.

9 April Arthur Michell & Peternell Bone
9 April Arthur Veale & Ruth Brewer
4 June James Bone & Katherine Davies
23 Sep. Henry Rescorla & Joane Downeing
8 Oct. William Lunye & Jane Thomas
10 Oct. William Merifeild & Bridgett Bounden
15 Oct. Thomas Trevithick & Mary Peters
7 Nov. Nathaniell Adams & Rebecca George
26 Dec. Nicholas Peters & Jane Thomas

ANNO 1688.

5 May Thomas Crapp & Rose Merifeild
2 June Phillip Harvey & Marrett Row

* He was son of Tho. Warne & Eliz. Lovell. His wife was a daughter of Arthur Broad and his wife, Margery Blake, of Mawgan.

8 Sep. William Clemens & Elizabeth Crews
21 Sep. Thomas Hoblyn,* gent., & Mary the daughter of John Carter, Esqr
16 Nov. Maryn Tom & Constance Bodye
22 Dec. Robert Husband & Mileent Retallack
31 Dec. ffrancis Pollard & Susanna Harris
9 Feb. Nicholas Grigg & ffrances Griggor

ANNO 1689.

20 July Elias Pollard & Ebbott Bray, wid.
9 Oct. Richard Langdon & Katheryn (*blank*)†
26 Oct. William Hornbrooke & Anne Merifeild
30 Nov. Edward Peters & Maudlyn Jeffery
14 Jan. Nathaniel Davies & Jane Richards
10 Feb. John Langdon & Jone Langdon
17 Feb. John Strongman & ffrances Launder

ANNO 1690.

6 June Thomas Mannell & Elizabeth Morcombe
9 June Phillip Ellot & Abbigall Jolly
29 Sep. Henry Mill & Joane Watts
6 Oct. Ezethill Retallack & Patience Brewer
7 Nov. Edward Richards & Blanch Jolly
28 Nov. Edward Williams & Temperance Skinner
5 Dec. John Richard & Mary Mill
15 Jan. John Davyes & Mary Blight
7 Feb. James Brear & Honor fford
20 Feb. Wm Minnow & Elizabeth Thomas
21 Feb. George Jolly & Ann Kent

* He was of Tresaddern, in St. Columb (son of Rob. Hoblyn, of Nanswhyden, by Grace Carew); his wife was the second daughter and coheiress of John Carter, of St. Columb, by whom he had an only son, John Hoblyn, of Kenwyn, from whom the present William Paget Hoblyn, Esq., of The Fir Hill, descends, and who still possesses some of the property acquired by this marriage, called the Carter Rocks, lying off the adjacent coast.

† A blank left.

ANNO 1691.

29 April John Collock & Joane Capell
16 May Thomas Callaway & Mary Bettenson, widow
20 May Thomas Starr & ffrances Oxnam
18 Sep. James Blake & Constance Troth
10 Oct. Jacob Tonkin & Elizabeth Bone
7 Nov. Joell Capell & Elizabeth Allen
9 Nov. John Eudye & Magdaline Eudye
28 Dec. Henry Cock & Mary Cock
2 Jan. Lancelott Clemens & Grace Tenny
9 Feb. James Merifield & Katherine Clemow

ANNO 1692.

30 April John Isabell & Grace Neele
21 Sep. Daniell Rapson & Margery Barnes
25 Sep. John Pill & Mary Hare
20 Oct. William Cock,* gent., & Mary the daughter of Robert Hoblyn, Esqr
18 Nov. Abraham Lee & Patienc James
31 Dec. Humphrey Benny & Jone Roberts
7 Jan. Anthony Callaway & Reddegon Trevenna
14 Jan. Henry Withell & Ursula Parrow
8 Feb. John Eastman & Jane Wills

ANNO 1693.

25 April Joseph Jane & Jane Merefield
6 May Henry Thomas & Jane Palmer
13 May John Cayzer & ffrances Strongman
8 Sep. Thomas Williams & Grace Cockaine
9 Sep. Isaack Nicholls & Jane Retallack
23 Sep. Joseph Merefeild & Jane Crawley
20 Oct. Richard Cowle & Thomas Trenennis
8 Dec. Stephen Warne† & Mary Jack Andrew

* He was of Helston, solicitor; his wife a daughter of Rob. Hoblyn, of Nanswhyden, by Grace Carew.

† He was son of Tho. Warne and Eliz. Lovell; they had several children, of whom Simon alone survived and married.

Anno 1694.

15 June Robert Vincent & Elizabeth Merefield
21 July Hugh Blake & Elizabeth Mitchell
27 Oct. William Harris & Frances Rawe
12 Nov. John Banger & Mary Pearse
1 Dec. Isaack Jenkyn & Ollive Westcott
15 Jan. Richard Webber & ffrances Jolley

Anno 1695.

1 April Henry Tenny and Priscilla George
25 May Richard Cornish & Phillippa Harris
15 June Thomas Hocken and Ann Brewer
17 Aug. Richard Manuell & Dorothy Pearse
12 Oct. Samson Gerrans & Christopher Arthur
5 Feb. Thomas Callaway & Juniphor Wills
25 Feb. Thomas Issabell & fflorence Harris

Anno 1696.

28 April Thomas Merrifield & Jone Watts
21 May Patherick Jelbert & Ann Mitchell
15 June Bernard Lobb & Elizabeth Jolley
20 June Mathew Ropstone & Marrian Cornish
26 June Richard Webber & ffrances Buckthought
7 Oct. Olliver Basley and Charity Capell
30 Oct. Blight Haycroft & M[rs] Honor Champion, married at St. Enoder
28 Nov. Olliver Rawe & Jane Scabeerian
16 Jan. Phillip King & Mary Robyns

Anno 1697.

22 May Edward Basley and Barbara Wolcock
1 Jan. John Perkins & Junifer Pollawyn
14 Feb. Henry Darr & Mary Rawe

Anno 1698.

14 May John Tenny & Temperance Hawking
14 June John Hilbron & Temperance Stephens
2 July James Adams & Margarett Punchard
7 July John Tenny and Elizabeth Arthur
18 Feb. Robert Merefield and Jane Hawke

Anno 1699.

27 Jan. John Lawrey & Jone Leckey
10 Feb. William Dennis, jun., & Jone Trenennis

Anno 1700.

29 May George Thomas*
5 Oct. Ralph Chynoweth & Joan Couch
7 Oct. Thomas Polkinghorne*
9 Nov. Christopher Tresteane*
26 Dec. Thomas Henry*
27 Dec. Richard Cowle*
28 Dec. John Jelbert & Katheryn May
4 Jan. Abraham Husband*
8 Feb. Richard Garlant & Dorothy Clemows
21 Feb. Charles Scraberrian & Margery Bonython

Anno 1701.

23 May Petter Best & Susanna Norwayel
10 Nov. Thomas Chapple & . . . . . *
13 Feb. Ralph Allen & Mary White

Anno 1702.

13 May Charles Jones, of S[t] Ives, in the county of Cornwall, gent., & Margery Keigwin, of Penzance
22 May Thomas Symons & Christian Gerans
25 July John Buling & Martha Pawle
24 Oct. William Withell and Mary Jolley
20 Dec. Peter Tremaine *al's* Cocking & Margery Kayling
31 Dec. William Resogan & Emblyn Day

Anno 1703.

18 April William Bone & Temperance Luley
16 May John Harris & Ann Hawke
13 Nov. James Moarshead and Ann Leverton
14 Feb. Samuel Williams & Honor Manuell

* Sic.

ANNO 1704.

20 April Jonathan Barrett & Catherin Barry
26 April Degory Keast & Pentecost Woodman
13 May Robert Husband & Joan Honey
27 May Methuselah Williams & Mary Harris
15 July John Gilbert & Dinah Best
23 July John Keast & Jane Philp, both of St Cue
23 Oct. Mr Francis Hawkinns, of Helston, & Mrs Margery Harris
23 Dec. Peter Pollard & Mary Tremain
23 Dec. Robt Philips of St Denis & Elizabeth Capell
27 Dec. Thomas Pearse & Margery Bounsell

ANNO 1705.

23 April Philip Michell & Phillippa Leeks
6 July Tho. Baseley & Frances Hicks
8 July Philip Callaway and Honr Andrews
22 July Popham Marrice & Catherin Langdon
17 Nov. Antony Godolphin & Mary Penrose

ANNO 1706.

25 Mar. Tho. Gilbert & Prudence Tregeare
27 Mar. Mr Walter Harris & Elizabeth ye dau. of Mr John King
19 Aug. Richard Arnold & Ursula Trevethan
5 Oct. John Meudon & Mary Tyre
9 Nov. Henry Lee & Eliz. Day
21 Dec. Richard Hambly & Eliz. Smith
26 Dec. William Baseley & Sarah Hockin
24 Feb. Daniell Sleep & Gerthurude Peters

ANNO 1707.

14 April John Parking & Mary Hodge
17 July Tho. Cornwall & Eliz. Brown
7 Sep. William Brewer & Mary Woolcock
8 Sep. George Wakeham & Jane Cockinn
31 Jan. Richard Lovell & Jane Oliver
11 Feb. Tho. May & Jane Callaway

ANNO 1708.

29 June John Hicks & Phillippa Tucker
29 Aug. John Chapell & Martha Lang
25 Sep. John Hawke & Joan Callaway
4 Oct. Richard Michell & ffrances Reth
13 Oct. William Williams & Barbara Clements
1 Jan. Stephen Tyer & Margarett Tyer
1 Jan. Faithful Cock & Joan Adams
3 Jan. Ishmael Pearse & Honor Cockyn
5 Feb. Anthony Langdon & Ann Nicholls
13 Feb. John Hendy & Ebat Jolly
20 Feb. James Cowling & Jane Haycroft

ANNO 1709.

3 June William Brewer & Elizabeth Hocken
20 July Tho. Hicks & Elizabeth Drew
6 Aug. Gilbert Merrifield & Mary Wheedon
24 Sep. Tho. Merrifield & Catherine Bromey
7 Nov. Philip Brewer & Sarah Honey
24 Dec. William Trevethan & Sarah Baseley
31 Dec. John Dingey & Eliz. Yelland
31 Dec. Robt. Brewer & Eliz. Wheedon
18 Feb. William Brown & Anne Lewarne

ANNO 1710.

28 May Francis Vivian & Joan Benallack
8 June Tho. Vivian,* Esq. & Mrs Sarah Dodson
5 Oct. Robt. Dunkin & Jane Isman
14 Oct. William Wilkin & Eliz. Bounsell
9 Nov. Henry Oxnam & ffforence Issable
17 Nov. John Werry & Hanna Grimes
30 Dec. Henry Blight & Eliz. Wills
3 Feb. John Tom & Joan Hendy

ANNO 1711.

18 May Tho. Mark & Honor Sarah

* He was of Truan (son of John Vivian, by his second wife Mary, daughter of Sir John Glanville). The above Sarah Dodson was his second wife, his first being Frances, one of the sisters of William Blathwayt of Ditham, county Gloucester; she died 16 March, 1707, and a mural monument remains to her memory in the chapel on the north side of the chancel (Jesus Chapel), on which are these arms, viz., or, a chev. az. betw. three lions' heads erased ppr., a chief gu., imp. or, two bends eng. sa.; crest, a lion's head erased ppr.

21 May Nath. Oliver & Sarah Jeffery
23 Sep. James Callaway & Grace Hocken
29 . . . Edmund Varkar & Diana Tonkin

ANNO 1712.

4 May Mr Blight Haycroft & Mrs Eliz. Edwards
18 May Peter Cockin & Joan Hobb
28 June Mr Stephen Williams & Mrs Jane Sawle*
29 June Gregory Nance & Wilmot Hawke
27 Dec. Richard Cundy & Catherine Leecher

ANNO 1713.

8 Aug. Samuell Bussow & Honr Couch
15 Aug. Arthur Rowe & Rebecca Wheedon
20 Dec. John Hambly & Joyce Evelyn
24 Dec. John White & Anne Brewer
26 Dec. John Wheedon & Mary Lawrey
28 Dec. Richard Peters & Petronell Brewer
31 Dec. Martyn Strongman & Joan Cook
6 Feb. Edward Prestige & Jane Oxnam

ANNO 1714.

11 July Robt. Strongman & Eliz. Pawley
15 Aug. Humphrey England & Eliz. Scaberrio
7 Oct. Arthur Strongman & Frances Strongman
5 Feb. Henry Garland & Mary Husband
6 Feb. Stephen Lovell & Mary Cook

ANNO 1715.

30 April John Harris & Dorothy Oxnam
26 May Gilbert Mealls & Joyce Husband
7 July James Champion & ffrances Godolphin
13 Aug. Tho. Callaway & Honer Grimes
15 Aug. Christopher Calf & Jane Gubbins
6 Nov. Robert Hambley & Anne Bolithoe
14 Nov. John Keys & Eliz. Trevarton of St Breock
19 Nov. Richard Peters & Philippa Philips
11 Dec. Robert Manuel & Mary Rawlyn
29 Dec. John Bone & Mrs Jane Day
9 Feb. Ben. Chalwell & Frances White
14 Feb. Henry Veale & Alice Retallack

ANNO 1716.

19 June Wm. Evelyn & Prudence Mathews
23 July John Sprey & Anne Stephens
23 Oct. Samll Litticot & Jane Heritage wid.
11 Nov. John Gilbert & Mary Tom
15 Dec. John Hawke & Joan Hawke, wid.
27 Jan. William Blake & Margarett Roch, wid.
3 Jan. Peter Pollard & Eliz. Inch, wid.
2 Mar. Nichs. Butson of Padstow & Honor Law

ANNO 1717.

20 Oct. Tho. Williams & Eliz. Symons
20 Nov. John Nichols & Eliz. Martyn
24 Nov. William Rawe and Mary Stephens
30 Nov. Michaell Cornish & Eliz. Veall
14 Feb. Shadrack Tremain & Jane Hawke
17 Feb. Mr Joseph Chubb & Jane Champion

ANNO 1718.

17 April Tho. Litticott & Mary Udye
9 June Wm. Angove & Susanna Bernallack
22 Nov. Richard Whitford & Anne May
17 Jan. Robt. Litticot & Mary Scaberio
8 Feb. John Hockin & Catherine Whitford

ANNO 1719.

30 Mar. Francis Rundle & Jane Stephens
6 June Francis Keyes & Martha George

* She was a daughter of Joseph Sawle of Penrice, Esq. Her sister Ann married the Rev. James Beauford, M.A.; another sister, Mary, married John, son of John Vivian, Esq., of Truan. She made her will as Mrs. Jane Williams of St. Austell, widow, 3 February, 1732, in which she names her sisters Ann and Mary Beauford; brother Francis Sawle, his son Richard and daughter Mary; brother Joseph Sawle, his son John; nieces, Polly and Agnes Sawle; sisters-in-law, Mary Sawle and Jane Carthew, and her husband John Carthew; nephews, John Harris and Thomas Shute; cousin, Tho. Vivian; brother-in-law, Hugh Williams; sister, Mary Vivian.

14 Sep. Henry Veall & Anne Thomas
23 Sep. John Tom & Mary Fleming
3 Oct. John Buckingham & Mary Harvey
13 Nov. Daniell May & Eliz. King
28 Nov. Mr Philip Spernon & Mrs Dorothy Hoblyn,* by licence
23 Dec. Wm Stephens & Jane Tremeane
23 Dec. William Robarts & Honor Tippett
4 Mar. Jno. Cock of St. Wen & Grace Basely of ys p'ish

ANNO 1720.

18 April Francis Pearse & Catherine Wms
19 June Jacob Slade & Eliz. Blake
25 June James George & Mary Benny
11 July John Bolitho of Redruth & Margery Godolphin
24 Sep. Ezekiell Retallack & Anne Williams
27 Oct. John Burgess & Grace Day (by licence dated ye 22nd Oct.)
29 Oct. Tho. Litticott & Ebat Lambe
5 Feb. Robt. Kent of Lower St Columbe & Mary Slogget
18 Feb. Henry Oxnam & Mary Darr

ANNO 1721.

16 April Henry Knight & Judith Lobb
18 May Samll Grimes & Mrs Mary Beauford (by licence dated May 13)
25 May Tho. Rawling & Anne Dancaster
23 July Daniel Thomas & Eliz. Wynne
10 Aug. Nicholas Opie & Jane Rawe
15 Jan. John Tremain & Anne Merrifield

ANNO 1722.

28 Mar. Thomas Glanfield & Eliz. Clemow
31 Mar. Wm Olver & Eliz. Tremain
3 April John Brewer & Amy Adams
29 April Stephen Silicock & Mary Lee
6 May Tho. Drew & Mary Glanfield
12 May Richard Glanfield & Jane Muffet (by licence dated April 30)

* She was daughter of Tho. Hoblyn of Tresaddern, by his second wife Joan, daughter of ..... Tresaddern.

31 May Mr James Bishopp* & Mrs Sarah Long (by licence dated ye 17 May)
4 June Wm Bear & Mary Symons
7 July Richd Solomon & Jane Hockin
15 Sep. William Rawe & Eliz. Baseley
16 Dec. Arthur Callaway & Mary Bone
23 Dec. Hugh Bullock & Mary Day
24 Dec. William Parkin & Jane Cockin
27 Dec. John Peters of Guenap & Anne Champion of this p'ish
23 Feb. Joseph Glanfield & Joyce Rows

ANNO 1723.

20 April Wm Dancaster & Jane Hoskyn
3 June Humphry Abraham & Jane Perry
14 July Robt. Manuell & Catherine Nyles
20 July John Mitchell & Mary Woon
8 Oct. Wm. Luney & Eliz. Rawe
15 Oct. Edward Inch & Catherine Harris, wid.
7 Nov. William Pound & Jane Metter
9 Nov. Jacob Grigg & Mary Service
1 Jan. John Whitford & Grace Eastman
25 Jan. John Lewarne & Mary May

ANNO 1724.

20 April Tho. Husband of Newlyn & Mary Pearce
22 July John Retallack of Ladock & Catherine Bone
23 Aug. Francis Cowling & Patience Robyns
29 Oct. John Mill & Ruth Langdon
5 Oct. Robt Strongman & Ann Adams
17 Nov. Edward Merifield & Elizabeth Hals
23 Jan. Thos. Warne & Eliz. Davis
2 Feb. Samuell Williams junr. & Frances Lawrey
2 Feb. Wm Antron of Kea & Catherine Gilbert
6 Feb. George Bond & Joan Merrifield

ANNO 1725.

22 April Joseph Dunkin & Mary Lewarne
24 April Solomon Baseley & Mary Harris
16 May John Rapson & Eliz Champion

* He was son of the Rev. John Bishop, rector of St. Columb, by his second wife. They had issue several children, for whom see their baptisms.

26 May — Mr George MacLaskey & Hannah Archer, wid., both of Falmouth (by licence dated June 19)

8 Aug. — John Cobbledick of St Evall & Margery Newell of this p'ish

10 Aug. — Henry Solomon & Honor Law

3 Dec. — Henry Barnicott & Honor Tinney

19 Feb. — William Stephens & Mary Opie

19 Feb. — William Williams & Mary White

Anno 1726.

13 Oct. — Robert Symons & Eliz. Hornabrook

6 Nov. — John Rowe of St. Teath & Eliz. daughter of Benjamin Chalwell of this parish (by licence dated Oct. 29)

9 Feb. — Mr John Tregenna,* rector of Maugan, & Mrs Eliz. Carkeet of this p'ish (by licence dated Jan. 28)

Anno 1727.

22 June — Tho. Carne & Jane Eudye

6 July — John Gummow & Eliz. Whitford

23 July — John Tippet & Mary Harding

21 Oct. — John Whetter & Dorcas Pascoe

7 Jan. — John Husband & Alice Rowse

19 Jan. — John Drew of Ladock & Jane Blight of this p'ish

11 Feb. — William Tinney & Eliz. Clemow

21 Feb. — Thomas Gill of this p'ish & Eliz. May of St. Clear

5 Mar. — Richard Davis & Mary Rows, wid.

Anno 1728.

15 May — Arthur Mitchell & Mary Oxnam

19 May — Wm. Lanyon & Honor Pearce

* Par. Reg. Mawgan in Pydar :—
Edw. Tregenna, gent., buried 16 Sep., 1707.
Mr. John Tregenna. gent.. buried 31 May, 1718.
Mrs. Joan Tregenna, buried 1 March, 1732.
John, son of John Tregenna, rector, buried 15 Sept., 1745.
Rev. John Tregenna, buried 13 April, 1752.
Mrs. Eliz. Tregenna, buried 14 Jan.. 1781.

Sarah Tregenna, youngest daughter of the Rev. John Tregenna. rector of Mawgan and Roach, died 10 May, 1807, aged 61. Monumental inscription on a tomb in the churchyard of St. Columb Major.

22 June — Wm. Davies & Anne Brabyn

1 July — James Rawling of St. Minver & Jennefayr James of this parish

27 Oct. — Stephen Carhart & Prudence Trevethan

12 Nov. — John Inch & Jane Chapell

27 Jan. — Richard Austin & Eliz. Couch

2 Feb. — Simon Warne & Hannah Bilkey

Anno 1729.

6 June — Wm. Bullen & Joan Gilbert

8 June — Richard Rows & Jane Yolton

14 June — Thomas Hawke & Anne Hoskyn

16 July — Arthur Mitchell & Grace Sampson

20 July — Henry Sanders & Martha James

11 Nov. — Wm. Antron of Kea & Avice Nichols

3 Jan. — John Husband of St. Austle & Blanch Rawling

Anno 1730.

18 May — Robt. Pascoe & Anne Yolton

19 June — Henry Blight & Constance Kente

4 July — Richard Brewer & Thomasin Gummow

27 July — Anne Pearce & Elizabeth Rosomond

24 Aug. — Mr William Collier, son of Phillip Collier, rector of this parish & Mrs Anne Toller, daughter of Mr Wm Toller* of ffowey (by licence dated Aug. 21)

5 Nov. — John Lamb & Mary Morish

26 Dec. — Tho. Bate of Helland & Sarah Brewer of this parish

27 Feb. — John Parnall & Jane Langdon

1 Mar. — James Harris of Probus & Grace Cock of this parish

Anno 1731.

19 April — Wm. Luncy & Rachel Langdon

27 May — John Martyn & Joan Thomas

31 May — Mr Walter Elford, rector of Milton Damarell in Devon, & Mrs Phillippa Collier of this parish (by licence dated the 29 May)

3 July — Wm Retallock & Matilda Tinney

* William Toller was son of John Toller of Fowey, by Jane daughter and eventual heir of Tho. Trefry of Place.

31 July John Jenkin of Illogan & Avice Lewarne of this p'ish
7 Nov. Adam Thomson & Mary Keast (by licence dated 24 Oct.)
30 Dec. Christopher Warne* & Honor Lee
24 Jan. Peter Mitchell & Jane Hicks
29 Jan. Phillip Gilbert & Eliz. Taylor
2 Feb. Pascoe Kestell of St Wen & Jenefaire Lawrey of this parish

ANNO 1732.

11 June Thomas Baseley & Eliz. Slogget
8 June John Merifield & Dinah Warne
27 Aug. James Hendy & Grace Edwards
27 Aug. Wm Mitchell & Emeliu Edwards
6 Oct. John Johns & Mrs Margarett Tanner (by a licence dated ye 8th Sep.)
24 Dec. Wm Evelyn & Grace Treugove
3 Feb. Wm Vivyan of St. Austle & Anne Vivian of this parish

ANNO 1733.

7 July Thomas Keast & Anne May
14 July John May & Jane Treugove
5 Sep. James Oliver, junr. & Eliz. Callaway
18 Oct. Joseph Kelly & Jenefaire Merifield

ANNO 1734.

3 May Samson Brown & Jane Rawe
18 May Nicholas Husband & Eliz. Kestell
23 June Nathaniell Lockett & Mary Bounsell
28 July James Trenerry & Eliz. Adams
29 Sep. Rich. Carne & Mary Brewer
8 Dec. John Wilton & Mary Trenerry
15 Dec. Richard Stephens of St Blazey & Grace Basset of St. Columbe
30 Dec. John Best & Anne Harris
31 Jan. William Harris & Elizabeth Baseley
2 Feb. Henry Endean of St. Agnes & Catherine Keast of St. Columbe
7 Feb. William Rickard of St Stephens in Barnwell & Mary Leacher *al's* Hoskyn of St. Columbe (by licence dated Jan. 18)

* Son of Christopher Warne and Jane Hichen, see note p. 84. His wife was a daughter of Hen. and Eliz. Lee; they had several children, of whom Catherine married William Rawlings of Padstow, and Grace married John Dungey; they were eventual co-heirs.

18 Feb. John Harris of St. Mewan & Anne Tinney of St. Columbe

ANNO 1735.

13 April Wm Capell & Jane Noddren
14 April Richard James of St. Mey & Anne Lawrey of St Columbe
18 April Jonathan Barrett & Sarah Williams
19 April John Rawlin & Catherine Daw
11 May James Johns of St. Mewan & Rachell Solomon of St. Columbe
11 May Joell Capell & Trephenea Bartlett
30 May Jonathan Daw & Margery Barry
7 Sep. Phillip Hornabrook & Mary Bullock
25 Sep. Thomas Perot & Anne Hornebrook
11 Feb. Stephen Carhart & Frances Best
21 Feb. Thomas Langdon & Catherine Austin

ANNO 1736.

26 April William Gilbert & Anne Jane
26 April Rich. Austin & Mary Luney
29 April Henry Baker & Rachell Basely
27 June Michaell Barrett & Jane Tippett
3 July Edward Merifield & Eliz. Ball (by licence dated June 30)
20 July John Buckingham & Grace Godolphin
13 Sep. James Commins & Dorothy Michell
3 Oct. Thomas Couch & Grace Harris
15 Oct. William Tinney & Gr Brewer
6 Nov. Michaell Cornish & ffrances Hobb
10 Nov. John Dungey & Jane Hawke
25 Feb. Mr Rich. Betty & Mrs Dorothy Tanner (by licence dated Feb. 7)

ANNO 1737.

17 April William Wilson & Margarett Adams
17 July Richard Jane & Anne Rowse
29 Aug. Rich. Pascoe & Alice Champion
29 Sep. Stephen Tyer & Anne James
26 Oct. Thomas Stephens & Anne Cundy
6 Nov. Thomas Morrish & Eliz. Merifield

13 Nov. Richard Page of St. Giles in ye ffields, Middlesex, & Phillippa Allen of this p'ish (by licence dated ye 11 Nov.)
25 Nov. Mr Daniell Copley Byrne of St. Clement Danes, London, & Mrs Mary Sawle of this p'ish (by licence dated the 25 Nov.)
27 Dec. Mathew Kirkland & Mary Parsons
19 Jan. Nicholas Brenton & Jane Thomas
22 Jan. Mark Nichols & Loveday Rowse
4 Feb. John Mark & Elizabeth Merifield

Anno 1738.

5 April Richard Bidgood & Mary Sandford
29 April Wm Cockyn & Mary Lawe
16 May Morice Newlyn & Elizabeth Crowts
22 June Wm Williams & Jane Eddy (by licence dated the 21st)
12 Aug. Stephen Daddow of Goran & Catherine Brown of this parish
20 Oct. Bernard Wetsford & Elizabeth Roch
28 Oct. Jude May & Eliz. Richards
2 Nov. Wm Binnick & Jane Hopgood, both of Padstow
3 Feb. John Hockin & Margarett Tinney

Anno 1739.

23 April Rich. Wilton & Dorothy George
23 April Antony Henry Cock & Thomasin Cock
24 April Thomas Harry of Morva & Elizabeth Harris of St. Columbe, wid. (by licence dated 14 Feb.)
24 June John Mewdon & Grace Hornabrook
28 July Richard Austin & Mary Westcote
10 Dec. Stephen Brewer & Ann Perrot

Anno 1740.

7 April Richard Oliver of Probus & Mary Rowse of ys parish
24 April Richard Husband & Eliza Adams
24 May John Tippet & Eliz. Coad
31 May Edward Lawrey & Ann Dennis
7 June John Symonds of St. Mewan & Mary Vivian
16 Sep. George Sowden & Mary Burn
20 Sep. John Varcoe & Mary Tomm
25 Sep. William Basely of Milton Damerell, Devon, & Eliz. Raw
4 Oct. Christopher Dennis & Mary Morshead
19 Oct. Thomas Willy & Margarett Blake
9 Nov. William Willis & Eliz. Raw
6 Jan. Edward Brokenshire of Roach & Jane Best
7 Feb. Methuselah Williams & Eliza Martyn

Anno 1741.

22 May William Fortune & Eliz. Opie
21 Sep. Chudleigh Cock of Stoke Damerell, Devon, & Eliz. Pearce of this parish, by licence dated 16 Sep.
8 Oct. John Cundy & Margarett Davies
5 Nov. James Stephens & Sarah Elford
2 Jan. James Pollard & Ann Mewdon
28 Feb. Richard Bullock & Jane Pollard of Mevagisy

Anno 1742.

18 April Thomas Coad, junr & Catherine Nicholls
20 April John Strongman & Mary Davies
24 April Thomas Watts & Elizabeth Tredween
21 May Mr Thomas Trethewy of St Austle & Mrs Mary Collier of this parish (by licence dated April 26)
5 June Edward Tremaine & Elizabeth Muffet
9 Sep. Robert Hawke & Joan Raw
6 Nov. Samuel Parkin & Elizabeth Betteson
8 Nov. Thomas Salmon & Dorothy Pollard
12 Feb. Richard Veal & Jane Whetter
15 Feb. Thomas Langdon & Catherine Mills

Anno 1743.

4 April James Coad & Jane Drew
5 May Edward Hesterbrook & Mary Hooper

24 July Thomas Sweet & Mary Inch
22 Oct. William Richards & Jane Carhart, both of Roach
29 Oct. Richard Carno & Catherine Thomas
3 Nov. John Walkey & Margarett Garland
4 Nov. Samuel Harris & Mary Cock
6 Nov. James May & Eliz. Hawke
6 Nov. Samuel Retallock of St Agnes & Ann Retallock of this parish
9 Nov. Nicholas Couch & Margery Grey, both of St Lawrence

ANNO 1744.

12 May Richard Martyn & Mary Raw
16 Nov. George Strongman & Ann Leddicote
2 Jan. Edward May & Prudence Evelyn
29 Jan. John Pearce of Roach & Cath. Nichols of this parish

ANNO 1745.

26 April John Arscott of this parish & Jane Strongman of St Enoder
25 May Robert Grace & Mary Harris
3 June Francis Tomm & Mary Thomas
7 July John Mark & Joyce Endyvean
29 July Francis Evans of Perranzabuloe & Honour Bullock of ys parish
20 Nov. Edward Hicks & Alice Coad
1 Jan. John Rawling of Kea & Elizabeth Tippet of this parish
3 Feb. Mr Thomas Sanders Allen of St Justin, Penwith, & Mrs Mary Lawrence of this parish, by licence dated Jan. 24

ANNO 1746.

30 Mar. Mathew Olliver & Margarett Willy, widdow
13 June Thomas Tamblyn of Crowan & Eliz. Autron of this parish
21 July John Bullen & Jane Brokenshire
26 Feb. Jonathan Rowse & Catherine Pearce
27 Feb. John Rogers of St Erth & Ann Hawke of this parish
9 Mar. Mr Hugh Rogers of Hellstone & Mrs Ann Bishop of this parish (by licence dated 3 Jan.)

ANNO 1747.

20 April Thomas Buckingham of Gweenap & Thomasine Brewer of ys parish
30 Oct. John Eva of Trigony & Philippa Hicks of this parish
24 Oct. Nicholas Reed of St Agnes & Patience Retallock of this parish
27 Dec. Richard Cornish & Elizabeth Brown
27 Dec. John Retallock & Elizabeth Sandy

ANNO 1748.

13 April William Brewer & Mary Garland
20 May Andrew Maubin & Amey Brewer
29 May Francis Rundle & Catherine Rundle
24 July James Hodge of St Agnes & Mary Tremayne of ys parish
20 Aug. William Merrifield & Frances Eudy

ANNO 1749.

5 May Jonathan Chapman & Mary Hawke of St Issey
14 May Francis Trelevin & Grace Cornish
16 May John Tomm & Mary Hicks
19 May William Skinner & Mary Lewarne
23 May Philip Cornish & Mary Merrifield
23 July Humphry Toms & Elizabeth Roberts
24 Sep. Thomas Westcote & Mary Glanvill
15 Oct. Benjamin Kent of St Dennis & Jane Opie of this parish
19 Nov. George Tremain & Elizabeth Oxenham
19 Jan. Ralph Busson & Mary Ham

ANNO 1750.

21 April Isaac Smith, a soldier, & Joan Strongman
5 May John Pearce & Jane Oxenham
21 June Humphry England, junr, & Susanna White
22 June George Champion & Elizabeth Chubb
6 July John Mitchell & Charity How, both of St Mary's in Truro
19 Oct. Richard Hogg, a soldier, & Catharine Dancaster

1 Nov. Samuel Grimes & Martha Lang (by licence dated 2nd Oct.)
10 Nov. William Lanyon, junr, & Ann Bullock
12 Nov. Thomas Glanvill & Julian Gummowe
29 Dec. William Hicks & Elizabeth Hicks
19 Feb. John Humfries, a soldier, & Elizabeth Nowlyn, widow

ANNO 1751.

20 June Edmund Varco & Mary Tippett
24 June John Crapp & Elizabeth Rapson
29 June Richard Luke & Elizabeth Boundy
24 Aug. William Leddicote *al's* Gregor & Jane Chapell
14 Sep. John Buckingham & Grace Cock
22 Sep. James Calaway of Mawgan & Mary Opie of this parish
4 Nov. Nicholas Leddicote & Mary Chapman
10 Nov. Isaack Grigg & Elizabeth Glanvill
15 Nov. Thomas Bate & Mary Bishop
26 Nov. Richard Lawrey & Mary Thomas

ANNO 1752.

31 Mar. William Drew, a soldier, & Elizabeth Jackson
1 April Timothy Eslem, a soldier, & Jane Pascoe of Endellion, widow
26 April Degory Trescott & Alice Veal
26 June James Jolly of St Maugan & Mary Pennaleggaw of this parish
6 July Mr Richard Cross of Plymouth, Devon, & Mrs Mary Drew of this parish (by licence dated June 30)
17 July Pasco Davis & Elizabeth Harris
15 Oct. James Pearce & Ann Jane
19 Nov. Richard Veal & Mary Cowling
3 Dec. George Raw & Elizabeth Mark
12 Dec. Peter Kendall & Jane Brewer

ANNO 1753.

7 Jan. George Pett, a soldier, & Margarett Rosewarne
24 June Philip Harris & Margarett Teddam
17 Nov. Philip Harvey & Mary Saunders
26 Dec. John Webber & Grace Oliver

ANNO 1754.

. . . . . John Buckingham of this parish & Jane Oliver of St Breock, 16, 23, & 30 June
25 Sep. Richard Chapman of this parish & Elizabeth Pinch of this parish
19 Nov. William Parkin & Elizabeth Inch
. . . . . Edward Pearse of this parish & Ann Arthur of the parish of St Ervan, 27 Oct., 3 & 10 Nov.
. . . . . James Jolly of St Enoder & Philippa Clemow of this parish, 3, 10 & 16 Nov.
. . . . . Thomas Mill of this parish & Mary Harris of Padstow, last time 8 Dec.
22 Dec. Richard Manuell & Mary Blight, both of this parish

ANNO 1755.

21 Jan. Nicholas Clemoe & Sarah Pearce
13 Feb. James Stephens & Joan Whetter, both of this parish
29 June Jasper Richards, a sojourner in this parish, & Barbara Binick of Truro
10 July John Peters & Mary Kelly, both of this parish
21 July Thomas Luney & Mary Dingle, both of this parish
20 Nov. Samuel Clymoe & Thomasine Basely, both of this parish
. . . . . John Chapman & Mary Corra of St Eval, last time 16 Nov.
. . . . . James Williams of this parish & Mary Benny of St Columb Minor, the last time 7 Dec.
. . . . . Richard Solomon of this parish & Martha Saundry of Little Colan, the last time 8 Ap., 1756.

ANNO 1756.

28 Jan. Richard Hawke & Sarah Tippet
7 June William Gass & Elizabeth Tregiddier, both of this parish

7 June Francis Penberthy of St Issey & Sarah Bishop of this parish

4 July William Andrew of this parish & Agnes Solomon* of St Columb Minor

5 July Robert Keam & Grace Rowe, both of this parish

17 July Peter Retallack & Margarett Bullen, both of this parish

. . . . . Hugh Davy of St Agnes & Jane Williams of this p'ish, last time 5 Sep.

13 Sep. William Rawlings† & Catherine Warne, by licence

14 Dec. John Rundle & Ann Brewer, both of this parish

17 Dec. John Whitford & Catherine Hoar, both of this parish

ANNO 1757.

5 Jan. Richard Gummo, labourer of this parish, & Elizabeth Williams of the parish of Key

29 Dec. Richard Stribley* of St Wenn, widower, & Catherine Merrifield, by licence

30 Jan. John Tamblyn & Blanch Retallack, both of this parish

. . . . . John Bullen & Susanna Basten of St Stephens, published the last time 10 April

. . . . . Thomas Jasper, a sojourner, & Patience Vreane of St Stephens by Launceston, published the last time 8 May

11 Sep. William Swan & Thomasin Prowte, both of this parish, by licence

. . . . . John Broad† of Maugan & Mary Hotten of this parish

3 Oct. William King & Sarah Stephens, both of this parish

ANNO 1758.

30 April William Crapp & Ruth Basely, both of this parish

3 June Thomas Williams, butcher, & Joan Tomm, both of this parish, by licence

3 June Hezekiah Bunt & Jane Daves both of this parish

13 June Joseph Merrifield, yeoman, & Mary Woon, both of this parish, by licence

20 July Richard Basely, tinner, & Elizabeth Basely, both of this parish

7 Aug. Henry Row & Elizabeth Stevens both of this parish

17 Aug. Thomas Hamley‡ & Grace Tregenne, both of this parish

* Colan Par. Reg. :—
Francis Solomon of St. Columb Major and Honour Cornish married 19 Aug., 1734.

St. Enoder Par. Reg. :—
Tho. Solomon of St. Columb Major and Amey Carveth, married Feb. 11, 1753.
Eleanor, daughter of Michall Carveath, bap. 29 March, 1579.

† He was son of Tho. and Elizabeth Rawlings of St. Columb. She was a daughter and co-heir of Christopher Warne, gent., of St. Columb, see note p. 102. They settled at Padstow, where their son and heir Thomas Rawlings built the mansion of Saunders Hill, and was High Sheriff of Cornwall in 1803; he married Margery, daughter and co-heir of Tho. Price, gent., of Tregolds, by Jane, daughter of William Phillips, gent., by whom he had issue several children.

William, the second son of the above William and Catherine Rawlings, was M.A. of Exeter College, Oxon, for fifty years Vicar of Padstow, and married Susanna, daughter of Peter Salmon, Esq., by whom he had several children. See Sir J. B. Burke's *Landed Gentry*.

Davies Gilbert gives their arms, quarterly, viz., 1 and 4 sa. three swords erect in fesse, arg. hilts and pomels, or. for Rawlings 2 and 3 sa. a cross or, cantoned in the first and fourth quarter, a martlett of the second, in the second and third a chaplet arg. for Warne. Crest, an arm embowed in armour, the elbow resting on the wreath, holding in the gauntlet a falchion arg. hilt or. Motto *cognosce teipsum, et disce pati.* The coat in the first and fourth quarters appears on some monuments to the family in Padstow church.

* St. Wenn Par. Reg. :—
Mr. Richard Stribley and Mrs. Ann Drew of St. Columb Major, married 24 Dec., 1748.
The name of Stribley occurs in the registers of Mawgan in Pyder as early as 1683, the earliest date existing there.

† The marriage is entered at Mawgan 26th Sep., 1757, he is there called "fuller," and her name is spelt Houghton. Thomas, son of John Broad and Martha his wife, baptised 20 Feb., 1687. Mawgan in Pydar Par. Reg.

‡ He was in holy orders, son of Giles Hamley and Grace Hoblyn his second wife. Grace Tregenna was daughter and co-heir of the Rev. John Tregenna, rector of Mawgan in Pydar; they had issue Thomas Tregenna Hamley, who married Mary, daughter of Hen. Braddon of Camelford. She died 19 April, 1761, aged 23 years. He died 9 June, 1766, aged 35. Monumental inscription on ledger stone at St. Columb Major. Thomas Tregenna Hamley, Vicar of St. Ervan and St. Eval, died 23 Dec., 1818; ledger stone placed by

2 Dec. John Jane & Grace Anthorn, both of this parish

ANNO 1759.

18 Feb. William Glanvile & Mary Retallock, both of this parish

16 April John Leddicoat & Mary Luke, both of this parish

26 June Robert Manell & Mary Hawke, both of this parish

26 June William Lawrence & Frances Drew, both of this parish, by licence

5 Sep. James Jane & Margaret Hooker, both of this parish

11 Nov. Bennet Retalick & Frances Salmon

18 Dec. John Symons & Joan Drew, by licence

ANNO 1760.

2 Jan. William Rowse and Mary Hawke both of this parish, licence

5 Mar. John Francis of S[t] Stephens & Grace Lydacote of this parish

7 April William Williams of this parish & Ann Cooke of S[t] Issey

13 May William Besly & Sarah Tippet, both of this parish

18 June William Lewarne & Elizabeth Mitchell

25 June John Bond & Mary Brewer

1 July The Rev. Jonathan Peters, clerk, of S[t] Clements, & Elizabeth Peter, of this parish, by licence

14 July William Moon of Liskeard, & Nancey Thomas of this parish

2 Aug. William Olliver & Mary William, by licence

26 Aug. William Haly of Broadoak & Jane Burley of this parish

29 Sep. Richard Bettinson & Mary Kerhart, both of this parish

24 Oct. John Lilycrap & Catherine Daves, both of this parish

John Clode Braddon, gent. of Camelford. Monumental inscription in St. Ervan church. Mary, wife of the Rev. Tho. Tregenna Hamley, curate of this parish, died 12 Dec., 1813, aged 57. Floor slab, St. Ervan church. This was the second wife of the Rev. Tho. Tregenna Hamley, by whom he had issue Edward and Giles.

27 Dec. Peter Courtenay & Elizabeth Husband, both of this parish

ANNO 1761.

1 Jan. William Bond & Grace Cowling, both of this parish

24 Jan. William Harris & Dorothy Retallack, both of this parish

28 Mar. John Rundel & Catherine Minnow, both of this parish

5 April Thomas Bulo & Joan Brewer, both of this parish

2 May James Snell & Mary Wilsford, both of this parish

11 May The Rev. Thomas Biddulph of Truro & Martha Tregenna* of this parish, by licence

20 June John Stephen, sojourner, & Mary Buckingham

8 Aug. Robert Bateman, Rector of this parish, & Elizabeth Hamley,† by licence

3 Oct. John Cooke of S[t] Columb Minor & Jane Warne of this parish

10 Oct. Thomas Bettinson & Jane Eveling, both of this parish

19 Nov. William Varcoe & Ann Hicks, both of this parish, by licence

24 Nov. Thomas Stick, of S[t] Stephens in Barnwell, tinner, & Jane Grigg of this parish, by licence

7 Dec. John Row, labourer, & Hannah Stephens, both of this parish

8 Dec. John Hand, mason, & Honnor Lamb, both of this parish

18 Dec. Thomas Trethewey, of S[t] Dennis & Wilmot Hicks of this parish

24 Dec. Francis Cornish, blacksmith, & Grace Williams of this parish

* She was daughter and coheiress of the Rev. John Tregenna, and the second wife of the Rev. Tho. Biddulph, who was for nineteen years vicar of Padstow; his first wife was a daughter of . . . . Townsend.

† She was a daughter of Giles Hamley, of St. Columb, gent., by his second wife Grace Hoblyn. Their daughter, Frances Bateman, married at St. Columb 8 Feb., 1797, to Rev. Richard Paul, rector of Mawgan in Pydar. The Rev. R. Paul died 7 Dec. 1805, aged 42; his widow died 25 Oct. 1819, aged 51, *vide* M.I. at Mawgan.

Dec. 26 John Morish, labourer, & Elizabeth Cundey, both of this parish

Anno 1762.

2 Feb. William Thomas & Margery Prideaux, both of this parish

22 Mar. Frances Hawkey, tinner, & Edith Harris, both of this parish

16 Oct. Richard Sampson & Frances Callaway, both of this parish

21 Oct. Charles Rickard & Mary Peters, both of this parish

Anno 1763.

23 Jan. John Buckingham & Margaret Piper, both of this parish

4 April John Tregillgass, labourer, & Elizabeth Watts, both of this parish

6 June Peter Palmer, a soldier, a sojourner, & Mary Twogood, of Kettleby, in Leicestershire

15 July Edward Hodge, of Stoke Damarel, co. Devon, glazier, & Martha Wills, by licence

21 Nov. Thomas Baker, a soldier, a sojourner, & Ann England, of this parish

21 Nov. Robert Sampson of Kenwyn, co. Cornwall, & Mary Martyn

24 Dec. William Austin & Elizabeth Spear, both of this parish

Anno 1764.

16 Mar. Arthur Capel & Ann Buckingham, both of this parish

10 May Abraham Walters & Elizabeth Pound, both of this parish

11 June Richard Hards, a soldier, & Aplin Thomas, both of this parish

29 June Michael Carveth of St. Cuthbert & Catherine Sampson of this parish, by licence

3 July Mr. Elias Hiscutt & Mrs. Mary Arthur both of this parish

23 July John Buckingham & Jane Oliver, both of this parish

5 Aug. Edward Gummow & Elizabeth Paskow, both of this parish

17 Aug. Benjamin Chalwell Rowe & Elizabeth Merifield, both of this parish

20 Aug. Alexander Mitchell & Elizabeth Stephens, both of this parish, by licence

28 Oct. John George & Jennefaire Mannell, both of this parish

6 Nov. Robert Mannel & Elizabeth Tippet, both of this parish

11 Nov. Peter Hilton a soldier, & Agnes Locke of this parish

16 Feb. Nicholas Lakeman of Mevigissy, & Jennefaire Brokenshire of this parish

Anno 1765.

16 April William Basely & Frances Woon, both of this parish

23 June William Tom & Susanna Pengelly, both of this parish

6 July Thomas Whitford & Mary Whitford, both of this parish

. . . . . Joseph Hatcher, a soldier, & Catherine Barrett, both of this parish, published the last time 23 June

27 July Thomas Buller of St. Agnes & Jennifer Sandy, of this parish

5 Sep. Francis Symonds & Elizabeth Martin, both of this parish

9 Oct. John Hardin & Elizabeth Turner, both of this parish, by licence

18 Oct. Thomas Hutchings of Mawgan & Ann Rundle of this parish, by licence

12 Nov. Richard Best & Elizabeth Sampson, both of this parish

15 Dec. John Veal & Sarah Stephens, both of this parish

Anno 1766.

7 Jan. Gawin Irwin, a soldier, & Rosamond Elvins

10 Jan. John Sheldon, a soldier, & Frances England of this parish

24 Jan. William Bone & Mary Tonkin, both of this parish

22 April John Merifield & Joan Veal, both of this parish

9 May Edward Nock, a soldier, & Catherine Barret, both of this parish

29 June Thomas Hicks & Prudence Cureb, both of this parish

6 July John Dungey & Grace Warne* both of this parish, by licence

25 Aug. Henry Warne† & Elizabeth Dungey both of this parish, by licence

31 Aug. William Benny, husbandman, & Margaret Berryman, both of this parish

15 Sep. Charles Faro of Roach & Betty Thomas both of this parish

23 Sep. George Colwell & Elizabeth Drew, both of this parish

24 Nov. Thomas Rowse & Mary Traer, both of this parish

ANNO 1767.

25 Jan. Francis Jane & Jane Hore, both of this parish

19 April Methuselah Barrett & Mary Best, both of this parish

27 April Robert Taylor of Crewkerne, co. Somerset, & Joanna Bishop, of this parish

18 May Zacharia Luke, of Redruth, & Mary Husband of this parish

16 June Richard Bullen & Mary Oliver, both of this parish

17 Aug. James Dennis & Elizabeth Jane, both of this parish

25 Sep. Nicholas Guenes & Elizabeth Rowse, both of this parish

4 Oct. Richard Grigg & Temperance Rowe, both of this parish

2 Nov. John Cowling & Mary Gilbert, both of this parish

22 Nov. Richard Landon of this parish, & Ann Maine of St Merran, published the last time

ANNO 1768.

1 Jan. Edward Stephens & Elizabeth Thomas, both of this parish

* She was daughter and co-heiress of Christopher Warne, of St. Columb. gent.; they left issue several children. She was buried a widow 13 March. 1789.

† He was son of Christopher Warne, gent., and died 3 Jan., 1813, age 71. His wife was buried 9 Dec., 1798, aged 59. He had issue Betsey Dungey, died unmarried 12 Feb., 1835, aged 66; Patsey Jane, died unmarried 9 Aug., 1819, aged 46; Mary, died unmarried 21 June, 1827, aged 51; Harry, died unmarried 12 Feb., 1780; and Sophia Grace, baptised 14 July, 1782, married 22 Dec., 1808, Nicholas Truscott Ball, of Mevagissy, and died 18 Oct., buried 21 Oct., 1809, aged 28. Tomb in churchyard at St. Columb.

16 Feb. John Ternery & Garthred Williams, both of this parish

20 April John Gwennap of Falmouth & Mary Dungey of this parish, by licence

24 April John James & Constance Tonkin, both of this parish

26 May John Harvey of Illogan & Elizabeth Vivian

. . . . . Samuel Jolly & Sibella Penrose of Newland, published the last time 19 June

21 Aug. Joseph Dyer & Barbara Hosking

25 Sep. Robert Tabb & Elizabeth Barrett

17 Oct. Philip Buckthought of Withiel, & Elenor Cayzer of this parish

16 Dec. Robert Drew & Jane Glanville, both of this parish

24 Dec. William Bennet & Elizabeth Raw, both of this parish

ANNO 1769.

20 Jan. William Car, a soldier, & Mary Barret, both of this parish

22 Jan. Ephraim Stephens & Susanna Oliver, both of this parish

1 Feb. John Whitford of Mawgan,* & Nancey Thomas, of this parish

4 Feb. Charles Liddicoat & Ann Tyer, both of this parish

. . . . . John Trescouthick & Elizabeth Ellery of Newlin, published the last time 21 May

. . . . . Luke Thomas of this parish & Elizabeth Cowling of Peranzabuloo, published the last time 1 Oct.

ANNO 1770.

24 Jan. Henry Barnacoat, yeoman, & Mary Beale, by licence

* John Whitford and Elizabeth Muffat of St. Columb Minor, married 11 Nov., 1726. Mawgan parish register.

Thomas Whitford, of St. Columb Major, widower, and Elizabeth Hobbs, of Mawgan, spinster, married Aug., 1788. Mawgan parish register; see his first marriage, ante 6 July, 1765.

John Whitford and Martha Vingo married 5 June, 1791.

Richard Whitford and Rachael Austin married 8 May, 1802.—St. Columb Major register.

Wm Trecontbick of this parish & Susanna James of St Enoder, published the last time 15 April

John Coal of St Enoder & Grace Bullock, published the last time 22 April

20 May James Dennis & Mary Gill

27 May Nicholas Tamblin & Dorothy Martin

6 Aug. John Mewton & Philippa Rawling

Francis Hill of this parish & Ann Hobb of St Eval, published the last time 17 June

John Julyan of this parish & Rebecca Drew of St Austle, published the last time 17 June

11 Nov. John Tonkyn & Charity Capell

ANNO 1771.

7 April Thomas Jenkin of this parish & Ann Curveth of Gurran in this county

8 July Thomas Williams, a soldier in the 20th regt, & Margaret Adams, late of St Warie in Shrowbury

20 July John Pascoe & Mary Treverton

28 July Arthur Strangman & Elizabeth Udy of Roche

10 Nov. Richard Jane & Elizabeth May

24 Nov. Nicholas Donnithorne* & Jane Drew

15 Dec. Peter Pollard of this parish & Jane Best of St Wenn

ANNO 1772.

9 Feb. John Martin & Jane Harris

3 Mar. William Henwood & Jane Kelly

11 April John Oxenham & Elizabeth Cornish

Henry Rowe & Frances Mitchal

Francis Cundy & Grace Mannel

5 July Joseph Kelly & Mary Hobb

Mark Thomas of this parish & Mary Hicks of St Wenn, published the last time 28 June

* Nicholas Donithorne, attorney-at-law, and Mary Swan married 15 March, 1782. Amelia, daughter of Mr. Nicholas Donithorne and Mary his wife, baptised 9 Jan., 1783. Mary, wife of Mr. Nicholas Donithorne, buried 25 Jan., 1796. —St. Columb Major Par. Reg.

26 July William Drew & Phillippa Tom

John Liddicot of this parish & Joyce Woon of Roach, published the last time 16 Aug.

12 Oct. Thomas Ball & Ann Morlen

19 Oct. Richard Lawry & Margaret Rawling

ANNO 1773.

2 Jan. Edward Kendall of Newland & Joan Bulling of this parish

18 Jan. Charles Clerk Dix, a soldier of St Mary's, Gloucester, & Mary Verren of this parish

13 Feb. John Truscott & Loveday Hancock

17 Mar. William Brewer & Elizabeth Rawe

12 April Richard Cundy & Mary Sowden

James Pearce of this parish, & Elizabeth Scowdrick of Falmouth, published the last time 14 Feb.

19 April Charles Rickard & Jennifer Retallack

20 May George Daw & Mary Brabyn

30 May Nathaniel Hender* & Elizabeth May

Edward May & Elizabeth Whiteford of St Austle, published the last time 1st August

16 Oct. Anthony White & Amey Williams

Stephen Brewer & Catherine Morrish

ANNO 1774.

13 Jan. Hugh Hopper of Holsworthy, Devon, a batchelor, & Sarah Jane of this parish, by licence

29 Jan. Thomas Bullock & Ann Basely

15 Feb. John Tippet & Frances Champion

20 Feb. John Jolly of Newlyn & Catherine Strongman of this parish

13 Mar. Henry Hoskin & Fanny Oxenham

* Their daughter Maria Hender married by licence 11 Oct., 1801, Tho. Retallack of St. Columb. Nathaniel, s. of Nathaniel and Elizabeth Hender, of Camelford, baptised 15 July, 1782.—St. Columb Major Par. Reg.

27 Mar. Arthur Langdon & Rebecca Lawry
4 April John Mill of St Wenn, & Jane Clifft of this parish
22 April Josias Williams of St Wenn, & Eleanor Tabb of this parish
23 April Michael Jenkin of St Just, & Honour Colwill of this parish
12 May James Tabb & Elizabeth Jones
5 July John Varco & Johanna Wilsford
22 July Edward Chaple of St Stephens in Branwell, & Ann Tippet of this parish
4 Sep. Alexander Shirp, a soldier of 3rd reg^t of foot, & Mary Strongman of this parish
John Solomon & Elizabeth Kaie of St Dennis, published the last time 18 Sep^t.
7 Oct. John Bryant of Stoke Damerel, co. Devon, & Johanna Keast of this parish
18 Oct. John Bellerby, corporal 11th reg^t of foot, & Mary Retallock of this parish
13 Dec. William Tremain & Elizabeth Grigg
25 Dec. Richard Veal & Mary Grigg

ANNO 1775.

30 Jan. Edward Gummo & Rachel Liddicoat *al's* Grigor
John Roberts of this parish & Prudence Giles of Roach, published the last time 9 Ap.
16 April Abraham Grigg & Joan Allen Rowe
25 April Joseph Rowe of this parish, & Susanna Gully of Cornelly
20 May Thomas Harvey & Joan Coad, by licence
6 June Henry Brenton of St Wenn, & Rose Grigg of this parish
John Eveling of this parish, & Mary Pearce of Bodmin, published the last time 30 July
19 Nov. Francis May & Catherine Gass
26 Nov. Thomas Salmon & Johanna Pascoe
19 Dec. Edward George & Jane Bulling
24 Dec. John Church Nichols & Jane Strong
Philip Brown of this parish & Ann Stephens of Withiel, published the last time 17 Dec.

ANNO 1776.

. . . . . John Drew of this parish & Mary Abbot of Little Petherick, published the last time 7 Jan.
23 Mar. Wm Truscott of Colan & Mary Williams of this parish
16 June John Stephens, husbandman, & Joanna Cundy, by licence
7 Sep. William Hocken of St Ervan & Mary Husband of this parish
13 Oct. William Buckingham & Mary Husband
5 Nov. Peter Rowe & Frances Cornish
26 Nov. William Rouse & Jane Clymows
10 Nov. Richard Hicks of this parish & Elizabeth Francis of St Enoder
22 Dec. Charles Bennet & Ann Rowe
27 Dec. Henry Brewer & Mary Jane

ANNO 1777.

6 Jan. Richard Carveth & Elizabeth Hicks
20 Jan. John Treverton of Bodmin & Elizabeth May
16 May Richard Grigg, husbandman, & Gertrude Cornish, widow
14 June William Rawling & Honour Bullock
6 July Richard Rowe & Ann Jenkins
8 July Thomas Loggett of Perranzabuloe, & Margery Tippet of this parish
5 July John Cock of Roach & Hannah Rowe
7 Sep. Christopher Raines & Jane Eveling
8 Nov. Richard Lobb & Grace Husband
19 Nov. John Grose of St Kew & Mary Thomas of this parish
23 Nov. John Carhart & Rosamond Ellery
21 Dec. Walter Teppit & Ann Sweet

ANNO 1778.

5 Jan. Michael Cornish & Elizabeth Gass
. . . . . Arthur White of this parish, & Alice Merifield of St Wenn, published the last time 7 Dec., 1777

17 Jan. Henry Stephens of St Austle, mariner, & Ann Truscott of this parish, by licence

30 Jan. Francis Tomm & Mary Husband

24 Feb. John Bullock of St Enoder & Jane Rowse of this parish

27 April William Ivey of St Merran, yeoman, & Elizabeth Rowse of this parish

30 May Richard Mewton & Elizabeth Thomas

13 July James Hodge & Martha Webber

19 July Richard Grigg & Elizabeth Grigg

19 July Joseph Hamm & Elizabeth Teppit

15 Nov. Oliver Adams Carveth of Truro & Elizabeth Drew of this parish, by licence

Anno 1779.

17 Jan. John Arthur of Bodmin & Elizabeth Jane of this parish, by licence

5 April William Rawling & Ruth Veal

6 April John Kent & Mary Morlin

24 April John Cornish, widower, & Ann Drew, spinster

23 May George Thomas & Mary Warne

16 July George Reynolds & Joyce Hoar

31 July John Gass of St Issey & Ann White of this parish

6 Aug. Barnet Falck, of Falmouth, merchant, & Elizabeth Harvey of this parish, by licence

14 Aug. Henry Mitchel & Ann Rowse

6 Sep. John Whitaker, rector of Roun Lanihorne, & Jane Tregenna of this parish, by licence

16 Oct. William Trebilcock & Elizabeth Martin

Anno 1780.

8 Jan. William Currah of St Eval & Jane Rowling of this parish

James White of this parish & Elizabeth Trebilcock of St Enoder, published the last time 19 Dec., 1779

17 April James Mitchell of St Agnes & Mary Bullin of this parish

. . . . . William Jane of this parish & Philippa Jolly of St Enoder, published the last time 12 March

11 May Williams Hicks of the parish of Tywardreath & Elizabeth Husband of this parish

23 May Stephen Brewer & Ann Clemoe

22 June William Ivey of St Merran, farmer, and Mary Rowse of this parish, by licence

24 June William Skinner & Catherine Brabyn

15 July John Truscott & Jane Blight

7 Oct. Richard Pasco & Mary Inch

Lord Arundell of WARDOUR.

BURIALS.

Here followe the names of suche as were and have byne buried in the said p'ish of St. Columb the over sythene the laste daie of Maye, in the one and theirteith yere of the reigne of Kinge Henrie the Eighth.

ANNO 1539.

1 June	Anne d. of John Moylle
3 June	Agnes d. of Henrie Arthur
4 June	Richard s. of Robert Tregona
6 June	Henry s. of Richard Typpet
16 June	Tamson d. of John Edward
16 June	Katherine, a bastard to Robert Lavyn
6 July	James s. of Robert Thomas
24 July	Emanuell s. of Richard Grosse
10 Aug.	John s. of John Lavyn
30 Aug.	John s. of John Melynnet
8 Sep.	Richard Watte
15 Nov.	Elizabeth Cregoe, widow
16 Dec.	Johan Norlyn, widowe
12 Jan.	Reighnold Bawden
16 Jan.	Johane a base child christyned at Hom
17 Jan.	Jane Carter wiffe of Richard Carter
19 Jan.	Margerie Pawle, widowe
7 Feb.	John s. of Udie Gene, christyned at Hom
22 Feb.	Alson Walis, widowe
3 Mar.	Katherine d. of John Sampson

ANNO 1540.

2 April	Margerie Weryn,* widowe
3 April	Alson d. of Marke Jobe
11 April	Agnes Will'ms, wydowe
12 April	Will'm Gascoyne
15 April	Ursula d. of James Nauskevell
12 May	John Julyn single man
19 May	Jane d. of John Cregoe
23 May	Marke s. of Thomas Bendy
30 May	Jenken Horken
13 June	Tamson d. of James Tybott
1 July	John s. of John Edward
4 July	Johane d. of Pearse John
1 Aug.	John Mayhowe
7 Aug.	Margerie d. of John Hopkyn
18 Aug.	John s. of John Sawle
20 Aug.	Agnes Rawlynge, wydow
22 Aug.	Alson the wiffe of Thomas Bendy
1 Sep.	John, a bastard to one Jane d. of L. Pethericke*
10 Sep.	Richard s. of Marke Williams
15 Sep.	Will'm Potter
17 Sep.	Will'm Manaduc
20 Sep.	Robert Uryn
2 Oct.	Bennett Potter
12 Oct.	Richow Arnger, widow
24 Nov.	John s. of Edward Meryfeild
11 Dec.	Richard s. of John Lawrenc
23 Dec.	Richard Rawlynge
6 Jan.	Will'm s. of Dennys Irishe
20 Jan.	Will'm s. of John Molhynnocke
6 Feb.	John Robynn, single man
4 Feb.	Maude Penpoll, widowe
12 Feb.	Harrie s. of John Chapleine
20 Mar.	Richard Hodge
20 Mar.	Bennett Benny

ANNO 1541.

2 April	Jane d. of John Horken
4 April	Ellen d. of Reynold Bodye
6 April	Robert Laven
9 April	Margaret the wiffe of Thomas Tomoow
10 April	Thomas Tome
13 April	Beatrix the wiffe of Renold Bodye
13 April	Isbell the wiffe of Lawrenc Skeberoon
14 April	Rawlinge Bennett
19 April	John Stephen the younger
12 May	Will'm Peryn, widower
14 May	Will'm Pawlle
16 May	Alson Towen, widow
17 May	Mawde Copithorne
11 June	Mabe Andrwe, widow
20 July	Jenken Symon

* More correctly Warne, sometimes spelt Warren, a family long seated in the neighbourhood.

* An initial letter only in the original, which was copied from entries made at the time of the funeral, etc.

24 July Agnes d. of Robert Gwynnowe
7 Aug. Ursula d. of Thomas Powlle
22 Aug. John* s. of James John Jane
20 Sep. Widow Darr
12 Oct. John Bennett
10 Nov. Johane d. of Will'm Sprey
12 Dec. Will'm s. of John Moylle
4 Jan. Thomas s. of Stephen Janye
13 Feb. Harrie s. of John Moylle of Treleved
15 Mar. Jane d. of John Crickley

ANNO 1542.

29 April Jennett Clement, widow
3 May Jane ffalmoth, widowe
4 May Margeriet† the wieff of John Jenken
18 May John s. of Thomas Dasow
1 June Jenken Bodie
29 July Jane d. of Richard Watt
10 Aug. Margaret d. of John Fraunce
28 Aug. Jane d. of Nicholas Stephen
9 Sep. Jane d. of Robert Uryn
23 Sep. Jane d. of James Bovyll
12 Oct. James s. of John Knight
23 Oct. Thomas, a bastard of Rawlinge Britton
2 Nov. Jannett Pearse, widow
16 Nov. Tamson Davye, widow
18 Dec. Reynold Trenocke
18 Dec. John Toker *al's* Newlyn
22 Jan. Pascatt d. of Harrie Joll
25 Jan. Agnes Glyne, widowe
25 Jan. Agnes d. of Thomas Meryfeild
23 Feb. Thomas Bostrong, single man
26 Feb. Margerie d. of John Spray
27 Feb. John‡ s. of James John Jane
28 Feb. Elizabeth Wylkie, singlewoman
5 Mar. Denys d. of Robert Gwynnow
8 Mar. John, a bastard of Rawlinge Brytton
8 Mar. John Phillepp
9 Mar. Sr Richard Payne, preist and custos
19 Mar. Margerie the wyff of Thomas Lambaran

ANNO 1543.

26 Mar. Sr Udie Pengwyne, chapleyne
27 Mar. John s. of Will'm Chapleman
29 Mar. Richard Rowse
22 Aug. Pascatt d. of John Clemow
23 April John Michell of Peryn, widoer
24 April Jane d. of Joan Brytton
25 April George* s. of Thomas Jenken
1 May Thomas s. of John Tome
6 May Will'm Darrservant to Richard Tremayne
10 May Joan Brytton
12 May John s. of John Sandowe
12 June Harrie s. of Will'm Smyth
14 June Stephen Rawe
15 June Thomas Jenken†
14 July Tamson d. of Richard Watte
24 July Harrie s. of James Nanscavoll
10 Aug. Margerie Page, widow
21 Aug. Richard s. of John James
2 Oct. Jane, the bastard of Katherine Vyncent
3 Oct. Denys Coswarne, widow
4 Oct. Lawrenc s. of Alexander‡
3 Nov. Jane the wieff of Richard Darr
10 Nov. Tamson the wieff of Richard Tremayne
27 Nov. Jane d. of John Stephen
26 Dec. Emblen Coble, widow
31 Dec. Margaret Benny
14 Jan. Johane d. of John Cornish
17 Jan. Jane the wieff of Harrie Typpett
22 Jan. John Olyver
1 Feb. John a bastard, father John Perkch
9 Feb. Katherine d. of Stephen Jenyn
9 Mar. Alson the wieff of John Tregleith
13 Mar. Alson Torker, widow
13 Mar. Thomas Pearse, widoer
23 Mar. John s. of John Gylberd

ANNO 1544.

30 April Michael Pascow, young man
2 May Pascatt d. of Thomas Dasow
5 May Phillepp d. of John Treharie
21 May John Pethericke
23 May Agnes the wieff of Robert Tregrear
25 May Alson d. of James John Jane
8 June John Dyar
27 June Will'm s. of John Moylle
18 July Jenken Rawlinge, widoer
24 July Udie Thomas, single man
14 Aug. Michael Thomas

* The baptism of this child does not appear in the register. See baptism of his brother of the same name, and note, p. 2 *ante*.

† She was his first wife; he married secondly Phillippa Vivian; see marriages 1550. He was probably a son of Tho. Jenkin, and grandson of John Jenkyn *al's* Pendyne of St. Columb Major.

‡ See his baptism, p. 2 *ante*.

* By his wife Katherine Pube.

† He was probably one of the sons mentioned without name in the will of John Jenkyn *al's* Pendyne of St. Columb Major, which will was proved 12 Dec., 1504.

‡ Surname left blank.

20 Sep. Jane d. of John Davye
4 Oct. Jane d. of John Menhire
4 Oct. Vivian s. of Edward Meryfeild
8 Oct. Thomas Tremain
15 Oct. Tamson, a bastard of Thomas Jenken
7 Nov. James s. of Saundry John
11 Nov. Johane d. of Richard Tom Nicholl
17 Nov. Richard Laven
11 Dec. Alson d. of James Horken
12 Dec. Love d. of Richard Osborne
22 Dec. Udie Brytton
22 Dec. Richard s. of Will'm ffere
23 Dec. Margerie wieff of Jenken Tremaine
7 Jan. Marren Tresannow
15 Jan. Marren the wieff of Richard Osborne
17 Jan. Marren the wieff of Udie Brytton
31 Jan. Arthur s. of Thomas Teage
20 Feb. S[r] John Arundell,* knight
22 Feb. John s. of Will'm Spray
24 Feb. Katherine d. of John Cregoe
28 Feb. S[r] John Bushe, chaplaine in Jess Chappell†
28 Feb. Johane d. of Udie Geyne

ANNO 1545.

5 April Thomas Tomewoo, widoer
6 April Johane d. of John Hawke
15 April Will'm Watte
17 April Ebbet the wieff of Thomas Rawlinge
26 April Roger Harper
28 April Wyllmott d. of Thomas Carter
29 April Stephen s. of Will'm Phillep
17 May John s. of Will'm Phillep
20 May Mellior d. of John Renold
12 June John s. of John Pearse
19 May Richard s. of Udie Myll
28 May Thomas Norton
13 July Alse d. of John Jenyn
23 Aug. Jane d. of Marke William
25 Aug. Richard Nanstaven
1 Sep. Margaret a bastard to Thomasine Tynckler
15 Sep. Richard Rvnell
5 Oct. Tamson a bastard to Jane Symon
8 Oct. John Vivian* *a'ls* John Trenowth
21 Oct. Remfrey Robert
21 Oct. Jane d. of Harrie Rowse
1 Nov. Peternell d. of Thomas Merifeild
3 Nov. John Williams
4 Nov. John a bastard to Christian servant to M[r] Tregose
24 Nov. George s. of John Thom
26 Nov. Katherine† d. of Will'm Trenowth
2 Dec. John Nauswyddon†
2 Dec. Elizabeth wieff of John Horkie
9 Dec. Jane d. of Richard Osborne
10 Dec. Margerie d. of Thomas Seys
17 Dec. Water Sandowe
31 Dec. Rawlinge s. of Richard Cocker
4 Jan. Harrie s. of John Pearse
16 Jan. Emblen Denys, wydow
26 Jan. Marren Phillep, wydow
3 Feb. Dorothie wieff of William Marke
14 Feb. John s. of John Menhire
14 Feb. John a bastard to John Chapelman
14 Feb. Henrie a bastard, mother Mary Pynock
27 Feb. John Fyrand‡

* This Sir John Arundell was of Lanherne, the son and heir of Sir Thomas Arundell of Lanherne, by his wife Catherine, daughter of Sir John Dinham and sister and co-heir of John, Lord Dinham. He was aged 11 years at his father's death in 1485. He married first, Lady Elizabeth Grey, daughter of Thomas Grey, first Marquis of Dorset (by his second wife Cecilia, daughter and heiress of William, Lord Bonville and Harrington), by whom he had issue, Sir John Arundell of Lanherne; Sir Thomas Arundell, ancestor of the Lords Arundell of Wardour; Elizabeth, married Sir Richard Edgcumbe; Jane, died unmarried, buried with a monumental brass at Mawgan. Sir John married secondly, Catherine, daughter of Sir Thomas Grenville, k[t], (by his first wife Isabella, daughter of Otes Gilbert), by whom he had issue one daughter, Mary married first to Robert Ratcliffe. Earl of Sussex, K.G., and secondly to Henry FitzAlan, 18th Earl of Arundell, K.G. There is a fine monumental brass to the memory of this Sir John in the church of St. Columb Major, fully described in the notes on the monuments remaining in the church; see introduction.

† Jesus Chapel, on the north side of the chancel, beneath it is the vault of the Vivians of Truan.

* He either purchased Trenowth, or has some think succeeded to it by descent, his father having probably married the heiress or coheiress of Trenowth, it being not uncommon at that period to use the *alias* in such a case. His will was proved Sep. 27, 1550. He was father of Richard Vyvyan, of Trenowth, who names him as "lately deceased."

† These names were probably acquired, like some others, by residence on lands so called in this parish.

‡ See burial of his widow in Dec. 1546.

27 Feb. Ebbott wieff of John Bennett
5 Mar. Thomas s. of John Pabe
10 Mar. John Edward
12 Mar. Jane wieff of John Pabe
21 Mar. Alson Sandow, widow

ANNO 1546.

25 Mar. Johnne wieff of John Renold
28 Mar. Agatha wiff of Michell Pabe
28 Mar. Phillep Avan
29 Mar. Catherine wieff of John Hawke
31 Mar. Robert Retallack
31 Mar. Johane d. of Robert John James
3 April S[r] John Lucow custos of O[r] Ladie Chapple*
3 April Walter s. of Thomas Nanscavan
4 April Jane d. of Udie Hodge
6 April Emblen Dawe, widow
7 April John s. of Thomas Carter
21 April Thomas s. of Thomas Beard
21 April Siblie Williams, widow
16 May Nicholas s. of John Trebodie
20 May John Opie
27 May Emblen d. of John Chaplaine
3 June Jane d. of Ote Dyar
13 June Niccholas Norton
25 June Alson Payne, widow
28 June Antonie s. of John Edward
2 July Remfrey s. of Will'm Ryse
10 July Will'm s. of John Sprayе
19 July Michell servant of John Richard
25 July Thomas Carter
27 July Robert s. of Stephen Pascowe
8 Aug. John Pearse
15 Aug. Jenken Kellyvreth†
22 Aug. Tybott Jacke Williams
26 Aug. Thomas Williams
13 Sep. Michell Mayhow
20 Sep. Larrie s. of Will'm Hawkie
23 Sep. Richard Tyar
23 Sep. John Rawe
15 Sep. Tamson wieff of John Sandowe

* The Lady Chapel is on the south side of the chancel, and belonged to the Arundells of Lanherne, who have a vault beneath it, and their monuments formerly stood within it. Although this is the last entry in the registers of a priest with the old title of "Sir," we find in the parish "Green Book," the style in use as late as 1585, in which year an entry records that Sir Robert Veale, clerk, and John Grace, were to keep the keys of the poor man's box *pro temp.*

† See entry 23 April, 1550.

2 Oct. Vivian s. of Luke Pollard
6 Oct. Elizabeth wieff of John Fraunce
6 Nov. John s. of James Rosogan*
8 Nov. Marie d. of John Darr
11 Nov. Niccholas Renolde
18 Nov. Janneth wieff of Udie Myll
21 Nov. Pascowe Spraye
8 Dec. Denys d. of Udie Hodge
8 Dec. John s. of Udie Hodge
14 Dec. Margerie the wieff of Michell Calwaie
15 Dec. Richard s. of Stephen Jenyn
17 Dec. Jane the wieff of Will'm Gascoyne
18 Dec. Jannett fferand, widow
4 Jan. Isett wieff of John Dyar
7 Jan. Richard s. of Richard Rowe
20 Jan. John Thomas
22 Jan. John a bastard to Johan Kembie
26 Jan. Jane the wieff of Udie Geyne
22 Jan. John s. of Udie Geyne
3 Feb. Jannett the wieff of Pearse, servant to R'frey Pascow
5 Feb. Michell Pabe
11 Feb. ffraunces Josse
14 Feb. Agnes the wieff of Thomas Whytte
14 Feb. Richard s. of Nicholas Grove
15 Feb. Tamson d. of John Olyver
23 Feb. John Bernard a bastard
26 Feb. Jane d. of Richard Ospren
9 Mar. Melliar Grove, widow
10 Mar. Melliar the wieff of John Trehare
16 Mar. Udan Vyncent the wieff of John Vyncent

ANNO 1547.

30 Mar. Jannett Manaduc, widow
2 April James Reskorlow, widoer
3 April Johane & John the children of John Pabe
15 April Will'm s. of Thomas Robert
27 May Jane d. of Henrie Rowse
17 June Margerie d. of John Jenken†
20 June Thomas s. of Otes Dyar
22 June Otes s. of Will'm Prowse
29 June Janet† d. of John Jenken
29 June John s. of Pascow Hey
2 July Water Tregase
5 July Humphrey s. of Marke Jobe
6 July Johane d. of Marke Jobe

* Rosogan, the name of a farm in the parish.

† Daughter of John Jenkyn (grandson of John Jenkyn *al's* Pendyne) by Margerie his first wife.

12 July Water Hey
14 July Pernall servant to John Rawe
15 July John a bastard to Bennett Wilkie
18 July Rawlinge s. of Robert Torway
18 July Tamson servant to Bennett Mawna
19 July Will'm s. of Robert Vages
20 July Nora servant to Rawlinge Teage
20 July Jane d. of Richard Trenock
20 July Elizabeth d. to Stephen Browne
20 July Elen a bastard to Will'm Bawden
20 July Thomas s. of Rawlyn Jeffery
21 July James s. of John Knight
21 July Will'm s. of John Stephen
23 July Thomas s. of Will'm Prowse
23 July James s. of Edward Island
23 July Alce d. of Robert Torway
24 July Jane d. of Richard Bawden
24 July John s. of John Stephen the younger
25 July Pearse Bodie
25 July Richard s. of Thomas Merifeild
25 July Jane d. of Robert Vyvian*
27 July Jane & Jane, daus. of Pears Marten
28 July John s. of John Edward
29 July Antonie s. of Richard Tocker
29 July Richard Pearse, singleman
29 July Stephen s. of Nicholas Dyar
30 July Jannett the wieff of John Clerk
30 July John s. of John Clerk
30 July Nicholas s. of John Kembre
1 Aug. John s. of Bennett Bone
1 Aug. Marie the wieff of Thomas Braye
3 Aug. Margaret d. of John Vyncent
4 Aug. Agnes servant to Thomas Merifeild
4 Aug. Agnes d. of Pearse Marten
5 Aug. Dorothie the wieff of Richard Pearse
5 Aug. Jane d. of John Clerke
6 Aug. John Clerke
6 Aug. Michell* s. of Thomas Jenken
7 Aug. Remfrey servant to Richard Carter
7 Aug. John s. of John Clark
7 Aug. Melliar the wieff of Pascow Pearse
7 Aug. Jane servant of Jane Keyser
8 Aug. Pascow Pearce
8 Aug. Richard Tremaine
9 Aug. Jane d. of Richard Rawlinge
9 Aug. Jane d. of John Laustone
9 Aug. Richard s. of Robert Torwey
10 Aug. Thomas s. of Udie Putford
10 Aug. Harrie s. of John Mayhow
10 Aug. Richard s. of John Melhynnock
12 Aug. John s. of Robert Symon
13 Aug. Edward s. of Emanuell Roger
13 Aug. Jane d. of John Hetherd
13 Aug. Mariott the wieff of Robert Symon
13 Aug. Jane d. of Richard Trenock
13 Aug. Stephen s. of Will'm Upcott
13 Aug. Will'm s. of John Molhynnock
14 Aug. Thomas s. of Remfrey Grosse
14 Aug. John Blackdom a stranger
15 Aug. John Ryse
16 Aug. Otes Dyar
16 Aug. John Monndaie†
17 Aug. Will'm Gascoyne
17 Aug. Jenken s. of Robert John
18 Aug. Will'm s. of Robert Gwynnow
18 Aug. Nicholl d. of Richard Trenorth
19 Aug. James s. of Jenken Vian
20 Aug. Edward s. of Pearse Bodye
20 Aug. Agnes d. of Jenken Vyan
22 Aug. Agnes d. of Thomas Treluddow
23 Aug. George s. of Ote Nawan
23 Aug. Phillep d. of Harrie Roswalsters

* This Robert was probably the brother of Michael Vivian, of Trelowarren, and if so his wife was Margaret, daughter and co-heiress of John Durant, of Trevarrion; he was a J.P. in 1523, and left issue James, Michael, and Margaret, who married first, Walter Kestell, and, secondly, Michael Hill. James continued the male line, but Michael left a daughter and heiress. Christian married William Fortescue, of Mawgan; her mother, Jane, daughter of Rob. Hill, married again to Nicholas Fortescue, father of William Fortescue.

* By Katherine Pube his wife.

† John Mondaie of St. Columb Minor, gent., gave by will money to the poor of St. Columb Major. (Green Book, 1585.) This family had the manor of Rialton, in Lower St. Columb, through the means of Tho. Munday Prior, of Bodmin, whose brother, John Munday, first settled there about 1540; they retained their position at Rialton for several generations, but eventually became very much reduced in circumstances.

23 Aug. Richard s. of Robert John
23 Aug. Will'm s. of Bennett Mawna
23 Aug. John s. of John Sandowe
23 Aug. Richard s. of Udie Myll
24 Aug. Richard s. of Will'm Upcott
24 Aug. Harrie s. of Remfrey Carter
24 Aug. Richard d. of Thomas Trenowth
25 Aug. Udie servant to John Moylle
25 Aug. Jane d. of Will'm Upcott
26 Aug. Thomas s. of John Hetherd
27 Aug. Richard Hainett, a stranger
28 Aug. Remfrey s. of John Jeffery
28 Aug. Luke s. of Richard Pluygie
28 Aug. Jane d. of John Jeffery
28 Aug. Elizabeth d. of Robert Gwynnowe
28 Aug. Brehard a bastard to Will'm Ryse
29 Aug. Henric s. of Robert Gwynnowe
30 Aug. Will'm Ryse
30 Aug. Nicholas s. of Remfrey Carter*
31 Aug. Richard s. of Will'm Hawke
31 Aug. Thomas s. of Thomas Carter*
31 Aug. Thomas Irish s'vant to John Nanconan
1 Sep. George s. of Thomas Wyll
1 Sep. Margerie d. of Thomas Teage
1 Sep. Tamson d. of John Lawrie
1 Sep. Phillip d. of Robert John
2 Sep. Jane d. of John Clemowe
3 Sep. Stephen s. of Henric Tybett
4 Sep. Agnes Irish s'vant to John Nanconan
4 Sep. Phillep servant to John Typett
6 Sep. Phillip d. of Harrie†
6 Sep. Remfrey s. of John Moylle
7 Sep. Thomas s. of Richard Tremain
8 Sep. Remfrey s. of Remfrey Carter
8 Sep. Katherine d. of John Hawke
8 Sep. John s. of Richard Watte
9 Sep. Isabell d. of Robert Sexton
9 Sep. Tamson d. of Nicholas Trelego
9 Sep. Elizabeth the wieff of John Sandow
10 Sep. Margerie d. of Thomas Benny
10 Sep. Alson, a bastard to Remfrey Carter
11 Sep. Thomas s. of Thomas Davie
11 Sep. Bennett s. of Thomas Treluddrow
11 Sep. Jane d. of John Stephen
13 Sep. Ursula d. of William Feyre

* Their relationship, if any, to the family of Carter in the *Heralds' Visitation* does not appear.

† No surname.

14 Sep. Alson servante to Thomas Conssoer
18 Sep. Margaret d. of Will'm Spraye
18 Sep. Jane d. of John Jeffery
18 Sep. Katherine s. of John Davie
19 Sep. Richard s. of Richard Vyncent
19 Sep. Richard s. of Will'm Ryse
19 Sep. John Irish servant to John Nanconan
21 Sep. Robert Jollye
21 Sep. Mariott d. of Thomas Tremaine
21 Sep. Thomas Davie
22 Sep. Johane Gove, widow
23 Sep. Elizabeth wieff of John Bodrogoe
24 Sep. Udie the servant of Stephen Robert
25 Sep. Richard Nicholas
25 Sep. Alson the wieff of James John
26 Sep. Richard s. of John Sewalsters
1 Oct. Walter servant to Janet Tremaine
2 Oct. John s. of John Tremaine
3 Oct. Vivian s. of John Browne
4 Oct. ffraunces s. of Will'm Phillep, and three others*
8 Oct. Richard s. of Will'm Jollye
8 Oct. Will'm s. of John Jane
9 Oct. John s. of Allen Whyte
11 Oct. Marie d. of Harrie Pluygie
15 Oct. Richard Falmouth, s'vant to Stephen Robert
15 Oct. Richard s. of John Lanyne
15 Oct. George s. of John Typett
20 Oct. Jane d. of Michell Mayhowe
21 Oct. Thomas s. of Will'm Bennett
22 Oct. Jane d. of Allen Wyott
22 Oct. Pascett d. of John Toker
25 Oct. Marie d. of John Trohare
6 Nov. John Gayffe
8 Nov. Tamson d. of John Typett
8 Nov. James s. of Richard Typett
12 Nov. John s. of Udie Myll
15 Nov. Richard s. of John Toker the elder
15 Nov. Elizabeth d. of Robert Jollie
23 Nov. Jane d. of Richard Rawe
26 Nov. Elizabeth d. of Richard Rawe
27 Nov. John s. of Stephen Jenyne
3 Dec. Phillep d. of Robert Tregona

* In this year the parish was evidently suffering from one of those epidemic diseases, which the unsanitary state of the social habits of the age so greatly tended to extend. The number of deaths registered in this year is 187, the usual number being from 30 to 40; the latter part of the year 1546, and the early part of 1548, are also affected.

4 Dec. Harrie bastard to Anne Hengcocke
21 Dec. Water s. of Richard Reiff
27 Dec. John Vyncent
10 Feb. John s. of Robert Tregona
19 Feb. Harrie s. of Harrie Arthur
24 Feb. Alson Jefferie, widow
28 Feb. John a bastard to Elizabeth Marten
18 Mar. Harrie s. of Thomas Teake

ANNO 1548.

26 Mar. John Rowse, singleman
3 April Anne wiffe of Udie Bawdyn
15 May Wenefred d. of Humphrey Tyfford
1 June Richard s. of John Tyake
4 June Pethericke servant to Thomas Cower
15 July Thomas Pascowe
29 July Richard Rawlinge
4 Aug. Will'm s. of Robert Gwynnow
Tooe whose names are torne out of the book were buried the 2nd and 3rd Sep.*
4 Sep. John s. of Thomas Tyar
27 Sep. Jane d. of John Mell
2 Oct. Thomas s. of Richard Weaver
18 Oct. Thomas s. of Robert Calway
21 Oct. James s. of Will'm Wattye
2 Nov. Grace servant to Phillep Tom
11 Nov. Jane Ryse, wydow
12 Nov. Margaret d. of John Tyake
Will'm s. of Luke Pollard
12 Jan. John Michell
16 Jan. James Corver
3 Feb. Thomas Sampson
20 Feb. Richard s. of John Tynckler
28 Feb. Nicholas Dyar
12 Mar. Jane d. of Udie Geno
19 Mar. Thomas Melhynnock
22 Mar. Robert Trepronye
22 Mar. J. . . .* whose name is worne out of the booke

ANNO 1549.

26 Mar. James s. of Manuell Roger
28 Mar. Richow wieff of John Wylky
5 April Elizabeth wieff of John Lavyn
7 April Constanc d. of Richard Nicles
13 April Thomas Adam
15 April Jenken Tom
19 April Anne wieff of Thomas Tyake

* The existing register being a copy of an earlier one, hence omissions and the occurrence of an initial only in some places, the name itself being illegible to the person then employed to make a copy of the entries.

3 May Tamson the wieff of Thomas Warren*
5 May Alson Norton, wydow
25 May Margerie wieff of John Kestell
25 May Elizabeth the wieff of John Richard
2 June James bastard to †
9 June Robert s. of Richard Rawe
31 July Harrie s. of James Younge
31 July John s. of James Younge
24 Aug. Jane d. of Robert John
25 Aug. James Rosogan
21 Sep. Emblen d. of James Vyncent
2 Oct. John‡ whose name is worne out of the book
18 Oct. Margerie d. of Thomas Benny
24 Oct. Will'm Kellie servant to Remfrey Strongman
19 Nov. Syslie d. of John Moylle
29 Nov. Jane d. of John Yedde
12 Dec. Richard Weaver
15 Dec. Melliar wieff of John Moylle
31 Dec. Pacience d. of Will'm Mar
2 Jan. Jane d. of Water Merifeild
16 Jan. Harrie s. of Remfrey Carter
17 Jan. John s. of Stephen Pascowe
17 Jan. Ursula d. of Thomas Richard
9 Feb. John, one out of Mayhowes howse
19 Feb. Anne the wiff of Will'm Salpyn
26 Feb. Richard Calwaie
9 Mar. John, bastard to Lallow Jolle
21 Mar. Water Merifeild§

ANNO 1550.

23 April Harrie Kyllywerth,‖ p'son of this p'ish
5 May Mollier Donne, widowe
9 May Margaret d. of Richard Kawlye
21 May Jane d. of Richard Kawlye
14 June Harrie s. of John Nankevell¶
27 May John Leprise *al's* Prest

* Warne, more correctly.
† Left blank.
‡ Entered thus; see note p. 176 *ante*.
§ Water for Walter occurs often.
‖ See entry 15 Aug., 1546; these two are the only entries of the name in the register. About 1600 a Hen. Kelverth married Elizabeth, daughter of Rich. Roskrowe of Gluvias.
¶ The pedigree of Nankevell in the Heralds' Visitation of Cornwall, 1620, gives the descent thus,—John Nankevill *al's* Tipott of St. Wenn, living in 1620, s. of Rich. N. of St. Wenn, s. of Mark N. of Colomb Maior, s. of Jenkin N. of C. M., s. of John N. of C. M., s. of Tipett N. of C. M. The above John N. living 1620, married Kath. daughter of Humph. Arscott, and had Richard aged 13, Joane aged 18, Katherine aged 16 in 1620.

2 July Jenet the wiffe of Remfrey Strongman
10 July Will'm s. of Thomas Marke
7 Sep. Anne bastard to Water Crips
27 Oct. Elizabeth wiff of Water Wil-l'ms
7 Nov. Udie Nancollas
3 Dec. Richard Nicholl
14 Dec. Richard Osburne
26 Dec. Will'm Prowse
24 Jan. Jane d. of John Robert
26 Jan. Richard a bastard
12 Feb. Alse Hockye, widow

ANNO 1551.

30 Mar. Michaell Davie
19 April ffraunce s. of Richard ffisher
29 May Margaret wiff of Thomas Cor-nish
14 June Jane d. of ffraunce Adam
18 June Umfrey s. of James Vyncent
12 Aug. Marren wiffe of Harrie Arthur
17 Sep. Alson Torware, wydow
25 Sep. Thomas s. of Stephen*
5 Oct. Jane d. of John Pearse
6 Oct. Stephen s. of Antonie Rawe

The name of those wch were buried the rest of the yere 1551 were lost or not registered, and from that yere untyll the theirtene yere of the reigne of our most gracious soveraigne Ladie Quene Elizabeth that nowe ys were lykewyse lost or not wryten, but here followe the names of those that were buried sythene the yere of our Lord God 1571.

ANNO 1571.

9 April Will'm s. of Thomas Calway
9 April Paskow Frapp
10 April Alice Dingle
12 April Marke Williams
12 April Margaret Roche
21 April John s. of Arnold Gennet
25 April Harrie s. of Renold Lavyn
25 April John Tyfford
25 April Tamson Symner
4 May Richard Bryent
4 May Johane Pascow, widow
5 May Katherine Vyncent, widow
16 May Constanc Tyfford
2 June Tamson Burlace
4 June John Marke
5 June Marten Collys
8 June Thomas s. of Thomas Teage
20 June John Cardewe
6 July John Cornish
10 July Clarye Younge

* No Surname.

15 Aug. John Trigen
15 Aug. Stephen Benny
22 Aug. Elizabeth Moylle
3 Oct. Tamson Pawle
20 Oct. Richard Lallowe
3 Nov. Richard Edye
4 Dec. Johane Adam
18 Dec. Columbe Stephen
29 Dec. Margerie Heycrafte
18 Jan. Johane Clarke
30 Jan. Johane Boscastell
3 Feb. Marie James, widow
6 Feb. John s. of Robert Marke
3 Mar. Harrie Hynder
19 Mar. Johane Vyvian*
22 Mar. John Collinge

ANNO 1572.

30 Mar. ffraunce Williams
10 April Margaret Rawe
13 April John Cockinge
18 April Johane Browne
22 April Margerie Pearse, widow
1 May Margaret James, widow
6 May Stephen Allen
14 May Bawden Seryvenor
24 May Constanc Typpett
2 June Paskow Tooker
2 June Johane Nawne
9 June John Hawke
12 June John Dawe
13 June John Othruge (?) of Alternone
28 July Thomas Hockinge
3 Aug. Richowe Spraye
12 Aug. Humphrey Mayhow
22 Aug. Thomas Hawke
8 Oct. Jannett Marten
18 Oct. Harrie Haycreft
28 Oct. Richard Allen
28 Oct. John Trescalett
7 Nov. Richard Oxnam
28 Dec. Amye Cerra (?)
29 Dec. Katherine Adam
30 Dec. Will'm Bettye
22 Jan. Johane Treluddrow
28 Jan. John Langdon
13 Feb. Mablye Morcombe
22 Feb. Alce Laven
28 Feb. Wylliam Spraye
1 Mar. Elizabeth Kood
6 Mar. Phillep Browne
11 Mar. Elizabeth Mayhowe
22 Mar. Stephen Browne
23 Mar. Johane Browne
24 Mar. Johane Allen

* Probably daughter of Richard Vivian, named in his will 1550.

ANNO 1573.

27 Mar. Margaret Rawlinge
8 April Margerie Geene
9 April Alse Hey
12 April Marye Rowse
13 April Hugh Hawke
14 April John Stephen
24 April Stephen Dyngell
29 April Manuell Cornish
30 April John Hockie
20 Mar. Will'm Sadlier
26 June Richard Hockie
3 July Honor Luke
5 July Phillepp Retalleck
6 July John Manuell
3 Aug. Elizabeth d. of Humphrey Ryse
7 Oct. Johane Manuell
7 Oct. Johane Marke
11 Oct. Richard Typpett
21 Oct. John Maben
4 Dec. Edward Calwaie
28 Dec. John Chaplinge
30 Jan. John Glanfeild
20 Feb. Humphry Symon
22 Feb. Luke Jenken
29 Feb. James Carter*
29 Feb. Jane Colle
30 Feb. John Nanconan

ANNO 1574.

20 April Harrie Joll
10 May John Bennet a bastard
9 June Thomas Manuell
20 July Will'm Upcott
14 Aug. Willmot Wylliams
3 Oct. Christen Calwaie
8 Nov. Katherine Treluddrow
19 Nov. Elizabeth Sexton
1 Dec. John Williams
26 Jan. Richard Watte
27 Jan. Elizabeth Tregenhay
10 Feb. John Davie the elder
20 Feb. Alse Nawne
10 Mar. Margerie Vyvian†

ANNO 1575.

5 April Johane Lyttacott
13 June Peter Rysse
20 June Nichlas Hockinge
23 June Ursula Rawe
12 July Johane Cocke
21 July Richard Maben
20 Aug. Radigan Luke
16 Sep. Alse Penputford
23 Sep. Alse Johns
14 Oct. Honor Gavrigan, widow**
26 Oct. Alse Pawlle
5 Nov. John Inhaye
1 Jan. Harrie Rawe
15 Jan. Marie Calwaie, bastard
16 Jan. Richard Trusoe
16 Jan. Richard Mevasoe
30 Jan. Johane Thomas
2 Feb. Elizabeth Spraye, widow
5 Feb. Johane Edye
2 Mar. John Mathew

ANNO 1576.

11 April John Menhynnett
28 April Margerie Lethe, bastard
11 May Johane Lukie
6 June Anne Trevithan
14 June John Moyses
23 June Will'm Bosello
23 June Johane Edward
28 June Christian Geene
11 July Umphrey Grosse
10 Aug. Johane Moylle
19 Aug. Johane Marten
9 Sep. Ollie Copithorne
27 Sep. Will'm Pell
12 Oct. Margerie Cocke
25 Oct. Richard Grosse
18 Nov. John Valleys
25 Nov. Will'm Benny
26 Nov. John Pascow
2 Dec. Johane Knight
18 Jan. John Collinge
20 Jan. Thomas Abraham
22 Jan. Blanch Spray
30 Jan. Agnes Darr
9 Feb. John Cockinge

ANNO 1577.

March, Apriell and Maye nothing registered.
6 June Richard Jenken
13 June John Ryse
13 June Johane Tremaine
13 June John Gobell
18 June Richard Edward
20 June Will'm Mayhowe
21 June Henrie Trevethan
22 June Umphrey Tremaine
30 June Johane Haycroft
3 July John Edward

* Son of Richard Carter, gent.; he married Honour, daughter and coheiress of John Newman, by whom he had issue several children.

† Probably daughter of Richard Vivian, named in his will dated 1550.

** She was daughter of John Michell, of Truro, and wife of John Gaverigan of Gaverigan.

9 July Anne Calwaie
15 July Elizabeth Calwaie
30 July Alse Jane
17 Aug. Katherine Illarie
21 Aug. ffraunce Snell
24 Aug. Johane Jobb
28 Aug. Marke servannt to John Illarye
30 Aug. Thomas Howell
7 Sep. Katherine Carvannell
15 Sep. Johane Jelon
15 Sep. Katherine Opie
26 Sep. Elizabeth Nanconan
26 Sep. Richard Nanconan
27 Sep. John Abraham
28 Sep. Christable Jenken
30 Sep. Edward Edwards
3 Oct. Pascae Sadler
8 Oct. Thomas Sadler
12 Oct. Elizabeth Sqere
12 Oct. John Browne
15 Oct. Johane Thomas
19 Oct. John *al's* Jenken Nanconan
20 Oct. John Pabe
26 Oct. Elizabeth Rowse
3 Nov. Richard Vesey
10 Nov. Lawrenc Browne
11 Nov. Tamson Rowse
12 Nov. Stephen Williams
17 Nov. Richard Rowse
17 Nov. Humphrey Skynner
22 Nov. Thomas Skynner
23 Nov. Johane Kinge, bastard
24 Nov. Johane Robert
30 Nov. Honor Williams
30 Nov. Honor Browne
3 Dec. Robert Indye
4 Dec. William Browne
8 Dec. John Robert
8 Dec. Harrie Batt
12 Dec. Richard Robert
12 Dec. John Robert
23 Dec. George Mayhowe
24 Dec. Elizabeth Trembeth
26 Dec. John Thomas
27 Dec. Richard Adam
29 Dec. James Williams
7 Jan. Marke Hocken
7 Jan. Tamsone Hocken
22 Jan. Johane Edward
16 Feb. Johane Jenken
2 Mar. Richard Bylkie
15 Mar. Agnes Palmer
18 Mar. Agnes Nicholas
20 Mar. Richard Bennye
21 Mar. James Striblie
23 Mar. Johane Dawe
23 Mar. Pascow Tremon

ANNO 1578.

10 April Johane Nankevell
16 April Tamson Pawlle
16 April Margerie Norton
30 April Nicholas Pawlle
3 May John Merifeild
15 May Thomas Carvannell
29 May John Chaplinge
3 June Anne Putford, bastard
16 June Richow Browne, widow
26 June Pethericke Snell
6 July Ebbie d. of Richard Maye
3 Aug. Elizabeth wieff of George Cardewe
29 Aug. Thomas s. of Richard Blake
5 Sep. Marke Penquite
16 Sep. Edward s. of Roger Maben
21 Oct. Thomas Teage
25 Oct. Alson Cocke
25 Oct. Margaret Cardew
30 Oct. Pentecost Marke
31 Oct. Margaret Whyte, widow
18 Nov. Jane Bennett
24 Nov. Thomas Langdon,* gent.
19 Dec. Margerie Jenyne, widow
2 Jan. John† s. of John Bonython
13 Jan. Sylvester a bastard
14 Feb. Robert s. of Lawrence Jobbe
23 Mar. John s. of Richard Spraye
24 Mar. John a bastard to John Symon

ANNO 1579.

28 Mar. Johane Rowthan
17 April Harrie Cost
4 May Thomas Jenken‡
8 May Tamson the wieff of Thomas Hawke
9 May John Nawne servant to Richard Jenyne
17 May Richard Dasowe
4 Aug. Jane Marten *al's* Scryvener
16 Aug. Tamson d. of George Mayhowe
19 Oct. Robert s. of George Mayhowe
13 Dec. Harrie s. of Richard Sampson

* He was fourth son of John Langdon, of Bicton, co. Cornwall, by Elizabeth, daughter of Sir William Godolphin. He married Katherine Rosuggon.

† By his wife Eleanor, daughter and coheiress of William Mylyton.

‡ He was probably son of Thomas, and brother of Henry Jenkin, who married Thomasin, daughter and co-heiress of Wm. Harry Watt, gent. He married in 1542 Katherine Pabe, or Pube.

17 Jan. Richard s. of John Vesey
10 Mar. Alse Browne, widow
15 Mar. Tamson d. of the saied Alse
19 Mar. Johane the wieff of Richard Benny
22 Mar. Henrie Gwynnow *al's* Roskigian
24 Mar. Johane d. of Robert Renolde

ANNO 1580.

11 April Johane d. of Harrie Gwynnowe
14 April Johane d. of John Cardewe
18 April John a bastard to Emblen Reede
19 April Dorothie d. of John Strongman
24 April John s. of William Clerke
24 April Jannett Tanner an old woman
9 May Richard d. of John Menhire
27 May Nicholas Lane
29 May John s. of John Cocken
10 June John s. of Harrie Adam
15 June Barbara d. of Richard Willm's
15 June Thomas s. of John Adam
4 July Elizabeth Reed, widow
14 Aug. Jane the wieff of Richard Carter*
14 Aug. ffranscis s. of John Snell
15 Aug. Milson d. of Robert John
22 Aug. Elizabeth d. of Thomas Vivian†
4 Sep. Agnes d. of Robert John
28 Sep. John s. of Will'm Copithorne
15 Oct. Jane the wieff of John Manuell
16 Oct. Walter servant to Richard Oxnam
29 Oct. Nicholas s. of Bastyian (no surname)
15 Dec. John s. of Richard Rowe
16 Dec. John s. of Humphrey Vyncent
16 Dec. Johane d. of Robert Custoller
17 Dec. John s. of Michell Harrye
16 Feb. Pascoe an old woman

* Daughter of (John ?) Nanconan. Her husband was the second son of Richard Carter, gent., and brother of James Carter, gent., who married the co-heiress of Newman.

† By his wife Anne, daughter and co-heiress of Peter Lower, of Truro.

15 Feb. Reskeen a widow woman
17 Feb. Margerie the wieffe of Richard Jane
29 Feb. William Brown an old man
13 Mar. John Moylle th'elder

ANNO 1581.

27 Mar. Tamson Upcott, widow
15 April John Gross, a verie old man
18 April Johane Jane
1 May Christian the wieff of Roger Servir
3 May John Stephens
22 June Harrie Sexton
10 Oct. John s. of John Skynner
27 Nov. Phillep d. of Renold Grosse
9 Dec. John Sandow
12 Dec. Richard s. of Thomas Vesey
16 Jan. John s. of William Wylls
11 Feb. John s. of Pascow John
23 Feb. Alse one dwellinge in the churchayrd
24 Feb. Elizabeth Trenowth *al's* Vivian*
2 Mar. Oliff d. of Degorie Stubs
3 Mar. ffranscis s. of Sampson Morcombe
14 Mar. Syslie the wieff of Richard Jane
14 Mar. Elinor d. of Harrie Opie
24 Mar. John s. of John Tocker

ANNO 1582.

9 April Will'm s. of Lawrence Jobb
9 April Honor bastard to Margaret Edwarde
10 April William Striblie
16 April John Norton the younger
20 April Jane the wieff of Paskow John
21 April Nicholas s. of Richard Hand
21 April John s. of Edward Weaver
22 April Margerie Typpett, widow
30 April John s. of Will'm Striblie
3 May Marren Striblie, widow
5 May Elizabeth d. of William Clerk
18 May Jane the wiff of William Gylberd
20 May Johane Bodye, widow
18 July Johane Nanconan, widow
21 July John Moyses

* Widow of Richard Vyvyan, of Trenowth, named in his will dated 27 Sept., 1550.

4 Aug. Richard Carter, gent.*
19 Aug. Thomas s. of Harrie Hawke
23 Aug. Katherine d. of Umphrey Nankevell
26 Sep. Agnes Reskigian, widowe
16 Oct. Tamson Hawke, widowe
25 Oct. John bastard to Katherine Engrosse
26 Oct. Marten s. of John Valleys
5 Nov. Alse Davie, widowe

The second daie of the saied November there was buried a woman unknown

12 Dec. Honor d. of Harrie Sexton
15 Dec. Tamson Typpett
18 Dec. A child to Robert Darr
20 Dec. Symon a bastard to Amye (*sic*)
27 Dec. A man child to John Roskigian
5 Jan. John s. of Thomas Hockie
5 Feb. Peternell d. of Davy Congdon
24 Feb. Elizabeth wiff to Gregorie Trenoage
28 Feb. Thomas Bennye

ANNO 1583

27 Mar. Margarett the wiff of John Epplett
10 April Honor d. of John Pollard
5 May John s. of John Brabyn
15 June Jane d. of Richard Moylle
15 July A bastard to Roches†
17 July J. d. of Harrie Adam†
31 July Oliffe d. of Thomas Merifeild
1 Aug. Honor d. of John Retallacke
18 Aug. John Copithorne, constable
19 Aug. fflorenc d. of Thomas Burges
1 Sep. John s. of Thomas Tyer
6 Sep. William s. of Lawrence Jobb
12 Sep. Johane the wiffe of Thomas Tyfford
27 Sep. Alse d. of Thomas Lukye
1 Oct. John s. of Thomas Daye
18 Oct. Will'm s. of Harrie Hawke
18 Nov. Richard s. of Will'm Michell
23 Dec. Katherine d. of Will'm Upcott
14 Jan. Charles s. of John Carter*
24 Jan. Anne d. of John Langdon, gent.
3 Feb. Jane d. of Robert Locke
17 Feb. Johane d. of John Brabyn
11 Feb. Margaret the wiffe of Richard Tresawlle†
24 Feb. Alse the wiffe of Thomas Weaver
11 Mar. John s. of John Leveton
15 Mar. Ollie d. of Pethericke Pernell

ANNO 1584.

25 April Margaret the wiffe of Roger fflamack‡
20 April Antonye s. of John Davye
3 June fflorence d. of Bennett Calwaie§
3 June Richard Reve
23 June Johane d. of John Mayhow
26 June Margaret a bastard
28 June Johane wiffe of Antonie the Smyth
28 July Udie Gene
28 July Anne d. of Thomas Vivian‖
7 Aug. John Lukie
11 Aug. Johane d. of George Marke
30 Aug. Umphrey Symon
8 Sep. William s. of John Hockie
24 Aug. Richard s. of Christopher Tresawlle¶
30 Oct. John Rowse the elder
10 Nov. Harrie s. of Will'm Trethunyck
10 Nov. Margaret d. of Marten Rawe
26 Nov. Marie d. of John Rawe
17 Dec. Johane a bastard to Syslie Tyer
25 Dec. Richard a bastard to Margerie Trevithan
27 Dec. Margaret Ollie
12 Jan. Honor Rowse, singlewoman
27 Jan. John Nankevell the younger
30 Jan. Mylson a bastard to the young Cocken

* He was second son of Richard Carter, gent., and married Jane, daughter of (? John) Nanconan, but died s. p.; his nephew, John Carter, was his heir. Richard Carter had as appears "by the old book" a grant by the twelve men in 1573 "for 21 yeres of vi shoppes, two stiles, the standing under the pentyses, and all the standings before the pyshe house for the yerelye rent of 53s. and 4 pence." In 1583 they were in the hands of John Carter as executor of Richard Carter, (vide Green Book.) The "old book" named above no longer exists; the one remaining commences in 1585.

† Sic.

* By his wife Jane, daughter of John Vivian, of Truan.

† There are in the parish two farms, Upper and Lower Tresawle. In 11 Ric. II. Ralph Vivian, of Trevidren, held Tresawell in right of his wife, widow of . . . . Tresawell.

‡ He was one of the Constables of the parish in 1585. Rog. Flamancke, gent., was one of the twelve men in the same year.—Green Book.

§ Bennet Callway, warden of the poor in 1588.—Green Book.

‖ By Anne his wife, daughter and co-heiress of Peter Lower, of Truro.

¶ Christopher Tresawell, one of the wardens of the parish in 1585.

1 Mar. Elizabeth servaunt to Lawrence Jobb
8 Mar. Alson Hawke, widow
8 Mar. Arthur s. of Sampson Morcombe
24 Mar. Agnes Grylls, widowe

ANNO 1585.

29 Mar. Nowell s. of John Phillepp
14 May Robert a bastard to Thomas Weaver's daughter
11 June Peter Heycrefte
20 July John Grysson
26 Aug. Harrie s. of Thomas Cock
6 Sep. Marie d. of John Davie
12 Sep. George s. of John Heydon
13 Sep. John Lawrie
15 Sep. Jane the wieffe of Will'm Thomas
26 Sep. Jefferie Uryn
30 Sep. Richard s. of Richard Rove
22 Oct. Constanc wieff of Edward Cardewe
24 Oct. Johane d. of Ann Edward
24 Oct. Johane d. of Will'm Calway
3 Nov. George Cardew
9 Nov. Johane the wieff of Nicholas Treluddrow*
18 Nov. Johane d. of Richard Spray
20 Nov. Johane Jane, widow
24 Dec. Elizabeth Hengcock
27 Dec. James Vyncent
7 Jan. John Spray th' elder
7 Feb. John s. of Will'm Tredynnick†
7 Feb. Pascow s. of Richard Norton
9 Feb. Barbara d. of Humphrey Evans
15 Feb. Johane Copithorne
3 Mar. Nicholas s. of John Phillepp
20 Mar. Jennett Moylle, widow
21 Mar. Reynolde s. of Richard Marten

ANNO 1586.

9 April Thomas Cocken
18 April John Pollard the younger
3 May Jane d. of Johane Lukie, widowe
4 May John s. of Will'm Browne
7 May Jane, the wiffe of Remfrey Rowse
9 May Umfrey Nankevell
13 May Richard Luke
23 May Emblen d. of ffrausces Calway

* Paid Nicholas Treluddrow for two years' wages, for keeping the bells at 12 pence a year, 2s., 1589.—Green Book.

† Wm. Tredinnick, buried 7 Feb., 1585. The Tredinnicks were seated in the parish of St. Breock near St. Columb, where their monuments still remain.

29 May Phillep* the wiff of John Langdon
1 June Elizabeth Nankevell, widow
13 July John Valleys
27 Aug. John s. of John Cardewe
8 Sep. John s. of Thomas Myll
6 Oct. Christopher s. of Robert Darr
8 Oct. Alse a poore old woman
13 Oct. John s. of Robert Darr
16 Oct. Jane the wieff of John Chapman
28 Oct. John Darr
4 Dec. fflorenc the wiffe of Wm Calway, and her two children
5 Dec. Will'm s. of William Clerk
12 Dec. Umphrey Evans
15 Dec. Jane d. of John Heyden
24 Dec. John Betty
27 Dec. John the bastard of one Rawe
29 Dec. John Payne
30 Dec. Katherine d. of Marten Rawe
4 Jan. Richard Bryent
15 Jan. Umfrey Manuell
18 Jan. Marie d. of Richard Gylberd
19 Jan. Elizabeth d. of Thomas Teage†
20 Jan. John s. of John Toker
21 Jan. Jane Bonithon,‡ gent.
24 Jan. Alson Clemow
30 Jan. Roger a poore boye
30 Jan. Lowdie d. of ffrances Calway
31 Jan. John Jenynge
31 Jan. Margaret d. of George Hockye
4 Feb. Katherine Polgreue
10 Feb. Margerie d. of Thomas Phillep
18 Feb. Melliar Gwynnowe

ANNO 1587.

31 Mar. John Menhire
6 April Jefferie Otes
8 April John s. of John Nankevell
11 April A poore man that dyed in Bostarnan's stable
23 April Elizabeth Bray, widow
23 April Margerie Trelowgan
5 May John Williams

* She was a daughter of .... Mountjoy, and her husband was fifth son of John Langdon of Bickton, by his wife Elizabeth, daughter of Sir William Godolphin. John Langdon, gent., was one of the twelve men in 1585.—Green Book.

† In 1586 Thomas Teage was paid 6s. 8d., a year's wages, for trimming the town clock.—Green Book.

‡ This was Jane, daughter and heiress of John Durant of Pensinans, co. Cornwall, and wife of Richard Bonithon of Bonithon. We learn from the parish green book that her son John Bonithon, Esq., paid to the parish for her burial 6s. 8d. and 6s. bequeathed by her.

10 June Elinor Nanconan
5 Aug. Richard Gyllerd
12 Aug. Antonie Rawe
13 Aug. Thomas Nankevell
26 Aug. Jane Harrie
27 Aug. Arthur Carter*
31 Aug. Margaret Lawrie, widow
2 Sep. Johane d. of Christopher Manuell
13 Sep. Johane d. of the younger Baylie
8 Oct. Agnes Grace
25 Oct. Katherine the wiff of John Rawe, glover
28 Nov. Elizabeth Drew
28 Nov. Nicholas a servant to Mr Goldsmyth of St. Kew
8 Dec. Johane Amye single woman
10 Dec. Luke Lyttacott†
23 Dec. Tamson Bettye
5 Jan. Thomas Tynckler
7 Feb. Grace, the wiffe of James Lawrence
10 Feb. Thomas Lukie
15 Feb. Robert Tregona
5 Mar. John Jefferye
7 Mar. Johane Peane
8 Mar. John Bennett
9 Mar. James Rawe
10 Mar. John Rowse s. of Harrie Rowse
18 Mar. George Trenowth

ANNO 1588.

4 April Johane, the wiff of Will'm Kerne
5 April Robert Moyses
8 April John Edie‡
15 April Christopher a bastard to Margerie Rawe
17 April Emblen the wiff of Marten Dyer
18 April John s. of John Heycrefte
20 April Thomas Hawke§
21 April Elynor‖ d. of John Carter, gent.

* Son of John Carter and Jane Vivian; he died s.p.

† Luke Litticotte, buried in the church, for which Sampson Morcombe paid 5s. (Green Book.) Sampson Morcombe was son-in-law to Luke Litticotte.

‡ In 1586 John Edye of Trevarren paid 3s. 4d. not to be a warden.—Green Book.

§ Tho. Hawke of Hellwone, and Harry Hawke of Trevarren in this parish, paid 25s. rent of coppice let to their late father. Harry Hawke of Halwoone was one of the wardens of the poor in 1586.—Green Book.

‖ By his wife Jane, daughter of John Vivian of Trenowth.

21 April Margerie Tocker
22 April Johane d. of Marke Dyer
24 April Thomas Lahacke
24 April Udie Taylor
24 April John s. of Robert Williams
25 April Richard Calwaie
1 May Anne Jenyn
5 May Marie d. of Lallow Jolle
6 May Thomas Tyer the younger
29 May Pethericke Pernall
31 May Thomas s. of Robert Moyses
10 June Richard Blake
27 June Tamson the wiff of John Geyne
28 June John Chapman
2 July Thomas s. of Richard Scryvener
27 July A child of Thomas Hodge
1 Aug. Stephen, Michell, and Richard Bennett *al's* Roskeen
7 Aug. Richard s. of Richard Oxnam
7 Aug. John s. of John Spraye
27 Aug. Alse d. of Thomas Baylie
15 Sep. John a bastard to Johane Rouseveil
21 Sep. Milson Rowse, widow
29 Sep. John Clemow
2 Oct. Jane the wiffe of Remfrey Rowse
7 Oct. Will'm bastard to Margaret Rawe
9 Nov. George Kure
15 Jan. Arthur Pollard
21 Jan. John Tresawlle *al's* Rawlinge
1 Feb. John Vincent
5 Feb. Emblen Pernell
12 Feb. Dorothie d. of John Phillpe
13 Feb. ffrausce, servant to Thomas Tyfford
15 Feb. ffrisoe d. to younger Abraham
2 Mar. John s. of Marke Lawrie
4 Mar. John s. of John Calwaie
15 Mar. James Jenken
21 Mar. Stephen Abraham*
22 Mar. John s. of John Hicks

ANNO 1589.

6 May Wylmot servant to Margerie Dyer
19 May Johane d. of Richard Copithorne†
21 May Emblen d. of Richard Pollard
23 May Marie d. of Thomas Treblefeild
15 June Marie Vallis
5 July Johane Menhynet

* Stephen Abraham the younger, one of the churchwardens in 1586.—Green Book.

† Richard Copithorne, one of the twelve men in 1587.—Green Book.

7 Aug. John Langdon,* gent.
13 Aug. Phillep d. of John Skynner
28 Aug. Richard Calway
30 Aug. Elizabeth wiff of John Jane
8 Sep. John s. of Degorie Stubbs
5 Oct. Will'm s. of Humphrey Vyncent
23 Oct. Johane Philp
27 Oct. Johane Grosse
17 Nov. Alse, one of almes women
3 Dec. Elizabeth d. of George Collinge
10 Dec. Johane Paver
24 Dec. Jane the wiff of John Thomas
27 Dec. John Strongman
15 Jan. Anne Putford
20 Jan. Johane the wiff of Bennet James *al's* Reskean
2 Feb. Elizabeth d. of John Tresawlle
7 Feb. ffransce s. of Richard Hawke†
12 Feb. Johane Bawden
2 Mar. Margaret Gallo
3 Mar. John Renold *al's* Williams
5 Mar. John s. of Walter Smyth
6 Mar. Richard s. of John Payne
11 Mar. Johane the wiff of Will'm Boscarvan
17 Mar. Margaret Hatter
24 Mar. Will'm Boscarnan

ANNO 1590.

15 April Jane Nicholl
17 April Margerie the wiff of John Norton
20 April Thomas s. of R. Inde
28 April Thomas Daye *al's* Rosogan
6 May Harrie Opie
6 May Harrie s. of John Tubb
8 May Marren Chaplen
11 May Thomas Trelowgan
1 June Edward Bettie
1 June Alson, the wiff of ffransce Rawe
4 June Johane the wiff of John Udie
17 June John Nankevell
19 June Johane d. of John Will'ms
13 July Tamson d. of Richard Seryven[r]
17 July Barbara d. of Richard Pollard
21 July Hugh s. of Richard Oxnam
14 Aug. Nicholas s. of Nicholas Will'ms
28 July Jane d. of Austyn Millen
17 Oct. Emblen d. of Marten Slogatt

* Fifth son of John Langdon of Bickton; see note. p. 187 *ante*. The baptisms of several of his children appear in the register.

† Richard Hawke, one of the constables in 1586.—Green Book.

18 Oct. Margaret Sexton
21 Oct. John s. of ffransce Rawe
21 Oct. Ebbet Will'ms
14 Nov. Katherine d. of Harrie Adam
6 Dec. Sir John Arundell, knight*
31 Jan. George Browne†
2 Jan. Richard Cardew
11 Mar. Jennet Rowse *al's* Jenken, widow
17 Mar. Jane d. of ffransce Behednow
21 Mar. Harrie s. of John Heycrefte
21 Mar. Johane Battye, widow
22 Mar. Elizabeth the wiff of John Moylle

ANNO 1591.

7 April Johane Willm's
21 April Richard s. of John Cockie
25 April Agnes wiff of John Tocker
3 May John Baylie
18 May Johane Torke
18 May Harrie Anhay & Kathrine his wiff
26 May Katherine Valleys
6 June Richard s. of Richard Cardewe
11 June Harrie s. of Nicholas Drew
13 June Pascow Anhay &his wieff
15 June Jone ffeare
17 June Jane Darr
22 June Constanc d. of John Pearse
1 July Andrew Darr
3 July Jane servant to John ffeare
9 July John Yeoman
10 July Richow d. of Bawden Moylle
15 July Dolorye s. of Bawden Moylle
20 July James Mayhow
31 July Dennys the wiff of Stephen Abraham
5 Aug. Will'm s. of James Mayhowe
20 Aug. Barbara the wiff of James Udie
23 Aug. Alse the wiff of Harrie Gascoyne
28 Aug. Katherine servant to M[r] Bonithon
26 Sep. Richard Pearse
29 Sep. Marke Lawrie

* He was son and heir of Sir John Arundell of Lanherne, by Elizabeth, daughter of Gerald Danet, Esq. of Danet's Hall, and was aged 30 at the death of his father in 1557. He married Lady Anne, daughter of Thomas, Earl of Derby (by Anne daughter of Edward, Lord Hastings of Hungerford), and relict of Charles, 7th Lord Stourton. He died the 17th Nov., 1590, and is recorded on a monumental brass still remainins in the church at St. Columb.

† Geo. Browne, one of the churchwardens in 1586.—Green Book.

11 Oct. Marian Syse
12 Oct. Jane d. of Marke Lawrie
13 Oct. Marie d. of Marke Lawry
13 Oct. Katherine d. of Rescoll*
16 Oct. J. d. of Marke Lawrie
17 Oct. Margerie d. of John Lawry
20 Oct. Anne d. of John Carter, gent.*
20 Oct. Elizabeth d. of Harrie Dyar
24 Oct. Marke s. of Marke Lawrye
24 Oct. Emblen d. of Thomas Myll
25 Oct. Margerie servant of Thomas Myll
24 Oct. ffransce Typpett
10 Nov. Thomas s. of Julian Rescollwas
10 Nov. Grace servant of Thomas Daye
5 Dec. John s. of Thomas Myll
5 Dec. Alse d. of Bennet Calway
1 Jan. Elizabeth d. of John Browne
1 Jan. Jane Browne
19 Jan. Elizabeth wiff of Degorie Stubbes
23 Jan. John s. of Degorie Stubbes
29 Jan. Mr Docter Rennalls
30 Jan. Edward Servir
20 Feb. Thomas Weaver
22 Feb. Thomas Jeninge
24 Feb. Thomas Jenken
26 Feb. ffransce Brytton Miller
2 Mar. James Younge

Anno 1592.

1 April Agnes d. of Will'm Braye
3 April Alse Escott
12 April Katherine Rawlinge
13 April Marie d. of Petherick Pernell
14 April Ollie d. of Nicholas Holman
23 April Thomas Nuttle
7 May Elizabeth Inde
20 May Thomas s. of Thomas Myll
21 May Jane d. of John Knight
2 July John Snell
22 July John s. of John Tyer
25 July Anne wiff of Thomas Carthew
31 July Margaret d. of Wm Gylberd
7 Oct. Johane d. of Will'm Jane
7 Oct. Phillep d. of John Darr
16 Oct. Robert Hawke
18 Oct. Thomas Rushona of Crantocke
24 Oct. Richard s. of John Heycrafte
7 Nov. Margaret the wiff of Will'm Browne
24 Nov. Elizabeth Rawlinge
13 Jan. Margerie d. of Wm Edward
23 Jan. Katherine wife of John Cocken
23 Jan. John s. of Marten Bishopp
6 Feb. Bennett s. of John Mayhow
10 Feb. Richard Copithorne the elder
10 Feb. Marie Seryvener
10 Feb. Marke Will'm
12 Feb. Phillep Hawke
14 Feb. Stephen Lovell
15 Feb. John Nicholas *al's* Norton
18 Feb. Joyes wiff of Marke Will'm
18 Feb. Jenken s. of John Moylle
24 Feb. Phillep wiff of John Dawbyll
24 Feb. Harrie s. of Richard Pollard
29 Feb. Robert Gwynnow
29 Feb. Anne d. of John Tocker
29 Feb. Thomas s. of John Younge
12 Mar. Richard s. of John Skynner
20 Mar. Marie d. of Robert Calway
21 Mar. Elizabeth d. of John Moylle
23 Mar. John Hendra

Anno 1593.

31 Mar. Christian Hendra
31 Mar. Elizabeth d. of John Moyll
5 April Will'm s. of Nicholas Thomas
7 April Marie d. of Stephen Lovell
7 April Bawden s. of John Jane
9 April John Vyncent
9 April Nicholl a bastard of William Bodie
12 April James s. of Edward Teage
12 April John a bastard to Johane Typpett
20 April Johane wiff of Bennett Pollard
28 April Agnes a poor woman in the churchyard
7 May John Thomas
10 May Peter Wylson
12 May Richard Carter
15 May Richard Teage
18 May Barbara the wyff of Harrie Hawke
22 May Honor wyff of John Knight
29 May Thomas Tyfford
2 June Richard Service
5 June Thomas a bastard to Margaret Calwaye
6 June Honor d. of Robert Calwaye
8 July Agnes wiffe of Austen Hosken
13 June Elizabeth d. of Steven Abraham

* Sic.
† By his wife Jane, daughter of John Vivian.

15 June Elizabeth d. of ffrancis Nanconan*
2 Aug. Thomas s. of John Pearse
10 Sep. Marten a bastard to Margaret Pell
12 Sep. Jane Nankevell
20 Sep. Johane d. of Stephen†
20 Sep. John s. of Gregorie Lyttacott
5 Oct. Agnes Trusoe
13 Oct. Katherine Beard
15 Oct. Johane Nankevall
2 Nov. William s. of Richard Gylian
8 Nov. Alson Copithorne
20 Nov. Katherine Reskigian
21 Nov. Elizabeth Teage
22 Dec. Jefferie Allen
2 Jan. Richarde Rawlinge
13 Jan. Humphrey Knight
15 Jan. Robert Kent
26 Jan. Alson Opie
27 Jan. John Brabyn, gent.‡
29 Jan. Johane d. of John Will'ms
2 Feb. Margaret the wiffe of John Thomas
7 Feb. Katherine the servant of John Calway
7 Feb. Alse d. of Alson Rawe
3 Mar. Thomas Benny
6 Mar. Agnes d. of John Nankevall
19 Mar. Will'm Nanconan
23 Mar. John Rawe, glover

In Aprioll, Maye and June none registered.

ANNO 1594.

28 July Jane wiff of George Collinge
31 July John s. of Pascow Tyfford
7 Aug. Willmot Jylls
14 Aug. Thomas Baylie
14 Aug. Richow d. of ffrancis Engrosse
30 Aug. Thomas s. of Thomas Daye
25 Sep. Michaiell servant to Mr John Carter
8 Oct. Will'm s. of Will'm Upcott
10 Oct. Will'm s. of John Heycrafte
1 Nov. Alse a bastard to John Phillop
9 Nov. Richard s. of Will'm Troblefoild
13 Nov. Phillop the wiffe of Richard Spray

* Francis Nanconan, warden of the coffer in 1585, also one of the twelve men in that year.—Green Book.

† Surname left blank.

‡ He was one of the twelve men in 1585-87. —Green Book.

9 Dec. Jane wife of Thomas Jenken*
18 Jan. Elizabeth wiffe of John Nankevall
19 Jan. Thomas s. of John Pollard
3 Feb. Elizabeth the wiffe of John Hawke
17 Feb. Johane the wiffe of John Bodie
16 Mar. Johane Myllone
19 Mar. Robert Dayo
23 Mar. Jane Yeoman

ANNO 1595.

20 May Johane d. of Lallow Nicholas
25 May John a bastard to Agnes Bawden
20 June Harrie Heycrafte
12 July Elizabeth d. of Robert John
25 July Margerie d. of Stephen Trevethan
26 July Marten s. of Will'm Strongman
11 Aug. Elizabeth d. of John Norton
5 Sep. John Gene
9 Sep. John Sheapeard & Kente his daughter
16 Sep. Johane Cardewe
18 Sep. Elizabeth d. of Thomas George
23 Sep. Richard Davie *al's* Moylle
26 Sep. Will'm s. of John Snowe
27 Sep. John s. of Thomas Symons
5 Oct. Jane d. of Richard Blake
8 Oct. Tamson d. of Will'm Bewes
9 Oct. Johane wiffe of Nicholas Trehemban
11 Oct. John Potter
15 Oct. John Snow
11 Nov. John Cornish
30 Nov. Marian the wiffe of Will'm Rendall
30 Nov. John, a poor man
11 Dec. Richard Spray
27 Dec. John s. of J. Rawe
28 Dec. Roger ffamacke, gent.†
29 Dec. Thomas Gatte
10 Jan. John James

* She was daughter and heiress of John Moyle, by Jane, daughter of John Retaller. See also burial of her husband in 1613.

† He was probably, Roger, fourth son of John Flamank (second son of Richard Flamock, by Jane, daughter and heiress of Thomas Lucomb of Bodmin), and his wife, Joyce, daughter of Sir Richard Nanfan, who had a grant of lands from his brother, Gilbert Flamock of Boscarne; *vide* Cart. Harl: 50, C. 44, 32 Hen. VIII.

15 Jan. Nowell s. of John Cornish
10 Feb. Buckland *al's* John Davies
15 Feb. Tamson the wiffe of ffransces Rawe
25 Feb. Will'm a bastard to Richard Williams
7 Mar. Richard Watte
13 Feb. Will'm s. of Richard Scryvener
14 Mar. Peter a bastard to M[r] Boskarnon
20 Mar. Johane wiffe of Richard Scryvener
21 Mar. Jane d. of Richard Dunscone

ANNO 1596.

28 Mar. Mylson Bennye
24 April Humphrey Vyncent*
25 April Thomas s. of Christopher Stradford
27 April Ann d. of Pascow Tyfford
6 May Nicoll d. of Will'm Rendall
10 May Johane d. of Robert Ryse
16 May Raff Michell
17 May George s. of Stephen Tubbe
20 May Maude Thomas
23 May Elizabeth d. of John Browne
27 May George s. of Reynold Engrosse
9 June Robert Calway
14 June Richard Spray
14 June John Bennye
15 June William s. of Robert Calway
9 Sep. Margerie wiffe of Marten Rawe
16 Sep. Nicholas s. of Harrie Trebenban
7 Oct. Thomas s. of James Valleys
12 Oct. John s. of Richard Hawke the elder
24 Oct. Lallow Jolle
23 Dec. Elizabeth d. of Nicholas Rendall
24 Dec. Collan Pollard
8 Feb. Johane the wiff of Edward Carthewe
14 Feb. John Rawe, junior
20 Feb. Hugh s. of Thomas Cocke
28 Feb. Alson d. of Nicholas Holman
1 Mar. Thomas s. of Harrie Hawke
2 Mar. Elizabeth Gene, widowe
7 Mar. Elnor Cocking, widow
12 Mar. Nicholas s. of John Bennett
14 Mar. John Pabe
17 Mar. Marten Behennow
20 Mar. John s. of John Bennett
23 Mar. Marie the wiffe of John Hockie

* Humph. Vyncent, one of the wardens in 1585.—Green Book.

ANNO 1597.

28 Mar. ffransces Lukie*
1 April Elizabeth the wiffe of John Bennett
2 April John ffeare
4 April Honor d. of Pascaw Rawe
7 April Reynolde Laven
12 April John, servant to Harrie Adam
13 April Johane the wiffe of John Grace & her child
25 April John Grace†
7 May Will'm s. of Nicholas Perken
8 May Richard Michell
14 May John Will'ms
17 May Richard s. of Marten Behennow
22 May Elizabeth a poore woman
15 June Katherine Jenken a poore mead drowned
25 June Anne a poore woman
29 June Thomas s. of Thomas Daye
12 July John Benny
12 Aug. Elizabeth Cornish, widowe
21 Aug. Ollyffe Vyvian, widowe‡
24 Aug. John Jolle
26 Aug. Elizabeth Cornish, widow
2 Sep. Johane d. of John Cocke
6 Sep. Constance the wiffe of Robert Cornish
15 Sep. Alson Braye
15 Oct. Marren the wiffe of Marke Retallack§
18 Oct. Roger s. of Thomas Wythell
2 Dec. Remfrey Jenken
2 Dec. Thomay Calway
24 Dec. Manuell Roger
8 Jan. Richard Tocker
3 Feb. Richard Hodge
3 Feb. J. Calwaie‖
13 Feb. Agnes a poore woman
13 Feb. Jane Rawe
23 Feb. John Keles
25 Feb. ffransces Rawe

* John Lukie paid 12d. for a knell in 1598.—Green Book.

† John Grace, churchwarden in 1585.—Green Book.

‡ She was daughter and heiress of . . . . Tresaster, of St. Wenn, and widow of John Vivian, of Trenowth; see marriages in 1546. She is named with their children, Thomas, John, Pascaux, Johane (married John Carter), and Emlin, in the will of her husband, dated 4 June, 1589.

§ Mark Retallack, churchwarden in 1589.—Green Book.

‖ Sic.

ANNO 1598.

26 Mar. Melliar Vyncent
28 Mar. Harrie s. of Thomas Cocke
3 April Richard s. of John Menhire
15 April Marton Tome
15 April John Mayhowe
30 April Typpett Heard
4 May Tamson Riche
23 May Harrie Dennys
3 June Johane the wiff of Thomas Stephens
10 June Johane Hodge, widowe
16 June Johane d. of Wm Thomas
20 June Marie d. of Harrie Treman
29 July John s. of * . . . . Jollie†
21 Oct. Richard Stratford, unmarried, s. of Christopher Stratforde
11 Nov. Joahne Priddyes wife of Will'm Priddies
24 Nov. Petronell Marke wiffe of John Marke
26 Nov. James Hawke, unmarried
13 Dec. Johane Browne, widow
15 Dec. Christopher Dar, widower
18 Dec. Alice Luke,‡ widow
19 Dec. Johane Wills wiffe of John Wills
29 Dec. John Roscarlow, maried
15 Jan. Margery Thomas wiffe of Will'm Thomas
25 Jan. Roger Day, unmarried, s. of John Day
26 Jan. Jane Williams
1 Feb. Richard Lovesse, unmarried, s. of Richard Lovesse
6 Feb. Will'm Upcott, married
11 Feb. John Williams s. of Will'm Williams
13 Feb. John Rise, married
20 Feb. Joane Grudgeay
25 Feb. Honory Williams wiff of Will'm Williams
16 Mar. Thomas Manton & his son John borne dead
19 Mar. Alice Girlower, widow

ANNO 1599.

28 Mar. John Perkins unmarried, s. of Michell Perkins
5 April Cicely d. of William Strangman

* Obliterated.
† After this entry comes the first entry in 1600, but it is scratched out, the rest of page left blank, and the year 1598 continued on the next page.
‡ Probably Lukie; see p. 196, 28 March, 1597.

11 April Honory Newell d. of John Newell
29 April Richard Gillian, married
1 May Robert Darr, married
5 May Thomas Brabant, married
6 May Margaret Roe, widow
8 May A man child of Will'm Tennyes, unchristened
14 May Thomas unchristened, a base s. of Jane Rogers
17 May John Lavan, unmarried, s. of Thomas Lavan
17 May Henry Haycrofte, unmarried, s. of John H.
27 May Thomas, unchristened, s. of George Daw
27 May Johane wiffe of Will'm Tenny
17 June Humphry Law, unmarried, s. of John Law
30 June Joane Rise, widow
3 Aug. Agnes Clerke wiffe unto Will'm Clerke
11 Aug. Mary Stevens, unmarried, d. of Henrie Stevens
29 Aug. Joane Jane, unmarried, d. of Will'm Jane
11 Sep. Richard Jane, widower
11 Oct. A daughter unchristened, base born to Jane Pearce
1 Nov. A daughter unchristened, base borne to Joane Nicholas
5 Nov. Honory Mill wiff to Thomas Mill
27 Nov. Joane, unmarried, d. of John Day
28 Nov. Thomasine Pollard, an old woman unmarried
20 Dec. Aulson Cawlaway wiffe of John Cawlaway
20 Dec. German Day s. of John Day
3 Jan. Joane Horrell, widowe
10 Jan. Joane Stubs wiffe of Diggory Stubs
11 Jan. John Body, married man
15 Jan. Rawlen Geene, an old man
4 Feb. Amy d. of Thomas Dassowe
7 Feb. Mary Grace
10 Feb. Elizabeth Coles
15 Feb. Wylliam Will's s. of Wyllm Williams
3 Mar. Wylliam Bronne, an old man
2 Mar. Richard s. of Thomas Beneto
7 Mar. Mary Growes wiffe of Reynolde Growes
20 Mar. Thomas Groves

ANNO 1600.

1 April Elizabeth Lolow, wedow

5 April Keye Mychell, wedow
5 April Pacience d. of Degory Stubes
10 April John s. of John Thomas *alias* Trobolfild
17 April Renalde s. of Thomas Lavin
26 April Mary Upcote
27 April James Jenken *alis* Chaplin
28 April Constance Coken
12 May William Hockye
17 May Alson Pellowe
18 May Jane the wife of Richard Rive
9 June John Body the servant of Mr Beskowen
4 Aug. Joane Williams d. of Thomas Williams
10 Aug. A child s. of Christopher Stratforde, beeinge baptized by the midwife at home the 7th day of Aug.
19 Aug. A child the s. of Henry Trehenban, beeing baptized at home & presently dead
30 Aug. Mary Brabrant, widow
15 Sep. Thomas a base child, s. of Dorothey Kent
3 Oct. Michaell Moyle s. of John Moyle
5 Oct. James Tenny a childe, s. of Will'm Tennye
24 Nov. ffrancisco a base childe, d. of Marest Bawdon wido
27 Nov. Alice Collyns d. of Thomas Collyns of St Wen
7 Dec. Elizabeth Martyn* d. of Thos. Martyn
14 Dec. Thomas Nicholas s. of John Nicholas
14 Dec. Elizabeth Dasso d. of Henry Dasso
17 Dec. Nicholas Trehymban
17 Dec. Agnes Younge, widow
20 Dec. Nowell Nicholas s. of John Nicholas
20 Dec. Joane Edwardes, widow
21 Dec. ffraunsce Bennye
22 Dec. Jane Nicholls wiffe of John Nicholls *al's* Natelan
8 Jan. John Knight
9 Jan. Walter Browne, a child
10 Jan. Elizabeth Hollman, a childe
12 Jan. Richard Tifforde, m'chaunt
18 Jan. Jane Vincent, widow
19 Jan. Will'm Engraws s. of Renold Engraws
23 Jan. Anthony Dey s. of John Dey

* Thomas Martyn's child, for a knell 4d.—Green Book

1 Feb. Henery Hawke s. of Henery Hawke of Hawloone
5 Feb. Thomas Syms an old man
14 Feb. Margaret Cottey the wife of Will'm Cottey
15 Feb. Jane Drew, widow
21 Feb. Richard Taproll, a base child
1 Mar. Mary Michell d. of Anthony Michell
2 Mar. Margerie Netherton the wife of John Netherton
4 Mar. Elizabeth Locke d. of Katherine Locke
6 Mar. Hughe Rowse s. of Henry Rowse
14 Mar. John Hawke s. of Anthony Hawke
19 Mar. John Browne s. of John Browne

ANNO 1601.

25 Mar. Edward Teague s. of Edward Teague
28 Mar. John Lukye s. of William Lukye
2 April Richard Victor a childe
4 April Emblen Trevaughen, widow
6 April Diggory Stubbes
7 April Richard Bennett a childe, s. of Thomas Bennett
12 April Michele Rogers *al's* Manuole, a pore woman
20 April Richard Coppithorne a childe, s. of William Coppithorne
5 May John Valloyes s. of James Valloyes
12 May John Body the sexton
12 May Richard Hindra
17 May Margaret Rogers the wife of John Rogers *al's* Manold
25 May Pascha Edy *al's* Rawe, widow
26 May Joane Simons, widow
27 May Cicely Rise, the wife of Rob. Rise *al's* Lawrence
5 June Joane Strongman, widow
15 June John Cocken thyounger (unmarried)
18 June Joane Wilson, widow
18 June Jane Hickes the wiffe of John Hickes
20 June A childe s. of James Jenken, gent., not baptised in the churche
23 June Margery Guylbert d. of William Guylbert
24 July Elenor Myll d. of Thomas Myll
5 Aug. Joane Wynne, unmarried

17 Aug. Thomasine Morcombe d. of Sampson Morcombe
26 Aug. Mary Bennett d. of John Bennett
29 Aug. John Woodde, a childe, s. of a strange gentle woman*
1 Sep. Anstace Cardew the wife of Thomas Cardew
5 Sep. Henry Williams s. of John Williams *al's* Reskigion
15 Sep. Gynnye Abraham, an olde woman
15 Sep. Richard ffrenche s. of John ffrenche
20 Sep. Jane Hughes the wiffe of James Hughes
26 Sep. Anne Cornishe, an almswoman
3 Oct. John Mayhow of Trevethicke, juxta Tregoose
14 Oct. Ebbett Morcombe, a childe, d. of Sampson Morcombe
2 Nov. Hughe Sexton, pemtercy†
12 Nov. ffrancisco Arundell d. of Thomas Arundell, Esqr.‡
18 Nov. Margaret Dasow, widow
28 Nov. Elizabeth Curdew, widow
3 Dec. Richard Tucker, of Tolskithye§
11 Dec. Dorothy Simons d. of Thomas Simons, deceased
12 Dec. Thomas, a base childe, s. of Bridgett Basely
21 Dec. John Hawke, a childe, s. of James Hawke
29 Dec. Nicholas Lovys s. of Richard Lovys
4 Jan. John s. of John Williams *al's* Reskigian, beeinge baptized at home by the mydwiffe same day
5 Jan. Thamsyne Wyse
19 Jan. John Callway of Tregaswith§
21 Jan. John Nuttle, of Tregomeere§
2 Feb. Dyonye Allen, widow, an almeswoman

* This entry is rather indefinite; possibly it was a son of John Wood. Esq., of Brixton, near Plymouth, and his wife, Elizabeth, daughter of Geo. Northcote of Calverley.

† Sic.

‡ This Thomas Arundell, Esq., was of Trevithick in St. Columb. son of Thomas Arundell of Tremere, by Elizabeth, daughter and co-heiress of . . . . . Tringove of Nance, and grandson of Sir John Arundell of Lanherne, and Elizabeth, daughter of Gerald Danet of Danet's Hall, Esq. His wife was Rachell Mompesson, sister of Sir Giles Mompesson.

§ A hamlet in this parish.

2 Feb. Thomas a base childe of Kowdye Trelogan
26 Feb. Elizabeth Allen the wyffe of ffrancesse Allen
12 Mar. Alice Duggoe the wyffe of Thomas Duggoe
20 Mar. Katherine Jollye the wife of Henry Jollye

ANNO 1602.

26 Mar. Elizabeth Jollye the wyfe of Will'm Jollye
28 Mar. Joane Stevens d. of Thomas Stevens thyounger
28 Mar. Joane Nicholas of Trewga*
4 April Joane Williams the wyfe of Will'm Williams
5 April Elizabeth Chapleman of Lanhimsith†
9 April Margery Roondell wife of John Roondell
10 April John Lukye s. of Will'm Lukye
13 April Roger Hockye
16 April Margarett Judde wyfe of John Judde
21 April Agnes Moyell d. of Richard Moyell
23 April John Collys the elder
24 April Elizabeth Morcombe d. of Sampson Morcombe
11 May Paschase Meryfielde widow
2 June Joane Burlace the wife of Anthony Burlace
10 June Mellison ffyne d. of David ffyne
11 June Elizabeth Collys d. of John Collys
23 June Richard Lovys, smith
24 June Tiffony Hawke d. of Henry Hawke, of Hollwoone
27 June Joane Carter d. of Richard Carter, gent.‡
2 July Joane Pollarde wif of Bennett Pollarde
13 July Jane Allen, widow
25 July Robert Jollye of Trewga
3 Aug. Jane Carter the wyfe of John Carter, gent.§
9 Aug. Katherine Smith, widow
11 Aug. Jane Rescarlow, widow

* A hamlet in this parish.

† A farm in this parish.

‡ By his wife Elizabeth, daughter of Sir John Arundell of Talverne.

§ She was a daughter of John Vivian of Trenowth, by his wife Olyff, daughter and co-heiress of Tresaster of St. Wenn; she is named in the will of her father.

6 Sep. William Abraham s. of Stephen Abraham
16 Sep. Martine Rowse d. of Richard Rowse
21 Sep. Richard Vanson
29 Sep. The worshipfull Ralphe Keate* barchelaw of lawe, officiall of the Archdeaconry of Cornwall and parson of St Ermet†
2 Oct. The Right Honorable Lady Anne Stoorton, widow‡
7 Oct. Elizabeth Lawrey d. of James Lawrey
9 Oct. Jane a base child, ye d. of Tamson Trevethyn
18 Oct. William Bownshall s. of Nic'las Bownshall
11 Nov. Joane Will'ms the wife of Richard Will'ms
30 Nov. John Dyer s. of Martine Dyer
23 Dec. Thomas Cocken s. of William Cocken

* He was the second son of William Kete. of Hugborne, co. Berks, by his wife Elinor, daughter of Thomas Augers. He married Anne, daughter of John Clarke, of Arrington, co. Berks, by whom he had Ralph, of St. Columb: William, of Heldrop, co. Wilts; John, of St. Enoder; Gilbert, of London; Sarah, married Richard Bossawsack, and another daughter. married Roger Squyer.

St. Enoder Par. Reg.

Mr. John Kete and Ann Willoughby, married 17 Nov., 1607.

Zachary Arundell, gent., and Anne Keate, widow, married, 1610.

Mistris Emline Keate, buried 16 Nov., 1605.

A child of Zachary Arrundell, gent., buried before baptized, 2 May, 1617.

Mistris Ann Arundell, wife of Zachary Arundell, gent., buried 17 June, 1665.

Zachary Arundell, gent., buried 11 August. 1665.

There is in the church of St. Enoder a monument to Dorothy, daughter of the above Zachary Arundell, and wife of Anthony Tanner, gent., who died 2 Feb., 1634; it has three shields of arms, first, on a chief three moors' heads side-face couped (Tanner); second, the same, with a crescent for difference, imp. six martlets, 3, 2, and 1, with a mullet for difference (Arundell); third, fretty (Willoughby).

† Entry much obliterated.

‡ She was a daughter of Thomas, 2nd Earl of Derby, by his wife Ann, daughter of Edward, Lord Hastings of Hungerford. She married, first, Charles, 7th Lord Stourton, by whom she was ancestress of the present Lord Stourton, after whose death she married Sir John Arundell of Lanherne; she is commemorated with her husband and children on a brass in the church at St. Columb.

2 Jan. Richard Keyther
11 Jan. ffrancis Allen
17 Jan. Elizabeth d. of Anthony Rawe
19 Jan. John Marke of Nanswhyddon
25 Jan. Joane Stephens, widow
17 Feb. Thomysyne Olver the wyffe of Thomas Olver
17 Feb. James Scoble a child
19 Feb. Richard Oxenham th'elder of Treprony
27 Feb. Joane Robyns d. of Ralphe Robyns
28 Feb. Maria Davye, unmarried woman
13 Mar. Henery Hawke s. of James Hawke
13 Mar. James Williams s. of Richard Williams
13 Mar. Margaret Daw wiffe of Geordge Daw
18 Mar. Martyne Trescotte s. of Gwalter Trescotte
24 Mar. Thomas Cocke th'elder, of Ruthevos*
23 Mar. Thomasine Jollye, widow

ANNO 1603.

25 Mar. Richard Service
30 April John Williams *al's* ffrancisce
4 May Patience Trefeys servent & kinswoman to Thomas Marke, gent
7 May Elizabeth Renfrey, widow
13 May Joane Tyar the wyfe of John Tyar
15 May Joane Allen the wyfe of John Allen
17 May Juliane West d. of Richard West
26 May Thomas Marke of Trevolvas*
27 May Emblen Manuell
1 June Thomas John of Lanhynswith*
3 June Margaret Lawrey the wyfe of Ambrose Lawrey
12 June Will'm Coppithorne
23 June Elizabeth Valleys a childe, d. of James Valleys
26 June Robert Rogers, an olde man
3 July John Dunstone (unmarried) s. of Richard Dunstone
25 July Thomas Trussell s. of Steven Trussell
25 July Margaret Staple the wyfe of John Staple

* A farm in this parish.

8 Aug. Alice Hawke d. of Richard Hawke, of Hallwoone
5 Sep. John Bate
9 Sep. Eleanor Hawke d. of Richard H., of Hallwoone*
10 Sep. John Browne *al's* Woe
13 Sep. Ambrose Hawke s. of James Hawke
15 Sep. Henery Baylye, of Trepodanawt†
6 Oct. Marye a child base d. of Jane Vincent
20 Oct. Joane Bodye d. of John Bodye
23 Oct. Maude Mabyn the wyfe of Roger Mabyn
24 Nov. Margerie Service
28 Dec. Margerie Horwell the wyfe of John Horwell
1 Jan. Nicholl Hand the wife of Richard Hand
18 Jan. John Arundell s. of Thomas Arundell, Esq.‡
19 Jan. Martin Blake s. of William Blake
25 Jan. Margaret Harrie d. of Mikell Harrie
27 Jan. John Tippet s. of William Tippet
1 Feb. Richard Cornish a chrisomer
5 Feb. Armunis Nicholas
7 Feb. John Michaell
8 Feb. William Clarke
9 Feb. Avice the wife of Robert the farrier
15 Feb. Nicholas Bousols, a child
16 Feb. William Williams s. of John Williams
20 Feb. John Williams
12 Mar. Ann Moile d. of Mr Moile§

Anno 1604.

25 Mar. Robert Cornish, Mr Vivians man
6 April Pascal Benny
20 May Jane the wife of William Jane
7 June Elizabeth Langdon
23 June Margery Dier
17 Aug. Olly d. of Halke‖
4 Sep. John s. of Joane Kettoe
21 Sep. Alice d. of George Daw
10 Oct. Gregory Vanson

* Sic.
† A hamlet in this parish.
‡ See note, p. 199.
§ He was Richard Moyell, of St. Austell, gent., and his wife, Emblin, daughter of Thomas Vivian, of Trenowth.
‖ Sic.

11 Oct. Jane Roe
15 Oct. John s. of ffrancis Jonas
15 Oct. Catherine the wife of ffrancis Jonas*
1 Nov. Tamsin John the wife of Thomas John
21 Nov. Jane d. of Anthony Rowe
28 Nov. Margery West the wyfe of Thomas West
28 Nov. Mary the wife of Pascow Vyvian†
30 Nov. William s. of John Trembeath
8 Dec. Hugh Besconan, gentleman‡
22 Dec. Chaia§
23 Dec. John Jeffery
17 Jan. John s. of Pascow Tifford
25 Jan. A stranger out of Lancashire
7 Jan. John Marke
22 Jan. John Turcker
23 Jan. Richard Cocken
11 Mar. William Norten
12 Mar. Thomas s. of Richard Williams
18 Mar. Joane d. of Sampson Rosivarrn
24 Mar. Martha the wife of Thomas Tyer

Anno 1605.

26 Mar. Martine Slaggat
26 Mar. Amy poore¶
27 Mar. Ursula Carnamell, widow
11 April Adam Tristean
25 April James s. of John Heicraft
25 April Elizabeth d. of John Taylor
2 May Donice Uida
6 May Agnice d. of Nicholas Bounsall
22 May Edward Teage

* This is the last entry on the page, and is followed by the signature of Thomas Smallridge, curate.

† She was a daughter of . . . . Flamock, see marriage 1601, and her husband was a son of Thomas Vivian, of Trenowth, gent., and Ann Lower, his wife.

‡ He was one of the twelve men in 1595-1600; his widow, Mary Boscowen, was buried 29 March, 1611. Who this Hugh Besconan was is not quite clear; the only person of the Tregothnan family whom, according to Col. Vivian's pedigree, it could possibly be, was Hugh Boscawen, who married Mary, daughter of Thomas Tredinnick, and who, according to the Inq., p.m., died 20 May, 1608 (6 Jas.) He held (*inter alia*) Tregamere, in St. Columb Major. his son and heir Hugh being then (20 May, 1608) aged 16 years. *Vide* Inq. p.m., 15 Jas. W. and L., B. 27, No. 152.

§ Sic.

‖ Being the last entry on the page, it is signed Tho. Smallridge, curate.

7 June Thomas Harrice
8 June Thomas s. of Ralpe Hooper
7 July Cisly the wife of Richard Holland
17 July Margaret Clemon
1 Sep. George Collins
8 Sep. David Fine
11 Sep. James Lawrie
17 Sep. Henry s. of Richard Browne
19 Sep. Richard s. of Richard Moyle of St. Austell, gent.*
21 Sep. Mary Medlyn w'th her chealure†
29 Sep. Richard Moyle
29 Sep. The d. of Richard Williams
14 Oct. William Colly
27 Oct. John Littycott
3 Nov. John Benett *al's* Davie
1 Dec. Joane Gine
9 Dec. The s. of Steven Abrame†
9 Dec. Richard Norton
22 Jan. Margerie d. of William Roskorlar
27 Jan Radish Cooper, widow
1 Feb. Margery d. of John Rescuegian
7 Feb. Thomas s. of John Reeve
14 Feb. Edmund Heine‡
15 Mar. Emline Michell

ANNO 1606.

1 April Steven Truscott
14 April Jane d. of Reinold Grosse
21 April John Darre
29 April Mary d. of John Retallacke
30 April John Skinner
14 May Margery the wife of Thomas Williams
19 May Katherine Rawe d. of William Rawe
25 May John Netherton
5 June Joyce d. of Robert Allen
15 June Elizabeth the wife of Richard Bounsall and her creature the day before
1 July William s. of John Allen
7 July Katherine the wife of Thomas Withiell
7 Aug. William Truscott§
19 Aug. Jane d. of John Heidon

* By his wife Emblin, daughter of Thomas Vivian, of Trenowth.
† Child.
‡ Last entry on page, signed Thomas Smallridge, curate.
§ In 1596 Wm. Truscott paid the rent of his shop, 12s.; he also paid for a steer 25s., for a ewe 6s. 8d., to the parish.—Green Book.

19 Aug. Oliver s. of Richard Pollarde
20 Aug. Philip Sloggatt, vid.
16 Sep. John a base s. of Mary Paskow
22 Sep. Petronell d. of Rob. Lawrence *al's* Row
3 Oct. Elizabeth d. of Edmund Nicholls
15 Oct. John Heidon
19 Oct. John Addam
3 Nov. Nicholas s. of John Gwine
17 Nov. George Horckye*
21 Nov. William s. of William Jane
4 Dec. A base child of Joyce Darr, being dead in the bearth
6 Dec. Henery s. of James Cornish
13 Dec. Darathe the wife of Thomas Williams
13 Dec. John s. of William Tenny
17 Dec. Agnes the wife of Stephen Harvey
20 Dec. Elizabeth d. of John Heycroft
21 Dec. Rainold s. of William Tenny
22 Dec. Alice d. of John Phillip of Ruthas
23 Dec. Walter s. of John Browne
23 Dec. George s. of Thomas Arundell, gent.†
27 Dec. Jane Lavinn wid.
23 Jan. Katherine d. of Henry Rowse
26 Jan. ffranses Grose*
31 Jan. Thomas Mayhoe
5 Feb. John s. of John Body
14 Feb. A poore traveller
16 Feb. Tamzen the wife of John Menheare
21 Feb. Jane the wife of William Browne
27 Feb. . . . . . d. of Ralph Hooper
28 Feb. Roger Carnier
11 Mar. Richard s. of Henry Calway
17 Mar. James s. of John Trembeth
20 Mar. Jane the wife of Thomas Withiell

ANNO 1607.

25 Mar. Henry Tine
29 Mar. Mary the base d. of Honor Sprey
9 April Agnes the wife of John Heycrofte
19 April Reinald Harrice
22 April Henry Hawke of Hallowne*
25 April Dorathe Parking servant to Mr. Hobline

* Being the last entry on the page is signed Thomas Smallridge, curate.
† See page 199, *ante*.

1 Mar. Avice Harrice, wid.
6 May Charity a base d. of Jane Vincent
12 May Nicholas a base s. of Tamzin Havent
14 May Elizabeth d. of John Williams
16 May Thomas s. of William Jollyfe
24 May Thomas Tucker
10 June Katherine the wife of John Merifeild, gent.*
19 June John s. of John Davie *al's* Bennet
30 June Martine Dyer
20 Aug. Henry Hawke
12 Sep. Katherine d. of Thomas Oxnam
16 Sep. Elizabeth. d. of Richard Browne
25 Sep. James Searle a pore wandering man
11 Oct. John Tier
1 Nov. Thomas Mill†
16 Nov. Jane Nuttell, wid.
15 Dec. Christopher s. of Humphrey Hawke
29 Dec. Stephen s. of Thomas Lavin
2 Jan. . . . . d. of Tho. Hooper‡
8 Jan. Grace the wife of Thomas Raw
23 Jan. Mary the wife of Thomas Simon
25 Jan. Elizabeth the wife of William Williams
27 Jan. John s. of John Smith, gent.
26 Jan. Darathe the wife of Richard Pollard
11 Feb. Joane d. of Thomas Cocke
25 Feb. William s. of Sebastian Trevethan
3 Mar. Thomas Stephcen
3 Mar. Elizabeth d. of Walter Cocke
7 Mar. Joane Tregennow, wid.
12 Mar. Katherine Grose
12 Mar. A young chrisomer of Mr. Thomas Arundells

ANNO 1608.

26 Mar. . . . . ||s. of Reinold Litticott
9 April John s. of William Ricard
19 April Jane Skinner, poore
22 April John s. of Richard Addams *al's* Rowse

* John Meryfield, gent., one of the twelve men in 1587.—Green Book.

† Thomas Myll, one of the twelve men in 1600.—Green Book.

‡ The last entry on the page, and is followed by the signatures of Tho. Smallridge, curate, and R. Cornish, R. Donacomb, churchwardens.

|| Blank.

22 April Maximillian base s. of Margery Grose
22 April John Staple
8 May A young chrisomer of Peeter Johnes
19 May Solome d. of John Menheare
13 May Elenor d. of Renfreid Hawke
16 May John Merifield, gent.
23 May Vrsula the wife of John Menheere
13 June Peeter Addams
16 June John Moile, sen^r
22 June Alice d. of William Rowe, a poore wanderer
27 June Julian Blacke
30 June John s. of Thomas Duggoe
8 July Joane d. of William Tippet
15 July Embline Bate, poore
18 July Henrie s. of Henrie Rowse
23 July Margaret d. of Reinald Grose
26 July Marke s. of Richard James
12 Aug. Dennes a base d. of Mary Cocke
23 Sep. Thomas s. of John Davie *al's* Benett*
10 Oct. Agnes d. of William Roscudian *al's* Williams
13 Oct. Agnes Pawly
13 Oct. Henrie s. of Nicholas Napparoe *al's* Roe
14 Oct. Edward s. of John Nankevall
16 Oct. A chrisomer of Thomas Withiell
20 Oct. Reinold Grose
8 Nov. Henrie s. of Richard Cornish
15 Nov. Paule Drue *al's* Rawe
12 Dec. A chrisomer of Thomas Tankins
19 Dec. Constance d. of Thomas Barnett
21 Dec. Cislye d. of William Jane
26 Dec. Jane the wife of John Retallock, gent.†
26 Dec. Susanna the wife of Richard Browne
27 Dec. John s. of Edward Benett
5 Jan. Emblin the wife of John Benett
7 Jan. Joane Cotty, poore
14 Jan. Susanna d. of ffransces Jones
25 Jan. A chrisomer of Henrie Calwayes

* The last entry on the page, and is followed by the signatures of Tho. Smallridge, curate, and Francis Jones, John Hugh, wardens.

† John Retallack, gent., one of the twelve men in 1585.—Green Book.

28 Jan. Joane the wife of Edward Carthew
23 Feb. Renfreid s. of William Rowse
19 Mar. John Benett sen^r
20 Mar. Richard Stephens

ANNO 1609.

26 Mar. Joane Dar, wid.
26 Mar. Darathe d. of John Willes
4 April Petronell wife of John Menheare
6 April Eleanor a base d. of Thomasine Wimbole
13 April John Calway
14 April Margaret the wife of John Tippett
15 April Katherine d. of Alexander Warne
19 April Elizabeth the wife of Humphry Treuowth
28 April Jane d. of Richard Hawke, sen^r
9 May John Cockin
12 May John Ivory servant to Thomas Merifield, gent.
16 May Walter Simon
22 May Bridgett the wife of John Nicholas *al's* Nantallen
30 May Agnes a base d. of Joane Holman
28 June Thomas Olver
5 July Mary the wife of Thomas Menedue
14 July Benett John*
19 July John Lae
22 July Joane, one of the poore of the pis'h
22 July Grace d. of Walter Cocke
17 Oct. Edw. Hockye
24 Oct. Katherine d. of Henrie Trewman
25 Oct. Tamzen the wife of John Cocke
11 Nov. Avice d. of Richard Paskow
15 Nov. John s. of Edward Merifield
10 Dec. Joane Miller the elder
29 Dec. John Tanken
29 Dec. Joane the wife of William Kendall
2 Jan. Mary d. of John Rise
26 Jan. John Benett *al's* Davie
15 Feb. Daniell Teage
17 Feb. John s. of Walter Bishop
19 Feb. John Manuell *al's* Roger

* The last entry on the page, and is signed by Tho. Smallridge, curate, and John Allen and Edward Benett, wardens.

24 Feb. Mathew s. of John Smith, gent.
3 Mar. Ursula the wife of Will'm Williams *al's* Roskugian

ANNO 1610.*

3 April Margarete Rowe vid.
18 April John Hix
24 April Mary the wife of Edmund Cray
28 April Joane the wife of Nicholas Lallow
3 May A chrisomer of Mr Thomas Arundells
19 June (*blank*) s. of William Williams *al's* Reskuegion
20 June A base childe unchristened of Joane Holman
10 July Alice d. of Thomas Varcoe
29 July William s. of Richard Addam
8 Aug. John Troblefeild†
29 Aug. Joane d. of Henry Sprey
5 Oct. Robert Darr‡
7 Oct. Rosa the wife of Walter Cocke
23 Oct. John Nantallen
31 Oct. Melissa the wife of John Daw§
2 Nov. Alice the wife of Henrie Trelevan
22 Nov. ‖ . . . . s. of Benett Pollarde who was drowned
1 Dec. fflorance d. of Reinold Litticott
4 Dec. Maud d. of John Rouse
17 Dec. A chrisomer of ffrancis Jones
20 Dec. Launcellott Eedy
23 Dec. An‖ Grosse
20 Jan. John s. of Robert Darr
6 Feb. Elizabeth the wife of John Julian
21 Feb. Katherine Locke
21 Feb. Joane d. of Walter Cocke
23 Feb. A servant maid to John Day
6 Mar. Ambros, Mr Vincents miller
6 Mar. Lavinea a base d. of Johan Darr

ANNO 1611.

25 Mar. Roger Carpenter

* Samuel Paul of St. Columb Major; buried 7 Dec., 1610. Par. Reg., St. Andrew's, Plymouth.

† John Troublefield was one of the wardens in 1609.—Green Book.

‡ Rob. Darr one of the wardens in 1596.—Green Book.

§ Last entry on the page, signed Thomas Smallridge, curate, Anthony Hawke and John Troblefield.

‖ Blank.

25 Mar. Andrew Simons
29 Mar. *Mary Boscowen, vid.
13 April Thomas Tior, a man as the comon report goeth 122 years of age
16 April Philip the wife of Renfreid Hawke
18 April Margaret Collins, vid.
23 May James s. of John Browne
26 May Alice d. of Richard Retallack
3 June John s. of John Davis *al's* Benett
4 June Julian the wife of John Copithorne
6 June Thomas s. of William White
15 June Tiffany d. of Sampson Bray
25 June † . . . . d. of Reinold Hawkin
26 June Philipp Knight, vid.
26 June Jane Bray, vid.
1 July Joane the wife of Richard Addam *al's* Rowse
10 July John Copithorne
13 July Jane d. of Richard Addam *al's* Rowse‡
15 July Elizabeth the wife of John Rowse
23 July James Roscudgion
25 July Katherine d. of ffrancis Dayowe
12 Aug. Katherine d. of Thomas Merifeild
23 Sep. Robert Rice
30 Sep. Joane Tucker, vid.
22 Oct. Joane Gwine
24 Oct. Michaell Cay
4 Nov. Tamazen the wife of John Day
30 Nov. John Rattenbury
2 Dec. Grace Lathy
13 Dec. John s. of ffrancis Lill *al's* Lar
17 Dec. Richard Rowse
17 Dec. Humphrey Hawke
18 Dec. Thomas Benett
25 Dec. An§ Tucker
26 Dec. Margery the wife of ffrancis Trehemban
19 Jan. The ould Paskow *al's* Polkinghorn
9 Feb. A pore wandering woman

* See note, p. 201 *ante*.
† Blank.
‡ Being the last entry on the page, is signed by Thomas Smallridge, curate, John Rescorler and Thomas Dayoe, wardens.
§ There is a blank space between the Christian and surname in the original.

12 Feb. Joane the wife of John Lill
15 Feb. Nicholas Lalloe *al's* Joll
7 Mar. John Hawke elder
22 Mar. Margarett Davie *al's* Benett
23 Mar. Joane d. of Martine Strangman*

Anno 1612.

27 Mar. Mary d. of John Cundy
31 Mar. Hugh s. of Benett Pollard
5 April James s. of John Gwine
18 April John Lill *al's* Lyon
8 May Henry Addam *al's* Rowse
5 June Elizabeth the wife of Thomas Hodge
8 June Nicholas Drewe
11 June Alice the wife of William Croode†
19 June Elizabeth Kent
21 June Jane Nuttle
26 June Mary d. of Thomas Benett *al's* Davie
27 July Margaret d. of John Taylor
10 Sep. John Julian bein slaine in a buce work
6 Oct. John s. of Thomas Hocky
9 Nov. Joane the wife of John Randle
27 Nov. William s. of James Mayhoe
29 Nov. William Body
11 Dec. William Strangman
22 Jan. Margerie the wife of James Hawke

In ffebruary & March were none buried. Thomas Smallridge, curate.

Anno 1613.

13 April Thomas White
14 April Ambrose Lawry
19 April Thomas Jenkin,‡ gent.
21 April Ursula the wife of Martine Hambly
25 April Martine Hambly
18 May Katherine Abraham
In June were none buried.
10 July Annice the wife of John Bayly
7 Aug. Elizabeth the wife of Will'm Benett

* The signature of Tho. Smallridge, curate, follows this entry, being the last on the page.
† Followed by the signatures of Thomas Smallridge curate, John Cocke and Sampson Morcombe, wardens.
‡ He was son and heir of Henry Jenkin of Trekinning in St. Columb, gent., by his wife Thomasine, daughter and coheir of William Harry Watt, gent. He married Jane, daughter and heir of John Moyle, by whom he had several children.

3 Sep. Agnes the wife of Richard Bastard
5 Nov. Katherine Moile
8 Nov. ffrancis* the wife of John Vivian, gent.
19 Nov. Melior one of the pore of the p'ish
15 Dec. Rainold Littycott
30 Dec. John Roger
5 Jan. Christopher Manuell *al's* Roger
12 Jan. Joane Lanyn, vid.
23 Jan. George & ffransces s. & d. of John Smith, gent.
5 Feb. Jane Darr, vid.
11 Feb. fflorance the wife of John Cundy
16 Feb. Michell Manuell *al's* Roger, vid.
20 Feb. Thomas s. of Reinold Littycott
26 Feb. Grace Day *al's* Mark†

ANNO 1614.

31 Mar. John Troblefeild‡
16 April Elizabeth the wife of Edward Bamlett
19 April Richard Reeve
3 May Tamazen Stribly
7 May Joane d. of ffransces Trehenban
8 May Joane the wife of Nicholas Carthew
13 May William Jane of Ruthvest
31 May Mary Carthew
23 June Philipe Tresole
4 July Alice the wife of Richard Drewe *al's* Jeffery
10 Aug. Grace d. of John Brounc
12 Aug. John s. of John Willes
19 Aug. * . . . . . Hockyn, one of the poore of the p'ish
18 Sep. Alexander Jolley
28 Sep. Joane d. of Richard Williams *al's* Baswalloe
4 Oct. John s. of Henry Calway
8 Oct. Margarete Genning
11 Oct. Agnes d. of John Hawke
13 Oct. Susan the wife of Paskell Tifford
16 Oct. * . . . . . A kinswoman of James Steephens
25 Oct. Richard s. of Thomas Bayly
10 Nov. Anna the wife of Ralph Keat, gent.†
21 Nov. John Lucky
28 Nov. A chrisomer unbaptized, d. unto M[r] John Beard
20 Dec. Melissa the wife of Thomas Merrifeild, gent.
10 Jan. Richowe Adam. vid.
20 Jan. Joane Adam
9 Feb. William . . . . .‡ a servant to M[r] Thomas Merrifeild
13 Feb. John Steephens
16 Feb. Katherine Day, vid.
17 Feb. Jane Knight
20 Mar. A chrisomer, unbaptized s. of William Beabre
25 Mar. John a base s. of Margaret Michell§

ANNO 1615.

22 April Maude Addam *al's* Rowse
27 April Dorathe Vanson, vid.

* She was the fifth daughter of Francis Buller of Shillingham, Esq., by his wife Thomasine, daughter of Thomas Williams, Esq., of Stowford, co. Devon. She was his first wife, and had an only child Anne.

† The signatures of Tho. Smallridge curate, John May and (blank), wardens, follow this entry.

‡ John Troublefield, one of the churchwardens in 1690. This name appears in these registers as early as 1589 (see p. 14), and remained in the parish for several generations, sometimes as Troublefield *alias* Thomas. The name occurs prior to this date in a gentle position in Devonshire and Dorset. James Troublefield, born in Dorsetshire, was consecrated Bishop of Exeter 1 May, 4 of Mary, 1556, and died 1 Nov., 1559. In an old heraldic MS. in the Plymouth and Cottonian Library, the arms of Troublefield (Turbervill or Turbervile of Samford) are given as, 'Erm. a lion ramp. gu., crowned or, langued and armed az.' It also states that the Bishop bore the same arms, giving for his motto "La famiglia des Justes deliavera." John Turbervile, Esq., was sheriff of Devon, 29 Hen. VI. 1451. The name of Turbervile occurs once in these registers.

* Blank.

† She was a daughter of Wm. Arscott of Holsworthy, co. Devon, by Julian, daughter of William Hender of Botreaux Castle, and the first wife of the above Ralph Kete, gent. Her husband was buried at St. Ervan, 14 April, 1636, aged 69, in which church there is a tablet to his memory. He married secondly, Sephronia, daughter of . . . . . Colman and relict of Peter Beare of St. Ervan. By his first wife he had (1) William, married and left issue; (2) John, vicar of Madron, married Elizabeth, daughter of Tho. Flemyng of Madron, and had nine children; (3) Ralph of St. Columb, married and had issue; (4) Rebecca, married Geo. s. of Peter Beare of St. Ervan; (5) Eliz.; (6) Ann, married 1631 Edw. Ashe.

‡ Blank.

§ Signed, Tho. Smallridge curate, Tho. Oxnam and John Brabyn, wardens.

4 May	Mary d. of Richard Smith, junr
27 June	Steephen Harvey
7 July	Jane Lucky, vid.
10 July	Thomas s. of John Rowe
6 Aug.	Elizabeth d. of Joell Jewell
7 Aug.	Alice d. of William Pelleane
9 Aug.	George Champian
13 Aug.	Elizabeth Vallice
18 Aug.	Edward s. of John Langdon
23 Aug.	Honor d. of Robert Allen
10 Oct.	Elizabeth d. of Henry Dyar
13 Oct.	A chrisomer unbaptized, s. of Paskowe Bawden
20 Oct.	Alice the wife of Paskowe Bawden
2 Nov.	Joane the wiffe of Robert Manuell
10 Nov.	Richard Donstone
13 Nov.	Agnes d. of Thomas Merrifield, gent.
14 Nov.	Joane Berry, vid.
3 Dec.	Elizabeth d. of Anthony Burlas
5 Dec.	Richard Beard
6 Dec.	Elizabeth d. of ffransces Lyon *al's* Lill
10 Dec.	Alice Benett, vid.
13 Dec.	Elizabeth d. of Richard Marke Williams
17 Dec.	John s. of Thomas Benett *al's* Davyes
22 Dec.	Joyce Tankyn
29 Dec.	John s. of John Taylor
30 Dec.	John Merrifeild of Talskythy
5 Jan.	Dorathe the wiffe of Richard Williams *al's* Pensalt
8 Jan.	Philipe the wife of Henry Merrifield
13 Jan.	Alice d. of Henry Sprey
15 Jan.	John Wills the potter
16 Jan.	Emblyn d. of John Nicholas *al's* Chune
17 Jan.	Margery the wife of William Typpett
18 Jan.	Alice d. of Anthony Randle*
19 Jan.	John s. of Edmund French
21 Jan.	Henry s. of William Jane
23 Jan.	John Nicholas *al's* Chune
23 Jan.	Gawen s. of Richard Carveith
25 Jan.	Darathe base d. of Katherine Moyle
27 Jan.	Joane d. of John Reskorler
27 Jan.	Henry Merrifeild

* Signed Thomas Smallridge, curate, Tho. Oxnam and John Carthew, wardens. The same names occur at the foot of the next page.

28 Jan.	Nicholas Duggoe
31 Jan.	Mary d. of John Hockyn
3 Feb.	John Dawe
8 Jan.	John Strangman, merchant
9 Feb.	Joyce d. of Richard Bowen
10 Feb.	Robert Allyn
11 Feb.	Thomas Simons
15 Feb.	Honor d. of Henry Sprey
18 Feb.	Margaret d. of John Stribly
25 Feb.	Joane d. of John Metheren
26 Feb.	Nicholas s. of John Geene
26 Feb.	Patience Oxnham
8 Mar.	Henry s. of Thomas Rawe
10 Mar.	Annice d. of John Reskorler
12 Mar.	Jane d. of James Mayhoe
13 Mar.	Joane d. of Nicholas Duggoe late deceased
22 Mar.	John Strangman s. of William Strangman

ANNO 1616.

26 Mar.	Nicholas d. of Steephen Knight
12 April	Charles s. of Christopher Pedler
2 May	Ann d. of Nicholas Duggoe
1 June	Eleanor Day *al's* Marke
7 June	Elizabeth Jolley, vid., being of the age of 107
20 July	Gilberte s. of Thomas Hockyn
15 Aug.	Joane Edward
17 Aug.	Margery Peerse, vid.
18 Aug.	Joane Myners servant to Mr Thomas Hoblyn
8 Sep.	A chrisomer of John Srivner, junr
10 Sep.	ffransces Lyon *al's* Lill
19 Sep.	Grace d. of Reynald Hawkyn
20 Sep.	Joane the wife of John Kent
21 Sep.	John Rowe
6 Oct.	Anstes Hawke, vid.
15 Oct.	Melior, one of the poore of the Churchyarde
17 Oct.	Alice Parking
27 Oct.	John Hayden
3 Nov.	Olife d. of John Mayoe
20 Nov.	Richard Drewe of Rothos
22 Nov.	Elizabeth Sprey, vid.
26 Nov.	Alice Stoky, vid.
2 Dec.	A chrisomer to Christopher Pedler
6 Nov.	Mary Yeoman
7 Dec.	Elizabeth the wife of Henry Sprey
9 Dec.	Thomas Tregeare
15 Dec.	Elizabeth Mayhowe, vid.
25 Dec.	William Typpett
6 Jan.	Eleanor the Weaver
8 Jan.	William Browne

13 Jan. Thomas Hodge
13 Jan. Alice the wife of John May
19 Feb. Alice Cockyn, vid.
24 Feb. William Ricard

ANNO 1617.

25 Mar. Agnes the wife of Thomas Symon
19 April Stephen a base s. of Jane Tubby *al's* Benett
26 April Richard Udy *al's* Skeberin
1 May Nicholas s. of John Trehenban
18 May Thomas Vivian, gent.*
20 May Jane d. of John Hawkey
21 June Nicholas s. of Edmond ffrench
In Julie were none buried
2 Aug. Mary d. of Reinald Hawkey
In September were none buried
1 Oct. Elizabeth d. of Thomas Brabyn†
14 Oct. Agnes, one of the poore in the church yeard howses
16 Oct. Judith d. of Edward Hoblyn, gent.‡
1 Nov Margery Dungie *al's* Tankyn
13 Nov. Elizabeth the wife of Thomas Retallack
21 Nov. Rosa Rawe
19 Dec. Thomas s. of John Hockyn
1 Jan. John s. of Gilbert Rawe
6 Jan. Nicholas Tubbe
8 Jan. Edward s. of Richard Behednoe
15 Jan. Richard s. of John Bond, gent§
26 Jan. Henry Darr
5 Feb. John Nicholas, a poore man who dyed in Nowell Mayhoes barne
15 Feb. Richard s. of Richard Fowler
15 Feb. James Cornish
22 Feb. Katherine Dunstone, one of the poore of the p'ish
28 Feb. Jane d. of Robert Allen
10 Mar. William Olver
17 Mar. Dorathea d. of Oliver Jagoe
19 Mar. Alice Conocke, vid.

* He was son and heir of John Vivian of Trenowth, gent., by Olive, daughter and heir of ..... Tresaster of St. Wenn. He married Ann, daughter and heir of Peter Lower of Truro, by whom he had (with other issue) John, who succeeded him.

† Followed by the signatures of Tho. Smallridge, curate, Hugh (H.L.) Lawrie and John Drewe, wardens.

‡ By his wife Mary, daughter and coheiress of Robert Apley of Barnestaple, co. Devon.

§ By his wife Honour, daughter of John Carter, gent., of St. Columb Major.

ANNO 1618.

27 April Anne Benett, one of the poore of the p'ish
27 April * A young child, one of the p'ish poore likwise
15 May A chrisomer of William Rawlyn
11 June Thomas Williams *al's* Roscudgion
8 July Joane Cocke, vid.
8 July Olife the wife of John Martyn *al's* Skinner
11 July Mary d. of John Williams
21 July Joane Rowse, vid.
9 Aug. Joane d. of Richard Daddoe
14 Aug. John a base s. of Jane Moylet†
8 Sep. Roger Mabyn
20 Oct. Nicholas Parking
2 Nov. Henry Offe
17 Jan. Mary the wife of John Body
21 Jan. Mary d. of John Body
28 Jan. John Nowell‡
1 Feb. Jane d. of Robert Pollard
26 Feb. A chrisomer of William Jolley
7 Mar. Tamazen Diamond, wid.
17 Mar. A chrisomer of Thomas Skynner

ANNO 1619.

3 April Katherine d. of John Mayhoe
8 April John Jenninge
11 April Anna d. of Oliver Jagoe
18 April Sislie,* wid., one of the poore of the p'ish
26 May Richard Rogers
12 June Elizabeth Jenkyn, one of the poore of the p'ish
13 July John Dyer of Tripcony
19 Oct. Richoe Chapleyn
5 Nov. Henry Young
9 Nov. Jane the wife of Thomas Grose
10 Nov. William s. of William Tresaddern
6 Dec. John s. of John Langdon
24 Dec. Joane the wife of George Juell
1 Jan. Jane the wife of William Williams

* Name blank.

† At the foot of the page, and followed by the signatures of Tho. Smallridge curate, Nathaniel Croode and Robert Drewe, wardens.

‡ Paid John Nowell for the carriage of post letters 6d., 1608.—Green Book. John Nowell paid 4d. for a knell for his daughter in 1599.—Green Book.

29 Jan. Cissillea d. of George Juell
11 Feb. Richard s. of Richard Rowse
12 Feb. Emblyn the wife of Jonathan Juell
22 Feb. Jane Rawe, spinister
16 Mar. Ann d. of Pascow John
23 Mar. Eleanor d. of Jonathan Juell

ANNO 1620.*

23 Mar. Henry s. of William Rowse
27 Mar. Adam s. of John Metherell
9 April Alison wife of John Tenny
19 April Thomas† s. of Edmond Nicolls
23 May Honnor‡ d. of John Bond, gent.
31 May Margaret wieff of Rob'te Callawaye
9 June John Spraye
29 June Richard Williams
12 July Christian the wiffe of Will'm Williams
12 July Margaret d. of John Geane
15 July Margaret the wife of James Maihowe
6 Aug. Avis wife of John White
6 Aug. Marye wife of John Lavyn
8 Aug. William s. of James Hawke
21 Aug. Richard s. of Reskynner Spray
24 Aug. Mary Dyer, widow
5 Sep. Emmanuell Meyhew
8 Sep. James Hawke
11 Sep. Gregory Litticotte§
25 Sep. Thomas James
10 Oct. Johane d. Mathew Wills
9 Jan. John Maye
27 Aug. Katherine‖ wiffe of James Jenkyn, gent.
23 Mar. Alice Edward

* Signed, Sa. Starr, who was apparently the successor of Tho. Smallridge as curate.

† Here a leaf of the register of burials is bound up in the original among the weddings.

‡ By his wife, daughter of John Carter of St. Columb Major. The above John Bond was son and heir of William Bond of Earth in St. Stephen's by Saltash, by his wife Margaret, daughter and coheiress of Hugh Fountaine of Ugborough, co. Devon.

§ In 1621 John Smith paid for the burial of Gregory Littacott 6s. 8d.—Green Book.

‖ She was a daughter of James Carter, gent., of St. Columb, by his wife Honour, daughter and coheiress of John Newman. She married first John Brabyn, gent., of St. Columb, by whom she had several children. By her second husband James Jenkin, gent., of Trekinning she had Honour, married James Praed, and Peter, who married in 1628 Anne, daughter of Andrew Pomeroy of St. Columb, Esq.

26 Mar. Baldwyne Moyle
31 Mar. Emblyn d. of Hugh Sexton

ANNO 1621.

2 April Sampson Morcombe*
4 April Elizabeth Bennye
20 April Jane Trewman
20 April Another poore woman
1 May John s. of Henry Husband
26 May Johan ffrancys†
9 Aug. Marye d. of John Martyn
9 Oct. Robert s. of ffrancis George
24 Jan. Katherine the wife of Bennet Calway
4 Feb. Will'ms s. of John Rowe
12 Feb. Rose d. of Henry Moyle
13 Feb. Katherine wife of Immanuell Mayhoe
20 Feb. Will'm Gilbert
5 Mar. Thomas s. of Thomas Skynner
13 Mar. Elizabeth d. of John Rise
17 Mar. Martyn s. of Williams Bewes
22 Mar. Thomas s. of Henry Calway

ANNO 1622.

25 Mar. Agnes Jolle
28 Mar. Johane d. of Francis Lille
8 April John Martyn servant to Penyndur‡
31 May John Cocke
1 June Margaret Geene
2 June Robert s. of Thomas Bennet
15 June Susan d. of Luke Pollard
19 June Joane d. of William Bond
24 June Joyce d. of John Jones
1 July John Jones
10 July Julian wiff of William Blake
8 Aug. Richard Besrenow
12 Aug. Elizabeth wiff of Thomas Cocke
21 Sep. §(. . . .) of Reinold Peter
23 Sep. William Cornish
16 Oct. Mary d. of Hughe Lawry
1 Nov. Mary d. of Robert Cockin
2 Nov. Henry s. of William Brus
3 Nov. Jane wiff of John Drew
10 Nov. Garderet d. of William Bond
20 Nov. Grace d. of Richard Pennow
24 Nov. Thomas s. of John Harvy
29 Nov. Jane d. of John Will'ms

* Sampson Morcombe, one of the wardens in 1589, in 1587 he had paid 3s. 4s. not to be churchwarden.

† In 1594 Widowe Frances of Penhale gave 3s. to the poor, and William Frances of Penhale gave 3d. to the poor the same year.—Green Book.

‡ Sic.

§ Blank.

29 Nov. Lowdy d. William Trekeene
2 Dec. Johan Brown, vid.
10 Dec. Alles Tippett
15 Dec. Christian d. of William Blake
19 Dec. Peter s. of John Adam
1 Jan. John s. of Richard Rowse
2 Jan. Catherine d. of William Brabin
7 Jan. John s. of Robert Tippit
9 Jan. Philip d. of Richard Jenkin
12 Jan. Tomson d. of John Moyor
14 Jan. Jane Simon, widdow
17 Jan. John s. of * Retollicke
17 Jan. James Stevens
23 Jan. Grace Tresteene, wid.
23 Jan. John s. of Robert Manwell
25 Jan. Richard Smith
7 Feb. Robert Manwell
20 Feb. Joane d. of Anthony Borlace
22 Feb. Arthur s. of John Meyo
27 Feb. Lowdy d. of ffrancis Huitt
13 Mar. John s. of Anthony Borlace
15 Mar. Nicholas Hollman
17 Mar. Jone Henscocke
17 Mar. John s. of John Maihow
19 Mar. Richard Hellier
19 Mar. Pascha s. of Thomas Dozor

ANNO 1623.

28 Mar. Henry Rowse
5 April John Randoll
8 April Peternell d. of Richard Hitchros
9 April Alles Nicholas
12 April Elizabeth the wiff of Thomas Michell
13 April †(. . .) d. of William Rouse
14 April Renold Peter
17 April William Tubb
20 April Joane Rescorlaw
20 April William s. of Thomas Wiat
2 May Ann d. of John Trivithicke
4 May Joane d. of William Jane
7 May John s. of John Martin
18 May ffrancis Trenoughe
7 June Thomas George
9 June John s. of Pascha John
9 June Joell Moyle
9 June Oliver Robinns
13 June Anthony Hawke
8 July Thomas s. of Thomas Wiat
13 July Thomas Merifeild, gent.
15 July Jenepher the wiff of John Colles
19 July John s. of Will'm Brabyn
4 Aug. Marvin Moyle
6 Aug. Nicholas s. of Thomas Jane

* Obliterated. † Blank.

2 Sep. Will'm s. of Thomas Skin'er
6 Sep. Richard Pollard
24 Sep. Grace d. of John Staple
6 Oct. Jane wiff of Henry Husband
14 Oct. Jenniphret Norton, widdow
5 Nov. Richard Martin
9 Nov. Alice Jenninge, widow
22 Nov. Margery d. of Henry Moyle
24 Dec. Mary d. of Thomas Trenibere
24 Dec. Robert West
29 Dec. Adam s. of Martin Trisven
30 Dec. Elinor the wiff of John Nankevell
16 Jan. Henry Tippet
20 Jan. Will'm s. of Jerman Retallacke
16 Mar. Tomson Simon, widow
16 Mar. Ann Cornish

ANNO 1624.

29 Mar. ffrancis d. of Nicholas Bounsall
20 April John Moyle
28 April ffrancis Luas
5 May Joane d. of Richard Cerveth
27 May Elizabeth the wiff of Richard Copithorne
30 May Alice wiff of ffrancis Row
30 July Sidwell Williams, widow
6 Aug. William Jane
10 Aug. Mary d. of Thomas Brabyn
10 Sep. John s. of John Bayly
15 Sep. Joane d. of John Mayoh
19 Oct. Johan the wife of Remphrey Joll
20 Oct. William Mitchell
28 Oct. Will'm s. of Reignold Weekes
24 Nov. Alice Oxenham, wydow
27 Nov. Agnes Tifford, wyd.
1 Dec. Margerye Behedna, wydow
2 Dec. Katherine wiffe of Nicholas Peor
9 Dec. Katherine Edwarde
6 Dec. Mary d. of Reynold Peter & Joane his wife
21 Dec. Alice d. of Will'm & Elizabeth Cocke
24 Dec. Richard Hanna
3 Feb. Steeven Knight
6 Feb. Mellarye Reeve
12 Feb. Katherine Polkinhorne*
28 Feb. Joane d. of Richard Tregeare
2 Mar. ffrances d. of John Brabyn
4 Mar. Remphrey s. of Alexander Penfound

* This name is very indistinct.

11 Mar. Katherine d. of Litticott*
16 Mar. fflorance Scantleburye, wydow

ANNO 1625.

31 Mar. William Edwards
1 April Christian d. of Thomas Bennett
12 April Richard Williams
21 April Emblyn Sadler
10 May Marye d. of Peter Morcombe
24 May John s. of Richard Hanne
25 May William s. of John Cocking
31 May Henry s. of Reynold Peter
5 June Will'm Wills
10 June Richard s. of John Marke
18 June Rowse Edwards, wydow
22 Oct. William s. of William Ketengen (?)
25 Oct. John s. of Immanuell Harric
25 Nov. Elizabeth Banner †
9 Dec. John Trehenban
12 Dec. John Bounsoll
16 Dec. John Moile
22 Dec. Alice Cock
7 Jan. Richard s. of Richard Carveth
2 Mar. Thomas base s. of ‡ . . .
3 Mar. Jane Harvey, widowe
20 Mar. William base child of . . . ‡

ANNO 1626.

19 April Alice Amy
29 April Thomas Parnell
1 May James Mayhowe
5 May John a base child of . . . . ‡
6 May Alice Williams
6 May John s. of Henry Moyell
10 June Blanch Daye, widowe
18 July Anne wiff of Regnold Hawkey
1 Aug. Jone wiff of Thomas Allen
10 Aug. Nicholas s. of John Cockin
18 Aug. Mary d. of Henry Harvey
19 Aug. Henry s. of Emmanuell Harvey
30 Aug. Symon s. of Jo. Trehemben
9 Sep. William Jolliffe
16 Sep. Jone wife of William White
16 Sep. Joice d. of Thomas Stephens
18 Sep. John Langdon
2 Oct. James Harris
6 Oct. Jane wife of Thomas Stephens
16 Oct. Phillip Jolliffe, widow
3 Nov. John s. of John Harvey
25 Nov. Richard s. of Ric. Rowse

* Obliterated.
† Spelt thus in the original, but query if it should not be Tanner.
‡ Blank.

ANNO 1627.

12 May Jane Edye
17 May John Hocken
1 June Will'm Bowerman
27 June Thomas s. of John Geene
24 Dec. Jone Kittowe*
10 Jan. Katherine wife of Thomas Day* gent
27 Jan. Robert Lock*
7 Feb. Ellenor Grosse, widow*
20 Mar. Henry Browne*
17 Mar. Will'm Williams*
13 April Anne d. of Gilbert Row
4 June Peter s. of John Adam
16 June Margery Gwynnow, widow
3 July Henry s. of Thomas Skynner
20 July John Horwell
3 Aug. Edward Teage
12 Aug. Alice wife of John Daye
15 Aug. John Pollard
. . . . . Honor d. of † . . . & Tamson his wife
. . . . . Richard† s. of . . . ah Coppithorne
. . . . . John s. of Thomas Tom & Dorothe his wife
. . . . . (*blank*)† d. of . . . . . Lawry & Philip his wife
23 Sep. John s. of Thomas Merifeild, gent. & Jane his wife
14 Oct. John s. of William Calway & Jane his wife
21 Oct. John s. of John Legge & Julian his wiffe
21 Oct. Joane d. of Beniamyn Stranford (?) & † . . . his wife
19 Oct. John Moyle
16 Oct. Edward Coxwith‡
30 Oct. Remphrey Trenouth
31 Oct. Edward s. of Henery Moyle
4 Nov. Catherine Peline wife of William Peline
24 Dec. William s. of John Dyer
4 Jan. Ann Edwards
13 Jan. Johan wife of † . . . Moile
19 Jan. Richard Sprey§
3 Feb. Thomas Stephens
8 Feb. Jane d. of James Reskigian
12 Feb. Will. Congdome

* These names were forgotten to be put down in their right place. Entered thus in the original.
† Obliterated. From the 15th Aug. to the latter part of Oct. following the entries are more or less completely obliterated, the whole page being much rubbed.
‡ Query if not Cosworth.
§ In 1627 Hugh Sprey paid 6s. 8d. for the burial of his uncle Richard Sprey.

18 Feb. Allise d. of Will'm Thomas
19 Feb. Margery Drewe
28 Feb. Johan Reskiggian
20 Mar. Allice James, widdow

ANNO 1628.

28 Mar. Henry Harvey
18 April Joane d. of John Harvey
21 May Honor d. of Marten Tier
3 June Sampson Browne
7 June Mary Bowell
11 June Grace wife of John Browne
18 June Thomas s. of Kouddye Terlogan
26 June Anne wife of Richard Retallack
2 July James Vallyes
12 July George Nanceckevell
19 July James Jenking,* gent.
26 Aug. Martyn s. of Phillipp Yeemon
28 Aug. John Tubb
28 Aug. Thomas Trimbeare
5 Sep. Tamsonn wife of John Rice
13 Sep. Cateren wife of John Trenege
4 Oct. John s. of David Walkey
3 Nov. John Phillipp
11 Nov. Jone wife of Richard Doone
17 Nov. Tiffieny wife of Richard Hawke
19 Nov. Mary Stevens
3 Dec. John Williams
4 Jan. Thomas Hocky
1 Feb. Honnor d. of John Arter
10 Feb. Henry Randall
12 Feb. John Daw
16 Feb. William Merifield
22 Feb. John Retallock, junior
4 Mar. Water Bishop

ANNO 1629.

6 April fflorence Michell
1 May John s. of Abraham Martyn
24 May Grace d. of Jonn Coppithorne
30 May John Doble
31 May Paskow Hawke
24 June Johan Martyn, wid.
27 June ffrances Roe
12 July Thomas Wiatt
19 July Thomas s. of John Brabyn
21 July Priscilla d. of Thomas Kent
27 July Richard Pernall
22 Aug. Beaten d. of Thomas Bayly
26 Sep. John Browne
27 Sep. Gilbert Rowe

* He was son and heir of Thomas Jenkin of Trekinning, by Jane, daughter and heir of John Moyle. He married Katherine, daughter of James Carter, gent., and relict of John Brabyn, gent. See note, p. 209 ante.

9 Oct. Alice Onffe
12 Oct. Peternell the wife of Michaell Thomas
19 Oct. Henry Jenkyn,* gent.
1 Nov. Thamsyn d. of Robert Bosparta
3 Nov. Anne the wife of John Kent
5 Nov. Grace d. of Barbara Merifeeld
13 Nov. Thomas s. of Anne Harvey
15 Nov. Ales Collins, widowe
2 Dec. Humphrey s. of John Laury
26 Dec. Susan the wife of Hugh Sprey
26 Dec. Katherine Hawke
28 Dec. Peter s. of Robert Pollard
3 Jan. William Pawland
30 Jan. Adam Trestean
22 Feb. John Jolliffe
23 Feb. Mellery Williams
5 Mar. John Sprey
13 Mar. John Warne† of Ervan
30 Mar. Alice Abraham

ANNO 1630.

2 April Richard Carter‡ Esquire
16 April Thomas Williams
20 April William base s. of Ame Hocks
20 April Hugh s. of John Grace
18 May Elizabeth d. of Henry Harry
19 May Agnes d. of Robert Dunken
26 May Christopher s. of Henrye Moyle
4 June John s. of Thomas Wyott
18 July Marye Charly
18 July Marye d. of William Dancaster
7 Aug. Honor d. of Thomas Wyott
14 Aug. Grace the wyfe of Anthony Whitford
31 Aug. Honor d. of John Harry
3 Oct. Richard s. of Robert Dunken
10 Oct. Beaten d. of Richard Cornishe
24 Oct. Hugh Norten
5 Nov. Jane d. of Patiente Williams

* He was the second son of Thomas Jenkin, gent., of Trekinning, by Jane Moyle his wife. He married Margaret, daughter and coheiress of Oliver Carminow, Esq., and relict of Philip Cole, Esq.

† He was most probably a son of John Warne of St. Columb, his baptism being lost through the loss of the registers from 1554 to 1571, as were probably Alexander Warne, who married Joan Drew, and Katherine Warne, who was married at St. Cubyn 25 June, 1594, to William Jolly, Clerk, Vicar of Enoder; the marriage is entered at St. Enoder.

‡ Son and heir of John Carter, gent., by Jane, daughter of John Vivian, gent. He married Elizabeth, daughter of Sir John Arundell of Talverne and his wife Ann Godolphin; and had an only child Joane, who died young.

28 Dec. Annes Truboddy
9 Jan. John Young
19 Jan. ffrances Trear
11 Mar. Joane wife of John Torker

ANNO 1631.

22 Mar. Prescylla d. of Henry Bligh
22 Mar. Tamson wyfe of John Phillip
27 Mar. Richard Oxnam
14 April Elizabeth Pinnow
23 May Bennett Pollard
27 May John Striblye
12 June Thomas s. of Thomas Pearse
21 June Grace d. of Anthony Whitford
30 July Richard Ruze
6 Aug. Marye Williams
4 Oct. Siblye wife of John James
4 Oct. Elizabeth Littlejohn
21 Oct. Mark Retallack
3 Nov. John Reeve
10 Nov. Jane Morcombe
19 Nov. John Tooker
30 Nov. Grace Congdon
1 Dec. Julyan Wyatt
16 Dec. Marye Tacye
19 Dec. Gilbert Libbye
26 Dec. Marye d. of Jone West
14 Jan. John s. of Thomas Bayliffe
26 Jan. John Roscorloe
31 Jan. fflorence d. of Walter Coryton
3 Feb. Johane Nuttinge
4 Feb. Wilmote d. of Patient Wilmote
13 Mar. John Spraye
21 Mar. Jane Pinnowe

ANNO 1632.

8 April Jane Stribley
14 April Jane Stribleye d. of David Stribly
5 May Richard Ruze* of Trebadanon
16 June Joane wiffe of John Bettye
27 July Katherine d. of James Mayhowe
26 Sep. Arthur Orchard
19 Sep. Alice d. of Robert Dunkyn
27 Sep. John Yolton
27 Sep. Joane d. of Luke Pollard
5 Oct. Jane Lovyne wydow
16 Oct. Phillip d. of Richard Laytye
19 Oct. John s. of Thomas Hawke
31 Oct. Alice d. of William Calway

* In 1633 Barbara Rowse, widow, paid a legacy of £6 left by her late husband Richard Rowse deceased. John Rowse was treasurer in the same year.—Green Book.

8 Nov. Jane d. of Martyn Dunnacombe
24 Dec. Barbara d. of John Dyar
8 Jan. George s. of Martyn Edwards
23 Jan. Lowdye Terlogan
25 Jan. Elizabeth Cocke wydow
25 Jan. Marye Geoffrye
28 Jan. Tho. Arundell* Esqr
2 Feb. Rebeccah d. of Henrye Lee
20 Feb. Richard Dunnacombe
29 Feb. Jonah s. of William Bewford
24 Feb. Edward s. of Rawlyn Merfeild
25 Feb. Alice Stribley wydow
6 Mar. Elward wiffe of John White

ANNO 1633.

5 April Honor Parkyn, wydowe
8 April John White
10 April John Launder
11 April Olive d. of John Darr
17 April Richard Hawke
24 May Nicholas Lang
22 May Elizabeth d. of Thomas Lawe
8 June Patience wife of John Grimes
12 June Henry Dyer†
9 July Ebbot d. of Walter Coryton
14 Aug. John Arrundell‡ Esqr
19 Aug. Thomas Symons
4 Sep. Thomas Allen
6 Sep. Digory s. of John Metherell
23 Sep. Elizabeth d. of Mathew Willes
30 Sep. Mathew Willes
18 Nov. Bennet Calley
24 Nov. John Treneag
11 Dec. Elizabeth Symons, widow
30 Dec. John Cocking
6 Jan. John Day
10 Jan. Richard Carter
30 Jan. Richard s. of George Lane

* He was of Trevithick in St. Columb, and was son and heir of Thómas Arundell of Tremere, Esq. (by Elizabeth daughter and coheir of ...... Tringove of Nance), who was the second son of Sir John Arundell of Lanherne, knt., by his wife Elizabeth, daughter of Gerald Danet, Esq., of Danet's Hall. He married Rachell Mompesson, sister to Sir Giles Mompesson, by whom he had issue several children.

† In 1634 John Dyer paid 20s., a legacy from his late father Henry Dyer, deceased, to the poor. John Dyer himself left 3s. 4d. to the poor of the parish.

‡ He was of Lanherne, being son and heir of Sir John Arundell of Lanherne, by his wife Lady Ann, daughter of Thomas Stanley, Earl of Derby, and relict of Charles, seventh Lord Stourton. He married Ann, daughter of Henry Jerningham, Esq., of Costessey, co. Norfolk.

7 Feb. John Marten
18 Feb. John Heycraft

ANNO 1634.

13 April Edward Meryfold
20 April William Williams
2 May John Dawe
31 May Mathew Pomery*
22 June Jone Spettygrue
25 June Peter s. of Thomas Tome
6 Aug. Pascow Vivian,† gen.
17 Aug. Olive d. of Thomas Allen
28 Sep. Margery Cornish, widdow
9 Oct. Jone Tregere
20 Oct. William Strongman
25 Nov. Maryan Betty
20 Jan. Richard Copithorne
6 Feb. Penelope d. of Mark Tyer
9 Feb. Jane Moyle, widow
18 Feb. Eliner Jagoe
22 Feb. Thomas Brabyn
23 Feb. Mathew s. of John Mayhow
6 Mar. Micaell Thomas
20 Mar. Thomas Vencent
17 Mar. John s. of John Luky
18 Mar. Johan Pollard, widdow

ANNO 1635.

27 Mar. Elizabeth Spray, widdow
27 Mar. Zenoby Hichens, widdow
31 Mar. Alice Nankevall, wydow
1 April Margaret John
4 April Thomas Duggoe
6 April Dennys Westcott
12 April Johan Hocky, wydowe
16 April Marye d. of John Rouse
21 April John Rouse
3 May Anthony‡ s. of Anthony Whitford
6 May Anthonye Whitford
10 May Dorethye Lukye
16 June John Grace
17 June Jane Holman
2 Aug. Luke Harvye
3 Aug. Honor Dyer, wydowe

* He was son of Edward Pomeroy and Julian his wife, daughter of ...... Forster, which Edward was third son of Andrew Pomeroy of Colliton, Devon, and uncle to the Andrew Pomeroy buried in 1639. Mathew Pomeroy above is named in the will of John Pomeroy of St. Clere, gent., dated 16 June, 1618.

† He was son of Thomas Vivian of Trenowth, gent., by Anne, daughter and coheiress of Peter Lower. He married Mary Flamocke (see marriages 15 Dec., 1601), and had several children.

‡ Being the last entry on the page, it is followed by the signatures of S. Legg, curate, John Day and Tho. Richards, wardens.

1 Sep. Elizabeth Oxenbam*
5 Sep. Margaret Bennett
21 Sep. Anne Brabyn
22 Sep. Thomasyn d. of William Basely
26 Sep. Henrye Spraye
5 Oct. Elizabeth Wyatt
13 Nov. Anne d. of Michaell Davye
25 Nov. Sydrack Retallack
24 Dec. Edward Carter,† gen.
29 Dec. Anne James
2 Jan. Thomas Hoblyn,‡ gen.
6 Jan. Katherine Mason
30 Jan. Johane Younge,§ wydow
6 Feb. Alice Braye
15 Feb. Charles & Elizabeth s. & d. of John Vivian, gent.||
21 Feb. Ursula Phillip
22 Mar. John s. of Sampson Roscorla
25 Mar. Anne Vyvean,¶ wydow

ANNO 1636.

30 Mar. Phillipp d. of William Bond
22 April Catherine Bettye
1 May Marye the wyfe of Michaell Davye
18 May Petter s. of Robert Pollarde
19 May Richard Williams
21 May John Pollarde s. of Bennett Pollarde
27 May Johane the wyfe of Henrye Nanparrowe

* In 1636 Thomas Oxenham paid 6s. 8d. for the burial of his wife.—Green Book.

† He was a younger son of John Carter of St. Columb, gent., by his wife Jane, daughter of John Vivian, gent. He died unmarried. John Carter, Esq. paid to the parish for the burial of his brother 20s.

‡ He was of Nanswhyden, being son and heir of Richard Hoblyn, gent. (who purchased Nanswhyden from John Nanswhyden), by his wife Philippa, daughter and coheir of John Pye. He married first Judeth, daughter and heir of Edward Trevalcois of Goran, and secondly Dorothy, daughter of John Dinham, but she died s.p. By his first wife he was ancestor of the present family. There is a ledger stone to his memory, which is fully described with the other monuments in the church elsewhere.

§ John Young for the burial of his grandmother paid 6s. 8d.—Green Book.

|| By his second wife Mary, daughter and coheiress of William Cavell and Jane his wife, daughter of William Pomeroy, Esq. These children are recorded on a monumental slab in the church, which will be found described with the other monuments; on it Charles is said to be aged 5 years, and Elizabeth one year and a half.

¶ In 1636 Mr. William Vivian paid 20s. for the burial of his wife, (but the burial does not appear to have been registered.)—*Vide* Green Book.

30 May Honnor d. of Abraham Husbande
26 June Jenever wyfe of Steven Lovell
26 June Nicholas Mason
28 June Alls the wyfe of Christopher Morcombe
3 July Thomas s. of John Copithorne
5 July John Cockyn
6 July Johane d. of William Calwaye
10 July Dorothie d. of Emanuewell Harvye
14 July Marye d. of Beniamyn Strongman
19 July John s. of William Calwaye
17 July Margaret d. of John Gremes
25 July Dorothye wyfe of John Motten
30 July William Libbye
6 Aug. Thomas Tom
7 Aug. Mary wyfe of William Bennye of Maugan*
21 Aug. Ann Vallis p^r
30 Aug. Thomazin the wyfe of Martyn Edwarde
11 Sep. James s. of Martyn Edwarde
13 Sep. Rytchaud Trenowth
4 Oct. Phillipe Robyns
22 Oct. Marye d. of Henry Blighe
30 Nov. Steven Abrahame
1 Dec. Johane the wyfe of John Joll†
2 Dec. Thomas James
3 Dec. Anthonye s. of John Kinge
27 Jan. Henrye s. of Jozies Daye
9 Mar. Precylla Bryantt
2 Feb. John Retallacke
9 Mar. Petter s. of Rob. Pollard

Anno 1637.

28 Mar. Henrye Cocke
16 April A childe to Ralph Keatt
16 April Nicholas Petter
18 April Donnett, a base child to one Maddocke
7 May Marke s. of John Grace
23 May Richard s. of John Joule
31 May Margaret Penfound
17 June Thomas s. of Reynolde Hawke
25 June Elizabeth Prist
27 June Thomas s. of Thomas Allen
6 July Ellener Pell
13 July Beaten d. of John Hoswell
5 Aug. Grace Robyns
13 Aug. Joane Row
18 Aug. Grace Roseware
28 Aug. Katherine Jenkyn
19 Sep. John s. of Thomas Law
24 Sep. Anthony Row
28 Sep. Margaret d. of John Dyer
11 Oct. Grace Marshall
4 Oct. Henry s. of John Reandall
5 Oct. Honoar d. of John Dyer
9 Oct. Joane wife of William Way
17 Oct. Joyce d. of Henry Bray
6 Dec. Elloner Lange, widow
26 Dec. Richard s. of Martyn Edwarde
31 Dec. William Cocken
6 Jan. Johane White
9 Jan. Mary White
11 Jan. Dorothie Hoblyn, widdow*
30 Jan. Elizabeth Ulcock
3 Feb. Alls West
5 Feb. Joyce Blacke
16 Feb. Ann Arundell, widdow†
5 Mar. Grace the wife of Thomas Williams
6 Mar. Thomas Witholl
21 Mar. Mary d. of Thomas Westcott
22 Mar. Katherine d. of John Jenkyn

Anno 1638.

11 April William s. of Giles Truscot
14 April Jane Tenney, widow
17 April Jermin Retalack
17 April Jone a base d. of Jone John
19 May William Dancaster
11 June Henry John
17 Aug. Donot Duncomb
26 Aug. Nicholas Parkyn
7 Sep. Richard s. of Beniamyn Strongman
8 Sep. Ann d. of John Copithorne
17 Sep. Edward s. of Thomas Michell
18 Sep. Jonathan s. of John Vivian,‡ Esq.
19 Sep. William Beauford§
20 Sep. Lewes s. of William Beard
26 Sep. Honor Stepston, widow

* In 1637 received 6s. 8d. for the burial of William Bennye's wife of Mawgan.

† In 1619 Kemfrey Joll paid 12s., owed to the parish by his brother John Joll.—Green Book.

* She was relict of Thomas Hoblyn of Nanswhyden, Esq., being his second wife, and daughter of John Dynham. She died s.p.

† She was daughter of Sir Henry Jerningham (or Gernigan), first bart., of Costessy Hall, by his wife Eleanor, daughter of Thomas Throckmorton, Esq., of Throckmorton, and granddaughter of Henry Jerningham, Esq., of Costessey, by his first wife Eleanor, daughter of William, Lord Dacre of Gillesland. She married John Arundell, Esq., of Lanherne, who died in 1633, leaving several children.

‡ By his wife Mary, daughter and coheiress of Wm. Cavell, Esq.

§ William Beauford the elder, treasurer of the parish, son of William Beauford the elder, who died the previous year while treasurer, and who left £5 to the poor of the parish.—Green Book.

12 Oct. Ric. s. of Richard Hawke
28 Oct. William Lukey
6 Nov. Jone Copithorne
3 Dec. William Jeffery
4 Dec. John Moyses
7 Dec. Ann Merifeld
20 Dec. Ann Vivian* wife to John Vivian, junr., Esq.
27 Dec. Jone Kent
5 Jan. John Kent
6 Jan. Katherine Mayow
9 Jan. Anthony s. of John Lawry
6 Feb. Tamson Tregonwen
11 Feb. Henery Beauford
11 Feb. John Parkyn
11 Feb. Jone d. of Nico. Jane
3 Mar. Amey Rowse
17 Mar. John† s. of John Vivian, Esq.
24 Mar. John s. of Martyn Stevens

ANNO 1639.

7 April Denes s. of Richard Langdon
8 April Barbara John
10 April Martyn s. of Martyn Stevens
11 April Paskow Tafford
13 April Jane Williams
21 April Ann d. of Robert Litticot
3 May Patience Trenethan
6 May Reynold Hawke
16 May Nicholas Stribly
20 May Nicholas Pearse
20 June Annies May, widdowe
18 July John s. of John Dar
6 Aug. Hugh Lawry
23 Aug. John Hoblyn,‡ gent.
31 Aug. John s. of John Jollye
16 Sep. Emlyn d. of John Oxnam
22 Oct. John Day, gen.
24 Oct. Barbara d. of Nicholas Peter
20 Nov. Lewes s. of William Hawkyn
21 Nov. Elizabeth Tucker
22 Nov. Andrew Pommery,§ gen.
30 Dec. Peter Martyn

* She was a daughter of Sir John Trelawny, first bart., by his wife Elizabeth, daughter of Sir Reginald Mohun, bart., of Boconnock, and aunt of the well-known Right Rev. Sir Jonathan Trelawny, Bishop of Winchester. She was the first wife of John Vivian of Truan, Esq.

† By his wife Ann, daughter of Sir John Trelawny, bart.

‡ He was the eldest son of Edward Hoblyn of Nanswhyden, Esq., by his wife Mary, daughter and coheiress of Robert Apley of Barnestaple, and died unmarried, v.p.

§ He was son of William Pomeroy of Colliton, co. Devon, by his wife Mary, daughter of John Bevill of Killgarthe. He married Jane, daughter and heir of Digory Hext of Launceston, by whom he had several children.

30 Dec. Joahie Hockie
4 Jan. John Nacolas
17 Jan. John Nankevall
18 Jan. Christopher Knight
18 Jan. Henry s. of William Cock
2 Feb. Roberta d. of John Dyer
4 Feb. John Baylie
11 Feb. William s. of Henry Tregare
22 Feb. Anthony Burlase
28 Feb. Nicholas Smith
28 Feb. Alls Hawke, widowe
7 Mar. Mary d. of Sampson Roscorla
11 Mar. Senobie widow of Joell Juell
11 Mar. Walter s. of Barnabas Bettye
12 Mar. John Coppithorne

ANNO 1640.

26 Mar. Henry s. of Henry Nanparrow
27 Mar. Marke s. of John Tenny
9 Mar. Superan Edgcomb, vid.
13 April John Heycraft
4 May William Rawlyn
23 May Thomas s. of Thomas Lawe
24 May Agnes Pernal, vid.
25 May Katherine Service
6 June Thomas Jolly
14 July Joane wife of John Martyn
25 Sep. Richard Richards
26 Sep. Richard James
1 Oct. Elizabeth d. of Henry Naparrow
8 Nov. John Adam
27 Nov. Richard Skynner
15 Dec. Margaret d. of Thomas Baly
27 Dec. Mary Cockyn, widdow
29 Dec. Annes Lane
6 Jan. Elizabeth Yolton, vid.
28 Jan. James Trebell
27 Jan. Joane d. of John Martyn
3 Feb. Elizabeth d. of Edward Hoblyn* gent.
10 Feb. Richard Crawly
22 Feb. Phillipp the wife of John Baylife
23 Feb. Alice Law, widdow
17 Mar. Richard Rowse†

ANNO 1641.

6 April John Phillipp
12 April Catheryn wife of Andrew Chapell
24 April Honor Geene

* By his wife Mary, daughter and coheir of Robert Apley, Esq.

† Richard Rowse *al's* Jenkyn, one of the twelve men in 1627. Richard Rowse *al's* Adams, churchwarden in 1644, and one of the twelve men in 1630.—Green Book.

28 April Jane Phillipp
24 May David s. of Mark Tire
24 May Jane d. of John Carthew
28 May William Boan
28 May Richard s. of John Kendall
6 June Jane Nicholls
14 June William* s. of John Vivian, Esq.
18 July Elinor Luny, vid.
24 July Elizabeth d. of Walter Coriton
4 Aug. Sissilla Westcott, vid.
19 Aug. James s. of Marten Rowe
13 Sep. Bernard* s. of John Vivian, Esq.
5 Oct. Olive Teage, vid.
13 Nov. Peter s. of Thomas Richards
30 Nov. Mary Tregeare
1 Dec. Jane the wife of John Marshall
1 Dec. Rose d. of John Tenny
8 Dec. William John
8 Dec. Honor d. of Sampson Rescorla
22 Dec. Tamsin d. of James Cockin
10 Mar. Katherine Naparow, vid.
16 Mar. Melliar Gilbert
25 Mar. Richard Bowen
31 Mar. Katherine wife of Robert Trehimbam
31 Mar. Jane James
4 April Mark s. of Mark Tire

ANNO 1642.

2 May Nicholas Moore
5 May Digory s. of John Stephens
14 May Mary Hixt
26 May Olive Roe
2 June Elizabeth Jolley
8 June Richard Carter
23 June John Bettey
3 July Constance Bettey
15 July John Arundell† of Lanhearon, Esqr
12 Aug. Barnard a duch man
27 Aug. Phillipp d. of Richard Langdon
25 Aug. Jane wife of John Hals, gent.
29 Aug. Joane Champion
16 Sep. Tho. Rawlinge of Mylor
10 Oct. Jo. Langdon
22 Oct. Radigon Brabond
28 Oct. Peeter Horswell
3 Nov. Tho. Hawke
11 Nov. ffrances Crues

* By his wife Mary, daughter and coheiress of William Cavell of Treharrock.

† Son of John Arundell, Esq., of Lanherne, by his wife, Ann, daughter of Sir Henry Jernigan, Bart. He married Elizabeth, daughter of William Brock, Esq., by whom he had one son, Sir John Arundell, of Lanherne.

17 Nov. Emblinge Bayly
24 Nov. Marten Tresteane
28 Nov. Jane Cornish
6 Dec. Elizabeth Behedno
18 Dec. Peternell Nichols
20 Dec. Allce Williams*

ANNO 1644.

26 Dec. John Leeckey
10 Dec. John Gommo
19 Dec. Anies Leeckey
15 Feb. Honnor Moyle, widow
22 Feb. John Allien
4 Mar. Elizabeth Rowse, widow
7 Mar. Heneney Moyle
18 Mar. Susan Evans†

ANNO 1645.

28 Mar. Joice d. of Archibald Rowse
18 April Cheston the wife of Theodorus Harvy
1 May Rozee d. of Henry Bligh
2 May Ellenor Morcomb
2 May Michaell s. of Mich. Davy
9 May Archibald Rowse
13 May Joane d. of Reskymer Sprey
29 May Mellier wife of Jo. Geene
1 June Patience Cocking
4 June John s. of David Larence of Pearan
14 June Remphrey Michell
10 July Grace wife of Degory Marsiall
20 July Jane Moyle
20 July ffrances d. of Thomas & Grace Littacott
29 July Jane wife of John Staple
10 Aug. Richoe Pollard
13 Aug. John s. of John Kendall‡ & Grace his wife
29 Aug. Thomas Nicholas
30 Aug. Judeth d. of Edward Hoblyn,§ Esq.
3 Sep. John s. of Henry & Thomazin Brey
9 Sep. Jo. Staple
1 Dec. William Bewis

* Here, in the original, come the weddings, after which follow two or three years of baptisms, weddings, and burials, very irregularly kept. The year 1643 is altogether wanting, also parts of 1642 and 1644.

† The foot of a page, and signed J. Beauford, rector, Richard Rowse and William Lanyon, churchwardens.

‡ Query if this John Kendall the father was not the John aged 19 at the Heralds' Visitation of 1620, son of Thomas Kendall of Treworgie by his wife Dorothy, daughter and heir of Thomas Cosworth of Cosworth.

§ By his wife Mary, daughter and coheiress of Robert Apley of Barnestaple.

2 Dec. Joane d. of Richard & Joane Copithorne
15 Dec. Jo. Day,* gen.
17 Dec. Thomas s. of Richard Hawke
26 Jan. Geo. Veale
31 Jan. Elizabeth the wife of Richard Cornish
3 Feb. Sissilla Hann
16 Mar. Thomsin Strongman, widdow

ANNO 1646.

26 Mar. Henry s. of John & Grace Jenkyn
29 Mar. Richard s. of John Daye, merch.
30 April Marke s. of Jane Facy
6 May Thomas Allen
13 May Alice Langdon
15 May Joane wife of Edward Knight
22 May Undie Amie Vivian
16 July Sibella d. of Reskim[r] Sprey, junr., & Jone his wife
30 July John base s. of Eliz. Gillingame
5 Aug. Ann West
3 Sep. Ellinor Steephens
5 Sep. Richard Hawke†
5 Sep. Thomas Tyer
6 Sep. Joane wife of Richard Langdon
1 Oct. John base s. of Judeth Harvey
8 Oct. *(blank)* s. of Thomas Endry
15 Oct. Humphrey the s. of Richard Edwards
29 Oct. Richard the s. of Hugh & Katherne Sprey
3 Nov. Richard Dunne
3 Dec. Thomas s. of W[m] & Lowdy Cockyn
10 Dec. Ruth d. of Jerman & Honour Retallack
17 Dec. Alice Donacomb
1 Jan. John s. of Robert Berry
21 Jan. Mary d. of Anthony & Janiver Pollewyn
23 Jan. Julyan wife of William Rowse
23 Jan. Winifred Husband
27 Jan. Constance Thomas
10 Feb. Richoe wife of John Mayow
24 Feb. Elizabeth wife of Lallow Nicholas
12 Mar. William Taylor
16 Mar. Elizabeth d. of John & Jane Jane

ANNO 1647.

29 Mar. William White
1 April James Oxnam
7 April Richard Polkinghorne
14 April Joane wife of John Lawry
25 April Mary Duggo
1 May Lowdy wife of Walter Vivian*
18 May William Trekeane
27 May Thomas Baylie
1 June Joane Bishop
16 June Elizabeth wife of Thomas Allen
15 Aug. Thomas s. of Adam† & Jone Day
17 Sep. Ann wife of Henry Rowse
4 Oct. Honour Danger
28 Oct. Francis Trehemban
17 Nov. Mary wife of John Retallack
24 Nov. Francis Tome
29 Nov. William Nankevall
10 Dec. William s. of John & Eliz. Williams
17 Dec. William Cockin, jun[r]
21 Dec. Thomas s. of Gilbert & Judeth Calway
29 Dec. John Adams
18 Jan. Thomas Oxnam
21 Jan. John s. of Xtopher & Peternell Hendy
23 Jan. Annis Trenhayle
28 Jan. John Treneage
1 Feb. Thomas s. of Mathew Allen
6 Feb. Philip Moore
13 Feb. Jane Edgecombe
18 Feb. Barbara Joll
28 Feb. Rachall Arundell,‡ widd.
9 Mar. Tho. Retallack

ANNO 1648.

25 Mar. David Floyd
29 Mar. Catherine d. of Hen. & Mary Tregeere
1 April Nicholas s. of W[m] & Anstes Thomas
2 April Philip d. of James & Eliz. Moyle
11 April Lallow Nicholas

* John Day of Tresadderne, churchwarden in 1637. Mr. John Day gave by will £5 to the poor of the parish, 1646.—Green Book.

† Richard Hawke in 1630, as one of four of the ancient men of the parish, elected William Kete, gent., to be one of the twelve men in place of Richard Carter, Esq., deceased. Richard Hawke churchwarden in 1637.—Green Book.

* Walter Vivian and Loveday Carlyon. See marriages, 1630.

† Adam Day, gent., one of the twelve men in 1650.—Green Book.

‡ She was sister to Sir Giles Mompesson, and relict of Thomas Arundell, Esq., of Trevithick in St. Columb, who died in 1633 (see note to his burial). They had several children, of whom Thomas and William both left issue.

25 April John base s. of Ann Veale
4 Mar. Elizabeth d. of John & Eliz. Lawry
5 Mar. Jane d. of John & Catherine Brewer
15 Mar. Thomas Calaway
28 June John s. of Robert Drew
5 July Regnald Hawkey
13 July John s. of Richard* & Joane Copithorne
3 Aug. John s. of John & Jane Jane
6 Aug. Joane Tregeare
8 Sep. Barbara wife of Thomas Basely
19 Sep. John s. of George Humphrey†
27 Oct. Honor Rescorla
2 Nov. Henry Littacott
5 Nov. Susan Crewes
6 Nov. Joh s. of John & Susan Hendra
8 Nov. Presilla Jane
20 Nov. Joice the d. of Henry & Joice Rescorla
5 Dec. John Strongman‡
14 Dec. Grace d. of Thomas & Mary Nanparrow
24 Dec. Marke Oliver
7 Jan. William s. of John & Anne Stephens
12 Jan. Michaell Carter,§ gent.
17 Jan. Tho. Dyer
26 Jan. Mary Wills
27 Jan. Giles Dadagell
30 Jan. Olive Brabyn
9 Feb. John Cornish
12 Feb. Mary d. of Henry & Margery Bligh
17 Feb. Charles s. of Michaell Bany
21 Feb. Mary Stephens
28 Feb. Margarite Bawden
3 Mar. Joane Jane
3 Mar. Johes filius mulieris Peregrine (nominis nobis incogniti), baptizæno erat Decimo Die Maii an. dm. 1601, P. J. W. curate, St. Columbe Maioris, in Domo Thomæ Merrifeild, gent.‖
10 Mar. Dorothy d. of Wm & Jane Salter
16 Mar. Theophilus Leekey

* Rich. Copithorne, one of the ancient men of the parish in 1629.—Green Book.

† George Humphrey paid rent of shop, 18s. in 1632.—Green Book.

‡ In 1616 Joyce Rowse paid 5s. 4d. owed by her son, John Strongman the younger. See marriages, 7 Aug., 1616.

§ Son of John Carter gent., and his wife, Mary, daughter of Robert Moyle of St. Germans, gent. He died unmarried v.p.

‖ Entered thus in the register.

19 Mar. William Thomas
23 Mar. William Williams
23 Mar. John the s. of Peter & ffrances Rescorla

Anno 1649.

29 Mar. Thomas s. of John & Grace Miller
2 April Jerman Retallack
10 April Thomas s. of Robert & Ebbett Husband
13 April Jane d. of Henry Roe
16 April John Husband
27 April Thomas s. of Tho. Bayley
2 May Willmott Tubb
6 May . . . * wife of Marke Williams
18 May John Jolley†
18 May Eliz. Cornish
22 May Jo. s. of Christopher & Peternell Hendey
26 June John Lawry
27 June Annis Moyle
21 Aug. John Parkyn
4 Sep. Barbara Tifford
4 Nov. Richard Retallack
10 Nov. John s. of Theophilus Lawe
19 Nov. Richard s. of Richard Cornish
27 Nov. . . . . * d. of Ric. Copithorne
3 Dec. Remphrey Moyle
12 Dec. Elizabeth Cowle
30 Dec. ffran. d. of William James
31 Jan. Mary d. of Robert Drew
5 Feb. James Moyle
20 Feb. Henry Rescorla
24 Feb. John s. of John Hendra
27 Feb. Emblyn George
1 Mar. Grace Littacott
16 Mar. Blanch Day
16 Mar. Bridgett Basely

Anno 1650.

28 Mar. Ric. s. of Hen. Nanparow
31 Mar. Honor d. of William James
2 April Ric. s. of Jo. Litticott
4 April Will'm s. of Tho. Rickerd
11 April Wilmot Littacott
15 April Mary d. of Mathew Wills
24 April Eliz. Dancaster
9 May Honor Tresseane
25 May (*blank*) d. of Dorothy Co'mon
15 June Ric. Copithorne
17 June Peternell Trenenge
15 July Mary Dyer
15 Aug. Mathew s. of Ro. Husband

* Obliterated.

† In 1618 John Jolly paid 3s. 4d. not to be warden.

23 Aug. ffran. s. of John Stephens
29 Aug. John s. of Anthony Roe
15 Oct. Margarite Law
9 Nov. Ebott Dungey
16 Nov. Mary d. of Jo. Williams
21 Nov. James Strongman
25 Nov. Henry Trehemban
22 Jan. Joell Juell
25 Jan. Katherine d. of Pascho Laugdon
3 Feb. John Mayhow
9 Feb. Mary Kinge
19 Feb. Katherine Tippett
21 Feb. Elizabeth Merrifeild
6 Mar. John Marshall
23 Mar. Henry Nanparrow
24 Mar. Emanuel Dungey

ANNO 1651.

6 April Mary Cocke
19 April Anne d. of John Steephens
20 April Edward s. of Anthony Pawly
23 April Thomas Basely
26 April Jane d. of Henry Roe
27 April Eliz. d. of Joane Copithorne
30 April Lewis s. of Lewis Godfrey
3 May Jo. s. of Robert Hoblyn,* gen.
25 May Anne Moyle
7 June Katherine Nutton
16 June Emblyn Godfrey
22 June Edward Knight
26 July Edward s. of David Hambly
29 July Edward s. of Ben. Strongman
7 Aug. Marke Jolley
9 Aug. Jane d. of Stephen Lovell
16 Sep. Thomas s. of Mathew Allen
17 Sep. Thomas s. of Thomas Hawke
18 Sep. Anne Troth
11 Oct. Beaton Strongman
14 Oct. Stephen base s. of Thomazine Harvey
27 Oct. Samuel s. of Mr Tho. Trevare
25 Nov. Mary d. of Robert Strongman
9 Dec. Jane wife of Henry Wills
10 Dec. Jane the d. of Ric. & Agnes Moyle
16 Dec. Katherine Libby
26 Dec. Alice Retallack
30 Dec. Eliz. d. of Annastatius Burne
31 Dec. Eliz. d. of John Vivian,† Esq.
11 Jan. Dorothy Roe
13 Jan. Grace d. of James Steephens
20 Jan. Philip wife of John Moyle
10 Feb. Richard Jolley

* By his wife Grace, daughter and coheiress of John Carew, of Penwarne, Esq.

† By his second wife Mary, daughter and coheiress of William Cavell of Treharrock

25 Feb. Honor Beauford
8 Mar. John Oxenam
15 Mar. William Rowse
24 Mar. Honor d. of Tho. John

ANNO 1652.

26 Mar. Margarite the wife of Richard Carter
1 April Beaton d. of Antho. Ellery
3 April Joice wife of Henry Rowse
19 April Henry Lee
26 April William s. of John Watt
29 April Katherine d. of John Sandow
1 May Peternell wife of Jo. Lawe
5 May Jo. s. of Pet. & ffra Rescorla
22 May Will'm Brabyn,* gent.
24 May Grace d. of Luke James
24 May Sissely wife of David Hambly
1 July Em wife of John Hendy
8 Oct. Elizabeth wife of Thomas John
11 Oct. John Carthew
5 Nov David Retallack
16 Dec. Katherine d. of Jo. Roe
25 Dec. Thomas s. of Robert Hoblyn,† gent.
2 Feb John s. of Nich. Basely
10 Feb. John Jane
12 Feb. Anne Humphry

ANNO 1653.

8 April Henry Oliver
8 April Thomas Leckey
11 April Mrs Mary Carter‡
26 April Mary John
26 April Mary Dawe
12 May Richard Vivian,§ gent.
19 May William s. of Josias Day
25 May William Basely
30 June James Jenning
2 Sep. Anthony s. of Isack Jenkyn
3 Sep. Thomas s. of John Lawry
6 Jan. Anne Retallack
16 Jan. Thomas Trekeene
16 Jan. Honor d. of Lewis Godfrey
31 Jan. Richard Cornish

* William Brabyn (son of John Brabyn, gent., and Katherine Carter, his wife), married, 14 Dec., 1613, Radigon, daughter and heiress of Thomas Tonkin, of Trevalack, in St. Kevern, by his first wife, Mary, daughter of Henry Dulyn, of Newton Ferrers, in Devon.

† By his wife, Grace, daughter and coheir of John Carew, of Penwarne, Esq.

‡ She was a daughter of Robert Moyle, of Bake, in St. Germans, by Ann, daughter of Henry Lock, of Acton, co. Middlesex, and wife of John Carter, of St. Columb, gent.

§ Son of Thomas Vivian, gent., of Trenowth, and Ann Lower, his wife. His will, dated 18 April, 1653, names a large number of relations.

2 Feb. Thomas Adams
9 Feb. Anthony s. of Anthony Pollawyn
16 Feb. Richard Hawke
19 Feb. Daniel s. of Humfry Oxnam

ANNO 1654.

26 Mar. Honor d. of George & Honor Champion
27 Mar. Richard s. of Richard Troth
31 Mar. Phillipp Carthewe
12 April Jane Sprey *al's* Ivye
13 April Grace d. of Peter & Elizabeth Warne
13 April John Benallack of Penzance
17 April John Kent
12 May Oliffe wife of Thomas Vincent
13 May Edward Hoblyn,* Esq.
17 May Will'm Cock
23 May Honor Browne
25 May William Cocken
12 June Mary Hoblyn,† widowe
13 June John Jolly
24 June James s. of Gabriel Cock
7 July Thomasine the wief of Henry Bray
10 July Grace d. of Stephen Lovell
10 July John s. of Simon Lae
25 Sep. Richard Trebilcock
30 Oct. John s. of Daniell Couch
6 Nov. Data d. of Luke James
18 Nov. Jane Wescott
20 Nov. James s. of Richard Moyle
23 Nov. Anastatius Burne
26 Nov. John Rous
5 Dec. Joane Adams, widowe
20 Jan. George s. of Richard Troth
21 Jan. Katherine Wills, wid.
29 Jan. Sarah wief of Emmanuel Harvye‡
12 Feb. Peter s. of Peter Jane
17 Feb. Mary Allyn, widow
24 Feb. Henry Oxnam
7 Mar. Alexander Wills
10 Mar. John Cundye
13 Mar. Marie wief of Thomas Napparoe
19 Mar. Patience Tresteane

* He was of Nanswhyden, being son and heir of Thomas Hoblyn, Esq., of Nanswhyden, by his wife, Judeth, daughter and heiress of Edward Trevalcois, of Goran, and married. Mary, daughter and coheiress of Robert Apley, of Barnstaple, which lady was buried just a month after him.

† Daughter and coheiress of Robert Apley, Esq. See preceding note.

‡ Emanuel Harvye paid rent of his shop, 15s. 6d., in 1652.—Green Book.

ANNO 1655.

14 April Elianor d. of William Keate,* gent.
17 April Dorothy wief of John Merifeild
28 April John Evans
2 June Richard Moyle
3 June Beniamyn s. of Beniamyn Harvye
13 June ffrancis s. of John Beafford
17 June Ellenor d. of Beniamyn Harvye
20 June John s. of James Wyett
22 June Sampson Stevens
6 July Hester d. of Susan Lae
7 July Grace d. of James Moyle
21 July John Dyer†
21 July Henry Rickard
21 July Thomas s. of Robert Husband
26 July Margaret Langdon
26 July Richard Litticott
7 Aug. John Bayly
13 Sep. Honour d. of Gabriel Cock
30 Oct. Mary the wief of Nathaniell Adams
15 Nov. Emanuel Harvye
27 Dec. James Trembeth
29 Jan. Peter s. of Peter Calway
29 Jan. ffranis the wief of Peter Rescorlae
4 Feb. Joane d. of William Brym
6 Feb. Elizabeth d. of John Berry
6 Feb. Elizabeth d. of Thomas Merifeild
7 Feb. Henry Nankilly *al's* Rowse
8 Feb. Mary wief of William Brym
24 Feb. Ruthen d. of Richard Slade
22 Feb. Thomas s. of Richard Troth
23 Feb. Richard s. of John Grymes
22 Feb. John Cripps
25 Feb. Jane Tregenza

ANNO 1656.

28 Mar. William s. of William Mill
4 April Honor‡ d. of John Beauford, clerke
7 April Alice the wief of Henry Heycraft
8 April The Lady Arundell§ of Lanherne

* This William Kete was son and heir of Ralph Kete, by his first wife, Ann, daughter of William Arscott, of Holsworthy.

† John Dyer, one of the twelve men in 1650.

‡ Probably by a first wife. See Burials, 1663.

§ She was Elizabeth, daughter of William Brock, and relict of John Arundell, Esq., of Lanherne (buried in 1642), and mother of Sir John Arundell, buried in 1701.

20 April Beaten the wief of Thomas Hawke
21 April Julyan d. of Sampson Rescorla
21 April Peter s. of Henry Trehembam
8 May Margery Wheare
19 May Ann d. of John Beauford, clerke
28 May William s. of Thomas Rickard
29 May Joane d. of Anthony Pawlye
2 June Gilbert s. of Humfry Oxnam
4 June Richard Retallack
6 June Catherine Williams
9 June Francis s. of Francis Richards
13 June Thomas s. of Humphry Harvye
11 July Thomas George
12 July John s. of John Merifeild
13 July Ebbott the wief of Benjamin Harvye
20 July Gilbert s. of Gilbert Calway
21 July Jane Williams
22 July George s. of Stephen Lovell
30 July Nicholas s. of Thomas Langdon
8 Aug. Ebbott d. of Christopher Hendye
9 Aug. Phillippa d. of Robert Hoblyn Esquire*
27 Aug. Mary wief of James Rowse
23 Sep. Henry s. of John Browne
3 Oct. Ollive d. of Hugh Sprey
10 Oct. Jonathan the s. of William Cundy
24 Oct. Thomas Lawrye†
2 Nov. Pascowe Browne
28 Dec. David Hambly
6 Jan. Joslyn d. of Anne Kent
26 Jan. Henry s. of James Rous
2 Feb. Elizabeth Jule, widow
6 Feb. Elizabeth the wief of William Lanyon
19 Feb. George Sprey
27 Feb. John s. of Robert Hoblyn,‡ Esquire
5 Mar. Joane Langdon
21 Mar. John Copithorne

ANNO 1657.

26 Mar. Margery Leekye
29 Mar. James s. of Thomas Bounsell
8 April John Rowse of Nankilly

* By his wife, Grace, daughter and coheiress of John Carew, of Penwarne, Esq.

† Thomas Lawry, one of the twelve men, and Treasurer of the parish in 1631-1645.—Green Book.

‡ By Grace Carew, his wife.

11 April James Wyett
18 April Charitye the wief of Thomas Carter
30 April Jane the wief of Richard Pinnow
19 May Katherine Kentall
8 July Grace d. of Pascowe Brabyn
16 July Ellenor Hawke
18 July Thomas s. of Mathew Allen
21 July Jacob s. of Isaac Jenkyn
5 Aug. Jane Trehare
6 Aug. Mary Tyar
11 Aug. Anne d. of William White
14 Aug. Hugh Sprey
25 Aug. Elizabeth d. of William Cruse
3 Sep. John s. of John Carter, gent.*
22 Sep. John s. of Robert May
1 Oct. John Jolly
7 Nov. Jane the wief of Nicholas Baseley
8 Nov. Anne wief of Thomas Crosman
9 Nov. Thomas Allyn
19 Nov. Alexander s. of Richard Jolly
23 Nov. Joane Williams
19 Nov. Elias s. of Richard Jolly
29 Nov. Honor Carvannell
12 Dec. John Harvye
20 Jan. John Hendye
27 Jan. Joane Williams
4 Feb. Elizabeth d. of John Merifeild
6 Feb. James s. of William Bone
18 Feb. Nicholas Chapell

ANNO 1658.

27 Mar. Reskymer Sprey
27 Mar. Sarah Beckett
29 Mar. Thomas s. of Stephen Lovell
1 April Anthony s. of Anthony Pollawyn
6 April John s. of John Kent
7 April Elizabeth Daw
23 April Barbara the wief of Ralph Williams
26 April Catherine d. of William Arundell,† gent.
30 April Mary d. of Robert Code
3 May Catherine Niclas
9 May Thomas Abram
11 May John s. of Nathaniel Adams
12 May Pascowe s. of John Browne
23 May Martyn s. of Edward Hocken
24 May Barbara d. of Josias Day

* Only son of John Carter and Honor Lawry, his wife; by the death of this John in infancy his sisters became coheiresses to their father.

† By Jane his wife; see his burial in 1675.

27 May Anne d. of John Beauford, clerk
4 June John s. of Richard Moyle
8 June James Jenkyn,* Esquire
25 June Jane Jenkyn† his wief
27 June John Netton
10 July Debora servant to John Munday
6 Aug. Gyles Lovell
19 Aug. Margaret d. of John Hendra
21 Aug. ffrances d. of James Jenkyn, Esqr
28 Aug. Emlyn d. of Lewis Godfrey
2 Sep. John s. of John Williams
19 Sep. Anthony Calway
24 Sep. Mary d. of Robert Hoblyn,‡ Esqr
5 Oct. Rawlinge Merifeild
15 Oct. Jane Benny
19 Oct. Jane d. of John Beauford, clerk
25 Oct. Jenefer d. of Henry Warne§
6 Dec. Jone d. of John Beauford, clerk
9 Dec. Jone James
15 Dec. William Salter
18 Dec. Anthony Pollawyn
29 Dec. Thomas Husband
3 Jan. Edward Langdon
6 Jan. John Lawry
3 Feb. Thomas Bilson
9 Feb. Rose d. of William Edwards
19 Feb. ffrances d. of Agnes Harvye
26 Feb. Philip Calway
8 Mar. Robert Cockyn
17 Mar. Susanna wief of John Hockyn

ANNO 1659.

9 April Susanna wife of Elias Pollard
18 Mar. Alce Merefeild
25 Mar. Walter Sprey
6 May William Vivian‖
16 May Margery Bounsall

* He was son and heir of Peter Jenkyn of Trekenning, by his wife Anne, daughter of Andrew Pomeroy, of St. Columb. He married Jane, daughter of John Fortescue of Filleigh, and she died a few days after her husband. They had issue five daughters, coheirs, viz. :— Anne, married Sir John St. Aubyn, bart.; Mary, married Sir Nicholas Slanninge, knt. and bart.; Katherine, married John Trelawny; Elizabeth, married Sir George Cary of Clovelly; and Frances, died unmarried the same year as her father, on 21 Aug.

† See preceding note.

‡ By Grace Carew his wife.

§ By Diana Philpe his wife. She was twin with Christopher, who married Jane Hichens.

‖ Son of John Vivian of Truan and Mary Cavell his wife.

20 May Mary wief of Thomas Richards
20 May Martyn s. of John Ingland
21 May Thomas Richards the elder
23 May Mary Kelway
3 June Elizabeth Brewer
3 June Jone Pynnoe
13 June Robert West*
24 June Grace Tom
25 June Jone wief of William Jolly
17 July Lewis Salter
21 July Grace Arundell†
30 July Arthur Jolly
11 Oct. Margaret Robins
10 Nov. Mary ffloyd
24 Nov. Anne Kent
9 Dec. Thomas s. of Richard Dancaster
10 Jan. Thomas Tremayne
5 Feb. Rose wief of Richard Edwards
10 Feb. Ruth d. of John Slade
23 Feb. John s. of John Steephens
5 Mar. Joane Lawry the younger
6 Mar. Joane Slade

ANNO 1660.

28 Mar. Loer d. of Gabriel Cocke
29 Mar. John Littacott
7 April Sampson Rescorla
14 April Henry s. of Theophilus Law
19 April Margaret Humphry
24 April Rodger s. of Rodger Jonas
4 May Mathaniell Trembeare
10 May Elizabeth the wief of Gilbert Launder
12 May Elizabeth d. of George Lunye
1 June Grace d. of John Brewer
17 June Mary d. of John Steephens
21 June Margery d. of Giles Edwards
25 June Barbara Oxnam
3 July Honor d. of John Horswell
27 July Edward Guyr of Minver
30 July Peternell Gregor
6 Aug. Anne Baylye
6 Aug. Grace d. of Paschow Brabyn
11 Aug. Edward s. of John & Beaton Merrifeild
15 Aug. Elizabeth d. of Peter Kendall
31 Aug. William s. of Henry Trehemban
21 Sep. Jane wief of Anthony Jenkyn
22 Sep. Christian Sprey
28 Sep. Margaret Wills, widd.
6 Oct. Richard s. of Edward Crawly

* Robert West, churchwarden in 1638.

† She was a daughter of Thomas, son and heir of Thomas Arundell of Trevithick, who was grandson of Sir John Arundell of Lanherne, and Elizabeth Daniel his wife. Her father married at Gorran in 1625, Johanna Pye.

16 Oct. Henry Wills
26 Oct. Richard s. of John Vivian,* Esqr
24 Nov. Mark Williams
5 Dec. John s. of Thomas Wills
22 Dec. John s. of Nathaniel Adams
30 Jan. Grace wief of Mathew Allen
4 Feb. Nicholas Basely
11 Feb. Richard Pinnow
22 Feb. Katherine Stribly
25 Feb. Elizabeth d. of William Merifield
28 Feb. Temperance the wife of Richd Edwards
3 Mar. John s. of William James
5 Mar. Margaret wief of James Watts
22 Mar. Thomazin Skynner

ANNO 1661.

27 Mar. Mary wief of Richard Grea
3 April Annis d. of Hugh Tranerson
5 April William Cocke
20 April Sampson s. of Humphry Trehemban
1 June Richard s. of Richard Grea
10 June Elizabeth d. of John Best
30 June Hannah d. of John Slade
3 Aug. Thomas Didman
13 Aug. John Edwards
18 Aug. Elizabeth Litticott
9 Sep. Richard Langdon
14 Oct. ffrancis Benny
11 Nov. Philip d. of Gilbert Lawnder
16 Nov. Susanna d. of John Lawry
20 Nov. Margaret† wief of William Keate, gent.
20 Nov. Edward s. of Peter Kendall
24 Nov. Avis d. of John Beauford, Rector
23 Nov. Constance d. of Henry Morcombe
10 Dec. Blanch Slader
21 Dec. John Kent
24 Dec. Philip s. of Humphry Oxnam
11 Jan. Samuel s. of John Roe
15 Jan. Susan Hawkey
4 Feb. Mary Coode, wid.
4 Feb. Alice d. of William Merifield
8 Feb. Thomasin Adam, wid.
8 Feb. Margery d. of Henry Tregeare
10 Feb. John Merifield
10 Feb. Elizabeth d. of Ralph Crawley
14 Feb. John Williams
21 Feb. John Slade
21 Feb. Ralph s. of Humphry Trehemban
23 Feb. Mary d. of John Napparrow
8 Mar. Hono^r the wief of Francis Richards
13 Mar. Mary d. of Anthony Roe

ANNO 1662.

27 Mar. Elizabeth the wife of William Randell
2 April Lowdy Olver
6 April Susan d. of Henry Bray
7 April Phillip Trembeer, widdow
4 May Joane d. of Oliver Basely
8 May George Knight
7 June William s. of Thomas Richards
11 June Elizabeth Bowen
12 June Mawde the wief of William Strongman
21 June William s. of Robert Coode
24 June Margrett Cornish, widow
20 July Phillip Nicholls
30 July Edward s. of Thomas Merifeild
20 Aug. Mrs Olive Vivian*
23 Aug. James s. of William Samble
7 Sep. John Geene
3 Nov. The Lady Grace Hals†
16 Nov. Margery the wife of John Thomas
17 Nov. Grace Nutten
21 Nov. William Laugdon
23 Nov. Peter s. of Christopher Inch
10 Dec. Alice d. of William Mill
12 Dec. Joane d. of Pascowe Brabant
13 Dec. Henry Blighe Esqr‡
20 Dec. Mary the wife of Theophilus Law

* By his wife Mary, daughter of Sir John Glanville of Tavistock.

† Her husband, William Kete, was son and heir of Ralph Kete, of St. Columb by Anne Arscott his first wife. Her maiden name does not appear; they had issue, Ralph, William, d. Young, William, Nicholas, George, Jane, Eleanor, and Margaret; of these Ralph died s.p. and William left a son Ralph. See Burials, 1667.

* Named in the will (1617) of Thomas Vivian, and in that of her brother Richard Vivian the elder of St. Columb (1653).

† She was relict of Sir Nicholas Hals, knt., and grandmother of William Hals, the author of a history of Cornwall, who was buried at St. Wenn. 16 July, 1737.

‡ He was the second son of Digory Bligh of Truro, by his wife, daughter of .... Tresillian. He was of Tresaddern in St. Columb Major, and married Margaret ....., by whom he had Gilbert, who had Halwin and Trerowa in Crantock; John, who had Tresaddern; Peter, who had Trevella in Crantock, by the will of their father 16 May, 1663; in it he also names his daughters, Elizabeth and Jenifer.

21 Dec. Stephen s. of Stephen Capell
4 Jan. Joane Edwards, widow
24 Jan. Isack s. of John Mill
31 Jan. Henry Blighe, gent.*
2 Feb. John Moyle
14 Feb. John s. of William Richards
14 Feb. Joane Abraham, widow
16 Feb. Elizabeth wife of Thomas Polkinghorne
21 Feb. Tristram s. of Christopher Hendy
24 Feb. ffrancis Trisk
28 Feb. Katherine wife of John Day, gent.
4 Mar. Stephen s. of Humphry Harvey
8 Mar. fflorence wife of Thomas Gilbert
9 Mar. Mathew base s. of Avis Burlace
16 Mar. Thomas ffosse
20 Mar. Barnabas Betty

ANNO 1663.

6 April Joane d. of John Young
8 April Luke Pollard
11 April Elizabeth the wife of John Williams
14 April Thomas Rickard of Tolskithy
23 April Agnes Young, widow
9 May Agnes d. of Henry Brewer
17 May Ann the wife of John Gillingham
11 June Joane Knight, wid.
14 June Mathew s. of Thomas Wills
14 June Elizabeth wife of John Tenny
18 June Thomas Lawe
19 June Christian Callaway, wid.
23 July Jane d. of John & Grace Miller
28 July Robert s. of Gilbert & Judeth Callaway
19 Aug. Eliz. d. of John & Eliz. Browne
30 Aug. Jane d. of Anthony & Beaton Ellery
4 Sep. Margery d. of Nicholas & Anne Bounsell
1 Sep. John s. of Simon & Honorr Lawe
17 Sep. Thomas s. of Giles & Margery Edwards
19 Sep. Peter Jenkyn,† Esq[r]
21 Sep. ffrances d. of John Beauford, Rector
11 Oct. Anne* the wife of John Beauford, Rector
16 Sep. John s. of Martin Stephens
17 Oct. William Callaway
24 Oct. John Martin
13 Nov. Honor[r] d. of Abraham & Elizabeth Husband
17 Nov. Peter Treneage
4 Dec. Richard s. of Ralph & Eliz. Crawley
22 Dec. Joane the wife of David Walkey
30 Dec. Thomas s. of George & Mary Lune
4 Jan. Peter s. of Christopher & Joane Inch
6 Jan. Elizabeth Williams
12 Jan. Michael Davey
7 Feb. John Kendall
7 Feb. John s. of William & Mary Bone
10 Feb. Anne Harvey
17 Feb. John Metherill
27 Feb. Mary d. of John & Susan Lawrey
29 Feb. Joane d. of Garterid Kent
29 Feb. Sarah d. of Sarah Litticott
11 Mar. Melior the wife of Thomas Withell
17 Mar. ffrancis George *al's* Ben'y
19 Mar. John s. of John & Jane Day
19 Mar. Philip Olver, wid.
20 Mar. Richard Rescorla

W[m]. s. of John Vivian, Esq[r], was buried the 26 June, 1663, being omitted in its right place.†

ANNO 1664.

30 Mar. Thomas Bounsell
30 Mar. . . . .‡ s. of Mary Rickerd
31 Mar. Joane d. of Gilbert & Judeth Callaway
1 April Jacob Punsher
5 Mar. Sarah d. of Theophilus Law
8 Mar. Mary May

* Henry Blighe, one of the twelve men in 1650.—Green Book.

† He was son and heir of James Jenkyn and Katherine, daughter of James Carter, and relict of John Brabyn, gent. He married Anne daughter of Andrew Pomeroy, of St. Columb, by whom he had an only son James, who left issue five daughters and coheirs.

* She seems to have been his first wife, for a marriage license was granted 27 Jan., 1664, between John Beauford, clerk, and Anne, daughter of Henry Nance.

† By his second wife, Mary, daughter of Sir John Glanville, entered thus.

‡ Blank.

12 April Barbara & Elizabeth ds. of Wm & Margt Hawkey
16 April Jane wife of William Arundell, gent.*
16 April Isack s. of Humphry & Sibella Harvey
18 April Grace John, widow
23 April Thomas s. of Richard Rowse
2 May Richard Pinnow
3 May Walter s. of Walter & Jane Tyer
11 May Cheston d. of Richard Rouse
13 May John s. of John & Jane Best
15 May Precilla d. of Peter & ffrancis Callaway
15 May George s. of George & Jane Humphry
25 May William s. of Paschow & Jane Brabant
25 May John s. of Sarah Litticott, wid.
28 May Marrian d. of William & Anne Hockyn
5 June Alice d. of Ralph & Anastatia Chenoweth
5 June Peter s. of Richard & Margaret George
6 June Symon s. of Humphry & Cissily Trebemban
11 June Jane d. of John & Bridgett England
12 June Anne d. of Gartrude Kent, wid.
15 June Anne d. of William & Frances White
7 July Honour Trekeane, widow
7 July William s. of Richard & Margaret George
8 July Frances d. of James & Joane Stephens
10 July Elizabeth d. of Daniel & Elinor Couch
19 July William Bettyson
24 July Elizabeth the wife of Reskymer Allen
29 July Susan the wife of Thomas Richards
5 Aug. John Upcott
17 Aug. George Cundey
18 Aug. Jane d. of Thomas & Mary Westcott
2 Sep. Mary d. of Theophilus Law
5 Sep. Alice the wife of Arthur Common
7 Sep. Em. d. of John & Margarett Truscott
23 Sep. John Mill
30 Sep. George Bayley

* See burial of her husband in 1675.

6 Nov. John s. of Nathaniel & Joane Adam
9 Nov. Bernard s. of Bernard & Elizabeth Rowse
20 Nov. John s. of Nicholas Withell
25 Nov. Patience the wife of George Cropp
1 Dec. Grace d. of Edward & Mary Steephens
5 Dec. Elizabeth the wife of Gabrill Cocke
18 Dec. Jane d. of John & Jane Best
25 Dec. Elizabeth d. of Leonard May
6 Jan. Alice Tonkyn
20 Jan. Henry s. of Gartherid Kent
28 Jan. William s. of Giles & Margery Edwards
2 Feb. Catherine Tyer
5 Feb. Lovdey the wife of William Cockyn
17 Feb. Margaret Browne, widdow
21 Feb. Christopher Inch
28 Feb. Alice Merifield, widdow
1 Mar. Joane d. of Thomas & Marriott Cockyn
6 Mar. Honor d. of Ralph & Joane Lambe
7 Mar. Thomazine the wife of James Cockyn
8 Mar. Maude Hockey, widdow
19 Mar. George s. of John & Grace Luke

ANNO 1665.

27 Mar. Mary & Udy d. & s. of Thomas & Grace Wills
24 April Margery Rawlin, widdow
13 May Andrew Beauford
22 May Jane Litticott
29 May Elizabeth base d. of Olive Williams
10 June Suson wife of John Hendra
20 June Thomas s. of Anthony & Joane Pawley
9 July Hannah d. of John & Thomasine Berry
26 July Robert Drew senr
24 Aug. Thomas s. of Isack & Elizabeth Nicholls
17 Sep. English Robins
29 Sep. Anne d. of John & Katherine Retallack
10 Oct. Anne wife of Francis Hearle, Rector of St. Erme
19 Oct. Grace d. of John & Thomasine Arthur
31 Oct. Thomazin Edwards, widdow
6 Nov. Margery Cockin, widdow

10 Nov. Alice Rescorla, widdow
27 Dec. Marriott d. of Paschow & Jane Brabyn
27 Dec. Peter* s. of Richard Vivian, gent.
29 Dec. Elizabeth the wife of Thomas Salter
11 Jan. John Allen
12 Jan. Mary d. of Peter & Joane Gibbs
2 Feb. John Merifield
20 Feb. Jane d. of John & Jane Best
28 Feb. Wilmot Cockyn, widdow
3 Mar. Mary Allen, widdow
5 Mar. Stephen Lovell†
17 Mar. George s. of George Crapp
21 Mar. Arthur Boddy

ANNO 1666.

4 April Mary d. of George & Alice Daye
5 April Joane wife of Ralph Lambe
9 April Peternell the wife of Richard Nicholl
27 April Elizabeth Dadgell, widdow
30 April Elizabeth Westcott
9 May ffrancis s. of Elias Pollard
10 May Edward Tubb
23 May Philip s. of Daniell James
2 June James s. of William & Alice Beauford
2 June Elizabeth Mill
9 June James Watts
19 June Catherine d. of John Luke
1 July Charity d. of Thomas Hocky
8 July Em. wife of W[m] Laniou‡
13 July Catherine d. of Peter Callaway§
17 July Joane d. of Henry Gill
18 July Anne d. of John Rowe
9 Aug. Elizabeth d. of Stephen Banger
22 Aug. John s. of William Samble
1 Sep. Peter Rescorla
18 Sep. Elizabeth Moyle, widdow
23 Sep. Edward s. of Edward Lawry
26 Sep. Elizabeth d. of Nicholas Jane
28 Sep. John Rowe
4 Oct. Anthony Ellery
13 Oct. Honor d. of James Rowse
19 Oct. Gilbert Richards

* Son of Rich. Vivian. See p. 220.
† Stephen Lovell paid rent of his shop. 5s., in 1639; in 1644, 10s.; in 1656, 24s. 9d.—Green Book.
‡ In 1644 William Lanyon paid rent of his shop, 20s.—Green Book.
§ In 1645 Peter Callaway paid rent of his shop, 10s.

17 Nov. Susan Williams
5 Dec. Phillip d. of Gidion Cockyn
11 Dec. John s. of James Hawkey
5 Jan. Hester d. of George Crapp
20 Jan. Anne d. of W[m] Allen
6 Feb. Henry s. of John Burnard
5 Mar. James s. of John Napparrow
12 Mar. Bridgett Allen
20 Mar. Elizabeth d. of Paschow Brabyn
24 Mar. Elizabeth Trehemban

ANNO 1667.

25 Mar. Honor d. of Richard Moyle
30 Mar. Richard Troth*
1 April John s. of John & Jane Daye
15 April Honor d. of John Metherill
16 April Thomas s. of Stephen Stephens
26 April William Hawkyn
1 May William Keate,† gent.
1 May Anne d. of Thomas Hawke
2 May John Tenny
18 May Richard Nicholls
26 May Thomas Bayley
26 May Alice Burlace
12 June Mary d. of John Brewer
12 June Phillip d. of John Brewer
4 July John Arnold
10 July Anne wife of Martyn Rowe
3 Aug. Hester Rescorla, widdow
3 Aug. Catherine Rickerd
14 Aug. John Dungey
15 Aug. Jacob Bayley
23 Aug. Hannah d. of John Berry
5 Sep. Elizabeth d. of John Best
14 Sep. Duens‡ d. of John Dodge, Esq.
19 Sep. Richard Daye
2 Oct. Ebbott wife of Robert Husband
5 Nov. Robert s. of Remphry Rowse
12 Nov. John Cannidge
13 Nov. Maude d. of James Stephens
30 Nov. Joane Pollard
7 Dec. Jane Pierce
18 Dec. Joane Upcott
26 Dec. Alice d. of Ralph Chenoweth
19 Jan. Joane West
30 Jan. Thomas Litticott
31 Jan. John Browne
9 Feb. Charles s. of John England

* In 1642 Richard Troth paid rent of his shop 6s. 8d.—Green Book.
† See note, p. 221. He was one of the twelve men, and Treasurer of the parish in 1651.
‡ John Dodge, Esq., and Dionyse, daughter of the Rt. Worshipful Sir Francis Glanville, Knt., married at Tavistock in 1635.

14 Feb. Mary White
14 Feb. Richard s. of Edward Crawly
19 Feb. Anthony s. of Anthony Rowe
27 Feb. Elizabeth Stephens
18 Mar. Mary d. of Thomas Westcott
24 Mar. Honor d. of John Merifield

ANNO 1668.

27 Mar. Anne Beckett
5 April George s. of Giles Edwards
12 April Grace Kendall
24 April Jane d. of Tho. Michell
29 April John s. of John Brewer
11 May Mary Hawkey
25 May Cissily wife of Richard fford
1 June William s. of Wm Jolley
4 June Jane Allen
18 June Anthony Jenkyn
27 June Ureilla the wife of Edward Chapell
28 June ffrancis s. of Robert Hoblyn,* Esq. & Grace his wife
6 July Elizabeth Wills, widdow
3 Aug. John s. of William Evelin
18 Aug. Christopher Morcombe
6 Sep. John Western
19 Sep. Marryan the wife of Daniell Phillips
3 Oct. Joane Jolley, widd.
6 Oct. Honor d. of John Rouse
9 Oct. John s. of James Metherill
11 Oct. Margaret the wife of John Truscott
22 Oct. Richard Richards
23 Nov. Elizabeth d. of John Browne
27 Nov. Susan wife of John Lawry
29 Nov. John Thomas
13 Dec. Julian Baylye
31 Dec. Hopson Davy
18 Jan. John Davis
19 Jan. Elizabeth the wife of Richard Hawke
29 Jan. Richard† s. of John Carter, Esqre

* He was twin with Carew Hoblyn, whose only daughter and heiress, Mary, married to Sir Vyal Vyvyan, Bart.

† This Richard was aged two years at the Heralds' visitation, in 1620, but this baptism does not appear in the register; he was a J.P., and M.P. for Mitchell. He sold the greater part of his estate to his brother, John, and died s.p., having married Elizabeth King, *alias* Lucas, *alias* Shepard, of London. His father, John Carter, Esq., of St. Columb, who had married Mary Moyle (see her bur. in 1653), was buried, according to Col. Vivian's pedigree, 2 Feb., 1668, but the entry does not appear to be in the Register.

13 Feb. William s. of Edward Crewse
20 Feb. Maudlyn d. of Wm Tenny
2 Mar. Joane the wife of Gilbert Coode
4 Mar. Richard s. of Edward Merifeild
7 Mar. Jane d. of Gilbert Coode
7 Mar. Rebecca Baylife
12 Mar. John s. of Gilbert Coode
16 Mar. Phillip d. of Tho. Crewse
21 Mar. Mary d. of Ralph Chenoweth
22 Mar. Martin Rowe
24 Mar. Alice Strongman

ANNO 1669.

26 Mar. Mary* the wife of John Vivian, Esqre
4 April Mary d. of John Tenny
5 April Nicholas s. of Nathaniel Adams
12 April Elizabeth d. of George Luney
20 April Joane d. of Ralph Crawley
19 May Jane Beauford
23 May John Retallack
23 May John Steephens
23 May John s. of Richard Rouse
24 May John s. of Robert Coode
25 May Rose Trebilcock
27 May Honr d. of Wm: Cockyn
31 May Mary d. of Wm: Cockyn
2 June Elizabeth d. of Arthur Jolley
19 June Jane Salter, widdow
2 July Wm Keate,† gent.
5 July Elizabeth d. of Nicholas Bounsell
25 July Rose Williams
27 July Dorcas Copithorne
1 Aug. Anne d. of Henry Brush
18 Aug. Thomas Richards
30 Sep. James Rowse‡
16 Oct. Barbara the wife of Henry Brewer
20 Oct. John s. of Wilm Delbridge
1 Nov. Christopher Rawlinge
2 Nov. Julian wife of Richard Bond

* She was a daughter of Sir John Glanville, Knt., and second wife of John Vivian, of Truan, Esq.,; married at Tavistock, 18 Oct., 1642.

† He was son of William, son and heir of Ralph Kete and Ann Arscott, and married, 1st, ... daughter of Richard James, of Crantock, by whom he had an only child, Ralph. He married, 2ndly, 13 July, 1667, at Cubert, Isabell, daughter of . . . . . Rillston, who survived him without issue.

‡ James Rowse, one of the twelve men in 1650 and in 1669, when he died, and Hen. Dyer, gent., was elected in his place.

3 Nov. Nicholas Bounsell
10 Nov. James Cockyn
30 Nov. Mary* d. of John Vivian, Esq[r]
30 Nov. Hon[r] Renorden
1 Dec. John Younge
29 Dec. Charles Thomas
16 Jan Edward s. of Edward Crawly
17 Jan. Jane d. of W[m]: White
26 Feb. John s. of Stephen Cavell
8 Mar. Joane Pollard

ANNO 1670.

27 Mar. Alice Gilbert
29 Mar. ffrances the wife of John Brabyn, gent.
29 Mar. Jane John
23 May Samuel† s. of Robert Hoblyn, Esq[re], & Grace his wife
26 May Elinor wife of Thomas Geach
29 May Hugh s. of W[m] Cocke
9 June Henry Thomas
13 June William Cockyn
16 June Emblyn d. of John & Jane Daye
18 June William Crewse
25 June Audry wife of Richard fford
5 July Stephen Banger
18 July Elizabeth d. of Giles Edwards
21 July George Champion‡
6 Aug. Dorothy d. of Richard Slade
19 Aug. Grace Lavers
22 Aug. Grace Litticott
24 Aug. Gidion Cockyn
5 Sep. Elizabeth wife of John Rowse
13 Sep. Joane Beauford,§ widd.
15 Sep. Richard Slade
21 Sep. William s. of Robert Skynner
26 Sep. Mary wife of Henry Tregeere
2 Oct. Henry Litticott
2 Oct. Joane Betty, widd.
2 Oct. Jane d. of George Luney
9 Oct. Richard Hawke, blacksmyth
16 Oct. John Rowse of Trevarren
22 Nov. Anne wife of W[m] Jenninge
22 Dec. John s. of Edward & Margery Lawry
28 Dec. John s. of John & Alice Pierce
5 Jan. Rebecca d. of Walter & Anstis Pierce
15 Jan. Henry Upcott
24 Jan. Abraham Husband
27 Jan. John s. of John Truscott
2 Feb. Jane Hicks
4 Feb. Richard s. of Nathaniel Adams
14 Feb. Jane d. of Henry Thomas
17 Feb. Anthony s. of Thomas Pollowyn
1 Mar. John s. of James Rowse
1 Mar. John s. of Thomas Chapell
3 Mar. Anne the wife of Stephen Steephens
12 Mar. Ralph Keate,* gent.
13 Mar. Ralph Williams
14 Mar. William s. of Walter Tyer
14 Mar. Elizabeth d. of John Retallack

ANNO 1671.

27 Mar. Abell s. of John Lockett
7 April Margaret Libby
10 April Eliz. wife of Walter Coryton
10 April John s. of Richard Rawe
12 April Alice Jolley, widow
24 April Ralph s. of George Luney
27 April Stephen s. of Richard Lovell
1 May William s. of Richard Clemow
2 May Hughe Blake
8 May Jane d. of John Brabyn
11 May Joane Dungey, widdow
17 May Eliz. d. of W[m] Delbridge
24 May Jane Haycreft
25 May Cissily Gross
27 May James s. of James Moyle
31 May Grace wife of Robert Cock
1 June Symon s. of Henry Trehemban
6 June John s. of W[m] Trennennis
8 June Samuel s. of Edward Crewse
14 June ffrancis s. of John Tenny
22 June Mary d. of Richard Rawe
23 June Anne d. of John Pollard of this parish and Loveday the d. of Thomas Rosevere of St. Enoder, were

* By his second wife, Mary, daughter of Sir John Glanville, Knt.

† By his wife, Grace, daughter of John Carew, of Penwarne. Baptized in 1669.

‡ In 1643 George Champion paid rent for his shop. 10s.—Green Book.

§ Joane Beauford, widow, was a witness to the will of Olive Vivian (daughter of Tho. Vivian and Ann Lower), in 1662; her brother, Richard Vivian, names in his will his godson "Edw. Beauford."

* Third son of Ralph Kete, of St. Columb, and Ann Arscott, his wife. He married, first, Gertrude, daughter of . . . . . . by whom he had issue, John, Ralph, Philip, Ann, and Gertrude, married 3 April, 1665, at Cubert, to Reskymer Allen. He married, secondly, Grace, daughter of . . . . . . but she died s.p.; her will, dated 4 April, 1681, was proved 21 Oct., 1685.

both most barbarously murthered the day before in the house of Capt Peter Pollard att the Bridge, by one John the sone of Humphrey & Cissily Trehemban of this parish, about 11 of the clock in the forenoone, upon a market day*

28 June Thomas s. of Thomas Crewse
3 July Thomazine d. of Henry Morcombe
4 July Mary d. of Henry Gill
10 July Wm s. of Ralph Chenoweth
15 July John Lawe
21 July Joane Petherick
4 Aug. Honr d. of Richard & Emblyn Edwards
6 Aug. Eliz. wife of Edward Pollowyn
16 Aug. Maude wife of Thomas Kestlack
18 Aug. Anthony Michell
23 Aug. John Dyer
27 Aug. Thomas Michell
4 Sep. Henry Trehemban
8 Sep. Catherine the wife of Philip Oxnam
21 Sep. Anne wife of Thomas Pollard
5 Oct. George Luney
3 Nov. Henry Morcombe
8 Nov. John Rowe
11 Nov. Olive Cornish
14 Nov. Nicholas s. of Amey Basely, wid.
19 Nov. David Walkey
21 Nov. Margaret the wife of Richard George
26 Nov. ffrance s. of Edward Crewse
13 Dec. William s. of Wm Merifield
6 Jan. James s. of Robert Litticot
8 Feb. ffrances Strongman
9 Feb. John Brabyn, junr
14 Feb. Luke s. of Luke Edmonds
20 Feb. Gilbert s. of John Richards
24 Feb. Margarett† d. of Sir ffrancis Godolphin, knight of the Bathe, deceased
25 Feb. Hugh Harvey
27 Feb. John Coode
11 Mar. John s. of John Blighe,* gent.
15 Mar. Patience Williams
20 Mar. Richard Steevens
21 Mar. Richard Cornish

ANNO 1672.

29 Mar. Giles Truscott†
31 Mar. Jane d. of Michaell Cowlinge
5 April Joane Cornish, widdow
19 April Jane wife of John Best
22 April Honor Dyer, widdow
1 May Jane wife of Adam Daye, gent.
7 May Mary d. of William & Honor Tinney
13 May Elizabeth wife of Richard Blake
21 May Anne d. of John Horswell
22 May Thomas s. of Richard Williams
24 May Elizabeth Crewes, widdow
27 May Anne Stephens, widdow
25 June Margarett wife of Charles Kinge
28 June Julian d. of Adam Daye, gent.
4 July John s. of John & Anne Merifield
16 July Judeth d. of Robert Hoblyn,‡ Esq., & Grace his wife
24 July Richard Edwards the younger
26 July John§ s. of John Carter, gt, deceased
29 July Emblin d. of John & Anne Merifield
4 Aug. Matilda‖ d. of Reskimer & Gertrid Allen
19 Aug. James s. of Josias & Dorothy Daye

* Thus entered; traditions relative to the murder still exist in the parish. The Bridge referred to is at the lower end of the town.

† She was a sister of Sidney, 1st Earl Godolphin. Her father Sir Francis (son and heir of Sir William Godolphin, of Godolphin, by Thomasine, daughter and heiress of Thomas Sidney, of Wrington, co. Norfolk), married Dorothy, daughter of Sir Henry Berkeley, of Yarlington, co. Somers.

* This John Blighe, gent., was son of John Blighe, of Tresoddern, in St. Columb, and to which the son succeeded by his father's will, dated 28 Jan., 1663.

† Giles Truscott, churchwarden in 1638.—Green Book.

‡ Baptized in 1649, her mother was daughter and coheiress of John Carew, of Penwarne.

§ His mother was Mary, daughter of Robert Moyle, of St. German's, gent. He married in 1647, Honor, daughter of Sampson Lawry (see note p. 152 *ante*.) He left issue three daughters, coheiresses, viz., Honor, born in 1650, married, in 1676, William Silly; Mary, born in 1655, married, 1688, Thomas Hoblyn, gent., of Tresadderne, issue an only son, John Hoblyn, of Kenwyn, from whom descends the present William Paget Hoblyn, of The Fir Hill, Esq., M.A., J.P.; and Jane, born 1661. married, 1684, Giles Risedon. See Reg. Ext. appended.

‖ Reskimer Allen and Gertrude, daughters of Ralph Kete and Gertrude his wife, married at Cubert, 3 April, 1665.

19 Aug. Anne d. of Thomas & Hester Merifield
27 Aug. James s. of Ellonor Rowse, widow
4 Sep. John England
6 Sep. Richard s. of Richard & Emblin Slade
24 Sep. Ralph s. of Reskimer & Gartrid Allan
29 Sep. Samuel* s. of Henry & Elizabeth Jolley
13 Oct. Henry Gill
21 Oct. Cisily Drew
24 Oct. George Crapp
26 Oct. William Beauford
29 Oct. John s. of Thomas Callaway
9 Nov. Bridget wife of Richard Raw
10 Nov. John s. of Thomas & Eliz. Callaway
14 Nov. Anthony s. of Simon & Mary Trehemban
6 Dec. Margaret Blighe, widdow
6 Dec. Mary Roach
7 Dec. Mary d. of Henry Gill, deceased
22 Dec. John s. of Simon & Honor Lee
1 Jan. Gilbert Bligh†
6 Jan. John Watts
8 Jan. fflorence Sprey, widdow
25 Jan. Jane d. of George & Mary Luney
12 Feb. John s. of Peter & Jane Bligh
22 Feb. Mary d. of James & Mary Merifield
28 Feb. Gilbert Launder
3 Mar. John ffriggens
7 Mar. Johan d. of Richard & Emblin Slade
11 Mar. Junifer the wife of Lawrence Kendall
19 Mar. Mary Wills, wid.

ANNO 1673.

28 Mar. Diana wife of Henry Warne
29 Mar. Peter Bligh, gent.‡

* In 1666 Richard Jolly paid for the rent of his shop, 8s., 13s. 4d. being allowed for repairs, Henry Jolly to have the same next year at 28s.—Green Book.

† He was son of Henry Blighe, of Tresaddern, and Margaret his wife; he had, by his father's will, Halwin and Trevowa.

‡ He was son of Henry Blighe, of Tresadderne, in St. Columb, and Margaret his wife; he had, by the will of his father, Trevella in Crantock.

31 Mar. Paschow Vivian, gent.*
12 April Peter Retallack
17 April John Miller
17 April Joan Leckye
23 April Grace Miller
27 April Hugh Trethue
4 May William Dellbrige
4 May John s. of Christopher & Peternell Ulcock
7 May Edward s. of Edward & Mariery Lawrye
23 May Richard s. of Henry & Joan Trehemban
25 May Ralfe Crawlye
31 May Grace Steephens, widd.
16 June Alice d. of Remphry & Jane Rowse
26 June Rebecka Bayly
17 July Richard Moyle
21 July Dorothy Lander
28 July Elloner Rowse, widd.
4 Sep. James s. of George & Mary Lunye
8 Sep. Mary Glydon, widowe
11 Sep. Nehemiah s. of John Best
13 Sep. Richard Pinnowe
14 Sep. Honor Lee, widowe
28 Sep. John s. of Petherick & Joane Gilbert
1 Oct. Thomazine d. of ffrancis Richards
2 Oct. Peter Gibbs
4 Oct. James s. of Peeter & Jane Bligh
27 Oct. Alice Drewe, widd.
28 Oct. ffrances d. of ffrancis & Mary Manell
31 Oct. John Edwards of Roch
6 Nov. Joan d. of Elizabeth Cralye
11 Nov. Richard Tinne
17 Nov. Edward base s. of Thomazin Richards
21 Nov. Mary d. of Elizabeth Cralye, widdow
12 Dec. Henry base s. of florence Trenimes
20 Dec. Thomas ye base s. of Millson Merefeld
11 Jan. Bridget England, widd.
20 Jan. Elizabeth Truscott, widd.
8 Feb. Ann Williams, widdow
12 Feb. James Daye,† gent.

* He was a son of Thomas Vivian, of Trenowth, gent., and Ann Lower his wife. He married, in 1601, Mary Flammacke, gent., widow.

† James Day, gent., one of the twelve men in 1650-1672.—Green Book.

12 Feb. Hals s. of John & Jane Daye
14 Feb. Francis Thomas
3 Mar. Elizabeth d. of Thomas & Elizabeth Chapell
8 Mar. Beniamin Strongman
16 Mar. Luke James
24 Mar. Robert Cock

ANNO 1674.

8 April Judeth d. of Christopher Wolcock
19 April John s. of Robert & Moete Skynner
22 April Thomas Finch,* gent.
26 April Mary wife of Henry Cock
26 April Joan wife of John Lockett
25 May Agnes d. of Thomas & Clary George
19 June Jane d. of Giles & Margery Edwards
20 June Alice wife of John Pierce
22 June Lovedy Watts
22 June Elizabeth d. of Richard Moyle, deceased
14 July Richard s. of Paschow & Cisily Williams
29 July Grace wife of Richard Hawke
31 July John s. of John & Matilda Dunkyn
7 Aug. Mary Lecky, widdow
19 Sep. Walter Coryton
20 Sep. Jane wife of George Reignolds
24 Oct. Mary Strongman, widdow
22 Nov. Dorothy Langdon, widdow
22 Nov. Philip White
15 Dec. Elizabeth d. of William Delbridg, deceased
18 Dec. Prudence d. of John & Abigall Udy
18 Jan. Joice wife of William Cundey
28 Jan. Cissly d. of Thomas West
29 Jan. Henry Husband
2 Feb. Honor wife of Thomas Prestridg
28 Feb. Elizabeth d. of Ralph Crawly, deceased
3 Mar. Elizabeth d. of William & Grace Edwards
4 Mar. Ralph s. of Ralph Crawly, deceased
5 Mar. John & Richard s. of John & Margery Williams
7 Mar. Alice Richards, widdow
23 Mar. Peter s. of Peter Rescorla, deceased

ANNO 1675.

28 Mar. Elizabeth d. of Anthony & Mary Callaway
30 Mar. John Edwards
6 April John s. of Stephen & Joan Stephens
13 April Pascas wife of Henry Roe
20 April Anne Baly, widdow
14 May Lewis Godfrey, gent.
31 May Wilmot Hawk, widow
21 June Richard s. of Richard & Beaton Clemow
21 June Anne Allyn
22 June Josias Day
23 June Grace d. of William & Grace Edwards
5 July William s. of Richard & Emblyn Slade
8 July Richard s. of John & Honor Richards
11 July William s. of William & Mary Lanyon
29 Aug. Mary d. of Robert & Maud Skynner
25 Sep. Thomas s. of Richard & Maud Skynner
15 Oct. John Pierce *al's* Naparrow
28 Oct. Mary d. of Samuel & Jane Pryn
1 Nov. Richard Wills
27 Nov. Thomazine d. of Peter & Honor Cocking
28 Nov. Barbara d. of Thomas Prestridge
11 Dec. Pascow Williams
12 Dec. Joan Strongman, widdow
3 Dec. Margaret d. of William & Grace Edwards
14 Dec. William Arundell,* Esq.
27 Dec. M[rs] Margaret Woone, widow
5 Jan. Martyn Dunnacomb
17 Jan. John s. of John & Catherine Moyle
17 Jan. John base s. of Grace Tonkyn
24 Jan. Jane d. of Richard & Mary Lovell
29 Jan. Luke s. of Luke & Honor Giles
9 Feb. James s. of Daniell & Hester Ropson

* James Finch, of St. Germans, appears in the list of those whose claims were disallowed by the Heralds at Bodmin, 30 Sept., 1620, as "Ignobilis."

* He was son of Thomas Arundell, of St. Columb, and Rachael Mompasson his wife. See note, p. 213. He married Jane, daughter of . . . , by whom he had issue Catherine and William.

12 Feb. Honor Mayhow
19 Feb. Elizabeth d. of Richard & Christian Retallack
23 Feb. Elizabeth d. of Nathaniel & Johan Adams

ANNO 1676.

30 Mar. Thomas s. of Nathaniel & Johan Adams
25 April William s. of William & Grace Edwards
9 May William s. of Simon & Alice Rawling
11 May Mary Moyle, widow
24 May Frances the wife of Richard Colley
2 June Priscilla Martyn, widdow
4 July Theodosia d. of Josias & Elizabeth Grimes
13 July Charles Thomas
24 July George Humphry
29 July Bernard Salter
5 Aug. Johan Jenkyn, widdow
24 Aug. Bridget England, widdow
9 Sep. Thomas Kestlack
29 Sep. Johan Trehemban, widdow
30 Sep. Mary d. of William & Jane Eveling
1 Oct. Martyn Stephens
10 Oct. Thomas s. of Peter & Honor Cocking
12 Oct. William Michell
22 Nov. John Hicks
29 Nov. Margarite the wife of Thomas Michell
7 Dec. John Jane
10 Dec. Alice Harvey
10 Dec. Isaac s. of Isaac & Elizabeth Nicholls
24 Dec. Florence the wife of William Minnow
4 Jan. Alice d. of Walter & Eustis Pierce
9 Jan. Michaell Strongman*
9 Jan. Rebecka d. of Walter & Eustis Pierce
17 Jan. John s. of Robert & Jane May
1 Feb. Margery wife of John Tyack
22 Feb. Richard Williams
22 Feb. William Minnow
24 Feb. Thomas Pollard
17 Mar. Anne Geene
18 Mar. Mary d. of William & Mary Lanyon

* Michael Strongman paid rent of his shop 11s 2d. in 1655.—Green Book.

ANNO 1677.

1 April Humphry Chaple
9 April John s. of John & Anne Merifield
11 April Edward s. of Edward & Margery Lawry
14 April Thomas Prestridge
17 April Peter s. of Nicholas & Jane Bounsell
18 April John Tyack, gent
19 April W^m s. of Marke & Anne Tyer
29 April John s. of Philip & Johan Kinge
1 May Mary wife of John Allyn
8 May Peter s. of Sr John Seyntaubyn,* barronet
9 May Francis s. of Thomas & Grace Crewes
15 May Mary d. of William & Mary Bone
16 May Tobias base s. of Christian Michell
21 May Arthur s. of W^m & Honor Jolly
23 May John s. of Wm Parkyn
2 June Martyn Strongman
5 June Pentecost Cocking
7 June Wm Cocking
13 June James s. of Robert & Jane Litticott
13 June Ralph s. of John & Margery Williams
15 June Margery Grace, widdow
26 June Enstis the wife of Ralph Chenoweth
29 June Bridget d. of Wm Crewes, deceased
9 July Thomas s. of Thomas & Elizabeth Scaberio
17 July Jacob s. of Jacob Puncher, deceased
19 July Anne d. of Thomas & Elizabeth Scaberio
20 July John s. of John & Johan Truscott
22 July John s. of Daniell & Elloner Couch
24 July Elizabeth d. of Nathaniel & Margarite Champion
3 Aug. Thomas Merifield, gent.
7 Aug. Margery wife of John Burne
7 Aug. Petherick s. of Petherick & Johan Gilbert

* This Sir John St. Aubyn was the first baronet. See note, p. 60.

13 Aug. Frances d. of Thomas & Alice Stephens
25 Aug. Anne d. of Thomas Litticott
2 Sep. Thomazine d. of . . . Saundere*
5 Sep. John Brabyn, gent.
8 Sep. John Daye,† gent
1 Oct. Sarah d. of John & Elizabeth Kinge
17 Oct. Dennis s. of Dennis & Agatha Westcott
28 Oct. John Mill
1 Nov. Catherine Sprey
4 Nov. Mary d. of John & Alice Benallack
9 Nov. M[rs] Johan Hore,‡ widdow
9 Nov. Thomas s. of John & Mary Langdon
13 Nov. John s. of John & Mary Langdon
14 Dec. Richard Edwards
18 Dec. Anthony Thomas
19 Dec. W[m] s. of John & Honor Richards
21 Jan. Beaton Ellery, widow
29 Jan. John s. of John & Millicent James
31 Jan. Isabella d. of Peter Rescorla, deceased
1 Mar. Christian the wife of Sampson Burt
7 Mar. W[m] s. of W[m] & Johan Launder
10 Mar. Enstis Thomas, widdow

ANNO 1678.

28 Mar. John Jolly
7 April Temperance, base d. of Dorothy Launder
21 April Elizabeth Blake, widdowe
25 April Agnes Harvey
26 April Charles Rescorla
27 April Johan d. of W[m] & Honor Jolly
7 May Thomas s. of Richard & Elizabeth Jolly
23 May Mark Cocking
28 May John s. of John & Johan Truscot
2 June Mary wife of Rich[d] Lovell
3 June Margery Thomas, widow
11 Sep. Christian d. of Ralph Burt
1 Oct. Mary Gill, widdow
7 Oct. John Allen y[e] elder
24 Oct. Jane Cocking, widdow
31 Oct. Honor d. of Ralph & Mary Lambe
16 Nov. Nicholas s. of Thomas & Mary Cocking
17 Nov. John Carbiss
6 Dec. Alexander Woone
13 Dec. John Richards *al's* Body
4 Jan. John s. of Francis & Mary Mannell
11 Jan. Tobias Olliver
18 Feb. Eliz. d. of Anthony & Mary Callaway
1 Mar. John s. of John & Frances Allen
5 Mar. Thomas George
21 Mar. M[rs] Alice Beauford, widdow

ANNO 1679.

2 April Johan Lawry, widow
4 April Bernard Rowse
10 April Anne Stephens
8 May Marrien wife of John Peter
14 May John Beauford,* rector
29 May William Trekeane
4 July Ann d. of John & Joan Sprey
2 July Richard Edwards the elder
1 Nov. Thomas s. of William & Audrye Hawke
10 Dec. Dorothy the wife of William Mare
31 Dec. Jane Humphrye, widdow
2 Jan. John Grimes
6 Jan. Ann wife of Nicholas Rodgers
25 Jan. fflorence the wife of Thomas Lawe
4 Feb. A dedd borne childe of S[r] John Seyntaubin, Knight & Barronett
15 Feb. Lowdye d. of Simon & Alice Rawling
24 Feb. Mathewe Allin†
25 Feb. Margaret d. of M[r] Nathaniel and M[rs] Margaret Champion
7 Mar. Elizabeth d. of John & Sibbella Lee
9 Mar. Jane Hawke, widdow

* Blank.

† John Day, gent., one of the twelve men in 1672.—Green Book.

‡ Richard Hore, gent., and Phillippa his wife. He died 4 July, 1610. She died 22 Jan., 1602; Richard, son of the above, died 22 Jan., 1593; Katherine, daughter of the above, died 21 June, 1599. Ledger stone at St. Ervan.

* Son of William Beauford. See bap. 1617, April 13. He married first, Ann, daughter of . . . . , by whom he had several children. He married secondly, Ann, daughter of Henry Nance; marriage licence granted 27 Jan., 1664.

† He paid for rent of a shop 17s. in 1642.—Green Book.

11 Mar. Marye d. of Anthony & Marye Callwaye

ANNO 1680.*

30 Mar. Thomas s. of William & Grace Edwards W
31 Mar. Samuel s. of William & Joane Laundero W
6 April Dorothy Daye, widdow
9 April Thomas s. of Thomas & Marrin Cockin W
16 April Margery Hosswell W
29 April Sariah d. of Methuselah & Sariah Williams W
3 May† Thomas s. of Thomas & Elizabeth Scibberrio W
9 May Honor Retallack, widdow W
15 May Elizabeth Bullock, widow W
5 June Ann d. of Philip Harrye‡ W
25 June Thomas Williams, sen^r W
16 July Joane d. of Methuselah & Sarah Williams W
18 July George s. of George & Alice Day W
23 July Henry s. of William & Hon^r Tinney W
8 Aug. Peter s. of Joan Gibbs, widow W
21 Sep. Thomas Benny Taylor W
27 Sep. Amy Williams, widdow W
29 Sep. William s. of William & Agnis Cock W
24 Oct. John Brewer W
8 Nov. Israel s. of John & Elizabeth Harris W

* With this year commence the certificates of burials in woollen; they are contained in a long narrow folio volume, written on paper, with limp parchment covers with, in place of clasps, pieces of cord to tie when the volume is closed. At the end of each year the officiating clergyman certifies its correctness, and it is signed by the justices.

It was originally intended to print these certificates in full at the end of the regular Register, but on account of the large amount of repetition involved it has been deemed best to mark the entries, which also appear in the certificates, with a W, noting any variations, etc., in foot notes. The certificates give the date of making the oath, which was generally a few days after the burial, and they were not entered regularly; thus, an entry in September precedes July, and one in June between two in October.

† This is the first certificate in the book. It is here given in full as an example of the others, which follow the same form: "There was oath made before John Vivian, Esq., by Christian Crap and Elizabeth Stevens that Thomas Skibbearow was buried in wollen only."

‡ . . . . Harris in the certificates.

12 Nov. Jane d. of Roger & Joan Ellery W
20 Nov. John s. of John & Alice Benallack W
22 Nov. Peter Pollard, sen^r W
2 Dec. Hon^r wife of William Tinnye W
5 Dec. William Salter W
25 Jan. Joan Metherill, widdow* W
2 Feb. Elizabeth Copithorne W
5 Feb. John s. of John & Mary England W
3 Mar. Katherine wife of Richard Troth †W

ANNO 1681.

27 Mar. Elinor Steevens W
5 April Hon^r Richards, widdow W
9 April Elizabeth d. of Jacob & Mary Husband
12 April Symon Trehenbam‡
20 April Susanna d. of Will & Agnis Cock W
28 April Martha d. of Will & Joyce Dennis W
11 May John Stevens, shoomaker W
14 May John s. of James & Jennifer Beauford§ W
15 May Julian wife of Henry Harvy W
19 May Edward s. of Edward & Sarah Shorton
24 May Margaret the wife of Richard Congdon W
26 May James s. of Stephen & Elizabeth Capell W
29 May Jane d. of Dan & Eliz^th Couch W
2 June Grace Harris

* Spelt Meddern in the certificates.

† "This is a true catalogue of all such certificates as have been brought to me of all such persons which have been burried in wollen only in this parish of Columb Major, since the 13th day of Aprill last unto this present time. Witness my hand the sixth day of Aprill, 1681.

"JOHN BISHOP, Rector.

"JOHN TRUSCOTT, JOHN MARTIN, } Churchwardens.

HENRY DYER, RICHARD KESTELLE, WILLIAM MOORE, HENRY BLAKE, } Overseers of the Poore.

"Thee 1st of April, 1681.

"Seen and allowed by us,

"JOHN SEYNTAUBYN.
JOHN VIVIAN."

(Vide certificates.)

‡ He paid rent of his shop 16s. in 1666.—Green Book.

§ The certificate says, "James Beauford, Clearke."

5 June	Mary d. of Gilbert Coode	W
14 June	Methusalah Williams	W
23 June	Lawrence Peeters	W
2 July	Mary Mayhow*	W
4 July	Alice Cornish, widdow	W
10 July	Thomas Rouse	W
16 July	Grace d. of John & Frances Allen	W
25 Aug.	Walter . . . .†	W
27 Aug.	Jane d. of Thomas & Mary Cockyn	W
2 Sep.	Thomas s. of Jacket Burne‡	W
11 Oct.	Layar wife of John Arthur	W
25 Oct.	Stephen Dungye was found dead upon ye downs	
27 Oct.	Benjamin Harvye	W
6 Nov.	Jane d. of Humphry & Jane Harvy§	W
7 Nov.	Nicholas Langdon	W
8 Nov.	An d. of Roger & Joane Ellery	W
15 Nov.	Elizth d. of James & Marriu Nettle	W
16 Nov.	John Hawky Tanner	W
25 Nov.	Daniel s. of Joan Rouse, widdow‖	W
6 Dec.	Gilbert Cood	W
22 Dec.	Richard s. of James & Mary Cock	W
22 Dec.	Mary Williams, widdow	W
9 Jan.	Hesther d. of Benjam. James	W
14 Jan.	Elizbth base child of Ann Jolley	W
16 Jan.	James s. of Nicholas & Jane Bounsell	W
19 Feb.	Henry Bray	W
4 Mar.	Thomas Polkinhorn	
7 Mar.	Mrs An Jenkyn, widdow¶	W
13 Mar.	Elizabeth Darr* the wife of John Darr**	

Anno 1682.

26 Mar.	Charles Gummow	W
29 Mar.	Luce English	W
7 April	Mary d. of Jacob Husband	W
22 April	Grace Cornish	W
23 April	Philip Hoskyn, widdow	W
3 May	Agnes Treneage	
4 May	John s. of William Cock	W
19 May	An wife of Mr John Vivian, Junr*	W
20 May	Thomas Oxnam	W
24 May	Margaret the wife of Richard May	W
4 June	Honour d. of Arthur Jolley	
9 June	Joan Gumow, widdow	
2 July	William Jeffrye servt to Mr John Bligh	W
1 Aug.	Hugh s. of John Langdon	

* She paid rent of her shop 21s. 4d. in 1658. —Green Book.

† Surname omitted; the certificate gives it as "Walter Evan."

‡ Berten in certificate.

§ The certificate, affirmed by Jane Harvey and Diana James, calls her Julian Harvey.

‖ Humphry in the certificate. made on the oath of Joan Rows and Joan Strongman.

¶ She was a daughter of Andrew Pomeroy, of St. Columb, by Jane, daughter and sole heiress of Digory Hext, of Launceston, co. Cornwall; she married, 27 Oct., 1628, Peter, son and heir of James Jenkyn, of Trekenning. They had an only son James Jenkyn.

** "This is a true catalogue of all such certificates as have been brought to me of persons buried in wollen only, in this parish of Columb Major, since the sixth day of Aprill last, 1681, to this present time. Witness my hand this 19th day of Aprill, 1682.

"John Bishop, Rector.

"Christopher Best, John Pollawin, — Churchwardens.
Henry Rows, Peter Richards, Henry Jolley. Nicholas Woodman, — Overseers of the Poor.

"Seen and allowed by us,

(A blank, apparently for the signature of Sir John St. Aubyn, Bart.)

"John Vivian."

(Vide certificates.)

The following is omitted from the regular register, but is among the certificates, Edward Stephens oath made 27th May that he was buried in wollen only.

* She was a daughter of Math: Halse, of Efford, and first wife of John Vivian, of Truan, second son of John Vivian and Mary Glanville.

Parish Register of Egg, Buckland, co. Devon.

Baptisms.

Thomas s. of William Hals. Esq., Dec. 8, 1653.
An d. of Mathew Hals, Esq.. Sep. 3, 1655.
Mathew s. of Mathew Halse, Esq., Feb. 2, 1657.
Sabina d. of Mathew Halse, Esq., Sep. 2, 1658.
Rebeckah d. of Mathew Halse, Esq., Sep. 15, 1659.
Rebeckah d. of Mathew Hals, of Efford, Esq., and Rebeckah his wife, 22 Oct., 1661.
Charles s. of Mathew Hals, Esq., and Rebeckah his wife, 11 Nov., 1662.
Amy d. of Mathew Hals, Esq., and Rebeckah his wife, 29 March. 1665.

Weddings.

Mr. John Tendale, minister, and Ann Halse, daughter of Mathew Halse, Esq., 18 Dec., 1655.
Thomas Sture. Esq.. and Amy. daughter of Mathew Halse, Esq., 27 March, 1656.
John Cosh, Esq., and Sabina, daughter of Mathew Halse, Esq., 22 March, 1656.

19 Aug. Matilda wife of John Dunkyn* W
1 Sep. Mr John Day of Tregaswith W
2 Sep. Melliar Trehenbam W
27 Oct. Elizabeth d. of John Udy† W
13 Oct. Elizabeth‡ d. of John Whitford W
3 Nov. John Allen W
9 Nov. William s. of Wm Moor W
10 Nov. Nathaniel s. of Nathan Champion
17 Nov. Jane wife of Nicholas Hodge W
10 Dec. John Row *al's* Michell
19 Dec. ffrancis Strongman, widdow W
31 Dec. Joseph s. of Samuel May§ W
17 Jan. Elizabeth Cock, widdow W
29 Jan. Elizabeth d. of Charles Bounsell W
31 Jan. Thomas s. of Isaac Nicholls W
31 Jan. Thomas Carter W
3 Feb. Gartret d. of Reskimer Allen W
4 Feb. Morgan Oliver W
15 Mar. Henry Jolley W
20 Mar. Elizabeth, base child of Jane Moyle‖ W

Mr. Charles Lambe, minister of the Gospel, and Mrs. Elizabeth Halse, daughter of Mathew Halse, Esq., 29 May, 1660.

Mr. Thomas Hele and Mrs. Elizabeth Hals, 22 April, 1670.

John Vivian, Esq., and Mrs. Ann Hals, 10 Nov., 1679.

Mr. Jonathan Elford and Mrs. Amy Hals, 5 Jan., 1681.

Burials.

Thomas Halse s. of Mathew Halse the younger, 2 Feb., 1654.

Mathew Halse the elder, Esq., Aug. . . . 1656.

Rebeckah d. of Mathew Halse, Esq., 24 Sep., 1659.

Charles Hals. 17 Nov.. 1662.

Mrs. Sabina Hals, Dec. 4. 1665.

Amy Hals d. of Mr. Edm. Hals, 20 Sep., 1673.

Mathew Hals, Esq., 25 Feb., 1675.

A female child of Mr. Edmund Hals, 16 Aug., 1677.

Dr. Edm. Hals, 21 March, 1678.

Sarah Hals d. of Sarah Hals, widow, of Plymouth, 19 May, 1679.

Mrs. Sabina Hals, 15 Dec., 1682.

Mrs. Amy Sture, 16 Dec., 1682.

Mathew Hals, Esq.. 29 June, 1684.

Mrs. Rebeckah Hals. 21 Nov., 1684.

* John Dunkyn, gent., in the certificates.

† Certificates say Edy.

‡ Certificates have Katherine.

§ Samuel May, gent., in the certificates.

‖ The usual declaration by the clergyman is attested by the signatures of John Seyntaubyn and John Vivian.

The following burials are not in the register; oath was made 25th July that Joan Burne was buried according to the Act.

Oath was made the 5 Feb. on the burial of John Whiteford.

Anno 1683.

2 April Jane wife of Michaell Cowling W
11 April Elizabeth d. of Henry Blake W
23 April John s. of Henry Haycraft W
30 April Ann d. of Peter Gibbs W
11 May Grace wife of ffrancis Godolphyn W
17 May William s. of Will'm Hosken W
18 May Ann d. of John Allyn W
20 May Joane d. of Henry Blake
20 May Grace d. of Giles Edwards W
21 May Patience d. of Richard Pollard W
21 May Anthony s. of Roger Ellery
26 May Anthony s. of Thomas Callaway W
28 May Elizabeth d. of Samuel May
31 May Thomas Hendye
31 May Ann Holman W
21 June John Cowle W
1 July Thomas s. of Thomas Skebberrio W
3 July Honour d. of Thomas Esbell W
9 July Ann Bounsell
29 July Mary d. of Thomas Hawke W
30 July Hestor d. of Benjamin James W
2 Aug. Peternell the wife of John Thorne W
17 Aug. Grace d. of John Metherel W
21 Aug. Grace d. of Nathaniel Champion* W
27 Sep. Joan wife of Arthur Jenkyn W
8 Oct. Robert Hoblyn, Esq.† W
10 Oct. Pentecoste Grymes W
12 Oct. Alice Rowse
12 Oct. Gatherude d. of John Husband
31 Oct John sonne of Arthur Broad W
15 Nov. William s. of Richard Greeby W
25 Nov. Rebecca Langdon W
5 Dec. Peter Callaway W
5 Dec. Alice Husband W
7 Dec. Elizabeth Anthorne‡ W
7 Dec. Jane d. of John Michael
12 Dec. Ann wife of Peter Kendall
19 Dec. Richard Blake W
20 Dec. Henry s. of Richard Veale W

* The oath adds "gent."

† He was of Nanswhyden, son and heir of Edw. Hoblyn and Mary Apley. He married Grace, daughter and co-heiress of John Carew, of Penwarne, by whom he had issue fifteen sons and five daughters.

‡ In the certificate spelt "Ounter," oath made by Temperance Ounter.

24 Dec. Margaret d. of Nathaniel Champion
24 Dec. Katherine wife of John Retallack W
23 Jan. Richard May
24 Jan. John s. of Hendye Langdon
26 Feb. James s. of Peter Day, gent, W
13 Mar. John Retalleck W
19 Mar. Richard s. of John Polkinhorne W
22 Mar. Nicholas Jane* W

ANNO 1684.

28 Mar. John Berrye† W
4 April Mary the wife of William Minnoe W
14 April Christian Woolcock
29 April John Lawry Sexon W
3 May Honour d. of Daniel Couch W
9 May Joane d. of Petherick Gilbert W
16 May Richrad Stapell W
20 May William Cundye W
30 May Honour Sprey W
1 June John Crawly W
2 June John Browne W
12 July Giles s. of John Truscott W
26 July Honour d. of Henry Morcombe W
31 July William Bone W
20 Aug. Edward Hoblyn, Esq.‡ W
29 Sep. John Dennis W
8 Oct. Sarah d. of Samuel May§ W
13 Oct. Jonathan Collins, a poore man of Illogan
8 Nov. Wilmott d. of William Browne W
9 Nov. John Beauchampe Esqre* W
15 Nov. Joice Hawke W
19 Nov. Mary d. of William Richards W
31 Dec. Thomas Richards W
6 Jan. James s. of Adam Day, gent. W
12 Jan. Richard George
13 Jan. Thomas s. of Samuel May W
16 Jan. William s. of William Minnoe
30 Jan. Mary d. of John Langdon
6 Feb. Margaret d. of Anthony Michell
19 Feb. Anstes wife of Walter Pearse, being murdered by him W
23 Feb. Henry s. of John Grymes W
26 Feb. Patience Carter
2 Mar. John Arthur
2 Mar. Persilla Stephens W
3 Mar. Mary d. of Thomas Richards
7 Mar. Honour d. of William Tynny W
9 Mar. Jane wife of Thomas Hawkey W
18 Mar. Robert s. of Thomas Rowse W
19 Feb. John Dart† W

ANNO 1685.

31 Mar. Honour Arthur‡ W
31 Mar. Robert s. of William Michell
23 May William s. of Roger Ellery W
31 May Thomas Hendra W
21 June William Allen W
30 June Joane Halse W
15 July Mary d. of Michell Cowling
16 July Grace Keate, widow§ W
30 July James Common‖ W
23 Aug. Dorothy the wife of Thomas Day W

* The usual declaration by John Bishop, rector, but not signed by the magistrates. The following names are not in the register: Tho. Hawke, oath by Mary Hawke, 7 April; Jane, wife of Humphrey Harvey, 29 Mar.; William Richard, Aug. 22; . . . . Jane Rowe, 10 Dec.; Alice Nichols, 16 Oct.; Grace Chapple, 31 Dec.; Richard, son of Robert Harris, 21 Feb.; Thomas Bounsell, 28 Feb.

† "John Berry, gent.," in certificate.

‡ He was the second son of Robert Hoblyn, of Nanswhyden, Esq., by Grace Carew, his wife. He married Damaris. daughter of . . . . Avant; she re-married Edward Hoblyn, of Croane (who died 27 April, 1704); she was burried at Egloshayle, 8 Dec., 1713. The above Edw. Hoblyn, Esq., had an only daughter, Diana, baptized at St. Columb, 18 Dec., 1683, and was married to William Bickford, of Dunsland. In the footnote at page 72, Edw. Hoblyn, of Croane, who married the widow of the above Edw. Hoblyn, is inadvertantly given as the father of Damaris, wife of William Bickford, which error is here corrected.

§ Certificates add "gent."

* He was probably the John Beauchamp baptized at St. Enoder, 24 Sep., 1644, and father of John Beauchamp, who married in 1684. at St. Columb Major, to Emblyn Edwards. Certificate says Capt. John Beacham.

† The usual declarations regarding the burials follow the certificates, but it is signed by John Bishop, rector, only.

The following entries are omitted from the register itself, viz.:—

Ann d. of Littleton Weymouth; oath made 5 May.
Joan Gummow, June 14.
Ann Bounsell, 15 July.
Thomas Michell, 21 Nov.
Patience Bastine, 2 March.
Thomas Michell, 21 Nov.
Alice Martin, 9 March.
Robert s. of William Rowe, 3 April.

‡ Certificate adds, "daughter of John Arthur."

§ She was the second wife and relict of Ralph Keate, Esq. (third son of Ralph Keate, Esq., by Anne Arscott, his wife); she died s.p. Her will dated 4 April, 1681; proved 21 Oct., 1685.

‖ Certificate adds, "son of Arthur Common."

26 Aug. Charitye Edwards W
26 Aug. Mary d. of William and Jane Dennis
13 Sep. James Skeberrio W
22 Sep. Peter s. of Elias Pollard W
11 Oct. ffrances s. of Margaret England W
14 Nov. John Hellier W
13 Dec. Florenc wife of William Tucker* W
15 Dec. Richard s. of John Lee W
25 Dec. John Lekey
26 Dec. William s. of John and Lidia Champion W
29 Dec. John s. of Luke Giles W
30 Dec. Remphry s. of Thomas Skeberrio W
8 Jan. Ann Hawkyns† W
15 Jan. Tamsin d. of Jonathan Rowse W
28 Jan. James Edwards, a labour man W
14 Mar. Margaret d. of John Tom‡ W

ANNO 1686.

6 April Richard Congdon W
19 April John Cocken W
30 April Edmond Dunridge
23 May James Cock W
28 May Mary Trekeane
26 June Mary Harvey
29 June Dennis Westcott W
10 July Margery wife of John Dunkyn, gent. W
11 July § . . . . . d. of Degory & Mary Williams W
5 Aug. Joane Skeberriow
6 Aug. Alice Hicks W
11 Sep. Margery d. of Honour Jolly W
1 Oct. Thomas Westcott W
2 Oct. Margery Daw W
4 Nov. Thomas Cocken
8 Nov. Nicholas s. of Nicholas Harris of St Muan W
10 Jan. Leonard Tyack W
5 Feb. Mary Searell ‖ W
6 Feb. Mary d. of Nicholas Bounsell W
17 Feb. Mary wife of John Merifeild W
18 Feb. Joane d. of Jonathan & Ann Daw W

* The certificate calls her " Dewens."

† Certificate by Ann Hocken, and that Ann Hocken was buried in woollen.

‡ The usual declaration by John Bishop, rector, and attested by W. Kendall and H. Countenay.

§ Mary, *vide* certificates.

‖ Mary Searle, widow, in certificates.

1 Mar. Humphry Trehemban
8 Mar. Jane Dennis, widdow W
23 Mar. Constance James, widdow* W

ANNO 1687.

2 April Samuel May, gent.
30 Mar. Jone d. of Richard & ffrances Callaway W
23 April Eliz. d. of Roger & Jone Ellery W
29 April William White
29 April John Peters *al's* Perthy W
8 May Thomas Merifeild, gent. W
8 May Elizabeth d. of Thomas Tibb W
14 May Michaell s. of Michaell Strongman W
20 May Petherick s. of Peth. Gilbert W
3 June Arthur s. of William Warren† W
8 June John s. of Isaac Nicholls W
29 June Mary wife of ffrancis Mannell
30 June Ann d. of Bernard Lobb
10 July Elias Pollard W
10 July Mary d. of Jacob Husband W
21 July James Moyle
6 Aug. Richard s. of Henry Blake & Jenifer his wife
31 Aug. Avis Jolly‡ W
10 Sep. Philip s. of George Tom W
12 Sep. Jone Pawley
24 Sep. Eliner wife of Daniell Couch W
10 Oct. Jone wife of Roger Ellery W
20 Nov. John s. of James Cowling W
8 Dec. Walter Vivian§ W
23 Dec. Anthony Couthlay, servant to Richard Hoblyn, Esqre‖ W
28 Dec. Walter Tyer
12 Jan. John s. of John Tyer
14 Jan. Philip Hornibrook W
20 Jan. Dorothy wife of Richard fford W
30 Jan. Marke s. of John Truscott W
1 Feb. Elizabeth d. of William Merifield W

* Here follows the declaration as before signed by John Bishop, rector, Geo. Kinge and Robert Benny, overseers of the poor.

H. COURTENAY & JOHN VIVIAN, Magistrates.

The following is omitted from the regular register :—

Mary Bastyn, July 1.

† Certificate says, Warne, made by Ann Warne; he was the only child of Wm. Warne and Ann Broad his wife. See Weddings, 1686.

‡ Certificate has Philip Jolly.

§ The certificate adds " Junior."

‖ The certificate spells the name " Curchoby."

4 Mar. William s. of William Tucker* W
11 Mar. John Horsewell W
21 Mar. Elizabeth d. of John Drew
22 Mar. Henry Rescorla W
23 Mar. Richard s. of Henry Jolly W
24 Mar. Jone d. of James Metherill†

ANNO 1688.

12 April John Jenkyn W
17 April Katherine d. of Peter Champion‡ W
17 April William s. of Richard Greby W
30 April Honor Champion, widdow W
30 April ffrancis Mannell W
13 May Emblyn wife of Richard Slade
27 May Elizabeth d. of Anthony Michell W
26 June Mr Philip Keate§ W
8 July Edward Crews W
21 July Nicholas Withiell W
28 July Mary wife of Peter Bounsell
3 Aug. Symon s. of Daniell May W
17 Aug. Anne the wife of John Bishop, rector W
17 Aug. Elizabeth d. of William Basely
15 Sep William Tucker‖ W
21 Sep. Lydia wife of John Champion¶ W
8 Nov. Daniell s. of Daniell May
12 Nov. . . . . wife of William Mill** W
17 Nov. Adam Day,†† gent. W
18 Nov. John Richards W
30 Nov. Elizabeth d. of James Cowling
14 Dec. Alice Gregor, widdow W
19 Dec. Theophilus Lawe W
22 Dec. James s. of Peter Husband
24 Dec. Sarah d. of Henry Michell
25 Dec. Nathaniell s. of Thomas Launder
29 Dec. Joane Hawke, widdow
1 Jan. William Dancaster
5 Jan. William Lanyon
13 Jan. Peternell the wife of Xpher Hendy
14 Jan. Philip Withiell & Christopher Withiell W
16 Jan. Jane d. of John England W
18 Jan. Edward s. of ffrancis Godolphin
20 Jan. William Richards W
29 Jan. Susan d. of Gilbert White
30 Jan. Philip wife of William Reynolds
4 Feb. Peternell Peters W
16 Feb. Milecent Burne
29 Feb. Jenifer Thomas, widdow*

ANNO 1689.

29 Mar. Avis Jolly
1 April Elizabeth wife of John Strongman
10 April Susanna d. of Nicholas Philpp
24 April Jane d. of John Husband
27 April Elizabeth d. of Thomas Skeberrio
12 May Thomazin Berry, widdow
28 May Stephen s. of Marke Tyer
10 May Philip s. of John Gilbert
11 May Thomas s. of Dennis Westcott
3 July Margaret England
14 July Eustice the wife of John Langdon
26 July Henry Tregear
31 July Nathaniel s. of Samuel Champion
15 Aug. James s. of William Luny
30 Aug. Margaret wife of Nathaniel Champion† W
19 Sep. Sarah d. of Peter Champion‡ W
22 Sep. Joane wife of Petherick Gilbert
23 Sep. Epiphany d. of William Dennis

* Certificate adds "gent."

† The following entries do not appear in the regular register:—
Charles s. of Robert Lithicott, oath made 11 April.
John Langdon, 20 July.
An, wife of Arthur Jolly, 9 Sept.
John Williams, 20 Oct.
The usual declaration is signed by John Bishop, rector.
"JOHN VIVIAN, SAMUEL BATTEN, HENRY HAYCROFT, } Overseers of the Poor.
"April 19th, 1688, allowed by us,
"H. COURTENAY, JOHN VIVIAN."

‡ The certificate adds "gent."

§ He was third son of Ralph Keate, by Gertrude his first wife; he died unmarried. Admonition granted to his sister Gertrude Allen, wife of Reskymer Allen, 28 July, 1688.

‖ The oath made before William Silly, Esq., styles him "gent."

¶ In the oath which was made before William Symons, vicar of St. Enoder, he is styled "Mercer."

** The certificate gives the name of the wife as Thomasine.

†† He was one of the twelve men in 1678.—Green Book.

* The usual declaration has been omitted here, and the following do not appear in the regular register:—
Mary d. of James Oliver, 2 June.
Julian Hawkey, 5 Jan.

† The certificate describes him as "Mercer."

‡ In the certificate he is described as "Attorney."

12 Oct. Jane d. of Thomas Cocken
20 Oct. John Williams, sen[r] W
3 Nov. Henry s. of William Dennis
11 Nov. Marryn Harris W
3 Nov. James s. of James Stephens
3 Nov. ffrançis s. of Martyn Tom
11 Dec. John s. of Benjamin James
17 Dec. Reskimmer s. of Charles Allen
17 Dec. A child to Robert Husband
21 Dec. Jane d. of Michaell Cowling W
30 Dec. Katherine Brewer, widdow W
3 Jan. Ann wife of Thomas Stephens
5 Dec. The d. of Honour Jolly,* widdow
6 Jan. ffrances wife of John Buckthorpe†
9 Jan. Katherine Williams
9 Jan. William s. of William Launder W
11 Jan. Richard Hoblyn, Esq[re]‡
14 Jan. Elizabeth Mill, widdow
15 Jan. Robert Husband W
20 Jan. Thomas s. of Thomas Skeberrio W
21 Jan. Thomas Crapp
26 Jan. Mary Williams, widdow
7 Feb. Joan d. of Robert Elford W
16 Feb. Elizabeth wife of Henry Blake
21 Feb. Thomas s. of William Merifeild W
12 Mar. Reskymmer Allen§ W
22 Mar. ffrancis s. of Daniell May
23 Mar. Ann Cocken‖

ANNO 1690.

1 April Walter Vivian, sen[r]
1 April Charity Jenkin, wid[o]
11 April Xtian Crapp
24 April Katherine d. of John Sprey W
26 April Mary wife of William Bone
1 May Ann d. of Bernard Lobb

* The certificate calls her Alice Jolly.
† In the certificate spelt Buckthought.
‡ He was a son of Robert Hoblyn, of Nanswhyden, by his wife, Grace, daughter of John Carew, of Penwarne. He married Martha, daughter of . . . . Stribblehill; she remarried Charles Holt. This Richard Hoblyn died s.p.
§ He married at Cubert, 3 April, 1665, Gertrude, daughter of Ralph Keate, of St. Columb.
‖ Here follows the usual declaration by John Bishop, rector, Joseph Hawkey and John Rous, overseers of the poor. "Seen and allowed by us the 13th daye of May, 1690,
"JOHN VIVIAN, HUM. NICHOLL."
The following are not in the regular register:—
Joan d. of Francis Tom, 2 June.
Katherine Williams. 9 Jan.
Grace d. of Thomas Day, 4 Feb.

6 May Grace May, vid.
11 May Isabell Hawkey, vid.
15 May Susanna d. of W[m] Dennis
21 May John s. of John Sprey W
3 June Hester wife of Daniell Ropson W
25 June William Metherell W
2 July Phillippa d. of Edward Rickard W
12 July Eliz. d. of John Grimes
23 July . . . d. of Phillip King
Aug. Richard s. of Thomas Phillips* W
17 Aug. ffrances d. of John Tom W
21 Aug. Mary d. of Humphry Oxnam W
3 Sep. Ralph s. of John Day, gent. W
12 Sep. Joane wife of W[m] Minnowe W
25 Sep. . . . d. of Phillip King
15 Oct. Richard fford
25 Oct. Joane d. of James Moyle
5 Nov. Peter s. of John Allyn
17 Dec. Walter s. of Philip Harvey
20 Dec. Ann d. of John Rouse† W
1 Jan. Joane Pennan
28 Jan.‡ Tho. s. of John Watts W
30 Jan. ffrancis Cocken W
4 Feb. Melior Launder W
17 Feb. Lewis Day, gent. W
19 Feb. Mary wife of Arthur Broad
21 Feb. Joane Richards
23 Feb. Henry & Richard ss. of Henry Rowse
5 Mar. Ann d. of Luke Jolly W
10 Mar. Joane wife of Henry Cock W
14 Mar. W[m] Lanyon
17 Mar. Tho. Callaway§ W
19 Mar. W[m] Mill
18 Mar. John s. of Peter Kendall
20 Mar. Agas Westcott, vid.
22 Mar. John Strongman‖

ANNO 1691.

27 Mar. Jane Chapell, widd. W
29 Mar. Philip King, gent. W
30 Mar. Julyan Strongman, widd. W

* The certificate gives the date 22 Aug.
† The certificate says John Rouse, gent.
‡ The oath was made before Thomas Wolridge, curate of St. Wenn.
§ Tho. Callaway paid 10s. rent of a shop in 1683.—Green Book.
‖ The declaration signed John Bishop, rector, John Oxnam and James Edwards, overseers of the poor.
JOHN VIVIAN, H. COURTENAY, } Magistrates.
Omitted from Registers:—
Mary d. of Richard Jolly, 10 Nov.
Joan wife of Hen. Mill, 16 Feb.

1 April Stephen Stephens W
5 April Elizabeth d. of Edward Lawry W
6 April John s. of Mr John Huddy* W
11 April Katherine d. of Mr Peter Champion W
21 April Martha Jolley, widdow W
22 April Johan Rouse, widd. W
23 April Honnor Bounsell† W
24 April John s. of Mr William Lamb W
24 April Jenipher wife of John Watts W
29 April George Cockaine W
30 April Ann d. of John Strongman W
3 May Nathaniel s. of Edward Lawry W
7 May Dorothy wife of Humphry Benny W
12 May John‡ Vivian, Junr, Esqre W
13 May Elizabeth the wife of Josias Grimes§ W
14 May Edward Lawrey
19 May George Tom W
28 May Margaret wife of John Pill W
29 May Jane Daye, widd. W
1 June Ollive Jones,‖ widd. W
3 June Henry Mill W
19 June Ann Daye¶ W
20 June Richard Edwards, weaver W
21 June Abigall the wife of John Edye W
29 June Thomasine the wife of Thomas Issbell W
29 June Maude Mitchell W
3 July Sarah Williams** W
7 July Jone Pawley W
21 July William Hawkey, junr W
15 Aug. Mary wife of William Browne W
11 Sep. John Thomas W
13 Sep. Mrs Honor Carter†† W

* The certificate describes the father as Mr. John Huddy, apothecary.

† The certificate adds, "widow."

‡ "This John was the eldest son of John Vivian, Esq. by his second wife, Mary, daughter of Sir John Glanville. He married first. Ann, daughter of Math. Halse, of Efford, co. Devon, she died s.p., and he married secondly, Mary, daughter of Joseph Sawle, of Penrice, Esq., by whom he left issue several children."

§ The certificate has Joseph Grimes.

‖ The certificate has Alice Jones.

¶ The certificate adds, "daughter of John Day, gent.

** Certificate has "Grace Williams, widow."

†† The certificate adds "relict of John Carter, gent." She was a daughter of Sampson Lawry, See note, p. 152.

28 Sep. Maude wife of Robert Skinner W
8 Nov. Mary d. of James Bone W
14 Nov. Ann the wife of Mr James Edwards* W
4 Dec. Ralph Lamb† W
5 Dec. Jacob Blake W
9 Dec. Jone d. of Arthur Crews W
11 Dec. James Stephens W
12 Dec. Mrs Agnes Tregear, widd. W
19 Dec. ffrancis s. of John Tom
22 Dec. Jone Stephens, widdow W
16 Jan. John s. of George Jolley W
27 Jan. Loveday d. of Nicholas Hawke W
21 Feb. Elizabeth Withiell, widdow W
24 Feb. . . . . . s. of Thomas Adams‡

ANNO 1692.

27 April Jone Stephens, widd. W
29 April Richard Caball W
17 May Mary wife of Thomas Hoblyn, gent. W
23 May John s. of James Tenny W
20 June Beaton wife of Richard Clemens W
23 June Mary Cowle W
30 June Joseph s. of John Hocker, gent. W
20 July Elizabeth d. of William Basley W
27 July Mathew Johns W
11 Aug. Amye Basley, widd. W
12 Aug. Ann Lovell, widd. W
23 Aug. Thomas s. of Thomas Callaway W
31 Aug. Paschow Browne§ W
20 Sep. Scicilley Williams, widd. W
13 Oct. John s. of William Browne W
22 Oct. Honnor d. of Robert Manuell W
24 Oct. Mary Trehembam, widdow W
4 Nov. Jane Dancaster, widdow W
5 Nov. Henry s. of Edward Rickard W
11 Jan. ffrancis White, widd. W
21 Jan. Thomas s. of Thomas Lander W
8 Feb. Ebbot Jolley, widdow W
11 Feb. Ann Nicholls, widdow W
14 Feb. William s. of Joall Cabell W

* The certificate describes him as 'mercer.'

† The certificate styles him 'gent.'

‡ The declaration signed by John Bishop, rector, John Kinge and Richard Rawe, overseers of the poor, and allowed by H. Courtenay John Vivian.

Omitted from the regular register:—
Blanch d. of John Harris, 24 Jan.

§ Paschow Brown, in 1642, paid rent of his shop 4s., for his other shop 5s.—Green Book.

21 Feb. Mary wife of Thomas Callaway W
2 Mar. Martyne Tresteane W
6 Mar. Richard Scruner W
7 Mar. Benjamin James
10 Mar. Margaret Richards W
12 Mar. Margery the wife of William Hawkey W
16 Mar. Ann Pollard, widdow W
24 Mar. Samuel s. of William Basley* W

Anno 1693.

3 April Margaret d. of Martine Tom W
8 April Elizabeth d. of John Rowe *al's* Mitchell W
16 April John s. of John Benallack W
18 April William s. of James Cockaine *al's* Tremeane W
21 April William s. of Isaac Nicholls W
22 April Paschow s. of Paschow Browne W
3 May Henry s. of Henry Lee W
7 May Ann d. of Peter Husband W
12 May Patience Letticott W
22 May Martine s. of John England W
31 May Mary Johns, widdow W
4 June Edward Pollawyn W
13 June Arthur Jolley W
16 June Haniball Hosken W
22 June Blanch the wife of Edward Richards W
27 June Theoder s. of John Issabell W
30 June Ann d. of Thomas Stephens W
2 July John Rescorla† W
8 July Mary d. of Thomas Lawe W
15 July Nathaniel s. of James Olliver W
22 July John s. of Benjamin James W
8 Aug. Mary d. of M[r] Robert Berry W
14 Aug. Avies Kevall, widd. W
31 Aug. Humphry Harvey W
17 Sep. Dorothy Day W
4 Oct. Ruth Peters W
10 Oct. Henry Wills W
15 Oct. Thomas s. of Thomas Pearse W
10 Nov. Richard West W
19 Nov. Margaret Sheeres W
20 Nov. Margaret the wife of Richard Veale W
13 Dec. Elizabeth the wife of Isaack Jenkyn W
16 Dec. William Bennett W

* Declaration signed Thomas Hoblyn and Nath. Champion, overseers of the poor. Allowed by Humph. Courteney and John Vivian.

† John Rescorla, churchwarden in 1641.—Green Book.

17 Dec. John s. of Edward Peters W
22 Dec. Ann wife of Peter Husband W
2 Jan. Maddam Grace Hoblyn,* widd.
4 Jan. Reddigon the wife of Anthony Callaway W
8 Jan. Mary d. of Arthur Mitchell W
17 Jan. Thomazine Wilkin W
17 Jan. Rose Cockaine W
19 Jan. William s. of William Minnow W
21 Jan. Nicholas s. of Nicholas Woodman W
23 Jan. Susanna Tresteane W
25 Jan. Sibella wife of William Hals,† gent. W
25 Jan. Henry Haycraft, merchant W
31 Jan. Alice Hellyar, widdow W
12 Feb. William Tremeane of S[t] Allen W
21 Feb. Honor d. of Edward Richards W
22 Feb. Christian Rowe, widdow W
19 Mar. Thomas s. of Lancelott Clemens‡ W

Anno 1694.

30 Mar. John s. of John Ball W
25 April Cardelia Bennett W
26 April Richard Hawke W
15 June Thomas Wills W
20 June Henry Blake W
23 June Elizabeth d. of Thomas Tonken W
17 July ffrances wife of John Drew W
4 Aug. Joane d. of Henry Blake W
27 Sep. Katherine d. of Mr. John Huddy W
28 Sep. Thomas Langdon W
4 Oct. Josias Grimes W
21 Oct. ffrances d. of Humphrey Harvey W
27 Oct. Grace Hendey W
3 Nov. Ann wife of John Eustis W
15 Nov. Jane d. of Humphry Harvey W
5 Jan. John s. of John Day, clerke W

* Oath was made Jan. 2, that "Maddam Grace Hoblyn, widdow, was buried in Linen; according to an Act of Parliament the fine was paid. She was relict of Robert Hoblyn, of Nanswhyden, and daughter and coheiress of John Carew, of Penwarne, Esq., (second son of Richard Carew, of Anthony, Esq., and his wife Julian, daughter of John Arundell, of Trerice, and coheiress of her mother, Katherine Cosworth,) by his wife Alice, daughter of John Hilman, of Furland. See note to her husband's burial in 1683.

† See extracts from parish registers of St. Wenn, *post*.

‡ Declaration by John Bishop, rector.

9 Jan. Grace wife of Thomas Crewes W
10 Jan. Philip Oxnam W
12 Jan. Maude Lawry, widdow W
22 Jan. Agnes wife of Thomas Hockin W
28 Feb. Jane Thomas Widdow W
20 Feb. Nathaniel Adams W
18 Mar. Charles King* W

Anno 1695.

7 April Rachell Banger W
19 April John s. of Mr James Edwards W
23 April Thomazine wife of Emanuell Hawke W
8 May Jone Strongman W
6 June John Bishop, rector† W
10 June Margrett d. of Thomas Hawke W
16 June Grace Leckey, widd. W
26 June Mary Rowse W
2 July John Darr W
5 July Mary wife of Robert Manuell W
6 July Jone Callaway, widd. W
6 July Ann d. of Mr Edward Crews W
9 July Mary d. of Anthony Callaway W
22 July Henry Warne‡ W
1 Aug. Elizabeth Williams W
10 Aug. Richard s. of Thomas Manuell W
11 Aug. Patience Peters W
19 Aug. Edward s. of James Merefield, junr W
21 Aug. Mary d. of James Cock W
24 Aug. Dennis s. of Michael Strongman W
3 Sep. . . . . d. of ffrancis Merefield§ W
8 Sep. Jane wife of Bernard Lobb W

* The usual declaration, signed by (Mr. Bishop, the rector, being dead) Henry Dyer and Robert Retallack, overseers of the poor. Allowed by John Vivian and Tho. Darell. Dated 12 July, 1695.

† He was of a Dorsetshire family, and married first, Ann, daughter of Robert Hoblyn, Esq., of Nanswhyden, by whom he had issue—Ann, Robert, Johan, Edward; see baptisms, 1681-83-85-87. She died in 1688, and he married secondly, Mary, daughter of the Rev. Thomas Pendarves, and had issue—James, Samuel, Mary, Thomas, Jonathan, and Grace; see baptisms, 1690-91-92-94-95.

‡ Probably eldest son of John Warne, by his wife Ann Flamack. He was twice married (see weddings, 1656 and 1673), by his first wife he was ancestor of Catherine Warne, who married William Rawlings. See note, page 172.

§ "Hester" in the certificate.

27 Sep. Elizabeth Olver W
24 Oct. Ann wife of Mr John Merefield W
24 Oct. Jane wife of Philip Vincent W
1 Nov. John Moyle W
4 Nov. William White W
15 Nov. John s. of Thomas Mannell W
17 Nov. Ann d. of George Jolley W
20 Nov. Grace Hawke W
20 Nov. Elizabeth White, widdow W
22 Nov. Elizabeth the wife of Thomas Tibb W
26 Nov. Edward Peters W
13 Dec. Alice Cockaine W
3 Jan. William s. of James Nettle W
4 Jan. Henry s. of William Dennis W
16 Jan. Arthur s. of Arthur Broad, junr. W
20 Jan. John s. of John Drew W
5 Feb. ffrancis Godolphin W
17 Feb. Grace Priest W
22 Feb. Emanuell Hawke W
29 Feb. William Bayley W
10 Mar. Loveday Sprey W
14 Mar. Jone Tyer, widdow W
17 Mar. . . . . s. of . . . . Woolcock* W
28 Mar. Christopher Hendey†

Anno 1696.

5 April Peter Husband W
15 April Mr James Edwards‡ W
17 April Richard Pollard W
19 April Thomas s. of Arthur Mitchell W
20 April Phillippa Troth W
29 April Richard s. of Thomas Whitford W
8 June Mary Langdon, widdow W
10 June Jane wife of Mr James Beauford W
15 June Grace the wife of William Edwards W
18 June Joseph s. of Henry Cock W
26 June Barbara Hawke, spinster W
8 July Richard s. of Richard Cornish W
28 Aug. Richard Jolley W
24 Sep. Hugh Retallack W
28 Sep. Avies Cockaine, spinster W
6 Oct. John s. of William White W

* "Philip, son of Elizabeth Woolcock," in certificate.

† Declaration signed by Tho. Pendarves, rector, Henry Rowse, John Williams, Tho. Brewer, and Richard Hicks, overseers. Allowed by Jo. Molesworth, Jo. Vivian.

‡ James Edwards, churchwarden in 1678.—Green Book.

10 Oct. ffrances the wife of Michael Cowling W
27 Oct. Honor Retallack, widdow W
27 Oct. Robert s. of Edward Stephens W
9 Nov. Honor Jolley, wid. W
11 Nov. Elizabeth Capell, widd. W
15 Dec. John Vivian, Esqre* W
17 Dec. Philip Harvey W
19 Dec. Elizabeth d. of Mr Richard Rowse W
21 Dec. Petronell the wife of Nicholas Trevethick W
24 Dec. Joyce Rescorla, widdow W
30 Dec. Peter Hicks W
12 Jan. Phillippa wife of John Best W
13 Jan. Robert Mayo W
15 Jan. Mary the wife of Thomas Nicholls W
17 Jan. Jone Oxnam, widdow W
21 Jan. Enstis d. of John Jolley W
26 Jan. Elizabeth Crewes, widdow W
5 Feb. ffrances the wife of Edward Champion† W
3 Mar. Elizabeth Callaway W
10 Mar. James s. of Henry Rowse W
11 Mar. Elizabeth Higgins, widdow W
11 Mar. Samson s. of John Hicks W
15 Mar. Richard Hawke W
18 Mar. Philip wife of Arthur Comons‡ W

Anno 1697.

25 Mar. Barbara wife of Henry Lee W
26 Mar. Elizabeth d. of Michaell Cornish W
9 April Elizabeth wife of James Cowling* W
12 April Thomasine Martine, widdow W
1 May Johan d. of Richard Langdon W
2 May Henry Haycraft* W
9 May William Darr, junr W
12 May Michaell s. of Edward Richards W
31 May Edward Chapell W
15 June John s. of Robert Dunkin W
3 Aug. Peter s. of William Darr W
21 Sep. John Jolley W
23 Sep. Mary d. of John Buckthought W
26 Sep. Mary d. of George Jolly W
27 Sep. Thomas Hockey W
4 Oct. Elizabeth wife of John Blight, gent.
6 Nov. Jone Langdon, widdow W
6 Nov. Millicent Blake, widdow W
11 Nov. Mrs Dorothy Smally, widdow W
10 Dec. Ezekiell Retallack W
23 Dec. Mary Rickard, widdow W
28 Dec. Avis wife of William Moore W
10 Jan. Elias s. of Henry Cock W
22 Jan. Thomas s. of Thomas Day
25 Jan. John s. of James Rowse
20 Feb. Sarah d. of Thomas Day
22 Feb. Arthur Crewes
23 Feb. Honor d. of Henry Cock
12 Feb. John Johns†

Anno 1698.

7 April Mrs Jane Herle, widdow
29 April Alice Bruer, widdow
3 May John Merefield of Tolskeddy
3 May Mary d. of William Mitchell
8 June Ruth Crawley, widdow
25 June Robert s. of Robert Mannell
13 July John s of ffrancis Herle
18 July James s. of Mr Peter Champion
23 Aug. John Tom of Gaverigan
22 Sep. ffrancis Cockaine, spinster
25 Sep. Jane d. of Michaell Cowling
26 Sep. Grace Stephens, spinster
9 Oct. Nicholas Bodella, a poore man
18 Oct. Ann wife of William Hancock
29 Oct. Martine Tom
18 Dec. Mary d. of Richard Webber
8 Jan. Gartrude wife of Marke Lawry
10 Jan. Marian wife of Mathew Ropson
12 Feb. Elizabeth d. of William Browne

* The certificate adds, "of Trewan." He was son and heir of John Vivian, of St. Columb, Esq., by his second wife, Mary, daughter and heiress of William Cavell, of Treharrock. He was Sheriff of Cornwall in 1668. He married first, Ann, daughter of Sir John Trelawny, Bart. See note, page 216. Issue, John and Elizabeth, both died young. He married secondly, Mary, daughter of Sir John Glanville, Kt., by whom he had several children, of whom Thomas, died, s.p., in 1716; John died in 1691. See page 242; Francis, of Coswarth, whose only child, Mary, married Sir Richard Vyvyan, Bart. He married thirdly, Amy, daughter of ——— Speccott, relict of ——— Nicholls; she died s.p.

† Styled "Mr." Edward Champion in the certificate.

‡ Declaration signed by T. Pendarves, rector, after which this year comes the following: "All certificates of their being buryed in woollen ought to express ye p'son before whom ye severall affidavits were made as also under their hands or else tis voide and no certificate.

"Seen and allowed ye 8th Apr, 1697, by us,
"Jo. Molesworth,
Hum. Nicholl."

* The certificate styles him "Mr."

† Declaration signed by Tho. Pendarves, rector.

23 Feb. Nicholas Trevethick W
5 Mar. Johan wife of John Sprey W
11 Mar. Rachell Langdon W
13 Mar. Jonathan s. of John Bishop, rector W
14 Mar. Edward s. of Joseph Jane W
17 Mar. Jane May, widdow W
20 Mar. Honor wife of John Husband* W

ANNO 1699.

31 Mar. Thomas s. of Thomas Wills† W
31 Mar. Edward Moulton‡
18 April Elizabeth Husband, widdow W
24 April Mary d. of William Merefield W
24 April Theophilus Betty W
28 April Jone Kent W
5 May Jone Retallack, widdow W
6 May Jane d. of John Grimes W
10 May Honor d. of Thomas Whitford W
22 May Joseph Newman, a soldier W
28 May William Hawkey W
28 May Arthur Comons W
22 June Mary d. of William Lander W
7 July Jone d. of Robert Dunkin W
7 July Thomas s. of James Stephens W
16 July William Retallack W
12 Aug. John Tyer W
14 Aug. Richard Cockaine W
3 Sep. Elizabeth d. of John Lewarne W
13 Sep. Mr. Charles Clarke
15 Sep. Catherine the wife of Richard Cowle W
9 Oct. John s. of Jacob Husband W
11 Oct. Joseph s. of Thomas Day W
1 Nov. Richard s. of John Sprey W
4 Nov. Jane wife of Peter Best W
8 Nov. John s. of Mr. John Lifford W
8 Nov. Ann Varcoe, widdow W
20 Nov. John s. of Thomas Callaway
20 Nov. Henry Cock W
20 Nov. William s. of Margaret England W
22 Nov. Agnes d. of John Lifford† W
23 Nov. Richard s. of Samuel Champion† W
26 Nov. Ann d. of Robert Merefield W
28 Nov. Joan d. of Humphry Sloggett W
28 Nov. Elizabeth Browne, widdow W
3 Dec. Mellicent wife of Robert Husband W
8 Dec. Peter s. of Thomas Callaway W
1 Jan. Mary d. of John Bishopp, clerke W
6 Feb. Mary d. of Thomas Whitford W
11 Feb. John s. of Richard Gilbert W
17 Feb. Grace Husband, widdow W
4 Mar. John Thorne W
2 Mar. Henry Dyer*
11 Mar. John Blake W
26 Jan. Alice wife of Edward Merefield W
1 Feb. Grace the d. of John Bishop, clerke W
17 Mar. Edward s. of Edward Richards† ‡W

ANNO 1700.

12 April Henry s. of Nicholas Gregg W
9 May Mary d. of Robert Litticott W
11 May John Merefield W
27 May Robert Litticott W
18 June ffrances Couch, widd. W
20 June Anthony Lawry W
4 Aug. Mary Lamb, widd. W
23 Aug. Philip Kendall W
7 Sep. Jenifer Merefield W
16 Sep. Jane d. of Bernard Lobb W
17 Sep. Elizabeth d. of John Tenny W
28 Sep. Abraham s. of John Buckthought W
30 Oct. Jane wife of Peter Bounsell W
9 Nov. Judith Vivian, wid. W
10 Dec. Margaret Haweis W
12 Dec. Thomas Minnow W
19 Dec. Jaquett Burton, widd. W
4 Jan. Jane d. of Robert Dunkin W
7 Jan. Mary d. of Thomas Trevethick W
1 Mar. Ann Retalack, widd. W
12 Mar. William Jolley W
12 Mar. Jane Hawke W
14 Mar. Giles Williams W
17 Mar. Mary Mitchell, widd. W
24 Mar. Jane Cock§ W

ANNO 1701.

6 April Charles s. of John England W

* Declaration signed by Tho. Pendarves, rector.
† In the certificate styled "Mr."
‡ In Plympton Maurice church, Devon, is a partly obliterated floor slab for Mrs. Mary, wife of Edward Moulton, gent. She died in 1687.
Peter Moulton and Sarah Stone, married 23 May, 1677.—St. Andrew's Parish Reg.

* The certificate has Mr. Henry Dyer. Hen. Dyer, gent., one of the twelve men in 1670.—Green Book.
† According to the certificate Alice Blake was buried 12 April, 1699, but is not in the Register; also Richard s. of Tho. Callaway, Nov. 30.
‡ Declaration signed by Tho. Pendarves, rector, and allowed by Jo. Molesworth and Hum. Nicholls.
§ The declaration at the end of 1700 signed by

21 April Mary d. of James Cockaine *al's* Tremeane W
27 April Elizabeth King, spinster
2 May Grace d. of Thomas Scaberrian W
12 May William Hancock W
27 May Epiphany d. of Robert Manuell W
9 June Arthur s. of Arthur Broad* W
10 June John Evagh
18 June Peter Pollard W
24 July Catherine Crewes W
1 Sep. Honor d. of Joell Capell W
15 Sep. Remfrey Rows W
23 Sep. Mary d. of James Merefield W
6 Oct. Honor d. of Oliver Basley* W
13 Oct. Samuel s. of Robert Dunkin W
16 Oct. Ann d. of William Rowe *al's* Mitchell W
28 Oct. Mr Peter Day† W
31 Oct. Martyn s. of John England W
2 Nov. Sr John Arundell, Knight‡ W
6 Nov. Elizabeth d. of Bernard Rows W
22 Nov. Nicholas Keslick W
13 Dec. Reginald Haweis,§ apothecary W
18 Dec. Thomasine d. of William Dennis, Junr W
13 Jan. Philip Harris W
14 Jan. Jone the wife of Stephen Stephens W
24 Jan. John s. of Richard Rawe the younger W
20 Jan. Elizabeth Reynolds, widdow W
21 Feb. Thomas s. of Thomas Adams W

the rector, Tho. Pendarves, John Day, Hugh Pollard, John Davies, overseers of the poor. Allowed by Anth. Nicholl and Edm. Prideaux.

* Certificate adds 'Junr.'

† Peter Day one of the twelve men in 1693.—Green Book.

‡ He was son and heir of Sir John Arundell, of Lanherne, by Elizabeth, daughter of William Brock, and became of Lanherne. He married, first, Elizabeth, daughter of Lord Teynham; and, secondly, Anna, daughter of John Arundell, Trerice, and relict of John Trevanyon. By his first wife Sir John had issue two daughters, his coheirs, Frances, married Sir Richard Beling, Knt., and Elizabeth, married Sir Henry Bedingfield, Bart., of Oxborow, co. Norfolk.

§ Mr. Hawes paid for Mr. Reynold Hawes shop rent £3 in 1703.—Green Book. John Hawes, of Key, married Grace, daughter and heir of Edward Vivian, of Key (by his wife, Jane, daughter of John Trencreeke, of Key), and had issue John, son and heir, aged 9 years in 1620, Francis, Reginald, Mary and Elizabeth.

1 Mar. Jone wife of Inigoe Inch* W
2 Mar. John s. of John Parking W
10 Mar. Ann wife of George Jolley W
13 Mar. John s. of Richard Edwards, mercer W
23 Mar. Ann Crewes, widdow W
23 Mar. Jone wife of Thomas Tibb† W

ANNO 1702.

10 April John Lawrey‡ W
17 April Humfrey Sloggett W
10 April Mary wife of John Tenny W
18 April James s. of Thomas Adams W
22 April Ann d. of Nathaniel Wood§ W
24 May William Cocking W
10 July Richard s. of George Jolley W
12 July Catherine Box W
26 July James Metherell W
5 Aug. John Gilbert W
11 Aug. Robert Skiner W
11 Oct. John s. of Nicholas Woodman W
29 Nov. Robert Harris W
2 Dec. Gregory s. of John Lamb W
16 Dec. Ralph Keate W
21 Dec. Constance Blake W
3 Jan. Margery Wolcock W
8 Jan. Mary d. of John Davis
12 Jan. Honor d. of Thomas Langdon W
31 Jan. Edward Morish W
8 Feb. John s. of Charles Trestaine W
12 Feb. John s. of Robert Merifeild W
13 Feb. Jane wife of Arthur Jolley W
14 Feb. John s. of John Symons W
20 Feb. Joan Inch, widdow W
10 Mar. John s. of Richard Rowe, junr W
18 Mar. Margery wife of Arthur Broad ‖ W

ANNO 1703.

25 Mar. John s. of John Gummow W
15 April Elizabeth d. of Thomas Tibb

* The certificate has 'Enoder Inch.'

† Declaration signed by Tho. Pendarves, rector. Edw. Crewse, Rich. Rowe, James Day, Wm. Cundye, overseers of the poor. Allowed by Edm. Prideaux, J. Tregagle.

‡ The certificate says of Tregoe.

§ Mr. Nathaniel Wood was named by Ralph Keate in his will (proved 10 April, 1686) to be guardian to his nephew Ralph Keate.

‖ Declaration signed by Tho. Pendarves, rector, Edw. Crewse, John Tanner, Francis Peters, and John Nicholls, overseers of the poor. Allowed by Edm. Prideaux and Robert Hoblyn.

Omitted from the register:—
James Bragg, buried 23 July.

29 April Richard Slade
4 May Emblyn Metherill, vid. W
16 Mar. Henry Rowse, gent., of Trebadannon* W
18 May Elizabeth d. of John Bonallack W
21 May Ellinor wife of William Wilkins W
6 June Charity Litticoate W
8 June Elizabeth Wills, vid. W
15 June Susley Trehemban W
29 June William s. of Petter Champion, Attorney W
8 Sep. Giles Edwards W
23 Sep. Thomazine Michell, vid. W
29 Sep. Joan wife of Richard Cowle W
4 Oct. John Grimes, Junr† W
8 Oct. Rebecka the wife of Jonathan Barrett W
16 Nov. John Hayman, Junr‡ W
10 Dec. Ann Pearse W
23 Dec. Elizabeth Pell, vid. W
5 Jan. Edward Eade W
29 Jan. John Tinny W
7 Feb. Katherine wife of John Jelbert W
11 Feb. Reginald s. of Stephen Buckingham W
27 Feb. Elizabeth Lackey W
6 Mar. Petherick Jelbert W
13 Mar. Ralph Allen W
18 Mar. Thomas Pendarves, Rector W
21 Mar. Mary wife of John Symons§ W

ANNO 1704.

25 Mar. Jane Bennett W
1 April John Burn, junr W
7 April John Burn, senr W
12 April Richard Clemens W
24 April Alice d. of Mr Hugh Pollard W
29 April William Moor|| W
30 April Jane d. of John Lewarne W
3 May Richard Jolley W

* Henry Rowse one of the twelve men in 1678-93, 1703.—Green Book.

† John Grimes paid rent of a shop 20s., in 1698.—Green Book.

‡ Mr. John Hayman paid rent of his shop for seven years at 33s., and another shop at 36s.—Green Book.

§ The declaration is signed by James Edwards, curate, Jos. Hawkey, Rob. Berry, Francis Dazzo, and John Harris, overseers of the poor. Allowed by Edm. Prideaux, Rob. Hoblyn.

Overseers for next year—Mr. Rich. Rows, Mr. William Rosogan, James Oliver, John Gilbert.

|| Davies Gilbert mentions a monument in the church to the memory of some of this family with these arms—Sa. a swan close within a bordure eng. arg., but the monument does not now exist.

17 May Wm Hambly W
19 May Mary Wills W
18 June Joan Burn W
4 July Daniell s. of Richd & Jane James W
9 July Eliz. d. of Richd & Frances Webber W
3 Aug. Daniell s. of Nathaniel & Frances Woods W
6 Aug. John s. of John & Jennefaire Parkins W
8 Aug. Mrs Anne May W
17 Aug. Anne d. of Roger Reading in ye Queen's service W
25 Aug. Grace d. of Mr Richd Rowse W
6 Sep. Thomas Hawke W
20 Sep. Susana Phillips W
7 Nov. Hester Morkam W
9 Nov. Joane d. of Elizabeth Strongman W
28 Nov. James s. of Thomas & Jane Polkinhorn W
13 Jan. Dorothy Benny W
30 Jan. Mr John Pollard W
2 Feb. John s. of John & Temperance Tinney W
22 Mar. Temperance d. of Mary Cock, widow W
24 Mar. Petronell Woolcock* W

ANNO 1705.

29 Mar. Audrey Hawke W
29 Mar. John Buckthought W
30 Mar. Frances wife of Edward Champion W
8 April Mathias s. of Mathias & Mary Battrell
18 April Mary d. of Richard & Thomazine Gilbert W
23 April Joan Edwards, widow W
8 May Samuel s. of Mr John Bishop, deceased W
14 May Joan Wilkins† W
4 June Jane d. of Wm Baseley W
1 July Thomas Somersford, a soldier W
24 July Mrs Eliz. Rumbelow‡ W

* Declaration signed by Ph. Collier, rector. Overseers for next year—Rob. Hoblyn, clerk, Arthur Mitchell, Philip Harris, Joseph Merefield. Allowed by Edm. Prideaux, Rob. Hoblyn.

† Certificate adds 'widow.'

‡ Mr. John Tuchim, minister of the Gospel at Stonehouse, and Elizabeth, daughter of Mr. John Rumbelow, of Bigbury, married 5 March, 1654; Philip Fitz Williams, son of Walter Fitz Williams, of Plymouth, and Mary, daughter of Mr. John Rumbelow, of Bigbury, deceased, married 12 Jan., 1654.—Par. Reg., St. Andrew, Plymouth.

5 Aug. John* s. of John Blamey W
6 Aug. Tho. Hocken W
9 Aug. Thomas Lae W
13 Aug. John Truscott W
17 Aug. Honor Delbridge W
22 Sep. Mary d. of M[rs] Ann Vivian W
11 Oct. Mary fford W
22 Oct. Dorothy d. of W[m] & Dorothy Roe W
28 Oct. Charles s. of John Blamey W
1 Nov. Jane wife of Robert Duncan W
5 Nov. Francis Richards W
16 Nov. Anne d. of Peter & Honor Tremain W
29 Nov. James Adams W
2 Jan. Joan the wife of M[r] Richard Edwards W
2 Jan. Philippa wife of John Pollawin W
3 Jan. M[rs] Honor Oxnam W
6 Jan. Pentecost d. of Thomas & Sarah Cockin *al's* Tremayn W
17 Jan. Michaell s. of Edw[d] & Grace Richards W
21 Jan. Isaac Jenkinn† W
1 Feb. The Rev[d] M[r] Rob[t] Hoblyn‡ of Nanswhidon dyed at London y[e] 7th Jan[ry] W
8 Feb. Eliz. wife of M[r] John King§ W
14 Feb. John s. of Dan[ll] May|| W
1 Mar. Sybella Harvey W
17 Mar. W[m] s. of John & Joan Lawrey W
18 Mar. Michaell s. of Eliz. Strongman¶

ANNO 1706.

25 Mar. James Mitchell W
26 May Mary wife of Mathias Battrell W
26 May Tho. s. of W[m] Cockyn *al's* Tremayn W
28 May Margery Lawrey W
29 May Tho. s. of Robert & Jane Merrifield W
8 April Jeremy s. of Phill. Collier, rect[r], & Eliz. his wife, died y[e] 7th April W
18 April Richard Webber W
19 April Eliz. Rowse, widow W
19 April Anne Hocken, widow W
9 May James Nettle W
18 May Sampson s. of John & Joan Mill W
3 June Eliz. d. of Henry & Jane Rowse W
5 June Mary d. of Thomas & Mary Hawke W
7 June Rich[d] Pendarves, Esq. W
19 July Dorothy wife of Colan Mannell W
27 Aug. Eliz. d. of Philip Collier, rect[r], & Eliz. his wife, died 25th W
18 Sep. Jane d. of Peter & Jane Bounsell W
28 Sep. Archibald Rowse W
31 Oct. Eliz. Callaway W
20 Nov. Jane d. of Bernard & Eliz. Lobb W
25 Nov. Eliz. d. of Anthony & Eliz. Hoskyn W
2 Dec. Peter Sampson W
5 Jan. Alice d. of Tho. & Jane Pearse W
12 Jan. Charles Retallack W
20 Jan. Petronell y[e] wife of Arthur Mitchell W
31 Jan. John Rowse W
2 Feb. W[m] s. of W[m] & Jane Evelin W
7 Feb. Arthur Broad W
2 Mar. John Polkinghorn W
9 Mar. Dorcas Retallock W
15 Mar. Abraham s. of Abraham Husband W
17 Mar. Denys Strongman* W

ANNO 1707.

26 Mar. Judith d. of John & Jennofaire Parkin W
27 Mar. M[rs] Jane Blight† W
28 Mar. Anne wife of Henry Jolly W

* He is recorded on a ledger stone in the church, on which he is said to have died 4 Aug., 1705, aged 24, having been apprenticed to a merchant and sailmaker. His brother Charles died 27 Oct. following, aged 21.

† Isaac Jenkin, parish clerk in 1697.—Green Book.

‡ Son of Rob. Hoblyn of Nanswhyden, Esq., by his wife Grace, daughter and coheiress of John Carew of Penwarne. He was rector of Ludgvan, and married Judith daughter and heir of Francis Burgess of St. Erth, by whom he had issue— Francis, married Lady Penelope Godolphin, and Edward, died s.p. before his father

§ Mr. John King, one of the twelve men in 1693-1703.—Green Book.

|| Daniell May paid 16s. rent of his shop in 1693.—Green Book.

¶ Declaration signed Philip Collier, rector. Allowed by John Molesworth, Charles Trelawny.

* Declaration signed by Ph. Collier, rector, and allowed by John Molesworth and Edm Prideaux.

Overseers for next year: John King, Sam. Batten, John Drew, and John Arscott.

† Certificate adds "widow."

29 Mar. Richard Watts W
16 May John England W
13 June Susanna d. of Thomas Tremain & Sarah his wife W
19 June Eliz. d. of Tho. & Eliz. Inch W
21 July Tho. Brewer W
8 Aug. Reskymer Allen W
8 Sep. John s. of Tho. & Florence Issable W
20 Sep. Philip s. of John & Jennefaire Parkin W
7 Oct. Mary d. of Wm & Eliz. Youlton W
17 Oct. Daniell s. of Nathaniel & Frances Wood W
28 Oct. Edwd the s. of John & Jane Richards W
30 Oct. Peter Harris W
9 Nov. Catharine d. of Christopher & Jane Warne W
15 Nov. John s. of George & Jane Baseley W
24 Nov. Henry Brewer W
27 Nov. Jane d. of Mr Hugh* & Eliz. Pollard W
28 Nov. Anne Bounsell W
30 Nov. Symon Rawlinn W
6 Dec. Mary d. of Mr Timothy Chute W
7 Dec. Joan Denys W
27 Dec. Mr Peter Pollard W
26 Jan. Mary Williams W
1 Feb. Philippa Lee W
1 Feb. Florence d. of Charles & Eliz. Trestaine W
3 Feb. Joan wife of Tho. Merrifield W
5 Feb. James Lawrey W
6 Feb. Anne d. of Mr Hugh & Eliz. Pollard W
9 Feb. Joan Ford, widow
10 Feb. Eliz. wife of Charles Trestaine W
10 Feb. Grace Wills, widow W
12 Feb. Eliz. d. of Robt & Thomazine Creebar W
23 Feb. Honor wife of Mr Blight Haycroft W
27 Feb. Margery Williams W
28 Feb. Dorothy Davies W
29 Feb. Wm Rawe W
2 Mar. Joan d. of Peter Kendall W
10 Mar. Tho. Stephens W
14 Mar. Peter Tremayne W

* Mr. Hugh Pollard, churchwarden in 1703, and one of the twelve men and treasurer in 1711. He was cousin to Peter Champion.

9 Mar. Frances* wife of Tho. Vivian, Esq.† W

Anno 1708.

26 Mar. Honr d. of John & Susanna Jane W
7 April John s. of Oliver & Jane Rawe W
20 April Alice wife of Edwd West W
22 April Samll s. of Peter & Susana Best W
27 April Tho. Kelly W
27 April Eliz. d. of John & Mary Parkin W
29 April Mary d. of Philip & Philippa Mitchell W
9 May Catherine the wife of Oliver Basely W
11 May John Best W
11 May Priscilla Williams W
19 May Wm s. of Richard & Anne Hicks W
6 June Florence Day W
7 June Eliz. wife of Henry Jolly W
19 June Gartred Kent W
26 June Stephen s. of Charles & Jane Thomas W
2 July George Luney W
22 Aug. Alice Rawlin W
10 Sep. Henry Withiell W
17 Sep. Wm Darr W
22 Nov. Edwd s. of John & Jennefaire Richards W
28 Nov. Mary d. of Tho. & Eliz. Manuell W
7 Dec. Eliz. Lockett W
10 Dec. Frances wife of Tho. Baseley W
4 Jan. Jennefaire wife of Tho. Callaway W
18 Jan. Francis Philips W
20 Jan. Joyce Strongman W
21 Jan. Grace Rogers W
28 Jan. Mr James Day W
29 Jan. Sarah wife of John Williams W
29 Jan. Robert s. of Tho. & Candacia Litticoat W

* She was sister to William Braithwaite of Detham, co. Gloucester. She was the first wife of Thomas Vivian of Truan, Esq. There is a monument to her memory in the north chapel or chancel aisle.

† Declaration signed by Ph. Collier, rector; allowed by John Molesworth and Edm. Prideaux.

Overseers for the next year: Mr. Thomas Hoblyn, Mr. William Rosogan, Richard Hicks, and Thomas Hoskyn.

The following is omitted from the register: Peter Parrow, Feb. 7.

31 Jan. Susanna Bennet *al's* James W
31 Jan. Florence d. of Tho. & Florence Issable W
2 Feb. George Strongman W
7 Feb. Dorothy d. of James & Catherine Bone W
8 Feb. Anne d. of Tho. & Eliz. Inch
19 Feb. Henry Jolly W
19 Feb. Mr Wm Rosogan* W
21 Feb. Joan Moyle, wid. W
28 Feb. Joseph Jane W
4 Mar. Thomas Pollawin s. of John & Jennefaire Parkyn W
10 Mar. Martin Tomm & Constance his wife W
12 Mar. Marriot Cockyn, wid. W
16 Mar. John s. of Stephen & Mary Warne W
16 Mar. John s. of Archibald & Mary Rowse† W

ANNO 1709.

2 April Jaell wife of Tho. Drew W
9 April John s. of Tho. & Julian Polkinhorn W
11 April Mary wife of Wm Brewer W
15 April Susanna d. of Tho. & Joan Tonkin W
18 April Joan wife of Tho. Tonkin W
23 April Jane Teage W
24 April Jane Rowse W
8 May Peter Kendall W
11 May Thomazine wife of John Ball W
11 May Mary d. of Jane Jane, wid. W
23 May Eliz. d. of Tho. & Eliz. Cornwall W
19 June Tho. Drew W
1 July Mr John Blight W
17 July Wm Condy W
24 July Stephen Knight W
27 July Temperance wife of Wm Bone, junr. W
1 Aug. John Williams W
6 Aug. Joan Strongman W
15 Aug. John s. of Wm & Sarah Baseley W
18 Aug. Richd Veale W
23 Aug. Wm Baseley, junr W

* William Resugga, for his grave £1 6s. 8d.—Green Book.

† Declaration signed by the rector, and allowed by the same as the previous year. Overseers for the ensuing year: Tho. Vivian, Esq., Mr. John Edwards, Mr. Henry Rowse, and John Hicks.

Omitted from the regular register:
Joan, wife of Michaell Cowling, bur. Sep. 3.

28 Aug. Catherine d. of John & Dinah Gilbert W
1 Sep. Wm s. of John & Joan Lawrey W
18 Sep. Jonathan Rowse W
21 Sep. Tho. Wills W
13 Oct. Richard Pascoe W
13 Oct. George s. of Phil. & Mary King W
23 Oct. Mary d. of Joseph & Jane Merrifield W
25 Oct. Jane Sprey W
25 Oct. Jane Litticot W
27 Oct. Olive Jenkyn W
30 Oct. Gartrude d. of Temperance Stephens W
7 Nov. Antony s. of Antony & Eliz. Hoskyn W
12 Nov. John s. of John & Joan Lawrey W
1 Dec. John s. of Wm & Joan Williams W
1 Dec. Richd Day W
3 Dec. Rebecka & Margaret ds of Wm & Joan Williams W
3 Dec. Jane d. of Oliver & Jane Rawe W
5 Dec. Anne d. of John & Jennefaire Parkyn W
6 Dec. John Lamb W
8 Dec. Jane d. of Wm & Joan Williams W
9 Dec. Eliz. d. of widow Jane W
10 Dec. Rebecka Jacob W
16 Dec. John Mill W
17 Dec. Susanna d. of Charles Trestaine W
23 Dec. Henry s. of Antony & Elizabeth Hoskyn W
26 Dec. Eliz. Brown W
7 Jan. Mary d. of John & Grace Gunow W
11 Dec. Frances d. of Richd & Frances Webber W
13 Dec. John Best W
17 Dec. Eliz. wife of Tho. Couch W
18 Dec. Mary d. of Michaell Cornish, junr & Grace his wife W
22 Dec. Mary d. of Robt & Mary Retallock W
5 Feb. Robert s. of Mr Tho. Hoblyn* & Joan his wife W
6 Feb. Mr Richd Rawe W

* This Thomas Hoblyn was of Tresaddern in St. Columb, and Joan was his second wife. She was a daughter of ..... Tresaddern, and the son was one of several of their children who died young.

7 Feb. Eliz. d. of John & Jennefaire Parkin W
11 Feb. Jane* d. of Mr. Tho. Hoblyn & Joan his wife W
22 Feb. Judith d. of M[r] Thomas Hoblyn & Joan his wife W
23 Feb. Jane d. of Henry & Mary Mitchell W
5 Mar. Tho. Issable W
6 Mar. W[m] Wilkin W
13 Feb. Eliz. d. of John & Mary Hawke W
19 Mar. Christopher Reynolds† W

ANNO 1710.

4 April Charity wife of W[m] Roe W
5 April Mary wife of Peter Pollard W
13 April John s. of George & Jane Baseley W
30 April John Rickard W
7 May Joan Lobb W
15 May W[m] Cock W
20 May Anne d. of Joan Pascoe W
23 May John Ball W
31 May Rose Watts W
13 June Jennefaire wife of John Parkyn W
14 June Joan Adams, wid. W
20 June Tho. Warne‡ W
21 June Remfry s. of Archibald Rowse deceased W
22 July Eliz. Jolley, wid. W
7 Aug. Charles s. of Peter Pollard W
11 Aug. Hon[r] Cockin, wid. W
25 Aug. Hon[r] d. of Mathuselah Williams . W
21 Sep. Tho. Stephens W
1 Nov. Catherine Williams W
4 Dec. Margaret Richards W
6 Dec. Mary d. of W[m] & Jane Callaway W
8 Dec. Jane Pollawin W
27 Dec. Christian the wife of Sampson Ball W
20 Jan. Julian wife of James Callaway W
1 Feb. Daniel James W
15 Feb. W[m] s. of Stephen & Mary Warne W
6 Feb. Martin Eudy W

* See note on burial of Rob. on 5th of the same month.

† Declaration signed by the rector, and allowed by John Molesworth and Edm. Prideaux. The new overseers: Hugh Pollard, gent., James Bone, John Metherill, and John Nichols.

‡ See his marriage to Elizabeth Lovell in 1663.

16 Feb. Eliz. wife of Tho. Adams W
20 Feb. Margaret Betty W
22 Feb. Philip s. of Philip Collier, rector, & Eliz. his wife* W
2 Mar. W[m] Bone W
9 Mar. Frances Webber, widow W
11 Mar. Tho. Callaway† W

ANNO 1711.

11 May Eliz. Thom W
22 May Frances d. of John & Joan Hawke W
22 May Jane wife of W[m] Evelin W
23 May Florence wife of John Nicholls W
25 May W[m] s. of John & Anne Harris W
1 June John Parkyn W
14 June Sarah d. of Thomas & Mary Hawke W
10 July James Gilbert W
14 July James s. of Henry & Mary Penaluna W
17 July Joan base child of Mary Denys W
19 July Tho. s. of Tho. & Eli. Cornwall W
25 July Anne wife of M[r] John Edwards W
13 Aug. W[m] Tinney W
16 Aug. John Parkin, clerk of y[s] parish W
26 Aug. Mary d. of Mary Cock, widow W
1 Oct. Joan Tubb W
8 Oct. Jane Soper W
9 Oct. Sampson s. of John & Phil[a] Hicks W
14 Oct. Michaell s. of W[m] Baseley W
18 Oct. Margaret wife of Peter Cockin *al's* Tremain W
30 Oct. W[m] s. of W[m] Bone W

* The Rev. Philip Collier was son of the Rev. John Collier of Gluvias, by his wife ..., daughter of .... Worth of Trenwugh in Mabe, and sister of William Worth, Archdeacon of Worcester. He married Elizabeth daughter of ..... Allen, by whom he had, with other issue, John, vicar of Colan, married there 8th Jan., 1733, to Mrs. Mary Pollard of St. Columb Major, and left issue—William, a lawyer at St. Austell, married Ann Toller of Fowey, and left issue; Philippa, married Rev. Walter Elford, rector of Milton Damarel, co. Devon; and Mary, married Mr. Tho. Trethewy of Lostwithiel.

† Declaration signed by the rector, but not attested by the signature of the justices.

New overseers: Mr. Peter Champion, Robert Merrifield, Henry Lee, Isaac Nichols.

9 Nov. Francis Hoblyn,* Esq[re] W
11 Nov. James s. of Thomas & Jane Polkinhorn W
14 Nov. Susanna d. of Peter Best W
27 Nov. Tho. Callaway W
28 Dec. Eliz. Couch W
6 Jan. Nichola Heritage W
22 Jan. John s. of Rich[d] & Ursula Arnold W
29 Jan. Charles Thomas W
4 Feb. Eliz. Warne† W
19 Feb. M[r] Joseph Hawkey‡ W
25 Feb. Mary Chapell W
1 Mar. Eliz. d. of M[r] Rich[d] Rowse W
11 Mar. Arthur Jenkin W
20 Mar. Richard Jackoe W
23 Mar. Thomas Issable§ W

ANNO 1712.

13 April Agnes Cock W
17 April Joan Launder W
21 April Joan Pollard W
26 April Joan wife of W[m] Callaway|| W
6 May Anne d. of John & Joan Hawke W
18 May Degory s. of Deg[ry] & Pentecost Keast W
4 June Joan wife of Thomas Langdon W
28 June Margaret Hawke W
30 June Dorothy Grey W
24 July Richard Hawke W
2 Aug. Mary wife of Thomas Tonkin W
4 Aug. Dorothy Burlace W
4 Aug. William s. of John & Dinah Gilbert W
14 Aug. M[r] Charles Pollard W
19 Aug. Luke Giles W

* He was son of the Revd. Robert Hoblyn, a J.P., and one of the Stannators. He married Lady Penelope, daughter of Sidney Godolphin, first Earl Godolphin. She remarried 5 Sep., 1714, at St. Enoder, Sir William Pendarves.

† She was relict of Tho. Warne, and daughter of Stephen Lovell and Ann his wife, daughter of John Bayly.

‡ "Mr. Joseph Hawkey to be allowed to build a seat next Mr. Vivian's as high and as far forward."—1688. "Mr. Joseph Hawkey to build a seat by the entrance to Sir John Arundell's chauncel, as far forth as Sir John St. Aubyn's."—1698. He was one of the twelve men in 1689-1712.—Green Book.

§ Declaration signed by the rector, allowed by John Molesworth, Edm. Prideaux, and James Nicholls. Overseers for next year: John Vivian, Esq., William Callaway, Henry Brewer and Philip Brewer.

|| William Callaway was one of the overseers of the poor, 1712.—Green Book.

3 Sep. Margery Edwards W
4 Sep. Tho. Inch W
16 Sep. M[r] John Edwards W
20 Sep. Joan Kinge W
23 Sep. Tho. Tonkin W
8 Oct. M[rs] Catherine Dyer W
26 Oct. Eliz. d. of Roger & Mary Reading W
2 Nov. Mary d. of James & Grace Callaway W
11 Nov. John s. of John & Jane Richards
12 Nov. Jennefaire d. of John & Susanna Jane W
19 Nov. Maud wife of John Eudy W
23 Nov. Thomas s. of Thomas Tonkin, dec[d] W
29 Nov. George s. of Philip & Mary Kinge W
10 Dec. Catherine wife of James Bone W
31 Dec. John Husband W
1 Jan. John s. of John & Joan Lawrey W
13 Feb. Eliz. d. of Rob[t] & Eliz. Brewer W
15 Feb. Richard Harris W
23 Feb. Francis s. of John & Eliz. Dingey* W

ANNO 1713.

8 April W[m] Merifield W
14 April Arthur Broad W
20 April John Hawke W
25 April Anne Cundy, wid. W
26 April Joan wife of John Harvey W
8 June Hon[r] Harris, wid. W
13 June Charles Wheedon W
18 June Eliz. d. of Faithfull & Joan Cock W
6 July John Strongman W
30 July Mary d. of Faithfull & Joan Cock W
4 Aug. John Udy W
11 Aug. Jane d. of Robert & Eliz. Brewer W
19 Aug. W[m] Oxnam W
19 Aug. Eliz. d. of Henry & Thomazine Cock W
25 Aug. W[m] s. of Agnes Lifford W
26 Aug. Jane d. of Giles & Jane Williams W
19 Sep. Abraham Lee

* The certificates signed by the rector, but not attested. Overseers for next year: Mr. William Batten, John Boone, Richard Peters, Mark Nichols.

12 Oct. Mary d. of Thomas & Candace Litticott W
17 Oct. Joan d. of W^m & Eliz. Minnow W
20 Oct. Jane wife of Leonard Brewer W
19 Nov. Martha d. of Wm Youlton W
25 Nov. Mary Lanyon, widdow W
29 Nov. Philip s. of Thomas & Hon^r Benny W
15 Dec. Henry s. of Henry Thomas W
16 Dec. John s. of Philip & Anne Harris W
27 Dec. The Lady Frances Bellings died ye 6 Dec.*
30 Dec. Grace Stephens
19 Jan. Emeline Troth, widdow W
21 Jan. Tho. s. of Thomas & Jane May W
16 Feb. Frances Strongman, widow W
27 Feb. Jane d. of Robert Litticot W
17 Mar. Samuel Yeoman of Ladock† W

ANNO 1714.

5 April John s. of George Basely W
12 April Anne Tyer, widow W
17 April Rich^d s. of Rich^d & Eliz. Brabyn W
24 April Joseph Merifield W
29 April Grace wife of Stephen Buckingham W
30 April Wm Evelyn W
2 May Richd Williams W
11 May Anne wife of John Harris W
11 May Mary d. of Rob. & Anne Husband W
17 May Patience Lee W
26 May Mr Thomas Hoblyn‡ W
1 June James Merrifield W
7 June Mr Francis May W
13 June Mary Lawrey W
1 July Honor Giles, widow W

* The Lady Frances Bellings was buried in "linnen." Forfeiture to ye poor of ye parish 50s.

† "There have been no other forfeitures this year than what is before mentioned. March 27, 1714. Ph. Collier, rector. New overseers: Mr. Nathaniell Champion, Mr. Walter Harris, John Gummow, John Dingey."

‡ Son of Rob. Hoblyn, of Nanswhyden, by his wife Grace, daughter and coheiress of John Carew, of Penwarne. He was of Tresaddern, in St. Columb, and married first, Mary, daughter and coheiress of John Carter—issue an only son, John, of Kenwyn, for whose descendants see Col. Vivian's "Visitations of Cornwall." Thomas Hoblyn married secondly, Joan Tresaddern, by whom he had several children.

15 July Mr William Atkinson, curate of this parish W
1 Aug. Daniel Ropson W
12 Aug. Jane d. of Thomas & Jane May W
19 Aug. Robert s. of Mr Richard & Jane Edwards W
30 Aug. Dorothy d. of Charles Thomas W
7 Sep. Epipheny Oxnam W
12 Sep. John s. of Mr John King W
21 Sep. Eliz. d. of Henry & Eliz. Lee W
11 Oct. Charity wife of Oliver Basely W
12 Oct. Anne d. of William Bone W
14 Oct. Grigory d. of Archibald Rowse, deceased W
24 Oct. Abraham s. of Abraham & Eliz. Husband W
26 Oct. John s. of Mr Richd Rundle of Mevagissey W
31 Oct. Philip d. of Philip & Honor Callaway W
31 Oct. Eliz. d. of James Bone W
1 Nov. Stephen s. of Joell Capell W
2 Nov. Hannah Leverton W
4 Nov. Joell s. of Joell Capell W
9 Nov. John s. of Philip & Martha Slogget W
11 Nov. Honor Jolly, widow W
12 Nov. Gilbert Merrifield W
14 Nov. John s. of John & Mary Davies W
15 Nov. Humphry s. of Philip & Martha Slogget W
17 Nov. Thomasine d. of James & Grace Callaway W
20 Nov. Eliz. d. of Philip Collier, rect^r, & Eliz. his wife W
20 Nov. W^m s. of Tho. & Eliz. Hickes W
23 Nov. Ralph s. of John & Ebat Lamb W
26 Nov. Dorothy d. of John Banger W
27 Nov. Mrs Luce Pollard, widow W
27 Nov. Tho. s. of Robt Merrifield W
28 Nov. Margaret d. of Robert & Jane Merrifield W
30 Nov. Eliz. wife of Benjamin Chalwell W
1 Dec. Elizabeth d. of John & Joan Lawrey W
2 Dec. Petronell wife of Richd Peters W
4 Dec. John s. of John Banger W
7 Dec. John s. of Archibald Rows & Mary his wife W

11 Dec. Tho. s. of John & Mary Metherill W
18 Dec. Oliver Baseley W
21 Dec. Rich[d] s. of M[r] Rich[d] & Jane Edwards W
24 Dec. Mary d. of Michaell & Grace Cornish W
26 Dec. John s. of Tho. & Eliz. Cornwall W
31 Dec. Charles s. of Arthur & Rebecka Raw W
31 Dec. Alice d. of Francis & Joan Vivian W
4 Jan. William s. of John & Mary Metherill W
5 Jan. Alice Blake, widow W
6 Jan. Henry Rlake W
6 Jan. Honor d. of Philip & Anne Allen W
12 Jan. Edw[d] s. of Tho. Pearse W
18 Feb. John s. of Michaell & Grace Cornish W
19 Feb. Jane Issable W
27 Feb. Mary Cock, widow W
27 Feb. Methuselah s. of Methuselah & Mary Williams W
17 Mar. Tho. May W
19 Mar. Rich[d] s. of Michaell & Grace Cornish W
24 Mar. Eliz. d. of Henry & Thomasine Cock* W

ANNO 1715.

1 April Philip s. of Henry & Florence Oxnam W
4 April Bernard Lobb W
5 April Nicholas Honey W
12 April Edward Stephens W
5 May Temperance Stevens W
30 May Peter s. of Henry & Mary Blight W
3 June Anne d. of Henry & Mary Blight W
4 June M[rs] Anne Massey
10 June Rich[d] s. of Philip & Honor Callaway W
19 June Eliz. d. of John Nichols W
21 June Gilbert s. of Henry & Mary Blight W
26 June Henry Blight of Gavrigan W
26 June Tho. s. of Henry Benny W
10 July Mark Nichols W
11 July M[rs] Judith Hoblyn,* wid. W
26 July Mary d. of Thomas Hoskyn W
30 July Joan Dar, wid. W
14 Aug. Grace wife of Mich[ll] Cornish W
17 Aug. Edward s. of Philip & Martha Slogget W
12 Sep. Thomasine Whitford, wid. W
14 Sep. Jane Blight W
15 Sep. Joan wife of Rich[d] Clemow W
8 Oct. George Jolly W
11 Oct. Francis Darr W
2 Nov. Jane Tremain, wid. W
7 Nov. Jane wife of Oliver Rawe W
16 Nov. John s. of Tho. May, dec[d] W
17 Nov. Grace wife of Robert Litticot W
8 Dec. Jane wife of William Evelyn W
11 Dec. Peter Kendall W
13 Dec. William base child of Epiphany Oxnam W
27 Dec. Mary wife of Robert Retallock W
30 Dec. Eliz. d. of Gregory & Wilmot Nancey W
3 Jan. James s. of James & Grace Callaway W
6 Jan Henry Tinney W
8 Jan. Catherine Thomas, widow W
15 Jan. W[m] s. of Richard Cundye W
18 Jan. George Moore W
22 Jan. Margery Pooll W
29 Jan. Margery base child of Margery Pooll W
6 Feb. Jane Jane, widow W
10 Feb. W[m] Edwards W
20 Feb. Henry Lee W
12 Mar. John Harvey W
20 Mar. M[rs] Jane Day, widow† W

ANNO 1716.

7 April Eliz. d. of John & Joan Mill W
18 April Florence wife of Henry Oxnam W
26 April Lancelot Clemows W
4 May Margery Whitaker W
7 May Tho. s. of Joseph Martyn W
8 May Susanna d. of Faithfull Cock W
19 May Edward Richards W
26 May Ralph Williams W
29 May Jane d. of John & Joyce Hamly W

* The woollen certificates signed by the rector and attested by Edm. Prideaux, John Peter, John Willyams.

New overseers: Philip Collier, clerk, John Harris, William Glanville, Benjamin Chalwell.

* See note, p. 249.

† Certificates signed and attested by the same as last year.

New overseers: Mr. Walter Harris, Mr. John Tanner, Arthur Veall, Thomas Stephens.

1 June Morgan s. of Gregory & Wilmot Nancey W
8 June Tho. Vivian,* Esq[re] W
9 June Dorothy wife of Nich's Hawke W
11 June Philip s. of Henry Oxnam W
13 June W[m] s. of Archibald Rows
4 July Sibella wife of John Lee W
13 July Jane d. of John & Jane Jane, dec[d] W
21 July Catherine wife of W[m] Blake W
8 Aug. Edward Lawrey W
26 Sep. Mary Woon, widow W
27 Sep. Margery Rows, widow W
16 Oct. Mary Cock, widow W
30 Oct. Michaell Cornish W
1 Nov. M[r] John Kinge W
5 Nov. Mary d. of Robert & Mary Manuell W
9 Nov. Mary d. of Tho. Hawke W
15 Nov. S[r] Rich[d] Bellings,† knight W
22 Nov. John Grimes W
23 Nov. W[m] Foss, a traveller W
30 Nov. Eliz. d. of M[r] Rich[d] & Jane Edwards W
30 Nov. Mary Jewell, widow W
3 Feb. Humphry Harvey W
7 Feb. James Callaway W
17 Feb. Grace Rows, widow W
14 Mar. John Bullen W
14 Mar. Mary d. of W[m] Cockin W
18 Mar. John Matthews W
19 Mar. Catherine Crews, widow W
19 Mar. Philip Slogget W
21 Mar. Rich[d] base child of Eliz. Polkinhorne‡

ANNO 1717.

9 April Thomas s. of Rob[t] & Anne Hambly W

* He was son and heir of John Vivian, of Truan, by Mary, daughter of Sir John Glanville. He sold Treharrock in 1699. Married first, Frances, sister of William Braithwaite, of Detham, co. Gloucester, she died in 1707; he married secondly, Sarah, daughter of . . . . . . Dodson, of Haye, 8 June, 1710, but died s.p.

† Sir Richard Bellings, Knt., was buried without a 'certificate,' for which a fine of five pounds was paid. He was, according to "Le Neve's Knights," Secretary to Queen Katherine, living at Somerset House in 1698, and came out of the county of Dublin. He married Frances, daughter and coheiress of Sir John Arundell, of Lanherne, and had issue Charles, died unmarried; Richard took the name and arms of Arundell, succeeded to Lanherne, etc., married and left issue—John; Mary married Sir John Hales, of Tunstall, Kent, Bart., and died 24 Jan., 1701, and a child died young.

‡ Certificates signed by the rector, and allowed by John Peters and Edm. Prideaux.

24 April Edward s. of Antony & Mary Godolphin W
29 April Mary wife of Isaac Nichols W
21 May Mary d. of Edward & Anne May W
31 May Philip s. of W[m] & Anne Benny W
3 July Joan Pascoe, widow W
3 Aug. Henry Jolly W
11 Sep. Mary wife of John Tom W
15 Sep. Judith Edwards W
13 Oct. Elizabeth d. of Rich[d] & Eliz. Cornish W
13 Oct. Eliz. wife of W[m] Minnow W
19 Oct. Mary d. of John & Mary Turner W
23 Oct. Eliz. wife of Luke Jolly W
29 Oct. Petronel d. of Rich[d] Peters W
17 Nov. Rich[d] Clemoes W
18 Nov. Tho. Davies W
27 Nov. John s. of John Hendy W
16 Dec. Honor wife of Edward Kestlake W
28 Dec. Tho. Bounsall W
10 Jan. Anne d. of Faithfull & Joan Cock W
25 Jan. Catherine Warne,* widow W
28 Jan. W[m] Adams W
14 Feb. Jane d. of Tho. May, deceased W
24 Feb. Honor Bird W
22 Mar. M[r] Benjamin Spernon† W

ANNO 1718.

12 April Anne Young, widow W
22 April James s. of M[r] Rich[d] Edwards W
2 May Ruth d. of W[m] & Joan Denys W
9 May W[m] d. of Peter & Eliz. Pollard W
2 June John s. of John & Mary Wheedon
3 June Tho. Clemows W
7 June M[r] Rich[d] Rawe W
21 June Frances d. of Thomas & Honor Callaway

New overseers: Sir William Pendarves, Mr. John Tanner, William Drew, James Oliver.

The following is omitted from the regular register:

Mary d. of Wm. Cocking, March 14, 1716.

* She was daughter of . . . . Ivey, and relict of Henry Warne, having been his second wife. See marriages, 1656 and 1673.

† Certificates signed and allowed as in the previous year.

New churchwardens: John Day and Michael Cornish. Overseers: Mr. James Paynter, Mr. John Tanner, Richard Grigg, Arthur Rawe.

22 June Rich[d] s. of John & Anne Sprey W
3 July Jennefaire d. of Anthony & Mary Godolphin W
5 July Eliz. d. of Robt. & Eliz. Cock W
6 July Margery Edwards, widow W
15 July Alice wife of Henry Veall W
28 July W[m] Cocking* W
30 Aug. Edward Merrifield W
8 Sep. M[rs] Anne Arundell† the wife of Rich[d] Arundell of Lanhern, Esq[re]
25 Sep. Audrey Hawke, widow W
11 Oct. Catherine d. of John & Ebat Hendy W
9 Oct. Oliver Basely W
15 Oct. Nath. Wood W
26 Oct. John s. of Isaac Nichols W
5 Nov. Rich[d] s. of Michael & Eliz. Rundle W
9 Nov. Eliz. Withiell, widow W
17 Nov. John s. of John Drew W
22 Nov. Florence Rickard W
27 Nov. Thomas s. of Thomas & Prudence Gilbert W
8 Dec. Mary d. of Anthony & Mary Godolphin W
13 Dec. Jane base child of Eliz. Bounsell W
24 Dec. James s. of Francis & Mary Cowling W
25 Dec. Nicholas Woodman W
13 Jan. Eliz. Harris, wid. W
30 Jan. Grace d. of Henry Lee, dec[d], & Eliz. his wife
1 Feb. Eliz. d. of Francis & Joan Tomm W
2 Feb. Joan d. of Martin & Joan Strongman W
3 Feb. Eliz. wife of John Dingey W
18 Feb. Anne d. of Philip & Anne Allen W
27 Feb. W[m] s. of Thomas & Eliz. Williams W
2 Mar. Frances Rawe, widow W
5 Mar. Grace d. of Timothy & Mary Stephen W
9 Mar. Philip s. of Henry Thomas‡ W

* The certificate adds, '*al's* Tremain.'

† She was a daughter of Joseph Gage, of Sherborne Castle (and sister of Thomas 1st Viscount Gage, and 8th Bart.), by his wife Elizabeth, daughter and heiress of George Penruddock, Esq. She married Richard Beling Arundell, of Lanherne. The certificates state that no certificate being brought forfeit was paid to y[e] poor 50s.

‡ The certificates signed and allowed by the same as last year.

ANNO 1719.

29 Mar. Dorothy d. of John & Eleanore Opye W
2 April Eliz. d. of John & Eleanore Opye W
13 April Thomas s. of Thomas & Eliz. Hicks W
6 May Philip s. of William & Anne Benny W
8 May Sam[ll] s. of John Perkins, dec[d] & Margaret his wife W
26 May James Cowling, attorney W
8 June Methuselah s. of Methuselah & Mary Williams W
8 June Mary Oliver, widow W
20 June Mary wife of Stephen Warne* W
2 July Samuel Litticot W
23 July Christian Rawe, widow W
25 July M[rs] Anne Vivian, widow W
12 Sep. Jane wife of Thomas Pearce W
15 Sep. Jane wife of John Cornish W
1 Oct. Avis Rawe
4 Oct. Philip s. of Philip Collier, rect[r] & Eliz. his wife W
23 Oct. Grace d. of John Issabell W
19 Nov. Mary wife of William Hellier, a traveller W
1 Dec. M[r] Francis Burges W
12 Dec. Jane Bounsell, widow W
26 Dec. Robert Manuell W
6 Jan. Anne Harvey W
12 Feb. Frances Treninnys, widow W
18 Feb. Jane Pollard, widow W
22 Feb. W[m] s. of W[m] & Anne Benny W
26 Feb. Isaac Nicholls W
29 Feb. Eliz. Skynner W
5 Mar. Stephen s. of Richard & Jane Lovell W
9 Mar. Edward base child of Honnor Pollard† W

ANNO 1720.

6 April Grace wife of Francis Dungey W
9 April Frances Best, widow W
9 April Mary wife of W[m] Woolcock W
10 April John Harris W

New overseers: Tho. Vivian, Esq., Mr. John Tanner, Philip Harris and James Rowe.

Omitted from the register:

Ann Jacka, wid., 12 April.

* See Mar. 1693.

† The certificates signed and allowed as last year. Churchwardens continued.

Overseers: John Bone, Henry Brewer, Henry Veale and Tho. Merrifield.

13 April Frances Thorn W
18 April W^m s. of Anthony & Dinah Coad W
25 April Joan Merrefield W
1 May Thomas Tremeane W
6 May Alice wife of John Langdon, jun^r W
18 May Joan wife of Charles Bounsell W
7 Aug. Anne Bone, widow W
8 Sep. Hendy Langdon W
24 Sep. James s. of Robert & Jane Merrifield W
28 Sep. Frances the wife of Charles Thomas W
13 Oct. Pentecost d. of Henry Darr, dec^d & Mary his wife W
26 Oct. Pascow s. of Richard & Eliz. Brabyn W
28 Oct. Honor Tyer, widow W
3 Nov. Mary d. of John & Mary Mewdon W
4 Nov. Honor d. of Thomas Callaway W
10 Nov. Mary Tomm, widow W
19 Nov. Mary d. of John Buckingham W
20 Nov. Henry Blight W
26 Nov. Rich^d s. of Archibald & Mary Rows W
29 Nov. John Sprey W
5 Dec. Henry s. of W^m & Margaret Blake W
1 Jan. Rich^d s. of Thomas Callaway W
3 Jan. Peter Merrifield W
7 Mar. Isaac Husband* W
13 Mar. Jane d. of John Langdon W
22 Mar. Revd Mr James Beauford† W
22 Mar. Henry s. of Henry & Thomazine Cock‡ W

ANNO 1721.

24 April Eliz. wife of Joseph Osborne of St Denis W

* Isaac Husband paid rent of his shop 10s. in 1703.—Green Book.

† He was rector of Lanteglos, and married, first, Anne, daughter of Joseph Sawle, Esq., of Penrice (by his wife Amy Travanion, married at St. Mawan by Licence, date 21 March, 1660); he married, secondly, Jane, daughter of John Vivian, Esq. (by his second wife Mary Glanville). He is commemorated by a monument with his arms, described with the other monuments.

‡ Certificates signed and allowed by the same. New churchwardens: Robert Merrifield and Roger George.

Overseers: John Bone, Michaell Cornish, John Williams and John Saunders.

26 April Jane d. of John & Jane Bone W
4 May John Lee W
21 May Charles base child of Prudence Parnell W
10 June Thomas s. of John & Catherine Hockyns W
11 June Thomas s. of Faithfull & Joan Cock W
19 June Nathaniel Adams W
12 July Richard s. of W^m & Margaret Trembeth W
28 July Jane d. of Rich^d & Eliz. Brabyn W
31 July Mary wife of Robert Manuell W
10 Aug. Joan d. of John & Joan Drew W
11 Aug. Eliz. d. of John & Mary Gilbert W
15 Aug. Mary d. of John & Mary Gilbert W
12 Oct. Joseph base child of Eliz. Baseley W
14 Oct. Mr Nathaniel Champion W
26 Oct. Mrs Mary Bishop,* wid. of John Bishop, late rector W
2 Dec. John s. of John Harris, dec^d & Catherine his wife W
6 Dec. Jane wife of Philip Husband W
8 Dec. Eliz. d. of Gregory & Wilmot Nancey W
13 Jan. Eliz. d. of W^m & Honor Roberts W
17 Jan. Edward s. of Edward & Anne May W
27 Jan. W^m s. of Richard & Anne Cock W
20 Feb. John s. of W^m & Ursula Tom W
24 Feb. Humphry Oxnam W
3 Mar. John Bone† W

ANNO 1722.

4 April Jane Grimes, widow W
7 April Rich^d s. of John & Jane Buckingham W
12 April Wm Minnow & Eliz. d. of Tho. & Candace Litticot W

* She was a daughter of the Rev. Thomas Pendarves, rector of Mawgan and St. Columb, and second wife of the Rev. John Bishop, rector of St. Columb.

† Certificates signed and allowed by the same as the previous year. Churchwardens continued.

New overseers: Mr. Hugh Williams, Thomas Glanville, William Callaway and Samuel Williams.

19 April Mr John Oxnam W
25 April Wm Symons W
10 Mar. Eliz. d. of Thomas & Eliz. Cornwall W
5 June Sarah, d. of Samuel & Alice Pearse W
7 June Mary Luney, wid. & Anne d. of Thomas & Eliz. Cornwall W
20 June Anne d. of Wm & Eliz. James W
1 July Catherine d. of Richard & Eliz. Brabyn W
3 July Wm s. of Anthony & Dinah Coad W
7 July Wm Dennis W
15 July John Opie, of Halveor W
25 July Mary wife of Francis Cowling W
26 July James s. of Mathuselah & Mary Williams W
31 July Mary d. of Robt & Anne Hamley W
3 Aug. John Lawe W
8 Aug. Thomas s. of Richd & Anne Hicks W
9 Aug. Julian wife of Thomas Polkinhorn W
22 Aug. Eliz. Cowling W
20 Sep. Francis Dingey W
23 Sep. Mr Blight Haycroft W
30 Sep. Anne d. of Samuel & Anne Pearce W
7 Oct. Anne d. of Michll & Eliz. Rendle W
11 Nov. Anthony s. of Mr John & Emlin Tanner W
6 Dec. Joan wife of John Mill W
23 Dec. Mary d. of Henry Blight, decd W
23 Dec. Anne base child of Margaret Champion W
3 Jan. Mary d. of Philip & Philippa Michel W
21 Jan. Wm Rawe W
22 Jan. Henry s. of Faithfull & Joan Cock W
1 Feb. James s. of John & Grace Burges W
8 Feb. Wm s. of Philip & Philippa Michell W
16 Feb. Philip s. of Philip & Philippa Michell W
16 Feb. Mrs Emelin Beauchamp, wid.* W

* She was a daughter of Mr. . . . Edwards; married in 1684 John Beauchamp.

17 Feb. John Cornish W
1 Mar. Mary wife of Philip Oliver W
4 Mar. Joan d. of Jonathan & Catherine Barret W
4 Mar. James s. of Faithfull & Joan Cock W
10 Mar. Frances wife of Richd Callaway W
21 Mar. Thomas Trevithick* W

ANNO 1723.

28 Mar. Robt Wheedon W
2 April Robt Litticot W
6 April Joseph base child of Eliz. Minnow W
26 April Eliz. wife of Robt Strongman W
2 May Frances Pollard, widow W
6 May Charles Bounsell W
22 May Robt Hawke† W
1 June Jane d. of Robt & Eliz. Brewer W
2 June Mary d. of Thomas & Mary Litticot W
15 June Mrs Emeline Stephens W
24 June John s. of Thomas Polkinhorne W
12 July Eliz. wife of Robt Blake W
21 Aug. Wm Baseley W
8 Sep. Agnes d. of John & Mary Metherill W
13 Sep. Peter s. of Peter & Grace Best W
29 Oct. Anne wife of Jonathan Dawe W
29 Oct. Philip s. of Robt & Eliz. Brewer W
29 Oct. John s. of Philip & Mary King W
30 Oct. Judith wife of Henry Knight W
5 Nov. Wm Price W
6 Dec. Eliz. d. of Wm & Deborah Gatty W
13 Dec. Peter Tremain *al's* Cocking W
14 Dec. Stephen Stephens W
15 Dec. Shadrack s. of Shadrack & Jane Tremain W
25 Dec. John s. of Samll Grimes & Mary his wife W
26 Dec. Eliz. wife of John Cocking W
28 Dec. Tho. s. of John & Catherine Gass W

* Certificates signed and allowed by the same as in the previous year. New churchwardens: Benjamin Chalwell and John Williams.

Overseers: Mr. Edward Crews, William White, Richard Cundye and Thomas Kestell.

† He was one of the waywardens in 1710.—Green Book.

3 Jan. John s. of Mr James Bishop & Sarah his wife W
6 Jan. Tho. Crews W
8 Jan. Margaret wife of Wm Trembeth W
17 Jan. Francis Tom W
19 Jan. Thomas Vivian, Esqr* W
31 Jan. Charles Thomas W
6 Feb. Richd s. of John & Anne Sprey W
11 Feb. Mary d. of Methuselah & Mary Williams W
25 Feb. Mary wife of John Whetter W
1 Mar. Melicent wife of Wm Tinney W
5 Mar. John s. of Mr Giles Hamley & Barbara his wife W
9 Mar. Joan Elvans of Mawgan, wid. W
11 Mar. Hester wife of Augustine Julians of Mawgan W
18 Mar. Grace wife of John Buckingham† W

ANNO 1724.

20 April Florence Harris, widow W
24 April Barbara wife of Mr Giles Hamley‡ W
28 April Joan Gilbert, widow W
29 April John Langdon W
5 May Sibella Harvey W
11 May Anne Gilbert, widow W
12 May John s. of Petherick and Margaret Williams W
16 May Thomas s. of Mr Thomas Shepherd & Mary his wife W
25 May Wm s. of Gilbert & Joyce Meales W
2 June Humphry s. of Humphry & Eliz. England W
7 June Elizabeth d. of John & Mary Tom W
11 June Mary d. of Shadrack & Jane Tremain W
13 June Mary Merrifield, widow W

* He was son of John Vivian of Truan, Esq., by his wife Mary, daughter of Joseph Sawle of Penrice, Esq., and died unmarried.

† Certificates signed and allowed by the same as the last. New churchwardens: Tho. Merrifield and Jacob Grigg. Overseers: Mr. John Harris, Tho. Drew, William Bone, and Edward Inch.

‡ She was a daughter of Philip Hawkins of Pennence, and first wife of Giles Hambly of St. Columb, gent., by whom she had an only son who died an infant.

13 June Alice, d. of Francis & Joan Vivian W
13 June Tho. s. of Samll & Alice Pearce W
15 June Thomazine wife of Charles Allen W
1 July Mary d. of Henry and Mary Rows W
5 July John s. of John & Anne Sprey W
6 July Mr John Tanner* W
7 July Peter s. of Peter & Dorcas Pidwell W
10 July James Bone W
12 July Susanna d. of Peter & Grace Best W
16 July Robt Hocken W
17 July Degory s. of Degory & Pentecost Keast W
17 July Frances d. of Richd & Jane Grigg W
25 July Mary d. of Daniell & Elizabeth May W
25 July Caroline Ward W
1 Aug. Anne Trevithick, widow W
9 Aug. Peter & John sons of James & Frances Champion W
24 Aug. Tho. Brabyn W
6 Sep. Grace d. of Richd & Thomazine Cowle W
22 Sep. Thomasine wife of Richd Cowle W
1 Oct. Ann d. of Mr. Tho. Shepherd W
2 Oct. Richard s. of Richard Cowle W
7 Oct. Jane d. of Francis & Catherine Pearce W
12 Oct. John Opie W
14 Oct. Mary d. of Philip & Mary Rickard W
22 Oct. John s. of John & Dorothy Arscott W
27 Oct. John Pearce *al's* Francis Orchard, a vagrant W
7 Nov. Arice wife of John Rawe W
7 Nov. Alice wife of Samuel Pearce W
11 Nov. Mr Peter Champion† W
18 Nov. Thomas s. of Edmond & Dinah Varcoe W
21 Nov. Thomas Scaberrio‡ W
22 Nov. Robt s. of Robt & Catherine Manuell W

* Called 'mercer' in certificate.

† Styled 'Attorney-at-Law' in certificate. He was one of the twelve men in 1703.—Green Book.

‡ The certificate adds 'Sexton.'

23 Nov. Wm s. of Wm & Mary Tubb W
27 Nov. Susanna d. of Mr James Paynter & Anne his wife W
5 Dec. Philippa wife of Richd Cornish W
7 Dec. Mrs. Eliz. Champion,* widow W
13 Dec. Honor wife of Samuel Williams W
14 Dec. Mary d. of Giles & Jane Williams W
26 Dec. Margaret Haycroft, widow W
16 Jan. Degory Williams W
23 Jan. Anne Slade W
4 Mar. Mary wife of Philip Rickard W
5 Mar. Mrs Emeline Resogan, widow W
13 Mar. Eliz. Wheedon, widow W
16 Mar. Mrs Jane Champion,† widow W
19 Mar. Richd Arundell‡ of Lanhern, Esq. §W

ANNO 1725.

4 April Mrs Alice Rows, widow W
9 April John Eudy W
17 April Grace Bounsell, widow W
20 April Mary Polkinhorn, widow W
7 May Mariot Nettle, widow W
6 June John s. of John Bone, decd & Jane his wife
7 June Eliz. wife of Richd Tremaine W
21 July Mr Edward Champion W
25 July Ruth Blake, widow W
26 July Mary d. of Robt & Grace Cock W
23 Aug. Anthony s. of Anthony & Dinah Coad W
3 Sep. Thomasine Law, widow W
27 Sep. Mary d. of Abraham & Eliz. Husband W
22 Oct. Eliz. d. of Thomas & Eliz. Hicks W
9 Nov. Mrs Gartrude Allen, widow W

* Relict of Mr. Peter Champion.

† Relict of Mr. James Champion.

‡ Son and heir of Sir Richard Belling, knt., by his wife Frances, eldest daughter and co-heir of Sir John Arundell of Lanherne by Elizabeth Roper, daughter of Lord Teynham. He married Ann, daughter of Joseph Gage, Esq., (see note p. 247), by whom he had Mary, daughter and co-heiress, married Henry seventh Baron Arundell of Wardour; and Frances, daughter and coheiress, married Sir John Gifford, bart.

§ Certificates signed and allowed by the same as last year. Churchwardens continued. New overseers: Phil. Collier, clerk, Mr. Joseph Bishop, Colan Manuell, and Rob. Brewer.

15 Nov. Joan d. of Inigo & Eliz. Inch W
17 Nov. Susanna base child of Mary Merifield W
27 Nov. Henry s. of Henry & Mary Brewer W
10 Dec. Dorothe Jolly, widow W
11 Jan. Eliz. d. of Nichs Hawke W
14 Jan. Eliz. d. of William Youlton W
15 Jan. Wm Hoskyn W
16 Jan. Mr Beltezar Williams W
24 Jan. Thomas s. of Francis & Catherine Pearce W
25 Jan. George Thomas W
10 Mar. Mary Sloggct, widow W
13 Mar. Rachell Hooper, a vagrant W
18 Mar. Eliz. Harris* W

ANNO 1726.

25 Mar. Sarah ye wife of Mr Edward Crews W
13 April Anne Hocken, widow W
17 April Anne the wife of Henry Skinner W
10 May Mrs Hannah Partridge, wid. W
11 May Elizabeth d. of William & Ursula Tomm W
20 May Nicholas Grigg W
20 May Catherine Hendy, wid. W
4 June Grace Williams, widow W
11 June Catherine the wife of the Revd Mr John Day, Rectr of St Ervan W
11 June Mary wife of Bernard Rouse W
15 June Stephen s. of Stephen Buckingham W
17 June Eliz. d. of Henry Rows W
21 June Margaret Adams, wid W
22 June Henry Rows W
9 July Benjamin s. of Arthur Strongman & Frances his wife W
10 July Philip s. of Richard Cornish W
21 July Henry Brewer W
27 July John s. of Martyn & Joan Strongman W
23 Sep. Richard Lee W
11 Oct. William s. of William Woolcock W
26 Oct. Elizabeth d. of Gilbert & Joyce Mealls W
15 Nov. Mary Langmead, wid W

* Certificates signed and allowed by the same as last year. Churchwardens continued. New overseers: Mr. Samuel Batten, Richard Rawe, Thomas Warne and Solomon Baseley.

22 Nov. William s. of John & Philippa Hawke W
5 Dec. Jane Oxnam, widow W
11 Jan. Stephen Warne* W
13 Jan. Anne d. of Wm & Catherine Antron W
20 Jan. Hester Griffey, wid. W
20 Jan. James s. of Francis & Patience Cowling W
24 Jan. Mary d. of John & Mary Tom W
28 Jan. John Tom W
31 Jan. William Hanne W
3 Feb. Catherine wife of William Antron W
3 Feb. Alice the wife of John Benallock W
18 Mar. Jacob Robyns† W

ANNO 1727.

26 Mar. Elias s. of Anthony & Catherine Kendall W
30 Mar. Barbara wife of Edward Baseley W
31 Mar. John s. of William & Mary Worth W
2 April Thomas Langdon W
10 April Mary Gilbert W
14 April Mary d. of Methuselah & Mary Williams W
18 April Samuel s. of Mr Joseph Bishop & Loveday his wife W
19 April Benjamin s. of Arthur & Frances Strongman W
28 April Nathaniel Adams W
1 May Margaret Hall W
10 May Eliz. d. of Joseph & Joyce Glanfield W
12 May Catherine d. of Mr Hugh Pollard & Eliz. his wife W
14 May Anne d. of Mr Hugh Pollard & Elizabeth his wife W
21 May Grace Rawe W
29 May James s. of Samuel & Elizabeth Harris W
29 May Honor wife of Henry Barnicott W
5 June Stephen Buckingham W
27 June Dinah Langdon, wid. W

* Son of Tho. Warne and Elizabeth Lovell; he married in 1693 Mary Jack Andrew, and had several children.

† Certificates signed by Phil. Collier, rector, and allowed by William Glynn and John Peter. Churchwardens continued. New overseers: Mr. John Collier, Mr. John Thomas, Thomas Retallock and Robert Drew.

17 July Susanna d. of John & Joan Hawke W
22 July Wm Evelyn W
15 Aug. Grace wife of William Lawe W
29 Aug. John Remphrey W
31 Aug. Mary d. of Nicholas & Jane Opie W
11 Sep. Mrs Anne Day wife of John Day W
12 Oct. William Lawe W
23 Oct. Rebecka wife of Thomas Angollan W
2 Nov. Joan d. of Wm & Joan Pascoe W
7 Nov. Eliz. wife of Daniell Thomas W
9 Nov. Elizabeth Seaberriow, wid. W
12 Nov. Mrs Mary May, wid. W
25 Nov. Elias Pollard* W
7 Dec. John Day W
10 Dec. Mathew Grose W
26 Dec. Frances Grigg, wid. W
29 Dec. Anne d. of Richd Whitford W
30 Dec. Robert Austin W
10 Jan. Catherine wife of James Merifield W
21 Jan. Augustine Jennings, of Mawgan W
23 Jan. George Baseley W
28 Jan. Eliz. d. of Wm & Elizabeth Woolcock W
30 Jan. John Lewarne W
3 Feb. Nathaniel Thomas W
4 Feb. John Benallock W
8 Feb. Henry s. of Richd Whitford W
9 Feb. Robert Retallock W
10 Mar. Wm s. of William & Jane Stephens W
24 Mar. Richd Grigg† W

ANNO 1728.

28 Mar. Philip Husband W
28 Mar. Thomasine Hawke W
27 April Thomas Pearce W
13 May Henry s. of Benjamin Chalwell W
2 June John s. of Richd Whitford W
4 June John s. of Bernard & Temperance Rows W

* He paid the rent of his shop, 10s. in 1686.—Green Book.

† Certificates signed P. Collier, rector, and allowed by Edm. Prideaux and John Peter. New churchwardens: John Johns and Thomas Retallock. New overseers: Mr. William Williams, Bernard Rowse, John Brewer, and Tho. Stephens.

7 June William Adams W
17 June Elizabeth d. of James & Epiphany Trenerry W
21 June Jane Oxnam, wid. W
24 June Jane d. of Saml[l] & Mary Grimes W
2 July Jane d. of Shadrach & Jane Tremain W
10 July Susanna d. of Wm Blake W
23 July Saml[l] s. of Saml[l] & Honor Bussow W
26 July Mr George Wayte, Supervisor of Excise W
2 Aug. Philip s. of Robert & Mary Kent W
4 Aug. Anne d. of John & Anne Sprey W
29 Aug. Wilmot wife of Gregory Nancey W
18 Oct. Eleanor Owens W
9 Nov. Dorothy Manuell, wid. W
2 Dec. Anne wife of Arthur Mitchell W
12 Dec. Peter Bounsell W
13 Dec. Gregory Nancey W
16 Dec. Thomas s. of Wm & Deborah Gattey W
16 Dec. John s. of John & Amey Brewer W
20 Dec. Grace d. of Giles & Jane Williams W
21 Dec. Wm s. of William & Deborah Gattey W
12 Jan. Eliz. wife of Philip Hornabrook W
25 Jan. Honor wife of Thomas Benney
4 Feb. Frances d. of Richd Grigg, decd, & Jane his wife W
5 Feb. Eliz: wife of William Youlton W
18 Feb. Joan Tomm, wid. W
25 Feb. Mathew Davis W
27 Feb. Martin Tomm W
3 Mar. Thomas s. of Thomas Polkinhorn W
4 Mar. Mary Pollard W
9 Mar. Wm Gatty W
13 Mar. Mary d. of Thomas & Catherine Merifield* W

ANNO 1729.

1 April James s. of Saml[l] & Mary Grimes W

* Certificates signed by P. Collier, rector, and allowed by Edward Hoblyn and John Peter. New churchwardens: John Burges and Hen. Brewer. New overseers: Mr. Tho. Vyvyan, John Metherill, James Oliver and Hugh Bullock.

8 April Wm s. of Wm & Eliz. Olver W
16 May Grace Snell W
19 May Paschas wife of James Lanyon W
19 May Saml[l] s. of John & Mary Johns W
23 May Eliz. Rickard W
26 May Mary Pill, wid. W
16 June Michaell Cowling W
20 June Wm s. of Robt & Anne Hamley W
4 July Wm s. of John & Margaret Jackson
7 July John Cockin W
15 July James s. of Francis & Patience Cowling W
8 Aug. Francis Cornish, wid. W
31 Aug. William s. of Timothy & Mary Stephens W
1 Sep. John Nichols W
6 Sep. Wm s. of Solomon & Mary Baseley W
25 Sep. Pascow s. of Thomas & Margaret Kestell W
3 Oct. Margaret wife of John Saunders W
7 Oct. Frances d. of John & Mary Whedon W
14 Oct. Charles s. of John & Mary Whedon W
15 Oct. Jane d. of Shadrach & Jane Tremain W
17 Oct. Richd Truscot W
25 Oct. Catherine d. of Rev. Mr. John Day, rectr of St Ervan W
6 Nov. Michael s. of Mich. & Eliz. Cornish W
12 Nov. Elizabeth wife of Mr Hugh Pollard W
18 Nov. Mary wife of John Turner W
25 Nov. Jane Lewarne, wid. W
1 Dec. Eliz. d. of Wm & Anne Benny W
1 Dec. Margery wife of James Olver W
7 Dec. Thos. Merifield W
7 Dec. Grace wife of Thomas Couch W
11 Dec. Thos. Gill W
25 Dec. Jane d. of Daniell Thomas W
28 Dec. Eliz. Gill, wid. W
4 Jan. Grace base child of Anne Benny W
7 Jan. John Gass W
9 Jan. Richd s. of Jane Grigg, wid. W
7 Feb. Mary d. of Shadrach & Jane Tremain W
19 Feb. Jane Davis, wid. W

19 Feb. Jane d. of Henry & Gertrude Pollard W
26 Feb. Temperance wife of John Hailbron W
26 Feb. Grace d. of Martin & Joan Strongman W
3 Mar. John s. of John & Mary Best W
6 Mar. Richard Garland W
8 Mar. Robert Creebar W
11 Mar. Elizabeth Harris W
13 Mar. William Creebar* W

ANNO 1730.

3 April Anne d. of Mr Giles Hamley & Grace his wife W
20 April Margaret d. of John & Amy Brewer W
3 May Catherine d. of Methuselah & Mary Williams W
6 May Catherine d. of Thomas Reynolds W
9 May John Wetter W
10 May Elizabeth wife of John Rapson W
18 May Frances Woodman, wid. W
24 May Mary Cowling W
31 May John Bilkey W
5 June Jane d. of Saml[l] & Honor Bussow W
15 June Christopher Warne† W
16 June Mr James Paynter‡ W
22 June Emeline Husband, wid. W
23 June Richard Harris W
25 June Wm Dennis W
5 July Henry Skinner W
12 July Richard Davies W
17 July Wm s. of Wm & Mary Worth W
26 July Deborah Gatty, wid. W
1 Aug. Mary d. of Mary Davies, wid. W
10 Aug. Jane wife of Richd James W
11 Sep. Honor d. of Thomas & Ebat Litticot W
20 Sep. Francis Pearce W
12 Nov. Sarah d. of Wm & Eliz. Olver W
17 Nov. Mary wife of John Johns W
4 Dec. Wm s. of John & Mary Gilbert W
5 Dec. Mr James Edwards W
20 Dec. Wm s. of Robert & Anne Hambly W
22 Dec. George Day W
25 Dec. Mary d. of John Johns W
1 Jan. Richard Lovell W
1 Jan. Elizabeth Blight W
6 Jan. Richard s. of John & Catherine Hockyn W
11 Jan. Elizabeth Lee, wid. W
23 Jan. Peter s. of John & Mary Best W
24 Jan. Mary wife of John Davies W
25 Jan. Jane wife of Wm Luney W
27 Feb. Joan wife of Hugh Rawe W
1 Mar. Thomas s. of Edward & Eliz. Merifield W
5 Mar. Elizabeth wife of Mr Richd Ingledon W
8 Mar. Martha d. of Edward & Eliz. Merifield W
21 Mar. Joan Cocking, wid.* W

ANNO 1731.

2 April William s. of John & Joan Hawke W
4 April Henry s. of Arthur & Mary Mitchell W
4 April Grace d. of Thomas & Mary Litticot W
10 April Wm s. of William & Honor Robarts W
10 April Eliz. Strongman, wid. W
23 April Joan Minnow, wid. W
2 May John Davies W
6 May Patience Retallock, wid. W
11 May Eliz. d. of Wm & Anne Davis W
18 May Wm s. of Wm & Anne Benny W
30 June Mrs Jane Day, wid. W
14 July Prudence the wife of Stephen Carhart W
17 July Mary d. of John Turner W
21 July Thos. Benny W
30 July John Hendy W
10 Sep. Eliz. Baseley, wid. W
23 Sep. Mary wife of Wm Bear W
24 Sep. Florence d. of Saml[l] & Eliz. Harris W
22 Nov. Jane Cowling W

* Certificates signed by P. Collier, rector, and allowed by Francis Gregor and John Peter. Churchwardens continued. Overseers: Mr. Ed. Hoblyn, Mr. Robert Elford, James Rowse, and Tho. Rawlyn.

† He was son of Henry Warne, by his first wife Diana Philpe. He married at St. Enoder, 31 Dec., 1698, Jane Hichens, by whom he had several children.

‡ James Paynter, gent., one of the twelve men in 1717.—Green Book.

* Certificates signed and allowed as last year. Churchwardens continued. New overseers: Rob. Hoblyn, Esq., William Drew, Jacob Grigg, and William Hicks.

6 Dec. John s. of John & Philippa Hicks W
7 Dec. Jonathan Dawe W
12 Jan. Elizabeth d. of Humphry & Anne Oxnam W
20 Jan. Anne d. of Wm Beare W
22 Jan. Mary d. of Henry & Mary Brewer W
25 Jan. Thomasine Creebar, wid. W
13 Feb. John Lovell W
18 Feb. John s. of Nicholas & Jane Opie W
25 Feb. Richard Cock W
17 Mar. Mariot Harvey, wid.* W

ANNO 1732.

30 Mar. Agns d. of Arthur & Frances Strongman W
21 April Edward s. of Bernard & Temperance Rows W
26 April Honor d. of John & Ebat Hendy W
28 April Eliz. wife of Edward Merifield W
29 April Sarah d. of Mr James Bishop & Sarah his wife W
30 April Henry s. of Arthur & Mary Mitchell W
7 May Anne d. of Mr George Keigwin† & Ann his wife W
26 May Jane d. of Sam^ll & Mary Grimes W
10 June Mary base child of Rebeckah Ellery W
26 June Jane wife of James Cowling W
30 June Epiphany wife of James Trenerry W
3 Aug. Wm Bone W
7 Aug. Wilmot Hicks, widow W
5 Sep. Benjamin Rows W
17 Sep. John Hamley W
31 Oct. Joseph Best W
31 Oct. Richard Michell of St Austle W
8 Nov. James Husband W
13 Nov. Joan wife of Mr John Harris W
20 Nov. Thos. Tremaine W

* Certificates signed by P. Collier, rector, and allowed by John Molesworth and John Peter. New churchwardens: Mr. John Thomas and Mr. William Drew. New overseers: Mr. Hugh Pollard, Mr. George Mapowder, Rob. Merrifield, and Robert Retallock.

† He was of Mousehole and after of Crowan, (son of James Keigwin of Mousehole by Julian, daughter of George Musgrave of Nettlecombe), and his wife was a daughter of Tho. Hoblyn of Tresaddern.

24 Nov. Arthur Michell W
16 Dec. Thos. Manuell W
29 Dec. Rich^d s. of Thos. Polkinhorn W
11 Jan. Grace d. of John & Jane Parnall W
7 Feb. John Hawke W
11 Feb. Robt s. of Robt & Francis Woone W
14 Feb. Mary Mannell W
17 Feb. Mary wife of John Gilbert W
18 Feb. Mrs Elizabeth Champion, widow W
19 Feb. John base child of Margaret Congdon W
19 Feb. Ralph Chenoweth W
22 Feb. George s. of Charles & Blanch Retallock W
24 Feb. Mary Rawe, wid. W
24 Feb. Eliz. wife of Robt. Drew W
25 Feb. Sarah d. of W^m & Mary Lanyon W
26 Feb. James Stephens W
6 Mar. Dorothy d. of Daniell Thomas W
9 Mar. Peter base child of Mary Chapell* W

ANNO 1733.

2 April Lydia wife of Sam^ll Champion W
2 April James Merifield W
10 April Eliz. d. of Joell Capell W
21 April Jane wife of Wm Drew W
28 April Nathaniel Oliver W
6 May John Turner W
10 May Joan d. of John Turner, dec^d W
16 May Grace wife of John Cock W
26 May Jane d. of Antony & Eliz. Rawe W
4 June Richd Callaway W
4 June Joan d. of Henry & Thomazine Cock W
10 June Mrs Mary Beauford W
16 June Anne the wife of Humphry Oxnam W
24 June William Mitchell W
26 June W^m s. of Mr Giles Hamley & Grace his wife W
1 July Elizabeth Rows, wid. of Richd Rows
27 July Mary wife of Denys Tremaine W

* Certificates signed by P. Collier, rector, and allowed by John Molesworth & Edm. Prideaux. Churchwardens continued. New overseers: Mr. Walter Harris, Richard Brabyn, Christopher Warne, and Rich. Veale.

27 July Richard Cornish W
29 July Temperance d. of John & Susanna Jane W
14 Aug. Thomas Liddycott W
22 Aug. Mrs. Susanna Dell W
26 Aug. George s. of George & Eliz. Tippet W
30 Aug. John Rawe W
1 Sep. Wm Dancaster W
18 Sep. Philip s. of John* & Philippa Hawke W
3 Oct. Catherine Allen W
24 Oct. Edward s. of Wm & Honor Lanyon W
10 Dec. Wm Wilkin W
29 Dec. Faith Troth W
9 Jan. Jane d. of Wm Rows W
11 Jan. Pascaw Kestell W
11 Jan. Mrs Mary Hearle W
30 Jan. Mary wife of John Rescorla W
2 Feb. Mary d. of John & Catherine Hockyn W
4 Feb. Thomas Tamlyn W
16 Feb. Mr Edward Bishop† W
24 Feb. Edyth Pye W
8 Mar. Elizabeth d. of Edwd Merrifield W
12 Mar. Thomas Whitford‡ W

ANNO 1734.

31 Mar. Penelope d. of Peter & Grace Best W
9 April Anne Kittoe W
15 April Wm s. of William Michell, decd & Emeline his wife W
19 April Mathew Battrell W
21 April Eleanore Opie, widow W
27 April Catherine Wetter, widow W
2 May William s. of Humphry Oxnam W
5 May Elizabeth wife of Richard Austin W
10 May Mary d. of Susanna Tinney W
20 May Philip King W
20 May Thomas Angollan W
20 May Robert Best W
21 May Grace d. of John & Joan Martyn W
23 May Dinah Martyn W

* Certificate says, 'John Hawke of Ruthoes.'

† Son of the Rev. John Bishop, rector of St. Columb, by his first wife, Ann, daughter of Rob. Hoblyn, Esq.

‡ Certificates signed by P. Collier, rector, but signatures of the Justices have been torn or worne away. Churchwarden continued. New overseers: Mr William Williams for Mr. Day, Thomas Merifield, Michaell Cornish and William Callaway.

30 May Nicholas s. of Nicholas & Jane Opie W
3 June Frances d. of Arthur & Frances Strongman W
16 June Richard Hawke W
25 June Agas d. of Arthur & Frances Strongman W
2 July Elizabeth Lobb, widow W
7 July Mary d. of Robert & Anne Hamley W
16 July John Drew & Joan his wife W
1 Aug. Bridget Cowling W
9 Aug. Robert Husband W
14 Aug. Lucy d. of Mr Hugh Pollard W
19 Sep. Grace the wife of Mr John Burges W
29 Sep. Jane d. of Robert & Elizabeth Cock W
15 Oct. Mary d. of Henry & Mary Brewer W
24 Nov. Elizabeth d. of Robert & Anne Hamley W
28 Nov. Jane base child of Elizabeth Hicks W
11 Dec. John Banger W
27 Dec. John Saunders W
19 Jan. Anne d. of John & Jane May W
7 Feb. Samuel s. of Thomas & Joan Solomon W
7 Feb. Samuel s. of Ezekiell & Anne Retallack W
14 Feb. Pentecoste wife of John Sandowe W
17 Feb. Jane wife of Robert Merifield W
17 Feb. Jane Baseley, wid. W
14 Mar. Richard Whitford W
16 Mar. Mary d. of Joseph Dunkin* W

ANNO 1735.

31 Mar. Mary d. of Willm & Joan Merifield W
18 April Samson s. of Samsom & Eliz. Rawe W
19 April Ebat Lamb, widow W
21 April Mary d. of Mr John Lawrence W
24 April Joseph Dunkin W
1 May Elizabeth wife of Robert Cock W
5 May Elizabeth d. of John & Grace Whitford W

* Certificates signed P. Collier, rector, and allowed by Francis Gregor and Nicholas Donnithorne. Churchwardens: Mr. John Lawrence and Mr. Joseph Hawkey. New overseers: Edw. Crewes, Esq., Benjamin Chalwell, Henry Veal, John Hawke.

19 May Mary d. of Thomas & Catherine Merifield W
19 June John base child of Abigaill Corner W
3 July Jane d. of Mr John Lawrence W
22 July Jane Dunkin, widow W
30 July Arthur s. of Arthur & Mary Michell W
3 April John Hailbron W
4 April Thomas s. of James & Alice Stephens W
6 April John s. of Thomas & Catherine Merifield W
10 April James s. of James & Frances Champion W
23 April Philippa Tinney W
7 Sep. Elizabeth d. of Mr John Collier & Mary his wife W
30 Oct. Francis Cowling W
7 Nov. James Oliver W
22 Nov. Mary d. of Thomas & Mary Tamlyn W
24 Nov. Joan wife of William Crawley W
30 Nov. Temperance wife of John Tinney W
7 Dec. Wm s. of Thomas Barlow a soldier W
7 Dec. Dorothy* wife of John Willyams, Esqre W
7 Jan. Edward s. of John & Anne Sprey W
28 Jan. Thomas Gilbert W
13 Feb. Nicholas Hawke W
14 Feb. Samson Bastard W
20 Feb. Priscilla Tinney, wid. W
8 Mar. Anne Austin, widow W
10 Mar. John s. of Robt. & Frances Woon W
12 Mar. Frances wife of Thos Coad W
13 Mar. Robt s. of Robt & Frances Woon W
22 Mar. Elizabeth wife of Wm Tinney W
24 Mar. Wm Benney† W

* She was daughter and heir of Peter Day, Esq., of Resuggan, in St. Columb; she married John Willyams, Esq., of Roseworthy, as his second wife, the first being Bridgeman, youngest daughter and coheiress of Col. Humphry Noye, of Carnanton, and his wife Hester, sister of the last Baron Sandys of the Vine. By his second wife, Mr. Willyams had John; James, ancestor of the present Edw. William Brydges Willyams, Esq., of Carnanton, M.P.; and Bridgeman M... Haweis.

† Signed and allowed by the same as last year. Churchwardens continued.

Overseers: Mr. John Harris, Mr. John Burges, William White, Thomas Warne.

Anno 1736.

12 April Thos s. of Mr Wm & Mrs Jane Williams W
13 April Eliz. Blight, wid. W
16 April Honor wife of Henry Michell W
30 April Elizabeth d. of Wm & Anne Davis W
14 May Wm s. of Shadrach & Jane Tremaine W
15 May George s. of George & Joan Bond W
16 May John Philips W
29 May Thos. Reynolds W
7 June Richard Cock W
11 June John s. of John & Anne Sprey W
20 June Frances the wife of Richard Webber
25 June Joyce Denys, wid. W
27 June Eliz. d. of Robert & Catherine Manuell W
29 June Thos. Day W
4 July Jane wife of Thomas Carne W
7 July John Gilbert W
7 July Roger Couch W
11 July Ebat Pollard, wid. W
28 July Daniell May W
3 Aug. Grace Day, wid. W
15 Aug. Mary d. of John & Joan Martyn W
15 Aug. Jonathan Barret W
28 Sep. Eliz. Cockyn, wid. W
8 Oct. Sarah d. of Nathll Oliver, decd W
6 Oct. Richard Langdon W
21 Oct. Loveday wife of James Rows W
27 Oct. George Grimes W
31 Oct. Thos. Solomon W
11 Nov. Mary d. of John & Mary Wilton W
13 Nov. Solomon s. of Solomon & Mary Baseley W
16 Nov. Robt. s. of John & Blanch Husband W
4 Dec. Samuel Champion W
20 Dec. Peter s. of Michl & Margaret Ilive W
21 Dec. Pentecoste d. of George & Eliz. Tippet W
3 Jan. Arthur Veall* W
16 Jan. Richard James W
22 Jan. Jane d. of James & Elizabeth Oliver W

* Arthur Veall, one of the overseers in 1716.—Green Book.

3 Feb. Michaell s. of Jane Tippet W
25 Feb. Elizabeth Morish W
5 Mar. Ebat d. of John & Mary Lamb W
10 Mar. Catherine d. of Rob[t] & Catherine Manuell* W

ANNO 1737.

11 April Jane Gilbert, wid. W
15 April Eliz. Blake, wid. W
16 April M[rs] Mary Hawkey W
16 April Will[m] Wilton W
18 April John s. of Rich[d] & Elizabeth Husband W
25 April Eliz[th] d. of Rob[t] Strongman W
4 May John s. of Jane Pearce, wid. W
11 May Mary d. of Robert & Catherine Manuell W
12 May Joan Buckingham, widow W
13 May Mary wife of John Lewarne
6 June Rich[d] Merifield W
14 June Jennefaire d. of Tho[s] Cornwall, dec[d] W
15 June Honour wife of Henry Solomon W
8 July Tho[s] Perot W
13 July Eliz. d. of John & Dorothy Hockyn W
19 July Rich[d] Brabyn W
11 Aug. John White W
20 Aug. Mary d. of Henry & Catherine Endean W
4 Oct. Eliz. d. of Simon & Alice Law W
6 Oct. Mary Blight, wid. W
8 Oct. Philippa d. of Michael & Frances Cornish W
31 Oct. Alice Stephens, wid. W
1 Nov. Rich[d] s. of John & Grace Whitford W
12 Nov. Jane d. of Abraham & Joanna Turner W
24 Nov. John Parkyn W
1 Jan. Jane Best, wid. W
3 Jan. M[rs] Mary Wyat, widow W
10 Jan. Catherine wife of John Hockin W
23 Jan Rich[d] s. of Thomas & Mary Keam W

* Certificates signed and allowed by the same as last year. Churchwardens: Mr. James Bishop, Mr. Robert Drew.

Overseers: P. Collier, Francis Clemow, Tho. Glanfield, Wm. Varcoe.

The burial of John s. of Richard Bidgood, 14 March, 1737, appears among the certificates only.

1 Feb. Ebenezer & Henemar children of John & Eleanor Powell W
1 Feb. Leonard Brewer W
1 Feb. Joan Rowse, wid W
5 Feb. Eliz. Manuell, wid. W
10 Feb. Francis s. of Rich[d] Webber W
17 Feb. Rebekah Adams, wid. W
23 Feb. Mary Bilkey, wid. W
27 Feb. Elizabeth Bussow, wid. W
1 Mar. W[m] s. of William & Emelyn Buckingham W
14 Mar. John s. of Mary Sandford* W

ANNO 1738.

29 Mar. Jane wife of Nicholas Opie W
29 April Elizabeth d. of Jonathan & Margaret Dawe W
28 June Thomasine wife of Rich[d] Brewer W
20 July Hugh s. of John & Barbara Miners W
31 July Mary d. of M[r] James Bishop & Sarah his wife W
9 Aug. John base child of Susanna Tinney W
15 Aug. Mary wife of Rich[d] Austin W
16 Aug. Mary d. of Rich[d] & Eliz[th] Husband W
20 Aug. M[rs] Elizabeth Collier wife of Philip Collier, Rect[r]† W
22 Aug. Anne wife of Benjamin Chalwell, jun[r] W
14 Sep. Eliz. Pearce, wid. W
21 Sep. M[r] Giles Hamley‡ W
21 Sep. W[m] Tinney W
14 Oct. George s. of Rich[d] Austin W
23 Oct. Edward Crews,§ Esqre W
1 Nov. Grace d. of Rich[d] Brewer W

* The certificates signed by P. Collier, rector, and allowed by Francis Gregor and Edm. Prideaux.

Overseers: Mr. Samuel Batten, James Jenkin, Richard Evelyn, and John Rowse. Churchwardens: Mr. James Bishop and Wm. Varcoe.

† She was a daughter of . . . . . Allen.

‡ He was second son of William Hamley of Treblethick (by his wife Rebecca). He married first Barbara, daughter of Philip Hawkins of Pennenee, by whom he had a s. John, who died an infant. He married, secondly, Grace, daughter of Tho. Hoblyn of Tresaddern, by whom he had, —(1) Elizabeth, married Rev. Dr. Robert Bateman, rector of St. Columb; (2) Thomas, who married first Grace, daughter and co-heiress of Rev. John Tregenna, rector of Mawgan, and, secondly, Mary daughter of . . . . . . by both of whom he had issue; and others who died young.

§ He was one of the twelve men as the time of his death.—Green Book.

7 Dec. Loveday wife of Mark Nichols W
7 Dec. Robert Merifield W
17 Dec. Elizabeth wife of Richard Husband W
17 Dec. Sarah base child of Mary Tippet W
19 Dec. Samuel s. of Eliz. Pearce, wid. dec W
6 Jan. Elizabeth d. of John Hockyn W
20 Jan. Thomasine d. of Denis Treman W
1 Feb. Catherine d. of Thomas & Catherine Langdon W
14 Feb. Solomon Brewer W
4 Mar. Joan wife of Martin Strongman W
4 Mar. Grace d. of John & Anne Sprey W
9 Mar. Elizabeth the wife of William Luney, jun[r] W
20 Mar. Joseph Kensley, a traveller W
21 Mar. Elizabeth d. of Michael & Frances Cornish* W

ANNO 1739.

21 April Margaret May, widow W
28 April James Rowse W
2 May William s. of William & Joan Bullen W
4 May Jane Evelyn W
14 May Grace d. of William & Honor Lanyon W
6 June Mary King, widow W
8 July Jane wife of Giles Williams *al's* Pell W
8 July Rachael d. of Charles & Margaret Leddicote W
13 July Jane d. of Francis Cowling, deceased W
14 July Ann wife of Edward May W
6 Aug. Mary d. of Hugh & Mary Bullock† W
15 Aug. Elizabeth wife of Daniel May W
28 Aug. Dinah d. of John & Dorothy Arscott W
3 Sep. Gilbert Meals W
11 Sep. Mary d. of George & Joan Bond W
21 Sep. Petherick John s. of Petherick & Margaret Williams W
28 Sep. Dorothy wife of John Arscott *W
10 Oct. John Gummow W
10 Nov. Ann Hornabrook, wid. W
12 Nov. Elizabeth Brewer, wid. W
15 Nov. William Denis, jun[r] W
19 Dec. John s. of Thomas & Ann Perrot W
7 Jan. Thomas Stephens W
10 Jan. Joan Chenoweth, wid. W
11 Jan. James Merifield W
15 Jan. Joan Dancaster, wid. W
19 Jan. M[r] Hugh Pollard W
24 Jan. Luke Jolly W
24 Jan. Elizabeth wife of John Mark W
7 Feb. Richard s. of John & Margaret Hockyn W
10 Feb. William Pascoe of S[t] Mawgan †W
16 Feb. Jane d. of Gilbert & Joyce Meals W
23 Feb. Margaret Parkin, wid. W
26 Feb. Jane Thomas *al's* Trubbow, wid. W
29 Feb. John Jane W
5 Mar. Elizabeth d. of Samuel Pearce, deceased W
17 Mar. Philippa d. of M[r] John Collier & Mary his wife W
22 Mar. Elizabeth d. of James & Elizabeth Oliver W
23 Mar. Ann d. of Mary Tubb W
23 Mar. Mark base child of Elizabeth Blake‡ W

ANNO 1740.

27 Mar. Mary d. of William Bear W
27 Mar. M[r] Benedict Hamly W
28 Mar. Dorothy Champion, wid.
29 Mar. Mary d. of M[r] John Collier & Mary his wife W
29 Mar. Jane Bounsell, wid. W
2 April Margaret d. of John & Amey Brewer W
3 April Jane d. of Richard & Ann Raw W

* Certificates signed by P. Collier, rector, and allowed by J. Tremayne and Jo. D. Birkhead. Overseers: Mr. John Collier, Mr. James Tanner, Mr. Robert Drew, and Thomas Retallock.

† Hugh Bullock, one of the waywardens in 1727.—Green Book.

* John Arscott was one of the parish constables in 1706, when 6s. 9d. was paid to his account.—Green Book.

† The baptism of the children of William and Mary Paskow are recorded about 1690 at Mawgan.

‡ Certificates signed P. Collier, rector, allowed by J. Molesworth and Jo. Hoblyn. New churchwardens: John Brewer and John Metherell, junr. Overseers: Mr. John Lawrence, Tho. Coad, William Worth.

3 April Grace Williams W
5 April James s. of John & Ann Best
12 April Mary England, wid. W
12 April Nicholas base child of Catherine Rundle W
12 April Hugh s. of Mr Thomas Stephens & Elizabeth his wife W
13 April Peter s. of James & Frances Champion W
13 April Ann d. of Mr Giles Hamly, deceased & Grace his wife W
13 April Elizabeth d. of Mr John Lawrence & Mary his wife* W
23 April Mr John Harris† W
26 April Richard s. of Anthony & Elizabeth Raw W
28 April Ann d. of Thomas Carne W
28 April Ann d. of Anthony & Elizabeth Raw W
1 May Jennefaire d. of John & Jane May W
2 May Jane d. of William & Mary Rickard W
3 May Ann d. of John Lewarne W
4 May Frances d. of John & Mary Wheeden W
6 May Judith d. of Jude & Eliz. May W
9 May William Hornabrook W
18 May Benjamin Chalwell,‡ junr W
18 May John Pye W
22 May Mary d. of William & Elizabeth Harris W
26 May Joseph s. of William & Elizabeth Raw W
29 May Elizabeth d. of Nathaniel & Mary Lockett W
29 May John s. of Henry & Ann Crews W
2 June Frances base child of Ann Leddicoat W
2 June Elizabeth d. of Ezekiel & Ann Retallock W
6 June John s. of Richard & Philippa Page W

* Mr. John Lawrence, of St. Columb, married Gertrude, daughter and coheiress of Henry Bond (son of Wm. Bond, of Holwood, and his wife, daughter of Henry Spoure, of Trebartha), by his wife, Lucy, daughter of John Mathew, of Tresunger. She was baptized 8 Aug., 1701, at Endellion.

† He was one of the twelve men.—Green Book.

‡ A ledger stone in the church records that, Benjamin Chalwell, fuller and clothier, died 16th May, 1740, aged 27. Ann, his wife, died 21 Aug., 1738, aged 22.

10 June Ann d. of Philip & Mary Rickard W
17 June Thomas s. of William & Mary Raw W
17 June Henry s. of Christopher & Honor Warne W
19 June Mrs. Ann Gribby W
22 June Henry Betty W
23 June William s. of William & Eliz. Olver W
29 June Susanna d. of Richard & Mary Veall W
7 July Daniel May W
12 July Margaret d. of Isaac & Elizabeth Blake W
21 July Mr James Bishop* W
28 July Elizabeth d. of Inigo Inch W
30 July Sarah d. of Isaac & Elizabeth Blake W
12 Aug. Ann Broommey W
18 Aug. Trephana wife of Joel Caple W
13 Sep. Thomas Warne W
15 Sep. Mr James Tanner W
16 Sep. Mary wife of Methuselah Williams W
18 Sep. Mary wife of Thomas Morrish W
21 Sep. John s. of William Luney W
28 Sep. Mr Daniel Sullyvean† W
5 Nov. Margaret d. of Adam & Mary Thomson W
11 Nov. Catherine Langdon, wid. W
30 Nov. Richard s. of Richard & Mary Carne W
10 Dec. Jane d. of Richard & Mary Carne W
18 Dec. Mary d. of John & Mary Metherell W
18 Dec. John s. of Arthur & Mary Mitchell W
23 Dec. Francis s. of Richard & Jane Rowse W
23 Dec. Elizabeth Williams W
31 Dec. Richard s. of Thomas & Catherine Langdon W
31 Dec. Isaac Nichols W
7 Jan. Humphrey Abram W
9 Jan. Elizabeth d. of John & Eliz. Oxnam W
29 Jan. John Tomm W
2 Feb. Grace d. of Michael & Frances Cornish W
10 Feb. Elizabeth Stephens, wid. W
15 Feb. David Martyn W

* He was a son of the Rev. John Bishop and Mary his second wife. See note p. 244.

† Received for Mr. Sullivan's grave £1 6s. 8d. —Green Book.

26 Feb. John Oxnam W
10 Mar. Mary Geak W
11 Mar. Philip Elford W
22 Mar. Richard Rowse* W

ANNO 1741.

25 Mar. Mary wife of Richard Veall W
3 April Thomasine Edwards W
18 April John s. of Richard & Elizabeth Evelyn W
24 April Jane Hodge W
15 May Jane Peters, wid. W
17 May Robert s. of Robert & Elizabeth Bilkey W
24 May Grace Tinney, wid. W
24 May Jane d. of William & Elizabeth Baseley W
29 May Thomas Carne W
7 June Elizabeth d. of Wm & Elizabeth Baseley W
21 June Anthony Langdon W
4 July Jane Lanyon W
6 July Richard Michell *al's* Raw W
14 July Frances d. of Adam & Mary Thomson W
17 July Grace Betty, widow W
23 July Susanna d. of John & Dorothy Whetter W
27 July Margery the wife of Jonathan Daw W
15 Aug. Mary wife of Richard Carne W
16 Aug. Philippa Eudy, wid. W
17 Sep. Joseph s. of William & Elizabeth Willis W
29 Sep. Margaret d. of Richard & Elizabeth Husband W
2 Oct. William s. of Thomas & Elizabeth Glanville W
5 Oct. Susanna d. of Mr Wm Williams & Jane his wife W
25 Oct. Martyn Strongman W
4 Nov. Mary d. of William & Mary Mewdon W
7 Nov. John Hockins, a distributor of the *Sherbourn Mercury* W

* Certificates signed by P. Collier, rector, and allowed by Edm. Prideaux and Jo. D. Birkhead. Churchwardens: John Brewer, John Motherell. Overseers of the poor: Mr. Joseph Hawkey, Mr. William Williams, John Hawke, and Tho. Mark.

The following entries appear in the certificates of burial in woollen only, viz.:—

Elizabeth, d. of Anthony and Thomasine Cock, 7 Oct.

Jane, d. of Henry and Constance Tamlyn, 10 Oct.

Mary, wife of John Wheedon, 15 Oct.

Alice, wife of Roger George, 24 Oct.

Humphry, s. of Henry and Constance Blight, Oct. 26.

8 Nov. Jane wife of Christopher Calf W
23 Nov. Mary wife of William Mewdon W
24 Nov. Stephen Thomas W
8 Dec. Michael Cornish W
11 Dec. Grace d. of Mr Giles Hamley, decd, & Grace his wife W
1 Jan. Dinah Gilbert, widow W
2 Jan. Jane d. of John & Margaret Cundy W
22 Jan. Mary Whiteford, widow W
26 Jan. Joseph Robins, a soldier W
5 Mar. Mr John Withers W
7 Mar. Ruth Veal, widow W
21 Mar. Mary Husband, widow* W

ANNO 1742.

30 Mar. Sarah Tremain, widow W
13 April Margaret Buckingham, widow
8 May Marthah Slogget, widow W
31 May Mary Tippet W
11 May Colan Manuell† W
22 July Thomas Vivian W
23 July William s. of John & Grace Buckingham W
28 July Elizabeth Clemows, widow W
12 Aug. Jane wife of Mr William Williams W
13 Aug. Nicholas Guens W
27 Aug. Francis Vivian W
27 Aug. Elizabeth d. of William & Jane Capell W
29 Aug. Mary d. of Jonathan & Sarah Barret W
30 Aug. William s. of William & Jane Capell W
11 Sep. John s. of William & Grace Evelyn W
17 Sep. Honor d. of Mr George Mapowder & Jane his wife W
23 Sep. William Crawley W
5 Oct. Dorothy Garland, wid. W
10 Oct. Martha d. of John Hockyn W
10 Nov. Joan Bannier, wid. W
10 Nov. Mary d. of John & Prudence Merrifield W
12 Nov. Thomas s. of William & Joan Merrifield W
16 Nov. Prudence Gilbert, wid. W
17 Nov. John Whetter W
23 Nov. John Saudoe W
3 Dec. John Lawrey W
8 Dec. Susanna Rapson, wid. W

* Certificates signed by the rector, but not attested.

† Colan Manuel, one of the waywardens in 1710.—Green Book.

19 Dec. John s. of Thomas & Rachael Keam W
27 Dec. Gidgeon Slade W
15 Jan. Arthur Strongman* W
21 Jan. Elizabeth d. of Samuel & Honour Bussow W
1 Feb. Joan d. of William Drew W
5 Feb. James s. of James & Ann Pollard W
1 Mar. Jane d. of Richard & Grace Brenton W
18 Mar. Grace Blake, widow† W

ANNO 1743.

25 Mar. John Gilbert W
4 April Mary d. of John & Thomasine Rowse W
4 April Joan d. of Richard & Ann Hicks W
11 May William s. of Mr Thomas Merrifield & Cath. his wife W
15 May Susanna base child of Honour Roberts W
2 June John Chapell W
14 June Catherine d. of William & Margaret Blake W
12 July Michael Cornish W
19 July Joel Capell W
23 July Grace d. of Henry & Constance Blight W
30 July James s. of Robert Merrifield, deceased W
1 Aug. Joan Tomm, widow W
19 Aug. John Dungey‡ W
27 Aug. Ann wife of Philip Allen W
20 Sep. Elizabeth Cornwall, widow W
29 Sep. Robert Cock W
3 Oct. James s. of John Whetter, deceased W
9 Oct. Mary Rickard, widow W
29 Oct. William s. of John Retallock, deceased W
6 Nov. John Johnston W
22 Nov. Mrs. Jane Halse, widow W
1 Dec. Henry Thomas *al's* Trubboe W

* Arthur Strongman, waywarden in 1727.—Green Book.

† Certificates signed by John Collier, curate, allowed by Edm. Prideaux and F. L. Leach. New churchwardens: Mr. William Bone and William Hicks. Overseers of the poor: Mr. Robert Hoblyn, Richard Hicks, John Brewer in Town, and Mark Nicholls.

‡ In 1738 John Dungey paid the rent of the great shop, from June to Easter day, 5s.—Green Book.

14 Jan. Robert s. of James & Dorothy Jenkyn W
19 Feb. Susanna d. of Anthony & Elizabeth Rawe W
10 Mar. Thomas s. of Henry & Constance Tamblyn W
10 Mar. Frances d. of William & Florence Hicks W
23 Mar. Wilmot d. of John & Philippa Hicks* W

ANNO 1744.

26 Mar. Margaret Metherell W
29 Mar. Thomas s. of William & Mary Cockin W
1 April Jane d. of John & Jane Truscote W
3 April Nicholas Opie† W
1 May Thomas the s. of Thomas & Rachael Keam W
7 May Jane the wife of Mr Samuel Batten W
9 May Henry Mitchell W
11 May Mrs Mary Vivian,‡ widow W
31 May Mrs Emblyn Edwards W
27 June Mr John Johns W
23 July Mr William Williams W
18 Oct. Richard s. of Richard & Ann Jane W
27 Oct. Jane Nichols, widow W
8 Nov. Mrs. Joan Hoblyn,§ widow W
23 Nov. Dorcas d. of John Whetter, deceased W
25 Nov. John Merrifield W
7 Jan. Mary d. of James & Mary Hawke W
23 Jan. Joan Husband W
31 Jan. Mary wife of John Varcoe W
11 Feb. Mrs Mary Tucker, widow W
20 Feb. Thomas Leddicote W
25 Feb. Henry Cock W
18 Mar. Grace wife of John Whiteford‖ W

* Certificates signed and attested as last year. New churchwardens: John Merrifield and Thomas Mark. Overseers of the poor: Mr. Thomas Merrifield, Mr. William Daw, James George, and John Harris.

† Nich. Opie, waywarden in 1727.

‡ She was daughter of Joseph Sawle, of Penrice, and second wife and relict of John Vivian, of Truan, Esq.

§ She was a daughter of . . . . . Tresaddern, and relict of Thomas Hoblyn, of Tresaddern, Esq.

‖ Certificates signed John Collier, curate; allowed by Francis Gregor and Edm. Prideaux. New churchwardens: Christopher Warne and James Jenkin. New overseers: Robert Drew, John Mark, Benjamin Chalwell and William Brown.

ANNO 1745.

8 April Ann d. of Richard & Alice Pascoe W
16 April John Symonds W
26 April Henry Garland W
9 June Mary d. of William & Honour Roberts W
20 June Alice wife of James Stephens W
21 June Inigo Inch W
25 June Edmund Conzew* W
26 June Jacob Slade W
6 July Richard s. of Richard & Jane Veal W
15 Aug. Martha Bullen, widow W
13 Nov. William Pits of Crediton W
19 Nov. Eleanor Rowse W
25 Nov. William Pearce W
17 Dec. Matilda the wife of William Retallock W
21 Dec. Humphrey Oxenham W
26 Jan. John s. of Christopher & Honour Warne W
26 Jan. Jeremiah s. of Edward & Elizabeth Merrifield W
8 Feb. Thomas Couch W
15 Feb. Rev[d] M[r] Philip Collier, rector, died 12th Feb.† W
23 Feb. Robert s. of Robert & Mary Litticote *al's* Gregor W
25 Feb. Philippa wife of John Hicks W
1 Mar. Joan Hawke, widow W
10 Mar. Charles s. of John & Susanna Husband W
16 Mar. James s. of James & Honour Colwill W
22 Mar. M[r] Thomas Stephens W
22 Mar. Richard s. of W[m] & Mary Brabyn‡ W

ANNO 1746.

1 April William s. of John & Grace Buckingham W
9 April John James of S[t] Agnes, a soldier W
11 April Nathaniel s. of Nathaniel & Mary Lockett W
18 April Elizabeth wife of James Trenerry W
20 April Jane Rowse, widow W
21 April John base child of Abigaill* Soper W
3 May Mary Davis, widow W
10 May Mary wife of James George W
16 May Mary d. of William & Joan Bullen W
28 May John Hicks W
28 May Patience Crap W
28 May Ann d. of Rich[d] & Eliz. Husband W
3 June Mary wife of Richard Austin
10 June Joan wife of W[m] Merrifield W
22 June Elizabeth wife of Robert Bilkey W
23 June Thomas Polkinhorne W
30 June Jane wife of William Brewer W
7 July Mary d. of Richard & Elizabeth Evelyn W
9 July Jane d. of Anthony Henry & Thomazine Cock W
20 July Elizabeth Remfry, widow W
25 July Edward May W
26 July William s. of James & Jane Coad W
5 Aug. Honour Thomas W
26 Aug. William Olver W
10 Sep. Mary d. of Solomon & Mary Baseley W
16 Sep. William Pemberthy of S[t] Ives W
16 Sep. Henry Solomon W
18 Oct. Elizabeth d. of James & Honor Collwill W
25 Oct. James s. of James & Elizabeth May W
9 Nov. Eleanor d. of Isaac & Elizabeth Blake W
20 Nov. Ann d. of John & Ann Harris W
28 Nov. John Metherell W
12 Dec. Joanna d. of John & Joan Thomas W
15 Dec. Robert s. of Robert & Elizabeth Bilkey, dec[d] W
19 Dec. Elizabeth base child of Abagail† Connar W

* Carnsewe, he was probably a son of George Carnsewe (son of Geo. Carnsewe and Ann d. of Humphrey May) and Mary his wife.

† He was son of the Rev. John Collier, of Gluvias. See note, p. 252.

‡ Certificates signed John Collier, curate, and allowed by Francis Gregor and John Radcliffe Gregor. Churchwardens: Christopher Warne and James Jenkyn. Overseers of the poor: Mr. William Bone, Hugh Bullock, John Whetta, and Thomas Glanfield.

* In certificate she is called Abigaill Jones, while on 19 Dec., in the same year, the certificate calls her Abigaill Soper, but the register records her as Abigail Connar.

† See note on previous page.

22 Dec. Joyce Hambley, widow W
2 Jan. William Congdon of St Columb Minor W
16 Feb. Thomas Hawke W
7 Mar. Mary d. of William & Elizabeth Harris W
9 Mar. Richard Lovell W
9 Mar. Giles Williams *al's* Pell W
24 Mar. Elizabeth wife of James Olliver* W

Anno 1747.

2 April Ruth d. of Thomas & Catherine Langdon W
14 June John Whiteford W
26 July Alice wife of John Husband
5 Aug. Ann Crews W
10 Aug. Joan wife of William Dennis W
13 Aug. Edward s. of Dennis Tremaine W
16 Sep. Elizabeth d. of Philip & Elizabeth Gilbert W
5 Oct. Edward Baseley W
5 Oct. Mary Clemows W
28 Oct. Anthony the s. of Thomas & Rachael Keam W
28 Nov. Oliver Raw W
24 Dec. John Martyn W
2 Feb. Ann wife of James Morshead W
7 Feb. James Moreshead W
19 Feb. William Luney, junr
23 Feb. Patience Cowling, widow W
27 Feb. Mr Walter Harris† W
7 Mar. Peter Best W
10 Mar. Cicely Tippet, widow W
15 Mar. Mary‡ wife of Samuel Grimes W
21 Mar. Philippa wife of William Drew §W

Anno 1748.

13 April Henry Rowse W
18 April Jane wife of Francis Rundle W

* Certificate signed and allowed by the same as last year. New churchwardens: Thomas Glanville and William Browne. Overseers: Mr. William Drew, Henry Brewer, Henry Veal, and William Varcoe.

† Mr. Walter Harris was one of the twelve men at the time of his death.—Green Book.

‡ She was a daughter of Rev. James Beauford, baptized at St. Breock, 1689.

§ Certificates signed by J. Collier, curate, and allowed by Francis Gregor and John Radcliffe Gregor. Churchwardens: William Brown and Thomas Glanville. Overseers of the poor: Mr. Rob. Drew, Christopher Warne, James Jenkyn, and William White.

19 April The Revd Mr William ~~Searle~~, Searle rectr, died 16th April W
2 May Jennefair d. of Jude & Elizabeth May W
12 June John Tinney W
17 June Anthony Coad W
14 July Mr Robert Hoblyn W
6 Sep. Henry Oxenham W
18 Sep. Jane Merrifield, widow W
27 Sep. Ann Strongman W
8 Nov. Mrs Elizabeth Bishop W
27 Nov. Arthur Jolly W
30 Dec. Popham Morrish W
12 Jan. Mary Callway W
19 Jan. Mrs Sarah Bishop, widow W
18 Feb. Mrs Elizabeth Harris, widow W
19 Mar. Richard Webber* W

Anno 1749.

25 Mar. Henry Veal W
27 Mar. Honor wife of Thomas Mark W
21 April Alice d. of Edward & Alice Hicks W
2 May Margaret the wife of Mathew Oliver W
5 May Richard Hicks & Ann his wife W
31 May John s. of Samuel & Elizabeth Harris W
1 June Mr John Harris W
10 July Mary wife of Jonathan Law W
21 July Thomas Baseley W
1 Aug. Charles Thomas W
2 Aug. Thomas Liddicote *al's* Gregor W
4 Aug. Mary wife of John Mewdon W
25 Oct. Howard s. of John & Loveday Cowling W
26 Oct. Jane Thomas *al's* Trubboe, widow W
30 Oct. Adam Tomson W
13 Nov. Degory Keast W
19 Nov. John Mill W
3 Dec. Whitten Whiteford W
4 Dec. Elizabeth d. of Archibald & Mary Rowse W
13 Dec. Thomas Retallock W
24 Dec. Frances Wood, widow W
4 Jan. Edward Raw W
9 Jan. John Brewer W

* Certificates signed by J. Collier, but not attested by the Justices. Churchwardens continued. New overseers: Mr. John Bishop, John Metherell, William Hicks of Rosedinnick, and Rob. Grigg.

9 Jan. Ann wife of Mr Richard Stribley W
14 Jan. William s. of James & Susanna Hunson W
16 Jan. Nicholas Allen W
22 Jan. Aves Terries W
25 Jan. Mrs Blendina Moore, widow W
29 Jan. Catherine Jolly, widow* W

Anno 1750.

8 April Joan Eudy W
10 April John Isabell W
17 April Timothy Stephens W
28 April Mary Luney W
29 April Benjamin s. of John & Mary Strongman W
29 April Ann wife of John Sprey W
5 May Stephen Brewer W
3 June Jane wife of John Truscote W
8 June Grace d. of Thomas & Mary Westcote W
25 June Jane d. of William & Mary Brabyn W
5 Aug. Ann Jane W
18 Aug. Honour Pollard W
28 Aug. Mary Combe, widow W
10 Oct. Mrs Elizabeth Stephens, widow W
24 Oct. Jenefayre d. of Samuel & Mary Harris W
16 Nov. Ann d. of John & Florence Warne W
15 Dec. Joan Benny, widow W
19 Dec. John Watts W
1 Jan. Pentecoste Keast, widow W
8 Jan. Joan wife of John Thomas W
5 Feb. John Jackson W
6 Mar. John s. of Christopher & Honr Warne W
24 Mar. Benjamin s. of Bartholomew & Joanna Brown† W

Anno 1751.

1 April Mary Stephens, widow W
2 April Samuel Bussow W
23 April Grace Couch, widow W
24 April Mary d. of James & Joan Tabb W
30 April Thomas Benny W
5 May John Buckingham W
6 May Jane wife of John Buckingham W
21 May Elizabeth Brabyn, widow W
22 May John s. of Henry & Constance Tamblyn W
27 May Jane wife of Richard Manuell W
30 May Thomas Williams W
7 June John Brewer s. of Andrew & Amey Mawbyn W
18 June Samuel Haskey, a soldier in Col. Conway's regt W
20 June John Gass W
23 June John s. of John Brewer, decd & Amey his wife W
19 Aug. Frances wife of James Champion W
12 Sep. Charles base child of Thomazine Basclcy W
16 Sep. William Calawaye W
23 Sep. Robert Manuell W
29 Sep. Joan wife of Faithfull Cock W
28 Oct. John son of James & Dorothy Jenkin W
6 Nov. John son of William & Jane Liddicote *al's* Gregor W
19 Nov. Alice wife of Edward Hicks W
29 Nov. Charles and Jacob ss. of John & Susanna Husband W
19 Dec. Ann Martin d. of John & Ann Martin W
28 Dec. Nicholas s. of John & Florence Warne W
31 Dec. Christopher Calf W
1 Jan. Ann d. of John Brewer decd & Amey his wife W
2 Jan. John s. of John & Florence Warne W
3 Jan. William Luney W
4 Jan. John s. of Nathaniel & Mary Locket W
26 Jan. Catherine d. of Richard & Catherine York W
10 Feb. Catherine Morrish, widow W
18 Feb. Thomas s. of Mr Thomas Merrifield & Catherine his wife W
5 Mar. John s. of Samuel & Mary Harris W
9 Mar. Ann wife of Theophilus Williams W
11 Mar. Stephen Minnow W

* Certificates signed by J. Collier, curate, and allowed by Robert Hoblyn and John Willyams.
Churchwardens: Jude May and Wm. Hicks of Retallock. Overseers.: Dr. Robert Bateman, or Mr. Hawkey, Samuel Baseley, Richard Grigg, and John Cornish.

† Certificates signed by J. Collier, curate, and allowed by John Willyams and John Radcliffe Gregor.
Churchwardens: Wm. Brewer and Mark Nichols. Overseers: Tho. Vyvyan, Esq., John Hicks of Trenowth, Geo. Bond, and Francis Clemowe.

28 Mar. Lady Frances Gifford, relict of S[r] John Gifford, Bart., died February 28*
22 Mar. Ann d. of Peter & Petronell Wills† W

ANNO 1752.

27 Mar. Mary wife of Anthony Godolphin W
30 Mar. Margaret Craze W
31 Mar. M[r] Edward Arthur W
4 April Benjamin s. of Bartholomew & Joanna Brown W
8 April Nicholas s. of William & Jane Williams W
11 April Joanna d. of M[r] Edward Arthur dec[d] & Mary his wife W
20 April Mary d. of John & Mary Strongman W
23 April Catherine Cardell W
7 May Humphry s. of John & Ann Martyn W
19 May Dorcas Martyn W
20 May Mary Oxenham, widow W
21 June Philip Jolly W
24 June William s. of Andrew & Mary Mawbyn W
20 June Ann wife of Philip Harris W
25 June Honour d. of James & Honour Colwill W
28 June James s. of James & Honour Colwill W
2 Aug. William s. of William & Jane Lorrington W
10 Aug. Henry s. of Thomas & Joan James W
14 Aug. Elizabeth d. of Thomas & Susanna Brewer W
19 Aug. Olive Sprey W
21 Aug. Jane d. of William & Jane Lorrington W
27 Aug. Catherine wife of M[r] Thomas Merrifield W
30 Aug. Jane Lovell, widow W
21 Sep. M[r] Edward Bishop s. of M[r] Joseph & M[rs] Lovedy Bishop dec[d] W
9 Oct. John s. of William & Jane Lorrington W
20 Oct. Samuel Harris W
8 Nov. Joseph s. of Bartholomew & Joanna Brown W
14 Nov. Henry s. of Henry & Frances Oxenham W
24 Nov. Joan Solomon, widow W
25 Nov. Ann Langdon, widow W
18 Dec. Mary d. of Henry & Agnes Willsford W
19 Dec. Roger George W
25 Dec. Joseph s. of Bernard & Elizabeth Willsford* W

ANNO 1753.

11 Jan. Anthony Williams W
21 Jan. John Cockin W
21 Jan. Blanche Rescorla W
10 Feb. Edward Hicks W
19 Feb. John Peters W
5 Mar. Mary d. of Richard Manuell W
31 Mar. Catherine d. of John & Mary Lamb W
9 April Robert Walker W
1 May Mary base child of Eliz. Nichols, now wife of Charles Pearce W
2 May Benjamin Chalwell† W
4 May Ann d. of James & Elizabeth May W
16 May Susanna d. of Nicholas & Mary Liddicote W
9 June William Brewer‡
19 June Margaret d. of Andrew & Amey Mabyn W
23 June James son of James & Mary Hawke W
6 July Thomas Tomm

* Lady Frances Gifford buried in Linen, forfeiture paid to the poor 50s; *vide* certificates of burials in Woollen. She was dau. and heir of Richard Beling Arundell of Lanherne, Esq., relict of Sir John Gifford, Bart. She is commemorated by a small brass in the north chapel.

† Certificates signed and allowed by the same as last year. New churchwardens: James Coad and James Stephens. Overseers: Mr. Edward Hoblyn, John Merrifield, William Hicks of Retallack, Richard Rowse of Cross.

* Certificates signed J. Collier, Francis Gregor, and John Willyams. Churchwardens continued. Overseers: Robert Hoblyn, Esq., or J. Collier, clerk for him, John Metherell, John Varcoe, Thomas Glanville.

† A ledger stone in the church records: Elizabeth, wife of Benjamin Chalwell, fuller of this parish, died 29 Nov. 1714, aged 27; Dorothy Grey, sister to the above Elizabeth Chalwell, died 29 June 1712, aged 17 years; Henry, s. of Benj. & Eliz. Chalwell, buried 13 May, 1728, aged 20 years; the above Benjamin Chalwell, fuller and clothier, died 30 April, 1753, aged 67.

‡ Wm. Brewer, overseer of the poor in 1712. —Green Book.

11 July Robert s. of Thomas Vyvyan,* Eqre & Loveday his wife W
17 July Dinah Coad, widow W
19 July William Trembeth W
22 July John s. of Mary Thompson, widow W
23 July Ann wife of Richard Hawke W
27 July Mrs Elizabeth Williams, widow W
30 July Elizabeth d. Jonathan Law W
30 July Mary d. of Robert & Ann England W
2 Aug. Walter Watts W
2 Aug. Mary wife of Humphry Harvey W
4 Aug. Edward s. of Mr Edward Arthur decd & Mary his wife W
9 Aug. Mary & Philippa dd. of Mr John Collier & Mary his wife W
12 Aug. Elizabeth d. of Samll Retallock decd & Ann his wife W
16 Aug. Honour Lee W
18 Aug. Mary d. of James & Mary Hawke W
18 Aug. James s. of James & Mary Callaway W
24 Aug. William s. of John & Margaret Walkey W
3 Sep. John Trembeth W
4 Sep. John Inch W
9 Sep. John s. of Jonathan & Catherine Rowse W
9 Sep. Elizabeth d. of Eliz. Rickard, now wife of Theophilus Williams W
12 Sep. William & Jane children of Jonathan & Catherine Rowse W
16 Sep. Philip s. of John & Ann Olliver W
19 Sep. Ann d. of Richard & Elizabeth Husband W
29 Sep. Mary d. of William & Jane Capell W
19 Oct. Jane Abraham, widow W
25 Oct. William James W
13 Nov. Robert & James ss. of Robt & Eliz. Bilkey W

* He was fourth son of Sir Richard Vyvyan, third Bart., by Mary, daughter and heiress of Francis Vivian, of Cosworth (see note, p. 48.) He married Loveday, only child of Nicholas Bogans, by his wife Loveday, daughter of Charles Vyvyan, second son of Sir Richard Vyvyan, first Bart. of Trelowarren. They had several children, who all died s.p. The eldest son, Thomas, was of Truan, in which he was succeeded by Richard, son of his cousin Rich. Vivian.

5 Dec. Grace d. of Richard & Ann Jane W
15 Dec. John Pearce* W

ANNO 1754.

5 Jan. Jane d. of John Pearce decd & Jane his wife W
9 Jan. Honour† wife of Christopher Warne W
14 Jan. John Mewdon W
14 Jan. Elizabeth wife of Peter Pollard W
14 Jan. Abraham s. of Mark & Elizabeth Nichols W
20 Jan. John Nichols W
22 Feb. Elizabeth, d. of Thomas & Jane Giles W
4 Mar. Catherine Manuell, widow W
10 Mar. William Rawe W
17 Mar. Philip Olliver W
22 Mar. Joseph s. of John & Mary Strongman W
26 April Francis Godolphin W
26 April Joanna d. of Henry & Constance Tamblyn W
9 May Mary Brewer, widow W
3 June Joice d. of John & Ann Martin W
6 July Mary Chapman, widow W
18 July Thomas s. of Thomas & Sarah Drew W
6 Aug. Sarah d. of Mr Joseph Bishop decd W
27 Aug. William Pearce W
22 Sep. Ann White, widow W
28 Sep. Er. s. of Thomas & Jane Giles W
10 Oct. Nathaniel s. of Robert & Ann Strongman W
21 Nov. George s. of James & Ann Pollard W
27 Nov. Elizabeth Manuell W
15 Dec. Mrs Martha Atkinson, widow W
16 Dec. James Hawke W
29 Dec. Thomazine Cock, widow‡ W

* Certificates signed by J. Collier, curate, and allowed by John Willyams and Thomas Vyvyan. Churchwardens: Geo. Bond and John Mark. Overseers: John Collier, clerk, Christopher Warne, William Hicks of Criftoe, John Hawke.

† She was a dau. of Henry and Elizabeth Lee. See note p. 168, 1766, 13 May.

‡ Certificates signed by R. Bateman, rector, allowed by Robert Hoblyn, John Willyams. New churchwardens: John Rowse and Peter Wills. New overseers: Mr. William Lawrence, James Jenkyn, Walter Harris, Pascoe Davis.

ANNO 1755.

17 Feb. Martha d. of Philip & Mary Harvey W
27 Feb. Joan Scabberio W
8 Mar. Elizabeth wife of Henry Veall W
15 Mar. William s. of Pascoe & Elizabeth Davies W
17 Mar. Ann. d. of Thomas & Dorothy Salmon W
26 Mar. Mary Mercfield, widow W
29 Mar. Jane Dancaster, widow W
12 June Abraham Husband W
14 June Mary base child of Catherine Brensell W
23 July Matthew Sampson W
2 Aug. Grace Richards, *al's* Tanner W
14 Aug. Roger Tippit W
15 Aug. Grace Best, widow W
18 Aug. Mary wife of William Worth W
2 Sep. Mathew White, officer of excise W
25 Sep. Robert Elford W
7 Oct. John Rawlyn W
12 Oct. William Kendall W
9 Nov. Mr Samuel Withers W
28 Nov. Catherine Mercfield, widow W
9 Dec. Philip Harris* W

ANNO 1756.

29 Jan. Mary d. of John & Ann Martin W
4 Feb. Eleanor d. of Richard & Elizabeth Cundy W
6 Feb. John Thomas W
6 Feb. Frances Raw W
14 Feb. Joan Lawrey, widow W
24 Feb. Mary Parkin, widow W
28 Feb. Grace Cock W
2 Mar. William Brown W
11 Mar. John s. of John & Jane Pearse W
14 Mar. Jane Sowden W
3 April William Parkyn W
7 April Ann d. of Thomas & Thomazine Buckingham W
8 April Joseph s. of Thomas & Jane Giles W
15 April Alice Cockin W
25 April Peter Pollard W
2 May John May W

* The certificates are not signed at all this year. Mr. Peter Wills and Mr. Tho. Drew are given as churchwardens, and Mr. John Metherell as overseer, but the list is left incomplete.

4 June Francis s. of Degory & Alice Trescot W
8 June Jane Thomas, widow W
9 July Catherine Martyn W
18 July Mary wife of Francis Thom W
3 Aug. Jane wife of Walter Petherick W
25 Aug. John s. of John & Elizabeth Mean W
8 Sep. Ann Skinner W
12 Nov. John Bullen W
24 Nov. Jane Parkin, widow W
27 Nov. Mr William Drew* W
28 Nov. Elizabeth James *al's* Danell W
29 Nov. Robert Hoblyn of Nanswidden Esqre† W
14 Dec. Henry s. of Thomas & Elizabeth Baseley W
16 Dec. Henry Brewer W
25 Dec. Humphry Harvey‡ W

ANNO 1757.

22 Jan. James Ternerry W
4 Feb. Candace Grigor *al's* Lidicot W
7 Feb. Elizabeth Harris of the parish of Key W
21 Feb. John s. of Henry & Constance Blight W
27 Feb. Elizabeth d. of Richard Hicks decd W
26 Mar. Catherine Barret, widow W
31 Mar. Mary Leverton of ye parish of Merryn W
8 April Ann wife of John Olliver W
3 May Elizabeth Symons, widow W
13 May Ann d. of James & Honour Colwel W
22 May Samuel Clymos W
28 May Mary wife of Stephen Lovell W
1 June John Rogers W
27 June Richard Rowe W

* Mr. William Drew, one of the twelve men in 1746.—Green Book.

† He was the only son of Francis Hoblyn of Nanswhyden, Esq., by Lady Penelope Godolphin. He was M.P. for Bristol, etc.; he mar. Jane dau. of Thomas Coster of Bristol, Esq., who rem. William Quick of Exeter. Having d. s.p. the estates went under entail to the issue male of Thomas Hoblyn, Esq., of Tresaddern. For the descent and a full pedigree of Hoblyn, see Col. Vivian's *Visitations of Cornwall*, p. 234.

‡ Certificates signed by William Hill, curate, but not attested. New churchwardens: John Merrifield and John Rowse of Trekenning. Overseers: Mr. Christopher Warne, Thomas Solymou, William White, John Traher.

15 July Mr William Bone* W
19 July Mrs Mary More W
21 Aug. Simon Law W
5 Oct. John Jane W
8 Oct. Thomas Liddicot W
13 Nov. James Cowling W
14 Nov. Martha d. of James & Jane Coad W
24 Nov. William s. of Edward & Mary Arthur W
9 Dec. Ann Eudey of ye parish of St. Issey W
11 Dec. William Caple* W

A NEW REGISTER OF BURIALS BEGINNING JANUARY 1758.

ANNO 1758.

2 Jan. Ann wife of Robert Strongman W
10 Jan. Mary Tinney of St Tiddey† W
5 Feb. John Lamb W
15 Feb. William Retallack W
22 Feb. Johnathan Rowse W
24 Feb. Ezekiel Retallack W
1 Mar. Honour Busso W
2 Mar. Jane d. of John & Ann Harris W
4 Mar. Mary Eveling W
7 Mar. Elizabeth Wilsford W
15 Mar. Mary Mithrel W
20 Mar. John Brumpfield W
4 April Margaret ye wife of William Blake W
5 April Mary Nettel W
13 April Jane wife of Mr James Coad W
23 April Mary wife of Mr Hugh Bullock W
7 May Nicholas s. of Thomas & Jane Giles W
10 May Mrs Embyn Tanner, widdow W
13 May Grace Groase, widow W
21 May Ann Tier, widdow W
28 May Thomas s. of William & Elizabeth Hicks W
29 May Susannah Jane, widdow W
22 July William Dennis W
30 July Frances Chalwell, widdow W
15 Aug. William Dungey W
10 Sep. Dorothy wife of Charles Retallack W
7 Nov. Frances Strongman, widdow W
21 Nov. Mr John Drew W
24 Dec. Joyce Meals, widdow† W

ANNO 1759.

5 Jan. Mary wife of Thomas Luney W
7 Jan. Arthur s. of Richard & Elizabeth Cornish W
2 Jan. Judith d. of Richard & Elizabeth Tom W
8 Jan. Mary Withell W
25 Jan. Arthur a base child of Ann Jolley W
26 Jan. Jane d. of Mr Christopher Warne W
7 Feb. Peter s. of John & Margaret Cundy W
13 Feb. William Woolcock W
24 Feb. Jane Chub d. of George & Elizabeth Champion W
10 Mar. Richard Cundey W
23 Mar. Philippa Champion W
1 April John Pearce of Cubert W
8 April John Hawke W
12 May Catherine the wife of Edward Inch W
22 May John Lewarne W
25 June John Rundle W
28 June Mrs Grace Gummo, widow W
20 July Humphrey England W
28 July Mary d. of Philip & Mary Harvey W
10 Aug. William Lanoine‡ W

* Mr. William Bone, one of the twelve men in 1746.—Green Book.
† St. Tudy.

* The certificates this year have no declaration, only "Seen and allowed, John Willyams, Tho. Vyvyan."
The following entry appears in the certificates only: Jennefair Richards, widow, bur. 24 Augt.
† Certificates signed William Hill, curate, and allowed by John Willyams and Tho. Vyvyan.
Churchwardens: John Merrifield and John Rowse. Overseers: Mr. William Varcoe, Mr. William Rawlin. Mr. Thomas Drew, senr., and Mr. Richard Veal of Rosewastis.
‡ More correctly 'Lanyon.'

8 Oct. Mary d. of William & Anne Pearce W
26 Oct. William Perking W
7 Nov. John Eveling W
20 Nov. Archibald Rowse W
30 Nov. Ibbit Lydacote, widow W
22 Dec. Solomon Basely W
23 Dec. Bennett Retallock* W

ANNO 1760.

13 Jan. Jane d. of James & Elizabeth May W
15 Jan. Stephen Lovell W
15 Jan. Joan Isabell W
11 Feb. William Blake W
12 Feb. Daniel s. of John & Jane May W
26 Feb. Elizabeth Polkinghorne W
3 Mar. Anthony Godolphin W
16 Mar. Ann wife of Robert Hamley W
22 Mar. Mrs Elizabeth Wyate W
30 Mar. Frances d. of Francis & Grace Aver W
2 April Joseph s. of Jane Retallock W
13 April Elizabeth Husband, widow W
15 April Joyce Luney W
22 April John Husband W
10 May John Tremaine W
13 May Alice d. of Digory & Alice Truscot W
26 May Nicholas s. of Nicholas & Mary Lydacote W
26 May Miss Johanna Hamley† W
13 June Jane Warne d. of Mr William & Katherine Rawlings W
13 June James s. of James & Honour Colwell W
17 June William Mewdon W
11 July Elizabeth d. of Philip & Mary Harvey W
26 July Lewis s. of Mary Coombe W
6 Aug. William s. of William & Mary Oliver W
23 Aug. Jane wife of Peter Mitchell W
26 Aug. Robert Lydacote W
27 Aug. Ann Peters, widdow W
9 Oct. Thomas s. of John & Joan Symmons W

* The certificates signed and allowed by the same as last year. Churchwardens continued. Overseers: Mr. Thomas Hamley, Henry Brewer, William Beare, Mr. Mark Thomas.

† The certificate calls her 'Mrs. Johanna, daughter of Mr. Giles and Grace Hamley.'—See baptisms, 1727.

15 Oct. Philippa d. of Peter & Elizabeth Hawke W
2 Nov. Peter Mitchell* W

ANNO 1761.

15 Jan. William s. of Mr William & Catherine Rawlings W
11 Feb. Mrs Ann Paynter† W
18 Feb. Mrs Frances Rawe W
3 Mar. James s. of James & Dorothy Jenkings W
6 Mar. Bernard Rowse W
8 Mar. James s. of William & Mary Ivey W
20 Mar. William Thomas of St Columb Minor W
27 Mar. Mr John Lawrance‡ W
1 April John s. of John & Mary Bond W
3 April John s. of John & Mary Peters W
22 April Grace§ the wife of Mr Thomas Hamley W
26 May Joseph s. of Joseph & Mary Merifield W
29 May John Bendel s. of Joan Telbert of Gulval W
14 June Grace wife of John Buckingham W
26 June Ann Brown W
11 July Elizabeth d. of Richard & Mary Veal W
14 July John s. of Samuel & Mary Harris W
24 July Honour d. of Ralph & Mary Busso W
28 July Samuel s. of James & Margaret Jane W
1 Aug. John & William s^s^ of William & Mary Retallack W
17 Aug. Mary d. of Grace Helborne W
1 Sep. Margaret the wife of Stephen Tyre W
7 Sep. Elizabeth d. of Robert & Grace Edevean W
13 Sep. Mary d. of Robert & Grace Edevean W

* Certificates signed and allowed by the same as last year. This is the last year to which a declaration as to the burials is attached.

† The certificate adds, 'widow.'

‡ Mr. John Lawrence, elected one of the twelve men in 1740. Mr. Lawrence appointed surgeon in 1758.—Green Book.

§ She was daughter and coheiress of Rev. John Tregenna, rector of Mawgan, and first wife of the Rev. Tho. Hamley, son of Mr. Giles Hamley and Grace (Hoblyn) his wife. See note, p. 172.

15 Sep. Sarah d. of William & Ann Langdon W
23 Sep. Elizabeth Williams* W
15 Oct. Catherine d. of Humphrey & Susanna England W
18 Oct. Mary d. of John & Margaret Walkey W
21 Oct. Henry s. of Richard & Catherine Carne W
22 Oct. Ann d. of Theophilus & Elizabeth Williams W
31 Oct. James Trelivan W
3 Nov. William s. of William & Jane Lorrington W
4 Nov. William s. of William & Elizabeth Perking W
21 Nov. Ann d. of Thomas & Dorothy Salmon W
1 Dec. Thomas s. of Thomas & Mary Mill W
8 Dec. John s. of Richard & Elizabeth Cornish W
8 Dec. Margaret d. of Thomas & Mary Mill W
9 Dec. Ann d. of James & Elizabeth May W
12 Dec. Bridget d. of John & Grace Webber† W

ANNO 1762.

26 Jan. Elizabeth Allen W
26 Jan. Julian d. of Julian Davie of . . . . . W
28 Jan. Frances wife of Mr William Lawrence W
3 Feb. Ann d. of Philip & Margaret Harris W
6 Feb. Margaret Hicks, widdow W
12 Feb. Elizabeth d. of Philip & Mary Cornish W
15 Feb. Theophilus Williams W
3 Mar. Hugh s. of Hugh & Mary Bullock W
5 Mar. Ebbet Hendey, widow W
23 Mar. Mary Lydicote *al's* Grigor, widow W
9 April John s. of John & Elizabeth Stephens W
7 May Elizabeth Oxenham, widdow W
12 June John s. of Philip & Johan Gilbert W
14 Aug. Elizabeth Cornish, widdow W
27 Aug. John s. of Joyce Dennis W
13 Sep. Charles Lydecote *al's* Greger W
10 Oct. Meldred Basley, widdow W
25 Oct. Thomas Rawlings W
23 Nov. Martha wife of Michael Basley W
26 Nov. Mary wife of Richard Lawrey W
10 Dec. Dorothy Hocken, widdow* W

ANNO 1763.

16 Jan. Mary wife of Robert Manuel W
15 Feb. Samuel s. of James & Margaret Jane W
12 Mar. Mrs. Mary Rawe† W
14 Mar. Grace d. of Thomas & Mary Westcott‡ W
10 May Joan Merifield W
15 May Ruth Mill W
17 May Anne Cocking W
17 May Nicholas s. of Nicholas & Mary Lydacote W
19 May Mary d. of Andrew & Mary Niblet W
22 May Henry Tamlyn W
30 May Mary d. of Mr Thomas & Mary Williams W
10 June John Dean, a soldier W
26 June Richard s. of Richard & Sarah Bearsley W
26 June Stephen s. of Mary Helbourn W
27 June Elizabeth Wilken§ W
1 July Anne d. of John & Elizabeth Stephens W
8 July William Rawe W
8 July John s. of William & Jane Lydacote W
24 Aug. Henry Oxenham W

* Certificate adds, 'widow.'

† Mr. Christopher Warne, appointed rector's churchwarden by William Hill, curate, in the name of the rector. The twelve men appoint Mr. James Jenkyn their churchwarden. Overseers: Edw. Hoblyn, Esq., William Hamley, William Hicks of Retallick, Richard Grigg of Grairgran.

The following appears in the certificates only: viz., Jane Kelly, widow, buried 30 Sep., 1761.

* Mr. William Ivey, rector's churchwarden. The twelve men appoint Nicholas Clemoe their churchwarden. Churchwardens: Tho. Vyvian, Edw. Hoblyn, Rob. Drew, Christopher Warne. Overseers: Mr. Rich. Hicks, Mr. William Angove, Mr. Peter Hawke, Isaack Grigg.

† The certificate says, 'Mary, daughter of John Rawe, gent., and Elizabeth his wife, of Foye (Fowey), deceased.'

‡ Certificate adds, 'deceased' after Tho. Westcote.

§ The certificate adds, 'widow.'

13 Sep. John s. of John & Florence Warne W
12 Oct. Catherine wife of Richard Carne W
17 Oct. Catherine d. of Mr William & Catherine Rawlings W
9 Nov. Elizabeth Walkey* W
7 Dec. Dorcas Whetter W
13 Dec. Angelet d. of Edward & Ann Pearce W
19 Dec. Florence Rowse† W

ANNO 1764.

15 Jan. John Robarts W
1 Feb. Mathew Webster‡ W
3 Feb. Rachel Luney W
3 Feb. Martha d. of Jonathan & Mary Chipman W
6 Feb. Robert s. of Robert & Mary Mannel W
25 Mar. Elizabeth Wolcock W
28 Mar. Henry Blith W
30 Mar. William Pound W
2 April John s. of John Bishop§ & Susanna his wife W
3 April Joyce d. of John & Ann Martyn W
19 April Catherine Pearce W
7 May Elizabeth wife of James May W
9 May Charles Retallock W
16 May William Drew W
5 June Robert Woon W
5 June John s. of William & Elizabeth Harris W
16 June Dennis Tremayne *alias* Cockin W
3 July Nancy the d. of William & Dorothy Blight W
14 July Jane wife of Shedrack Tremayne W
22 July Catherine Basely W
25 July William§ s. of William & Ann Strowle W
25 July Methuselah Williams W
10 Sep. Robert Hamley W
31 Oct. John s. of Richard & Susan Rowse W
2 Nov. Margaret Guens W

* The certificate adds, 'widow.'

† William Swan, rector's churchwarden. The twelve men appoint John Mark as their churchwarden. Overseers: John Quick, Esq., William Ivie, Jeptha Whettar, William Rowse.

‡ The certificate adds, 'of Crowan parish.'

§ The certificate calls the father a 'soldier.'

18 Nov. Ursula wife of William Tom W
23 Nov. James England* W

ANNO 1765.

28 Jan. Elizabeth d. of Jane May† W
6 Feb. Joseph Woodman W
6 Feb. John Day
20 Feb. Mary d. of John & Joan Symons W
22 Feb. Elizabeth d. of William & Mary Pyper W
15 Mar. Grace d. of Edmund & Mary Varcoe W
26 Mar. Mary Brewer, widdow W
28 Mar. Robert Strongman W
30 Mar. Prudence Meriffeld‡ W
13 April Susanna the wife of Richard Rowse W
25 April Lydia Champion W
1 May John Husband W
1 May James Price W
5 May Elizabeth Slade, widdow W
27 May Margaret Cayzer W
12 June William Roberts W
10 July Jane d. of William & Jane Lorrington W
17 July Stephen Tyre W
18 Aug. Avis Cockin W
26 Aug. Susanna wife of William Angove W
27 Aug. Nathaniel Loggett W
17 Sep. Elizabeth Husband W
17 Sep. Grace d. of Richard Rowse W
21 Oct. Frances Tom W
21 Oct. Mary wife of Robert Kent W
9 Nov. Catherine d. of Anthony Kendall W
11 Nov. Nicholas Brenton W
24 Nov. Blanch wife of John Husband W
30 Nov. Ann Stephens W
1 Dec. Elizabeth d. of Thomas & Jane Bettinson W
28 Dec. Faithfull Cock§ W

ANNO 1766.

4 Jan. William the s. of William & Dorothy Blight

* Mr. John Dungey, churchwarden, appointed by R. Bateman, rector. The twelve men appointed John Cornish. Overseers: John Metherell, John White, James Jenkin. James Coad. Allowed by John Willyams and Tho. Vyvyan.

† Certificate styles the mother, 'widow.'

‡ The certificate adds, 'wife of John Merifield.'

§ Mr. Henry Hawkey and Richard Rowse, churchwardens. Overseers: Mr. Christopher

9 Jan. William Eveling
18 Jan. Grace Hoppey
20 Jan. Ann Benny
3 Feb. Thomas s. of Thomas & Ann Giles
7 Feb. James s. of Andrew & Amey Mabyn
19 Feb. William Kent
26 Feb. Elizabeth Retallock
28 Feb. Richard s. of Thomasine Teppett
17 Mar. John s. of Philip & Mary Cornish
21 Mar. William s. of Thomas & Amey Solomon
5 April Mary d. of Robert & Mary Grigg
10 April Elizabeth Rouse
12 April Mary Teppet, widow
19 April Ann Tremain, widow
27 April Elizabeth d. of William & El. Lewarne
28 April Ann Rawling, widow
30 April John s. of John & Joan Seymons
13 May Christopher Warne*
14 May Lovedy d. of Humphrey & Elizabeth Tom
23 May Robert s. of William & Elizabeth Austion
25 May Peternel wife of Peter Wills
28 May Ann Hawke, widow
11 June The Rev[d] M[r] Thomas Hamley†
14 June Thomas Rawe
26 June Arabella Trebilcock, widow‡
28 July Thomas s. of Edward & Ann Pearce

Warne, Richard Veale, John Rawlings, John Chapman. This is the last year there are any entries of certificates of burials in woollen.

* He was son of Christopher Warne and Jane Hichens, and married Honour daughter of Hen. and Eliz. Lee. (See baptisms, 1707; marriages, 1731.) He held the office of rector's churchwarden, one of the twelve men, and an overseer of the poor, for many years. He had issue: Catherine, married William Rawlings; Grace, married John Dungey; Henry, married Elizabeth Dungey; and others, who died young.—See also note, pp. 172, 175.

† He was a son of Mr. Giles Hamley of St. Columb. He married, first, Grace daughter and co-heiress of the Rev[d] John Tregenna, and secondly, Mary daughter of . . . . . By his first wife he had Rev[d] Thomas Tregenna Hamley; by his second wife he had Edward and Giles. —See also note, p. 172.

‡ In 1763 John Trebilcock paid £4 17s. 4d., one year's rent of the Rock Park, St. Issey. In 1807 the Roach Parks let to William Warne for seven years at £15 per annum, which lease was renewed twice.—Green Book.

12 Oct. John s. of William & Elizabeth Gass
17 Oct. Edward Inch
1 Nov. John Arscutt *
4 Nov. William Brown, soldier
7 Nov. Mark Nicholas
8 Nov. Elizabeth d. of John & Mary Peters
11 Nov. George Teppit
22 Nov. Elizabeth Briming
25 Nov. Edith Bishop, widow
29 Nov. Mary wife of Philip Rickard
6 Dec. Prudence May, widow
7 Dec. Peter Retalack
9 Dec. William Bear
17 Dec. Jane Rouse

ANNO 1767.

7 Jan. Elizabeth Capple
11 Jan. Elizabeth Harris, widow
26 Jan. Catherine wife of Anth. Kendall
30 Jan. Robert Thomson
30 Jan. Nicholas s. of John & Mary Tonkin
1 Feb. Catherine the wife of Thomas Langdon
5 Feb. John Husband
26 Feb. Elizabeth England, widow
15 Mar. Sarah Oliver, widow
18 April Richard s. of Richard & Mary Bettinson
30 June Shadrach Tremain
6 July Thomas s. of William & Thomasine Swan
13 July Thomas Mark
17 July James s. of William & Thomasine Swann
13 Aug. Ursula Mill of Colan
18 Aug. John s. of Joan Martin
25 Oct. John Mewton
15 Nov. Mary wife of Richard Manuell
20 Nov. Margaret wife of Petherick Williams

ANNO 1768.

7 Jan. Elizabeth d. of Jepthah & Grace Whitten
8 Jan. Reskimo Allen
26 Jan. Richard s. of William & Sarah Ellery
6 Feb. Ann Benny, widow
1 Mar. Mary Rowse, widow
15 Mar. Judith Howard
18 Mar. Methuselah s. of Methuselah & Mary Barret

* John Arscott, waywarden in 1728.

22 Mar. Joseph s. of Joseph & Elizabeth Tinney
30 Mar. Jane Dungey, widow
18 April John s. of Richard & Elizabeth Gummow
6 May Robert Howard
11 May Elizabeth Coomb of St Ervan
14 May Loveday* the wife of Thomas Vivian, Esqre
15 May Elizabeth wife of John Cowling
18 May Elizabeth the wife of James Dennis
4 June Elizabeth the wife of Richard Gummow
14 June Margaret d. of Revd Thomas Biddulph & Martha his wife
16 July Samuel s. of William & Catherine Rawlings
7 Aug. Elizabeth Teppit, widow
24 Aug. Grace wife of Richard Callaway
24 Sep. John† s. of Richard & Alice Hicks
26 Sep. Elizabeth d. of William & Elizabeth Peters
20 Oct. Joan Hill
3 Dec. Hannah d. of Ralph & Mary Bues
24 Dec. Ann d. of Richard & Elizabeth Basely

Anno 1769.

15 Jan. Elizabeth wife of Benjamin Jones
29 Jan. Jennifer d. of George & Elizabeth Colwell
9 Feb. Ann d. of John & Catherine Whitford
15 Feb. William Hicks
20 Feb. Jephthah s. of Jephthah & Grace Whitter
20 Feb. Alice d. of Francis & Edith Hawkey
1 April Nicholas Lakeman
13 April Ann Tremain *alias* Cocking
2 May Humphrey s. of John & Ann Martin
6 May Philippa wife of Henry Barnicoat
11 May Elizabeth the wife of Thomas Basely
22 May Peter Kendal
30 May Richard Hawke
27 June Sarah d. of John & Grace Jane
12 July Elizabeth wife of George Tremain *al'is* Cocking
18 July Elizabeth wife of William Raw
10 Aug. Ann d. of Philip & Margaret Harris
12 Aug. Jane d. of Philip & Joan Gilbert of St Enoder
22 Aug. Mark d. of George & Elizabeth Raw
26 Aug. Mary Tabb, widow
28 Aug. Ann d. of Thomas & Joan Williams
5 Sep. John s. of George & Elizabeth Raw
15 Oct. Mr William Lawrence,* gent.
28 Oct. Ann d. of Richard & Elizabeth Basely
30 Oct. Samuel s. of William & Catherine Rawlings
7 Nov. Elizabeth wife of Anthony Raw
15 Nov. John Bond
15 Nov. Thomas s. of Thomas & Joan Williams
21 Nov. Alice wife of John Cornish
30 Nov. Dinah Merifield widow
3 Dec. Mary Basely widow
4 Dec. Mary Hailburn
7 Dec. James Oliver
13 Dec. Ann ye wife of John Martin
16 Dec. Joan Vivian widow
21 Dec. John Sprey
24 Dec. Dorothy Keast
26 Dec. Richard Callaway
28 Dec. Honour England, widow

Anno 1770.

4 Jan. Robert Retallack
10 Jan. Mary wife of John Teppett†
12 Jan. Ralph Bues
17 Jan. Mary King widow
19 Jan. Ann d. of William & Margaret Benny
2 Feb. Elizabeth Blake
11 Feb. Elizabeth Warne
19 Feb. John s. of James May
24 Feb. Margaret Retallack widow
25 Feb. John Tippett†

* She was daughter and heir of Nicholas Bogans, Esq., by his wife Loveday, daughter of Charles Vyvyan, second son of Sir Richard Vyvyan, bart., of Trelowarren.

† A tomb in the churchyard records this John, who on it is said to have died 1st Sep., 1758, aged 5 years; also, Catherine Drew, daughter of the above Richard, died Jan. 1785, aged 25 years.

* William Lawrence, buried 23 Jan., 1781.—St. Columb Par. Reg.

† In 1766 John Tippet was governor of the workhouse.

7 Mar. William s. of Thomas & Rachel Keam
10 Mar. Elizabeth d. of Thomas & Ann Cook
13 Mar. William Blight
17 Mar. John s. of Jephthah & Grace Whitton
26 Mar. George s. of George & Elizabeth Champion
27 Mar. Bartholemew Brown
29 Mar. Joan wife of William Bulling
17 April Thomas Tyne *alias* Richards of ye parish of St Dennis
21 April Joan d. of James & Joan Tabb
3 May Elizabeth Williams widow
4 May Catherine d. of Thomas & Elizabeth Tabb
8 May Sarah Retallack
21 May Mary wife of Charles Rickard
24 May John Cowling
30 May Margaret Pill
1 June Hugh Bullock
8 June James Champion
11 June Elibabeth wife of Nicholas Husband
13 June Frances d. of Philip & Ann Beswarick of ye parish of Luxillion
24 June Ann wife of James Pearce
29 June Philippa Hawke widow
6 July Elizabeth wife of George Champion
17 July John s. of Nicholas & Elizabeth Guens
17 July Ann Rowe widow
18 July Elizabeth d. of Richard & Elizabeth Hawken
23 July Mary d. of Methuselah & Mary Barrett
5 Aug. Frances d. of Mr James Coad
12 Aug. Elizabeth d. of Thomas & Jane Giles
23 Aug. Henry s. of Richard & Elizabeth Basely
2 Sep. Frances Woon widow
8 Sep. Flizabeth d. of John & Elizabeth Stephens
15 Sep. Mary & Jennifer daughters of John & Elizabeth Stephens
26 Sep. Nancey d. of John & Elizabeth Stephens
18 Oct. Elizabeth d. of James Pearce
9 Nov. Richard s. of Richard & Elizabeth Luke
12 Nov. Richard s. of Thomas & Amy Solomon
5 Dec. William Worth

Anno 1771.

25 May Mary wife of Henry Pine
8 June Richard Carne
10 June Allice d. of Digory & Allice Truscutt
11 June William s. of William & Dorothy Harris
13 June Mathew King
14 June Catherine Rawling
20 June Joan the wife of Thomas Buse
23 June Elizabeth the wife of Humphrey Tomm
30 July Dorothy Blight, wid.
22 Aug. Thomas Langdon
2 Nov. Grace d. of Robert & Grace Keam
26 Nov. Ann d. of George & Mary Tippett
28 Nov. John Parnel

Anno 1772.

13 Jan. Joan Martin, widow
25 Jan. Mary ye wife of Henry Rowe
8 Feb. William s. of Nicholas & Dorothy Tamblyn
21 Feb. John s. of Richard & Frances Sampson
5 Mar. Ann Gill, widow
16 Mar. Allice d. of Peter & Elizabeth Hawke
22 Mar. William s. of William & Margaret Benny
13 April Margaret the wife of James Jane
20 April Thomas Luney
6 May Richard s. of Richard & Mary Williams
22 May Catherine Johnson, widow
15 June Peter Callaway
18 June Jonathan Daw
15 July Jane Brenton, widow
24 Aug. Daniel Thomas
25 Aug. Barnabas, s. of John Truscutt
12 Sep. John Martin
15 Sep. John Meryfield
28 Sep. Philippa d. of James & Elizabeth Inch
31 Oct. William Fordham, soldier in ye 7th Reg^t^ of Foot
13 Nov. Gilbert Cayzier of ye parish of Mawgan
23 Nov. Jane Parnel, widow
4 Dec. James Brewer
7 Dec. Elizabeth d. of Nicholas & Mary Liddicoat
12 Dec. John Helston

ANNO 1773.

6 Jan. Elizabeth Harris
7 Jan. William Teppet
22 Jan. Elizabeth Roberts, widow
4 Feb. Susanna Vivian
15 Feb. John King
10 Mar. Amy Brewer, widow
3 April Rebecca d. of William & Honour Blight
4 April Catherine Cundy, widow
30 April William s. of Elizabeth Lobb
4 May Honour Roberts, widow
5 May Mary d. of Mary Oliver
14 May Catherine d. of Robert & Elizabeth Manuel
30 May William Blight, postmaster
12 July Philip Gilbert
14 Aug. Sarah wife of William Jane
18 Sep. Mary d. of John & Constance James
26 Sep. Ann d. of John & Constance James
4 Oct. Philip Rickard
16 Oct. John Rowse
24 Oct. William Brabyn
28 Oct. Mary Husband
25 Nov. William Jane
16 Dec. Francis Solomon
19 Dec. Ann d. of John & Lovedy Truscutt
27 Dec. William d. of Robert & Jane Drew

ANNO 1774.

7 Jan. Thomas s. of Robert & Jane Drew
6 Mar. Mary wife of John Liddicoat
4 Mar. Jane Pound, widow
8 Mar. Harry s. of John & Elizabeth Oxenham
30 April Philip s. of James & Grace Gilbert
14 May Grace Mitchell, widow
24 May Ann Pearce, widow
26 May Mary Coad d. of James Coad
19 June Thomas Hutchings
11 July Abigal Corner
27 Aug. William s. of Francis & Jane Jane
4 Sep. William Davis
7 Sep. John s. of John & Margarett Walkey
12 Oct. Elizabeth Best
26 Nov. Elizabeth Williams
9 Dec. Catherine Hendy
11 Dec. Thomas s. of Robert & Elizabeth Manuel
24 Dec. Ann the wife of John Best

ANNO 1775.

25 Jan. Mary Lanyon, widow
8 Feb. Thomas s. of Richard & Grace Vivian
15 Feb. Jane wife of Richard Veal
17 Feb. Florence the wife of William Hicks
12 Mar. Anthony s. of Richard & Lydia Batten James
18 Mar. Catherine d. of James & Joan Tabb
23 Mar. Philip s. of Peter & Elizabeth Hawke
25 Mar. Thomas s. of Thomas & Prudence Hicks
2 April Rebeccah the wife of Francis May
1 May Joan Sampson of y[e] parish of Lower S[t] Columb
19 May Frances Woods
1 June Richard Pascoe
8 July James Callaway
11 July Thomas Sweet
3 Sep. Thomas s. of James & Dorothy Jenkins
18 Sep. William s. of William & Elizabeth Lewarne
25 Sep. William Angove, Esq[re]
30 Sep. M[r] John Burgis
12 Oct. James s. of John & Elizabeth Helston
24 Nov. Elizabeth wife of John Stephens
2 Dec. John s. of Thomas & Johanna Salmon
23 Dec. Thomas Gass

ANNO 1776.

4 Jan. Joyce wife of John Mark
8 Feb. Richard Austin
20 Feb. Elizabeth Cowling
3 Mar. John May
9 Mar. William s. of Richard & Lydia Batten James
30 Mar. Amy d. of William & Elizabeth Brewer
2 April Peter s. of John & Grace Jane
2 April Thomas Williams late officer of Excise
8 April William Lewarne
11 April Frances Evans, widow
3 May Joan wife of James Stephens
4 May Digory Truscott
18 May Frances d. of Peter & Elizabeth Hawke

5 June Richard s. of Richard & Elizabeth Basely
6 June Mark s. of Mark & Elizabeth Nichols
22 June Elizabeth the wife of Richard Husband
10 July James s. of James & Ann Pearce
11 July Elizabeth d. of Benjamin & Elizabeth Rowe
13 July Rev[d] D[r] Robert Bateman, rector of this & Mawgan parishes*
1 Aug. James s. of Arthur & Ann Caple
7 Aug. Jane Rowse, widow
3 Sep. Jane d. of Mark & Elizabeth Nichols
29 Sep. John Buckingham
29 Oct. Henry Tamblyn
17 Nov. John Harvey
18 Nov. Henry Barnicoatt
7 Dec. Richard Basely
25 Dec. Anthony Rowe
31 Dec. Lovedy wife of John Truscott

ANNO 1777.

11 Jan. Alice Pascoe, widow
12 Jan. John Cundy
22 Jan. Jane Bilkey
4 Feb. George Bond
9 Feb. William Merifield
13 Feb. Jennifer d. of Francis & Grace Cundy
18 Feb. John s. of William & Mary Glanvil
28 Feb. Andrew Mabyn
20 Mar. Thomas Giles
25 Mar. Frances wife of Stephen Carhart
3 April Jonathan & George ss. of George & Mary Daw
12 April John Hockin
22 April Lovedy Cowling, widow
28 May Joyce Dinnis
1 June Henry Hoskin
7 June M[rs] Martha Grimes
22 June John s. of Francis & Jane Jane
26 June Edward s. of Edward & Rachel Gummo

* Said by his representative to be a brother of Sir Hugh Bateman, Bart., of Hartington, but his name does not appear in any pedigree of the Batemans' of Hartington.

Mrs. Elizabeth Bateman, relict of the late Dr. Bateman, buried July 4th, 1800.—St. Columb Par. Reg

3 July M[rs] Grace Augove, widow
4 July John Strongman
10 July John s. of Peter & Elizabeth Hawke
17 July Emblyn wife of William Buckingham
21 Aug. Thomas s. of Richard & Lydia Batten James
21 Sep. Thomas s. of Nicholas Bree of Stoke
22 Oct. Enstees Hendy
24 Nov. William Tomm
27 Nov. Ann Retallack
27 Dec. James Shambles

ANNO 1778.

23 Jan. Henry Rowse
25 Jan. Robert Kent
27 Jan. Elizabeth d. of Michael & Susanna Basely
28 Jan. Mary Liddicoat
1 Feb. John Merifield
2 Feb. John s. of William & Dorothy Rounseval
6 Feb. William Crap
20 Feb. Peter Wills
20 Feb. Henry s. of Susanna Husband
15 Mar. Mary d. of Robert & Elizabeth Manuel
1 April Sampson Brewer
10 April John Cundy, soldier
13 April Mary d. of John & Jennifer George
20 May Margaret wife of John Cornish
23 May Edward Hoblyn, Esq[re]*
25 May Susanna wife of Michael Basely

* He was of Tresaddern, son of Thomas Hoblyn of Tresaddern, gent., by his second wife Joan daughter of . . . . Tresaddern. He married Anne, daughter of John Peter of Harlyn (she died s.p. in 1791), and died s.p. aged 69.

Mrs. Anne Hoblyn of Tresaddern, widow, buried 4 May, 1791.—St. Columb Major Par. Reg.

Miss M. Hoblyn of Truro, buried 22 April, 1796.—St. Columb Major Par. Reg. [She was a daughter of Samuel Hoblyn of Penheale (grandson of Tho. Hoblyn of Tresaddern and his first wife Mary Carter), who succeeded to Nanswhyden on the death of his cousin, Robert Hoblyn. He was buried at St. Columb, 12 May, 1790 his wife Joan, daughter of Enoder Hawke of Treugove, died 10 March, 1817, buried at St. Columb.]

Caroline, daughter of the Rev[d] Robert Hoblyn and Mary his wife, buried 31 Jan., 1800.—St. Columb Major Par. Reg. [Her father was son of Samuel, named above ; he was curate of Gwennap, and succeeded to Nanswhyden. He

25 May Temperance d. of Henry & Fanny Hoskin
27 May Elizabeth d. of Edward & Rachel Gummo
28 May Jennifer d. of Joseph & Mary Kelly
6 June Thomas s. of Edward & Elizabeth May
14 June Delia d. of John & Margaret Buckingham
3 July Rachel wife of Henry Keam
6 July John s. of Edward & Ann Pearce
7 July Thomas Keam
17 July Thomas s. of Thomas & Prudence Hicks
27 July Richard s. of William & Sarah Ellery
1 Aug. Elizabeth Solomon, widow
1 Sep. William s. of Joseph & Patience Hancock
29 Sep. James s. of Robert & Elizabeth Tabb
9 Oct. Frances d. of John & Rosamond Carhart
2 Nov. Elizabeth d. of Peter & Jane Pollard

ANNO 1779.

4 Jan. Richard Gummo
6 Jan. John Metheral
19 Jan. Margarett d. of Thomas & Thomazine Gass
9 Feb. George s. of Richard & Mary Veal
24 Feb. William Truscutt
27 Feb. Blanch Tom
6 Mar. Jane wife of Michael Barrett
15 Mar. Mary d. of John & Martha Jewell
5 April Mary d. of Mark & Elizabeth Nichols
25 May Elizabeth Nichols, widow
3 June Mary Simons, widow
16 June Wm.'s. of George & Mary Daw
21 June Mary wife of George Dawe
25 June Mr John Dungey*
5 July Sarah d. of Elizabeth Harris
8 July Mr Elias Hiscutt
14 July Samuel Hooker s. of James & Margarett Jane
16 July Ann Lee
22 July Mary wife of Robert Bilkey
24 July William s. of John & Grace Dungey
29 July William Williams s. of Ann Aver
2 Aug. William s. of Richard & Elizabeth Jane
6 Aug. John s. of Richard & Elizabeth Jane
8 Aug. Richard s. of Richard & Elizabeth Jane
17 Aug. Ann d. of John & Johanna Bryant
22 Aug. Robert s. of John & Joan Simons
31 Aug. James s. of William & Margaret Benny
3 Sep. William s. of Richard & Mary Williams
2 Oct. John s. of Nicholas & Ann Courtney
9 Oct. Richard s. of William & Sarah Basely
10 Oct. Susanna Jane d. of James & Ann Pearce
14 Oct. Thomazine d. of Nicholas & Ann Courtney
22 Oct. Elizabeth d. of Richard & Susanna Rowse
26 Oct. John s. of Samuel & Elizabeth Johns
12 Nov. Constance Bligth, widow
14 Nov. Philip s. of Philip & Joan Gilbert

ANNO 1780.

2 Jan. Thomas s. of Joseph & Mary Merifield
13 Jan. Jane Cowling
20 Jan. William s. of Thomas & Amy Solomon
8 Feb. Thomas Keast
9 Feb. George Hallway
12 Feb. Harry s. of Henry & Elizabeth Warne*
13 Feb. Gertrude Lawrence, widow
16 Feb. Samuel Hoskin
20 Feb. Margarett d. of Francis & Edith Hawkey
26 Feb. John Tregillgass

married Mary, daughter of Hugh Mallet of Millbrooke, by whom he had, with other issue, the Revd William Mallet Hoblyn, rector of Clipsham, co. Rutland, who, by his wife, Frances Laura, daughter of John Paget, Esq. of Cranmore Hall, was father of the present William Paget Hoblyn, of the Fir Hill, Esq.]

* He married Grace, daughter and co-heiress of Mr. Christopher Warne of St. Columb, by whom he left several children.

* Mr. Henry Warne was bur. Jan. 3, 1813, aged 71; his wife Elizabeth (Dungey) bur. Dec. 9, 1798, aged 59.

25 April Thomas Merifield
3 May Robert Helborn
6 May M[r] Nicholas Donithorn Arthur
16 May James Tabb
30 May Ann Veal, widow
29 June Joan Tabb, widow
5 July Rosamond wife of John Carhart
6 July Eleanor wife of Robert Tabb
12 Sep. Alice Law, widow
10 Oct. Mary wife of Henry Barnicott
13 Oct. Honor Oliver, widow
16 Oct. Anthony Kendall
26 Oct. Mary d. of Jane Giles
20 Nov. Richard s. of Richard & Mary Billing
25 Nov. John s. of James & Mary Snell
28 Nov. Henry s. of James & Mary Snell
29 Nov. Martha d. of Richard & Mary Billing
3 Dec. Frances Oxenham, widow
6 Dec. Cordelia d. of John & Margaret Buckingham
8 Dec. Margarett d. of John & Ann Cornish
9 Dec. John Hand
9 Dec. Ann d. of Edward and Elizabeth May
12 Dec. Ann wife of John Cornish
17 Dec. Frances Merifield, widow
23 Dec. William s. of Richard & Susanna Rowse
26 Dec. John Best

EXTRACTS FROM OTHER REGISTERS RELATING TO ST. COLUMB FAMILIES.

MAWGAN IN PYDAR.

BAPTISMS.

1686 Jan. 16 Wm s. of Hen. Haycraft & Margery his wife
1690 July 24 Wm s. of John Tom & Dorothy his wife
. . . Nov. 18 Wm s. of Tho. Pendarves, rector & Grace his wife
1695 Nov. 5 Alice d. of James Ivey & Eleanor his wife
1696 Dec. 15 Francis s. of Francis Jolly
1697 July 13 Grace d. of Benj. Devonshire, gent. & Dorothy his wife
1698 Jan. 25 Mary d. of Philip Vivian & Honor his wife
1701 Mar. 21 John s. of John Willyams gent. & Dorothy his wife

MARRIAGES.

1686 May 21 Peter Kendell & Margt Bary
. . . Dec. 27 John Addams & Mary Retallack
1688 Jan. 7 Mr Tho. Pendarves, rector & Mrs Grace Hoblin
1690 June 24 James Strongman & An Ginniens
1692 Nov. 14 James s. of John Day of St Columb & Martha d. of John Tregenna, rector
1696 Sept. 5 Archibald s. of Remfrey Rowse of St. Columb Major & Dorothy d. of Gregory May & Janewell his wife
1698 Nov. 26 James Row & Mary Rowse of St. Columb the higher
1704 Nov. 22 James Spry & Margaret Brewer
1706 June 8 Ric. Jolly & Johan Pollard
1709 June 3 Mr Wm Symons, vicar of Cornelle and Merder, & Mrs Trephena Williams (Willyams)
1709 July 29 Francis Dungey & Elizabeth Roberts
1709 July 26 Wm James & Hannah Jack Andrew
1711 April 19 Hen. Lawrence & Sarah Austen
1725 July 11 Wm Bilkey & Mary Vivian
1726 July 29 John Arthur & Honor Sleeman of St. Columb Minor
1729 May 26 Hen. Lawrence & Eliz. Hurt
1734 Nov. 11 John Whitford & Eliz. Muffat of St. Columb Minor
1736 June 5 John Pearse & Mary Dungey
1747 Dec. 23 Mr Wm Lemon, junr, of Truro & Miss Ann Willyams, by licence
1763 Jan. 31 Wm Kendall of this parish & Frances Retallack of St. Columb Major
1788 Aug. Tho. Whitford of St. Columb Major, widower & Elizabeth Hobb of Mawgan Spinster
1805 July 28 John Ball of this parish & Ann Warne of St Issey

BURIALS.

1698 Nov. 19 Hannabell Carhart
1741 Dec. 25 John Willyams, Esq.
1765 Feb. 4 Jane Arundell
1781 July 30 Mrs Jane Willyams
1784 Aug. 9 John Willyams, gent.
1790 July 3 Mrs Charlotte Willyams

COLAN.

BAPTISMS.

1670 Feb. 23 Diones & Katherine children of Colan Mannuell & Oner his wife
1677 Jan. 26 Luke s. of Colan & Alice Bettison
1680 Mar. 15 Peter s. of James Day, gent. & Joane his wife

1681 Sep. 28 Mary d. of Francis Vivian of Coswarth, Esq. & Ann his wife
1683 Feb. 19 Elizabeth d. of James Day, gent. & Joan his wife
1687 Jan. 17 Anna d. of James Day, gent. & Joan his wife
1688 Sep. 15 Charles s. of John Robins & Jane his wife
1689 May 8 Edw. s. of Rob. Hoblyn, clerk & Judeth his wife
1704 April 1 Eliz. d. of Anthony Whitford & Elizabeth his wife

MARRIAGES.

1661 April 15 Wm Thomas & Mary Glanville
1670 Jan. 15 Wm Cottle, gent. & Mrs Dorothy Hoblin of St. Enoder
1674 Feb. 2 Wm Tremean & Thomasine Sleeman
1686 Oct. 14 Timothy Berrie & Hester Poole
1688 Aug. 4 Francis Stephens & Beaton Hawke
1691 Nov. 14 Timothy Gully of St. Enoder, gent. & Ann Dodson
1694 Aug. 3 Christopher Hendra & Philippa Jolley
1703 Sept. 11 Philip Husband & Susanna Harris
1715 May 23 Anthony White of St. Columb Major & Mary Scagel of Lancast
1717 July 12 Mr Ric. Ingleton & Mrs Eliz. Courtenay
1718 June 24 John Trebilcock of St. Columb Minor & Ann Row, widow
1719 June 26 Wm Blake of St. Columb Major & Susanna Merson of Cullumpton, Devon
1719 Dec. 26 Francis Langdon & Jane Wilton
1720 April 18 Wm Thom & Ursula Hendra of St. Columb Major
1720 July 2 Jonathan Law & Mary Raw *al's* Mitchall of St. Columb Major
1722 Oct. 27 Hen. Pollard of Mawgan & Gartred White of Colan
1723 Feb. 17 Samuel Glanville of St. Columb Major & Grace Trebilcock of Colan
1725 Dec. 23 Edw. Richards *al's* Tanner of St. Columb Major & Grace Woon of St. Enoder
1726 April 28 Tho. Whitford & Elizabeth Sams of the parish of Charles Plymouth
1728 Jan. 26 John Row of Maker & Ann White of St. Columb Major
1732 Sept. 10 Robert Drew of St. Columb Major & Elizabeth Watts of St. Columb Minor
1735 Oct. 28 John Rowse & Thomasine Renfrey of St. Columb Major
1736 May 8 Ric. Whitford & Dorothy Hockings of St. Columb Minor
1736 Dec. 31 John Trescott of Breggur & Jane Cundy of St. Columb Major
1738 Aug. 2 Mr James St Aubin of St. Agnes & Mrs Mary Sleeman, by licence
1738 Sept. 5 Wm White of St. Columb & Ann Trebilcock

BURIALS.

1661 April 18 John Bluett
1668 April 25 Mrs Martha Bluett, widow
1668 June 21 Grace d. of Ric. Whitford
1671 Sep. 5 John White of Higher St. Columb
1672 Nov. 8 Richard Bluett, gent.
1673 Dec. 8 Mrs Elizabeth Day
1673 Sep. 3 Ann wife of Ric. Whitford
1677 Oct. 13 James s. of James & Joan Day
1690 Dec. 18 Madam Eliz. Blewet
1712 Sept. 13 Bridget relict of James Edwards of St. Columb the greater
1718 Jan. 23 Mr James Day, gent.
1725 April 8 Grace d. of John Bagwell, vicar & Grace his wife
1726 Sept. 11 Wm Glanville of St. Columb
1727 Aug. 22 Grace wife of John Bagwell, vicar
1736 July 6 Mr Ric. Kempe of Tregony

1737 Dec. 3 Mrs Anne Kempe of Tregony
1738 May 13 Ric. s. of Ric. Plint of St. Columb Major
1739 July 5 Mr James Kempe of Tregony
1740 June Mr Wm Kempe of Tregony
1740 July 14 Martha Sanders of St. Columb
1745 April 15 Revd Mr Bagwell, Vicar of this parish
1762 Feb. 27 Revd Mr Hoblyn

ST. ENODER.

BAPTISMS.

1576 April 11 Jone d. of John Champion
1579 Mar. 29 Margerye the d. of Rob. Pokenhorne
1579 June 10 Katherine the d. of Ric. Hodge

MARRIAGES.

1572 June 9 Wm Truebodye & Grace Rickarde
1574 Oct. 3 Ric. Cood, gent. & Jone Willoughby, widow at Morvall
1577 Jan. 27 Rob. Pollard & Tamsen Jenninge
1587 Sept. 30 Tho. Vivian & Ann Hall
1592 Nov. 7 John Willoughby & Katherine Collins
1592 Feb. 6 Ric. Penros, gent. & Jane France
1592 Sept. 24 John Dunstone & Johan Dawe
1594 June 25 Wm Jolly Clarke, vicar of Enoder & Katherine Warne at St. Cubyn
1607 Nov. 17 Mr John Kete & Ann Willoughby
1610 Zachary Arundell, gent. & Ann Keate, widow
1612 Mar. 7 Tho. Cook & Jane Willoughby
1619 April 14 John Tynny of St. Columb the higher & Alice Hoskyn
1624 Oct. 12 Ric. Hoblyn & Elizabeth Martyn
1641 Sept. 30 Hen. Lawrence & Thomasin Row
1642 April 25 Rob. Edy & Jone Buckingham, both of Ladock
1649 Nov. 19 Edw. Bluett & Christen Arthur
1649 Dec. 13 Wm Gully & Joane Jolly
1660 Dec. 13 John Rickard, gent. & Alice Hoblyn
1660 Dec. 18 Richard Thomas & Agnes Flamack
1669 Sept. 18 John Halle & Johan Jenking
1672 Nov. 21 Tho. Flammack & Elizabeth Maunder
1685 Sept. 4 Hen. Blake & Grace Ford of St. Columb Major
1691 May 28 John Massey & Ann Tanner
1693 April 29 Geo. Arundle & Ann Bice
1695 July 29 John Flamank, gent. & Ann Spernon
1697 June 19 Richard Hooper & Elizabeth Mooreshead
1698 Dec. 26 Rob. Strangways & Catherine d. of Anthony Tanner, gent.
1701 Nov. 20 Mr John Flamanke & Mrs Elizabeth Cardew
1709 May 7 Edm. Bullock & Mary Vivian
1709 June 14 Mr Francis Stephens of St. Ives & Mrs Grace Flamanke
1712 Nov. 10 Tho. Cardell & Jane Hooper
1714 Sept. 5 Sr Wm Pendarves, knt & Madam Bridget Hoblyn
1716 April 3 Lewis Cock of Mevegissy & Grace Warren (Warne)
1716 Nov. 27 Mr Joseph Beale & Mrs Anne Carthew
1734 April 17 John Warren (? Warne) & Margaret Legayzack
1742 May 3 Revd Mr Wm Penwarne of St. Veep & Mrs Grace Tanner
1743 Sept. 23 Francis May of St. Columb Major & Rebecca Harris
1751 Sept. 21 Wm Retallick of St. Enoder & Mary Row of St. Columb Major
1751 Nov. 2 John Cornish of St. Columb Major & Alice Hawke

BURIALS.

1590 Sept. 20 Robert Darr of St. Columbe
1590 Mar. 11 Nicholas s. of Geo. Willoughby
1605 Nov. 16 Mistres Emline Keate

1617 May 2 A child of Zachary Arundell, gent., before baptised
1626 Mar. 8 Geo. Willoughby, gent.
1628 May 29 Wm Jolly, vicar
1633 July 30 A d. of Anthony Tanner, gent., before baptised
1634 Feb. 5 Dorothy wife of Anthony Tanner, gent.
1638 Oct. 16 Judith d. of Thomas Hoblyn, Esq. & Alice his wife
1639 Dec. 10 John Willoughby
1643 Nov. 14 Thomas Dungey
1644 Mar. 11 Mrs Jane Willoughby
1665 June 17 Mistres Ann Arundell, wife of Zachary Arundell, gent.
1667 Aug. 11 Zachary Arundell, gent.
1675 April 24 Mrs Alice Hoblyn
1675 Jan. 6 Mary Flamanck wife of Robert Flamanck
1675 Mar. 16 Susanna Flamanck
1675 Aug. 1 Susanna Flamanck
1700 July 25 Anne wife of John Flamanck, gent.

ST. WENN.

BAPTISMS.

1709 Mar. 25 W^m s. of Wm Nankivel
1712 April 20 John s. of Sampson Anstes
1714 Mar. 29 Sampson s. of Sampson & Grace Anstes
1719 June 1 John s. of Ric. & Grace Retallack
1728 Jan. 25 Cornelius s. of Richard & Ann Green of St. Columb Major
1731 April 12 W^m s. of Ric. & Grace Retallack
1731 Jan. 21 James s. of James & Jane Retallock
1733 June 4 Grace d. of Ric. & Grace Retallick
1734 Oct. 7 Richard s. of James & Jane Retallack
1734 July 26 Christopher s. of Richard & Grace Retallick
1735 (gone) W^m s. of Tho. & Eliz. Dungey
1736 Dec. 27 Hen. s. of Mr Ric. & Margaret Hawkey
1737 Mar. 25 Elizabeth d. of James & Jane Retallick
1739 July 13 W^m s. of James & Jane Retallack
1746 May 19 Mary d. of John & Frances Blewett
1748 May 14 James s. of John & Frances Blewett
1752 Nov. 24 Ann d. of John & Elizabeth Retalick
1753 Oct. 15 W^m s. of James & Mary Merifield
1753 Nov. 23 Rich^d s. of Hen. & Eliz. Retallack
1762 Feb. 13 James s. of W^m & Eliz. Retallack
1787 July 1 Ric. s. of Joseph & Mary Warn
1790 June 7 James s. of Joseph & Mary Warn

MARRIAGES.

1707 Sept. John Edwards & Ann Mapowder
1709 Sept. 10 Tho. West & Mary Retalack
1709 Oct. 19 Sampson Anstics & Grace Williams
1712 June 15 John Loob & Mary Vivian
1715 Feb. 11 Peter Gilbert & Grace Olver
1716 July 9 Anthony Coad & Dianah Pollard
1721 Oct. 23 Wm Peters & Elizabeth Hoare of St. Columb
1722 Aug. 11 Wm Nankivall & Judeth Hoare
1724 Dec. 17 Peter Warne & Ann Best by licence
1725 Aug. 3 Wm Williams, gent. & Mrs Jane Resuggan
1726 July 24 James Retallack & Jane Bayley
1726 Oct. 5 Richard Veal & Mary Vincent
1727 June 13 Tho. Dungey & Elizabeth Penyligan
1742 Feb. 5 John Hicks of St. Columb Major & Mary Trembeth
1743 Mar. 27 John Retallack of Roache & Elizabeth Docken of St. Wenn
1745 Nov. 10 John Blewett & Frances Retallack
1748 April 21 Hen. Oxman & Frances Hawk both of St. Columb
1749 June 22 Benjamin Jones & Elizabeth Mewden, both of St. Columb
1749 Dec. 16 Tho. Giles & Jane Inch, both of St. Columb

BURIALS.

1707 Mar. 16 Grace Mapowder, gentlewoman
1712 Sept. 15 Dorcas Vivian
1713 April 10 Frances the wife of Edw. Brokensheer
1713 Dec. 5 Henry Stribley, gent.
1719 Nov. 27 Dorcas wife of Stephen Vivian, gent.
1719 July 16 Robert Berry, gent.
1720 Jan. 11 Robert Berry, gent.
1737 July 16 W[m] Hals, gent. (The historian of Cornwall)
1752 June 17 M[rs] Sarah Carew
1793 Mar. 2 Elizabeth Vyvyan

PARKHAM, CO. DEVON.

BAPTISMS.

1667 Nov. 4 Simon s. of Giles Risdon, Esq.
1668 Jan. 10 Frances d. of Giles Risdon, Esq.
1670 Aug. 26 Henry s. of Giles Risdon, Esq.
1685 July 12 Jane d. of Giles Risdon, Esq. & Jane his wife
1689 Oct. 1 Gyles s. of Gyles Risdon, Esq. & Anna his wife

BURIALS.

1676 Feb. 10 Grace wife of Giles Risdon, Esq.
1678 Mar. 24 Gyles Risdon, Esq.
1682 Sept. 14 Catherine wife of Giles Risdon, gent.
1685 July 23 Jane wife of Giles Risdon, Esq.
1697 Sept. 24 Gyles Risdon of Bableigh, Esq.

ALWINGTON, DEVON.

MARRIAGES.

1677 April 11 Giles s. of Giles Risdon of Bably, Esq. & M[rs] Katherine Coffin d. of Richard Coffin of Portledge, Esq.

ST. JOHN'S BY SALTASH.

BAPTISMS.

1683 Oct. 10 Richard s. of Richard Mapowder & Mary his wife
1735 Jan. 18 Edmond s. of Edmond Prideaux of St. Awstell & Ruth his wife

MARRIAGES.

1714 Sept. 4 Cap[t] Thomas Graves & Mary d. of M[r] William Warne of Anthony

MAKER.

BAPTISMS.

1709 May 20 Symon* s. of Symon Warn & Elizabeth his wife
1710 Oct. 25 William s. of Simon Warn & Elizabeth his wife
1710 Dec. 10 John s. of Tho. Hoblyn & Charity his wife
1711 May 1 Elizabeth d. of Hugh Mallet & Mary his wife
1712 Dec. 8 Thomas s. of Thomas Hoblyn & Charity his wife
1713 Sept. 29 Mary d. of Hugh Mallet & Mary his wife
1713 Dec. 9 Thomas s. of Thomas Hoblyn & Charity his wife

MARRIAGES.

1710 June Hugh Mallet & Mary Hawse
1741 Jan. 21 Simon Ward* & Johanna Little
1780 July 20 John Luckraft & Ann Priscilla Ward(Warne)
1781 Sept. 13 Simon Ward† (Warne) & Elizabeth Nodder
1786 Sept. 25 William Mallet & Loveday Warne

ST. BUDEAUX, DEVON.

BAPTISMS.

1631 July 24 Joane d. of John Vivian & Jane his wife

* He took the name of Ward. See his marriage below. He died 11 Oct., 1759, aged 50 years, and is buried under an altar tomb on the south side of the church, together with Johanna his wife, who died 29 May, 1776, aged 70. Thomasine their daughter, died 7 July, 1781, aged 44. She was wife of Capt. Edward Lower, R.N., who died 4 March, 1802, aged 67.

† Son of Simon Ward and Johanna Little. He had two daughters: Ann Priscilla, born 26 March, 1782, died an infant; and Mary, born 7 April, 1784, married at Maker, on Sept. 26, 1817, John Friend, Esq., Lieut. Royal Surrey Militia, and had issue,—John Simon, died unmarried; and Mary Anne Elizabeth, born 6 Jan. 1823, married 20 Jan., 1847, Frederick Arthur Jewers, son of Commander Richard Jewers, R.N., and had issue three sons and five daughters.

1772 July 14 Mary d. of John Arundell & Elizabeth his wife

MARRIAGES.

1555 June 9 Rich. Triscott & Ann Berrye
1689 June 11 John Pendarvis, gent. & Mary Beele, gen[t]

BURIALS.

1540 Aug. 10 Thomasyne Hornbrook
1551 Dec. 6 Thomas Blighte
1554 Feb. 20 S[r] John Hornbrooke, priest & curate of this parish
1621 Aug. 9 Elizabeth Leigh wife of Richard Leigh

PADSTOW.

BAPTISMS.

1599 Jan. 30 Catherine d. of William Opey, St. Delian
1600 June 19 Arthur s. of George Moyle, gent.
1602 Jan. 2 Margarete d. of William Flamock
1605 July 15 John s. of William Flamock, gent.
1631 Jan. 25 William s. of John Flamock, gent.
1633 Aug. 16 John & Catherine children of John Flamock, gent.
1638 Feb. 18 John s. of John Flamock, gent. & Ann his wife
1652 Aug. 28 Mathew s. of Mathew Webber, gent. & Jane his wife
1655 May 9 Elizabeth d. of Mathew Webber, gent. & Jane his wife
1655 June 19 Thomas s. of George Beare, gent. & Eliz. his wife
1656 Jan. 5 Mary d. of Mathew Webber, gent.
1681 Jan. 24 Grace d. of Hen. Vivian & Ann his wife
1683 Feb. 7 William s. of Hen. Vyvyan & Ann his wife
1685 Feb. 2 Jane d. of Hen. Vyvyan & Ann his wife
1692 July 24 Rich. s. of Hen. Vivian & Ann his wife
1722 Oct. 30 Rich. s. of John Vivian & Jane his wife
1725 Nov. 24 William s. of John Vivian & Jane his wife
1728 Feb. 5 John s. of John Vivian & Jane his wife
1731 Oct. 5 Hellen d. of John Vivian & Jane his wife
1740 Aug. 21 John s. of Edw. Day, gent. & Martha his wife
1743 Nov. 13 Ann d. of Edw. Day, gent. & Martha his wife
1744 Nov. 20 Edw. & Peter s[s] of Edw. Day, gent. & Martha his wife
1755 Oct. 10 John s. of John Vivian & Elizabeth his wife
1758 Rich. s. of John Vivian & Eliz. his wife
1758 Jane d. of John Vivian, jun[r] & Eliz. his wife
1760 Rebecca d. of John Vivian, jun[r] & Eliz. his wife
1761 Walter s. of John Vivian, jun[r] & Eliz. his wife
1762 John s. of John Vivian & Eliz. his wife
1763 James s. of John Flamick & Frances his wife
1771 Aug. 4 John s. of John Vivian & Mary his wife
1774 May 23 Eliz. d. of John Vivian & Mary his wife
1784 June 28 Kitty d. of Thomas Rawlings & Margery his wife
1785 Aug. 5 Jenny d. of Tho. Rawlings & Margery his wife
1785 Sept. 7 Frances Phipps d. of the Rev. Thomas Biddulph & Sarah his wife, born 22 April
1787 Jan. 8 Kitty d. of Tho. Rawlings & Margery
1788 May 19 William s. of Tho. Rawlings & Margery
1788 Sept. 12 Mary d. of Rev[d] William Rawlings & Susanna his wife
1789 Dec. 29 Charlotte Louisa d. of the Rev[d] Tho. Biddulph & Sarah his wife, born 10 Nov.
1790 Jan. 8 Nancy d. of Tho. Rawlings & Margery
1790 June 9 W[m] s. of William Rawlings, clerk & Susanna his wife, born 28 March
1791 Sept. 20 Moriel d. of Tho. Rawlings & Margery

1792 Mar. 20 Tho. s. of Rev[d] W[m] Rawlings & Susanna
1793 June 16 Suky d. of W[m] Rawlings, clerk
1793 April 20 Patsey d. of Tho. Rawlings
1795 Sept. 11 Harriet d. of Tho. Rawlings & Margery
1796 June 27 Henry Peter s. of W[m] Rawlings, clerk & Susanna
1797 May 5 Price s. of Tho. Rawlings & Margery
1798 Nov. 20 Anna d. of W[m] Rawlings & Susanna, born 20 Nov. 1797
1799 Sept. 17 Charlotte d. of Tho. Rawlings & Margery
1800 Mar. 20 Caroline d. of Rev[d] W[m] Rawlings & Susanna
1800 Aug. 17 John Day s. of Geo. Wilson & Martha his wife, born 20 Mar. 1799
1801 Jan. 22 John Bradford s. of John Vivian & Eliz. his wife
1802 Jan. 8 Peter Day s. of Geo. Wilson & Martha
1803 Jan. 15 Edw. s. of Tho. Rawlings & Margery
1803 May 17 Tho. s. of John Vivian & Eliz.
1803 May 25 James s. of W[m] Rawlings, clerk & Susanna, born 20 July 1802
1804 Dec. 8 Geo. s. of Tho. Rawlings & Margery
1805 Feb. 9 Esther Day d. of Geo. Wilson & Patty
1805 Mar. 20 Charles s. of Rev[d] W[m] Rawlings & Susanna
1805 Nov. 5 Jane Gilbert d. of Peter Vivian & Ann
1811 Sept. 18 Geo. s. of Stephen Vivian & Mary

MARRIAGES.

1607 Mar. 25 Robert Hoblyne & Tamson Vosprey
1621 Sept. 10 John Norman & Cheston d. of W[m] Flamock, gent.
1638 July 21 John Warne & Anne Flamock
1667 May 23 W[m] s. of Rich. Pendarves Esq. & Admonition d. of Edm. Prideaux, Esq.
1683 Nov. 20 Rich. Bolitha & Eliz. Edwards
1754 Dec. 11 John Vivian & Eliz. Pentyre
1765 Oct. 24 W[m] Northcote of Lanteglos & Ann Hoblyn
1767 Jan. 29 John Vivian, widower & Mary Mitchell
1767 Mar. 3 John Hoblyn of Newlyn, clerk & Ann Symon
1777 Aug. 19 Hen. Vyvyan, clerk, rector of Withiel & Ann Williams
1783 May 30 Thomas Rawlings & Margery Price
1785 May 19 Richard Hicks of St. Columb Major & Martha Peter
1785 Oct. 20 John Marshall of St. Austle & Frances Flamank
1787 May 14 William Rawlings, clerk & Susanna Salmon
1794 May 5 W[m] Pettigrew & Grace Vivian
1796 April 17 Tho. Hoblyn, Esq. of Truro & Peggy Martyn
1798 Jan. 13 Rich. Carveth of the parish of Elmor, co. Gloucester, clerk & Esther Day
1798 Feb. 20 Geo. Wilson & Martha Day
1801 Aug. 25 Edw. Upham of St. Martin's, Exeter & Mary Hoblyn
1802 Oct. 3 W[m] Vivian & Thomazine Parker of St. Minver
1803 Feb. 28 Edw. Arthur, gent. & Judith Rowse
1805 April 5 John Paynter of St. Stephen's, Coleman street, London, gent. & Nancy Rawlings
1805 April 5 Robert Bear & Joanna Vivian

BURIALS.

1606 May 11 Catherine wife of W[m] Flamank
1619 Feb. 2 William Flamack
1636 Sept. 21 Joan widow of William Flamock, gent.
1650 July 14 John Flammock, gent.
1663 July 7 Catherine d. of John Flamock, gent.
1670 Dec. 14 M[rs] Joan Vivian, widow
1673 June 17 M[rs] Margery Cavell
1674 Dec. 12 Stephen Pendarvis, gent.

1702 Feb. 13 William Devonshire
1724 Jan. 3 Dorothy Nanskeval
1743 May 15 Jane Vivian
1755 Oct. 19 John s. of John Vivian, jun[r]
1757 Nov. 11 Dorothy Pomeroy
1758 April 16 Rich. s. of John Vivian
1762 Aug. 12 Jenny d. of John Vivian, jun[r]
1764 Sept. 28 Eliz. Vivian
1766 Aug. 26 John Vivian
1768 Jan. 4 John Vivian
1768 July 26 Elizabeth Vivian
1780 Nov. 23 Mary Vivian
1782 Feb. 11 Eliz. d. of John & Mary Vivian
1783 Mar. 7 Martha Biddulph, wife of Tho[s] Biddulph, clerk, vicar of this parish
1795 Mar. 26 M[r] W[m] Rawlings, merchant
1805 June 6 M[rs] Catherine Rawlings
1808 Sept. 23 Mary d. of Will'm Vivian
1808 Nov. 15 John Vivian
1812 May 7 M[rs] Sarah Biddulph, relict of Rev[d] Tho. Biddulph, vicar of this parish

ST. BREOCK.

BAPTISMS.

1576 June 24 Andrew s. of Philip Pumerye
1578 Dec. 5 Mary d. of Philip Pumerye
1600 May 10 Nicholas s. of Christopher Teake, gent.
1600 Grace d. of George Beare, gent.
1601 Nov. 1 Ollye d. of Christopher Teake, gent.
1601 Dec. 16 Mary d. of Geo. Beare, gent.
1602 Dec. 13 Rawlin s. of Christopher Teake, gent.
1602 Mar. 16 Jane d. of John Beare, gent.
1604 Jan. 12 Robert s. of Christopher Teake, gent.
1606 April 15 Jane d. of Christopher Teake, gent.
1606 June 24 Thomas s. of Christopher Teake, gent.
1607 Aug. 7 Alexander s. of Geo. Beare, gent.
1607 Mar. 12 William s. of Christopher Tyacke, gent.
1609 Jan. 12 Christopher s. of Christopher Tyacke, gent.
1620 May 23 Dionisia Joh[is] Glanvill, Theologia Bachalorii
1625 Feb. 22 Edmund s. of Edm. Opye of St. Columb Inferior
1629 Feb. 19 Dorothy d. of Tho. Beare
1631 Feb. 19 Margaret d. of Thomas Beare
1638 July 30 Jane d. of Thomas Beare, gent.
1640 Feb. 19 John s. of Thomas Beare, gent.
1642 Oct. 16 Catherine d. of Thomas Bere
1643 Jan. 1 Otho s. of Obidias Blighe
1647 Oct. 16 Susan d. of Tho. Bere, gent.
1663 Feb. 16 Edw. s. of John Bere, gent.
1689 April 5 Mary d. of James Beauford, clerk
1700 Aug. 20 Peter s. of Stephen Warne, clerk & Elizabeth, his wife
1803 April 24 W[m] s. of W[m] & Tamson Vyvian

MARRIAGES.

1565 Feb. 7 M[r] W[m] Flammanke & Mary Carminow
1571 Oct. 10 W[m] Godolphin & Jane Tredinneck
1573 Feb. 16 Nicholas Bluet & Anne his wife
1584 Nicholas Keswell *al's* Kestell & Ann Tredinneck
1586 Nov. 3 Christopher Stratford & Eliz. Tredinneck
1586 Nov. 28 M[r] Giles Risedon & Mistris Eliz. Viell
1590 Nov. 17 Hugh Bescoane & Mary Tredinneck
1617 Sept. 13 John Carter, gent. & Mary Moyle, gen[t]
1617 Jan. 23 Joh'es Glanvell, Theologia Bachalarius, et D[na] Fleura Rillston
1686 Jan. 1 John Werry s. of Roger Werry & Johan Beauford
1689 June 30 John Bishop, clerk, & Mary Beauford
1721 Feb. 5 Rev[d] John Bagwell, A.M., vicar of Little Colan, & Grace Werry
1726 Oct. 28 George Jewell of St. Columb, Cornwall, surgeon & Catherine Nickel

BURIALS.

1590 July 1 George Beare
1595 Nov. 9 George s. of Geo. Arundell of Lanherne, Esq.
1604 May 2 Dorothy d. of Geo. Bere, gent.
1612 July 10 Walter s. of Christopher Tyack

1618 Oct. 12 James s. of Tho. Peters, rector of Mawgan
1621 Dec. 19 Eliz. d. of John Carter, gent.
1677 Dec. 10 Mary d. of Nicholas Opie, Esq.
1681 Feb. 24 Tho. s. of John Opie, clerk
1689 July 18 Richard Hoblin, gent.
1694 May 1 Katherine Hoblyn
1720 Feb. 16 Mary, wife of the Rev[d] M[r] Stephen Warne, clerk & minister of Crantoch
1722 Nov. 7 Jane d. of the Rev[d] M[r] Stephen Warne, clerk

ST. ANDREW, PLYMOUTH.

BAPTISMS.

1588 May 2 John s. of William Pumery
1590 July 15 Hugh s. & Jone d. of Thomas Pomeroy
1593 May 1 George s. of Francis Blewet
1604 Dec. 23 Richard s. of Arthur Hals, Esquire
1619 Aug. 9 Walter s. of Gabriell Arundell
1620 Jan. 7 Samuel s. of Gabriel Arundell
1626 Jan. 7 John s. of Gabriel Arundell
1634 Nov. 12 Susan d. of M[r] Geo. Pumeroy, preacher at Stonehouse, & Rebecca his wife
1634 Dec 28 Eliz. d. of M[r] Rich. Arundell & M[rs] Eliz. his wife
1635 Oct. 14 Robert s. of M[r] Robert & M[rs] Ann Arundell
1645 April 6 John s. of John Saint Abin, Esq.
1648 Dec. 15 Elias s. of M[r] Thomas Travers
1650 Aug. 9 Samuel s. of M[r] Thomas Travers
1663 April 2 W[m] s. of M[r] Tho. & M[rs] Mary Warne
1664 Dec. 23 Elizabeth d. of Nicholas & Jane Bagwell
1668 July 1 Eliz. d. of Dillimoor & Eliz. Arundell
1668 July 3 Ann d. of Nicholes & Jane Bagwell
1669 Mar. 25 Jane d. of William & Philippa Mountsteven
1670 April 26 Mary d. of Nicholas & Jane Bagwill
1673 Dec. 5 Abraham s. of M[r] William Pomroy
1674 June 5 John s. of Nicholas Bagwell
1674 Sept. 27 Jone d. of Gentle & Jone Godolphin
1683 Aug. 24 Mary d. of Gentle & Mary Godolphin
1687 Oct. 30 Jone d. of Rich. & Marg[t] Warne
1690 Mar. 24 Ruth d. of Steph. & Eliz. Retallick
1720 June 24 William s. of William & Jane Courtenay
1731 Mar. 16 Eliz. d. of M[r] John & M[rs] Eliz. Arundell
1732 Mar. 18 John s. of M[r] John & M[rs] Eliz. Arundell

MARRIAGES.

1589 Nov. 3 Henry James & Agnes Blewett
1590 Jan. 20 John Pomery & Flower Manke
1591 Aug. 3 John Bagwell, clerk, & Christian Jeffry, widow
1594 Dec. 1 William Pomery & Joan Luscumbe
1603 Sept. 19 John Leigh & Ann Hals
1605 June 14 John Hals, gent. & Mary Durrant
1618 May 3 Gabriel Arundell & Eliz. Holman
1625 April 17 M[r] Nicholas Pomerie & Agnes Barons
1625 Sept. 25 M[r] Nicholas Slanning & Gartered Bagg
1629 Nov. 16 Nicholas Rowze & Elizabeth Bewford
1634 Oct. 29 M[r] Robert Arundell & M[rs] Ann Ceeby
1643 Jan. 14 Gentle Godolphin & Ann Jole
1645 May 17 Gentle Godolphin & Martha Hooper
1652 Aug. 3 M[r] Thankful Owen & Loveday Virian
1652 Aug. 25 M[r] John Warne & Faith Ceely
1654 Feb. 12 John Beauford of Plymouth & Eliz. d. of James Dones of Plym., deceased
1675 Dec. 24 Rich. Addams & Grace Arundell
1681 Jan. 31 Gentle Godolphin & Mary Groot
1685 Sept. 27 Rich. Warne & Margaret Lane
1686 Aug. 4 Thomas Larrance & Constance Hals

1688 June 12 Tho. Pollard & Mary Warne of Eglesbayle
1693 Feb. 3 Cornelius Doyly, souldier, & Eliz. Carter of St. Columb
1694 April 6 Thomas Hoblin of Liscard & Mary Smaley of Minhinnit
1696 Mar. 3 Nicholas Bagwell & Ann Newton
1698 Oct. 3 William Warne & Melina Philp
1719 July 31 John Hobling & Mary Ash

BURIALS.

1581 June 19 M[r] John Hals
1593 May 24 Geo. s. of Francis Blewet
1610 Dec. 7 Samuel Paul of St. Collomb
1627 Feb. 6 W[m] Hawkinge of St. Collomb
1634 Oct. 18 Walsingham wife of M[r] Nicholas Opey, jun[r]
1635 Aug. 4 Susan d. of Geo. Pumeroy, preacher of God's Word at Stonehouse
1676 June 20 Delamore Arundell
1680 Feb. 18 Jone the wife of Gentle Godolphin
1691 Aug. 11 M[r] Christopher Tyack
1696 April 14 M[rs] Jane Tyack
1700 Jan. 31 M[r] Thomas Warne
1705 Nov. 13 Bennet Arundell

BRADFORD, CO. DEVON.

BAPTISMS.

1637 Nov. 29 Frances d. of M[r] William Bickford & Grace
1639 June 26 Elizabeth d. of M[r] William Bickford & Grace
1679 Nov. 14 Honor d. of Arscott Bickford, Esq. & Honor *(sic)*
1684 Sep. 2 William s. of Arscott Bickford, Esq. & Bridget
1685 Oct. 21 Edmond s. of Arscott Bickford, Esq. & Bridget
1689 Oct. 23 Nicholas s. of Arscott Bickford, Esq. & Bridget
1690 Feb. 13 Bridget d. of Arscott Bickford, of Dunsland, Esq. & Bridget
1712 Feb. 5 Arscott s. of W[m] Bickford, Esq. & Damaris
1714 Jan. 25 Edward s. of W[m] Bickford, Esq. & Damaris
1716 May 23 Damaris d. of W[m] Bickford, Esq. & Damaris
1717 June 12 William s. of W[m] Bickford, Esq. & Damaris
1718 Aug. 25 Edward s. of W[m] Bickford, Esq. & Damaris

MARRIAGES.

1634 Dec. 9 M[r] William Begford *(sic)* & M[rs] Grace Arscott
1699 Feb. 12 William Harris, Esq[re] & Honor Bickford
1733 Nov. 7 William Bickford, Esq. & Eliz. Richards

BURIALS.

1635 Mar. 20 Mary d. of M[r] W[m] Bickford
1659 Nov. 3 William Bickford of Dunsland, Esq.
1677 Sep. 30 Edward Bickford
1686 Jan. 13 M[rs] Grace Bickford of Dunsland, wid.
1689 May 22 Arscott s. of Arscott Bickford, Esq. & Bridget
1690 July 31 Nicholas s. of Arscott Bickford, Esq. & Bridget
1693 June 19 Arscott Bickford of Dunsland, Esq.
1693 Jan. 1 Bridget d. of Arscott Bickford, Esq. deceased, & Bridget
1695 Feb. 19 Arscott s. of Arscott Bickford, Esq. & Bridgett
1708 Feb. 11 Bridgett wife of W[m] Bickford, Esq[re]
1712 June 18 M[rs] Bridgett Bickford of Dunsland
1715 Jan. 21 Edward Bickford, gent.
1717 May 22 Damaris d. of W[m] Bickford, Esq. & Damaris
1729 July 25 Damaris late wife of W[m] Bickford, Esq.
1740 Feb. 26 William Bickford of Dunsland, Esq.
1743 July 12 Edward Bickford
1745 May 30 W[m] Bickford, clerk
1765 June 3 M[r] John Bickford of Oakhampton
1767 June 22 M[rs] Elizabeth Bickford of Oakhampton
1771 April 26 Arscott Bickford, Esq.
1795 May 27 Geo. Bickford, Esq., of Dunsland
1803 Nov. 10 Mary Bickford, relict of the late Geo. Bickford of Dunsland, Esq.

ADDENDA ET CORRIGENDA.

Page 16, Dec. 19, 1592, for Janne, *read* Jane.

„ 27, In the first entry, for Nymise, *read* Nynnise.

„ 28, Aug. 10, 1617. From this Thomas is descended Lord Vivian of Glynn ; his grandson, Tho. Vivian of Comprigney, by his wife Lucy Glynn, had a son Thomas, Vicar of Cornwood, co. Devon, from 1747 to his death at the age of 71, in 1793, and was buried with a monument in the church, having the arms of Vivian of Trewan on it. He was grandfather of the first Lord Vivian of Glynn.

„ 32, Nov. 23, 1625, Legge, *not* Lugge.

„ 36, Feb. 17, 1630, for Marryall, *read* Marshall.

„ 38, July 14, 1633. for John, *read* Degory.

„ 39, Feb. 9, 1633, for Agnes, *read* Ann.

„ 52, Note ; also note, page 54. This Isabella and Alice were sisters of Samuel Travers, Esq., M.P. The Isabella and Alice named in his will were daughters of his brother, the Rev. Elias Travers of Dublin. Their father, the Rev. Thomas Travers, matriculated at Cambridge and entered Magdalene College in 1637, took his B.A. in 1640-1, and M.A. in 1644. (He was the second son of the Rev. Samuel Travers, Vicar of Thorverton, Devon, who died in 1648, and grandson of John Travers, Rector of Farringdon, Devon, who married in 1580, Alice, daughter of John Hooker, Chamberlain of Exeter.) Thomas Travers married, according to Calamy, "a niece of the noble Lord Robartes," and, as Dr. Boyse tells us, his son Elias was nephew to John Lord Robartes ; and his son Samuel, the M.P., used the arms of Rous (or, an eagle displayed azure), quartered with those of Travers. It would appear that Tho. Travers, the Rector of St. Columb, must have married Elizabeth, daughter of William Rous of Halton, by Mary sister of John Lord Robartes ; this Elizabeth married first her cousin, Francis Rous of Wootton-under-Ridge, co. Gloucester. The Rev. Thomas Travers was lecturer at St. Andrew's church, Plymouth, prior to going to St. Columb, in which church were baptized his son Elias, and a son Samuel buried at St. Columb 27 Oct., 1651.

„ 74, Sep. 24, 1687, eodem die, inadvertently inserted as in the original, instead of the previous date being repeated.

„ 86, Note. Since this note was printed information has been received from Tho. Hoblyn, Esq., of Welshpool, from which it appears that this Penelope was not a daughter of the first Earl of Godolphin, as generally supposed, but a daughter of Col. Sidney Godolphin, Lord of Bron-e-arth (grandson of John Godolphin and Judith Meredith), who married Susanna, daughter and heiress of Rhys Tanat, Esq., heiress of Abertanat. In the register of Llanblodwell, Denbighshire, is the burial of Susanna, daughter of Francis Hoblyn and Penelope his wife, in 1711, having been born the same year ; her brother, Robert Hoblyn, was born in 1710.

Page 119, Note, third line from the bottom, *read* 1783 *not* 1782.

„ 121, Nov. 30, 1759, for Mason, *read* Mabyn.

„ 146, Sep. 30, 1609, for Saple, *read* Staple.

„ 146, Nov. 23, 1608, for Alce, *read* Alee.

„ 147, Dec. 19, 1612, for Juth, *read* Inch. This Ursula is named in the will of her brother, Richard Vivian of St. Columb, in 1655, who also mentions, "My cousin Wm Inches three children," he probably meant nephew. It was usual at that period to call a nephew or niece, 'cousin.' The Inch family lived at St. Kew.

„ 167, July 27, 1730, for Anne, *read* Sam^ll.

„ 185, Sept. 27, 1548, for Mell, *read* Melvis.

„ 228, Note. The entry of the burial of John Carter, the father, does occur in the register on the date given in the note, but was omitted in the transcript.

„ 234, May 14, 1679, add the following to the note : John Beauford matriculated from Exeter College, 21 June, 1633, aged 16, son of Wm Beauford of St. Columb, paying the fees of a Plebeian's son. William Beauford, aged 16, and James Beauford, aged 15, brothers, matriculated at Oxford from Exeter College, 10 July, 1668, as sons of John Beauford, minister of St. Colomb, Cornwall. They both took the degree of B.A., 20 April, 1672, and M.A., 19 Jan., 1674-5. There were no others of the name at Oxford.

„ 238, Note ‡ At the seventh line, for Diana, *read* Damaris, as elsewhere in the note. Damaris, daughter of John Avent, gent., and Damaris his wife, baptized 5 Dec., 1663, at Plympton St. Mary, and married there as Damaris Hoblyn to Edward Hoblyn, 8 Sep., 1692.

„ 287, Note. Though said by his representative to have been a brother of Sir Hugh Bateman, Bart., upon search being made no trace of Robert Bateman can be found in any pedigree of Bateman of Hartington. No one of this name was ever at Oxford, nor was his degree either from Cambridge or Dublin ; possibly it may have been from Edinburgh, or else an Archbishop's degree. There was a Robert Bateman, of Queen's College, Cambridge, A.B in 1721, A.M. 1725, M.D. 1732.

INDEX.

A

C

D

H

I

K

O

Q

R

S

T

U

V

W.

Y

ADDENDA ET CORRIGENDA.

Adams: after Richard, for 299 *read* 298.
Arundell: after George, for 298 *read* 297; after Grace, for 299 *read* 298.
Ashe: for Agnes *read* Anne.
Avant: *see* p. 300.
Bateman: after Sir Hugh and Robert, *add* 300.
Beare: after Dorothy and George, *dele* 298.
Beauford: after John, for 299 *read* 298; for additions, *see* p. 300.
Bickford: after Arscott, Damaris, Elizabeth, Mary, and William, *dele* 300; after George and John, for 300 *read* 299.
Brewer: after Margaret, *add* 290, after Mary, *dele* 290.
Carnsewe: *add* Mary, 273.
Carter: after John *add* 300.
Cely: for 299 *read* 298.
Clemow: after Nicholas *add* 281.
Dones: for 299 *read* 298.
Drew: after Thomas *add* 260.
D. G., 16; John, 16.
Godolphin: after Gentle, for 299 *read* 298; after Martha, *dele* 299; for additions, *see* p. 300.
Groot: for 299, *read* 298.
Hoblyn: for additions, *see* p. 300.
Hockey: after Jane, for 6 *read* 1.
Hooker: *add*, Alice 300, John 300.
Lawry: after John, for 44, 46, *read* 44-46.
Tanat, Rhys, 300; Susanna, 300.

London: Mitchell and Hughes, Printers, 140 Wardour Street, W.

www.ingramcontent.com/pod-product-compliance
Lightning Source LLC
Chambersburg PA
CBHW030905270326
41929CB00008B/587

9783337037741